GREEK NYMPHS

GREEK
Nymphs

MYTH, CULT, LORE

Jennifer Larson

OXFORD
UNIVERSITY PRESS

2001

OXFORD
UNIVERSITY PRESS

Oxford   New York
Athens   Auckland   Bangkok   Bogotá   Buenos Aires   Cape Town
Chennai   Dar es Salaam   Delhi   Florence   Hong Kong   Istanbul   Karachi
Kolkata   Kuala Lumpur   Madrid   Melbourne   Mexico City   Mumbai   Nairobi
Paris   São Paulo   Shanghai   Singapore   Taipei   Tokyo   Toronto   Warsaw

and associated companies in
Berlin   Ibadan

Copyright © 2001 by Oxford University Press

Published by Oxford University Press, Inc.
198 Madison Avenue, New York, New York 10016

Oxford is a registered trademark of Oxford University Press

Library of Congress Cataloging-in-Publication Data
Larson, Jennifer (Jennifer Lynn)
Greek nymphs : myth, cult, lore / Jennifer Larson.
p.   cm.
Includes bibliographical references and index.
ISBN 0-19-512294-1; ISBN 0-19-514465-1 (pbk.)
1. Nymphs (Greek deities)   I. Title.
BL820.N95 L37   2001
292.2'114—dc21   00-026246

9 8 7 6 5 4 3 2 1

Printed in the United States of America
on acid-free paper

In memory of

BARBARA HUGHES FOWLER

who was and remains an inspiration

PREFACE

Why a study of nymphs? The field of religious studies has seen a recent trend toward examination of popular traditions as opposed to elite ones, for example, the series Princeton Readings in Religions, edited by Donald Lopez, Jr. This approach can be applied fruitfully to the field of classics, where both the sources themselves and the preferences of scholars have favored the experiences of the elite and the city dwellers over those of the more numerous rural populations. The gap that until recently existed in the scholarship on Greek magic, an aspect of the culture seldom mentioned in canonical literature, illustrates this point. The worship of nymphs was conceptually aligned with the rural and non-elite populations, though not confined to these groups. In the literature of classical Athens, we find comparatively few references to nymphs, while in the rural areas surrounding the city, their cults thrived at this period. The Hellenistic interest in pastoral themes and local traditions, however, made nymphs fashionable subjects for the sophisticated scholar-poets of Alexandria. Hence, in addition to improving our perception of ancient Greek religion, a study of nymphs can also shed light on the relationship between popular and elite traditions in Greek culture as a whole. A further and related focus of interest is the contribution that the study of nymphs can make to our understanding of women's lives in ancient Greece. Much attention has been given to the roles of goddesses in the rituals and myths that surrounded female rites of passage, but little attention has been paid to nymphs, figures who were probably much closer to the everyday lives of the majority of women.

In this text, I sometimes speak of devotion or devotionalism, which has special relevance to the worship of nymphs (and of many other Greek deities). By this term, I refer to individual piety, especially as expressed outwardly and materially through, for example, ex-voto offerings. Devotionalism also implies an emotional, not merely intellectual, apprehension of the divine. Participation in group rituals, such as processions or sacrifices, may partake of devotionalism insofar as the individual's sense of personal relationship with the deity is engaged. Devotional practices are to be found in all the world religions, though they have received little scholarly attention in comparison with theology and sacred texts. In the past, Western scholars of world religions have erroneously attributed devotionalism primarily to non-elite populations and women, and they have subscribed to a hierarchical model that valued internal, intellectual apprehension of the divine over emotional experience and external, material expressions of piety.

A final reason for undertaking this project is that little beyond the information in standard handbooks has been published that specifically addresses the nature and function of nymphs, and no book-length works in any language currently exist. The materials available to readers of English are particularly few. Much information is scattered in archaeological reports, corpora of inscriptions, and scholarly studies of other subjects. Yet nymphs and their cults were ubiquitous in the Greek world before Homer and remained so through the Hellenistic period and beyond. The nymph, in the guise of the modern Greek *neraïda*, is one of the small number of ancient deities who survived the transition to Christianity. Few other aspects of Greek religion have been so pervasive yet so little studied.

What is a nymph? This question, which I first asked myself when undertaking the research for a book on Greek heroines, has rarely been discussed in a scholarly fashion. I believe it has escaped attention because the answer was assumed to be self-evident, but the question of definition is not a simple one. Chapter 1 begins with a section that addresses basic problems of definition and taxonomy. In order to discuss the roles and functions of nymphs in Greek culture, we must be able to distinguish them from other, similar figures. Second, I discuss the conceptual and physical contexts in which the nymphs pursue their activities—the archetypal landscapes of mountain, spring, cave, grove, and meadow—and I examine some of the taxonomic categories that were applied to the nymphs by ancient commentators. An important social dimension of nymph worship is introduced in the section on divination and nympholepsy. Finally, a brief review of nymphs in Greek poetry through the Hellenistic period helps to clarify the ways in which the characterization of nymphs changed over time or by author and addresses their relative popularity in various genres and periods. Classical scholars will already be familiar with most of the texts discussed in this section, but I hope it will form a helpful introduction for general readers.

The second chapter, "Ancient and Modern Narratives," explores the kinds of relationships between heroes (or heroines) and nymphs illustrated in antique literary sources, and it examines the striking parallels between these ancient narratives and their modern counterparts. The chapter argues for some degree of continuity between the ancient and modern materials, and it uses the insights of modern folklorists to provide an interpretation of the stories, focusing especially on the gender-related fears and desires expressed in them.

Chapter 3, "Gods, Goddesses, and Nymphs," shows how the nymphs interact in myth and cult with other deities of the Greek pantheon. Again, gender provides a strong organizational principle: the nymphs' relations with gods are usually envisioned in terms of sexual contact or familial relationship (lover, nurse, or daughter), while for goddesses they act as a supportive group of attendants who share a given goddess's functional and geographical sphere of influence. Both nymphs and goddesses are closely concerned with the stages of the female life cycle as these are conceptualized in Greek thought.

The fourth chapter, "Lore of the Nymphs in the Greek World," is a reference tool that summarizes the lore for each district of the ancient Greek world, excluding cave sites. To my mind, a geographical survey, illustrating the regional character of the myths and cults, is more useful for the present work than a chronological one. Though developments did, of course, take place over the centuries, they seem as a whole less helpful as a structural framework and less dramatic than regional differences. I balance this synchronic approach by summarizing chronological changes and by keeping the reader informed of and aware of chronological considerations throughout, particularly with regard to the dates of primary sources.

The final chapter, "Caves of the Nymphs and Votive Iconography," provides a detailed look at two important features of the nymphs' cult. The discussion of excavated nymph caves, arranged in roughly chronological order, examines the development and functions of these distinctive sites. The remainder of this chapter is a discussion of nymph iconography as it appears in the stone votive reliefs first popularized in fourth-century Attica. In this section, I examine the reliefs primarily from the perspective of content and function, and I am little concerned with the minutiae of attributions or dating (interested readers may further explore these issues through some of the sources in the bibliography). In order to provide context for the reader, I survey the iconographic antecedents of the votive reliefs, but considerations of space prevent a full treatment of the ways in which nymphs were visually represented in antiquity. Further iconographic information is scattered throughout the other sections, especially the geographical survey.

The chronological limits of the book are the eighth century B.C.E. through the Hellenistic period. Archaeological and art-historical evidence of the Roman period has generally been excluded, except where it could be assumed to cast light on previous ages (in this category, I would place, for example, the dedications to the nymphs in Roman Lykia and the funerary monument of Isidora in Egypt). Similarly, there has been no attempt at comprehensive coverage of Latin or late antique literature, but certain essential texts, such as Porphyry's *Cave of the Nymphs* or Longus' *Daphnis and Chloë*, receive selective treatment.

Like many authors of books on classical subjects, I have failed to achieve consistency in the transliteration of Greek names. Generally, I prefer a direct transliteration, but several familiar names retain familiar Latinized spellings (Delphi, Corinth, Muses, Oedipus). Names of ancient authors and titles keep the Latinized spelling commonly used in reference works. All dates are B.C.E. unless otherwise specified, and all translations are my own except where otherwise noted.

Writing a manuscript is a solitary enterprise, but many people contribute to the making of a book. I owe thanks to the Kent State University Research Council and the Center for Hellenic Studies, which supported my scholarly activities. The interlibrary loan staff at KSU were extraordinarily helpful during the five years it took to prepare this book. Rosa Commisso and Mark Rubin helped me to obtain photographs. Professor Hans R. Goette of the Deutsches Archäologisches Institut (DAI) generously offered me photos from his private collection. Rick Newton helped me with modern Greek. Christina Clark supplied useful references and encouragement. Finally, I would like to thank my dear husband, Bob, for his love and support.

August 2000   J. L.
Kent, Ohio

CONTENTS

GREEK NYMPHS

1 | WHAT IS A NYMPH?

1.1 Toward a Taxonomy

Scholars face a taxonomic dilemma in discussing the female figures of Greek mythology and cult. If the female under discussion is not a well-recognized goddess, one must decide (in the absence of convenient labeling by the ancient sources) whether to refer to her as a mortal woman (that is, a heroine), as a nymph, or as a member of some other group. Did the Greeks make a significant conceptual distinction between heroines and nymphs, and if so, what factors were used to distinguish them? No detailed discussion of these questions exists, and the matter of nomenclature has so far been idiosyncratic. It is, of course, made more tricky by the ambiguity of the term *numphê*, which can refer not only to the minor female divinities of the wild places but also to any nubile woman or, more commonly, to a bride.[1] The semantics of the term in the context of marriage is very close to the English *bride*, which describes a woman's status during limited periods both before and after her wedding. There is no necessary qualification of virginity. Occasionally, a *numphê* may be a mature, even matronly woman. In the *Odyssey*, Penelope is addressed as *numphê* by Eurykleia, and on classical Attic reliefs dedicated to the nymphs, the conventions permitted sculptors to show the three nymphs as women of various ages (though never as aged crones). The crucial point is that, when applied to a mortal woman, the term *numphê* points to her status as a sexual being.[2]

The Greeks at all periods do seem to have recognized a distinction between mythological females who were to be understood as mortal women and those who were divine nymphs, even when they did not invoke the terms *nymph* or *heroine*. In the sphere of cult, the same distinction applied. Below are enumerated the main criteria on which I base my understanding of this distinction.

1. Terminology used by ancient sources. Surprisingly often, the Greek sources take the trouble to identify nymphs. The clues are easy to miss if, for example, one passes over the formula "daughter of Asopos" without realizing that the father mentioned is a river god. More often, the terms *naiad* and *nymph* are juxtaposed in order to make the sense unmistakable. This practice begins in Homer and continues as a habit of diction through late authors. Similarly, certain names are typical of nymphs, particularly names containing the element *naïs* (naiad) or those ending in the suffix *-rhoê*, so that they describe the flowing movement of water. Such etymologies are suggestive, but not infallible, indicators.

2. Parentage. Nymphs are described with great frequency as the daughters of Zeus, of Ge, or of various river gods. Acheloös, to some degree a generalized river god, often figures as the father, but many others are also invoked, depending on the region. Heroines, on the other hand, are normally the daughters of heroes. One gray area in this regard, discussed below, involves the daughters of primordial and indigenous kings, such as the Danaids and the daughters of Kekrops.

3. Mortality and the death narrative. While the ultimate mortality of nymphs was debated among ancient authors (1.4.1, 2.4), it was clear to the ancients that they enjoyed a superhuman lifespan far outstripping that of mortal men and women. For practical purposes, they were immortal, while heroines were all too easily killed. In the myths of heroines, as in those of heroes, the manner and location of death is often a matter of great interest. This mythic emphasis on death is complemented by the focus of heroic cults at what were believed to be the tombs of the heroes and heroines.

4. Gender restrictions and vulnerability to mortal men. The nymph is a highly ambiguous figure. Though sexually desirable, she is usually free of the familial restrictions applied to mortal women and can rarely be fully domesticated. Nymphs may be sexually promiscuous, and they often act as the aggressors in ephemeral affairs with mortals. Furthermore, such affairs can be deadly to the male, as the cases of Daphnis and Rhoikos show. Unlike nymphs, mythological heroines who indulge in promiscuity or violence are usually punished in one fashion or another. Moreover, the narratives of cult heroines often emphasize their passive availability to men's use and their vulnerability to male violence.[3]

5. Role in heroic genealogies and narrative flexibility. The nymph often played a role in local genealogies as the earliest, autochthonous ancestor and provided a link to and an implicit claim upon the land and its resources. Nymphs likewise seem to figure significantly in mythic genealogies that deal with the period of the Great Flood and with colonization. The activities or characters of such nymphs are seldom described in a detailed narrative. This

is in contrast to heroines, who may be virgins, wives, or crones, admirable or villainous, and who play detailed roles in the local myths.

6. Association with a water source. Nymphs regularly personify and inhabit springs, rivers, and lakes. One of their main mythic and cultic functions is to provide fresh water. The same is not true of heroines, though they are sometimes associated with springs. When this is the case, there may be a parallel tradition that involves a tomb.[4]

7. Special functions in relation to the gods. A female who is part of Artemis' or Dionysos' mythic retinues or who takes part in the care of infant gods is likely to be a nymph. While the cult of heroines usually exists within a familial context, so that they are worshiped in conjunction with a husband or son, nymphs are associated with Hermes, Apollo, Pan, the river god Acheloös, and other deities. Their cult organization is not analogous to the family but to the relationship between a god and his *thiasos* or the chorus leader and chorus.

8. Cultic functions. Comparison of the discernable functions of nymph and heroine cults reveals some overlap. This is not surprising: Greek deities presided over a limited number of timeless human concerns, and no sharp division of labor existed. The main area of overlap encompasses human fertility, childbirth, and childcare. This kourotrophic function can be further divided into concern for young children and concern for those who are approaching adulthood, a group of special interest to the community as future warriors and fertile wives.[5] These concerns form a spectrum of life experiences with birth at one end and entry into adult status at the other. The participation of nymphs at each stage of this process is well documented (3.2). Heroines may play similar roles, especially when concerns about nurturance are given a civic focus, and the association of heroines with the Attic Arrhephoria and Arkteia has been much discussed.[6]

Some important divergences in function can also be discerned between the two groups. Nymphs, because of their association with springs, are often healing deities. Healing gods as a rule are close to a water source, preferably one that is heated or has interesting mineral properties, such as the sulfurous springs of the Anigrid nymphs at Samikon. Though there are several examples of heroes who heal, there is little evidence for heroine healers; Kearns suggests that this gap corresponds to the societal restraints on female physicians.[7] Another area that nymphs normally do not share with heroines is that of inspiration and, to a lesser extent, divination.

9. Physical setting and significance of the cult places. Heroines' tombs and shrines, like those of heroes, tend to be strategically located in central spots within the city walls, usually in the agora or, occasionally, at gates as protective guardians. Sometimes, they are literally focal points of the city. The tomb of Antinoë, founder of the city of Mantineia, was the *hestia koinê*, the "public hearth."[8] The cult places of nymphs, on the other hand, are as a rule associated with natural features: rivers, caves, and springs. Many, if not most, nymph cults are rural (unsurprising in view of their importance in pastoral

life), and the fact that they are tied to naturally occurring caves and water sources limits their spatial flexibility. However, it is too simplistic to say that nymphs are rural and heroines are urban, for exceptions abound.

Both nymphs and heroines contribute to the community's sense of itself in history (through the presence in the community of well-known water sources or natural objects and of heroic monuments, respectively). On the other hand, heroines are more likely to have civic functions of little concern to nymphs. The political importance of heroic relics is well recognized, and the relics of Alkmene and Hippodameia were prized and disputed in the same way as those of Orestes.

10. Objects commemorating cult. For fourth-century Attica, especially, two separate series of votive reliefs with well-developed iconography can be compared: one for heroic figures and one for nymphs. Sculptural conventions oppose the domestic setting of a banquet for heroic figures with natural settings in caves for nymphs, and familial relationships with "choric" ones. The fourth-century calendars of the Attic demes Erchia and Marathon honor nymphs and heroines separately, which suggests that even in the case of localized anonymous figures, the distinction still holds.[9]

11. Other narrative or cultic motifs. Satyrs or silens, herding and pastoralism, caves, trees, bees, and honey are all common motifs in the myths and cults of nymphs. None of these criteria should be employed alone or applied too rigidly, but taken as a whole they can provide a workable method for us to distinguish nymphs from heroines as well as from various minor goddesses, and they indicate that the Greeks generally did the same. Of course, there are hybrid cases of female figures who exhibit some characteristics of both nymph and heroine; there is no use attempting to force such individuals into one category or the other. Again, our picture of most mythic and cultic figures is built up from various ancient sources, which may or may not agree on essential points.

As mentioned above, the daughters of early kings are often ambiguous figures. In *Greek Heroine Cults*, I classified Aglauros, Pandrosos, and Herse as heroines because of their conformity to an Attic and Boiotian pattern in which the king's daughters willingly sacrifice themselves to save the city.[10] Yet the daughters are nymphlike in their association with Pan's sanctuary on the north slope of the Akropolis (4.2.1). The daughters of Danaus are closely associated with water sources and the myth of a drought in the Argolid. Amymone, in particular, shows several nymphlike characteristics. There is a spring or stream Amymone in which maidens bathe for ritual purposes. Amymone was sent to find water, pursued by a lusty satyr (a motif borrowed from the early iconography of nymphs), and impregnated by Poseidon, who showed her the springs of Lerna as a reward for her favors (4.4.2).

Dirke is another good example of a hybrid type. Dirke is a river that flows through Thebes and, in some accounts, a spring. She is described as a daughter of Acheloös by Euripides. Yet Dirke also infiltrates human genealogies as the wife of Lykos and rival of Antiope. She has an important death narrative, the story that she was trampled beneath a bull in punishment for her cruelty to Antiope. Finally, she had a tomb in Thebes, a secret spot where the old archon passed on his office to the new. Thus, Dirke with her human genealogy, tomb, and civic importance ends up looking more like a heroine than a nymph.[11]

Kallisto is often considered a nymph because of her companionship with Artemis. Yet Kallisto's tomb was a cult place in Arkadia; the ancient sources reflect the confusion over her status (4.4.3). Kallisto illustrates another problem in identifying nymphs: local goddesses were sometimes assimilated into the Olympian pantheon by demotion to the rank of nymph. This appears to be the case for Kallisto as well as for certain Kretan nymphs, such as Diktynna or Britomartis, both of whom seem to have been cult figures supplanted by Artemis.

Female pluralities, particularly triads, are ubiquitous in Greek mythology and cult. Some of these, like the daughters of Proitos or Minyas, are mortal women, and others are divine. The Okeanids are the daughters of the primordial river Okeanos and are hence an early generation of nymphs. Okeanids appear occasionally in myths (most notably as the companions of Persephone before her abduction), figure rarely in cult, and serve mainly as genealogical starting points.[12] Nereids are the daughters of the sea god Nereus and are the marine counterpart of the nymphs who live in springs and woods. The most famous of the Nereids is Thetis, who has an important cosmological status as well as being the mother of Achilles. The Nereids share many features with the nymphs who live on land, particularly their love of the dance and their occasional liaisons with mortals. I do not treat the Nereids at length in this book, because a detailed study of them already exists.[13] The Pleiades are the daughters of the Titans Atlas and Pleione. Their status as primordial figures is consistent with what we know of nymphs. Maia, the mother of Hermes, is a Pleiad whose name means "nurse." The Pleiads as a group are especially important in the genealogies of the Peloponnese (4.4.3), Samothrace, Boiotia, and Euboia. Sources disagree on the parentage of the Hesperides, though they always favor primordial deities, such as Night, Hesperis, and Atlas. These maidens, with the serpent Ladon, were the guardians of a tree of golden apples, located in the famous garden of the Hesperides at the western border of the river Okeanos, given to Hera as a wedding gift. Like other female pluralities, they were famous for their singing. Apollonius of Rhodes regarded them as tree nymphs and goddesses of vegetation.[14]

The Muses, Charites, and Horai are groups closely allied to the nymphs, and they fulfill under other names many of the functions otherwise attributed to nymphs (e.g., causing the crops to ripen or producing inspiration). They are primarily cultic entities, though we do find some mythic mentions of their choruses and their function as escorts of the gods and goddesses. There can be little doubt that the Muses and the Charites developed from the same ancestral stock as the nymphs and are in fact more specialized members of the same general group. Both had localized cults that spread within limited areas, yet they became known on a Panhellenic scale at an early date. The Muses' function (4.3.1, 4.7.1) as the catalysts of divine inspiration correlates with aspects of the more humble phenomenon of nympholepsy, and their associations with mountains, springs, and the pastoral milieu are definitely nymphlike.[15]

Later in this book, I discuss the convergence of nymph and Muse in Thrace, Attica, Boiotia, Lydia, Lykia, and Sicily. The Charites, or Graces, had important cults at Athens, Orchomenos, and Paros. Like the nymphs, they act as companions and attendants of certain Olympian deities, particularly Aphrodite and Hermes. They, too, are goddesses of vegetative abundance and moisture as well as creative inspiration. The most striking correspondences between Charites and nymphs, however, appear in iconography, where both groups are depicted as dancing triads. Charites and nymphs occasionally appear together in both poetry and iconography.[16] The Horai, or Seasons, said by Hesiod to be daughters of Zeus and Themis, resemble the Charites but are closer to simple personifications of natural abundance. They, too, act as escorts of the gods, and Homer describes them opening the gates of the sky for Hera. Like the nymphs and Charites, they are associated with weddings, childcare, and choruses.[17] Female pluralities are further discussed in the section on votive iconography (5.2).

1.2 Nymphs in the Landscape

In the Greek imagination, nymphs are inseparable from the landscape. To a greater degree than most other Greek deities, they are closely associated with certain topographical features. The most basic of these is the spring, for nymphs are above all deities of water. While many nymph names contain the transparent root -rhoê (e.g., Kallirhoë, "lovely flowing"; Okyrhoë, "swift flowing"), derivations from Indo-European roots describing the properties of running water have been proposed for nymph names as diverse as Peirene, Salmakis, Neda, Gargaphia, and Arethousa.[18] Nymphs are thought to inhabit all watery places, and the many collective designations for nymphs include those of the rivers (potamêides, epipotamides), springs (naiades, krênaiai), marshes (limnaiai, limnades, heleionomoi), and water in general (hudriades, ephudriades).[19] Although most of these terms are attested only after the classical period, the term naiad (naïs is related to the Greek verb naô, "flow") is used from the time of Homer forward as a substitute or qualifier for numphê.[20] From Homer to the late epigrams in the Greek Anthology, nymphs are consistently the inhabitants of water sources and providers of fresh water. Their cultural significance thus stretches far beyond the spring itself to all the symbolic and practical uses of water.[21]

The spring might be described as the microhabitat of the nymph; if this is so, the macrohabitat is the mountain, which is regularly defined in both ancient and modern Greece not by a specific height but by its opposition to "the plain." A "mountain," *oros*, need be little more than a hill in terms of altitude. Yet *oros* carries a consistent range of associations in Greek thought. In myth and cult, it is regularly the meeting place of gods and mortals (Hesiod and the Muses or Anchises and Aphrodite) and a place where societal norms undergo temporary reversal, as in Dionysiac revels. It is space beyond, and contrasted with, urban areas.[22] It is the setting for many activities of economic importance. To take Attica as an example, Parnes (like Pelion in Thessaly) was a source of timber and charcoal; Pentelikon and Hymettos were sources of marble; Hymettos was a site for apiculture. The economic significance of mountains also lay in the age-old practice of pastoral transhumance.[23] Herders of sheep and goats grazed their stock on the plain during the colder half of the year (September through March), and during the hot months, when the lower areas were barren and dry, they moved to the higher altitudes where green plants and water could still be found.

Goats and, to a lesser extent, sheep can be grazed well in the rocky scrub and wooded areas of the mountain slopes. They share part of this habitat with bees, who are dependent on the wildflowers in the open areas like the slopes of Hymettos. Finally, the hunt took place in the wild mountain spaces, particularly in the pine and oak woods. The nymphs are associated with all of these occupations at one time or another. The activities of herding, beekeeping, tree cutting, hunting, and even quarrying might fall under their purview because of their spatial and conceptual ties to the *oros*. Homer calls them *orestiades numphai*, and we hear later of *oressigonoi numphai* (mountain-born nymphs) and *oreades*.[24]

The third specific landscape feature associated with nymphs is the cave (also, of course, a feature of the *oros*). Geology has played a serendipitous role here, for the rocky karst landscape of Greece is riddled with caves created by the action of water (5.1). Caves large and small are likely to contain springs, and in fact the cave is the most common cult site of the nymphs, although by no means belonging exclusively to them. Again, caves were used in antiquity both as convenient homes for bees, who require shelter plus a water source, and as temporary shelters for herders and quarrymen. Caves had a symbolic value out of proportion to their minor economic value: they regularly appear in mythology as the birthplaces and homes of deities and monsters, the sites for sexual intercourse (usually of an illicit character), and the spots where heroic infants are exposed.[25] The nymphs, as cave deities, figure in many of these stories.

Finally, certain places characterized by abundant water, shade, and vegetation, often semicultivated vegetation, were imbued with the nymphs' presence. These places were above all pleasing to the senses; they invited passersby to stop and refresh themselves. The traditional motif of the *locus amoenus*, or pleasant spot, goes back to Hesiod's description of his midday rest beside a cooling spring.[26] Hesiod himself does not mention the nymphs, but many later versions of the *locus amoenus* include them. Homer, for his part, uses the characteristic triad of spring, cave, and vegetation, particularly poplar trees, to describe the lovely abodes of Kalypso, the Ithakan nymphs, and the nymphs of Goat Island, opposite the Kyklopes (1.4.1).

The classic example of a *locus amoenus* is Plato's description in the *Phaedrus* of a pleasant spot beside the Ilissos River. Sokrates and his companions reach a certain place marked by a plane tree and a spring, a shrine for the nymphs and Acheloös (the generalized river god who often appears with them in cultic contexts). Both the landscape and the time of day are significant. The plane trees and their cool shade, the riverbank, the grassy slope, the sound of cicadas all combine to create an inviting place to rest. The hour of midday, when one is inclined to seek shade beneath a tree, is also the hour when divine epiphanies are most likely.[27]

Such a place as this is never without a divine presence, which accounts for the appeal of the landscape and its strong influence upon the susceptible observer. As Sokrates says, "Truly the place seems divine [*theios*], so do not be surprised if I often seem to be *numpholêptos* as my discourse progresses, for I am already almost uttering dithyrambics."[28] The term *numpholêptos*, or "seized by the nymphs," has several possible meanings, but in this case it describes an access of poetic inspiration brought on by Sokrates' surroundings. Contrary to his usual custom of questioning his interlocutors, he is voluble, expressing himself in an elevated poetic fashion. The close relationship between poetic inspiration and prophecy in Greek culture is well known, and nympholepsy could also be manifested as a prophetic gift (1.3).

Any spot that is refreshingly cool, green, and pleasing to the eye might be the abode of nymphs. According to Dionysius of Halikarnassos, each natural space has a divinity appropriate to it. The spaces that belong particularly to nymphs, he says, are meadows and verdant areas. Some of these spots were unmarked places in the wild, but more often there was minimal cultivation and improvement on nature: the *pêgê*, or spring, in its natural state might become a *krênê*, a "fountain" with a basin or cistern.[29] There might be a shrine, an altar, or a grove set apart by a low wall as a sacred area. Such places were gardens of the nymphs, a more overtly erotic concept, which overlaps with that of the *locus amoenus*. Often the garden was located at the mouth of a cave, an arrangement well attested in both literature and cult.

With the "dear nymphs," unlike the Olympian gods, one could feel an intimate bond, and the nymphs had a sensual, sexual aura shared by none of the Olympian goddesses except Aphrodite. Aphrodite too was worshiped in gardens, and the fertile, moist parts of the landscape were associated with female anatomy in a metaphor that is probably universal. The words *kêpos* (garden), *leimôn* (meadow), *delta*, and *pedion* (plain) were all informal terms that referred to the female genitalia, and maidens picking flowers in meadows, like Kore or Europe, are archetypes of sexual vulnerability.[30]

The nymphs, as providers of water, are naturally associated with all types of vegetation, including grasses, flowers, and, above all, trees. The oak, the plane tree, and the black poplar are their special favorites, the latter two species being most abundant beside rivers and springs. While hamadryads and dryads (2.4) are most often mentioned in the late sources, we also hear of elm and ash nymphs (*pteleades*, *meliai*) as well as nymphs connected with fruit, nut, and other trees.[31] Other nymphs associated with vegetation include Syrinx (reed), Leiriope (lily), the Ionides (violets), Rhodos (rose), and the Pterides (ferns).[32]

Mnesimachus of Phaselis, with the gusto for classification characteristic of the Hellenistic period, comments that some of the nymphs are heavenly (presumably the Pleiades or Hyades), some are upon the earth, some are in the rivers, some on marshes, and some in the sea.[33] The tendency of generalizing late sources is to classify nymphs by the landscape features they inhabited, and while this concept certainly existed from Homer's time onward, we should also keep in mind the local character of nymphs. In poetry and cult, they were just as likely to be described with reference to specific rivers, islands, or mountains. Examples discussed in this book include the Leibethrides, Kithaironides, Anigrides, Amnisides, and Asopides.

1.3 Nympholepsy and Divination

The attribution of divinatory powers to the nymphs or to those inspired by them was not uncommon in the Greek world. The nymphs' fundamental association with water, the vector of prophecy and inspiration, and their close association with the mantic god Apollo were both salient factors. In a fragment of Aeschylus, we hear of nymphs who are *namerteis*, truthful or infallible. The word is also a favorite epithet for the watery prophets Proteus and Nereus.[34] Prophetic nymphs, though not abundant in mythology, appear regularly, including Daphnis, the nymph who first prophesied at Delphi before Apollo's arrival; Erato, the Arkadian nymph who gave oracles of Pan; and Oinone, the nymph who foretold her lover, Paris', death. The mothers of prophets tend to be nymphs, as Teiresias' mother is Chariklo, the favorite nymph of Athena.

Few actual oracles of the nymphs, in the sense of sanctuaries where oracular responses could be obtained, are known. An outstanding example is the oracle at the Korykian cave of the nymphs at Delphi (5.1.5). Amandry, the excavator, argued that the 23,000 astragaloi deposited at the cave had served an oracular function.[35] Astragaloi, the "knucklebones" of sheep and goats, were used for both gaming and divination in a manner similar to dice. Children formed collections of them, and they are found as grave gifts and as occasional dedications in sanctuaries. But in any sanctuary with such a huge number of astragaloi, the likelihood is that their dedication as gifts was incidental to their main purpose as divinatory tools. In antiquity, people consulted astragaloi as they might now use tarot cards or read tea leaves. The use of astragaloi, however, was a poor person's method of divination, much in keeping with the other offerings at the cave, which were almost uniformly humble and of poor quality. Those who could not afford consultation at the oracle of Apollo made the journey up to the cave to consult the nymphs, perhaps in conjunction with Hermes.

At the end of the Homeric *Hymn to Hermes*, Apollo bestows upon Hermes certain oracular bee maidens as a sort of consolation prize for his refusal to let the younger god share in his own mantic privileges. These three sisters live "beneath a ridge of Parnassos" and teach a form of divination that Apollo practiced as a boy when he still worked as a herdsman. Apollo cedes this method to his younger brother, Hermes, along with dominion over domestic animals but denies to him the loftier mantic privilege: knowledge of the will of Zeus. These bee maidens have long been identified with the Thriai, Parnassian nymphs who nursed Apollo and were the personification of divination with pebbles, *thriai*.[36] But the bee maidens are more probably the Korykian nymphs, whose cave corresponds to the *Hymn*'s description of an oracle near Delphi but "apart from" Apollo. Myths that identify bees with nymphs or that make bees the nymphs' proxies are plentiful enough to make this explanation plausible.[37]

In Apollodorus' version of the myth, Hermes trades his shepherd's pipes for Apollo's golden wand, which Apollo owned when he herded cattle, plus the rights to divination by pebbles.[38] Hermes' role as the god of cleromancy, a humble form of divination with small objects, such as lots, pebbles, dice, or astragaloi, fits the evidence from the cave well, but the oracle mentioned in the *Hymn* works only through the agency of prophetic bees, who must be given offerings of honey. Visitors to the Korykian cave probably began their consultation by making a libation of this liquid, then asked a question and cast their astragaloi in order to receive a simple yes or no answer. It is also possible that bees, whether wild or domesticated, inhabited the cave and played some role in the divination process.

The only other historical example of a nymph sanctuary that served as an oracle is the nymphaion at Apollonia in Illyria, which provided yes or no answers to petitioners who threw incense into its fires (4.5.3). Far from being the products of a fixed sanctuary, oracles inspired by nymphs were much more likely to circulate as verse collections under the name of the nympholept prophet Bakis. There were supposedly several individuals called Bakis, so that the name is actually a categorical term for male prophets, just as Sibyl is more a designation of occupation than a personal name and was applied to several different female prophets. The oldest of the Bakides was from Eleon in Boiotia and was inspired by the nymphs. Prophets called Bakis were also linked to Attica, Lokris, and Arkadia.[39] Though actual Bakides probably gave oracles firsthand in the early archaic period, by the fifth and fourth centuries the Bakides and Sibyls themselves had been largely replaced by wandering chresmologues, oracle mongers who compiled and offered access to collections of oracles attributed to famous seers. Attitudes toward the chresmologues varied. More sophisticated observers, such as the comic poets, made a practice of lampooning oracle mongers, their influence over the demos, and their manipulation by politicians. Herodotus quotes with credulous approval several oracles of Bakis that refer to the outcome of specific battles in the Persian war.[40]

Several further references to oracles of Bakis are preserved in the comedies of Aristophanes, most notably in the *Peace*, in which the chresmologue Hierokles arrives and declares the oracular authority of the nymphs in order to pour gloom over Trygaios' celebration of the return of Peace. These comic oracles take riddling and somewhat hackneyed forms, which are nevertheless not far in style from genuine examples: "timorous gulls, you have trusted the fox cubs" and "it is not pleasing to the blessed immortals that we cease the battle cry, until the wolf and the sheep be wedded." In the *Knights*, Kleon/Paphlagon attempts to use a collection of Bakid oracles to maintain control over Demos.[41] Such collections of oracles, which drew heavily upon bodies of popular wisdom, such as proverbs, could be easily interpreted and manipulated to serve political purposes. At the same time, the public had an inexhaustible appetite for supernatural pronouncements and predictions, and oracles were also held in high regard by many statesmen. Access to and control over oracles was a source of political prestige and authority throughout antiquity but appears to have been especially important in archaic Greece. The Athenian tyrant Peisistratos' political use of oracles and amassing of oracle collections is well known; he also is said to have gone by the epithet Bakis, as if he himself were a nympholept.[42] That the tyrant might have wished to take on himself the authority of the nymphs, in much the same way he did that of Athena, is not surprising.

This brings us to the term *nympholepsy*, which is a blanket word that can be used to describe several overlapping concepts. First and foremost, as Connor has shown, the term refers to a heightening of awareness and elevated verbal skills believed to result from the nymphs' influence on a susceptible individual. It is in this sense that Boiotian Bakis was inspired to produce oracles, and it is this form of nympholepsy to which Sokrates alludes when he playfully announces that he is on the verge of speaking in dithyrambs under the influence of the nymphs of Ilissos (1.2). In such contexts, poetry and prophecy, always closely related, cannot be separated, and the nympholept, like the poet, the Sibyl, or the Pythia, experiences a state of divine madness but not one that his or her contemporaries would regard as pathological. Similarly, Amelasagoras (or Melesagoras) of Eleusis, the reputed author of a history of Attica, claimed to be wise (*sophos*) and prophetic (*mantikos*) because he was *ek numphôn katochos*, "overpowered by the nymphs."[43]

In the postclassical period, however, possession by the nymphs began to be seen as an abnormal and dangerous state hardly distinguishable from illness, and this idea is the direct precursor of the fear, prominent in modern Greek folklore, of being beaten or stricken by the *neraïdes* (2.1, 2.3.2). Another sense of the term nympholepsy, also best attested in the postclassical period, is that of physical rather than mental rapture by the nymphs. In mythology and cult, we have Hylas, Bormos, and Dryope, who were snatched away into the company of the nymphs, and in funerary inscriptions, we find that children or young women were sometimes said to have been so abducted or received (2.3.1).

Finally, the term nympholept could be used to describe someone who exhibited an unusual degree of religious devotion to the nymphs. This state need not exclude the qualities of heightened sensation and expression described above but was not manifested primarily in poetic or prophetic utterances. Instead, it was evident in a person's extended commitment to the maintenance of a specific cult of the nymphs, especially through the embellishment of cave sanctuaries. The investment of time, resources, and physical labor needed for such devotions, which were highly personal in character, would have set the nympholept apart from the rest of the population.

Epimenides of Phaistos, the famous wonder worker of the archaic age, appears to have been a nympholept of sorts. His 57-year slumber in a cave is reminiscent of modern Greek folktales about men held captive in caves by the *neraïdes*. According to one account, he wished to build a sanctuary of the nymphs (a behavior typical of the nympholept) but heard a voice saying, "not a *hieron* of the nymphs, but of Zeus." Other stories have him receiving magic food from the nymphs, which he kept in a cow's hoof. This food, perhaps honey, allowed him to subsist with no other form of nutrition and was completely absorbed by his body. Finally, as in the case of many other prophets, his mother, Balte, was reputedly a nymph.[44] The neo-Pythagorean holy man Apollonios of Tyana argued that water was superior to wine as a beverage to facilitate divination "for we are nympholepts and Bacchants of sobriety."[45]

For a number of years, around the turn of the fifth century, the Attic cave of Vari (5.1.9, figure 1.1) was the haunt of a Theran immigrant named Archedamos, who thought of himself as a nympholept. Archedamos did a great deal of physical labor in order to improve the cave, cutting stairs, inscriptions, and sculptures into the rock, including a self-portrait. This relief, clearly an amateur work, shows him wearing a short chiton and holding stone-cutting tools. It is inscribed twice with his name, which appears a total of six times on inscriptions from the cave. Two rupestral examples appear near the first landing as one descends into the cave. One simply says "Archedamos the Theran," and the other states, "Archedamos the Theran, a nympholept, at the instructions of the nymphs [*phradaisi numphôn*] worked out this cave." A block of stone found near the large enthroned figure in the south chamber was probably once set up near the entrance to the cave. Each side recounts different activities of the nympholept. The first says that "Archedamos the Theran cultivated a garden for the nymphs." The other side, more difficult to interpret, says that Archedamos built a dwelling for the nymph (singular) and further describes him as *cholonodches*, an unknown word. Connor suggests that it might re-

Figure 1.1 Vari cave: Archedamos on left. Deutsches Archäologisches Institut, Athens.

fer to bile, *cholos*, since an Aristotelian medical text attributes inspired states to an abundance of hot bile.[46] Archedamos could have been referring to what he considered the physical basis of his condition, while the spiritual basis was possession by the nymphs. All three of the lengthier inscriptions have heightened, poetic diction and hexametric cadences. The inscriptions show variations in both dialectal and letter forms, which suggest that they were carved over a long period. Yet all could be accommodated within the lifetime of Archedamos.

Certain features of the evidence are worthy of comment. First, Archedamos seems proud of his physical exertions on behalf of the nymph(s); he does not share the elite aversion to manual labor. We do not know whether he was a freed slave or simply an immigrant, whether he supported himself through some trade or lived at the cave and was supported by the offerings of visitors. In any case, both his metic status and his retreat to this isolated rural spot make him marginal to Athenian society. The cult he oversees seemingly has no civic, tribal, domestic, or deme affiliation. His marginality is typical of visionaries across cultures, who either belong to an outsider class in the first place or deliberately remove themselves from the mainstream. This separation, however, does not imply complete disengagement from society. The nympholept, like possessed persons in other cultures, had a recognized social role that was enhanced by his withdrawal and isolation. Connor plausibly suggests that Archedamos, as a nympholept, prophesied for pilgrims to the cave.[47]

Second, Archedamos speaks twice of plural nymphs, at whose suggestion he worked out the cave and for whom he tended the garden, and once of an individual nymph for whom he built a dwelling. These activities have undertones that, in view of the erotic significance of gardens and enclosed chambers, might have been much more obvious to the ancients. One thinks both of Odysseus' sexual captivity in the cave and garden of Kalypso and of his building with his own hands a nuptial chamber and bed for his bride, the symbols of their marital intimacy. Onesagoras, another nympholept who filled a cave in third-century Cyprus with dedications to an individual nymph, referred to her as sister, daughter, and possibly as lover. Like Archedamos, Onesagoras created self-portraits, incised faces on the pots that he dedicated to the nymph. The nympholept's devotion is not self-effacing; on the contrary, he feels the need to proclaim his presence over and over, asserting the exclusive character of his relationship with the nymph(s).

Thessalian Pantalkes, a near-contemporary of Archedamos, similarly maintained a cave near Pharsalos and left inscriptions that detail his activities (5.1.6).[48] The earlier inscription, dating from the fifth century, announces that Pantalkes dedicated something ("this work" or, perhaps, "this tree") to the goddesses (i.e., the nymphs); a second sentence, difficult to interpret, mentions a laurel.[49] The later inscription belongs several decades later, sometime in the fourth century. Composed in dactylic hexameters of simple diction, it reads:

θεός
τύχα
Χαίρετε τοὶ προσιόντες, ἅπας θῆλύς τε καὶ ἄρσην,
ἄνδρες τε ἠδὲ γυναῖκες, ὁμῶς παῖδές τε κόραι τε,
χωρόνδ᾿ εἰς ἱερὸν Νύμφαις καὶ Πανὶ καὶ Ἑρμῆι,
Ἀπόλλωνι ἄνακτι καὶ Ἡρακλεῖ καὶ ἑταίραις,
Χίρωνος τ᾿ ἄντρον καὶ Ἀσκλαπίου ἠδ᾿ Ὑγιείας·
τούτων ἐστὶ τὸ χωρίον ἅπαν ἱαρωτά τ᾿ ἐν αὐτῶι
ἔμφυτα καὶ πίνακες καὶ ἀγάλματα δῶρα τε πολλά·
ἄνδρα δ᾿ ἐποίησαντ᾿ ἀγαθὸν Παντάλκεα Νύμφαι
τῶνδ᾿ ἐπιβαινέμεναι χώρων καὶ ἐπίσσκοπον εἶναι,
ὅσπερ ταῦτ᾿ ἐφύτευσε καὶ ἐξεπονήσατο χερσσίν,
ἀντίδοσαν, δ᾿ αὐτῶι βίον ἄφθονον ἤματα πάντα·
Ἡρακλέης μὲν ἔδωκ᾿ ἰσχύν, ἀρετήν τε κράτος τε
ὦιπερ τούσδε λίθους τύπτων ἐπόησ᾿ ἀναβαίνειν,
Ἀπόλλων δὲ δίδωσι καὶ υἱὸς τοῦδε καὶ Ἑρμῆς
αἰῶν᾿ εἰς τὸν ἄπαντα ὑγίειαν καὶ βίον ἐσθλόν,
Πὰν δὲ γέλωτα καὶ εὐφροσύνην ὕβριν τε δικαίαν,
Χίρων δ᾿ αὐτῶι δῶκε σοφόν τ᾿ ἦμεν καὶ ἀοιδόν·
ἀλλὰ τύχαις ἀγαθαῖς ἀναβαίνετε, θύετε πάντες,
εὔχεσθε, εὐφραίνεσθε· κακῶν δὲ ἐπίλησις ἀπάντων
ἐνθάδ᾿ ἔνεστ᾿, ἀγαθῶν δὲ..ρη πολέμοιο τε ν[ί]κη.

GOD
FORTUNE

Welcome visitors, every male and female,
men and women, boys and girls,
to a place holy to the Nymphs and Pan and Hermes,
Lord Apollo and Herakles and his companions [fem.],
the cave of Chiron, and of Asklepios and Hygeia.
Theirs is the place, and all the sacred things in it,
growing things and tablets and dedications and many gifts.
The Nymphs made Pantalkes a gentleman
they who walk these places; and made him overseer.
He tended these plants and shaped things with his hands
and in return they gave abundance for all his days.
Herakles gave him strength, excellence and power
with which he smote the stones and made a way up.
Apollo and his son Hermes give
health and prosperous living through the whole age;
Pan gave laughter and good cheer and righteous unrestraint;
Chiron gave him to be wise and a poet.
But go up with good fortunes. Let all sacrifice,
pray, and enjoy yourselves. Forgetfulness of all cares
is here, and a share of good things, and victory in strife.[50]

The first part of the inscription welcomes visitors and lists the deities who are honored in the cave. The second part recounts Pantalkes' role in the administration of the cave as a cult site: how he created a path to the cave opening, planted a garden outside it, and oversaw the votive offerings. The nymphs provided the original impetus for his actions, and other deities contributed to his efforts by giving him strength, health, a good living, and happiness. It has been suggested that Pantalkes and Archedamos are both legendary founder figures rather than historical persons, but their distinct, vivid personalities seem to belie this view. It is possible that some of the inscriptions were carved by followers rather than by the nympholepts themselves. Yet Pantalkes could have been the author of both of the inscriptions that bear his name, in spite of their apparent chronological separation. He might have begun his work as a young man with the shorter inscription and composed the longer one as a valedictory, summarizing his achievements and making it clear that he expected the cave to be maintained for posterity. (Onesagoras, the Cypriot devotee of the nymph at Kafizin, seems to have dedicated an inscribed pot after his retirement, in which he calls himself the good steward of the nymph.)[51] In that case, the age of the dedications in the cave, as at Vari, would indicate that votives were already being placed there when Pantalkes began his work.

Pantalkes does not refer to himself as a nympholept, and he seems more gregarious and self-confident than Archedamos, with his hearty invitation to visitors and his greater skill at versification. But, as in Archedamos' case, it was the nymphs who conferred a special status on Pantalkes, making him *anêr agathos* and *episkopos*. It is they who appear in the earlier inscription as the sole recipients of his attentions (the cults of the other deities must have accrued over the years as the cave's reputation grew). And, like Archedamos, he is proud of his physical labor. There have been attempts, none so far successful, to link the Vari and Pharsalos caves historically.[52] More likely than a direct influence from Thessaly to Attica is that there was a widespread, shared concept in the late fifth century of how devotion to the nymphs might manifest itself.

This religious mentality was still in force when Onesagoras worshiped a nymph at a cave in third-century Cyprus, though there are some noticeable differences. Onesagoras' cave, in spite of his own enthusiasm, did not become a place of pilgrimage like the caves of Vari and Pharsalos. The cult was of interest only within Onesagoras' own circle of associates and quickly faded when Onesagoras died (5.1.13). As late as the third century c.e., we find an unusual degree of devotion to the nymphs attested in the gravestone inscription of one Chrysogonos of Kos, who calls himself *latris numphôn*, "servant" of the nymphs.[53]

Gender and sexuality appear to be significant in the phenomenon of nympholepsy as a whole. It is certainly no coincidence that the male Bakid prophets were thought to be possessed by nymphs, while the Sibyls and the Pythia were possessed by Apollo. Possession may be understood in sexual terms, so that the possessing deity acts as an overmastering sexual partner (as in Vergil's famous description of the Sibyl's struggle with Apollo).[54] Obviously, male possession by female deities raises interesting questions of sex-role reversal. Though none of our sources explicitly address this aspect of nympholeptic prophecy, such a role reversal should not be surprising in view of similar reversals in the mythological material: not only is Hylas passively possessed by lustful nymphs, but Rhoikos and Daphnis are punished for indiscretions by their nymph mistresses (2.4.1, 2.5.1). For devotional nympholepts, similar dynamics might have been at work.[55] The use of titles such as *despotis* for the nymph and other language that suggests the subordination of the devotee to the nymphs' will might have had erotic connotations. There are no attested examples of female nympholepts except in the mythological and funerary materials, where they are thought of as joining the company of the nymphs.

One outstanding instance of nympholepsy remains to be discussed. Near Plataia on the border of Attica and Boiotia was a well-known cave of the nymphs, which today remains unidentified. According to Pausanias, it lay on Mount Kithairon about two miles down from the site of the altar for the Great Daidala. "There is the cave of the Kithaironides nymphs, called the Sphragidion, and there is a story that the nymphs used to give oracles [*manteusthai*] there in the old days." The cave came to the attention of authors like Pausanias not because of its oracles but because it figured in a Delphic oracle concerning the battle of Plataia. Upon Mardonios' invasion in 479, Aristides received a response from the Pythia assuring him that the Athenians would be victorious if they made prayers to Zeus, Hera Kithaironia, Pan, and the Sphragitic nymphs and sacrificed to seven heroes. These were all deities of the area around Plataia, where the battle was expected to take place.[56] After the war, the tribe Aiantis, because of its great valor in the battle, was chosen to conduct sacrifices for the Sphragitic nymphs on behalf of the whole city, with the victims and other paraphernalia provided at state expense. Thus, the state's interest in the cult developed only through a quirk of fate; had it not been for the war, the cave would have remained an obscure site of purely local interest, as described by Plutarch: "The cave was on one of the peaks of Kithairon facing the summer sunsets, and in it there was also an oracle [*manteion*] in former days. Many of the locals, whom they called nympholepts, were possessed [*kateichonto*]."[57]

This account is of particular interest because it brings together elements of the phenomenon of nympholepsy that remain separate in the rest of our evidence. Nympholepsy occurs as a result of the supernatural influence that emanates from a specific site, the Sphragidion. This recalls Sokrates' statement in the *Phaedrus* that his altered mental state was linked to the location itself: the shrine of the nymphs and Acheloös on the Ilissos River. As in that dialogue, not everyone who inhabits or visits the place is affected; only certain individuals seem susceptible to the state of nympholepsy. On the other hand, we hear of "many" possessed persons in connection with this cave, a fact that diverges significantly from the evidence of Archedamos, Pantalkes, and Onesagoras, all isolated individuals who associated themselves with caves. In the community around the Sphragidion, nympholepsy seems to have been, if not a group phenomenon, at least a recognized characteristic of the residents. Moreover, this characteristic probably worked to benefit the community, since outsiders would have visited and brought offerings for the purpose of consulting the oracle.

The name of the Sphragitic nymphs presents something of a mystery. Sphragidion, the name of the cave, derives from the word *sphragis*, "seal" or "signet ring." The same word is used in enigmatic fashion by Theognis, who speaks of placing a "seal" upon his utterances lest they be stolen or altered.[58] Ford has offered an interpretation of the Theognidean passage, which I think applies equally well to the Sphragitic nymphs. In his reading, the metaphorical application of the seal is not an assertion of authorship but of authority. The concern was not that verses be attributable to a specific author, but that their essential soundness, as products of divine inspiration, be identifiable.[59] Seals were used to guarantee the genuineness of documents, that of oracles in particular. The authenticity of oracles, which carried a great deal of political weight, was a matter of great moment in the archaic period. Hipparchos, for example, expelled the chresmologue Onomakritos from Athens when he was discovered tampering with an oracle of Musaios. Theognis, with regard to poetry, insists that no one shall "substitute an inferior thing for the genuine [*esthlon*] thing that is there." And later in the corpus, we hear of the duty owed by the *theoros* to whom an oracular response is entrusted: "You will not find any remedy if you add anything, nor will you escape from veering, in the eyes of the gods, if you take anything away." Poetic authority, which derives from the Muses, and oracular authority, which derives from other gods, such as Apollo or the nymphs, are two sides of the same coin.[60]

Thus it seems possible that the name applied to our nymphs and their cave referred specifically to their oracular authority. The symbolic power of the *sphragis* might also have been at work in the Korykian cave, where the excavators found an extraordinary accumulation of signet rings (5.1.5). These are uniformly of cheap quality, made of bronze or lead rather than gold and silver, but display a wide range of iconography, most of it not immediately relevant to the nymphs. Apparently, it was the dedication of the signet itself, not the scene upon it, that pleased the oracular goddesses.

1.4 Nymphs in Greek Poetry

1.4.1 *Homer, Hesiod, and the* Homeric *Hymns*

In the Homeric epics, our earliest literary sources, the nymphs already have most of their defining characteristics. The picture that we find in Homer, furthermore, proves to be remarkably stable through time, with only a few major developments occurring later. The word *numphê* is used from the beginning to mean both "bride" and "female water/landscape deity." In addition, both Helen and Penelope are addressed flatteringly as *numpha philê*, presumably referring to their status as sexually desirable wives.[61]

Toward the end of the *Iliad*, Zeus tells Themis to summon all the gods to a council. Even the gods who inhabit the surface of the earth are included, and virtually all come to the palace of Zeus on Olympos:

οὔτε τις οὖν ποταμῶν ἀπέην νόσφ' Ὠκεανοῖο,
οὔτ' ἄρα νυμφάων, αἵ τ' ἄλσεα καλὰ νέμονται
καὶ πηγὰς ποταμῶν καὶ πίσεα ποιήεντα. (Hom. *Il.* 20.7–9)

None of the rivers was absent, except Okeanos, nor any of the nymphs who inhabit the lovely groves and the springs of rivers and the grassy meadows.

The nymphs are listed together with the rivers, an association that will long continue. The homes of the nymphs are enumerated: groves, springs, and meadows. *Odyssey* 6.123–24 adds mountains to the formulaic list of places where one is likely to find nymphs. The standard Homeric parentage of the nymphs is provided somewhat earlier in this book, in the famous simile that compares Nausikaä among her maidens to Artemis surrounded by a chorus of nymphs:

τῇ δέ θ' ἅμα νύμφαι, κοῦραι Διὸς αἰγιόχοιο,
ἀγρονόμοι παίζουσι· γέγηθε δέ τε φρένα Λητώ·
πασάων δ' ὑπὲρ ἥ γε κάρη ἔχει ἠδὲ μέτωπα,
ῥεῖά τ' ἀριγνώτη πέλεται, καλαὶ δέ τε πᾶσαι· (Hom. *Od.* 6.105–8)

and with her dance the nymphs of the wild places, the daughters of aigis-bearing Zeus, and Leto is delighted in her heart; for above them all she holds her head and easily outshines them, though all are lovely.

The phrase "daughters of aigis-bearing Zeus" is the usual formula applied to the nymphs (though it is not exclusive to them), and the nymphs are provided no alternative genealogies in Homer except in special cases like those of Kalypso, whose father is Atlas, or the daughters of Helios, Phaëthousa and Lampetië.[62] The nymphs' association with Artemis will remain a fixture in epic contexts though rare in other genres and only occasionally attested in cult (3.2.2).

Returning to the *Iliad*, we find the earliest examples of what will later become a staple of folktales, the idea that nymphs sometimes couple with mortal men (2.2). Homer relates the genealogies of several Trojans and Trojan allies killed in battle, and he mentions that their parentage is unusual:

Δρῆσον δ᾽ Εὐρύαλος καὶ Ὀφέλτιον ἐξενάριξε·
βῆ δὲ μετ᾽ Αἴσηπον καὶ Πήδασον, οὕς ποτε νύμφη
νηῒς Ἀβαρβαρέη τέκ᾽ ἀμύμονι Βουκολίωνι.
Βουκολίων δ᾽ ἦν υἱὸς ἀγαυοῦ Λαομέδοντος
πρεσβύτατος γενεῇ, σκότιον δέ ἑ γείνατο μήτηρ·
ποιμαίνων δ᾽ ἐπ᾽ ὄεσσι μίγη φιλότητι καὶ εὐνῇ
ἡ δ᾽ ὑποκυσαμένη διδυμάονε γείνατο παῖδε. (Hom. *Il.* 6.20–26)

Now Euryalos slaughtered Opheltios and Dresos, and went after
Aisepos and Pedasos, whom the naiad nymph Abarbareë once bore to
noble Boukolion. Boukolion himself was the son of haughty
Laomedon, eldest born, but his mother conceived him in secrecy.
While herding his flocks he [Boukolion] made love with the nymph,
and she became pregnant and bore twin boys.

This is the first recorded use of *naïs* (naiad), a term indicating that Boukolion's
lover was a spring nymph. Boukolion, "the cowherd," was the illegitimate
son of the Trojan king Laomedon and the nymph Kalybe, according to
Apollodorus, and like his father sired offspring with a nymph (Abarbareë) in
an illicit encounter. Their sons, Aisepos and Pedasos, were eponyms of a river
and town in the Troad.[63] The description of Boukolion looks forward to
pastoral themes that would later become popular (4.9.1).

The motif of a mortal's sexual encounter with a naiad nymph recurs twice
more in the *Iliad*:

ἔνθα πολὺ πρώτιστος Ὀϊλῆος ταχὺς Αἴας
Σάτνιον οὔτασε δουρὶ μετάλμενος ὀξυόεντι
Ἠνοπίδην, ὃν ἄρα νύμφη τέκε νηῒς ἀμύμων
Ἤνοπι βουκολέοντι παρ᾽ ὄχθας Σατνιόεντος. (Hom. *Il.* 14.442–45)

First then, swift Aias, son of Oileus, rushed out and stabbed with his
sharp spear Satnios, Enops' son, whom the excellent naiad nymph
bore to Enops as he tended his herds by the Satnioeis River.

Ἰφιτίωνα
ἐσθλὸν Ὀτρυντεΐδην πολέων ἡγήτορα λαῶν,
ὃν νύμφη τέκε νηῒς Ὀτρυντῆϊ πτολιπόρθῳ
Τμώλῳ ὕπο νιφόεντι Ὕδης ἐν πίονι δήμῳ· (Hom. *Il.* 20.382–85)

[Achilles killed] Iphition, the noble son of Otrynteus and a lord
over many people, whom a naiad nymph bore to Otrynteus, sacker
of cities, under snowy Tmolos in the rich countryside of Hyde.

In all three of the passages I have cited, the nymphs or their offspring are
associated with specific local topography: the Satnioeis River, the eponyms
Aisepos and Pedasos, and Mount Tmolos in Lydia. In the *Iliad*, such encoun-

ters happen only to the Trojans and their allies and are absent from the genealogies given for the Achaians. Apparently, the motif of the mortal herdsman who is loved by a local nymph was at first confined to Asia Minor; Griffin has suggested that it is in origin a variation of the union of the Great Goddess with a mortal consort (2.5.2). Unions between nymphs and mortals, however, were not unknown to the Achaians, for Achilles was born of Peleus and the unwilling Nereid, Thetis.

In book 6 of the *Iliad*, we hear how Achilles killed Andromache's family, including her father:

κατὰ δ᾽ ἔκτανεν Ἠετίωνα,
οὐδέ μιν ἐξενάριξε, σεβάσσατο γὰρ τό γε θυμῷ,
ἀλλ᾽ ἄρα μιν κατέκηε σὺν ἔντεσι δαιδαλέοισιν
ἠδ᾽ ἐπὶ σῆμ᾽ ἔχεεν· περὶ δὲ πτελέας ἐφύτευσαν
νύμφαι ὀρεστιάδες, κοῦραι Διὸς αἰγιόχοιο. (Hom. *Il.* 6.416–20)

He killed Eëtion, but did not strip his armor, for he felt scruples at this. But he burned the body with its cunningly wrought armor, and piled a grave mound over it, and the mountain nymphs, daughters of aigis-bearing Zeus, planted elm trees about it.

The participation of the mountain nymphs in the hero's funeral is intriguing. Why did they honor Eëtion thus? Did Eëtion, like some of the other Asiatic noblemen, have a liaison with a nymph? Or is this an early example of the pathetic fallacy, whereby the natural world, personified in the nymphs, expresses its sorrow at his death? Certainly, the respect shown by the nymphs seems to parallel the actions of Achilles in seeing to Eëtion's funeral. Andromache's father was such a great man that even his enemy honored him, while the nymphs came out of the mountains to do the same. This passage is later imitated more than once, and the nymphs are said to plant trees on the graves of Protesilaus and other heroes (1.4.4).

In the last book of the *Iliad*, Achilles tells Priam the story of Lydian Niobe, who dared to compare herself to Leto and was punished by the loss of her children and by metamorphosis into a stone. Priam must eat in spite of his grief, for even Niobe once did so:

ἣ δ᾽ ἄρα σίτου μνήσατ᾽, ἐπεὶ κάμε δάκρυ χέουσα.
νῦν δέ που ἐν πέτρῃσιν ἐν οὔρεσιν οἰοπόλοισιν
ἐν Σιπύλῳ, ὅθι φασὶ θεάων ἔμμεναι εὐνὰς
νυμφάων, αἵ τ᾽ ἀμφ᾽ Ἀχελώϊον ἐρρώσαντο,
ἔνθα λίθος περ ἐοῦσα θεῶν ἐκ κήδεα πέσσει. (Hom. *Il.* 24.613–17)

But when she was worn out with weeping, she remembered her food. And now somewhere among the rocks, in the lonely mountains of Sipylos, where they say are the couches of the divine nymphs who dance around the river Acheloios, there even as a stone she nurses her sorrows from the gods.

Here again, the nymphs are at home beside mountain and river. They engage in one of their favorite activities, dancing, and they have "couches" or "beds," probably in a cave. The habitations of the nymphs were often imagined to contain furniture of a sort, perhaps suggested by the natural rock formations found in caves. This is the case with the cave of the nymphs on Thrinakia, the home of the Sun's cattle:

ἦμος δ᾽ ἠριγένεια φάνη ῥοδοδάκτυλος Ἠώς,
νῆα μὲν ὡρμίσαμεν, κοῖλον σπέος εἰσερύσαντες·
ἔνθα δ᾽ ἔσαν νυμφέων καλοὶ χοροὶ ἠδὲ θόωκοι. (Hom. Od.
   12.316–18)

As soon as early-born, rosy-fingered Dawn appeared, we dragged up our ship and drew her into a hollow cave, and there were the lovely dancing floors and seats of the nymphs.

And, again, in the cave of the nymphs on Ithake, there are wonderful furnishings:

αὐτὰρ ἐπὶ κρατὸς λιμένος τανύφυλλος ἐλαίη,
ἀγχόθι δ᾽ αὐτῆς ἄντρον ἐπήρατον ἠεροειδές,
ἱρὸν νυμφάων, αἳ νηϊάδες καλέονται.
ἐν δὲ κρητῆρές τε καὶ ἀμφιφορῆες ἔασι
λάϊνοι· ἔνθα δ᾽ ἔπειτα τιθαιβώσσουσι μέλισσαι.
ἐν δ᾽ ἱστοὶ λίθεοι περιμήκεες, ἔνθα τε νύμφαι
φάρε᾽ ὑφαίνουσιν ἁλιπόρφυρα, θαῦμα ἰδέσθαι·
ἐν δ᾽ ὕδατ᾽ ἀενάοντα. δύω δέ τέ οἱ θύραι εἰσίν,
αἱ μὲν πρὸς βορέαο καταιβαταὶ ἀνθρώποισιν,
αἱ δ᾽ αὖ πρὸς νότου εἰσὶ θεώτεραι· οὐδέ τι κείνῃ
ἄνδρες ἐσέρχονται, ἀλλ᾽ ἀθανάτων ὁδός ἐστιν. (Hom. Od.
   13.102–12)

At the head of the harbor is a long-leafed olive tree, and near it is a pleasant, shadowy cave sacred to the nymphs called naiads. In it are stone mixing bowls and jars and there too the bees store honey. And in the cave are long looms of stone, where the nymphs weave sea-purple cloth, a wonder to see, and there are ever-flowing springs. There are two doors: that toward the north wind is the way down for humans; but that toward the south wind is holy indeed. Men do not enter by that way, but it is the path of the immortals.

The elements of the Homeric nymph cave often reappear in later cult and literature. The nymphs' abode is always described as a pleasant, cool place. A tree or grove stands outside, while in or near the cave is a water source.

These scenes influenced the motif of the *locus amoenus* so familiar in later Greek literature. Here, too, for the first time, we see the close association of nymphs and bees in Greek thought. This link must be due to the fact that the wild bees' favorite homes were tree trunks and caves, also two principal haunts of nymphs. The two entrances, one for mortals and one for gods, reappear in later descriptions of nymph caves (1.4.5).

In the Ithakan portions of the *Odyssey*, we also get a first look at the cultic relationship between mortals and nymphs. As Odysseus begins to realize he has reached Ithake at last, Athena tells him that he will recognize his home beyond doubt by the landmark of the nymphs' cave:

> τοῦτο δέ τοι σπέος εὐρὺ κατηρεφές, ἔνθα σὺ πολλὰς
> ἔρδεσκες νύμφῃσι τεληέσσας ἑκατόμβας·
> τοῦτο δὲ Νήριτόν ἐστιν ὄρος καταειμένον ὕλῃ. (Hom. *Od.*
>   13.349–51)

This is the vaulted cave, where you used to offer to the nymphs many complete hekatombs; and here is Mount Neriton, clothed in trees.

According to Athena, it was Odysseus' regular practice to offer hekatombs, costly sacrifices that traditionally consisted of a hundred oxen. This is a generous offering indeed for nymphs, and one that is unparalleled in later literature and cult, though animal sacrifices for the nymphs are common enough. When Odysseus recognizes his home, he first kisses the earth, then prays to the nymphs:

> νύμφαι νηϊάδες, κοῦραι Διός, οὔ ποτ᾽ ἐγώ γε
> ὄψεσθ᾽ ὔμμ᾽ ἐφάμην· νῦν δ᾽ εὐχωλῆς ἀγανῇσι
> χαίρετ᾽· ἀτὰρ καὶ δῶρα διδώσομεν, ὡς τὸ πάρος περ,
> αἴ κεν ἐᾷ πρόφρων με Διὸς θυγάτηρ ἀγελείη
> αὐτόν τε ζώειν καί μοι φίλον υἱὸν ἀέξῃ. (Hom. *Od.* 13.356–60)

You naiad nymphs, daughters of Zeus, I never thought I would see you again, but now I greet you with loving prayers. And I will give gifts too, as before, if the daughter of Zeus, she that drives the spoil, will graciously allow me to live, and bring to manhood my dear son.

Clever Odysseus divides his prayer between the goddesses of his home and the powerful Olympian who stands before him. The Ithakan nymphs are never presented as active players in the narrative the way Athena is. We see places associated with them, and we hear characters praying to them, but they do not show themselves. Odysseus is now back in the "real" world as opposed to the fantastic world of his travels, and the only overt supernatural element in the Ithakan narrative is Athena herself. On the other hand, the unseen presence of the nymphs is constantly suggested. By a sort of divine metonymy, they are the island itself, and they represent all that Odysseus is struggling to regain, homecoming in every sense of the word—not merely a physical homecoming and reclaiming of the land but recognition of his true identity.[64] In spite of Odysseus' craftiness, there is a special poignancy about his prayer to the nymphs, native goddesses of the island. This scene is the first of a series of emotional reunions, which bring Odysseus ever closer to the ultimate meeting with his bride, Penelope. Near the town is another cult place of Ithakan nymphs, a classic *locus amoenus*:

ἄστεος ἐγγὺς ἔσαν καὶ ἐπὶ κρήνην ἀφίκοντο
τυκτὴν καλλίροον, ὅθεν ὑδρεύοντο πολῖται,
τὴν ποίησ᾽ Ἴθακος καὶ Νήριτος ἠδὲ Πολύκτωρ·
ἀμφὶ δ᾽ ἄρ᾽ αἰγείρων ὑδατοτρεφέων ἦν ἄλσος,
πάντοσε κυκλοτερές, κατὰ δὲ ψυχρὸν ῥέεν ὕδωρ
ὑψόθεν ἐκ πέτρης· βωμὸς δ᾽ ἐφύπερθε τέτυκτο
νυμφάων, ὅθι πάντες ἐπιρρέζεσκον ὁδῖται· (Hom. *Od.* 17.205–11)

They came to a fair-flowing wrought fountain, whence the towns-people drew water. Ithakos had made it, and Neritos, and Polyktor, and completely encircling it was a grove of water-nourished poplars. Cold water flowed down from the rock above, and on the top was built an altar of the nymphs where all passers-by made offerings.

Nymphs preside at the water sources used by the townsfolk as well as those in the rural and wild areas. This fountain is a *krênê*, a built fountain with a spout and basin, rather than a simple spring welling out of the ground. It was built by Ithakos, Neritos, and Polyktor, apparently the first colonists of the island. Ithakos is the eponymous hero of the island, while Neriton is one of its mountains. As in the Iliadic descriptions of nymphs in the Troad, the Ithakan nymphs here are closely associated with topography and aboriginal heroes. We learn that it was customary for anyone passing by to pay his or her respects to the nymphs; this also was true in later cult practice.[65]

In the humble hut of the swineherd Eumaios, we witness a private offering to the nymphs. A boar is slaughtered for the herdsmen's evening meal, and during the sacrificial ritual, "first offerings" of bristles from its head and bits of flesh and fat from its limbs are made to "the immortals." After cooking the meat, Eumaios carefully carves it:

καὶ τὰ μὲν ἕπταχα πάντα διεμοιρᾶτο δαΐζων·
τὴν μὲν ἴαν νύμφῃσι καὶ Ἑρμῇ, Μαιάδος υἱεῖ,
θῆκεν ἐπευξάμενος, τὰς δ᾽ ἄλλας νεῖμεν ἑκάστῳ· (Hom. *Od.*
14.434–36)

And dividing up the whole, he allotted seven portions. With a prayer he put down one for the nymphs and Hermes, son of Maia, and the others he distributed to each man.

It is appropriate for Eumaios, as a herdsman, to make an offering to the nymphs and Hermes together, for they are rustic gods who protect and increase livestock. (Note that Hermes is also evoked in the Ithakan landscape at the Hill of Hermes.)[66] When Odysseus meets the princess Nausikaä, the nymphs are described as a chorus flocking about Artemis, who is taller and lovelier than they. This epic simile has an aristocratic flavor in its themes of choral competition and physical beauty and presents the nymphs as chaste yet desirable. With the sacrifice of Eumaios, we have an entirely different picture of the nymphs as the objects of veneration by a humble herdsman (the swineherd being lower on the social ladder than any other). Nymphs were the sexual companions of Hermes, and their cultic linkage with him promoted fertility. These two opposed ways of looking at nymphs, in relation to Artemis and in relation to Hermes, continued to exist side by side in later Greek culture (3.2.2).

Homer also touches upon the role of the nymphs as guardians of herds in book 12, in which nymphs act as divine keepers for the flocks of their father Helios (*Od.* 12.131–36), and in book 9, when Odysseus and his men arrive on a game-filled island opposite that of the Kyklopes. The nymphs of the island are well disposed toward the visitors and allow them to partake of the island's wild livestock. Their abode is a *locus amoenus*, well watered and green with vegetation:

αὐτὰρ ἐπὶ κρατὸς λιμένος ῥέει ἀγλαὸν ὕδωρ,
κρήνη ὑπὸ σπείους· περὶ δ' αἴγειροι πεφύασιν.
  (Hom. *Od.* 9.140–41)

At the head of the harbor, a spring of bright water flows from beneath a cave. And round about it poplars grow.

ἦμος δ' ἠριγένεια φάνη ῥοδοδάκτυλος Ἠώς,
νῆσον θαυμάζοντες ἐδινεόμεσθα κατ' αὐτήν.
ὦρσαν δὲ νύμφαι, κοῦραι Διὸς αἰγιόχοιο,
αἶγας ὀρεσκῴους, ἵνα δειπνήσειαν ἑταῖροι. (Hom. *Od.* 9.152–55)

When early-born, rosy-fingered Dawn appeared, we walked around the island marveling at it. And the nymphs, daughters of aigis-bearing Zeus, roused the mountain goats, so that my comrades might dine.

Finally, there are Kalypso and Kirke, both of whom seem to have an odd intermediate status between the other nymphs in the Homeric poems and the major goddesses, like Athena. Of the two, Kalypso is by far the more nymphlike. In *Odyssey* book 5, she is called "nymph," "queenly nymph," and "lovely-haired nymph." She is also referred to numerous times as a goddess.[67] Later, in his account of his adventures, Odysseus refers to her as "dread goddess" and "dread goddess with human speech."[68] Kalypso lives on an extremely remote island, Ogygië, far from the areas where either mortals or other gods live, as Hermes ruefully remarks after his journey there. Like other nymphs, she inhabits a cave, which opens onto a garden so lovely it pleases even Hermes, with trees, birds, fruiting vines, wildflowers, and four fountains. Her cave dwelling, her garden, and her "abduction" of Odysseus for sexual purposes are her most nymphlike characteristics. On the other hand, her remote home contrasts with those of other terrestrial nymphs, who live in relative proximity to mortals.

That the nymph Kalypso is in fact immortal and ageless in the same way as the Olympian goddesses is integral to the narrative because of the choice she offers Odysseus between immortality and the chance to return home. His mortal condition (and that of Penelope) is several times contrasted with her divine status. At table, he eats regular food, while she partakes of nectar and ambrosia. He is forced to admit that Kalypso, as an ageless goddess, is taller and better looking than Penelope. And Kalypso complains to Hermes that goddess-mortal unions are always frowned upon by the gods (2.3). As we might expect from her unusual status, Kalypso does not have a typical nymph's parentage (daughter of Zeus, Gaia, or a river god) but is the daughter of Atlas, who holds up the sky at the borders of the earth. Hence it is fitting that she lives on such a remote island at an "untold" distance. She is part of the older generation of gods, the grandchild of the Titan Iapetos. Her status is similar to that of the Okeanids, daughters of the Titans Okeanos and Tethys, and Hesiod, in fact, lists her among the Okeanids (*Theog.* 359).

Kirke shares several epithets with Kalypso. She too is queenly, a goddess, and lovely haired. The appellation "dread goddess with human speech" (*deinê theos audêessa*), while it is used once of Kalypso, seems to belong more properly to Kirke. She is more obviously sinister, a sorceress (*polupharmakos*). Kirke is called a nymph only once, in a formulaic dressing passage that is duplicated at a similar point in the account of Kalypso (both dress in order to see Odysseus off). She lives not in a cave but in a house built of polished stone. Within, she sings and works the loom just as Kalypso does. Outside, there is no garden but a wood, and the house is surrounded by her metamorphosed victims. Kirke's parentage, however, is divine: she is the child of Helios and an Okeanid, Perse. Her rank seems to be confirmed by the handmaidens (*amphipoloi*) who serve in her house: "they are born of the springs and groves, and the sacred rivers that flow forth to the sea." In other words, Kirke is served by local nymphs. (Kalypso also has female servants, but their identity is not specified.)[69]

The Hesiodic corpus is much less comprehensive on the subject of nymphs than Homer and much more enigmatic. As for the origin of the nymphs, the *Theogony* says they appeared in the early stages of creation as the offspring of the Earth:

Γαῖα δέ τοι πρῶτον μὲν ἐγείνατο ἶσον ἑωυτῇ
Οὐρανὸν ἀστερόενθ᾽, ἵνα μιν περὶ πᾶσαν ἐέργοι,
ὄφρ᾽ εἴη μακάρεσσι θεοῖς ἔδος ἀσφαλὲς αἰεί.
γείνατο δ᾽ οὔρεα μακρά, θεᾶν χαρίεντας ἐναύλους
Νυμφέων, αἳ ναίουσιν ἀν᾽ οὔρεα βησσήεντα. (Hes. *Theog.* 126–30)

Gaia first bore starry Ouranos [Heaven], equal to herself, to enclose her on all sides and be an ever-steadfast seat for the blessed gods. And she brought forth long hills, lovely abodes of the goddess-nymphs who dwell up along the wooded hills.

Hesiod does not say explicitly that the nymphs are created along with their hills, though this is the most likely interpretation. On the one hand, it is unexpected for them to have such pride of place in the creation, yet as we have seen, they are inseparable from the landscape. Like Kalypso, these nymphs are not only *numphai* but goddesses (*theai*).

More puzzling is the passage in which Hesiod describes the creation of the Meliai immediately following Ouranos' castration:

ὅσσαι γὰρ ῥαθάμιγγες ἀπέσσυθεν αἱματόεσσαι,
πάσας δέξατο Γαῖα· περιπλομένου δ' ἐνιαυτοῦ
γείνατ' Ἐρινῦς τε κρατερὰς μεγάλους τε Γίγαντας,
τεύχεσι λαμπομένους, δολίχ' ἔγχεα χερσὶν ἔχοντας,
νύμφας θ' ἃς Μελίας καλέουσ' ἐπ' ἀπείρονα γαῖαν. (Hes. *Theog.*
183–7)

All the bloody drops that gushed forth Gaia received, and as the year moved round she bore the strong Erinyes and the great Giants gleaming in their armor, with long spears in their hands, and the nymphs whom they call Meliai upon the boundless earth.

If (as most commentators agree) the Meliai are ash-tree nymphs, this passage is the first specific reference to tree nymphs in Greek literature. Unlike the Homeric nymphs, daughters of Zeus, these deities are earthborn and belong to the earliest generation of gods. We also hear of Meliai in *Works and Days*, where they again play a role in the primordial creation:

Ζεὺς δὲ πατὴρ τρίτον ἄλλο γένος μερόπων ἀνθρώπων
χάλκειον ποίησ', οὐκ ἀργυρέῳ οὐδὲν ὁμοῖον,
ἐκ μελιᾶν, δεινόν τε καὶ ὄβριμον· (Hes. *Op.* 143–45)

Father Zeus made a third race of mortal men, a bronze race from the *meliai*, in no way like the silver race but terrible and strong.

Here, the term *meliai* seems to refer to ash trees themselves, though Proclus thought it meant ash-tree nymphs. Hesiod may be mingling the myth of the metallic races with another myth, which traced human origins to the trees.[70]

In a Hesiodic fragment, we have the earliest known discussion of the nymphs' lifespan. The primary characteristic of gods is their immortality, and nymphs are sometimes said to be goddesses or godlike. Yet Hesiod is clear that they do not have the same absolute immortality as the gods. We rarely hear of nymphs dying, and yet a spring could dry up, and even a mighty oak or ash tree is not immortal. According to the poet:

ἐννέα τοι ζώει γενεὰς λακέρυζα κορώνη
ἀνδρῶν ἡβώντων· ἔλαφος δέ τε τετρακόρωνος·
τρεῖς δ' ἐλάφους ὁ κόραξ γηράσκεται· αὐτὰρ ὁ φοῖνιξ
ἐννέα τοὺς κόρακας· δέκα δ' ἡμεῖς τοὺς φοίνικας
νύμφαι ἐυπλόκαμοι, κοῦραι Διὸς αἰγιόχοιο. (Hes. fr. 304)

A chattering crow lives out nine generations of mature men, but a
stag's life is four times a crow's, and a raven's life makes three stags
old, while the phoenix outlives nine ravens. But we, the rich-haired
nymphs, daughters of aigis-bearing Zeus, outlive ten phoenixes.

This is a riddling way of saying "untold numbers of years." Relative to
humans, nymphs were immortal, but relative to the Olympian gods, they
were not.

The *Theogony* catalogues the offspring of the Titans Okeanos and Tethys:
first is a list of their sons, the river gods, followed by a list of forty-one daughters, which is described as a partial accounting:

τίκτε δὲ θυγατέρων ἱερὸν γένος, αἳ κατὰ γαῖαν
ἄνδρας κουρίζουσι σὺν Ἀπόλλωνι ἄνακτι
καὶ ποταμοῖς, ταύτην δὲ Διὸς πάρα μοῖραν ἔχουσι . . . (Hes. *Theog.*
346–48)

And she bore a holy race of daughters, who bring up boys to men
with the help of Lord Apollo and the rivers; this they have as their
charge from Zeus . . .

αὗται δ' Ὠκεανοῦ καὶ Τηθύος ἐξεγένοντο
πρεσβύταται κοῦραι· πολλαί γε μέν εἰσι καὶ ἄλλαι·
τρὶς γὰρ χίλιαί εἰσι τανίσφυροι Ὠκεανῖναι,
αἵ ῥα πολυσπερέες γαῖαν καὶ βένθεα λίμνης
πάντῃ ὁμῶς ἐφέπουσι, θεάων ἀγλαὰ τέκνα. (Hes. *Theog.* 362–66)

These are the eldest daughters born from Okeanos and Tethys, but
there are many others. For there are three thousand neat-ankled
Okeanids, who scattered far in every place alike govern the earth and
the deep waters, glorious offspring among the goddesses.

The Okeanids are primordial nymphs, daughters of the first and greatest river.
In both myth and cult, nymphs regularly act as *kourotrophoi,* or protectors of
the young. In the case of infants, they are imagined as nurses, while for older
children and youths they (often in conjunction with the local river and Apollo)
are protective, nurturing powers (3.1.3). In mythology, nymphs are the nurses
of numerous divine and heroic infants, most notably Zeus himself, Dionysos,
and Aineias. In another Hesiodic fragment (fr. 145.1–2), Zeus entrusts a son,
probably Minos, to the nymphs of Ide.

A puzzling passage from the *Theogony* concerns Echidna, one of the many monsters in the family of Pontos. Echidna is a hybrid creature who lives, like a nymph, in a cave. She is

ἥμισυ μὲν νύμφην ἑλικώπιδα καλλιπάρηον,
ἥμισυ δ᾽ αὖτε πέλωρον ὄφιν δεινόν τε μέγαν τε
(Hes. *Theog.* 297–99)

half nymph, with glancing eyes and fair cheeks, and half monstrous snake, terrible and huge

The formless sea gives rise to monstrous shapes. Immortal and ageless like the gods and possessed of a terrible beauty, Echidna is yet a monster likely to devour anything that passes by her lair. In the *Odyssey*, the parents of the man-eating Kyklops Polyphemos are said to be Poseidon and a nymph, Thoösa, daughter of Phorkys, who lay with the god in hollow caves (Hom. *Od.* 1.71–73).

Moving on to the Homeric *Hymns* and fragments from the epic cycle, we come to the most detailed and lengthy description of nymphs in all of early Greek literature, which appears in the Homeric *Hymn to Aphrodite* (5.256–75). It reminds us more of Hesiod than Homer in its strong association of nymphs with trees and its insistence that nymphs are long-lived but not immortal. In the *Hymn*, Anchises meets the goddess Aphrodite while tending his flocks on Mount Ide. He does not realize that she has disguised herself with the intention of seducing him, but he speculates that such a lovely female must be a goddess of some kind. Just as Nausikaä seemed to Odysseus to be a goddess, this strange beauty seems more than human to Anchises:

χαῖρε ἄνασσ᾽, ἥ τις μακάρων τάδε δώμαθ᾽ ἱκάνεις,
Ἄρτεμις ἢ Λητὼ ἠὲ χρυσέη Ἀφροδίτη
ἢ Θέμις ἠϋγενὴς ἠὲ γλαυκῶπις Ἀθήνη
ἤ πού τις Χαρίτων δεῦρ᾽ ἤλυθες, αἵ τε θεοῖσι
πᾶσιν ἑταιρίζουσι καὶ ἀθάνατοι καλέονται,
ἤ τις νυμφάων αἵ τ᾽ ἄλσεα καλὰ νέμονται,
ἢ νυμφῶν αἳ καλὸν ὄρος τόδε ναιετάουσι
καὶ πηγὰς ποταμῶν καὶ πίσεα ποιήεντα. (Hom. *Hymn Ven.* 5.92–99)

Welcome to this house, lady, whoever of the blessed ones you are: Artemis, or Leto, or golden Aphrodite, or well-born Themis, or gray-eyed Athena. Or maybe you are one of the Charites, who bear the gods company and are called immortal, or else one of the nymphs who inhabit the lovely groves, or of those who haunt this lovely mountain and the springs of rivers and grassy meadows.

The poet of the *Hymn* uses the familiar Homeric list of nymph habitations but modifies it slightly to refer specifically to Mount Ide. This mountain was famous as a home of nymphs, perhaps because of its many springs and the rivers that flowed from it into the coastal plains. We find these same nymphs of Ide as companions of Aphrodite in a fragment of the *Cypria*, an epic poem that told of the Judgment of Paris and the beginning of the Trojan war:

ἢ δὲ σὺν ἀμφιπόλοισι φιλομμειδὴς Ἀφροδίτη
[lacuna]
πλεξάμεναι στεφάνους εὐώδεας, ἄνθεα γαίης,
ἂν κεφαλαῖσιν ἔθεντο θεαὶ λιπαροκρήδεμνοι,
νύμφαι καὶ Χάριτες, ἅμα δὲ χρυσῆ Ἀφροδίτη,
καλὸν ἀείδουσαι κατ᾽ ὄρος πολυπιδάκου Ἴδης. (*Cypr.* fr. 5)

And laughter-loving Aphrodite with her handmaidens . . . weaving sweet-smelling crowns, flowers of the earth, they put them upon their heads, the bright-veiled goddesses, nymphs, and Charites, and golden Aphrodite too, singing sweetly on the mount of many-fountained Ide.

The love goddess is of course a successful seductress and conceives a child with the Trojan hero. Ashamed of her association with a mortal, she wishes him to put it about that the child's mother is one of the beings called nymphs:

αἵ ῥ᾽ οὔτε θνητοῖς οὔτ᾽ ἀθανάτοισιν ἕπονται·
δηρὸν μὲν ζώουσι καὶ ἄμβροτον εἶδαρ ἔδουσι,
καί τε μετ᾽ ἀθανάτοισι καλὸν χορὸν ἐρρώσαντο.
τῇσι δὲ Σειληνοὶ καὶ εὔσκοπος Ἀργειφόντης
μίσγοντ᾽ ἐν φιλότητι μυχῷ σπείων ἐροέντων. (Hom. *Hymn Ven.*
5.259–63)

They belong neither with mortals nor with immortals. They live for a long time, and eat divine food and with the immortals they join the lovely dance. With them the Silenoi and sharp-eyed Argeiphontes [Hermes] mate in the recesses of pleasant caves.

The nymphs, we gather, are sexually promiscuous, for they welcome Hermes and the silens (horse men) alike, and nobody would be surprised if one of them lay with a shepherd and conceived a child. Note that the association with Hermes was made in the *Odyssey* and that the canonical spot for these amours is the "pleasant cave." This is the first time nymphs are paired with silens, though the connection is logical (silens are minor rustic *daimones*, or spirits). Early Athenian black-figure vases show nymphs and silens cavorting together (3.1.1). Aphrodite continues:

γεινομένῃσιν ἔφυσαν ἐπὶ χθονὶ βωτιανείρῃ
καλαὶ τηλεθάουσαι ἐν οὔρεσιν ὑψηλοῖσιν.
ἑστᾶσ᾽ ἠλίβατοι, τεμένη δέ ἑ κικλήσκουσιν

ἀθανάτων· τὰς δ᾽ οὔ τι βροτοὶ κείρουσι σιδήρῳ.
ἀλλ᾽ ὅτε κεν δὴ μοῖρα παρεστήκῃ θανάτοιο
ἀζάνεται μὲν πρῶτον ἐπὶ χθονὶ δένδρεα καλά,
φλοιὸς δ᾽ ἀμφιπεριφθινύθει, πίπτουσι δ᾽ ἄπ᾽ ὄζοι,
τῶν δέ θ᾽ ὁμοῦ ψυχὴ λείπει φάος ἠελίοιο. (Hom. *Hymn Ven.*
    5.265–72)

But when they are born, pines or high-topped oaks spring up with
them upon the fruitful earth, beautiful lush trees standing high on the
lofty mountains. They call them the sanctuaries of the immortals, and
mortals never cut them with an ax. But when the fate of death is
near, first those lovely trees wither where they stand, and the bark
shrivels about them and the twigs fall, and the soul of both [nymph
and tree] leaves the light of the sun together.

The concept of nymphs as tree spirits is ancient. As a belief in female tree
spirits (and spring spirits) is common to many peoples speaking Indo-
European languages, these nymphs might have a high pedigree indeed. The
terms *dryad* and *hamadryad*, though not used in this poem, became commonplace after the archaic period, and Pindar used the term *isodendron*, "equal
with the tree," to describe the lifespan of a nymph. The mention of the taboo
against cutting one of these trees brings to mind the folktale pattern of the
woodsman who either cuts the tree and is punished or spares the tree and is
rewarded by the grateful nymph (2.4).
    In keeping with one of their usual roles, the nymphs will act as nurses to
Aphrodite's infant son, Aineias:

αἱ μὲν ἐμὸν θρέψουσι παρὰ σφίσιν υἱὸν ἔχουσαι.
τὸν μὲν ἐπὴν δὴ πρῶτον ἕλῃ πολυήρατος ἥβη
ἄξουσίν σοι δεῦρο θεαί, δείξουσί τε παῖδα· (Hom. *Hymn Ven.*
    5.273–75)

They shall keep my son beside them and nurse him. And as soon as
he reaches lovely boyhood, the goddesses will bring him here to you
and show you the child.

ἢν δέ τις εἴρηταί σε καταθνητῶν ἀνθρώπων
ἤ τις σοὶ φίλον υἱὸν ὑπὸ ζώνῃ θέτο μήτηρ,
τῷ δὲ σὺ μυθεῖσθαι μεμνημένος ὥς σε κελεύω·
φασίν τοι νύμφης καλυκώπιδος ἔκγονον εἶναι
αἳ τόδε ναιετάουσιν ὄρος καταειμένον ὕλῃ. (Hom. *Hymn Ven.*
    5.281–85)

But if any mortal man should ask you what mother got your dear son
beneath her belt, remember to tell him as I bid you: say he is the
offspring of one of the flowerlike nymphs, they who inhabit this
forest-clad hill.

The forest-clad hill is Ide in the Troad, and the nymphs there seem eager for male companionship. We have already seen that nymphs from this area have intercourse with the silens and Hermes, and they bear to mortal lovers the Trojan heroes Aisepos and Pedasos and the Trojan ally Satnios. Paris, too, was supposed to have taken to wife a nymph of Ide (2.5.2).

Around the start of the fifth century, we find in the Homeric *Hymns* our first evidence of the nymphs' association with Pan, which was soon to become prominent in cult:

> Ἀμφί μοι Ἑρμείαο φίλον γόνον ἔννεπε Μοῦσα,
> αἰγιπόδην δικέρωτα φιλόκροτον ὅς τ᾽ ἀνὰ πίση
> δενδρήεντ᾽ ἄμυδις φοιτᾷ χοροήθεσι νύμφαις
> αἵ τε κατ᾽ αἰγίλιπος πέτρης στείβουσι κάρηνα
> Πᾶν᾽ ἀνακεκλόμεναι νόμιον θεὸν ἀγλαέθειρον
> αὐχμήενθ᾽ . . . (Hom. *Hymn Pan* 19.1–6)

> Muse, tell me of Hermes' dear son, goat-footed, horned, lover of the beat. He roams through wooded meadows with nymphs who delight in the dance, they who tread the peak of the sheer rock, calling upon Pan, the shepherd god, shaggy and rough . . .

The image of Pan as a musician surrounded by a chorus of dancing nymphs quickly became canonical.

The epic poets who succeeded Homer, such as Eumelus and Asius, used nymphs as literary devices in order to stake claims to territory and to assert prestigious genealogical claims (4.1). This practice was characteristic of the archaic period, and we will meet it again in the works of Pindar.

1.4.2 *Lyric and Choral Poetry*

The fragments of the Greek lyric poets are so meager that it is risky to generalize from them. In the fragments of Sappho, for example, nymphs are not mentioned explicitly. Sappho does pray to Kypris (Aphrodite) and the Nereids that her brother "may arrive safely."[71] The Nereids are here protectors of sea travelers, like Helen and the Dioskouroi. Yet the themes of Sappho's extant poetry overlap strikingly with the conceptual sphere of the nymphs: lush nature, eroticism, nuptials. An ancient commentator, in discussing Sappho's subject matter, wrote, "The charm is sometimes inherent in the object, such as the gardens of the nymphs, wedding songs, love affairs, all the poetry of Sappho."[72] These gardens of the nymphs (*numphaioi kêpoi*) epitomize motifs that Sappho used again and again: the sensuous appeal of natural objects and settings such as flowers, fruit, the splashing of cold water, light filtering through trees. Sappho's patron is Aphrodite, the goddess who made garlands of flowers with the Charites and nymphs on Ide. In a fragment of the *Anacreontea*, Aphrodite and the nymphs both bring to mind flowers, gardens, and blushes[73]:

ῥοδοδάκτυλος μὲν Ἠώς,
ῥοδοπήχεες δὲ νύμφαι,
ῥοδόχρους δὲ κἀφροδίτα
παρὰ τῶν σοφῶν καλεῖται. (Anacr. fr. 55.20–23)

Rosy-fingered dawn, rosy-armed nymphs, rosy-hued Aphrodite, so
the poets call them.

A moist garden of the nymphs is also described by Ibycus:

ἦρι μὲν αἵ τε Κυδώνιαι
μηλίδες ἀρδόμεναι ῥοᾶν
ἐκ ποταμῶν ἵνα Παρθένων
κῆπος ἀκήρατος . . . (Ibyc. fr. 286.1–4)

In the spring flourish Kydonian quince trees watered from flowing
rivers where [stands] the inviolate garden of the Maidens . . .

The Spartan poet Alcman described yet another such sacred spot, inhabited
by minor goddesses called Leukotheai:

Λευκοθεᾶν ἐρατὸν τέμενος
ἐκ Τρυγεᾶν ἀνιών, ἔχον
δὲ σίδας δύω γλυκήας.

ταὶ δ᾽ ὅτε δὴ ποταμῶι καλλιρρόωι
ἀράσαντ᾽ ἐρατὸν τελέσαι γάμον
καὶ τὰ παθῆν ἃ γυναιξὶ καὶ ἀνδρά[σι
φίλτ]ατα κωριδίας τ᾽ εὐνᾶς [τυ]χῆν (Alcm. fr. 4a.11–17)

[I came to] the lovely sanctuary of the Leukotheai by going up from
Trygeai, and I carried two sweet pomegranates, and when they [fem.]
had prayed to the fair flowing river that they achieve lovely wedlock
and experience those things that are [dearest] to women and men and
find a lawful marriage bed . . .

The Leukotheai, or White Goddesses, are closely related to nymphs because
of their association with the god whose river flows through their sanctuary
and the responsibility that they share in preparing the young for marriage.[74]
    The predominance of female sexual aggressors in Sappho, a pattern shared
with extant narratives about the nymphs (2.5.1–2), is also suggestive. In addition to Aphrodite, Sappho speaks of both Selene and Eos, goddesses famous
for their love affairs with mortals. Sappho is also thought to have written of
Phaon, an Adonis-like figure who was beloved of Aphrodite and who appears on Meidian vase paintings in a sensuous garden setting surrounded by
Aphrodite's female retinue.[75]

Sappho's compatriot Alcaeus seems to have referred to Achilles' mother, Thetis, as a naiad nymph (fr. 44), though she is more commonly considered a Nereid. In another fragment, possibly a hymn to the nymphs, he invokes the Homeric version of their parentage, though he avoids the explicit Homeric formulation of the nymphs as Zeus' daughters:

Νύμφαις ταὶς Δίος ἐξ αἰγιόχω φαῖσι τετυχμέναις . . . (Alc. fr. 343)

They say that the nymphs created by aigis-bearing Zeus . . .

A new development in lyric and choral poetry is the frequent appearance of Dionysos, who is accompanied by an ecstatic swarm of nymphs. The theme of Dionysiac nurses first appeared in the Iliadic story of Lykourgos (3.1.1), but now the nymphs appear as regular companions of the adult god, paralleling the popularity of the subject in contemporary vase painting. As early as Alcman, "naiads and Lampads and Thyiads" are juxtaposed.[76] In Anacreon, we find Dionysos invoked in an erotic context:

ὦναξ, ᾧ δαμάλης Ἔρως
καὶ νύμφαι κυανώπιδες
πορφυρῆ τ' Ἀφροδίτη
συμπαίζουσιν, ἐπιστρέφεαι
δ' ὑψηλὰς ὀρέων κορυφάς·
γουνοῦμαι σε, σὺ δ' εὐμενὴς
ἔλθ' ἡμίν . . . (Anac. fr. 357)

Lord with whom Eros the subduer and the blue-eyed nymphs and radiant Aphrodite play, as you haunt the lofty mountain peaks, I beseech you: come to me with a kindly heart . . .

We have already learned that the nymphs and Aphrodite are at home on a mountain top; Dionysos too is native to this milieu. In a fragment of Pratinas, the chorus imagines itself participating in the boisterous mountain revels with the god and his entourage[77]:

ἐμὸς ἐμὸς ὁ Βρόμιος, ἐμὲ δεῖ κελαδεῖν, ἐμὲ δεῖ
παταγεῖν
ἀν' ὄρεα σύμενον μετὰ ναϊάδων
οἷά τε κύκνον ἄγοντα ποικιλόπτερον μέλος. (Pratin. fr. 708.3–5)

Mine, mine is Bromios: it is for me to shout and stamp, racing over the mountains with the naiads singing a song of flashing wings like the swan.

That this image has become canonical is confirmed by a Pindaric dithyramb in which the ecstatic rites of Dionysos and the Great Mother are combined[78]:

ἐν δὲ ναΐδων ἐρίγδουποι στοναχαί
μανίαι τ' ἀλαλαί τ' ὀρίνεται ῥιψαύχενι
σὺν κλόνῳ. (Pind. fr. 70b.12–13)

there too the loud-sounding groans of the naiads and the ecstatic cries
are aroused in the agitation of tossing necks.

In the odes of Pindar, written for victorious athletes from various cities,
we see nymphs in a different light. An individual nymph is elevated to represent the city itself; she personifies at once the land, its familiar topographical features, and the local mythic genealogy. These nymphs take honored
positions at the beginning or end of many odes and are usually apostrophized,
or addressed directly, by the poet.[79] An ode for Psaumis of Kamarina begins:

Ὑψηλᾶν ἀρετᾶν καὶ στεφάνων ἄωτον γλυκύν
τῶν Οὐλυμπίᾳ, Ὠκεανοῦ θύγατερ, καρδίᾳ γελανεῖ
ἀκαμαντόποδός τ' ἀπήνας δέκευ Ψαύμιός τε δῶρα· (Pind. Ol. 5.1–3)

Daughter of Okeanos, with a glad heart receive this finest sweet
reward for lofty deeds and crowns won at Olympia, gifts of the
tirelessly running mule-car and of Psaumis.

The "daughter of Ocean" is the nymph of the lake also called Kamarina. If
it were not for this epithet, we would assume that Pindar was simply apos-
trophizing the city. In *Olympian* 4.10–12, similar ambiguity is present: "Psaumis
who, crowned with Pisan olive, is eager to arouse glory for Kamarina." Pindar
refers at once to both nymph and city.[80]

Often the nymph is the eponym of the city and is therefore a named individual. However, in an ode for Ergoteles of Himera in Sicily, Pindar refers
to a group of unnamed nymphs:

νῦν δ' Ὀλυμπίᾳ στεφανωσάμενος
καὶ δὶς ἐκ Πυθῶνος Ἰσθμοῖ τ', Ἐργότελες,
θερμὰ Νυμφᾶν λουτρὰ βαστάζεις ὁμι-
    λέων παρ' οἰκείαις ἀρούραις. (Pind. Ol. 12.19)

But now, having won a crown at Olympia, and twice from Pytho
and at the Isthmos, Ergoteles, you exalt the nymphs' warm baths,
living by lands that are your own.

"The nymphs' warm baths" is metonymy for Himera, famed then and now
for its hot springs. Hence the nymphs, even if not obvious personifications,
represent the city as a whole in one of its famous natural features. The nymphs
of the baths were important enough to be depicted on Himera's coins (4.10.4,
figure 1.2).

Another named example is Aigina, nymph of the island in the Saronic gulf
(4.3.3). Aigina was the most famous daughter of the river Asopos, which flows

Figure 1.2 Coin from Thermai Himereiai: three nymphs. Photo copyright British Museum.

south of Thebes. The myth had it that Zeus abducted Aigina and brought her to the island, which henceforth took her name:

> ὑδάτ<εσσ>ι δ᾽ ἐπ᾽ Ἀσ[ω-
> ποῦ π[οτ᾽ ἀ]πὸ προθύρων βαθύκολ-
> πον ἀγερέψατο παρθένον
> Αἴγιναν· τότε χρύσεαι ἀ-
> έρος ἔκρυψαν κομ[α]ι
> ἐπιχώριον κατάσκιον νῶτον ὑμέτερον,
> ἵνα λεχέων ἐπ᾽ ἀμβρότων . . . (Pind. fr. 52f. 134–40)

By the waters of the Asopos, he once carried off from her portal the deep-bosomed virgin, Aigina. Then the golden tresses of the air hid the shadowy ridge of your native land, so that in an immortal bed . . .

Aigina bore Aiakos, who had a great reputation for justice and was often said to be a judge in the underworld. Aiakos, in turn, mated with Cheiron's daughter Endaïs and sired Peleus and Telamon, the respective fathers of Achilles and Ajax. At the end of *Pythian* 8, the poet addresses this ancestral nymph and makes a request:

> Αἴγινα φίλα μᾶτερ, ἐλευθέρῳ στόλῳ
> πόλιν τάνδε κόμιζε Δὶ καὶ κρέοντι σὺν Αἰακῷ
> Πηλεῖ τε κἀγαθῷ Τελαμῶνι σύν τ᾽ Ἀχιλλεῖ. (Pind. *Pyth.* 8.98–100)

Dear mother Aigina, on its voyage of freedom safeguard this city, together with Zeus and king Aiakos, Peleus and noble Telamon, and with Achilles.

The nymph is here a sort of tutelary spirit, presumed to have the power to give (or at least encourage) prosperity in cooperation with the local heroes. In time of peril (here, on the eve of Aigina's loss of independence to Athens), a prayer to her is appropriate.[81] She is "mother" as the ancestor of a great line of heroes and also in the sense that she nourishes and watches over the land named for her.

Nagy has emphasized the importance of the ancestral hero in Pindar's victory odes; such heroes, he suggests, reflect the prestige of elite groups in the polis. In the Aiginetan odes (about a quarter of the total extant), we find "the notion of the Aiakidai [a local family] as a totality consisting of the body of the ancestor Aiakos and an unbroken succession of descendants."[82] What then is the significance of the nymphs whom Pindar so often invokes? They seem to represent the polis itself or the land it sits on, as opposed to the more narrowly defined, elite groups who claimed descent from the heroic ancestor. The eponymous nymph of the city, she who is represented on its coins, cannot be claimed by any one family.[83]

Pindar was not the first to make a point of genealogies; the Hesiodic *Ehoeae*, now fragmentary, was organized around a list of (mostly mortal) females who bore the great heroes. But Pindar does emphasize the connection between local nymphs and civic identity more than any previous author. This reflects a historical trend rather than Pindar's own eccentricity, for the coins of several cities show these local nymphs. Some, such as Aigina, are better attested than others, but the pedigrees of those mentioned by Pindar do not seem to stretch back very far (Aigina, for all the ancient sound of the myth, is not well attested as the mother of Aiakos until the fifth century, when she becomes prominent in Pindar and in vase paintings).[84] This special role of the individual nymph as city emblem is characteristic of the late archaic and early classical periods, when competition between *poleis* was perhaps at its strongest.

Genealogy could also be used to establish mythic links between friendly cities. By making Aigina and Thebe twin daughters of Asopos, Pindar alludes to Thebes' and Aigina's shared ideologies (both were conservative, aristocratic, and hostile to Athens). In another ode, a connection is established between Pindar's Thebes and the Arkadian city Stymphalis, homeland of the athlete Hagesias; Thebe had Arkadian roots, for her mother was Metope, a nymph of the river Stymphalis.[85]

The abduction of the nymph by a god and her relocation in a new home are popular mythic motifs because they establish links between mother city and colony, or they give a less-distinguished town a better pedigree by aligning it with a greater one. In these genealogies of the Greek families (as opposed to the Homeric ones we saw for the Trojans and their allies), the nymph usually has a divine partner, one of the major gods. Aigina was paired with Zeus, Kyrene with Apollo, and so on.[86] A fragment of the Boiotian poet Corinna tells of the daughters of Asopos, nine of whom were abducted by gods. Asopos is at first angry at this high-handed behavior, she writes, until a seer, apparently the local hero Akraiphen, explains to him the future of his family:

τᾶν δὲ πήδω[ν τρὶς μ]ὲν ἔχι
Δεὺς πατεὶ[ρ πάντω]ν βασιλεύς,
τρὶς δὲ πόντ[ω γᾶμε] μέδων
Π[οτιδάων, τ]ᾶν δὲ δουῖν
Φῦβος λέκτ[ρα] κρατούνι,

τᾶν δ᾽ ἴαν Μή[ας] ἀγαθὸς
πῆς Ἑρμᾶς· οὔ[τ]ω γὰρ Ἔρως
κὴ Κούπρις πιθέταν, τιὼς
ἐν δόμως βάντας κρουφάδαν
κώρας ἐννί᾽ ἑλέσθη·

τή ποκ᾽ εἰρώων γενέθλαν
ἐσγεννάσονθ᾽ εἰμ[ιθί]ων,
κἄσσονθη π[ο]λου[σπ]ερίες
τ᾽ ἀγείρω τ᾽· ἐς [μ]α[ντοσ]ούνω
τρίποδος ὤιτ[. . . . . . .]. (Cor. fr. 654.12–26)

And of your daughters, father Zeus, king of all, has three; and Poseidon, ruler of the sea, married three; and Phoibos is master of the beds of two of them, and of one Hermes, good son of Maia. For so did the pair Eros and the Kyprian persuade them, that they should go in secret to your house and take your nine daughters. One day they shall give birth to a race of heroes half-divine, and they shall be fruitful and ageless; so [I was instructed] from the oracular tripod.

With this explanation, Asopos is satisfied, and his anger changes to joy. The rest of the tale is too fragmentary to interpret, except that the local mountains Parnes and Kithairon join the conversation.

This notion of heroes mothered by nymphs plays a prominent role in the extant fragments of Corinna; she also speaks of

Ὠρί[ωνα] μέγαν
κὴ πεντεί[κοντ᾽] οὐψιβίας
πῆδα[ς οὕς νού]μφησι μιγ[ί]ς
τέκετο . . . (Cor. fr. 655.14–16)

great Orion and the fifty sons of high strength whom [he fathered] by intercourse with nymphs.

A look back at Corinna fr. 654.27–31 assures us that among these very sons of nymphs was the seer Akraiphen, who prophesied to Asopos. The same theme of heroes as the progeny of nymphs and gods appears in Pindar, who tells of the Okeanid consort of Apollo, Melia. She bore to Apollo the sons

Teneros, a prophet, and Ismenios, who gave his name to the local river and to the temple itself, the Ismenion (4.3.1).

For the Boiotians, then, the generation of heroes from whom they themselves were descended had been the result of unions between two categories of deities: first, the Olympian gods (or heroes of godlike stature, such as Orion) and second, the rivers and their female offspring. The first group provided a link to the other Greeks, who shared with the Boiotians Zeus, Apollo, Poseidon, and Hermes. The prestige of naming an Olympian god as one's progenitor cannot be underestimated, as Theseus' struggle to prove his divine paternity shows. Yet, in their own way, the humbler Asopos and his daughters, and Melia, are as important in the genealogies because they provide a crucial link to to the local landscape. Apollo is the god of the Ismenion, yet Pindar's attention is mostly bestowed upon Melia, who makes this temple of Apollo unique. According to Vivante, Melia, Metope, Asopos, and the others "underlie the delicate and elusive relations which bind places to the sense of divinity emanating from them."[87]

Pindar disagrees with Homer that the nymphs are "daughters of aigis-bearing Zeus." Instead, he gives them an older and thus more awe-inspiring history akin to that described in the *Theogony*. Kyrene's grandmother Kreousa is a daughter of Gaia; thus she belongs to the first generation of created beings. The Theban nymph Melia is a daughter of Okeanos, as is Kamarina.

1.4.3 *Tragedy and Comedy*

In the poetry of the classical period, which was dominated by cosmopolitan Athenian dramatists, the nymphs became less visible, even as their rural cults enjoyed a period of peak activity.[88] Tragedies, of course, dealt primarily with mortal heroes and heroines; most passages of interest to us here appear in the choral sections of the plays, which employ a wide spectrum of subjects for meditative commentary upon the characters and events in the plot. The tragedians, like most extant authors of the classical period, belong to Athens, but their treatment of nymphs echoes that of the more geographically diverse archaic materials. The picture presented in Homer, Hesiod, and other archaic poetry is not substantially changed (though city nymphs, like those in Pindar, are unusual). Nymphs continue to be linked with gods who have rural or pastoral associations: Dionysos, Hermes, Pan, and Apollo.[89] A chorus in Sophocles' *Oedipus Tyrannus* speculates on the mysterious origins of their king:

Τίς σε, τέκνον, τίς σ᾽ ἔτι-
κτε τᾶν μακραιώνων ἄρα
Πανὸς ὀρεσσιβάτα πα-
τρὸς πελασθεῖσ᾽; ἢ σέ γ᾽ εὐνάτειρά τις
Λοξίου; τῷ γὰρ πλάκες ἀγρόνομοι πᾶσαι
    φίλαι·

εἴθ᾽ ὁ Κυλλάνας ἀνάσσων,
εἴθ᾽ ὁ Βακχεῖος θεὸς
ναίων ἐπ᾽ ἄκρων ὀρέων εὑ-
ρημα δέξατ᾽ ἔκ του
νυμφᾶν ἑλικωπίδων, αἷς
πλεῖστα συμπαίζει. (Soph. *OT* 1099–1109)

Who of the blessed ones [i.e., nymphs] bore you, child, lying with mountain-roving father Pan? Or did a bedmate of Loxias [Apollo] give you birth? For all the grassy slopes are dear to him. Or was it the ruler of Kyllene [Hermes] or the Bacchic god dwelling on the high hills that received you as a foundling child from the dark-eyed nymphs, with whom he dances the most?

Thus Oedipus is imagined to be the offspring of a nymph and one of the gods with whom they consort. These idylls with gods of a pastoral or rustic character seem to belong to the lore of the humble, while myths of a nymph's union with Zeus or Poseidon to produce a city founder or heroic ancestor (as in Pindar) are products of the urban elites. This passage suggests a folkloric belief that an abandoned infant, perhaps found in the shelter of a cave, might be the child of a nymph.[90] In Greek myths, both nymphs and mortal women are said to expose their infants, though their motivations seem to be different. For a heroine, the motive is shame at an illegitimate birth or actual persecution (usually by her father or other relatives). Nymphs expose their children or give them into the keeping of others because they are by nature free of familial responsibilities. Paradoxically, nymphs often act as nurses, but the infants they care for belong to someone else. Typically, too, a group shares responsibility for the child, as in the cases of Aineias and the hero Rhesos (4.7.2).

Dionysos' divine nurses make an appearance in the *Oedipus at Colonus,* when the chorus characterizes their sacred grove as a place

ἵν᾽ ὁ Βακχιώ-
τας ἀεὶ Διόνυσος ἐμβατεύει
θείαις ἀμφιπολῶν τιθήναις. (Soph. *OC* 680)

where the reveler Dionysos ever treads, companion of the goddesses who nursed him.

In the *Hippolytus*, Euripides compares Herakles' unwilling bride, Iole, who was raped during the sack of Oichalia, to "a running naiad or a bacchant."[91] The nymph and the bacchant have in common their physical freedom, their wildness, and a certain sexual vulnerability that is associated with their "outdoor" status (though fight and flight are both possible options in the face of attack). The description of the running naiad, in the context of Iole's rape, recalls another Euripidean passage, which describes Pan's rape of a nymph in a cave:

νύμφα τις οἷα ναῒς
ὄρεσι φυγάδα νόμον ἱεῖσα
γοερόν, ὑπὸ δὲ πέτρινα {μύχαλα} γύαλα
κλαγγαῖσ<ι> Πανὸς ἀναβοᾷ γάμους. (Eur. Hel. 185–90)

Just as some naiad nymph, caught fleeing on the hills, voices with
shrieks beneath the rocky hollows her mournful song, crying out on
Pan's nuptials.

Shorter dramatic works, known as "satyr plays," were produced as a sort of
comic relief at the tragic festivals, one for every three tragedies. Though fragmentary, they yield a surprising variety of passages that concern nymphs and
their relations with the satyrs and Dionysos (3.1.1).

A sacrifice to the nymphs is an important plot point in Euripides' *Electra*.
Upon Orestes' arrival in Argos, he learns that Aigisthos has retired to a
sanctuary of the nymphs in order to prepare a feast (*erotis*) for them. He
asks:

τροφεῖα παίδων ἢ πρὸ μέλλοντος τόκου; (Eur. El. 626)

For the rearing of children, or for a birth soon to come?

Orestes goes to the well-watered garden, where Aigisthos and his men are
preparing to sacrifice a calf. Unrecognized, he is invited to participate in
accordance with the laws of hospitality. Aigisthos prays:

Νύμφαι πετραῖαι, πολλάκις με βουθυτεῖν
καὶ τὴν κατ' οἴκους Τυνδαρίδα δάμαρτ' ἐμὴν
πράσσοντας ὡς νῦν, τοὺς δ' ἐμοὺς ἐχθροὺς κακῶς. (Eur. El. 805–7)

Nymphs of the rocks, often may I sacrifice, and my Tyndarid spouse
at home, faring as we now do. And may it go ill for our enemies.

Aigisthos thus requests of the nymphs that they grant him peace and security
by freeing him from his greatest fear: that Agamemnon's son might return
to exact vengeance. Orestes meanwhile prays to the nymphs under his breath
for the opposite outcome. The sacrifice is carried out, but Aigisthos receives
an ill omen, for the slaughtered calf's liver is missing its lobe. As Aigisthos
stares at the calf's innards, Orestes strikes. Why does Euripides make the
sacrifice to the nymphs, described in great detail, the centerpiece of the play?
Aigisthos expects the nymphs, as kourotrophic deities, to aid in the care of
his young sons by Klytaimnestra (*El.* 61–62) or to further his dynastic hopes
through the conception of additional offspring. Hence, Orestes' question as
to whether the sacrifice is made for heirs already born or for heirs-to-be is
quite pertinent. The sacrifice of Aigisthos, as the omen shows, is rejected by
the deities of the land itself. A typical Euripidean moral ambiguity is intro-

duced, however, in the fact that Orestes, the putative hero, kills his host during a sacrifice, while Aigisthos meets his end during an act of piety.[92]

Above all, tragedy echoes the Homeric picture of nymphs as integral to the landscape, sometimes sharing in and reflecting the emotions of the principals in the drama through the so-called pathetic fallacy. The chorus in Euripides' *Heracles* calls upon the streams Ismenos and Dirke and the local nymphs to help celebrate the victory over Lykos:[93]

Δίρκα θ᾽ ἁ καλλιρρέεθρος,
σύν τ᾽ Ἀσωπιάδες κόραι,
     πατρὸς ὕδωρ βᾶτε λιποῦσαι συναοιδοὶ
νύμφαι τὸν Ἡρακλέους
καλλίνικον ἀγῶνα. (Eur. *Heracl.* 784–88)

Come, fair-flowing Dirke, with the nymphs, daughters of Asopos, leaving their father's waters; sing together the lovely victory of Herakles.

Because Dirke is emblematic of Thebes, this passage is similar in feel to the victory odes in which Pindar addresses the nymph of the city. Nymphs also live in the waters of exotic foreign rivers:

Νείλου μὲν αἵδε καλλιπάρθενοι ῥοαί. (Eur. *Hel.* 1)
These are the lovely-maiden streams of Nile.

And in *Iphigenia at Aulis*, the chorus visualizes the upbringing of Paris as a herdsman in a well-watered garden of the nymphs:

μήποτ᾽ ὤφελες τὸν ἀμφὶ
βουσὶ βουκόλον τραφέντ᾽ Ἀ-
     λέξανδρον οἰκίσαι
ἀμφὶ τὸ λευκὸν ὕδωρ, ὅθι κρῆναι
Νυμφᾶν κεῖνται
λειμών τ᾽ ἔρνεσι θάλλων
χλωροῖς καὶ ῥοδόεντ᾽
ἄνθε᾽ ὑακίνθινά τε θεαῖς δρέπειν. (Eur. *IA* 1291–99)

Would you had never reared Alexander, herdsman of cattle, to dwell by the silvery water, where the fountains of the nymphs lie, and the meadow blooming with tender shoots, and to pluck roses and hyacinths for goddesses.

The setting is the fertile and flowery Mount Ide from the Homeric *Hymn to Aphrodite*. In winter, the same mountain and nymphs reflect the terrible grief and isolation of Demeter after the loss of her daughter:

χιονοθρέμμονάς τ᾽ ἐπέρα-
  σ᾽ Ἰδαιᾶν Νυμφᾶν σκοπιάς,
ῥίπτει δ᾽ ἐν πένθει
πέτρινα κατὰ δρία πολυνιφέα· (Eur. *Hel.* 1323–26)

she crossed the snow-bearing watch-places of the Idaian nymphs and
in her grief flung herself down the stony thickets in deep snow . . .

Perhaps the most poignant use of the landscape theme appears in Sophocles'
Philoctetes, when the castaway hero must say farewell to the isolated spot that
has so long been his home.[94] In the last lines of the play, he enumerates the
features of the landscape, taking his leave nostalgically in spite of the suffer-
ing and the harsh life that he endured there:

χαῖρ᾽, ὦ μέλαθρον ξύμφρουρον ἐμοί,
Νύμφαι τ᾽ ἔνυδροι λειμωνιάδες,
καὶ κτύπος ἄρσην πόντου προβολῆς,
οὗ πολλάκι δὴ τοὐμὸν ἐτέγχθη
κρᾶτ᾽ ἐνδόμυχον πληγῆσι νότου,
πολλὰ δὲ φωνῆς τῆς ἡμετέρας
Ἑρμαῖον ὄρος παρέπεμψεν ἐμοὶ
στόνον ἀντίτυπον χειμαζομένῳ.
νῦν δ᾽, ὦ κρῆναι Λύκιόν τε ποτόν,
λείπομεν ὑμᾶς . . . (Soph. *Phil.* 1453–62)

Farewell, you cave that shared my vigil, you watery meadow
nymphs, and virile thunder of the sea's spur, where many a time, in
the inmost part of my cave, my head was drenched with the lashings
of the south wind, and you Hill of Hermes, which often in answer to
my voice, sent me back a groan as I labored under the storm. And
now, you springs and Lykian water, I am leaving you . . .

This passage brings to mind and reverses Odysseus' rapturous greeting of the
nymphs on Ithake, where there was also a Hill of Hermes. The nymphs are
the animating spirit of the coast of Lemnos, to which Philoktetes has grown
attached in spite of his sufferings. Yet, as for Odysseus, there are nymphs
waiting to receive Philoktetes beside the banks of the Spercheios, in his one
true home (Soph. *Phil.* 724–26).

In the Old Comedy of Aristophanes, with its fantastic yet often contemporary (as opposed to mythological) settings, we touch more closely
upon popular ideas of the nymphs and their role in everyday piety. In the
Thesmophoriazusae, the female herald leads a prayer to a long list of gods arranged just as they might be on a cultic inscription: "Demeter and Persephone,
and Pluto and Kalligeneia and Kourotrophos, and Hermes and the Charites."
The chorus answers with its own prayer to Zeus, Apollo, Athena, Artemis,

Poseidon, the Nereids, and the mountain-roving nymphs (Ar. *Thesm.* 325–26). The purpose of these litanies is to avoid offending any god by omission. The list opens with the gods of fertility traditionally invoked first, moves on to the Olympians, and finally covers the minor gods of sea and land. Later, the chorus invokes a traditional pastoral triad:

Ἑρμῆν τε νόμιον ἄντομαι
καὶ Πᾶνα καὶ Νύμφας φίλας (Ar. *Thesm.* 977–78)

I entreat Hermes Nomios and Pan and the dear nymphs

The use of the phrase "dear nymphs" indicates a level of familiarity, affection, and daily contact rarely found in relationships with other deities.[95] The affective element or feeling of emotional closeness to the deity, which we also see in Sappho's description of her relationship with Aphrodite, is a central aspect of religious devotion in many traditions.

The Aristophanic comedies contain several references to the nymph-inspired prophet known as Bakis (1.3). The nymphs, according to popular tradition, could inspire certain persons with supernormal abilities of prophecy or verbal expression. This idea, though it was undoubtedly very old, is particularly well attested in the classical period, and we find it in Aristophanes and Plato, whose works also have a contemporary setting, rather than in the tragedians.

In the *Birds*, the fanciful bird chorus reports that it spends much of its time with the nymphs:

Χειμάζω δ᾽ ἐν κοίλοις ἄντροις
νύμφαις οὐρείαις ξυμπαίζων·
ἠρινά τε βοσκόμεθα παρθένια
λευκότροφα μύρτα Χαρίτων τε κηπεύματα. (Ar. *Av.* 1097–1100)

I winter in the hollow caves playing with the mountain nymphs. In spring I feed on the virgin white myrtle and the gardens of the Charites.

Likewise, the chorus in the *Clouds*, who seem to be minor goddesses, are proper companions for the nymphs:

εἴτ᾽ ἐπ᾽ Ὀλύμπου κορυφαῖς ἱεραῖς χιονοβλήτοισι κάθησθε,
εἴτ᾽ Ὠκεανοῦ πατρὸς ἐν κήποις ἱερὸν χορὸν ἵστατε νύμφαις. (Ar.
Nub. 270–71)

whether you sit on the sacred snow-covered peaks of Olympos or set up the sacred chorus with the nymphs in the gardens of father Okeanos.

These Oceanic gardens of the nymphs are perhaps those of the Hesperides, who tended the apples of immortality.[96]

Our only (more or less) complete example of New Comedy is Menander's *Dyscolus*, "The Misanthrope." This charming play is set in the Attic deme of Phyle upon the slopes of Mount Parnes, beside a shrine of the nymphs and Pan, which has been archaeologically identified (5.1.9, figure 1.3). The shrine is represented onstage as a structure beside Knemon's house, though in reality it was a cave in the side of a steep gorge. As in Aristophanes, the local, contemporary setting and the lighthearted mood both contribute to an informal treatment of religious material (relative to tragedy or choral poetry).[97] The play illustrates for us a fourth-century Athenian citizen's view of the nymphs in his own backyard, as it were. Menander makes good use of the setting, allowing the local deities (naturally well disposed toward erotic love) to influence the outcome of the story. Pan begins the prologue:

τῆς Ἀττικῆς νομίζετ᾽ εἶναι τὸν τόπον,
Φυλήν, τὸ νυμφαῖον δ᾽ ὅθεν προέρχομαι
Φυλασίων καὶ τῶν δυναμένων τὰς πέτρας
ἐνθάδε γεωργεῖν, ἱερὸν ἐπιφανὲς πάνυ. (Men. *Dys.*1–4)

Imagine that this place is Phyle in Attica; that this nymphaion from which I come forth is the well-known shrine of the people of Phyle, they who can farm the rocks here.

He explains that he has caused a wealthy young man, Sostratos, to fall in love with the daughter of the farmer Knemon, in reward for her piety:

ἡ δὲ παρθένος
γέγονεν ὁμοία τῆι τροφῆι τις, οὐδὲ ἓν
εἰδυῖα φλαῦρον. τὰς δὲ συντρόφους ἐμοὶ
Νύμφας κολακεύουσ᾽ ἐπιμελῶς τιμῶσά τε
πέπεικεν αὐτῆς ἐπιμέλειαν σχεῖν τινα
ἡμᾶς· (Men. *Dys.* 34–39)

The maiden is like her upbringing, wholly innocent. By honoring and carefully tending my companions, the nymphs, she has caused us to care for her in return.

The irascible Knemon, however, takes a violent dislike to the would-be suitor. Various misadventures follow, which come to a climax when Knemon falls down the well. After being rescued by his stepson, Gorgias, and Sostratos, he has a change of heart and agrees to the proposed match. The play ends with a final teasing of Knemon, now defenseless, by the slave Getas and the cook Sikon, whom he had earlier insulted. All don garlands, and they carry Knemon into the shrine to participate in the revelry.

Though Pan is not seen again after the prologue, both he and the nymphs are represented onstage throughout by statues. The deities themselves are mentioned repeatedly in the text, so that their continuing presence and influ-

Figure 1.3 Area in front of entrance, east cave at Phyle. Photo courtesy H. R. Goette.

ence are not forgotten.[98] The influence of the nymphs is manifested particularly in Knemon's fall down the well, which Sikon attributes to them (Men. *Dys.* 643–44). This is the earliest known text to suggest that the nymphs were responsible for drownings in wells and springs, though the belief must have had a long folkloric history. The subject is treated in funerary epigrams, which usually feature toddlers and children (those most likely to suffer this sort of accident). There are also the myth of Hylas, the beautiful youth who was pulled by amorous nymphs into a spring, and the related myths of Narkissos and Hermaphroditos. Grouchy old Knemon's fall into the well is a comic reversal of the expected pattern, for the nymphs were known to prefer the young and beautiful.

1.4.4 *Hellenistic Poetry*

In the Hellenistic period, we find an increased interest in rustic and bucolic themes, even as the consumers of contemporary poetry become more urban and elite. The pastoral or bucolic genre is, of course, rooted in earlier literary motifs, such as the *locus amoenus*, as well as in poets' observations of the age-old practice of song competitions among herdsmen. Theocritus, credited with the invention of the pastoral genre, was influenced to some degree by his sixth-century Sicilian compatriot Stesichorus, who is thought to have composed "bucolic songs." Yet pastoral poetry thrives primarily in urban elite society, where the rural, the working class, and the mundane are idealized to provide readers with a fantasy of escape. This fantasy of an unchanging land of simple pleasures, under the eye of benevolent rural gods, was especially attractive to those experiencing the widespread social and political upheavals of the period.

One of Theocritus' forerunners was Anyte of Tegea, an Arkadian poet who was active during the early third century. Anyte was the first to import rural themes and female perspectives into the genre of epigram, which had previously celebrated the values of the male-dominated polis. Epigrams, as the term implies, began as funerary or dedicatory inscriptions that celebrated, for example, fallen warriors or the prizes donated to the gods by victorious athletes. During the third century, epigrams began to be collected for publication, and they emerged as a poetic genre independent of the carved stone. According to Gutzwiller, Anyte was the first to fashion an individualized persona and attach it to a collection of epigrams. As a woman of Arkadia, an isolated district known for its poverty, its pastoral economy, and its patron god, Pan, she was well positioned to appeal to readers through her novel emphasis on the hitherto marginal subjects of rural life, women, children, and animals. As these subjects later became central to the Hellenistic aesthetic, the influence of Anyte and her immediate successors, who also treated these themes, can hardly be underestimated.[99]

Two examples of Anyte's work illustrate her interest in animals and her feeling for the rustic landscape, of which the nymphs are a standard element:

Θάεο τὸν Βρομίου κεραὸν τράγον, ὡς ἀγερώχως
    ὄμμα κατὰ λασιᾶν γαῦρον ἔχει γενύων
κυδιόων ὅτι οἱ θάμ᾽ ἐν οὔρεσιν ἀμφὶ παρῆδα
    βόστρυχον εἰς ῥοδέαν Ναῖς ἔδεκτο χέρα. (Anyte 14, *Anth. Pal.*
    9.745)

Look at the horned goat of Bromios [Dionysos], how like a lord he
casts his haughty eye down over his shaggy face, glorying because
often in the mountains a naiad took the tuft of his cheek into her rosy
hand.

Φριξοκόμα τόδε Πανὶ καὶ αὐλιάσιν θέτο Νύμφαις
    δῶρον ὑπὸ σκοπιᾶς Θεύδοτος οἰονόμος
οὕνεχ᾽ ὑπ᾽ ἀζαλέου θέρεος μέγα κεκμηῶτα
    παῦσαν ὀρέξασαι χερσὶ μελιχρὸν ὕδωρ. (Anyte 3, *Anth.
    Pal.* 16.291)

For bristly-haired Pan and the nymphs of the grotto, the lonely
herder Theudotos placed this gift under the crag, because when he
was greatly weary from the summer heat, they refreshed him, offering
honey-sweet water in their hands.

Leonidas of Tarentum was another early epigrammatist who favored rural
themes. Taking a philosophical stance in support of the simple life, self-suffi-
ciency, and the dignity of physical labor, he seems to have been influenced
by the Cynics.[100] Several of his dedicatory epigrams are miniature vignettes
of the rustic sanctuaries and their gods:

Νύμφαι ἐφυδριάδες Δώρου γένος, ἀρδεύοιτε
    τοῦτον Τιμοκλέους κᾶπον ἐπεσσύμεναι,
καὶ γὰρ Τιμοκλέης ὕμμιν, κόραι, αἰὲν ὁ καπεύς
    κάπων ἐκ τούτων ὥρια δωροφορεῖ. (Leon. 6, *Anth. Pal.*
    9.329)

Nymphs of the water, offspring of Doros, quickly water this garden
of Timokles, for the gardener always brings you gifts in season,
maidens, from these gardens.

Πέτρης ἐκ δισσῆς ψυχρὸν καταπαλμένον ὕδωρ,
    χαίροις, καὶ Νυμφέων ποιμενικὰ ξόανα,
πέτραι τε κρηνέων καὶ ἐν ὕδασι κόσμια ταῦτα
    ὑμέων, ὦ κοῦραι, μυρία τεγγόμενα
χαίρετ᾽ · Ἀριστοκλέης ὅδ᾽, ὁδοιπόρος ὧπερ ἄπωσα
    δίψαν βαψάμενος, τοῦτο δίδωμι γέρας. (Leon. 5, *Anth. Pal.*
    9.326)

Hail, icy stream that leaps down from the split rock, and rustic images of the nymphs, and rocks of the fountain and these your myriad dolls moistened in the waters, maidens. Hail! I, Aristokles the wayfarer, give you as a prize this cup, which I dipped in the water to quench my thirst.

The rustic images (*poimenika xoana*) are those carved by the shepherds themselves. An anonymous epigram in Leonidas' style (*Anth. Pal.* 9.328) speaks also of *xesmata* (carved images) dedicated to the naiad nymphs. Dolls or doll-like votives were left in the water basins, much as we throw coins into fountains today (figure 1.4). Leonidas and other epigrammatists show a great deal

Figure 1.4 Athena washing at fountain with doll votives. Bibliothèque nationale.

of interest in the quotidian details of rustic shrines and devotions, but mythic elements are also present in some of the poems. The motif of the nymphs' chorus is a favorite:

Σιγάτω λάσιον Δρυάδων λέπας οἵ τ' ἀπὸ πέτρας
    κρουνοὶ καὶ βληχὴ πουλυμιγὴς τοκάδων,
αὐτὸς ἐπεὶ σύριγγι μελίσδεται εὐκελάδωι Πάν
    ὑγρὸν ἱεὶς ζευκτῶν χεῖλος ὑπὲρ καλάμων·
αἱ δὲ πέριξ θαλεροῖσι χορὸν ποσὶν ἐστήσαντο
    ὑδριάδες νύμφαι, νύμφαι ἀμαδρυάδες. (Plato 16, *Anth. Pal.* 9.823)

Let the bushy cliff of the dryads be silent, and the springs from the rock, and the mingled bleatings of the mother ewes, for Pan himself plays on his melodious pipe, running his moist lip over the joined reeds. All around they have started the dance with their fresh feet, the hydriad nymphs and the hamadryads.[101]

In the pastoral poems of Theocritus, rustic motifs and themes that had already been well established coalesced into a distinct genre. Readers could immerse themselves in an alternate universe of lovesick herdsmen, recalcitrant nymphs, and meditations on the nature of poetry, where the nymphs act as rustic counterparts of the Muses:[102]

Λυκίδα φίλε, πολλὰ μὲν ἄλλα
Νύμφαι κἠμὲ δίδαξιν ἀν' ὤρεα βουκολέοντα. (Theoc. *Id.* 7.91–92)

Dear Lykidas, many another thing have the nymphs taught me as I herded my cattle upon the hills.

Theocritus often combines erotic and rustic themes, in contrast to early Hellenistic epigrams, which tended to keep these areas separate. The myth of Sicilian Daphnis and his doomed love affair with a nymph is prominent in the corpus (*Id.* 1, 7, 8), and the erotic adventures of Polyphemos (*Id.* 11) and Hylas (*Id.* 13) are recounted.

The Alexandrian scholar-poets Callimachus and Apollonius of Rhodes found endless opportunities for the display of erudition in the vast mythological repertoire of nymphs. Unlike Theocritus and the epigrammatists, they wished less to evoke an ideal landscape than to recapitulate the roles the nymphs had played in archaic poetry, especially epic, and in the logographers, or early historians. With the great resources of the Library at their disposal, they had access to virtually limitless details of local rites and genealogies, which they deployed in sophisticated literary fashion for the delectation of fellow antiquarians.

Fragments 65–66 of Callimachus' *Aetia*, for example, deal with Argive water sources and their role in Hera's cult. They clearly illustrate the ambiguity of certain Danaids' status as heroines, on the one hand, and nymphs, on the other, a conundrum that probably exercised Callimachus as much as it does us (1.1). Fragment 66.1 appears to call the Danaids heroines (*hêrôissai*). In the next line, Amymone is addressed as *numpha Poseidaônos ephudrias*, "watery nymph/bride of Poseidon." There is a deliberate play on the double meaning of nymph, since Amymone is the bride of Poseidon, but the term *ephudrias* is elsewhere reserved for nymphs. Four water sources are mentioned, probably wells (3.2.4, 4.4.2): Amymone, Automate, Physadeia, and Hippe. In fragments 66.8–9, the four are hailed as "venerable homes of nymphs" (i.e., water), *palaitata numpheôn oikia*. These lines, which employ a metonymy of "nymphs" for water (see below), support the rationalizing view that the fountains are simply named after the Danaids and that they are not, in fact, their divine embodiments. Yet, the end of the line continues, "flow, brilliant Pelasgiades." Here, the Pelasgian maidens are simultaneously Danaids and fountains. Thus, Callimachus constantly exploits the ambiguities in both the term *numphê* and the concept of the personified water source.[103]

Apollonius' epic poem, the *Argonautica*, is a virtual encyclopedia of mythopoetic and genealogical themes pertaining to nymphs. Orpheus' cosmogonic song is reminiscent of Hesiod's account of the nymphs' origin; they come into being with the rest of the natural world:

οὔρεά θ᾽ ὡς ἀνέτειλε, καὶ ὡς ποταμοὶ κελάδοντες
αὐτῆσιν νύμφῃσι καὶ ἑρπετὰ πάντ᾽ ἐγένοντο. (Ap. Rhod.
   Argon. 1.501–2)

[He sang] how the mountains rose and how with their nymphs the sounding rivers and all the animals were born.

He also reworks the famous epic comparison of Nausikaä and her maidens with Artemis and her nymphs, applying the simile this time to Medeia and enumerating the homes of the nymphs in typical epic manner:[104]

τῇ δ᾽ ἅμα νύμφαι ἕπονται ἀμορβάδες, αἱ μὲν ἀπ᾽ αὐτῆς
ἀγρόμεναι πηγῆς Ἀμνισίδος, αἱ δὲ λιποῦσαι
ἄλσεα καὶ σκοπιὰς πολυπίδακας. (Ap. Rhod. *Argon.* 3.881–83)

The nymphs follow along with her as attendants, some flocking from the source of Amnisos, some leaving the woods and the high peaks with their many springs.

Apollonius recounts the familiar abductions of Kyrene by Apollo and Korkyra, daughter of Asopos, by Poseidon, but also provides several more obscure local genealogies, using formulas reminiscent of the pathetic genealogies in the *Iliad*:

τὸν ῥα Θόαντι
Νηιὰς Οἰνοίη νύμφη τέκεν εὐνηθεῖσα. (Ap. Rhod. *Argon.*
1.625–26)

[Sikinos] whom the naiad nymph Oinoie bore, when she lay with
Thoas.

Τίκτε δέ μιν νύμφη λειμωνιάς. (Ap. Rhod. *Argon.* 2.655)

Him [Dipsakos] a meadow nymph bore.

Τὸν μὲν Καυκασίη νύμφη τέκεν Ἀστερόδαια. (Ap. Rhod.
Argon. 3.242)

Him a Kaukasian nymph bore, Asterodaia.

Finally, he touches upon themes newly popular in Hellenistic poetry, such
as the erotic abduction of Hylas by the nymphs (2.3.1) and the pathetic fallacy, the depiction of nature as sharing in human emotions. A favorite means
of suggesting this harmony of natural and human feeling is to show nature
personified through the nymphs.[105] Thus, the nymphs fittingly bemoan the
suicide of the young bride Kleite:

τὴν δὲ καὶ αὐταὶ
νύμφαι ἀποφθιμένην ἀλσηίδες ὠδύραντο·
καὶ οἱ ἀπὸ βλεφάρων ὅσα δάκρυα χεῦαν ἔραζε,
πάντα τά γε κρήνην τεῦξαν θεαί, ἣν καλέουσι
Κλείτην, δυστήνοιο περικλεὲς οὔνομα νύμφης. (Ap. Rhod.
Argon. 1.1065–69)

The very nymphs of the woods mourned her when she perished, and
the goddesses made a spring of all the tears their eyes poured to the
earth for her. This they call Kleite, the far-famed name of the
unhappy bride [*numphê*].

We find similar mourning by the nymphs in the pastoral laments for Adonis
and Bion.[106] These mourning nymphs have their origin in the Homeric
themes of the Nereids' mourning for Achilles and of the nymphs' attendance
at Eëtion's grave (1.4.1).[107]

Alcaeus of Messene composed two funerary epigrams in honor of Homer
and Hesiod, portraying the nymphs and Nereids as mourners who have
physical contact with both corpses and tombs. In the first (Alcaeus 11, *Anth.
Pal.* 7.1), the Nereids anoint Homer's body (*nekun*) with nectar and bury it
beneath a rocky outcropping. In the second, nymphs care for the body of
Hesiod:

Λοκρίδος ἐν νέμεϊ σκιερῷ νέκυν Ἡσιόδοιο
νύμφαι κρηνίδων λοῦσαν ἀπὸ σφετέρων,
καὶ τάφον ὑψώσαντο. (Alcaeus 12, *Anth. Pal.* 7.55.1–3)

In the shady grove of Lokris, the nymphs washed the the body of
Hesiod from their own springs, and heaped up his grave.

Both poems emphasize the handling of the body and the intimate services
that are normally performed by the women of the family: anointing with
oil (here, nectar) in the first case and bathing in the second. Finally, the
nymphs in each poem prepare the tomb itself and lay the body to rest. It is
unclear whether the poet had in mind the Iliadic passage about Eëtion,
but certainly he sees nothing untoward in making the nymphs the poets'
morticians, in spite of the Greek gods' traditional aversion to contact with
the dead.

Mourning nymphs long continued to be a favorite theme in epic contexts. In the first century C.E., Antiphilus of Byzantium mentions that the
nymphs, in much the same fashion as for Eëtion, "tend and encircle with
overshadowing elms" the grave of Protesilaus, the first of the Greek heroes to die at Troy. The motif appears again in Quintus of Smyrna's description of the tomb of Memnon: when the body had been set down by
the winds, the daughters of the river Aisepos raised a mound, planted a
grove of trees about it, and lamented the hero. Similarly, Glaukos' body
was borne to Lykia, where the nymphs caused a stream to gush from the
rock under which he was entombed, and Paris was mourned by the nymphs
of Ide. Another tale, preserved by Photius, says that Euphorion, the winged
son born to Achilles and Helen in the Isles of the Blessed, was loved by
Zeus who, failing to seduce him, peevishly struck him with a thunderbolt.
The nymphs on the island of Melos buried him but were transformed into
frogs as punishment.[108]

In the late Hellenistic period, we find that the metonymic identification
of nymphs with water has solidified into a convention. Nicander, the second-
century poet of pharmacology, regularly uses the term *numphê* this way:[109]

ἢ νύμφαις τήξαιο βαλὼν ἁλὸς ἔμπλεα κύμβην. (Nic. *Alex.* 164)

Or cast a cupful of water into salt and let it dissolve.

γληχὼ ποταμηίσι νύμφαις
ἐμπλήδην κυκεῶνα πόροις ἐν κύμβεϊ τεύξας (Nic. *Alex.* 128)

Give as a posset doses of pennyroyal mixed in a cup with river water.

The later epigrammatists made more playful use of the convention, particularly in conjunction with Dionysos as the personification of wine, which the
Greeks normally drank mixed with water:

Αἱ νύμφαι τὸν Βάκχον, ὅτ᾽ ἐκ πυρὸς ἦλαθ᾽ ὁ κοῦρος,
    νίψαν ὑπὲρ τέφρης ἄρτι κυλιόμενον.
τοὔνεκα σὺν νύμφαις Βρόμιος φίλος· ἢν δέ νιν εἴργῃς
    μίσγεσθαι, δέξῃ πῦρ ἔτι καιόμενον. (Meleager 127,
    Anth. Pal. 9.331)

The nymphs washed Bakchos when the lad leapt from the fire after
rolling in the ashes. Therefore Bromios with nymphs is dear to men.
But if you prevent them from mixing, you shall receive a still-
burning fire.[110]

1.4.5 Excursus: The Cave of the Nymphs
in Later Greek Literature

Though it falls outside the chronological limits set for this book, we must
conclude with a brief discussion of the literary renaissance of the third century C.E. At this period, a renewed interest in the nymphs, and particularly
in the motif of the nymphs' cave is evident among Greek prose authors and
poets.[111] The nymphs' cave was at once a literary topos of great antiquity, a
familiar cult space, and, in the form of public baths modeled on grottoes, a
civic space in contemporary use. As a source of rebirth, an earthly paradise,
a meeting place of gods and mortals, or an exemplar of the cosmos itself, its
symbolic power was inexhaustible.

Longus' pastoral romance, *Daphnis and Chloë*, which belongs to the second or early third century C.E., draws upon New Comedy and lyric poetry
(primarily Sappho) as well as the Greek and Roman bucolic poets. Longus
recounts the romantic adventures of two abandoned children, who grow up
together in a rustic environment on Lesbos. Daphnis was found being suck-
led by a nanny goat, while Chloë had been left in a cave of the nymphs to be
cared for by a ewe. Throughout the amorous adventures of the pair, which
include erotic rivalries, kidnappings, and joyous reunions, the nymphs act as
patrons. It is through their agency that Daphnis and Chloë are destined for
each other in love and marriage, and the nymphs, with the gods Pan and
Eros, help the pair through all their travails.

The character Daphnis shares little with the mythic Sicilian Daphnis except his name and occupation, and the romance as a whole references relatively few classical myths (that of the nymph Echo being a prominent exception). On the other hand, the detailed descriptions of rustic sanctuaries
and devotional activities are quite valuable for our study, in spite of the
way Longus idealizes them in keeping with pastoral convention. The
nymphs regularly intervene by appearing to the characters in dream visions (a religious experience that was by no means uncommon in Longus'
time), and the entire work is filled with accounts of fervent prayers and
dedications to them. It is not known whether Longus himself was a native
of Lesbos or had actually seen there a nymphaion of the kind he describes,

but the constant, almost oppressive presence of the nymphs and Pan in the narrative hints that his interest might have been more than academic. In the proem, he says that the impetus for the writing of the romance was a painting he saw in a grove of the nymphs on Lesbos, and he presents the work itself as a dedication (*anathêma*) to Eros, Pan, and the nymphs.[112] The description of the nymphs' cave will suffice to convey the atmosphere of the whole:

νυμφῶν ἄντρον ἦν, πέτρα μεγάλη, τὰ ἔνδοθεν κοίλη, τὰ ἔξωθεν περιφερής. τὰ ἀγάλματα τῶν νυμφῶν αὐτῶν λίθοις πεποίητο· πόδες ἀνυπόδητοι, χεῖρες εἰς ὤμους γυμναί, κόμαι μέχρι τῶν αὐχένων λελυμέναι, ζῶμα περὶ τὴν ἰξύν, μειδίαμα περὶ τὴν ὀφρύν· τὸ πᾶν σχῆμα χορεία ἦν ὀρχουμένων. ἡ ὤα τοῦ ἄντρου τῆς μεγάλης πέτρας ἦν τὸ μεσαίτατον. ἐκ δὲ ἀναβλύζον ὕδωρ ἀπήει χεόμενον, ὥστε καὶ λειμὼν πάνυ γλαφυρὸς ἐκτέτατο πρὸ τοῦ ἄντρου, πολλῆς καὶ μαλακῆς πόας ὑπὸ τῆς νοτίδος τρεφομένης. ἀνέκειντο δὲ καὶ γαυλοὶ καὶ αὐλοὶ πλάγιοι καὶ σύριγγες καὶ κάλαμοι, πρεσβυτέρων ποιμένων ἀναθήματα. (Longus DC 1.4)

There was a cave of the nymphs, a great rock, hollow within and rounded on the outside. The images of the nymphs themselves had been made in stone; their feet were unshod, their arms bare to the shoulder, their hair loose to their necks. Their garments were tucked up at the waist, and there was a smile about their eyes. The whole scene was like a chorus of dancers. The mouth of the cave was in the middle of the great rock, and gushing water spouted from it, so that a hollowed meadow was created before the cave, and plentiful soft grass was nourished by the moisture. There were hung up milking pails, double flutes, and syrinxes and whistles, dedications of the elder shepherds.

Longus' description of musical instruments hung up as dedications is corroborated by finds from the Korykian cave at Delphi. At the end of the romance, Daphnis and Chloë discover their true identities and are married, but maintain their rustic mode of life. They give much of their time to the maintenance of the cave, adorning it and setting up statues and altars of the deities (Longus DC 4.39–40). This form of intense devotion to the nymphs also has historical precedent, as we have seen (1.3).

Longus appears to draw upon both literary models and direct knowledge of cult practice in describing the Lesbian cave of the nymphs. The ultimate source is, of course, the Ithakan cave in the *Odyssey*, but other wondrous caves had been described as well, particularly the famous cave of Nysa. Longus might have been acquainted with picturesque literary accounts, such as that of Diodorus Siculus. Here, Nysa is located in Africa on an island surrounded by the river Triton. The cave is circular in shape and fashioned of multicolored stone. Before the entrance is a grove of trees, and within the cave itself, flowering plants grow and exude a lovely fragrance.[113]

> ὁρᾶσθαι δὲ καὶ νυμφῶν εὐνὰς ἐν αὐτῷ πλείους ἐξ ἀνθῶν
> παντοδαπῶν, οὐ χειροποιήτους, ἀλλ᾽ ὑπ᾽ αὐτῆς τῆς φύσεως
> ἀνειμένας θεοπρεπῶς. Κατὰ πάντα δὲ τὸν τῆς περιφερείας
> κύκλον οὔτ᾽ ἄνθος οὔτε φύλλον πεπτωκὸς ὁρᾶσθαι.
> (Diod. Sic. 3.69.3–4)

In it are also to be seen several beds of the nymphs, formed of all sorts of flowers, made not by hand but by nature herself, in a manner fitting for a god. What is more, in the entire circular area not a fallen flower or leaf can be seen.

Longus' cave shares with Diodorus' the conventional elements of a nearby water source, lush vegetation, and a circular shape indicative of natural perfection, yet the cave at Nysa is a much more fanciful creation. Diodorus' account stresses that its contents have not been "made by hand" in the way devotees usually ornament sacred caves. Instead, all its decorations and furniture are wrought by nature. No cult or votive images are necessary because the cave is the abode of immortals alone. By contrast, Longus' cave is full of the signs of human devotion.

Quintus of Smyrna, in his epic *Posthomerica*, combines an *Iliad*-style pathetic genealogy with a description of a Paphlagonian cave reminiscent of that in Ithake:

> Λάσσον, ὃν ἀντίθεον Προνόη τέκεν ἀμφὶ ῥεέθροις
> Νυμφαίου ποταμοῖο μάλα σχεδὸν εὐρέος ἄντρου,
> ἄντρου θηητοῖο, τὸ δὴ φάτις ἔμμεναι αὐτῶν
> ἱρὸν Νυμφάων ὁπόσαι περὶ μακρὰ νέμονται
> οὔρεα Παφλαγόνων καὶ ὅσαι περὶ βοτρυόεσσαν
> ναίουσ᾽ Ἡράκλειαν· ἔοικε δὲ κεῖνο θεοῖσιν
> ἄντρον, ἐπεί ῥα τέτυκται ἀπειρέσιον μὲν ἰδέσθαι,
> λαΐνεον, ψυχρὸν δὲ διὰ σπέος ἔρχεται ὕδωρ
> κρυστάλλῳ ἀτάλαντον, ἐνὶ μυχάτοισι δὲ πάντη
> λαΐνεοι κρητῆρες ἐπὶ στυφελῇσι πέτρῃσιν
> αἰζηῶν ὡς χερσὶ τετυγμένοι ἰνδάλλονται·
> ἀμφ᾽ αὐτοῖσι δὲ Πᾶνες ὁμῶς Νύμφαι τ᾽ ἐρατειναὶ
> ἱστοί τ᾽ ἠλακάται τε καὶ ἄλλ᾽ ὅσα τεχνήεντα
> ἔργα πέλει θνητοῖσι, τὰ καὶ περὶ θαῦμα βροτοῖσιν
> εἴδεται ἐρχομένοισιν ἔσω ἱεροῖο μυχοῖο· (Quint. Smyrn.
>   *Posth.* 6.469–83)

Lassos, whom godlike Pronoë bore by the streams of the Nymphaios River near a wide cave. This wondrous cave was said to be a sacred place of the nymphs, all who inhabit the long hills of the

Paphlagonians and all who dwell by Herakleia rich in grape clusters.
It was a fitting cave for the gods, hewn from stone yet boundless to
the eye. Cold, crystalline water flows through the cave, and in niches
all round there are stone kraters on the rough rocks, seemingly
wrought by strong men's hands. And about them are Pans and
charming nymphs alike, looms and spindles, and all the other skillful
works that belong to mortals. And these things seem to be wonders
to the people who come within the sacred recess.

Quintus follows the Homeric precedent of having stone kraters and looms
in the cave, but he adds the images of Pan and the nymphs, which he would
have expected to see in a contemporary cult site. Like the cave on Ithake,
this cave has two entries: the north is the path for humans, while the south,
which opens onto a great chasm, is reserved to the gods. Such double entrances are not uncommon phenomena in caves, and observation of nature
probably lay behind the original Homeric description.[114]

The cosmological significance of this detail interested Porphyry, whose
essay *On the Cave of the Nymphs in the Odyssey* is a celebrated work of scholarly exegesis, discussing the *Odyssey* 13.102–12 from a neo-Platonic perspective. Porphyry interprets the cave and its contents allegorically. The cave,
both "lovely" and "murky," represents the cosmos. The naiad nymphs and
the bees are both representative of souls coming into being (*genesis*). It is
through the agency of moisture that souls become embodied:

ναΐδες οὖν νύμφαι αἱ εἰς γένεσιν ἰοῦσαι ψυχαί. ὅθεν καὶ τὰς
γαμουμένας ἔθος ὡς ἂν εἰς γένεσιν συνεζευγμένας νύμφας τε
καλεῖν καὶ λουτροῖς καταχεῖν ἐκ πηγῶν ἢ ναμάτων ἢ κρηνῶν
ἀενάων εἰλημμένοις. ἀλλὰ ψυχαῖς μὲν τελουμέναις εἰς φύσιν καὶ
γενεθλίοις δαίμοσιν ἱερός τε ὁ κόσμος καὶ ἐπέραστος καίπερ
σκοτεινὸς ὢν φύσει καὶ ἠεροειδής· ἀφ' οὗ καὶ αὐταὶ ἀερώδεις
καὶ ἐξ ἀέρος ἔχειν τὴν οὐσίαν ὑπωπτεύθησαν. διὰ τοῦτο δὲ καὶ
οἰκεῖον αὐταῖς ἱερὸν ἐπὶ γῆς ἂν εἴη ἄντρον ἐπήρατον ἠεροειδὲς
κατ' εἰκόνα τοῦ κόσμου, ἐν ᾧ ὡς μεγίστῳ ἱερῷ αἱ ψυχαὶ
διατρίβουσι. (Porph. *De antr. nymph.*11–12)[115]

Thus souls coming into *genesis* are naiad nymphs and so it is the
custom to call brides "nymphs" as well, since they are being married
for childbearing [*genesis*], and to pour over them water drawn from
springs or streams or everflowing fountains. For souls that have been
initiated into the material world and for the deities that preside over
genesis [i.e., the nymphs], the cosmos is both holy and pleasing,
though by nature it is shadowy and "murky": that is why these
beings are considered to have the substance of mist or air. For the
same reason an appropriate temple for them would be a "pleasant
grotto," a "murky" one, in the image of the cosmos in which souls
dwell as in the greatest of temples.

As deities of moisture and of birth, the nymphs preside over the embodiment of souls when children are conceived and born. At the same time, they themselves are representative of the soul, which enters material existence when it enters the "pleasant grotto" of the cosmos. Porphyry spends some time discussing whether the cave is Homer's fiction or historical fact, but he argues that ultimately it does not matter. His interpretation, as he observes, applies equally well to the literary text of the *Odyssey* and to historical caves of the nymphs (*De antr. nymph.* 5). Thus, his analysis uncovers hidden transcendence in the cult tradition itself, a transcendence that he believed Homer, in the capacity of theologian, wished to express.

2 | ANCIENT AND MODERN NARRATIVES

2.1 Modern Greek Folklore
and the Ancient Nymphs

The identification of continuities between ancient Greek and modern Greek culture is now controversial. In an influential article, Loring Danforth exposed some of the methodological pitfalls of this practice, which has long dominated modern Greek folklore studies. These include a failure to consider "survivals" as part of an integrated contemporary culture and failure to demonstrate continuity with evidence from the late antique, Byzantine, and Turkish occupation periods. The ideological underpinnings of the search for continuities have also been closely examined. The need for a national identity, specifically one that links the modern Greeks to the culturally prestigious ancient Hellenes, spurred the development of Greek folklore studies in the nineteenth century. This goal was openly avowed by Greek scholars, including Nikolaos Politis, the father of the modern discipline.[1] Works by many non-Greek scholars, such as Lawson's *Modern Greek Folklore and Ancient Greek Religion* (1910), followed the same path in attempting to show that contemporary beliefs and practices bear witness to "the genuinely Hellenic" character of the modern Greeks.[2] One often-cited example of the continuous survival of an ancient belief into modern times is the modern Greek *neraïda*. The term *neraïda* is derived from ancient *nêrêis* (a daughter of Nereus, i.e., a nymph of the sea), though it refers in modern usage to a group of supernatural females who inhabit not only the sea but woods, springs, and wild places in general.[3] The modern term *numphê,* meanwhile, has retained only the ancient meaning of "bride."

The object of comparisons between the ancient nymphs and the *neraïdes* is first of all to determine whether the *neraïdes* are in any sense the "descendants" of the classical nymphs. The second object is, from the classicist's point of view, to determine what light the modern material can shed upon the ancient. Since ancient sources are biased away from the viewpoints of women, the uneducated, the poor, and the rural, those for whom the cult of the nymphs was most important, we may profit by looking at modern material collected from analogous populations.

In the modern era, the *neraïdes* are only one category of a large population of supernatural beings known as *(e)xôtika,* "things outside or beyond."[4] Some of these beings have apparently classical origins, to judge from their names and functions, including Gello, the child-killing demon, and Charos, the lord of the dead; others are not as easily placed, such as the *kallikántzaroi* (goblins) or the *vrykólakes* (revenants or vampires). These exist alongside a host of saints, angels, and demons who belong to Christian cosmology. All of the *exôtika* have been profoundly influenced by Orthodox Christianity, and it is worth emphasizing that the *neraïda* exists within a Christian matrix of beliefs. This fact alone accounts for some significant differences between nymph and *neraïda.* Most informants in collected material on the *exôtika* indicate that the *neraïda,* like other *exôtika,* belongs to or is somehow allied with the devil.[5] The *neraïda* is more often a cause of misfortune and disease or death than prosperity and health, while precisely the opposite was true for the nymph.

Even a cursory look at the parallels between the *neraïda* and the classical nymph is suggestive of continuity. Many of the characteristics of the nymphs in antiquity are equally applicable to *neraïdes:* they haunt springs, caves, mountains, and groves of trees; they have the form of beautiful young women; they dance and weave; and so on.[6] Even more significant, postclassical sources can be marshaled to demonstrate the transition from nymph to *neraïda.* As the centuries passed, the more sinister and disturbing aspects of nymph beliefs in classical Greece were selected for emphasis. For example, the phenomenon of nympholepsy, which in archaic and classical times was a positive or, at worst, ambiguous event (1.3), eventually became a grievous attack. In the fourth century, we begin to find possession or inspiration by gods associated in both popular and intellectual opinion with pathological states. A medical text attributed to Aristotle suggests that those in whom black bile is both excessive and hot may be "affected by the diseases of madness or enthusiasm, which accounts for the Sibyls and Bakides [nymph-inspired prophets] and all inspired persons."[7]

While the cult of the nymphs remained strong in the Roman Imperial period, nympholepsy itself was widely considered an illness or madness with no positive connotations of inspiration. According to the lexicographer Festus, "Popular belief has it that whoever sees a certain vision in a fountain, that is, an apparition of a nymph, will go quite mad. These people the Greeks call

numpholêptoi and the Romans, *lymphatici*."[8] The shift toward negative interpretations of "seizure by the nymphs" seems to have been largely completed
during the Byzantine period, when the classical nymphs were syncretized
with malignant demons, both the fallen angels of Christian orthodoxy and
older Greek demons like the *lamiai* and *gelloudes*. A Byzantine demonological
text called *The Testament of Solomon* depicts a beautiful female called Onoskelis
(Donkey-leg), who lurks in caves and gorges and entice men sexually only
to strangle them. A much later magical text gives a protective spell against
the demons of night and day, including "the Fair One of the Mountains or
the Nereid Onoskelis." *Neraïdes* who are otherwise beautiful but with the
lower legs of donkeys or goats are sometimes mentioned in modern Greek
material.[9]

The Byzantine dialogue *Peri Daimonôn* attributed to Michael Psellus identifies the ancient nymphs as a class of demons: "those which live in damp
places and are fond of a softer way of life make themselves into the resemblance of women, wherefore these were also called in a feminine way by the
sons of the Greeks Naiads, Nereids, and Dryades."[10] While intellectuals argued that demons had no gender but merely assumed an outward male or
female appearance, popular belief continued to recognize certain classes of
demons who were not only female but whose activities were marked for
gender: the Gello type attacked pregnant women and babies, while the
Onoskelis type seduced, then harmed men. Both of these activities have been
attributed to *neraïdes* in the modern period.

The fourteenth-century preacher Joseph Bryennios attributed the rise of
the Turks to God's punishment of the Christians for their superstitious beliefs, including various forms of divination and the belief that "Nereids" lived
in the sea. Joannes Canabutzes, a Greco-Italian scholar who wrote a commentary on Dionysius of Halicarnassus in the first half of the fifteenth century, also produced a manuscript entitled "Concerning Nymphs, and What
Type of Demons Those Are which the Common People call Neragides."[11]
Seventeenth-century sources relate tales that both reflect Byzantine traditions and look forward to material collected in modern times. Hieronimo
Giustiniani, a Chian belonging to the Genovese nobility ousted from power
by the Turks, wrote a history of his native island in which he recounted much
of interest to the folklorist. He tells of certain spirits who inhabited water
and took upon themselves the appearance of females in order to lure men
into the river to drown. These he compares both to ancient Nereids or naiads
and to succubi. He also speculates that the Fair One of the Mountains (usually spoken of as the "queen of the *neraïdes*") might be a mountain or tree
nymph.[12] Another Chian of the same century, Leo Allatius, recounts a story
of a young girl who saw some lovely ladies in a well and climbed in at their
invitation. When the girl's father searched for her, he saw her sitting on the
water's surface. He too climbed in and was suspended in the same way.
Relatives then rescued the pair with a ladder. These strange events were
attributed to the *neraïdes*, whose home was in the well.[13]

The Byzantines and later observers through the seventeenth century, then, identified a specific kind of female demon with the nymph of the classical world. Furthermore, the ancient nymphs were inevitable candidates for such a transformation to the status of demons because of the well-known phenomenon of nympholepsy, which already in pre-Christian antiquity had lost its positive connotations. In antiquity, as in all later periods, nympholepsy could be manifested either as an abduction, a literal "rapture," or as an aberrant mental or physical state observed in an individual. According to Nilsson, *daimones* like the *neraïdes* survived because they resisted Christianity more successfully than the Olympians, being more basic to people's daily lives.[14] There is much truth to this, but observation of the role of *exôtika* in modern Greece suggests that certain classical *daimones* survived because they also fit comfortably within the developing Christian context. Concern with the malignant influence of evil spirits and demons and the dangers of interaction with them was a feature of the Hellenistic world, but it seems only to have increased with the introduction of Christianity and its emphatic division of the supernatural into the categories of good and evil.[15]

2.2 Patterns of Interaction

In the preceding section, I collected evidence that traced the historical development of the classical nymph into a Christian demon, the *neraïda*. The balance of the chapter takes a comparative approach to the questions of continuity and typological similarity by discussing parallels between ancient and modern stories about the interactions of these figures with mortals. As context, I include in the notes parallels from Thompson's *Motif Index of Folk Literature*. Comparison of *neraïda* and nymph lore with the huge body of world folklore in the *Motif Index* shows the greatest similarities with Celtic, particularly Irish tales, on the one hand, and those of India, on the other. (The majority of *MI* numbers cited below are Irish or Indian parallels.) Hence we may at least speculate that water and/or tree spirits who occasionally took human lovers were a feature of Indo-European mythology. A major distinction between the Irish and Indian material, on the one hand, and the Greek, on the other, is that the former deals with races of supernatural beings both male and female, while the Greek nymphs are exclusively female (male *neraïdes*, however, are attested). It is possible that the silens and satyrs, regular companions of the nymphs, were once their male counterparts (3.1.1).[16]

In the following discussion, stories that deal with abduction by and capture of nymph(s) fall naturally into one group, as do stories that involve nymphs and their trees. This leaves a somewhat heterogeneous group of narratives, which I have kept together on the basis of their common concern with herdsmen. I include a discussion of Anchises' encounter with Aphrodite in the Homeric *Hymn to Aphrodite* because it closely resembles and may be an adaptation of a stereotypical herdsman's encounter with a nymph. For each group, I discuss both the ancient context and the modern parallels. Here, the question of any particular narrative's continuity from antiquity becomes complicated, since we are occasionally dealing with folktale types and motifs that are not unique to Greek culture, ancient or modern (e.g., a supernatural wife).[17] Also, the folklore of the neraïda displays a strong admixture of European tale types and motifs that deal with supernatural beings; this factor, as well as the change to Christianity, accounts for many differences between the ancient nymph and modern neraïda.[18]

As we will see, typical interactions between nymphs and heroes reveal two main preoccupations. First is the possibility of sexual contact with a nymph or nymphs; such contact plays a role in the majority of the stories. With some notable exceptions (e.g., Aphrodite and Anchises or Eos and her various lovers), Greek goddesses do not engage in sex with mortals. In fact, aspiring to sex with a goddess is a prime example of hubris, as the cases of Iasion, Tityos, and Ixion show.[19] Yet, if we except the chorus of Artemis and certain other special cases, it would be reasonable to say of the nymphs that their habit of sexual relations with mortals constitutes a defining characteristic. Structuralists would say that the nymphs thus mediate between the divine and human conditions. Yet no mediation is required in the case of Olympian gods, who freely have intercourse with mortal maidens.

Perhaps this aspect of the nymphs has less to do with mediation than with the cultural significance attached to female sexuality and the adolescent girl. The nymphs combine the forbidden allure of the virgin Artemis with the lust of the sexually aware Aphrodite; yet as local deities believed to inhabit not Olympos but the caves, trees, and springs, they are much more accessible than these goddesses. The nymph is also an idealized mythopoetic version of the village girl at the peak of her sexual desirability, so that her interactions with mortal men can hardly avoid connotations of sexual attraction. Just as gods are attracted to nubile maidens, men are attracted to nymphs. But there is much more variety in tales of nymph-mortal liaisons than in those of gods and maidens. Typically, gods "consummate their desire on the spot, then leave the maiden to become the founding mother" of an elite family.[20] Nothing is said about the female partner's will or desire; she is a simple vehicle for the god's pleasure. The case is very different when mortal men interact with nymphs. The nymph's supernatural power balances or overwhelms the assumed superiority of the male, so that her desires are often central to the narrative.

Second is the danger of displeasing the nymphs; many nymph stories are similar in structure to the numerous myths of hubristic mortals (Niobe, Tantalos, etc.) insulting Olympian gods, who immediately take action to preserve their dignity. Mortal men occasionally display hubris in regard to the nymphs by cutting their trees or by boasting of relations with them. Simply aspiring to sexual relations with a nymph, however, is not a crime as it is in the case of other goddesses. The Daphnis pattern, in which the hero is initially the nymph's favorite, but later incurs her anger through his disobedience, will be revisited several times below.

2.3 Abduction and Capture

Abduction of mortals is a familiar motif in myths of the gods. Zeus' abductions of Ganymedes and Europe are among the most famous examples, but many others exist (Boreas, the North Wind, was famed for his abduction of the Athenian maiden Oreithyia). The abduction is usually erotic in nature, and the interest may be heterosexual or homosexual. Abductions of heroines (and nymphs) by gods are common and typically involve a journey to a different land, where the relationship is consummated (for example, Zeus brings Europe to Krete). Of course, heroes engage in abductions too: Laios abducts Chrysippos, and Theseus abducts Helen. What distinguishes the divine sort of abduction is that it involves immortalization and/or heroization when a mortal is the abductee. The gods made Ganymedes immortal and brought him to Olympos because of his surpassing beauty.[21]

Abduction (like the fulfillment of sexual desire) is the prerogative of the more powerful over the weaker: Olympian over nymph, immortal over mortal, older over younger, and male over female, to the Greek way of thinking. Thus abductions of mortals by nymphs fit the expected pattern in one way (immortal over mortal) and reverse it in another (female over male). The same is true for abductions of mortals by other goddesses, such as that of Tithonos by Eos.[22] The tension produced by the reversal of "normal" power relationships between the sexes is reflected in the outcomes of these myths. Tithonos suffers a terrible fate when he is given immortality without eternal youth. When Hermes brings Zeus' orders for Kalypso to set free her captive lover, Odysseus, she complains bitterly of unequal treatment (Hom. *Od.* 5.118–28) and cites the doomed relationships of Eos with Orion and Demeter with Iasion, which the gods swiftly ended by killing the male partners.

Abduction by a god or goddess is conceptually similar to death, for the abductee undergoes a transformation (heroization/immortalization) that is analogous to death. Certain categories of death are thought of as a kind of selection by the gods and are associated with heroization or transition into an immortal state: being struck by lightning, swallowed by the earth, or carried away in a whirlwind.[23] Drowning in a river or spring is another example, attributable to the nymphs as water deities.

2.3.1 *Hylas and Bormos*

The myth of the beautiful youth Hylas, though certainly of local Bithynian origin, was absorbed into the adventures of the Argonauts.[24] Apollonius of Rhodes relates that Herakles had carried off Hylas after killing his father in a raid. On the journey to Kolchis, he acted as Herakles' companion and servant. At a landfall near Kios, Hylas went to fetch water from a spring in the woods:

ἡ δὲ νέον κρήνης ἀνεδύετο καλλινάοιο
νύμφη ἐφυδατίη. τὸν δὲ σχεδὸν εἰσενόησεν
κάλλεϊ καὶ γλυκερῇσιν ἐρευθόμενον χαρίτεσσι,
πρὸς γὰρ οἱ διχόμηνις ἀπ᾽ αἰθέρος αὐγάζουσα
βάλλε σεληναίη· τῆς δὲ φρένας ἐπτοίησε
Κύπρις, ἀμηχανίη δὲ μόγις συναγείρατο θυμόν.
αὐτὰρ ὅ γ᾽ ὡς τὰ πρῶτα ῥόῳ ἐνὶ κάλπιν ἔρεισε
λέχρις ἐπιχριμφθείς, περὶ δ᾽ ἄσπετον ἔβραχεν ὕδωρ
χαλκὸν ἐς ἠχήεντα φορεύμενον, αὐτίκα δ᾽ ἥ γε
λαιὸν μὲν καθύπερθεν ἐπ᾽ αὐχένος ἄνθετο πῆχυν,
κύσσαι ἐπιθύουσα τέρεν στόμα, δεξιτερῇ δὲ
ἀγκῶν᾽ ἔσπασε χειρί, μέσῃ δ᾽ ἐνὶ κάββαλε δίνῃ. (Ap. Rhod.
   Argon. 1.1228–39)

The water nymph was just rising from the fair-flowing spring. She noticed him nearby, flushed with beauty and the sweet graces, for the full moonlight struck him as it shone from the sky. Kypris excited her heart, and in her confusion she could scarcely keep her spirit within her. But as soon as he dipped his pitcher in the stream, touching the surface crosswise, and the brimming water sounded loudly on the ringing bronze, she quickly put her left arm up and around his neck, longing to kiss his tender mouth, and with her right hand she pulled down his elbow. And he plunged into the pool's midst.

Hylas cried out for help but to no avail. The Argonauts set sail the next day, not realizing that Polyphemos and Herakles had been left behind, still searching for Hylas. Later, the sea god Glaukos informed them that a nymph had made Hylas her husband (*posis*).[25] Theocritus tells essentially the same story but has three nymphs in place of Apollonius' one:

ὕδατι δ᾽ ἐν μέσσῳ νύμφαι χορὸν ἀρτίζοντο,
νύμφαι ἀκοίμητοι, δειναὶ θεαὶ ἀγροιώταις,
Εὐνίκα καὶ Μαλὶς ἔαρ θ᾽ ὁρόωσα Νύχεια.
ἤτοι ὁ κοῦρος ἐπεῖχε ποτῷ πολυχανδέα κρωσσόν
βάψαι ἐπειγόμενος· ταὶ δ᾽ ἐν χερὶ πᾶσαι ἔφυσαν·
πασάων γὰρ ἔρως ἀπαλὰς φρένας ἐξεφόβησεν
Ἀργείῳ ἐπὶ παιδί. κατήριπε δ᾽ ἐς μέλαν ὕδωρ
ἀθρόος . . . (Theoc. *Id.* 13.43–50)

And in the water the nymphs were arraying the dance, the sleepless nymphs, dread goddesses for countryfolk, Eunika, and Malis, and Nycheia with her eyes of May. Eagerly the boy reached down to dip his great pitcher in the fount, but they all clung to his hand, for love of the Argive lad had fluttered all their tender hearts; and headlong into the dark pool he fell.[26]

Apollonius' account more closely approximates conventional relationships by making Hylas the husband of a nymph, while Theocritus eerily describes an erotic yet infantilized Hylas, the common possession of a group of nymphs: "There in their laps the nymphs sought to comfort the weeping lad with gentle words."[27] Both accounts describe the nymphs dancing immediately before the abduction takes place, and both set the scene at night, details that recur in modern accounts of abduction by neraïdes.

Just beyond the Bosporos, east of the site of Hylas' abduction, lay the territory of the Mariandynoi, who told a similar tale. According to a local historian:

ὁμοίως δὲ καὶ τῶν ᾠδῶν ἐνίας κατανοήσειεν ἄν τις, ἃς ἐκεῖνοι κατά τινα ἐπιχωριαζομένην παρ᾽ αὐτοῖς <ἑορτὴν> ᾄδοντες ἀνακαλοῦνταί τινα τῶν ἀρχαίων, προσαγορεύοντες Βῶρμον. τοῦτον δὲ λέγουσιν υἱὸν γενέσθαι ἀνδρὸς ἐπιφανοῦς καὶ πλουσίου, τῶι δὲ κάλλει καὶ τῆι κατὰ τὴν ἀκμὴν ὥραι πολὺ τῶν ἄλλων διενεγκεῖν, ὃν ἐφεστῶτα ἔργοις ἰδίοις καὶ βουλόμενον τοῖς θερίζουσιν δοῦναι πιεῖν, βαδίζοντα ἐφ᾽ ὕδωρ ἀφανισθῆναι. (Nymphis 432 F 5b)

Likewise one may note some of the songs which they sing during a certain festival that is held in their country, repeatedly invoking one of their ancient heroes and addressing him as Bormos. They say he was the son of an eminent rich man, and that in the beauty and perfection of his prime he far surpassed all others. While superintending work in his own fields, wishing to give the reapers a drink, he went to get water and disappeared.

Nymphis does not say who was responsible for the disappearance of the lovely youth Bormos, but the lexicographer Hesychius tells us that he was numpholêptos, snatched by the nymphs. Both Hylas and Bormos were heroized and commemorated in ritualized searches. Nymphis says that the Mariandynoi who lived in the countryside searched for Bormos "to the strains of a dirge with repeated invocation, which they all continue to use to this very day," while the people of Kios conducted a periodic sacrifice and "search" for Hylas in which the priest repeatedly called out Hylas' name.[28]

The affinity of the Hylas myth with that of Echo and Narkissos was recognized by Nicander, in whose Metamorphoses Hylas was transformed to an echo. The nymphs, having abducted Hylas, feared the wrath of Herakles and effected the transformation, which is recalled in Hylas' echoing voice during the ritual search at Kios. In both the Hylas and Echo myths, a nymph aggressively pursues a lovely youth, and one of the protagonists is transformed to a mere voice. A spring is central to both these myths as well as that of another enamored nymph, Salmakis. When the beautiful youth Hermaphroditos bathed in her spring, Salmakis embraced him and prayed that they might never again be separated. The gods answered this prayer, and Hermaphroditos, finding that his body had fused with hers, prayed successfully that any male henceforth bathing in the spring might find himself enfeebled and emasculated.[29]

There is some question as to whether the more torrid erotic myths about nymphs and mortals, such as those of Hylas, Echo, and Salmakis, are entirely products of the Hellenistic period. This book demonstrates that accounts of liaisons between mortal and nymph are found in sources from all periods, beginning with Homer. The accounts that can be traced to the archaic and classical periods, such as those of Daphnis, Rhoikos, and Arkas (discussed below), tend to be concerned with the genealogical fruits of these liaisons or with the powers and prerogatives of the nymphs in their relation to mortals. In stories known only from Hellenistic or later accounts, such as those of Echo or Salmakis, the focus has shifted to the erotic and psychological details of the liaisons, and there is a special emphasis on unrequited or thwarted female desire. Thus Ovid's versions of the Echo and Salmakis myths, as well as his tale of Galateia's disastrous love for the youth Akis, all tend to reduce the distinction between nymph and mortal by describing their psychological states in similar detail and in favoring accounts in which nymphs, like lovestricken mortal girls, are unable to fulfill their desires without help from "the gods." Echo does not spitefully punish Narkissos for his scorn. Instead, it is another scorned lover, a male, who implores Nemesis to punish the arrogant youth. Interestingly, Ovid does not treat the myth of Hylas, which emphasizes the nymphs' ability to choose and coerce their lovers, betraying an affinity with accounts of nymphs found in early sources.[30] It is impossible to tell when the Echo and Salmakis myths originated, but if of ancient vintage, they bear clear marks of modification to suit Hellenistic and Roman tastes.

Another abduction story is related in an epigram by the Hellenistic poet and scholar Callimachus:

Ἀστακίδην τὸν Κρῆτα τὸν αἰπόλον ἥρπασε νύμφη
    ἐξ ὄρεος, καὶ νῦν ἱερὸς Ἀστακίδης·
οὐκέτι Δικταίησιν ὑπὸ δρυσίν, οὐκέτι Δάφνιν
    ποιμένες, Ἀστακίδην δ᾽ αἰὲν ἀεισόμεθα. (Callim. Ep. 22)

A nymph carried off Astakides the Kretan goatherd
from the mountain, and now Astakides is holy.
No longer beneath the Diktaian oaks, no longer
shall we sing Daphnis, shepherds, but ever Astakides.

Interpretations of this little poem vary, since we do not know the identity of Astakides and cannot be certain whether the intent is humorous or serious. Callimachus is perhaps paying a compliment to the pseudonymous Astakides who, like Daphnis, composed pastoral songs and, like Hylas, was "abducted by a nymph." As in the cases of Hylas and Bormos, Astakides' abduction makes him *hieros* (holy), deserving of ritual commemoration. The repetition of Astakides' name in the epigram is reminiscent of the invocations for the two mythical abductees and of the repetitions found in Hellenistic pastoral laments.[31] The pastoral hero Daphnis, too, though he was not abducted, died a mysterious death after erotic involvement with a nymph, and a cult was instituted in his honor (2.5.1).

The idea that young people who died had been carried off by the nymphs became a popular conceit in funerary art and verse in the Hellenistic and Roman worlds. (Note that the funerary element was present from the start in the Hylas and Bormos myths and is emphasized in Callimachus' epigram.) Several epitaphs offer consolation to the bereaved in the belief that a loved one was "snatched by the nymphs" because of his (or her) beauty. For example, the second-century C.E. epitaph of a five-year-old girl states: "Not Death, but the naiads snatched the excellent child as a playmate." Similarly, the first- or second-century epitaph of a two-year-old says: "The spring nymphs snatched me from life." It is impossible to tell whether these deaths were due to drownings, but this seems likely in view of the emphasis upon water nymphs. The funerary epitaphs, however, seem to differ from the Hylas and Bormos myths in that they lack the erotic element and focus on the nymphs' abduction of children rather than of youths or men. They usually involve very young children, and many of the examples (perhaps the majority) were written for females. The epitaphs belong to a cosmopolitan, probably widespread funerary tradition that draws upon the abduction myths.[32] The dissemination of the Hylas myth in literary sources, such as Apollonius of Rhodes' *Argonautica*, must have been a major influence upon this tradition. An example is Isidora, an Egyptian girl whose funerary inscriptions explicitly compare her to Hylas (4.8.9).

A few atypical stories that involve heroines and nymphs are closer thematically to these funerary inscriptions than they are to the Hylas-Bormos pattern, since they express the belief that the nymphs desire a playmate rather than a lover. Dryope, the Thessalian shepherdess who bore a son, Amphissos, to Apollo, was such a favorite of the hamadryad nymphs that they later snatched her and made her one of themselves (4.6). Essentially the same pattern is present in the story of another Thessalian shepherdess, Kyrene (4.8.8).[33]

2.3.2 *Abductions by* Neraïdes

Both erotic abduction and the snatching of children are practiced by the *neraïdes*. In a Greek folktale from Kos, a young man is seized and "kissed all over" by the *neraïdes*. Weakened by their attentions, he is kept enchanted in a cave, where he is forced to dance with them every night until dawn. He finally escapes the enchantment with the help of a protective cloth marked with crosses.[34] In village lore, men or women are sometimes seized and forced to dance until they drop from exhaustion, or they are simply carried away by the nymphs to a remote mountain top. Sleeping outdoors, especially beside a spring or under a tree, is considered especially dangerous. The same verb, *(h)arpazô* ("snatch" or "seize"), is used in both ancient and modern accounts. One man who was walking with his wife was suddenly seized and carried away; he was later found dead by a fountain, his body covered with bruises.[35] Both the sudden seizure and the location of the body indicate the identity of his attackers.

Very much as in the epitaphs mentioned above, children who die or disappear are said to have been taken by the *neraïdes*. There is even a story, reminiscent of Dryope's myth, about an adolescent girl who used to run wild in the woods until she slowly sickened and died. It was said that the *neraïdes* wanted her, and neighbors told how they had seen her dancing with the *neraïdes* in the woods only days before her death. Another girl was cured of her desire to join the *neraïdes* only by a ceremony of exorcism. Leo Allatius' seventeenth-century Chian story about a pretty young girl enticed into a well bears a certain resemblance to the Hylas myth, and mothers are duly warned to keep children away from wells and springs, especially at the critical times of late night and midday.[36]

2.3.3 Capturing a Nymph: Thetis and the Swan Maidens

The capture of a supernatural creature is a common folklore motif in many cultures.[37] If a human succeeds in capturing the otherworldly creature, he or she can expect a reward for letting it go. In Greek myths, the motif was applied to deities of water such as Proteus, who commonly had the power both to shapeshift and to tell the future. The capture motif was used in some versions of the myth of Peleus and the Nereid Thetis. Thetis was an unwilling bride but had to marry Peleus after he hung on while she changed into a variety of terrifying shapes. A doublet of the myth is the conquest by Aiakos, Peleus' father, of another Nereid. Psamathe, whose name means "sea sand," turned herself into a seal while trying to escape Aiakos; their son was called Phokos, "seal."[38]

The earliest reference to Peleus and Thetis appears in the *Iliad*, where Thetis does not mention her actual capture by Peleus but gives a rather different explanation:

ἐκ μέν μ' ἀλλάων ἁλιάων ἀνδρὶ δάμασσεν,
Αἰακίδῃ Πηληῖ καὶ ἔτλην ἀνέρος εὐνὴν
πολλὰ μάλ' οὐκ ἐθέλουσα. (Hom. *Il.* 18.432–34)

Out of all the sea goddesses, he [Zeus] subjected me to a man,
Aiakos' son Peleus, and I endured the bed of a mortal man, though I
was completely unwilling.

There are in fact two distinct traditions about Peleus and Thetis. The version followed by Homer attributes the marriage to Zeus' command that Thetis marry a mortal, either out of spite, because she refused him in order to please Hera; or prudently, because an oracle that Thetis was destined to bear a son greater than his father made her a danger to the hegemony of the Olympians. This version is better suited to epic because of its cosmogonic significance.[39] The other version, naturally a favorite of vase painters and plastic artists because of its visual possibilities, emphasizes the physical trial endured by Peleus in the capture of his wife—surely unnecessary if Zeus had commanded her obedience. Pindar gives both versions of the tale though not in the same ode. In both cases, he makes the marriage to Thetis follow immediately upon Peleus' demonstration of superior virtue in refusing the lewd advances of Akastos' wife, Hippolyte.[40]

Peleus' capture of Thetis is an ancient example of what is known in modern folklore as the "swan maiden" type.[41] This is one of the most widespread of European tale types and indeed is often found in non-European cultures. In one common version, a man captures a bird maiden by stealing her coat of feathers while she bathes. Once a wild and free creature, she must now return home with him and be his wife. This she does and usually serves as a model wife and mother. However, she often is said to be completely silent during this period of captivity. (A fragment of Sophocles refers to the "voiceless marriage" of Peleus and Thetis.[42]) Eventually, she regains possession of the coat and disappears, though she may return periodically to check on or aid her children. In modern Greek folklore, a youth commonly captures a neraïda by stealing her scarf or another article of clothing and leads her home to be his wife. But, as in the case of the swan maiden, she always gets her scarf back and vanishes. One variant has the youth capturing the neraïda by holding onto her hair as she changes into different beasts. Later, he consults an old woman as to how he might make his wife speak; she recommends that he pretend to burn their child in the fire. When he does so, the neraïda screams, "Let go of my child, you dog!" and leaves forever, taking the child with her. This version clearly draws upon the myth of Thetis' shapeshifting and her attempt to immortalize Achilles in the fire.[43]

Capture of a neraïda would seem to be a reversal of the theme of abduction by nymphs and to reflect the "normal" power relationships between male and female. Such a capture of a fairy spouse is always effected by a man, never by a woman, thus coinciding with established gender roles. Why, then, are only two examples of this motif (Thetis and Psamathe) known from ancient Greek material, while it is one of the commonest stories about neraïdes? Certainly, the influence of European fairy-capture stories has played a role. Yet it also appears that the notion of a deity placed within a mortal's power was repugnant to classical Greek religious sensibilities.[44] The only explanation for such an anomalous reversal of the normal relations between mortal and god was the intervention of Zeus: Apollo is ordered to serve the mortal king Admetos as punishment for his disobedience; Thetis is made subject to a mortal husband to prevent the birth of rivals to Zeus' power. Furthermore, the claims of both Peleus and his father, Aiakos, to the mastery of divine brides were bolstered by their reputations for righteous behavior. Aiakos was among the "most pious" of men, able by his prayers to end a famine (Apollod. *Bibl.* 3.12.6), while Peleus virtuously rejected the advances of Akastos' wife (Pind. *Nem.* 5.25–34).

In contrast to the respect accorded these Nereids, the *exôtika* of orthodox Christianity are quite low in the hierarchy of supernatural power. They stand at the end of a long tradition of magical manipulation of demons and are powerless to resist certain talismans and prayers. Thus, it is not surprising that the swan maiden type thrives in modern Greek lore. On the other hand, the supernatural female always defies the mortal woman's role and ultimately rejects her wifely and motherly duties. The *neraïda's* inevitable escape shows that the mortal husband's power over her is temporary at best.

2.4 The Nymph's Tree

The simple idea that a hamadryad nymph is coeval with her tree is well attested in archaic and classical literature. The word hamadryad itself, a compound of *hama*, "together with," and *drus*, "tree," "oak," contains this idea. Plutarch suggests that the word was first used by Pindar, but the idea is attested as early as the Homeric *Hymn to Aphrodite* (1.4.1).[45]

Sources of widely varying date elaborate the basic motif of the hamadryad into narratives about heroes' encounters with these tree-dwelling nymphs. Sometimes, the hero observes that the tree is in imminent danger and preserves it, to be rewarded by the nymph. (Not surprisingly, sex comes into the picture here.) Other times, the hero wickedly cuts the tree in spite of the nymph's pleas and is duly punished.[46] Both stories are moral exemplars; the latter is probably the elder of the two, since it fits the ancient paradigm of hubris punished.

2.4.1 *Saving the Tree: Rhoikos and Arkas*

The hero Rhoikos is known to us from three sources. A fragment of the historian Charon of Lampsakos, who was roughly contemporary with Herodotus, is the fullest of these. It relates how Rhoikos, seeing that an oak was about to fall, had it propped up. The nymph, who had been doomed to perish with the tree, acknowledged her debt to Rhoikos and bade him ask for whatever he wished. When he asked to have sex with her, she told him to avoid relations with other women and said that a bee would act as a messenger between them. The bee flew by while he was playing draughts, and Rhoikos spoke so crudely that he angered the nymph, who "maimed" him.[47] (It is unclear whether the bee itself irritated Rhoikos or was simply the witness to his offensive speech.)

The second source is a scholiast to Theocritus 3.13, who tells us that Rhoikos, a Knidian by birth, saw in Assyrian Nineveh a well-grown tree that was leaning over and about to fall. He steadied it with a stake, and the nymph having witnessed this act thanked him, for she was coeval with the tree. She then bade him ask for whatever he wished as a reward. He requested sex, and she told him that a bee would announce the time of their meeting; here the story ends without mention of Rhoikos' punishment. The combination of the Near Eastern setting with the detail that Rhoikos is a Knidian is puzzling (perhaps arising from the period of Persian domination of Knidos).

The third source is a fragment of Pindar, unfortunately preserved only in a Latin translation of Plutarch's *Quaestiones Naturales*. Plutarch quotes the fragment in his answer to the question: "Why are bees quicker to sting those who have recently committed adultery [*stuprum*]?" He explains that those who are debauched are unclean and hence are quickly detected by bees, who are "devoted to cleanliness and neatness." To illustrate his point, he cites Pindar: "You little builder of honeycombs who struck Rhoikos, subduing with a sting his treachery."[48] This seems to imply yet another version, probably one in which Rhoikos, like the herdsman hero Daphnis, broke a promise not to consort with other women and in which his punishment was administered by the bee. The folklore of bees had it that they were pure, fastidious creatures (2.5.3), easily offended. The bee was angered by sexual infidelity or even the uncleanliness of a recent sexual act.[49] In Charon's version, however, the nymph is angered by the hero's "crude" speech, perhaps his boasting of his anticipated sexual conquest. As we shall see, both infidelity and indiscretion in speech are taboo for mortals who have affairs with nymphs.

On mainland Greece, the hero Arkas, eponymous ancestor of the Arkadians, is supposed to have married a nymph; Charon is again the earliest source for this tale. When hunting one day, Arkas came upon a hamadryad's oak in danger of perishing, about to be swept away by a snow-swollen stream. Arkas rerouted the stream and steadied the tree's foundation, and "the nymph, whose name according to Eumelus was Chrysopeleia, mated with him and bore Elatos and Aphidamas, from whom all the Arkadians are descended." Arkas' marriage to the nymph Chrysopeleia is also ascribed to the early epic poet Eumelus by Apollodorus, while Pausanias specifies that Arkas' wife was a dryad nymph, whom he calls Erato. He further describes a sanctuary of Pan in Arkadia where "in older days this god used to give oracles through the lips of the nymph Erato, the same Erato who married Arkas son of Kallisto" (4.4.3). Presumably, the prophetic nymph aided Arkas in his capacity as king.[50]

The idea that the hero who saves a nymph's tree is entitled to sexual relations with her has certain similarities to the Peleus and Thetis capture myth. In both cases, the hero does something that puts the supernatural female within his power, at least temporarily. Rhoikos forfeits his privilege by breaking a taboo, either of fidelity or of silence. Arkas, like Peleus, marries the nymph and sires offspring. A myth with interesting similarities to these is that of Thamyris, who challenged the Muses to a singing contest. If he won, he was to have had intercourse with one or all of them; his punishments upon losing the contest were blinding and the loss of his musical talent.[51] Here are the familiar elements of the mortal's desire for intercourse with the supernatural female, his attempt (in this case, unsuccessful) to gain power over her, and his ultimate punishment by blinding (2.5.1).

2.4.2 Cutting the Tree: Paraibios and Erysichthon

The most obvious way to offend a hamadryad nymph is to damage the tree that is the nymph's abode. The digression on nymphs in the Homeric *Hymn to Aphrodite* speaks of the respect in which men hold large pines or oaks on the mountains: "they call them holy places of the immortals; these trees no mortals cut with the ax." Similarly, in modern times, respect for trees remained strong. According to Lawson, the first days of August were regarded as sacred to *neraïdes* in many parts of Greece, so that both the cutting of trees and the use of water for washing was prohibited. In the forests of northern Arkadia, he adds, the woodcutters refrained from speech while a tree was falling, lest a *neraïda* hear them, and the cutting of the finest trees was the most dangerous, since they were more likely to harbor *neraïdes*.[52]

Apollonius of Rhodes relates the tale of Paraibios, whose father had cut a nymph's tree "in the pride of youth" in spite of the nymph's protests. This hubris resulted in a curse upon the man and his descendants, and apparently did not kill the nymph, as the description in the Homeric *Hymn* would lead us to expect. The seer Phineus advised Paraibios to erect an altar and sacrifice to "the Thynian nymph" in order to restore her good favor.[53] The same motif of tree cutting appears in Callimachus' *Hymn to Demeter*, in which Erysichthon, son of Triopas, attempts to cut down Demeter's grove in spite of her warnings (in the guise of the priestess Nikippe) and is punished by an insatiable hunger. Here, the goddess has been substituted for the nymph as the offended party, and Erysichthon attacks her sacred grove, not just one tree. Yet the nymphs have not been expunged completely from the story, and one tree in particular is singled out for attention and personified:

ἧς δέ τις αἴγειρος, μέγα δένδρεον αἰθέρι κῦρον,
τῷ δ' ἔπι ταὶ νύμφαι ποτὶ τῶνδιον ἑψιόωντο,
ἃ πράτα πλαγεῖσα κακὸν μέλος ἴαχεν ἄλλαις. (Callim. *Hymn*
    6.37–39)[54]

There was a certain poplar, a huge tree reaching to the sky, near which the nymphs used to play at noon. This was the first tree struck, and it wailed an anguished song to the others.

In Ovid's version of the Erysichthon myth (*Met.* 8.738–878), the tree nymphs are similarly present, as is the focus on an individual tree. One of the mighty oaks in a grove that belongs to Ceres is hung with fillets, garlands, and votive tablets. Around it, the dryads are accustomed to dance. When Erysichthon impiously attacks the "oak of Deo," blood flows from it, and the nymph within the tree cries out a prophetic curse as she dies. The dryads then petition Ceres for vengeance; Ceres sends an Oread nymph to fetch Fames (Hunger) from the Caucasus. The hideous hag Fames attacks Erysichthon, who proceeds to use up his patrimony, sell his own daughter, and finally to consume his own flesh.

A modern Greek folktale called "Myrmidonia and Pharaonia" is very similar to these ancient tree-cutting myths. The king of Myrmidonia loved a girl called Dimitroula, but she reserved her love for a humble plowman. The king had this man murdered, but "the spirits" (*ta stoichia*), an inclusive term for supernatural beings, caused the king and his men to be drowned in a hidden well. (This death by drowning in a water source provides a hint as to the identity of the offended spirits.) The king's son then had a nearby grove cut down in revenge (again, showing his awareness that a supernatural agent had caused his father's death). A great oak tree bled as it was cut, and Dimitroula was seen in its severed trunk, cursing the men. The king's son, crying out against "the female spirits" (*ta thêlika stoichia*), attacked her with his sword but could not draw it back because it was embedded in the tree. He left the sword sticking in the tree and ran away.

> Now all men were saying that this was either one of the *neraïdes* [*anerades*] or one of the Good Women [*tes kales gunaikes*] or in short some daughter of the spirits [*korê tôn stoichiôn*]. But in fact as for Dimitroula, everyone said that she was a daughter of the *neraïdes* [*neraïdopoula*]. And this was made the surer because the prince [soon after] suffered a great and unthought-of evil, and this because he had cut down her mother's trees, killing her [Dimitroula] also.[55]

The prince began to be plagued by dreams of the *neraïda* threatening revenge. She caused him first to be burned, then chilled to the bone, saying, "This and very much worse is the lot of those who cut my beautiful trees." Finally, he was visited by Ravening Hunger, personified as an old hag who struck him in the belly, using the sword with which he had killed Dimitroula. He ate so voraciously that he was forced to sell all his possessions, even trying to sell his son and daughter. Finally, he died, tearing at his own flesh. (There follows a long sequel, rarely discussed by classical scholars, in which the wicked prince's niece marries a neighboring king. Her brother, now the king of Myrmidonia, wagers his life on her chastity. Through a palace intrigue, the girl is accused of adultery, and her brother is ordered to give up his life. On the way to his execution, he reproaches Dimitroula that her enmity still haunts the family even though the third generation is innocent, and he is miraculously saved.)

Dawkins, who collected the folktale, comments that this story is not a widespread type; he knows of no modern parallels to this punishment for cutting a tree. The resemblance to the ancient story of Erysichthon, on the other hand, is striking. The question is whether this tale represents a continuous tradition or a literary borrowing; scholarly opinion has been divided on the issue since Dawkins first published the tale. In favor of the tale's antiquity is the fact that it includes details present in both the Ovidian and Callimachean versions of the Erysichthon myth. For example, the extended description of the haglike Hunger strongly recalls Ovid, while the description of the offender leaving his weapon behind and running off in a panic is present in Callimachus but not in Ovid.[56] Also pertinent are the facts that the modern tale was collected on Kos directly opposite the Knidian promontory, where the ancient myth was set, and that this area was continuously populated by Greeks since antiquity.[57] (Rhoikos, who saved a nymph's tree and asked for sex as a reward, was also a Knidian.) The most recent scholarship, however, has not accepted Dawkins's tale as an authentic survival. Fehling, followed by Hopkinson and others, has argued that the tale's similarity to the literary sources makes it suspect, since the centuries should have produced a dramatic divergence, and that there is no parallel for such a detailed correspondence between ancient and modern material. He concludes that the folktale is actually a nineteenth-century amalgam of Callimachus and Ovid.[58]

The tale's resemblance to Ovid, in particular, is suspicious, but if we are to identify Ovid as the source (perhaps in the Greek translation of Planudes),[59] we must then dismiss the locale near Knidos as a coincidence and accept Fehling's unlikely reconstruction of borrowings from *both* ancient authors. Furthermore, the degree of the tale's similarity to or divergence from the literary sources is a surprisingly subjective matter. Several important elements of the modern tale are present in neither ancient version, suggesting to me a plausible degree of divergence (for example, the entire prelude of Dimitroula's love for the plowman and his murder; the *neraïda* 's punishment of the prince with heat and cold; the long sequel to the tree episode that, like the Paraibios tale, emphasizes the curse through generations). Another possibility is that "Myrmidonia and Pharaonia" combines an authentic antique tradition with contamination from later sources, most likely Ovid in translation.

Fehling further argues that the modern tale has no internal coherence because Christian rationalization has transformed Ovid's Demeter and hamadryad into the human girl Dimitroula, leaving no reason for the cutting to be considered a crime.[60] He ignores the *neraïda*, who is clearly identified in the tale as the offended party. Christian rationalization admittedly caused the elimination of Demeter from the story (hence the awkwardness of the hunger punishment), but her place was easily taken by the *neraïda*, that is, one of the nymphs who in all versions are present at the tree. This change is quite natural, since the Erysichthon myth is itself a variation on a folktale about cutting or preserving a *nymph's* tree (we have the parallels of Rhoikos, Arkas, and Paraibios for the nymph's tree but no parallel stories of Demeter and trees). The early transference of the story to Demeter was probably the result of the influence of Demeter's prominent cult at Knidos.[61] With the advent of Christianity, Demeter must disappear, but there would have been little pressure to rationalize a nymph out of the story, since as we have seen, the nymphs were smoothly assimilated as *neraïdes* into the Christian system. The presence of a *neraïda* is exactly what we should expect in a modern version descended from the ancient myths.

2.5 Nymphs and Herdsmen

The ancient nymphs, with Apollo, Hermes, and Pan, were the favorite deities of herdsmen. They protected and increased the flocks; they were associated with the cooling water and shade of caves and areas with abundant vegetation; and they delighted in music, the pastime of the solitary herdsman.[62] And it was the herdsman (or the above-named gods) with whom the nymphs most often interacted. An account of a herdsman given by Nicander illustrates the benefits and hazards of the relationship. Kerambos, a Thessalian shepherd, was once a great favorite of the nymphs, who gathered about to hear his beautiful songs. Yet he rejected the kindly advice of their associate Pan to remove his flocks to lower ground for the winter. To this foolish whim, he added the offense of insulting the nymphs by denying that Zeus was their father. Thus, when winter came, his flocks froze to death and he was transformed to a wood-gnawing beetle.[63] The nymphs, with Pan and the other rustic gods, could aid the herdsman in protecting and increasing his flocks. But neglect or insult of these deities could lead to dire punishment, particularly for an erstwhile favorite. Kerambos' tale is similar to other stories of hubris punished but illustrates the specific sphere in which the nymphs were expected to act.[64]

Often the relationship between herdsman and nymph is complicated by a sexual liaison. Homer mentions several sexual encounters between princely herdsmen and local nymphs, which in every case lead to the birth of royal Trojans or their allies (1.4.1, 4.9.1). The Homeric examples and the case of Arkas who, with his nymph wife, was the progenitor of the Arkadian kings have genealogical raisons d'être that set them apart, as successful outcomes, from the prevailing pattern of disaster following sexual contact with a nymph. Sex with a nymph is always considered an alluring prospect, but these stories also focus on the inherent danger of a liaison with a female more powerful than the hero is. Moreover, unhappiness in love seems to be regularly associated with herdsmen, as with their patron god, Pan.[65] The Daphnis myth perhaps best illustrates the intersection between pastoral themes and the erotic danger of nymphs.

2.5.1 Daphnis

The Sicilian cowherd Daphnis was the nymphs' favorite, an exceptionally beautiful son of Hermes, according to several accounts derived from the fourth-century historian Timaeus. Parthenius' account is the only one explicitly ascribed to Timaeus' *Sicelica*:

> ἐν Σικελίαι δὲ Δάφνις Ἑρμοῦ παῖς ἐγένετο, σύριγγι δή τε δεξιῶς
> χρήσασθαι καὶ τὴν ἰδέαν ἐκπρεπής. οὗτος εἰς μὲν τὸν πολὺν
> ὅμιλον ἀνδρῶν οὐ κατήιει, βουκολῶν δὲ κατὰ τὴν Αἴτνην
> χείματός τε καὶ θέρους ἠγραύλει. τούτου λέγουσιν Ἐχεναίδα
> νύμφην ἐρασθεῖσαν, παρακελεύσασθαι αὐτῶι γυναικὶ μὴ
> πλησιάζειν· μὴ πειθομένου γὰρ αὐτοῦ, συμβήσεσθαι τὰς ὄψεις
> ἀποβαλεῖν. ὁ δὲ χρόνον μέν τινα καρτερῶς ἀντεῖχεν, καίπερ οὐκ
> ὀλίγων ἐπιμαινομένων αὐτῶι, ὕστερον δὲ μία τῶν κατὰ τὴν
> Σικελίαν βασιλίδων οἴνωι πολλῶι δηλησαμένη αὐτόν, ἤγαγεν εἰς
> ἐπιθυμίαν αὐτῆι μιγῆναι· καὶ οὕτως ἐκ τοῦδε ὁμοίως Θαμύραι
> τῶι Θρακὶ δι᾽ ἀφροσύνην ἐπεπήρωτο. (Timaeus 566 F 83)[66]

> Daphnis, the son of Hermes, was born in Sicily; he was skilled at
> playing the syrinx and exceptionally good looking. He did not enter
> into the company of men, but he lived in the open, herding his cattle
> winter and summer on Mount Aitne. They say that a nymph,
> Echenaïs, fell in love with him and forbade him to draw near to any
> other woman. If he disobeyed, he would become blind. For some
> time, he resisted strongly, although many women were mad for him.
> Finally, one of the Sicilian princesses caused his ruin with much
> wine, arousing in him a desire to sleep with her. As a result, like the
> Thracian Thamyris, he was blinded because of his foolishness.

We find the earliest attestation of the myth in Aelian's observation that the sixth-century Sicilian poet Stesichorus wrote about Daphnis, though we have little idea what his poems contained or whether they bore any resemblance to later accounts. Aelian tells a story identical in essentials to that of Timaeus and adds that "because of this incident, bucolic song was first heard and the blinding of Daphnis was the subject. Stesichorus began such poetry." A late tradition, perhaps due to Theocritus' influence, assigns to Daphnis himself the invention of pastoral, or bucolic, song. Other versions of the myth besides the Timaean exist, and the best known, that of Theocritus, is deliberately enigmatic.[67]

Theocritus' *Idyll* I depicts a series of visitors to Daphnis, who is wasting away with love. First, Hermes, the local herdsmen, and Priapos come, all asking Daphnis what ails him, but the youth is unresponsive. Finally, Aphrodite arrives and asks whether Daphnis admits defeat. She says with a smile, "Surely, Daphnis, you vowed that you would give Love a fall, but have you not yourself been thrown by cruel Love?" (the metaphor is from wrestling). Daphnis angrily reproaches her and insists that "even in Hades Daphnis will be a bitter grief to Eros." He scornfully taxes her with her love of the mortals Anchises and Adonis and her defeat at the hands of Diomedes. Last of all, Daphnis apparently dies in spite of Aphrodite's wish to prevent this; he bids his surroundings farewell, then "goes to the stream," or dies.[68] What relation this version has to Timaeus' Sicilian account is unclear, though theories abound. Most either attempt to reconcile the two or, conversely, see the Theocritean version as completely different from the Timaean and similar to the Hippolytos myth in that Daphnis dies after incurring the anger of Aphrodite with a vow of chastity.[69] (Diodorus Siculus' account mentions that Daphnis liked to accompany Artemis, though this detail is found in no other version.)

Gutzwiller, however, has convincingly suggested that Daphnis is more like Phaidra: he wastes away because he refuses to submit to his love for the mortal woman. Thus, Theocritus changes the ending so that Daphnis does not betray the nymph, but when he finds that his love for the mortal woman is incurable, he allows himself to die. Daphnis, in the position of being forced to choose between his communion with nature (represented by the nymphs, the landscape, and the animals) and his overwhelming erotic passion (represented by the mortal girl, referred to as Xenea in *Id.* 7), confounds Aphrodite by choosing death. Daphnis' bond with nature and rejection of human society is present even in the Timaean version, which says that he "did not enter into the company of men, but he lived in the open." This misanthropy is attributed to other mythical herdsmen as well. Essentially the same conflict is present in the Sumerian Gilgamesh epic, in which the wild man Enkidu, once in perfect harmony with nature, is seduced by the harlot from the city and is therefore rejected by his animal companions. Daphnis avoids this fate but dies prematurely, like Achilles, because of his unbending adherence to a pastoral version of the heroic code.[70] Theocritus' Daphnis, then, represents a major departure from the folktale pattern found in Timaeus. Daphnis' infidelity to the nymph and his resulting blindness, both characteristic folktale motifs, are jettisoned.

Yet, there might have been Sicilian versions of the Daphnis myth that spoke of his death. Because Daphnis was worshiped as a hero (Servius reports that the Sicilians sacrificed at a spring, which replaced Daphnis' translated body), an account of his death would have been an important part of the cult. There is also a tradition that Daphnis' hounds were buried with him, another probable reference to hero cult.[71] The folktale account, which emphasizes Daphnis' punishment of blindness, could have coexisted with a cult in which Daphnis' death was the principal focus.

The fact that blindness is not mentioned in Theocritus' account, while death is not mentioned by Timaeus and Parthenius, fits Devereux's observation that death, blindness, and castration, while usually mutually exclusive fates, are symbolically equivalent. Devereux's Freudian perspective on blindness is given a significant corrective by Buxton, who argues that blindness in Greek mythology has a much broader range of connotations than a strictly Freudian view allows.[72] For example, must we always interpret the blindness of singers and seers as a symbolic castration? On the other hand, Devereux provides a long list of ancient citations that link blinding with sexual trespass, and in this specific context, we must consider the possibility that blindness is a symbolic substitute for the dire fate of "unmanning" feared by mortals who cohabit with goddesses. Odysseus fears that Kirke will leave him "weak and unmanned"; Rhoikos and Daphnis are blinded; and Anchises after his encounter with Aphrodite is either "enfeebled" or blinded. Giacomelli has argued persuasively that Anchises' plea to Aphrodite not to leave him "living *amenênos* among men" refers to fear of lifelong impotence; she cites at the same time many examples of the association between the head (especially the eyes) and the male generative organs.[73]

There are many modern Greek accounts, moreover, of men who suffer illness, impotence, or death after a sexual encounter with a *neraïda*. Others enjoy a period of unusual prosperity followed by a disaster. The misfortune is the result of displeasing the *neraïda* by breaking a taboo: either having sex with someone else (as in the Daphnis myth) or boasting of the relationship (as in the Anchises myth).[74] Usually, those reported to have liaisons with *neraïdes* are herdsmen, whose long periods of isolation in the wild make the story plausible. Stewart collected some particularly horrifying accounts of this kind during his fieldwork on Naxos. In two cases, men who spoke of their relations with *neraïdes* sickened and died after enduring a painful swelling of the genitals. In another case, a man had so many sheep and goats that everyone wondered how he could tend them alone. He foolishly bragged to Kyría Sophía (Stewart's informant) that he kept company with *neraïdes*. She, in turn, told the man's wife, who determined to visit him on the mountain. The angry *neraïda* first abandoned, then destroyed both flock and herdsman, who died within a few days.[75]

2.5.2 Trojan Herdsmen: Anchises in the Homeric *Hymn to Aphrodite*

Segal, Clay, and others have illuminated the structural function of the nymph digression in the Homeric *Hymn to Aphrodite* (1.4.1): mediation of the contradiction between mortality and immortality, which forms the core of the poem. But other, external factors can also shed light on the prominence of the nymphs in the *Hymn*. A possible model for the *Hymn*'s interaction between a female divinity and a mortal man is the folkloric union of herdsman and nymph, a motif that appears, in spite of Sicilian Daphnis, to have been particularly characteristic of the Troad and is found as early as the *Iliad*.[76]

The best-known example of union between a nymph and a member of the Trojan royal family is that of Paris and Oinone. The story seems late because of its romantic features, but it can be traced back to Hellanicus, who mentions Paris and Oinone's son, Korythos. Paris meets and marries Oinone while working as a solitary shepherd on Ide, before his true identity is known. This nymph has divinatory and healing powers and warns Paris that if he is ever wounded, only she can cure him. He abandons Oinone for Helen and is ultimately punished when, mortally wounded by Philoktetes' arrow, he is refused treatment by the spiteful nymph. Hegesianax and Apollodorus say that she repented of her decision, but when she found that she was too late, she killed herself. We can see in this story, though tailored to fit the circumstances, the basic elements of the Daphnis pattern: hero meets and has erotic encounter with nymph, who enjoins fidelity; when he angers the nymph by his disobedience, he is punished.[77] Paris' marriage to Oinone and her suicide are details more characteristic of a heroine's story than a nymph's. Indeed, Oinone is not always identified as a nymph, though her special powers, her home on Ide, and her river-god father, Kebren, demonstrate her basic affinities.

In interpreting the relationship between Anchises and Aphrodite, most commentators have chosen between two models of immortal-mortal intercourse. The first is the abduction model, as practiced by Eos upon Tithonos and her other mortal lovers or by Zeus upon Ganymedes. As these examples are mentioned in the *Hymn* itself, we might expect them to be relevant. Structuralist analysis has shown that their significance lies in the contrast of the fate of Anchises, on the one hand, with Ganymedes' eternal youth and, on the other, with Tithonos' old age.[78] Anchises will remain mortal and will age normally; the point is that his case is, in fact, different from theirs. Unlike Anchises, both Ganymedes and Tithonos are permanently removed, spatially and temporally, from the world of mortal men. They are both swept away suddenly to a divine realm, whereas Anchises meets and is seduced by his divine lover on earth. Thus, while Tithonos and Ganymedes are important points of reference within the context of the *Hymn*, their myths are not parallel to that of Anchises.

The other obvious model for sexual contact between a goddess and a mortal is the great Near Eastern complex of Ishtar/Astarte and Tammuz (Sumerian Innana and Dumuzi) and, closer geographically to the setting of our *Hymn*, Anatolian Kybele and Attis. Since the relationship of Aphrodite's lover Adonis to Tammuz is well known, she might be expected, especially in the neighborhood of Phrygia, to play the counterpart to Kybele. This theory, that the Aphrodite of the *Hymn* was closely related to the Anatolian Great Mother (and hence that Anchises is a mythic relative of Tammuz, Adonis, and, particularly, Attis), was widely accepted in the first half of the twentieth century but has now largely fallen out of favor. Still, most scholars agree that certain details of the *Hymn* are suggestive of Anatolian and/or Near Eastern influence. The behavior of the wild animals that fawn upon Aphrodite calls to mind Kybele's status as *potnia therôn*.[79] Then, too, the motif of the young, beautiful herdsman-prince, so prominent in the myths of the Trojan royal family discussed below, is suggestive of the herdsmen Dumuzi, Tammuz, and Attis. (Dumuzi was both shepherd and king, a fact that is integral to his myth.)[80] On the other hand, in narrative terms, the Anatolian–Near Eastern pattern is no better a match for the Anchises myth than the Tithonos-Ganymedes pattern. Adonis, a herdsman or, more often, a hunter, dies and is mourned by Aphrodite; Ishtar/Astarte deliberately sends her lover to the underworld, then decrees mourning for him. Attis is driven mad by Kybele and castrates himself, then dies or is turned into a fir tree; again, mourning is a significant element of the myth. Anchises clearly does not fit this pattern, which has as its most significant element the death of the goddess's lover. He is killed by the bolt of Zeus only in Hyginus' account; in the other extant accounts, he lives out his life in an enfeebled state.

The tale of Aphrodite's union with Anchises, then, is a narrative match for neither of the proposed models of goddess–mortal interaction. Instead, it reproduces a folkloric story pattern that appears most often in accounts of nymph–mortal relations.[81] In this "Daphnis pattern" there is a rustic (mountain) setting; the goddess meets her lover, usually a herdsman, in a solitary location rather than snatching him away in the style of Eos[82]; the goddess places a restriction or taboo on her lover; and she threatens her lover with punishment if he disobeys (which he eventually does). All of these elements are present in the *Hymn*, and all are typical of narratives about nymph–hero unions. In addition, both the specific taboo of silence placed upon Anchises and his fear that his encounter will result in impotence have parallels in modern folklore about herdsmen's affairs with *neraïdes*.

All the accounts of goddess–mortal unions I have so far discussed have at their root the same male fear of placing oneself at the mercy of a more powerful female (with, perhaps, an attendant unconscious attraction to this idea). The reversal of expected gender roles creates a powerful anxiety that is completely absent when gods have their way with mortal maidens. The three models I have discussed, however, have quite distinct outcomes. Tithonos, Endymion, and Odysseus, who all experience variations of the abduction model, have their identities erased or threatened through senility, unconsciousness, and isolation, respectively. Dumuzi/Tammuz, Attis, and Adonis, on the Near Eastern model, are killed outright in horrifying ways and make trips to the underworld. Daphnis and Anchises, by contrast, are maimed physically but continue to live. Daphnis' death and lamentation, it is true, are certainly prominent elements of the later pastoral tradition. Yet the Timaean account, our earliest detailed source, speaks only of Daphnis' blinding, not his death, and blinding is prominent in most accounts of his fate. According to Aelian, "the first bucolic songs" had the blinding of Daphnis as their subject. We have seen that Theocritus' account of Daphnis' death is a poetic elaboration on the folktale, designed to lend the hero a tragic dignity and pathos. Hence, Anchises appears to have more in common with the Timaean Daphnis than with Dumuzi.

To return to the Homeric *Hymn*, Anchises is alone herding cattle on Mount Ide when Aphrodite arrives. In order to seduce Anchises, the goddess must make him believe that she is a mortal maiden ready for marriage. Thus, Anchises is enabled to assert himself sexually and take a dominant role, undressing the goddess while she coyly keeps her eyes lowered. After the sex, however, she wastes no time in abandoning the game and revealing her true identity to the terrified Anchises. She demands a cover story that will protect her identity and plausibly explain the origin of Aineias: Anchises' lover was a nymph of Mount Ide. In fact, no story could be more plausible in the context of the royal genealogy (4.9.1). Anchises is commanded to tell nobody of the true encounter; the *Hymn* alludes to his eventual punishment for disobeying this order. As we have seen, such a requirement of silence is common in modern tales of erotic encounters with *neraïdes*; the man who divulges the secret usually sickens and dies. The idea, emphasized in the *Hymn*, that Aphrodite is ashamed of her affair with a mortal and thus demands silence is a rationalization of the folkloric taboo against telling of a supernatural encounter, particularly one of a sexual nature. In the *Iliad*, there is no secrecy, and Aphrodite does not appear to be ashamed.[83]

Viewed in this light, the presence of the nymphs in the poem is less of a digression than a sign, perhaps a conscious recognition by the poet, of their pervasive influence on the narrative. The problem of the sexual politics of such a union is eased by placing it within a familiar paradigm. Three possibilities are envisioned in the poem: sex with a goddess (the true state of affairs and disturbing to Greek sensibilities), sex with a mortal woman (Aphrodite's ploy to seduce Anchises), and sex with a nymph, plausible because of the bucolic setting and the local tradition of unions between herdsmen and nymphs. The flowerlike nymphs of Ide not only provide the childcare for Anchises' son but the explanation of his origin.[84]

2.5.3 *Aristaios and the Helpful Nymphs*

Nymphs often act as nurses for young gods and heroes (as the Okeanids do in the *Theogony*) or as helpers in a hero's quest. Nymphs also play a minor role in several quest myths, as an intermediate source of helpful information or objects.[85] Aristaios, the herdsman–hero par excellence, enjoyed a relationship with the nymphs very different from that of the unfortunate Daphnis or any of the other heroes we have so far examined. The tale that Aristaios offended the nymphs when he attempted to rape Eurydike is familiar to readers of Vergil's fourth *Georgic*, but the connection with Eurydike (hence the offense) is generally thought to be Vergil's invention.[86] The Greek versions of the Aristaios myth do not include this episode. Instead, they depict

Aristaios as a benefactor of humanity, who has acquired knowledge of the rural arts as well as a virtuous lifestyle through the tutelage of the nymphs or from other figures prominent in rustic cult, such as Ge, the Horai, and Cheiron.

The myths of Aristaios are abundant, complex, and occasionally self-contradictory. This results in part from the fact that his cult, like that of Herakles, was more widespread than those of most other heroes. Unlike Herakles, however, Aristaios never quite achieved Panhellenic status, and there was no concerted attempt to rationalize his myths into a coherent narrative.[87] The traditions about Aristaios fall into two main groups, with some ancillary material. First (and probably oldest) is the Thessalian-Libyan account, which focuses on Aristaios' mother, Kyrene (4.8.8). In this version, Aristaios is born in Libya but reared in Thessaly by the Horai and Ge (Pindar) or by Cheiron and the Muses (Apollonius of Rhodes).[88]

The second group of myths belongs to the islands of Keos and Euboia.[89] In this view, the infant Aristaios was reared not by Cheiron or Ge but by nymphs, who taught him all of his famed skills: herding, cheesemaking, olive culture, and especially beekeeping. Kean bee nymphs called Brisai were the source of this last skill.[90] Pseudo-Oppian's Euboian account makes Aristaios the pedagogue, so to speak, of the young Dionysos. He lives in a cave on a mountain in Euboia at Karyai (i.e., Karystos) and is renowned for the same list of rustic skills as in the Kean myth. There, he receives from Boiotian Ino the infant Dionysos, whom he rears with the help of the Euboian women and the local nymphs, including the dryads and "the nymphs who have the care of bees," *melissonomoi numphai*.[91] Both Keos and Euboia, then, possessed myths that portrayed the nymphs as the source of Aristaios' knowledge about apiculture and other rural arts. Both might have claimed to be the hero's birthplace as well. It is interesting that a fragment of Aristotle makes the nymphs of Keos flee to Karystos when they are frightened by a great lion; perhaps this is an attempt to explain the dual traditions.[92]

There is a parallel to this picture of Aristaios as caretaker of the young god in Diodorus's account of Dionysos' birth, drawn from an Alexandrian source, Dionysius Scytobrachion. There, the Libyan god (Zeus) Ammon takes his son to the nymphs and to Nysa, "one of the daughters of Aristaios," to be reared in a miraculous cave on an island in the river Triton (1.4.5). Aristaios is appointed guardian of the child because of his understanding, learning, and self-control, *sôphrosunê*.[93]

Apollo, who is Aristaios' father in most accounts, was also taught by bee nymphs (1.3). The story of Apollo's tutelage by the nymphs in a herding context was transferred to his son, Aristaios, who shares Apollo's cult title of Nomios. Yet the similarity between Aristaios' nymph nurse-teachers and those of Dionysos is perhaps even more striking. Thus, we have a number of stories that share a basic outline: a rural culture hero/god is reared or receives tutelage from supernatural figures with similar rural associations:

God/Hero	Teacher	Skill Mentioned	Version
Apollo	bee maidens	divination	Hom. *Hymn* 4.555–57
Aristaios	Horai, Gaia	"guardian of flocks"	Pind. *Pyth.* 9.59–65
Aristaios	nymphs, bee nymphs	herds, cheese, honey, olives	Aristotle; Diod. Sic. 4.81
Aristaios	Cheiron, Muses	healing/divination, herding	Ap. Rhod. 2.509–15
Dionysos	Nysa, nymphs, Aristaios	ingenuity, self-control	Diod. Sic. 3.70
Dionysos	nymphs, bee nymphs, Aristaios	herds, olives, cheese, honey	Oppian 4.265–72

What is the role of nymphs in these accounts beyond the simple fact that nymphs are kourotrophic and belong to a large group of figures who have the care of the young as their purview? The nymphs appear to have a special function not merely as nurses but as the ultimate source of specific customs and skills, which are then passed to humankind through the conduit of a culture hero or god. Healing and divination may seem odd in tandem with cheesemaking and herding, yet their rustic origins are recognized in both the Homeric *Hymn to Hermes* account of Apollo's youth, which connects divination with herding, and the accounts of Cheiron's tutelage of heroes in healing.[94] For the survival of his flocks, the herdsman needed a working knowledge of both weather prediction and the properties of beneficial and harmful plants. The nymphs are variously said to teach divination and a range of pastoral skills; they are especially associated with beekeeping.

The folklore and mythology of the bee is extensive, and this insect is regularly associated with the civilizing virtues of order, cleanliness, and continence. The antiquarian Mnaseas' account of certain bee nymphs gives a good picture of their function in this respect.[95] He says that in the Peloponnese, *melissai* (nymphs) stopped men from eating human flesh and convinced them to eat instead the fruit of trees. At the same time, a certain one of these, named Melissa, first found a honeycomb, tasted it, then mixed it with water as a beverage. She taught others to do this, and thus the creature was named for her, and she was made its guardian. The scholiast quoting Mnaseas (*FHG* fr. 5) adds:

> Without nymphs there is no honoring of Demeter, for they first showed men the use of produce [*karpos*], how to avoid cannibalism [*allêlophagia*], and how to contrive coverings for themselves from the woods for the sake of modesty. Nor is any marriage celebrated without them, but we honor them first as a recognition, because they were the originators [*archêgoi*] of piety [*eusebeia*] and observance of divine law [*hosiotês*].

The bee nymphs here are regarded as teachers of the earliest skills and moral values that distinguished civilized humans from bestial savages.[96] They thus make fitting teachers of Aristaios, who brings humanity to the next level of civilization, pastoralism. (Perhaps because of the existence of pastoral nomads, the Greeks regarded pastoralism as an earlier stage than agriculture, though the archaeological evidence suggests that the two developed in tandem.)[97] Aristaios, in turn, acts in concert with the nymphs as the teacher of Dionysos.

Dionysos' various teachers presumably are not themselves the source of knowledge about viticulture but act as a moderating influence on the wild young god, just as the bee nymphs moderated the savage behavior of early humans. This, at least, is how Plutarch understood the function of the nymphs: "The ancients made Zeus' nurses two [Ide and Adrasteia], Hera's one [Euboia], and Apollo's of course two [Aletheia and Korythaleia] but gave Dionysos more, for it was necessary to make this god more gentle [*hêmerôteros*] and prudent [*phronimôteros*] by giving him nymphs in greater measure to tame and train him." Aristaios the bee master, who is famed for his *sôphrosunê*, was chosen as the guardian of the infant Dionysos for the same reason.[98]

The nymphs' role in the Aristaios myth thus diverges from the other patterns we have examined. First, the nymphs stand in a maternal relationship to Aristaios, and sex never enters the picture (unless one believes that the Vergilian Aristaios, would-be rapist of the nymph Eurydike, has a Greek antecedent).[99] Aristaios is never said to interact with one nymph in particular; the nymphs are always treated as an undifferentiated group. Because of his actual identification with Zeus and Apollo, as well as the spread of his cult throughout the Greek world, Aristaios seems to inhabit an august sphere far removed from the popular tales of Daphnis or Rhoikos. In fact, he has a close typological kinship with Dionysos, who similarly was reared by nymphs, benefited mortals with knowledge of a rustic art, and was raised to the status of a god. Not surprisingly, there are no close parallels for the myth of Aristaios in modern Greek folklore, because the *neraïdes* are rarely seen as a source of civilizing benefits. As we have seen, however, they have the power to increase or decrease a man's flocks.[100]

2.6 Interpreting Ancient and Modern Narratives

A dominant theme in both the ancient and modern accounts we have examined is that of actual or potential sexual relations between a mortal male and a supernatural female. Stewart observes that women often report hearing or seeing *neraïdes*, "but they do not have the same type of contact with them." *Neraïdes* occasionally accept a young girl into their society, but the majority of *neraïda* stories focus on their sexually charged relations with males. The same is true of the ancient examples collected here, which include only a few female protagonists, those who "join the nymphs." The relations of males and females to the nymphs in traditional narratives are qualitatively different because they are predicated on gender difference and the potential for sexual activity. As we have seen, moreover, stories about the *neraïdes* and nymphs seem to represent in their respective societies some of the same cultural concerns about the dangers of female sexuality and status. Several folklorists have theorized about the function of *neraïdes* and the *exôtika* in general in modern Greek culture. Stewart concludes that "an image such as the nereid is perhaps most of all an image that enables the expression and negotiation of sensitive issues of gender and sexuality."[101] It is in exploring the psychosexual significance of ancient stories about nymphs, then, that the comparative folklore approach can aid us most.

Again, we must allow for certain differences. The most important is the *neraïdes'* position on a spectrum of good and evil. In popular belief, they partake strongly of the devil's end of the spectrum. The nymphs, on the other hand, are neither good nor evil, for the gods of classical antiquity did not exist on a moral spectrum of the Christian type. Thus, while the spheres of interest of nymphs and *neraïdes* are largely identical, their activities are interpreted differently. The nymphs were generally seen as providers of benefits who were dangerous when provoked, but a certain malice is usually assumed to underlie the activities of the *neraïdes*. The second important difference is that the ancient nymphs possessed a dignity and cultural prestige as (mostly) beneficent goddesses, which their modern counterparts lack. Hence, the nymphs could play important roles in mythic accounts of the origin of basic institutions and skills, as in the training of the culture heroes Dionysos and Aristaios or the civilizing behaviors taught by the bee nymph Melissa.

In modern Greek culture, the *neraïdes* as well as other *exôtika* are associated with deviance from expected behavior, sexual or otherwise. Roaming about at times when others in the village are sleeping (i.e., at night or at midday) indicates an abnormal desire for sex, and it is not coincidental that these are precisely the times when the *exôtika* are active (the same was true of nymphs).[102] On the one hand, the *exôtika* embody fears about unfaithful spouses or unchaste offspring, who may be a danger to the order of family and village; on the other, they represent the desires that are held in check by social strictures. In the modern Greek setting, there is a strong overlay of Christian sexual mores, but there is no reason the nymph could not have functioned in much the same way for the ancients, especially since the strict control of female sexuality is of major concern for both cultures. The *neraïdes* appear, at first, to be wholly negative examples for women because of their license and freedom, while the Panaghia (the Virgin) seems to be the only sanctioned role model. But the picture is more complex than this, because beautiful girls or those accomplished at domestic tasks are often compared to *neraïdes*. Furthermore, the *neraïdes* themselves are often described as brides (*nuphes*), a state that is (and was in antiquity) the recognized goal for young women.[103] Thus, the *neraïdes* are at once the epitome of what the young Greek woman both should and should not be. The same paradox is present in the ancient conception of the nymph, who is sometimes a chaste companion of Artemis, sometimes a sexual aggressor, but always beautiful and accomplished.

The Blums and Stewart observe that *neraïda* stories are told by both sexes in a variety of contexts and that the context often affects the interpretation of a given story. In modern times, the men often tell each other those *neraïda* stories "which show how one controls a woman, refusing to allow her freedom, keeping her tokens (children, clothes, affection, responsibility, reputation) to prevent the flight of the wild bird." The women, by contrast, "in warning men of how nereids will harm them . . . indirectly express their own aggressive wishes and frighten the men into good behavior."[104] Versions of the Rhoikos myth told in antiquity, then, might have emphasized the titillating prospect of sex with a nymph when told in an all-male group, while in a group of women or a mixed group, the dominant element might have been Rhoikos' punishment for infidelity.

The Blums concluded from their fieldwork that *neraïdes* both embodied female fantasies, whether conscious or not, and were a projection of male anxieties about women.[105] Likewise, we can see that, as a sexually independent female, the nymph is a powerful figure of fantasy who arouses desires and fears in both sexes. Her beauty and eroticism make her a fantasy figure for men. The myths of capturing a nymph, on the one hand, and being abducted by one, on the other, appeal to different kinds of male fantasies. Yet she is also powerful enough to inflict punishment upon those who displease. The fear of being "unmanned" by such a female is translated into the mythical punishments of blinding or laming (though, in modern tales, impotence is mentioned openly).[106] The nymph's sexual aggressiveness is both attractive and repellent. Stories of handsome youths' abduction by nymphs, for example, express male desire for a passive sexual experience, yet the same desire cannot be separated from the fear that such a surrender is equivalent to death. Odysseus' experience as the captive and unwilling lover of Kalypso also fits this paradigm.

It is well recognized that Greek culture distinguished conceptually between females ready for or newly entered into the state of marriage (*numphai*) and wives (*gunaikes*). Unmarried girls were associated with the wild and compared to spirited horses who needed to be "tamed" or fields to be "cultivated."[107] Only through marriage could they be properly integrated into society. This idea is clearly operative in the physical domination of Thetis by Peleus, as in many of the modern swan maiden folktales. But the stories about heroes and nymphs provide a counterpoint to male complacency about the taming of women. If the bride truly belongs to wild nature, she may be as unpredictably powerful as the natural world. The state of cultivation only lasts as long as the farmer continues his efforts; as soon as land is neglected, it returns to its former wild state. Thus, Thetis and the swan maidens ultimately abandon their mates and leave their children in the care of others.

From a female point of view, the nymph represents different desires and fears. On the one hand, the nymph's sexuality can spell disaster in the wrong context. Myths of nymphs expelled from Artemis' chaste choruses when they are found to be pregnant by gods warn against spurning social expectations. The nymph can also represent "the other woman," the deviant member of the community who lures others' husbands into her bed and is thus a threatening figure (as Kalypso is Penelope's rival for Odysseus). On the other hand, the nymph embodies a fantasy of total female independence. Eternally young and lovely, she enjoys both sexual freedom and, equally important, the physical freedom that was denied most Greek women. The nymphs are most often represented in the dance, which combines the twin aspects of eroticism and physical activity. Only in dance could a Greek woman be the center of attention, both male and female. Thus, the nymph represents sexual pleasure without the restricting aspects of marriage and, what is more, without the duties of caring for children. Interpreting from the female point of view the material on *neraïdes* they collected in 1962, the Blums draw several conclusions.[108] First, there is a desire to be free of the subordination and responsibility of marriage. Second, there is recognition that even well-loved children are a burden that one sometimes would wish to overthrow. Finally, there is a wish for the ecstatic experiences of dancing and music, which might also include sexual license and, ultimately, doing violence to men.

The Blums collected two stories in which *neraïdes* forced women to dance naked with them until dawn, leaving them exhausted.[109] The detail of nakedness, in view of the strict standards of female modesty current in the Greek women's community, is a surprisingly candid expression of the fantasy of sexual and physical freedom. Finally, the nymph is able to demand the sexual fidelity of her mortal lovers and punish those who stray. While ancient Greek society as a whole condoned extramarital sex for husbands, it did recognize the sexual jealousy (and loss of dignity) of neglected wives. Jealous Hera, ever on the watch to punish Zeus' mortal lovers, is a figure of fun. Thus, the nymphs possessed a power for which many Greek women must have wished in vain. In stories of mortals and nymphs, the sexual double standard is turned on its head.

3 | GODS, GODDESSES, AND NYMPHS

3.1 Nymphs and the Rustic Gods

The nymphs' relations with the Olympian gods, particularly Zeus and Poseidon, are usually envisioned in terms of abduction and sexual contact, which lead to colonization and the birth of eponymous heroes. These relationships are discussed in chapter 4. The focus of the present discussion is the special attraction between the nymphs, deities of the untamed or partially tamed landscape, and those gods who have strong rural or pastoral associations. In these cases, the relationships are sometimes best described as familial (Dionysos and his nurses, the rivers as fathers of nymphs) and sometimes as sexual (nymphs and silens). A third category is one we might call choregic, which describes the relationship between a male chorus leader and his female dancers; this too can have a sexual subtext (Apollo, Hermes, or Pan and nymphs).

3.1.1 *Nymphs, Silens, and Dionysos*

Silens, or satyrs, are mythical horse-man hybrids, often depicted in vase paintings with a horse's tail and ears and, occasionally, with horselike legs and hooves instead of feet. Unlike centaurs, they do not have four legs; they also lack the centaurs' social organization and bellicose temperament. They are portrayed as cowardly, lazy, and sexually insatiable. On the François vase, the only vase to identify the creatures as a group, they are called *silênoi*, silens. Another name, often used in literary sources but absent from the vases, is *saturos*, satyr. Though the names were probably used synonymously in the classical period, I use the term silen in this discussion except where "satyr" is specified in the sources.[1]

In spite of the strong Dionysiac aura the silens possess in the classical period, some evidence suggests that in origin they were unattached to the wine god. There are numerous myths of silens who seem independent of Dionysos. For example, King Midas captured a silen, and a silen attempted to rape Amymone when she was searching for a spring. There are legends of towns terrorized by marauding satyrs, and satyrs are reported to have dwelled in distant, uncivilized lands.[2] In the mythic universe of the early archaic Greeks, silens and nymphs were natural companions for each other, lusty and boisterous beings of the wild who engaged in promiscuous sex and were unrestrained by the social conventions applied to mere mortals.

There is also evidence that the silens and nymphs formed part of a single phylogeny in early Greek myth. The earliest literary reference to the silens, in the Homeric *Hymn to Aphrodite*, describes them as mating with the nymphs in pleasant caves. The satyrs are identified in a fragment of Hesiod as cousins of the nymphs, and silens are said in various ancient sources to have nymphs as consorts, mothers, or companions.[3] Satyric drama also sheds some light on these relationships. Little remains of these plays, which portrayed Silenos and a band of mischievous silens intruding into various mythological stories. Yet, in this meager material, we find abundant references to nymphs. The plays often had rustic settings, for which the front door of the *skênê* represented the mouth of a cave.[4] In a fragment, perhaps from the *Oineus* of Sophocles, the silens describe themselves: "We come as suitors, children of nymphs, servants of Bakchos, neighbors of the gods." This is not the only text to call silens children of nymphs. A line in Sophocles' *Ichneutae* that mentions "any nymph-born wild creature of the mountains" seems also to refer to silens. Their father is usually considered to be Silenos, who brags of his achievements to his unruly brood in the same fragment: "Yet your father, you worthless creatures, in his manly youth set up many elaborate offerings in the nymphs' abodes."[5] It was customary to set up hunting trophies, such as skins or heads, as thank offerings to the nymphs or Pan; in this case, the offering can also be viewed as a love gift. A Hellenistic epigram witnesses a trophy of a boar's head and skin, dedicated to Pan and "the silens' mates that dwell in caves."[6]

Euripides' *Cyclops* reinforces our view of the close relationship between nymphs and silens, on the one hand, and Dionysos with both these groups, on the other. Silenos tells how he accompanied Dionysos on his youthful adventures: "first, when Hera drove you mad and you left your nurses, the mountain nymphs; then in the battle against the earthborn giants." Scholars think these lines refer to earlier satyr plays. One candidate is Sophocles' *Dionysiscus*, which probably told of Dionysos' persecution by Hera and his parting from the nymphs of Nysa. Later, the chorus of *Cyclops,* stranded in Sicily, laments the loss of their revels: "no more in Nysa with the nymphs do I sing the Iakchos song to Aphrodite." And Odysseus asks whether the silens want to escape their servitude to Polyphemos, return to their former haunts, and "live with the naiad nymphs in the halls of Bakchos."[7]

In spite of their own anthropomorphism, then, nymphs apparently shared their essence as beings of the wild with the various man–beast hybrids (satyrs or silens, centaurs, and Pan). At least in early times, silens and nymphs seem to have been male and female counterparts. Perhaps this symmetry was always limited to certain contexts, since both nymph and silen have unique qualities. Satyrs or silens are often characterized as worthless and lazy, qualities that are never attributed to nymphs. Nymphs, in turn, have a wide range of cultic and social functions, while the silens are usually not cult recipients nor did they develop specific roles outside of their familiar Dionysiac presence. Both display a robust sexuality, though in the silens' case it is comic and crude; in the case of the nymphs, seductive and awesome.

Hedreen has made an important contribution to our understanding of the silens' relationship with Dionysos by emphasizing the role of narrative context in interpreting vase paintings. Silens appear in certain literary and visual Dionysiac contexts and not in others. For example, silens are not among the characters in Euripides' *Bacchae*, nor do they appear in the other narratives of Theban and Argive resistance to the god. They are, however, prominent in visual representations of the return of Hephaistos and the union of Dionysos and Ariadne. Hedreen argues, in fact, that the silens of Dionysos were indigenous to Naxos, and that in Attic vase paintings, the silens appear primarily in mythic contexts associated with that island.[8] Whether or not one fully accepts this argument, the Dionysiac silens can be seen as a specialized subgroup of silens in general, albeit one that became predominant in the iconography of Dionysos by the archaic period.

Similarly, nymphs had no original association with Dionysos, but a subgroup of nymphs, whom we will describe as Dionysiac, became a part of the god's regular entourage at an early period. This was partly the result of their preexisting relationship with the silens and partly because of the myth that the god himself was reared by the nymphs of Nysa. The nurses (*tithênai*) of Dionysos are first mentioned in Homer's *Iliad* 6.132–35, where Thracian Lykourgos chases them down from Nysa with an ox goad (4.7.2). In terror, they throw down their *thusthla*, a word usually interpreted as an early equivalent of *thursos*, an ivy-tipped staff common in Dionysiac iconography.

Hermes, a regular companion of the nymphs, is supposed to have delivered the infant Dionysos to his waiting nurses, and this episode was a favorite subject in Greek art and poetry. Athenian vases generally show a mixed group of silens and nymphs on Nysa, and an elderly silen, or *papposilênos*, is sometimes shown receiving the divine infant while the nymphs stand by. At other times, an individual nymph, Nysa, is envisioned, as on an ancient plaster cast of classical Greek metalware, which shows a single motherly nymph opening the folds of her robe to accept the infant from Hermes. Among the many votive reliefs dedicated to the nymphs in Attica is an elaborate example given by the influential citizen Neoptolemos in the late fourth century. It shows Hermes presenting the infant to the nymphs, while Zeus presides overhead, and other gods, including Artemis, Apollo, Demeter, Pan, and Acheloös, witness the scene. All are depicted within a frame sculpted to resemble a cave.[9] This divine cave was also depicted in a renowned religious procession, which took place during the reign of Ptolemy Philadelphos at Alexandria. Among the other wonders of the procession were a tableau of the cave with springs of milk and wine, gold-crowned nymphs, and a twelve-foot statue of Nysa, which automatically stood and poured a libation of milk.[10]

Silens are especially plentiful in the black-figure vase paintings of the sixth century, where they are often accompanied by female figures, who must be nymphs. Dionysos does not appear on the earliest vases that show silens and nymphs together, and some scholars have suggested that these vases pre-date the silens' association with Dionysos. On the François vase, the first extant vase to illustrate this association, the silens who appear with Dionysos in the return of Hephaistos are accompanied by females labeled *nuphai*, nymphs.[11] On sixth-century vases, not only at Athens but in the Greek west, Ionia, and Boiotia, we find silens cavorting with nymphs in a fashion that strongly recalls the description of their sexual intimacy in the Homeric *Hymn to Aphrodite*. Silens dance with nymphs, they kiss and walk arm in arm with nymphs, and they carry them about on their shoulders. Some vases depict intercourse with nymphs. Cordial relations are the rule, and few examples indicate unwillingness on the part of the nymphs to engage in these activities. The nymphs themselves are sometimes fully clothed (even during intercourse) and sometimes nude. Their nudity, in my view, is an indication of their divine status, for female nudity is otherwise rare in Greek art of the sixth century. The nymphs are shown nude for the same reasons that Aphrodite is disrobed in later art: their divine nature frees them from the conventional standards of modesty otherwise applied to representations of females, and their overt sexuality is at this period, as later, a defining characteristic.

During the second half of the sixth century, the companions of the silens in Athenian vase painting gradually acquire a number of iconographic attributes associated with Dionysos: fawn- or panther-skin garments, snakes, thyrsoi, ivy crowns, and so on. These attributes, which correspond to those of the Dionysiac worshipers described by Euripides in the *Bacchae*, have led a number of scholars to identify the silens' female companions as maenads rather than nymphs.[12] Maenads may be defined either as mythic mortal women under the maddening influence of Dionysos, such as Agave in the *Bacchae* or the daughters of Minyas, or as participants in actual, historical ecstatic rites in honor of the god. Neither of these descriptions fits the figures on the vases well. The maenads in the myths that tell of resistance to Dionysos' cult have nothing to do with silens, and they are described in the *Bacchae* as chaste. Historical maenads, on the other hand, are unattested until the Hellenistic period, and while there has been a great deal of debate over whether maenadic celebrations could have taken place in classical Attica, the only evidence for them is the vase iconography, so that a circular argument becomes unavoidable.[13]

It remains doubtful, too, whether historical maenads would have been depicted dancing with the mythic silens in the presence of the god; it seems much more likely that all the figures in these compositions are to be regarded as mythical. The best argument we can make for retaining the term *maenad* is to say that the maenads of the vases are mythic counterparts of the putative historical celebrants but that their ontological status (as mortals or immortals) is unclear. In fact, no such logical contortions are necessary. The possession of Dionysiac attributes does not automatically exclude the identification of the silens' companions as nymphs, particularly not if we think of the nymphs as Dionysos' former nurses, who seem to be equipped with thyrsoi even in the *Iliad*. Furthermore, the depiction of the silens' companions in black-figure vase painting belies any conclusion that they are "maddened" in the destructive, frenzied fashion of the maenads in literature. The personal name Mainas ("madwoman") does occasionally appear as a nymph name on the vases, as do Methuse ("drunken woman"), Choreia ("dancer"), and Thaleia ("blooming"). These names express general Dionysiac concepts, and nothing iconographically distinguishes the individuals named Mainas from the other nymphs.[14]

Over the past few decades there has been an ever-growing tendency to recognize the silens' companions in Attic vase painting as nymphs, even when they possess Dionysiac attributes.[15] In the case of red-figure iconography, the argument is more difficult, because the companions of the silens undergo a significant change in behavior at the end of the sixth century. Far from welcoming the sexual advances of the silens, they begin first to resist and then to repel them aggressively. This iconographic shift has been interpreted in the past as indicating a change in the identity of the silens' companions from promiscuous nymphs to chaste maenads. Yet nothing about their behavior precludes identifying them as nymphs; the vase painters might simply have tired of the archaic cliché about the lusty nymphs. Inspired perhaps by contemporary satyric drama, they might have seen more interesting possibilities in the portrayal of sexually frustrated silens, humiliated by their erstwhile partners. A similar iconographic shift took place during this period in the depictions of silens and nymphs on northern Aegean coins, but in this case, the nymphs were at first resistant and later compliant (4.7.2).[16]

To conclude, the companions of the silens on Attic (and other) vase paintings, whatever amount of Dionysiac paraphernalia they may boast, should in general be considered nymphs. Though there are certain important parallels between nymphs and maenads, in that the latter have rejected male authority and have abandoned their normal sphere of the *oikos*, or home, for the wild mountains, still it is possible to maintain a distinction even when the nymphs are garbed in maenadic attire. The skins, thyrsoi, and ivy leaves indicate recognition and acknowledgment of the god, not necessarily a maddened state; and they are, of course, not exclusive to maenads. In the *Bacchae* (175–77), old Kadmos and Teiresias dress themselves in full Dionysiac gear in order to honor the god, and they experience not madness but a state of heightened energy. Thus the nymphs, both as age-old companions of the silens and as nurses of the god, are a regular part of his mythic entourage, just as nymphs in different contexts form escorts for and act as companions to other gods and goddesses.

3.1.2 *Nymphs and the Pastoral Gods*

In keeping with Greek conceptual ties between the rustic life and certain forms of song, pastoral (in the socioeconomic sense) and choral themes are regularly combined in literary, iconographic, and cultic representations of the nymphs. Above all, the nymphs act as a chorus, dancing to the music of a male choregos and/or musician. The gods Apollo, Hermes, and (later) Pan, who all share important pastoral functions with the nymphs, appear as divine musicians or leaders in the dance. Though the earliest clear-cut iconographic examples of such musical scenes are black-figure vase paintings of the late sixth century (5.2.1), the cultic affinity of these gods with the nymphs is doubtless of great antiquity. The seventh-century poet Semonides, echoing the Homeric account of Eumaios' sacrifice, told how shepherds sacrifice to the nymphs "and to the offspring of Maia [Hermes]; for these have kinship with the herdsmen."[17] And the oldest extant cult relief that shows the nymphs pairs them with Apollo Nymphagetes, who holds his lyre (4.7.2). Nymphagetes is a widespread epithet of Apollo, attested in Thasos, Attica, Phokis, Kyrene, and Samos.

At least in the archaic and classical periods, Dionysos' relationship with the nymphs seems to be more or less chaste because it is based on their motherly services as his nurses and because his erotic energies are directed primarily toward his consort, Ariadne, while theirs are shared with the silens. In contrast, the pastoral gods Apollo, Hermes, and Pan relate to the nymphs in a more overtly sexual manner. Their potential sexual partnering, whether or not it is depicted, seems to be an important ingredient in the chemistry of cult, and the familiar literary juxtaposition of these deities certainly derives from cultic practice. Perhaps its ultimate origin lay in a form of sympathetic magic, by which the sexual arousal of the pastoral gods themselves, whether frustrated or fulfilled, was understood to stimulate the animals they protected. (An erotically stimulating effect was attributed to their music as well; Apollo is supposed to have played "pastoral wedding songs" on the syrinx during his time as a herdsman for Admetos.) While Hermes is a regular sexual partner of nymphs in the Homeric *Hymn to Aphrodite*, Apollo and, especially, Pan are often portrayed as unsuccessful lovers. Pan's fruitless pursuits of Syrinx, Pitys, and Echo recall—and in their late literary forms were probably modeled upon—Apollo's pursuit of Daphne.[18]

Just as cultic heroines are usually subordinated to their heroic consorts, there is a potential for the nymphs to be conceptually subordinated to the dominant figure(s) with whom they are linked.[19] This phenomenon is manifested most dramatically in the case of Pan. The cult of the nymphs received a great deal of attention when the god Pan was introduced to Attica after the battle of Marathon in 490. According to Herodotus 6.105, the herald and trained runner Philippides was sent to the Spartans and, on his way through Arkadia, was accosted by the goat-footed god, who asked why the Athenians did not honor him, since he had often helped them before and would do so again. Afterward, the Athenians, believing that the Arkadian god had aided them at Marathon, installed Pan's cult in a cave on the north slope of the Akropolis. The sudden surge in the number of Attic rural sites devoted to Pan and the nymphs in the second quarter of the fifth century, including a site near Marathon, may or may not be the result of official encouragement but was certainly due to this new interest in Pan. Once Pan made his entrance, he became exceedingly popular, and he was associated with the nymphs first in Attic caves, then at virtually every Greek nymph cave, with the old sanctuary at Pitsa in the area of Sikyon (5.1.4) being a rare exception.

How well established was the cult of the nymphs in Attica before the coming of Pan? Urban cults of the nymphs, such as those at the springs Empedo and Kallirhoë, certainly existed at Athens before Pan's arrival, as did the archaic cult of Nymphe (3.2.3). Nymphs also appear in the Attic deme calendars, while Pan is entirely absent from these, which suggests that the former belonged to older traditions of worship. Three of the Attic cave sites that showed classical deposits also yielded a few black-figure sherds and archaic-looking terra-cottas (Vari, Phyle, and Daphni). This evidence confounded excavators, who believed that the cave cults could not have been established until after the Persian wars.[20] Yet an archaic cult of the nymphs might have existed at these sites, just as it did in many cave sites outside Attica, including the Korykian, Pitsa, and Pharsalos caves. The Attic cave sites were probably not established specifically for Pan, since Pan does not appear to have inhabited caves in his homeland; instead he was honored there with manmade shrines and temples.[21] Nymphs are present at every classical Attic Pan cave, with the important exception of the state-sponsored Akropolis cave (this, however, seems to have been associated with the Klepsydra spring and with the daughters of Kekrops). Hence, Pan seems to have been grafted onto a preexisting Attic tradition of nymph worship in caves, but he quickly became equal in status with his cult partners and, in several cases, overshadowed them.

Borgeaud has shown that Pan's installation took place in caves because the god's significance for the urban-oriented Athenians diverged from his previous role as tutelary god of the Arkadians. Pan's symbolic power lay in his evocation of an imagined primitive past, a period of protocivilization that, while harsh and savage, was also in some sense an idealized golden age. He was a stranger who belonged to the physical and psychological frontiers of civilized life, a bestial god who shared the erotic urges and frustrations of the silens, yet transcended their comic antics.[22] Pan, the savage cave dweller, is both beast and god. He is far more than a mere cultic projection of the shepherd, just as the nymphs themselves are not merely divine realizations of the bride.

Like Hermes and Apollo, Pan had a natural affinity with the nymphs as a musical and pastoral deity. After 490, he quickly began to accompany or even supersede these gods as the nymphs' regular companion in poetry and iconography. Typical is the addition of Pan to the cultic group of Hermes Nomios and the nymphs in an Aristophanic prayer.[23] On the Attic votive reliefs of the fourth century, Hermes and Pan are equally in evidence, while the round dance of Pan and the nymphs (with Hermes no longer present) dominates the relief sculptures thereafter. Pan and the nymphs share the quality of immanence in the landscape; they both inspire a sense, alternately reassuring and unsettling, of the presence of the supernatural in everyday life. Both are considered responsible for altered states of consciouness linked to the influence of the landscape itself: in Pan's case, the phenomenon of "panic" might strike the herdsman alone in a wild, isolated spot, or it might appear during battles. "Panolepsy" is attested as a counterpart to the better-known phenomenon of nympholepsy.[24]

3.1.3 *Acheloös and the Rivers*

The longest river in Greece, located in Akarnania, is the Acheloös, which has a special prominence among mythic rivers and is called the eldest of Okeanos' sons. The earliest literary source to refer to the nymphs as his daughters is Plato; he is also named as the father of individual springs or streams, like Dirke and Kastalia.[25] Acheloös' association with the nymphs is of great antiquity. As water deities, the nymphs are often said to be daughters of Acheloös, Okeanos, or other river gods. Hesiod says that Tethys bore the world's rivers to the greatest and eldest river, Okeanos, and also the nymphs known as Okeanids, "who over the earth bring men to adulthood with Lord Apollo and the rivers." Acheloös became a generalized river god, who stood in much the same relation to the nymphs as the Hesiodic Okeanos. Yet, while Okeanos is rarely, if ever, the object of cult, Acheloös is widely honored in conjunction with the nymphs and other gods, perhaps as a result of active propaganda by the ancient oracle of Zeus at Dodone. Together with the nymphs and the other rivers, his function is to ensure the successful nurture of the young, particularly young males. The *koureion* ritual, in which youths at their maturity cut and dedicate their hair to the local river, is well attested.[26]

In archaic thought, the local river often stands in preference to district or town as a man's birthplace. Heroes are conceived and born beside a river, which thereafter represents the land of their nurture and is an important focus of their loyalty and identity.[27] Rivers were usually, though not universally, imagined as male deities with the physical and sexual vigor of bulls. In rivers, the bull's fertility, physical power, and aggressive unpredictability are recognizable, and the standard iconography shows rivers either as horned men or as bulls with human faces. Like Apollo, Hermes, and Pan, they enjoy a natural sexual chemistry with their companions, the nymphs. Such cult groupings, bringing male and female generative powers together, were probably felt to increase the efficacy of prayers and offerings. Myths of sexual contact between the river gods and the nymphs vary in popularity by region. The best known in mainland Greece is the tale of Alpheios' lust for Arethousa, but in the western Greek colonies, the rivers seem regularly to have had nymphs as consorts. Many rivers of the Greek mainland, on the other hand, such as Asopos, Peneios, Inachos, and Kephisos, were thought of as progenitors of nymphs, in spite of the observable fact that rivers arise from springs and not the reverse.

Acheloös, with Hermes and Pan, appears by convention in the iconographic schemes of most Attic votive reliefs to the nymphs (5.2.2, figure 3.1). Noticeable, however, is the fact that he is never fully depicted but always appears either as the front half of a human-faced bull who protrudes into the cave frame or simply as a masklike face against one wall. Acheloös, like Dionysos and the silens, often appears in other media as a protome or mask. A series of roof antefixes from Sicily shows the heads of horned river gods alternating

Figure 3.1 Quirinal relief: dedicant, Hermes, three nymphs, and Acheloös. Staatliche Museen zu Berlin, Preussischer Kulturbesitz, Antikensammlung.

with those of nymphs, and the head of Acheloös is also a popular motif for jewelry (which might have functioned as amulets). It is possible that Acheloös protomes, such as a marble mask found at Marathon, were normally hung in Attic cave sanctuaries as a symbol of the nymphs' affinity with the river gods, though there is no independent evidence of such a practice.[28] The protomes in the votive reliefs could be iconographic symbols of the relationship rather than attempts to depict the furniture of the caves realistically.

3.2 Nymphs, Goddesses, and the Female Life Cycle

The Greeks conceptualized a woman's life as a series of stages and events related to reproduction. A young girl was a potential bride and mother, a wild creature who needed to be socialized and reconciled to the culturally approved restrictions on female behavior, a goal that was achieved in part through participation in rituals. Young girls learned about gender roles through maturation rituals, like the Athenian Arkteia, and through the use and dedication of doll-like votives. A girl near puberty joined her first chorus or made dedications to mark her entry into the pool of marriageable females. The wedding itself and its preliminaries involved sacrifices and a nuptial bath. The consummation of the marriage was considered secondary in significance to the birth of a child, but ritual baths were in order after both of these events. With the birth of the first child, the all-important transformation from *korê* to *numphê* to *mêtêr* or *gunê* was complete. This process, far from being of merely personal significance, was recognized as a fundamental and crucial requirement for social continuity. Abundant myths illustrate the drama of the young woman's resistance to her forfeiture of freedom and her inevitable, necessary submission to the requirements of the group.[29]

These areas of female life were under the purview of major goddesses, for example, Artemis, Hera, Persephone, and Eileithyia. Each district and city had its own customs in this regard and relied on its own combination of deities and rituals to achieve essentially the same ends. The elasticity of the concept of the nymph, coupled with the almost universal presence of water in ritual contexts, allowed the nymphs, unlike the major goddesses, to play important roles at one locale or another in most of the acculturative stages and events I have just described. The nymphs in various contexts could represent the wild prepubertal girl, the chaste chorus member, the bride before and after consummation, and even the mother, whereas the sexual and familial identities of the major goddesses were more firmly fixed. While the nymphs were ubiquitous, moreover, the cults of goddesses such as Hera or Persephone tended to dominate certain geographical areas, so that we find a recurrent pattern of one great goddess who is attended and aided by nymphs. The nature of the evidence makes it difficult to reconstruct fully a picture of the female ritual cycle for any one area, but it is clear that goddesses and nymphs sometimes functioned separately and sometimes in concert.

In the following sections, I juxtapose female rites of passage, rituals performed in the worship of goddesses and nymphs, and accompanying myths in order to show how they are related. Goddesses and nymphs, as divine exemplars, enacted at both mythic and ritual levels the choruses, baths, and other symbolic events of the female life cycle. Girls and women, in turn, believed they were emulating the deities by their participation in these events, while the community as a whole celebrated and affirmed gender expectations through the deities' public cults. My intent is not to claim or provide a full account of any one cult or myth but to point out areas of contact and to identify recurrent patterns with regard to the concept(s) of the *numphê*.

3.2.1 *Dolls and Female Socialization*

Several Attic grave reliefs show young girls, some clearly prepubertal, who appear to be playing with dolls or holding doll-like objects. These objects fall into three categories: clothed, seated figures; full-length nude figures; and nude figures truncated at the shoulders and thighs. Though all the figures have traditionally been called "dolls," Reilly has argued that the naked figures are not to be considered toys but votives dedicated by the girls to help ensure their sexual maturation.[30] She interprets them as "anatomical votives" analogous to those dedicated in sanctuaries of Asklepios and other healing deities. True dolls can be identified by their articulated limbs, and examples of dolls with articulated limbs are not found on the reliefs. The dedication of anatomical votives also had a socializing function as they taught the girls that the important parts of their bodies were the womb and breasts: that their identities and destinies were inseparably bound to reproduction.

While Reilly's insights about the votive and socializing functions of the figures are surely correct, no such strict distinction between toy and votive is supportable or necessary. Several of the reliefs show the girls in conventional "play" contexts: for example, the young Melisto in a relief at the Sackler Museum holds the truncated figure with her left hand while she teases her small pet dog with a bird held in her right hand (figure 3.2). Reliefs carved for boys show the same dog-bird iconography, while the boy holds a toy corresponding to the girl's doll: a ball, wheeled toy, or astragaloi. Attic grave reliefs of females normally show domestic scenes of daily life, not special ritual occasions. Finally, the strict interpretation of the truncated figures as anatomical votives and not toys leaves unanswered the question of why both fully-formed naked figures and seated, clothed figures also appear on the reliefs. These admittedly are less common, but they share the same conventional play iconography as the examples with truncated figures.[31]

There is no reason why all the doll-like objects should not be interpreted as both toys and (potential) votives. Perhaps, in the case of the truncated figures, the eventual votive use was more obvious, but we know that a wide

Figure 3.2 Grave stele of Melisto: girl with doll and pet dog. Arthur M. Sackler Museum, Harvard University Art Museums.

range of articles from daily life, including toys, could easily be turned to votive use. Articulated dolls, which were clearly used as toys, turn up regularly as dedications in caves of the nymphs and other sites. We probably ought to think not of a strict dividing line between toy and votive but of a spectrum along which some objects to our eyes have more votivelike characteristics and some seem more toylike. Yet either category could easily fulfill the function of the other. Terra-cotta dolls and votive figures of seated or standing women share many stylistic features because they were produced by the same craftspeople. Clothing, hairstyles, and the modeling of face and body all progressed in parallel fashion, reflected equally in votives and dolls. There is also reason to believe that many of the same terra-cotta figurines we would consider votives if found in sanctuaries were bought and kept as personal possessions by adults and children.[32]

The fact that some of the figures are naked and/or without limbs does not preclude their use as toys, though it might strike us initially as an oddity. The category "doll" can and has included a wide range of objects, from clothespins and corncobs to the anatomically exaggerated fashion dolls of the modern West. To qualify as a doll, an object need not realistically reproduce the full human figure.[33] The socializing function attributed to these objects, moreover, could be fulfilled equally well whether they were dolls or votives. The socializing functions of dolls across cultures are well recognized and, as Reilly notes, many of the fully-formed naked figures look to modern eyes like an ancient version of the American perennial favorite, the Barbie doll (figure 3.3).[34] They are roughly the same size: the length varies from twelve to twenty-five centimeters (truncated examples have the same size torsos as the full-figure dolls). Like the Barbie, they approximate the adult proportions culturally favored as ideal for the nubile female. This fact is of special interest because ancient sources tell us that one of the words for *doll* was *numphê*.

Literary references to dolls are surprisingly scarce compared to the archaeological evidence. A fragment by the poet Erinna on her dead friend Baukis contains poignant lines describing the two girls' childhood play with dolls and juxtaposing the word *dagus* with *numphê*. With Bowra's supplements, the lines read, "When we were young we held our dolls [*dagudes*] in our rooms, like *numphai* free from care." In Theocritus' *Idyll* 2.110, the speaker, Simaitha, recalls how her body stiffened like that of a doll (*dagus*) when her lover appeared on the threshold. The scholia explain that a *dagus* is a *numphê* or *korokosmion*, which girls dress (*kosmountai*); among the Athenians, a doll formed from wax was called a *plangôn*. Hesychius further defines the word *datus* (apparently a doublet of *dagus*) as a little *korê* (*kourallion*) or a doll of white wax (*numphê leukokêros*). Clement of Alexandria speaks of wax and clay images and *korokosmia*, which the scholiast defines as "figures modeled from wax or chalk of *numphai* or *parthenoi*, which the Dorians call *dagudes* and the Athenians *korokosmia*."[35] The abbreviated term *kosmion* also appears as a synonym for doll or doll-like votive in the *Palatine Anthology* 9.326.3, which describes dedications placed in or around a fountain of the nymphs. *Korai*, too, could be both dolls and small votive images; both were supplied by the terra-cotta craftspeople known as coroplasts. *Korai*, probably doll-sized, were among the dedications in the shrine of Acheloös and the nymphs on the Ilissos (Pl. *Phdr.* 230b). Thus, there were several terms signifying "doll," among which *numphê* seems to have been widely recognized. Dolls were made of a variety of materials, although generally only the terra-cotta examples have been preserved.

The sources above also suggest that dressing dolls was a common pastime for girls. The naked doll, as we have seen, had its own significance, but the

Figure 3.3 Grave stele: girl with doll. National Archaeological Museum, Athens.

dressed doll must also have had an important socializing function. Like Aphrodite (to images of whom the term *dagus* could be applied),[36] the nymphs appear in Greek visual media sometimes naked and sometimes carefully ornamented. Both the naked and ornamented states, as well as the process of ornamentation itself, had archetypal significance. (In this regard, we think of Aphrodite's special toilet before her meeting with Anchises or the dressing of Pandora by the gods.) The ornamentation, or *kosmêsis*, of the doll corresponds to the value placed upon conventional measures of female beauty, especially in the contexts of chorus and wedding. An ensemble taken from a fifth-century Athenian tomb illustrates this point. A nude terra-cotta doll in a permanent seated position can be placed on a matching *thronos*, a chair elaborately fashioned with female heads supporting the armrests. Her miniature accessories include a pair of shoes, an *epinetron* (knee piece over which wool is worked), and a *lebês gamikos*, a ritual vessel with special nuptial connotations (figure 3.4). It is highly likely that the accessories also included a textile wardrobe suitable for an Athenian lady, now long since disintegrated. All of the objects are ones that elite Athenian brides might have expected to receive as wedding gifts. This girl's toys, then, had specific relevance to what

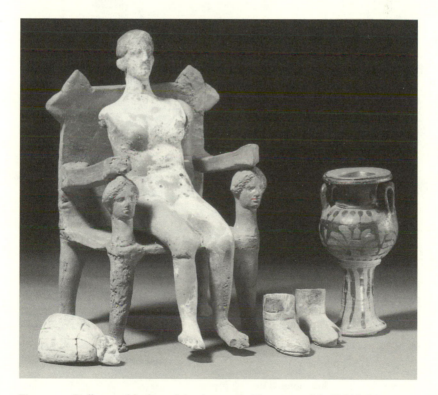

Figure 3.4 Doll ensemble from Athenian tomb. Photo copyright British Museum.

should have been her future state as a bride. It is no wonder that dolls were called *numphai*.

Another point is that articulated terra-cotta dolls often hold castanets (*krotala*) or tambourines (*tumpana*) in their hands, indicating that they were conceived of as dancers or chorus members. Many articulated dolls were designed to be dangled on a string so that their limbs could move as in a dance. These details reflect both the mythic ideal of the dancing, musical nymph and the young girl's expectation that she would one day emulate the nymphs by becoming a member of a chorus. Many dolls wear a tall crown (*polos*) or other special headgear, which indicates they were representations of goddesses (figure 3.5).[37] The only goddess for whom we have direct evidence of doll versions is Aphrodite, but it is likely that dolls often repre-

Figure 3.5 Corinthian jointed doll with *polos* and *krotala*. Photo copyright British Museum.

sented nymphs and goddesses, and this possibility will be explored further below. We can at least note here that the *kosmêsis* of sacred images was a serious matter in Greek religion and that the dressing of dolls could have been seen as a form of play with close analogies to the ritual dressing and ornamentation of cult images often undertaken by older girls and women.

A Hellenistic epigram that describes the dedication of Timareta has often been cited to support the idea that girls dedicated dolls in connection with the *proteleia*, or prenuptial sacrifice. Before marriage, Timareta dedicates to Artemis a *tumpanon*, a ball, and other objects interpreted either as her dolls and dolls' dresses or her hair and girl's clothing (the latter comes from the reading of *komas* instead of the emendation *koras*). As Daux has shown, the latter reading is preferable in this epigram; hence we can claim no specific tie between the dedication of dolls and the prenuptial ceremonies.[38] On the other hand, dedications of dolls and doll-like votives are widely attested in the archaeological record, and this epigram and others show that toys such as Timareta's tambourine and ball were common gifts to the gods. (Boys dedicated their toys to the ephebic gods Apollo and Hermes.)[39] As such, they must have marked the child's entry into adult status or, perhaps, particularly in the case of the dolls, represented hopes for successful maturation. Other possible links among dolls, deities, and nuptial rites are discussed below.

3.2.2 *Handmaidens of Artemis?*

Traditionally, the nymphs have been pictured as a band of lovely, chaste maidens who surround Artemis, herself a youthful virgin. This familiar image owes much to the famous Odyssean simile that compares Nausikaä and her companions to Artemis and the nymphs. Artemis is hunting on Mount Taygetos, or Erymanthos, and about her the nymphs dance, and Leto is glad at heart because Artemis stands out as the most beautiful of all. As Burkert says, the Artemis simile "became the definitive picture of the goddess: Artemis with her swarms of nymphs, hunting, dancing, and playing on mountains and meadows." Apollonius of Rhodes uses a similar comparison with Artemis and her nymphs to describe the beauty of Medeia going to meet Jason, and Vergil speaks similarly of Dido about to meet Aeneas.[40] Yet, this "definitive" image of Artemis belongs almost exclusively to epic, and outside of Homer, the association of Artemis and the nymphs is surprisingly limited in Greek literature before the Hellenistic period. In Hesiod, the Homeric *Hymns*, Pindar, Bacchylides, and the extant lyric poets, both Artemis and the nymphs are mentioned frequently but not in the same breath. Instead, we find the nymphs linked with Dionysos, Aphrodite, Hermes, and Pan.[41] The Homeric *Hymn to Aphrodite* yields one exception (119–20), when the goddess claims to have been abducted by Hermes from a chorus where Artemis was dancing with "nymphs and marriageable maidens." This motif appears to be borrowed from the Iliadic description of Polymele's abduction from an Artemisian chorus by Hermes (Hom. *Il.* 16.179). The sole example in extant tragedy occurs in the *Trachiniae*, where the chorus sings a joyous song that praises Artemis Ortygia and her neighbor nymphs. Clearly, the *numphê* in tragedy is primarily the human bride rather than her divine counterpart.[42]

Hellenistic and Roman depictions of Artemis with her band introduce the idea that the nymphs are the maidservants of Artemis and perform various menial tasks. In Callimachus' *Hymn to Artemis*, the goddess chooses nymphs to care for her boots and dogs, like a Hellenistic matron selecting suitable help, and the parents, Okeanos, Tethys, and the Kretan rivers Amnisos and Kairatos, seem glad that their daughters have secured such good employment. Similarly, in Ovid's version of the Aktaion myth, Diana has nymphs with the special tasks of caring for her armor, disrobing her, dressing her hair, and fetching water for her bath.[43] This notion of the nymphs as maidservants also seems to derive ultimately from the Odyssean simile, though it recalls the description of Nausikaä and her handmaidens as much as that of Artemis and her chorus.

While the association of Artemis and the nymphs is surprisingly limited in early Greek poetry, in the sphere of cult, it is equally so. In spite of the fact that Artemis is regularly associated with woods, lakes, trees, hot springs, and so on, nymphs are not a part of the widespread cults of Artemis Agrotera or Limnaia or any other Artemis cults, with certain important exceptions.[44] Our sources mention numerous sacrifices to Artemis, but the nymphs are never included in these. Nor is Artemis normally honored in nymph cults. Greek inscriptions to Artemis and the nymphs together are extremely rare; the few examples of which I am aware list Artemis and the nymphs among other deities and not contiguously, so that no special relationship can be inferred. The hundreds of votive reliefs dedicated specifically to the nymphs do not depict them with Artemis but with Hermes, Pan, and Acheloös. Dedicatory and other kinds of epigrams that mention the nymphs are plentiful in the *Palatine Anthology*, those mentioning Artemis somewhat less so, but they are never mentioned together.[45] Again, in the most prominent cult sites of the nymphs, the caves of Parnes and Vari in Attica, the Korykian cave at Delphi, and so on, we find no explicit links to Artemis. Instead, the nymphs are worshiped independently, or they have various cult companions, especially Hermes and Apollo. In Artemis' own cults, she is linked unambiguously to the nymphs only in the Peloponnese: at Karyai in Lakedaimonia (4.4.3) and at Letrinoi near Elis (4.4.4).[46] These two examples of Artemis and the nymphs as cult partners are the only certain ones attested, and in both cases it is clear that the primary expression of their link is the choral dance, not a sacrifice, a dedicatory relief, nor even a shared sanctuary.[47]

Ritual bathing is another possible point of contact, and a link between Artemis and the nymphs might have existed in this context at Kyrene. In a late fourth-century inscription of Kyrene's cathartic laws, we learn that during the festival of the Artemisia, newly married women were expected to "go down to Artemis" to the nymphaion, presumably for a purifying bath after the loss of their virginity. Pregnant women were also required to visit the nymphaion and to give an animal skin to the priestess of Artemis. Here, the rites of passage that accompany the transition from maiden to wife and mother are, as often, within the sphere of Artemis. But they take place in a location called the *numphaion*, which would normally be translated as "shrine of the nymphs" but in this context has been called "the bride room." Both translations may be appropriate, if the nymphaion has been correctly identified as the cave to the northwest of the spring of Apollo. A series of steps leads down into this apparently manmade grotto, which would explain the odd expression "go down to Artemis." Within the cave are a number of hollowed depressions in the stone, which served as basins, apparently for ritual bathing.[48] Nothing here explicitly links Artemis to the nymphs, but the term nymphaion, the fact that the nymphaion is a grotto with a water source, and the proximity of the cave to an attested cult site of Apollo Nymphagetes and the nymphs (4.8.8) are all suggestive.

Unlike the chorus of Artemis, which attempts to preserve sexual purity, the nymphs in general are likely to engage in sexual sport with Hermes, the silens, or even a bemused shepherd. In relation to the chaste Artemisian nymphs, Hermes is an outsider who resorts to abduction, but for other nymphs, he is a welcome sexual partner and fellow reveler. He himself leads the dance on most nymph reliefs, and he shares with these nymphs the concerns of pastoral deities (from which Artemis is, for the most part, excluded). Dancing is a major activity for both kinds of nymphs, but the dance has a different significance in each case. When Artemis is present, the dance takes on special associations of courtship, sexual initiation, and the tensions between the requirement of maidenly chastity and the force of male desire—hence the constant theme of threatened rape and abduction. Artemis' nymphs are bound to chastity by the same conventions that expect the dance to be, for their human counterparts, a stage of courtship that will lead ultimately to socially approved marriage and motherhood.

The nymphs, then, have two functions in relation to Artemis. First, they serve as a divine escort of the type that many other deities, such as Aphrodite, Apollo, and Dionysos, have. Second, as has been well recognized by Calame and others, they, like Artemis herself, are mythopoetic representatives of the Greek maiden at adolescence. Artemis has a special relationship with her chorus: she herself is one of the chorus members, the most beautiful and outstanding, the one who leads the dance. As Burkert notes, her virginity is not asexual, like that of Athena, but is highly eroticized, just like that of the Greek maiden of marriageable age. Nymphs in their relations with Artemis are not themselves objects of cult, nor do they give or withhold blessings, but they are representative of the social rituals by which females come of age and take their place in society.[49]

The word *numphê*, paradoxically, can refer to the Greek maiden as a virgin bride and her divine counterpart in the chorus of Artemis, or it can refer to a local fertility deity, often manifestly unchaste, who presides over the spring and woodland.[50] Of course, it is neither possible nor desirable to keep these two conceptions of the nymph completely separate. Indeed, the woodland nymph worshiped by the shepherd has some of the same combination of forbidden sexual allure, innocence, and capricious cruelty that we see in Artemis. The goddess is a sort of über-nymph and might have begun as a local nymph who became differentiated from the rest, just as she stands out from her companions in the Homeric simile.[51] Why then is her association with nymphs expressed primarily in narrative (epic) and choral contexts, rather than through the sharing of votives or sacred space?

Part of the answer may lie in the early development of sacred space, because Artemis was one of the principal temple deities. The significance of temples in the religious life of the polis tended to draw the worship of Artemis into the city sphere, a somewhat paradoxical development in view of her traditional associations with the wild. This conflict is illustrated as early as the Homeric *Hymn to Aphrodite* (20), which states that Artemis not only liked hunting but the "cities of just men." Similarly, in Callimachus' *Hymn to Artemis*, we find the young goddess stating that she will only visit cities when women in labor cry out for help, but her indulgent father, Zeus, later promises that thrice-ten cities will be named for her, and many others both inland and on the islands will honor her. Later in the poem, she is apostrophized as "lady of many shrines and many cities."[52] The cults of nymphs have no necessary association with cities and require no large outlay of resources but are tied closely to a particular natural feature, whether spring, cave, or mountain, which makes their location arbitrary and tends to favor rural sites. Thus, a cultic separation of Artemis and the nymphs was inevitable from early times. Hermes, it should be noted, was one of the gods least often honored with a temple, coming sixteenth in frequency after Eileithyia and the Dioskouroi.[53] Instead, he had a rustic monument: a pile of stones amassed by travelers and, eventually, the outdoor herm of the classical period. Finally, Artemis' insistence on virginity results not only in the mythic expulsion of pregnant nymphs from her band but has a corresponding effect of separation in all cultic contexts except those in which sexual purity or virginity are themselves central themes. The maiden chorus is one such cultic context; ritual bathing is another.

The Artemisian nymphs, then, can be seen as a subgroup whose function is to act as a mythic paradigm of the community's adolescent, marriageable girls. This affects their cultural manifestation since, unlike other nymphs, they are sexually chaste, and as mythic counterparts of Artemis' worshipers, they do not themselves receive offerings or confer blessings, as nymphs do in other contexts. The Artemisian nymphs had their origin in the institution of maiden choruses to the goddess, which were imaginatively transformed into divine choruses in epic. The image of Artemis surrounded by nymphs, though not traditional in cult or in other literary genres, was disseminated through the authority of epic to become definitive in the Hellenistic and Roman periods.

3.2.3 Nymphe and the Prenuptial Bath

The prenuptial ritual bath is similar to the chorus in that both have archetypal significance (that is, both are represented extensively in myth and enacted by goddesses), both can be rites of passage, and both are communal activities in which the focus falls upon one member of the group. There exist numerous myths of bathing goddesses; we can be confident that many of these reflect rituals in which the cult image was bathed.[54] The mythic nymph attendants, who provide water for bathing goddesses and act as their escorts, are sometimes paralleled in ritual by priestesses, who carry water or otherwise assist at the rite. Bathing is an important part of the *kosmêsis* before a sexual encounter, as the Homeric *Hymn to Aphrodite* shows. Aphrodite's constant companions, the Charites and nymphs, are cosmetic and bathing attendants. While examples of the bathing of both male and female cult images are known, goddesses predominate in these rituals, and, in the case of images bathed in rivers, all the attested examples involve goddesses.

Beside the river, the concepts of chorus and bath are melded together, as in Helen's chorus dancing by the river Eurotas, the chorus of Artemis Alpheiousa daubed with mud, or Nausikaä's maidens at their washing and games. The primary purpose of the maiden's bath is fecundating: all the river deities, including the river gods and their offspring, the nymphs, aid in conception as well as in nurturing children after birth. The mythic dance of the chorus beside the river partakes of a complex of interlocking ideas about the generative powers of water, its relationship to the young woman's life cycle, and, not least, the ties between an individual and the water sources that help define local identity (3.1.3).[55] Thus, when Iphigeneia goes to be married at Aulis, her bathwater must be brought from her home town.

Not only the goddesses but the nymphs are enthusiastic bathers. Bathing nymphs are a frequent subject in black-figure vase painting. On an amphora by the Priam painter, seven nymphs bathe in a grotto with fountains, a diving platform, and two trees. More often, communal outdoor bathing by nymphs is overtly erotic, as silens creep up to spy on the naked bathers.[56] This scene is an earthier version of the myths in which goddesses' baths are interrupted or otherwise violated.

Plutarch speaks of a girl, Aristokleia, making a *proteleia* to the nymphs at the spring Kissoëssa in Boiotia. It is unclear whether the word here indicates a sacrifice, the ritual collection of water from the spring for a prenuptial bath, or both.[57] There is some question as to the exact details of the *proteleia*, a ceremony that, like the bath, preceded the wedding banquet and consummation of the marriage. Artemis is the goddess for whom the *proteleia* is best attested. In her case, sacrifices are specifically described as the payment of a penalty for the bride's loss of virginity. Other gods, however, are known to have received *proteleia*, including Hera and Zeus, the Tritopatores and Athena at Athens, and the Erinyes, as well as the nymphs;

the significance of these prenuptial sacrifices must have been understood differently.[58]

Ritual bathing was an indispensable part of prenuptial celebrations. In Attica, the primary symbol of the prenuptial bath—and indeed of the wedding itself—was the loutrophoros, a long-necked vessel used to carry the bathwater. The water had to come from a running source, a river, spring, or fountain, and we are told that in Athens the traditional source was Kallirhoë (4.2.1). The loutrophoros was such an important symbol of transition to the wedded state that it was also used to mark the graves of those who had died before marriage, standing as a sort of compensatory substitute for the rite.[59] After the wedding, some loutrophoroi might have been kept as souvenirs. Vase paintings often show loutrophoroi proudly displayed among the wedding gifts. Others were certainly dedicated to the gods, particularly to the nymphs. Some were full-sized, though miniature versions were also popular (perhaps as a substitute for the genuine article, which the bride wished to keep). They are regularly found in votive deposits of the classical period in Attic nymph caves. Others come from the shrine of Artemis Brauronia on the Akropolis, that of the hero Amynos, and finally, that of a personage called Nymphe, whose shrine lay in the agora.

The shrine of Nymphe is significant because of its age: though no literary sources mention it, votives were being deposited there from at least the seventh century. It has yielded some of the earliest loutrophoroi found in Athens. It was a large, open-air enclosure, located near the present-day Odeion of Herodes Atticus. In the fifth century, an ellipsoid building was added. The deposits, not only loutrophoroi (though these are the most numerous) but aryballoi, lekythoi, plates, lamps, plaques, masks, and terra-cotta figurines, continued until the third century. The recipient of the cult, Nymphe, is identified on pot graffiti and on a marble boundary stele.[60]

The shrine is unlike other Attic shrines to the nymphs not only because the cult is directed toward a single nymph but because of its earlier date and because it lacks association with a special natural feature, such as a spring or cave. Nevertheless, a clear association of some kind exists between Nymphe and the nymphs because of the similar deposits of loutrophoroi in Attic caves. Nymphe should probably be thought of as a personification of the Bride, a divine being in some ways parallel to Hera Nympheuomene in Boiotia or Persephone in her Western cults. A chthonic association has been attributed to Nymphe because a fourth-century stele dedicated to Zeus Meilichios, which shows a snake, also belonged to the sanctuary. Perhaps Nymphe was thought of as the consort of this Zeus.[61] Also of interest is the fact that Nymphe had her own priestess. A late Hellenistic inscription, now extant only in a sketchbook copy, records a decree of the Athenian *genos* Theoinidai in honor of this priestess, and she had a special seat in the theater of Dionysos.[62] These late notices indicate that the cult of Nymphe continued even after votive deposits were no longer made at the agora site.

3.2.4 *Hera and the Nymphs: Boiotia, Argolis, Paestum*

Hera and the nymphs share an important sphere of influence: the marriage of young girls and the attendant concerns of fertility and childbirth. Hence, it would be surprising if their cults never overlapped with respect to the preparations for marriage, the purifications after childbirth, and so on. Hera's cult sphere overlaps with that of Artemis in the area of transition from adolescence to adulthood, but Hera in her virginal, prenuptial guise of Parthenos is always paired with Hera Teleia, the goddess fulfilled by marriage. In certain areas, such as Boiotia and Argos, Hera's influence is such that she overshadows Artemis as a guardian of adolescent girls.[63]

The Daidala, the Boiotian festival of Hera conducted at Plataia and Mount Kithairon, had much in common with the festival of the goddess on her ancient stronghold of Samos. Both involved the ritual clothing of an aniconic wooden image. Both probably included a procession in which the statue was carried to and from a river, where it received a ritual bath. The Daidala festival itself involved the bathing and dressing in bridal gear of a roughly carved log or plank. This plank was then placed in a cart with a bridesmaid and ceremoniously conducted from the river Asopos to the top of Kithairon, where it was burned along with sacrifices, a specially made wooden altar, and other *xoana*, or wooden images, contributed by the Boiotian towns. The festival itself was named for these wooden figures, which were locally termed *daidala*. The etiological myths attached to this ritual say that Hera had become angry with Zeus and had hidden herself away. To bring her back, Zeus arranged a sham marriage with Plataia, or Daidale, the wooden plank. The hymeneal was duly sung, the nymphs of the local river Triton brought water for the nuptial bath, and the procession began. Hera, getting news of the impending wedding, rushed down from Kithairon with the women of Plataia and ripped the clothes from her rival. Then, laughing at the ruse, she accompanied the procession to the top of Kithairon, where she insisted that the impostor be burned.[64]

O'Brien has made a strong case that the major cults of Hera underwent a transformation about 600, partly as the result of the influence of Homeric epic, from celebrations of a powerful nature goddess of the *potnia therôn* (mistress of animals) type, to a more limited depiction of Hera as bride of Zeus and guardian of marriage. The wild nature goddess was tamed according to the contemporary understanding of marriage as the acculturation of the female; the clothing and bathing of the image, in earlier times a devotional activity and a ritual renewal of the goddess's powers, now took on the more specific denotations of the bridal raiment and bath. Hera's high crown, the *polos*, came to be shared by brides, and her fertility symbol of the pomegranate also gained (or was narrowed to) a nuptial significance.[65] In this context, Hera becomes an Olympian counterpart to the nymph, who shares the same duality of the wild, unconstrained embodiment of nature and the bride who must be tamed and acculturated. Thus, Hera has her own cadre of nymphs, who are specifically concerned with the wedding preparations. On a sixth-century Boiotian ceramic *polos*, the goddess is shown wearing her *polos*, standing in a hieratic pose with both arms extended to the sides. Two birds fly down toward her, reminding us of the *potnia therôn*. On each side are two female attendants, also wearing the *polos* and bringing ritual vessels to the goddess. These are apparently nymphs, and as we learned in the etiological myth of the Daidala, nymphs of the river Triton (running into Lake Kopaïs) brought water for the bath of the impostor bride.[66]

The myth, then, is more than a simple rationalization of the Daidala ritual. It reflects the imposition of Hera's new role as bride of Zeus and her subordination to him as husband. It has the same comic tone as the Homeric stories of Hera's schemes, jealousies, and chastenings by Zeus. Hera's paramount concern, like that of the Plataian women, is now to assert and preserve the rights of the wife: though husbands might have sexual freedom, they could have only one wife at a time. The wife's legitimacy and social status was thus enshrined. Hera, while allowing herself to be acculturated and returned to Zeus, insists on her privilege of exclusivity and primacy. Hera had two cult statues in her sanctuary at Plataia, one as Nympheuomene (Led as Bride) and one as Teleia (Fulfilled). The Daidala, then, while ostensibly the burning of Hera's rival, also becomes a celebration of Hera's own nuptials, and the focus of the cult is Hera as Bride, or Nymphe. Though the myth as recounted by Plutarch mentions the nymphs of Triton as bridal attendants, there existed on Kithairon a cult of the nymphs, which could have been associated with Hera in this capacity.[67]

It has been suggested that a certain type of archaic Boiotian terra-cotta figure, planklike and decorated with *polos*, pomegranate, and double waterbirds, represents the wooden Daidala used in the ritual.[68] Some of the earliest Greek articulated dolls are from geometric Boiotia and share the double bird motif. Other examples are decorated with fish, vegetation, or a female chorus. They have bell-shaped bodies with strange, elongated necks and movable legs attached under their skirts; their sexual maturity is indicated by small but protruberant breasts.[69] If indeed these are dolls, it is possible that they represented the goddess Hera for their young owners.

In a fragment of Aeschylus, Argive Hera approaches young women in the guise of a priestess to solicit a donation for the Inachid nymphs, who concern themselves with wedding hymns, "newly bedded, newly wedded girls" (*koras neolektrous artigamous te*), and the fruitful engendering of children. Robertson convincingly argues that the fragment is from a play entitled *Xantriae* (Wool Carders), and that it deals not with Semele, as was previously thought, but with the daughters of Proitos.[70] He shows that the ritual begging practiced by the disguised Hera has parallels at Delos and Kos and is especially concerned with marriage, fertility, and childbirth. In the Hesiodic myth of the daughters of Proitos, the girls were punished for their scorn of Hera (and their rejection of marriage) by the destruction of their "bloom," disfigurement caused by a loathsome skin disease. The affliction, in later versions conflated with Dionysiac madness, was cured by Melampous, and the Proitid sisters went on, significantly, to marry him and his brother, Bias.[71] Several places in the Peloponnese claimed to be the site of the cure, including the healing springs of the Anigrid nymphs (who specialized in skin diseases). This association of springs with the Proitid myth indicates that the girls were thought to have been cured by a ritual bath. The Proitids' bathing is not merely a healing ritual but a prenuptial one, which reconciles them to Hera and her expectations of young women. In an alternative version, they are reconciled to Hera with the help of Artemis, to whom they institute choruses (as we have seen, the chorus is a motif closely analogous to the ritual bath).[72]

Baths of goddesses play an important cultic role in Argolis, where statues of both Athena and Hera were periodically bathed. The nymphs who accompany Athena in Callimachus' *Hymn* on the goddess's bath had their counterpart in the human *numphai* who washed the statue in the river Inachos. The hymn is sung by a chorus of girls, who invoke Athena as protector of Argos. Athena Akria, goddess of the Argive citadel, seems to have functioned as the sponsor of adolescent girls in their relationship to the polis, while Hera's concerns were more directly connected with marriage, fertility, and birth. There were special priestesses in the Argive cult, *korai* known as the Eresides, who carried Hera's bathwater.[73] Hera's annual bath to restore her virginity in the Kanathos spring at Nauplia, like the bathing of Hera's image at the Argive Heraion, was considered a mystery, not to be revealed to the profane.

These mythic baths of the goddesses were reenacted through ritual baths for Argive women: nuptial baths for fertility, purifying baths after childbirth, and other purifications. Callimachus mentions the spring Amymone's role in the cult of Hera (1.4.4): the women who are to weave the robe for Hera must purify themselves beforehand by sitting on the "sacred rock" of the fountain and bathing in the water. The rock is perhaps associated with the one that Poseidon strikes in a vase painting of the Amymone myth, causing fresh water to flow.[74] Water is drawn from Automate, on the other hand, for the purpose of bathing slaves after childbirth.

The nymphs of Argos are drawn from two different mythological strata, both associated with Hera. There are the daughters of Inachos, autochthonous nymphs who are invoked by Hera in the *Xantriae*. Then there are the daughters of the primordial king Danaos, certain of whom are identified with water sources and associated with Hera in cult. Both groups are concerned with women's rites of passage, and the two strata are linked in the person of Io, priestess of Hera and the ancestor of the Danaids, who is often called "daughter of Inachos."

At Poseidonia (Paestum), an important cult center of Hera in Magna Graecia, an enigmatic structure was built in the late sixth century. It is a hypogaeum, or underground shrine.[75] The surrounding stone is flush with the structure on three sides, while the fourth side, on the east, is free. It takes the form of a rectangular building, with a gabled roof in two layers, one of stone and one of terra-cotta tiles. When completed, the structure was completely sealed off, with no doors or windows, and apparently covered with earth to form a mound. The excavators entered through the roof and found the contents undisturbed: six hydriai and two amphorai of gilt bronze, filled with honey; an Athenian black-figure amphora that depicts the apotheosis of Herakles and a Dionysiac scene (Dionysos, Hermes, satyrs, and nymphs); and in the middle of the room, two travertine blocks upon which were laid five large iron spits, with fragments of wood, iron netting, and textiles.[76] The only clue as to the purpose of the building comes from a vase found outside, which is decorated with a flower and two marsh birds and incised with the dedication "I am sacred to the *numphê*."

The hypogaeum has been the subject of much discussion, and the evidence is simply not decisive enough to support any one interpretation conclusively. The three main schools of thought hold that the structure is a shrine to a hero, that it is a shrine to the nymphs, or finally, that it is devoted to a goddess under the epithet of Nymphe.[77] In any case, a chronological connection can be established with the destruction of Sybaris (c. 510). Because the hypogaeum is extraordinary in that it was completely sealed at the time of its construction, it is thought to be a one-time offering, perhaps made by Sybarite refugees who were received at Poseidonia. That the spot continued to be held in reverence is indicated by the remains of an enclosure wall that was built in the late fourth or early third century.

If we take the pot graffito as solid evidence that a Nymphe of some description was the object of the cult, several features of the hypogaeum call for more detailed discussion. First, there is no satisfactory parallel for the worship of nymphs in a subterranean structure (as opposed to a cave); the hypogaeum itself naturally brings to mind tombs and cults of a chthonic (underworld) nature and is, in fact similar in structure to local tombs.[78] The closest parallel is the archaic cult similarly addressed to a singular Nymphe in the Athenian agora (3.2.3). The Athenian cult was not, however, conducted in a hypogaeum but within a sacred enclosure. Furthermore, the site contained votive deposits over a long period, which do not seem to be in evidence at the Paestan shrine, in spite of the spot's continuing sacredness as attested by the later enclosure wall. (The earth fill of the enclosure did, however, contain fragments of votive vases from the end of the sixth century.)[79]

The contents of the hypogaeum are similarly ambiguous. Both the hydriai, water vessels decorated with lion motifs, and their contents point to the nymphs; one cannot help thinking of the vessels of honey stored in the cave of the nymphs on Ithake. On the other hand, the richness of the dedication (a large number of bronze vessels) is unparalleled for the nymphs, and the significance of the Athenian amphora, which was included in spite of prior repairs to its base, is unexplained. Again, the hydriai are distinctly feminine in character: according to Sestieri, such vases are found at Paestum in women's graves but not men's. The most curious feature is the arrangement of blocks, spits, and textiles at the room's center, which has been interpreted as the remains of a bed. If this is correct, parallels can again be drawn with the model beds attested as dedications to the nymphs from the Phyle and Caruso caves (5.1.9, 5.1.12). The bed could be a nuptial couch, but it could also be interpreted as the couch on which heroes recline in the feast of the afterlife. The most likely of the possibilities is that the hypogaeum was built as an offering to either Kore or Hera in the guise of Nymphe, or Bride. The combination of nuptial and chthonic themes in cult is, after all, characteristic of Magna Graecia and Sicily, most notably in the case of Persephone, who is at once the archetypal bride and the goddess of the dead. The location of the hypogaeum at Paestum, however, points to Hera, who also has a strong claim to the title of Nymphe. The vase on which the graffito was inscribed was decorated with a flower and water birds, possibly as references to Hera's sanctuary in the Sele estuary. Athenaeus records that Hera was angered at the conduct of the Sybarites, and the construction of the hypogaeum might have been an attempt to propitiate the angry goddess.[80]

3.2.5 *Other Goddesses*

Sicily and Magna Graecia afford numerous examples of minor mythic and cultic links between the nymphs and the major goddesses Hera, Artemis, Athena, and above all Persephone (4.10). An important group of terra-cottas from the Caruso nymph grotto in Lokroi Epizephyroi, represented by several hundred examples, depicts seated females, nude except for a *polos* (figure 3.6).[81] Most of these date from the third and second centuries, though a few are thought to belong to the fourth century. The figures are molded in a sitting position, with their arms close to their sides. No chair or throne is depicted, though separate thrones were found, on which some of the figurines fitted. The majority appear to have lacked a throne, and they are able to be placed in an upright position because the legs end at the knee. This gives the impression that the figures are kneeling with legs tucked underneath, though there is no indication of lower legs or feet in the modeling. Some examples have obviously had their lower legs broken off, but others are deliberately modeled so that the legs taper off smoothly at the knee. The situation is similar with regard to the lower arms: some figures have complete arms with hands held in a relaxed position along the thighs; others are missing lower arms but show insertion points for them, and still other examples were simply abbreviated, with no lower arms at all.

The Caruso terra-cottas as a group constitute a remarkable parallel to the dolls of the previous two centuries in Corinth and Attica, which similarly depict nude, *polos*-wearing women, sometimes as complete figures and sometimes with limbs truncated at the upper arm and thigh. There are further close parallels to a subcategory of seated dolls, well attested from Attica, the area of Kyrene, Taras, and Sicily.[82] These, like the Caruso figures, are nude, wear only a *polos* or jewelry, and are molded in a seated position. They are sometimes

Figure 3.6 Seated "nuptial" figure from Caruso cave. Museo di Reggio Calabria.

provided with their own *thronoi* and sometimes not. They always have articulated upper limbs, a feature found on only a few of the Caruso examples.

The majority of the figures are roughly contemporary with the semicircular basin built in the last stage of the sanctuary's long life, and most were found in the basin itself. Similar nude figures have been found at Morgantina in Sicily and at several sites in Magna Graecia; some were placed in the graves of young women.[83] The most likely interpretation is that the figures are nuptial dedications, given to the nymphs on the occasion of the ritual bath before marriage (or placed in the grave in the case of premature death).[84] Whether or not they were played with by girls is unclear, but their superficial similarity to dolls is surely significant. Their nudity is erotic yet formal and stylized; they seem to represent the concept of the bride, *numphê*, rather than any specific goddess.

But their appearance in the cave is probably related to the fact that both Persephone and Aphrodite have a cultic presence there (5.1.12).

Another interesting assemblage of seated figures with jointed arms comes from the Hellenistic cemeteries at Myrina in Asia Minor. Some of these examples are nude, seated figures with no special attributes, of the kind usually accepted as dolls (figure 3.7). Others, however, are provided with elaborate adornments. While some are nude and some draped, they all wear elabo-

Figure 3.7 Seated, jointed doll from tomb at Myrina. Photo by M. and P. Chuzeville. Louvre Museum.

rate, tall headdresses and high platform shoes of the type worn by actors. Some have large circular pendants between the breasts. These figures, in spite of their jointed arms, are usually not considered dolls. They are thought to be representations of an oriental Aphrodite, derived perhaps from a cult image. Because the figures were found in graves and were the personal possessions of the deceased, it has been suggested that they were "decorative" or, on the basis of the jointed arms, that they were used in miniature theatricals along with similarly jointed figures of boys, probably intended to represent Adonis.[85] Objects such as these show how nebulous the distinction between toys and religious articles can be, and it is probably unwise to insist on a strict one. As we have seen, certain dolls referred to as *dagudes* were thought to be images of Aphrodite, and it would not be surprising if playing with Aphrodite and Adonis toys contributed to girls' socialization in this part of the Greek world, just as dolls that represented Hera might have existed in Boiotia alongside analogous sacred images.

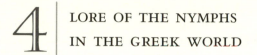

4 LORE OF THE NYMPHS
IN THE GREEK WORLD

4.1 Introduction to Sources and Chronology

In the sections that follow, I draw upon a wide spectrum of evidence to reconstruct, as far as possible, the nymph lore that belongs to each part of the
ancient Greek world. The most useful literary sources for this task are the
Greek poets, especially Homer, the Hesiodic corpus, the fragments of Greek
epic, and Pindar; the fragments of the classical and Hellenistic Greek logographers and historians; and finally, the numerous histories and compilations
of mythological, linguistic, and geographical information produced during the
Roman Imperial period. Other evidence is provided by excavation reports,
inscriptions, and above all, coins.

A few words are in order regarding the role of the logographers in the
collection and preservation of materials that relate to the nymphs. The logographers, who wrote prose works treating the myths, legends, and popular
history of the Greek world, were the fifth-century predecessors and contemporaries of Herodotus. They especially delighted in genealogies and in
founding stories, or *ktiseis*, and to them we owe much of our knowledge of
the roles nymphs played in local traditions as ancestors and founders. They
made use of a variety of sources, including official civic records, epic poetry,
and folk traditions. In part because the logographers were not popular at
Athens, their voluminous works now exist only in fragments. Herodotus and
Thucydides both claim complete independence from them but were clearly
familiar with their work.[1]

Hecataeus inaugurated the tradition, producing mythographic and geographical works in prose. These two subject areas provided the guiding organizational principles for later logographers. The most important of them, Hellanicus, wrote mythographic studies, such as the *Deucalionea* and *Phoronis*; ethnographic studies arranged by region, such as the *Aeolica*, *Argolica*, and *Lydiaca*; and studies of mythohistorical chronology, such as the *Atthis* and *Priestesses of Hera*. Discussing the Pelasgian colonization of Italy, Hellanicus gives the genealogy of the founder, Nanas, in detail, beginning five generations back with the union of Pelasgos and the nymph Menippe, daughter of Peneios. His method contrasts with that of Herodotus, whose treatment of the Pelasgians excludes genealogical concerns completely.[2] Herodotus' love for anecdote and ethnography, however, are logographic characteristics.

Relationships between peoples and places are expressed mythically through eponymous heroes and genealogies: this is a Mediterranean practice, as prominent in the Old Testament as in Greek mythology. Endemic to Greek mythology from a very early period, it is well established in the *Iliad*, in which Homer uses nymph genealogies to express the relationships between land and people in the Troad. Hellanicus and the other logographers systematized the genealogical lore of the Greek world, reconciling contradictory versions and filling in missing generations. Doubtless, some elements of these accounts were fabricated by the logographers, and it is now virtually impossible to distinguish between materials of local origin and those that resulted from rationalization and extrapolation on the part of the logographers.

The Ionian logographers and a wide variety of local historians who followed their lead were enthusiastically taken up by the Alexandrians, who were equally attracted to the minutiae of local cults and family trees. Both the logographers and their Hellenistic successors favored *ktiseis*, *aitia* (founding stories of cities and customs), eponymous heroes, and of course, local nymphs. Callimachus, for example, drew extensively on local histories for his poem entitled *Aetia*, or *Origins*. In his account of Akontios and Kydippe, he even cites "old Xenomedes," a fifth-century Kean chronicler, as his source. Later, many of the mythographers used these classical sources for their compilations. The *Bibliotheca* attributed to Apollodorus of Athens, a compendious library of myths often cited in the discussions below, makes extensive use of Hellanicus and Pherecydes of Athens. Other important sources of Roman date, the periegete Pausanias and the geographer Strabo, are in spirit the successors of the logographers and had access to many of their works. They, the lexicographers, and the scholiasts, who provide other materials for our study, draw upon a body of tradition that was substantially formed by the fifth and fourth centuries.

Finally, it is helpful to keep in mind that our goal is not to ascertain one "correct" version of any myth or custom. We may attempt to distinguish between earlier and later versions, but pronouncements on the relative value of these obscures an important point. Mythic genealogies were always laden with serious political and social significance and were subject to manipulation from the earliest times. Indeed, manipulation and fabrication of these stories for the purpose of gaining prestige were probably the norm in the archaic period, whereas later would-be manipulators were more likely to be inhibited by respect for older, written sources. I quote Huxley's discussion of a genealogy from the sixth-century epic poet Asius of Samos:

> The naming a daughter of the Meander river Samia reflects Samian interest in the Asiatic mainland on the Mykale peninsula not far from the river; this interest culminated in a series of bloody battles with the mainland Ionian city Priene for land on Mykale early in the sixth century B.C. By making Samia a daughter of the great river of southern Ionia, Asios was, in the Eumelian manner, asserting a claim to territory long in dispute. Samia and her child Samos also compensated a little for the neglect by Homer of Asios' native island.[3]

Perhaps as early as the eighth century, the epic poet Eumelus had asserted Corinthian interests in the Black Sea by making Sinope, an important promontory on the south coast, a daughter of the Peloponnesian river Asopos. Because of their identification with water sources and other landscape features, nymphs provided a useful mythographic shorthand for peoples, villages, and cities. Thus, Athenian vase paintings of Aigina's abduction by Zeus have a political dimension (4.3.3), and stories of a god's intercourse with a local nymph often underlie colonization narratives.[4] The same strategy was used regularly throughout the Hellenistic period. The founding of the Bithynian city of Nikaia by Antigonos I saw the appearance of stories about a corresponding nymph, the beloved of Dionysos. Presumably, the existence of an eponymous nymph gave the foundation an instant aura of venerable antiquity.

Our first archaeological evidence for cultic activity addressed to the nymphs belongs to the sixth or perhaps the seventh century. It is difficult to draw general conclusions from archaeological patterns of cult distribution in the sixth century, because the evidence is randomly or arbitrarily preserved. Mainland Greece and, particularly, Attica have, of course, been more thoroughly explored, while other areas apparently crucial to the early development of the cult of the nymphs, such as the northern Aegean and Ionia, have received much less attention. These areas abound with late evidence of nymph worship, but archaic and even classical evidence is rare.

Mythic and cultic recognition of the nymphs is well attested in Homer, especially in the *Odyssey*. The Homeric testimonies to the cult of the nymphs (on Ithake at a fountain, in a cave, and in the sacrifice by Eumaios) are important evidence that the cult was known in the eighth century, in much the same forms it would take during the classical period. The similarity of the Odyssean descriptions to later practices raises the question of what influence the *Odyssey* had in shaping these. The Homeric portrait of the cave as the nymphs' abode has counterparts in archaeologically established cult practice in the early archaic period (Pitsa cave, the Korykian cave), but these are spotty at best. It is only in the fifth and, especially, the fourth centuries, the periods when the cave cult of the nymphs was at its height, that we begin to suspect the influence of the *Odyssey* and its cave. We may then conclude that the effect of the Homeric poems on this particular aspect of Greek religion was weak during the archaic period but grew as the poems became canonized, stable, and accessible on a Panhellenic scale.

The earliest and most accurately datable objects that represent nymphs are coins and black-figure vases (3.1.1, 4.7.2, 5.2.1). The coins correspond to the literary and archaeological evidence suggesting that the cult of the nymphs in the archaic period was often focused on water sources, particularly those abundant, accessible sources that were desiderata for the formation of urban spaces, and for the establishment of colonies. Individual nymphs, as personifications of springs, made excellent emblems for the new medium of coinage. The vogue for nymphs on coins began in the northern Aegean in the mid–sixth century and continued throughout antiquity with much imitation of motifs from one city to the next. This extensive cross-fertilization might lead one to think that the use of nymphs was a mere decorative convention, but we can see from the poems of Pindar and Bacchylides that certain nymphs had important roles in their cities' self-definition and self-advertisement. Each city had a unique water source or sources, often linked to a local nymph and an etiological myth. In those regions especially noted for nymph emblems on coins, such as Magna Graecia and Thessaly, we find abundant evidence of nymphs in local myth and cult. The individuality of water sources was further enhanced by the archaic boom in the building of waterworks and fountain houses. Carried out in some celebrated cases by tyrants, this activity was as competitive as the construction of the gods' temples and could give cities, as in the case of Megara, comparable fame.

There is also some reason to believe that the cult of the nymphs achieved broader diffusion throughout the class structure of Greek society as the centuries passed. The archaeological evidence suggests that, in the archaic period, the worship of nymphs was primarily the concern of the rural poor. This conclusion rests in part on negative evidence: we know from Homer that certain assumptions about the cult of the nymphs were widely shared and that the cult existed in the eighth century or before, yet the offerings they received and, indeed, the sanctuaries where they were worshiped are archaeologically invisible. In cases where archaic nymph sanctuaries have been identified, the durable votive offerings are invariably of poor quality and usually of local manufacture. There were some exceptions to this general rule. First, nymphs could be important in cases of colonization or public works that involved water sources. Second, some of the best evidence for worship of the nymphs in the archaic period results from their association with nuptial rites, which might have crossed class lines but were certainly important for elites. Finally, as we will see, archaic worship of the nymphs seems to have come under state sponsorship earlier in Ionia than in Attica.

During the classical period, elites began to take a strong interest in rural cults of the nymphs, and the durable offerings found in sanctuaries rose in quality and quantity. In Attica, this phenomenon came about because of the new popularity of Pan's cult after the Persian war, in conjunction with a strong wave of devotionalism in which elites participated by purchasing and dedicating stone monuments. The wide range in quality of fourth-century Attic votive reliefs suggests that, while the worship of the nymphs and other "assisting gods" had become fashionable for the well-to-do, it also remained a concern of the less affluent. Attic votive iconography and techniques were exported throughout the Aegean, and the stone relief remained a well-established form of votive gift to the nymphs throughout the Hellenistic and Roman periods.

The Hellenistic kingdoms saw a renewed interest in devotionalism directed toward assisting gods, those who might be expected to aid the individual in the travails of daily life. By this time, the cult of the nymphs had become widely diffused both geographically and socially and was beginning a process of urbanization and secularization in the establishment of a new form of nymphaia, highly ornamented public waterworks. While the poets put forth an idealized, antiquarian vision of the nymphs in their rustic idylls and scholarly dissertations on customs and genealogy, the cultic reality had evolved. In some cases, the nymphs were identified with indigenous deities (hence, with non-elite populations) through a process of syncretism; in other cases, the nymphs represented Greek culture (hence, the elite classes). The clearest examples of the latter phenomenon appear in the period of the Ptolemies, when the deified Arsinoë Philadelphos could be envisioned as a nymph, and Dionysiac nymphs appeared in the extravagantly luxurious Grand Procession of Ptolemy Philadelphos (3.1.1).

The relationship of Hellenistic poems (such as the *Hymns* of Callimachus or dedicatory epigrams) to lived religion is still unclear. What is notable is that aspects of Greek religion formerly perceived for the most part as unremarkable and quotidian began to attract the interest of fashionable, intellectual, and royal circles. Part of this cultural ascent was the tacit assumption that subjects such as the lore of nymphs, by their very mundaneness and their rural, local connotations, somehow distilled an essential, authentic quality of Hellenism—much as the customs of nineteenth-century European peasants were thought by Romantics to embody "true" European identity. The vogue for nymphs was part of a broader antiquarian movement that sought to maintain ties to Greek cultural roots.

The following sections discuss the archaeological and literary evidence geographically, beginning in Attica and traveling in an outward spiral through mainland Greece, the northern Aegean, and so on. This arrangement is somewhat arbitrary; I could just as well have begun with the Peloponnese or Thessaly. I chose a geographical organization over a diachronic one because only in this way can the distinctive local character of nymph lore be demonstrated for the reader: the city nymphs of Sicily and Thessaly, the Muse-like plural nymphs of Boiotia, the solicitous nurses of the Peloponnese, and the partially Hellenized nymphs of Lykia, Thrace, and northern Africa. Though chronological developments did take place, notably the fluctuations in the popularity of the nymphs in different social sectors as described above, the cults and lore of the nymphs were remarkably stable and conservative over the centuries. Three basic themes are sounded over and over: the nymphs' presence in the landscape (including their connections with water supplies and the concept of the nymphs' garden); rites of passage and the social dimension of the *numphê* as bride; and lastly, genealogy and local identity, a major focus of interest in the following sections. In an oft-recurring pattern, we find the nymphs as daughters or consorts of the local rivers and as mothers and wives of primordial heroes.

4.2 Attica

4.2.1 *Athens*

In the mythic accounts of Athens' earliest period, as in foundation stories of other cities, nymphs are often incorporated into the genealogies, though cult activity is not necessarily attested for these figures. According to Apollodorus, both Erichthonios and his son, Pandion, married naiad nymphs. Perhaps they were daughters of the Kephisos River, like Praxithea, the wife of Erechtheus. The daughters of the primordial king Kekrops have some characteristics in common with nymphs, particularly their manifestation at the cave of Pan on the northwest slope of the Akropolis, discussed below.[5]

Excluding the shrine of Nymphe on the south slope of the Akropolis (3.2.3), the earliest known sites of the nymphs' cult at Athens are three water sources: Empedo, Kallirhoë, and a spring or springs by the Asklepieion. At the base of the Akropolis on the northwest side, a spring was located in a deep cleft. According to ancient sources, this spring once had the name Empedo but was renamed Klepsydra when a spring house was constructed about 470–60 in order to collect its waters. (The Klepsydra cave seems to have been first cleared and used as an outlet for the spring as early as the Bronze Age.)[6] The spring house incorporated the natural rock overhang of the cave and consisted of rectangular poros walls, a drawbasin, and a nearby paved area designed to collect rainwater pouring off the Akropolis. The fact that special care was taken to preserve the natural rocky appearance of the spot (even to the point of preserving the cave by supporting the roof with wooden posts) suggests the sanctity of the place. A poros boundary stone found in the agora, inscribed *numphaio hiero horos* ("boundary of the sacred nymphaion") and dating to the first half of the fifth century, has been ascribed to the Klepsydra area and assumed to belong to a shrine of Empedo.[7]

The name Empedo is formed from *empedos*, meaning "firmly set," hence "in the ground" and, by extension, "steadfast" or "continual." Parsons, who excavated the Klepsydra, observed that all these senses are appropriate to the spring, which is both set deeply in the ground and reliable as a water source. The name given to the new construction, Klepsydra, or "water hider," refers to the fact that the spring is hidden deep within the cave. Overlooking the area are the Akropolis caves, which contained shrines of Apollo Hypakraios, and Pan's shrine, formally established after the battle of Marathon.[8] The rock in this area contains many niches cut to receive votive offerings. The complex of caves is also the mythical site, mentioned in Euripides' *Ion*, of Apollo's rape of Kreousa, and it also seems to be connected with the daughters of Kekrops who, according to the *Ion*, threw themselves from the Akropolis upon seeing the infant Erichthonios but still haunt the cliffs, dancing in the neighborhood of Pan's cave. The four small caves and the spring below probably made up a single sacred precinct.[9]

Another important spring is the famous Kallirhoë, "lovely flowing," the spring that supplied water for the nuptial baths of Athenian brides (3.2.3).[10] In the time of the tyrants, a spring house known as the Enneakrounos, or Nine Spout, was built over Kallirhoë. The name Kallirhoë appears on some black-figure vase paintings that depict women at a splendid fountain house, though the vases cannot reliably tell us much about its actual appearance.[11]

The location of Kallirhoë/Enneakrounos is a long-debated mystery. The majority of ancient sources, including Thucydides, refer to a site south of the Akropolis on the Ilissos, where a fountain known as Kallirhoë has existed up until the present day; yet Pausanias' description of the famous Enneakrounos makes it clear he is standing in the agora near the Odeion. Hence we are left with two candidates for the site: one is the spring on the bank of the Ilissos by the church of Ayia Photeini. Here, there are two or three small cavelike shelters and ancient cisterns, but no obvious remains of a sixth-century spring house. Across the river from this Kallirhoë is a small shrine of Pan, with Pan's figure carved in a relief of the fifth century or later, now almost weathered away. The second possible site is a sixth-century fountain house in the agora (the Southeast Fountain House), which has been firmly identified with the Enneakrounos seen by Pausanias, although the excavators were unable to confirm the nine spouts.[12] Every imaginable solution has been brought to bear on the riddle, including the possibilities of a corruption in the text of Thucydides, the existence of two springs named Kallirhoë, and the removal of the Ilissos fountain house to the agora in the Roman period.[13]

Thucydides' account suggests that Kallirhoë was the main souce of water for the early city, which included the Akropolis and the Ilissos area to the southeast. As the urban area expanded, the use of water from Kallirhoë for nuptial baths and other rites became a matter of cultic conservatism rather than convenience. Kallirhoë's cult is attested in a fourth-century relief dedicated by Xenokrateia (4.2.2), and figures of Kallirhoë and Ilissos are thought to have filled the opposite corners of the west pediment on the Parthenon.[14]

About 500 meters upstream from Kallirhoë, on the far side of the river, is the hill of Ardettos at the foot of which the shrine of the nymphs and Acheloös mentioned in Plato's *Phaedrus* was probably located.[15] The spot where Sokrates and his companions sit down is shaded by a large plane tree and a willow; a spring of cool water flows beneath the plane tree; a grassy bank is convenient for resting; and it is identified as a shrine of the nymphs and Acheloös by the presence of *korai* and *agalmata*. The *korai* are probably not statues, like the famous Akropolis maidens, but smaller, doll-like figures placed in or near the spring. The *agalmata* might be stone reliefs fitted to bases, though they could also be other objects pleasing to the resident gods. Interestingly, it is between the dramatic date of the *Phaedrus* (c. 414) and the approximate date of composition (c. 370) that the first known Attic votive reliefs to the nymphs were carved.[16]

Kallirhoë and the shrine of the nymphs and Acheloös on the Ilissos are part of a group of shrines and cults that could be said to exist on the margin of the old city, in a quasi-rural setting where one would expect to find nymphs. Even in Sokrates' time, the trip to the shrine involved exiting the city gates and strolling in a parklike area rather than an urban one. Across the Ilissos, on the stadium side where the shrine of the nymphs lay, the district was known as Agrai, "the Field," and many of the cults of the Ilissos area had a rustic character. Thucydides (2.15.3–6) mentions five landmark sites in the southeast area: the shrine of Zeus Olympios, the shrine of Apollo Pythios, the shrine of Ge, the shrine of Dionysos at Limnai, and Kallirhoë. In Agrai itself, we have Zeus Meilichios, Artemis Agrotera, Demeter and the Lesser Mysteries, Meter, and the shrine of the nymphs and Acheloös. These cults were interconnected to some degree, and it is no surprise to find the nymphs in this company.

Near the stadium and by the Ilissos riverbank was found a relief dedicated to the nymphs and "all the gods" by an association of launderers, men and women who worked in and beside the river (figure 4.1).[17] The relief is divided into two registers: the top shows an abbreviated version of the conventional iconography for the nymphs (Hermes leads the dance while Pan and Acheloös are in attendance). The lower and larger register, however, depicts Demeter and Kore, who are approched by a bearded hero (perhaps Demophon) leading a horse. This relief recognizes the neighborly relationship between the Ilissos cult of the nymphs and the Lesser Mysteries of Demeter and Kore, whose initiates bathed in the Ilissos.

The shrine of Dionysos at Limnai was also in the southeast district of the city, and it has been suggested as the most likely site for the sanctuary of the Horai with its altars of Dionysos Orthos and the nymphs. The association of Dionysos with the Horai is also attested from copies of a relief sculpture (the original was perhaps of the fourth century), which depicts the god leading a dance of the Horai much as Hermes leads the nymphs on Attic nymph reliefs. The sanctuary of the Horai is mentioned in a fragment of the Attic historian Philochorus, who considered the altar of Orthos the oldest monument of Dionysos in Athens. The name Dionysos Orthos presumably refers to an ithyphallic, hermlike cult statue, and the associations of the Horai, the

Figure 4.1 Launderers' relief from area of the Stadium, Athens. Staatliche Museum zu Berlin, Preussischer Kulturbesitz, Antikensammlung.

nymphs, and the sanctuary *en limnais* ("in the marshes") all suggest a cult of vegetative fertility. Philochorus further connected the site with a myth about King Amphiktyon, who was the first to mix wine with water and who founded the altars. The Horai, it is said, are responsible for the ripening of the grapes; the nymphs provide water; and Dionysos, of course, presides over the whole process. If Philochorus is recording an ancient tradition about this site, we may have here unusual evidence of the cult of the nymphs in the sixth century or earlier. On the other hand, the story of Amphiktyon is uncomfortably reminiscent of Hellenistic epigrams on the mixing of wine, many of which equate "nymphs" with "water" in a fashion that we rarely find until that period (1.4.4). An undated Attic inscription to the Horai and nymphs might have belonged to this sanctuary.[18]

A third area that contains sacred springs is the site of the Asklepieion, on the south slope of the Akropolis. There are two candidates for the spring of the Asklepieion, both associated with nymphs: the Round Spring House to the east and the Slouth Slope Spring House to the west. If the nymphs were the earliest inhabitants at either spring, the introduction of Asklepios to Athens will have followed a pattern (also known from Lebena in Krete) of incorporating an earlier nymph cult, probably one that had a healing emphasis. Abundant water, of course, was necessary for the god's healing operations, and the logical place to establish his cult would be on a spot already associated with healing, as nymphs' springs often were. Asklepios' cult was introduced to the site in 420–19, when Telemachos donated the first Asklepieion building. Two small caves, an upper and lower, were incorporated into the shrine at some point. The lower cave contains a spring and was built into an early third-century Doric stoa as the Round Spring House. In this area were discovered the earliest known Attic nymph relief, dedicated by Archandros (figure 4.2), and other nymph reliefs, including one dedicated by a priest of Asklepios.[19]

Another spring to the west was provided with a spring house (the South Slope Spring House) in the late sixth century. Travlos suggests that this archaic spring house was associated with the Asklepieion and had been the site of a shrine of the nymphs and (later) Pan. The Isis inscription (to Hermes, Aphrodite, the nymphs, Pan, and Isis) and the remains of a small temple of Isis were found nearby. Aleshire has provided convincing arguments that the first Asklepieion was indeed the establishment to the east, so that we are left

Figure 4.2 Archandros relief. National Archaeological Museum, Athens.

with a choice of counting this area as a late addition to the precinct or of considering it merely a neighbor to the Asklepieion, a sacred precinct that contained, at various periods, shrines of the nymphs, Themis, Aphrodite, Hermes, Pan, and Isis.[20]

North of the Pnyx is the Hill of the Nymphs, on which stands the Church of Ayia Marina, encompassing an older church with a large cavity in the rock beneath. West of the church is a fifth-century rupestral inscription that marks the shrine of the nymphs and Demos (the hill derives its modern name from this inscription). The cult of Demos, the personification of the Athenian citizenry, is more often attested in association with the Charites.[21] Another old (perhaps sixth-century) inscription, located thirty meters below the church, refers to the boundary of Zeus (probably Zeus Meilichios, to judge from dedications found on the north slope). A rock on the hill, highly polished and slippery from long wear, used to be employed as a slide for pregnant women, a charm for encouraging easy labor. Ervin has suggested that the juxtaposition of the slide and the Church of Ayia Marina, a saint who aids in childbirth, with an ancient cult site of the nymphs is not coincidental. Also found in the general vicinity was a fourth-century relief dedicated to the *numphai ompniai*, which shows three nymphs in a cave, Pan, and a seated male deity, probably Zeus. The adjective *ompnios* refers to grain or, more generally, to abundance and prosperity.[22]

4.2.2 *Peiraieus and the Demes*

Moving outside of the main urban center toward Peiraieus, we find many indications of the nymphs' popularity, even excluding the rural cave sites (5.1.9). In the area between the Long Walls known as New Phaleron, near the ancient hippodrome, lay a sanctuary of the river god Kephisos. The district was called Echelidai after an old hero, Echelos, and the river itself was adjacent to the spot chosen for the sanctuary. A dam of sand and pebbles was constructed to prevent the river from flooding the sacred precinct. Here, at various times, have been found several remnants of the sanctuary's contents, including two votive reliefs with their bases and a small stone inscribed with a sacrificial regulation. These objects belong to the last decade of the fifth century or, perhaps, a few years later. Two dedicators and founders are named: Xenokrateia of the deme Cholleidai and Kephisodotos of the deme Boutadai. The river Kephisos runs through both demes, and Kephisodotos' name ("gift of Kephisos") further attests his personal connection to the river god (3.1.3).

Xenokrateia, who claims to have founded the sanctuary, set up a votive sculpture (figures 4.3 and 4.4) to Kephisos and "the gods of the same altar" on behalf of her son, Xeniades, and for the sake of his education (*didaskalia*). Accompanying the relief, which shows a crowded throng of figures reminiscent of those on the east frieze of the Parthenon, was an inscription on a separate stone that listed (probably) twelve gods to whom sacrifice was indicated. There is a rough, inexact correspondence between the list of gods in

Figure 4.3 Xenokrateia relief. National Archaeological Museum, Athens.

the cult regulation and those portrayed on the relief. The list below shows the names and their corresponding figures on the relief (the numbers refer to figure 4.4), according to the interpretation of Edwards.[23]

Regulation	Relief
not present	Hermes (no. 3)
not present	Xenokrateia (no. 4)
not present	Xeniades (no. 5)
not present	Echelos? (no. 7)
not present	Hekate statue (no. 13)
Hestia	not present
Kephisos	no. 6
Apollo Pythios	no. 1
Leto	no. 8
Artemis Lochia	no. 2?
Eileithyia	not present
Acheloös	no. 12
Kallirhoë	not present
Geraistai Nymphai Genethliai	nos. 9, 10, 11
Rhapso	not present

Those who appear on both the cult regulation and the relief, then, are Kephisos, Apollo Pythios, Leto, Artemis Lochia, Acheloös, and the Geraistai Nymphai Genethliai, "the Geraistian Nymphs of Birth." The order of the

Figure 4.4 Xenokrateia relief. Line drawing by author.

cult inscription seems significant, for after the preliminary sacrifice to Hestia, Kephisos is honored first as the main god of the sanctuary. Then, the Apolline triad takes pride of place in what looks like a descending order of precedence. Apollo Pythios had a cult in the old southeast sector of Athens,[24] and he is also included in a Marathonian inscription concerned with the well-being of youths, discussed below. Eileithyia is a venerable goddess but not an Olympian. Acheloös precedes Kallirhoë, and the Geraistian nymphs and Rhapso, perhaps a nymph of healing, come last. All these gods and goddesses received sacrifice on the same altar.

The discrepancies between the cult regulation and the relief are explained by their different functions. The regulation ensures that the correct gods will receive sacrifice in the correct order, while the relief depicts the relationship between Xenokrateia, her son, and the gods of the sanctuary. Hermes appears to escort Xenokrateia and the tiny Xeniades toward the welcoming figure of Kephisos, who bends toward her. The attention of Apollo Pythios and Artemis Lochia has already been drawn to Xenokrateia, while the deities to the right of Kephisos have not yet become aware of the visitor. Since there was insufficient space to include all of the minor goddesses, the Geraistian nymphs were included as a representative group. The presence of Acheloös in profile with the group of three nymphs brings to mind the standard composition of fourth-century Attic nymph reliefs; this arrangement was already becoming canonical (a similar Acheloös appears on another early nymph votive, the Quirinal relief; see figure 3.1).[25]

The objects contributed by Kephisodotos are a double-sided relief (known as the Echelos relief) and an inscribed stele, which served as its base. Side A of the relief, inscribed to Hermes and the nymphs, shows six figures: an unidentified figure (who may be Artemis), a bearded male (perhaps a mature Echelos), a horned river god (presumably Kephisos), and three nymphs. Side B shows the abduction of Iasile by the local hero Echelos, depicted as a youth, while Hermes looks on. Thus, both Hermes and Echelos are gods of this sanctuary and rightly appear in the iconographic welcome for Xenokrateia. They do not appear in the cult regulation, however, because they had a separate altar of their own.[26] Kephisodotos speaks of setting up an altar in his dedicatory inscription, but his altar was distinct from the one Xenokrateia must have contributed to serve the gods listed in her regulation. Edwards suggests that side A depicts the introduction of Kephisos and the nymphs, as occupants of the new sanctuary, to Artemis, who had an important shrine at Mounychia near the Peiraieus and who also was honored in the regulation as Lochia, a goddess of childbirth. Echelos is represented on side A in "the present," as a local hero seeing to the well-being of his district, and his bearded aspect is consistent with depictions of the heroes feasting on votive reliefs. In side B, an episode from his earthly life is depicted, and he is shown as an energetic youth.

The founding and care of a sanctuary required a degree of piety somewhat beyond the normal, and the dedications themselves reflect highly personalized choices. It is likely that Xenokrateia and her associate, Kephisodotos, felt a heightened sense of devotion to the local deities, analogous to the nympholepsy that caused Archedamos to care for and embellish the cave shrine of Vari. This type of devotion had its origin in the individual psyche and was different in kind and degree from the piety expected of everyone. It both was and was not conventional. The expression of piety must take place within certain parameters recognized by all, including sacrifice and setting up gifts to the gods. But most Athenians did not found sanctuaries. Moreover, the flexibility of Greek polytheism permitted a personalized selection of gods. The primary gods of the place appear to have been Kephisos, the nymphs, and Echelos (with Iasile), while Artemis or Bendis resided nearby. The others are included based on the personal preferences of the dedicators and the context surrounding the dedications. Xenokrateia's choices consist primarily of deities who concern themselves with birth and the well-being of children (Leto, Artemis Lochia, Eileithyia, river gods, nymphs). Kephisodotos' choices complement those of Xenokrateia and, like hers, fulfill gender expectations. He is interested in the hero Echelos and in Echelos' demonstration of his male prowess by abducting a bride. He also takes an interest, appropriate to a founder, in the proper introduction of the cult to the site and incorporates Echelos into this scheme.[27]

In the Peiraieus, the harbor of Athens, several finds of votive reliefs indicate the presence of a cult or cults of the nymphs. A nymphaion is also attested in a third-century inscription, which deals with the procession of Bendis witnessed by Sokrates at the opening of the *Republic* (c. 380). Those in charge of the Thracian orgeones are to meet the procession of Bendis on its arrival in the Peiraieus. The participants in the procession will be furnished with sponges, basins, and water in the nymphaion and will then partake of a meal in the Bendideion (the decree was not motivated simply by the need for water, for the Bendideion had its own supply). The link between Bendis' cult and that of the nymphs is confirmed by an earlier votive relief to Bendis (figure 4.5).[28] The goddess stands with her consort, Deloptes; they look down at the smaller figures of two men, who are being honored for their administration of the Bendideion. Above the heads of the honorees is carved a small scene borrowed from the iconography of nymph votives: Hermes leads three nymphs, while Pan looks on. What was the significance of this cult association with the nymphs? Examination of Thracian cult reveals a close relationship between the goddess Parthenos (apparently, an epithet of Bendis) and local nymphs (4.7.2, 4.8.1).

Yet another exotic god linked with nymphs was the Phrygian moon god Men. Men's cult arrived in Athens via the Peiraieus by the third century, and his votaries, for the most part slaves and metics, associated him with Pan and the nymphs. A second-century relief from Athens depicts Pan, Men, and a nymph within the same rocky cave frame used in conventional votives to the nymphs and Pan. About a century later, an inscription from the rim of a well, found beside the Dipylon gate, invokes Pan, Men, and the beautiful nymphs as bringers of rain. Men was also associated with nymphs at his principal sanctuary in Antioch.[29] In general, the rich evidence for the worship of nymphs in the Peiraieus reflects their popularity in non-elite, including noncitizen, portions of the population.

Each Athenian belonged not only to the polis but to one of the local neighborhoods, or demes. Sacrificial calendars from several demes, first inscribed during the fourth century in imitation of the city calendar, record offerings to a range of obscure heroes and deities about whom we might otherwise know nothing. It is likely that, were we able to examine the traditions of the more than 130 Kleisthenic demes, we would find abundant cults of the nymphs. Of the five extant calendric inscriptions, two mention nymphs, those of Erchia and Marathon.

At Erchia, the nymphs exist in a cult partnership with Acheloös, Alochos, Hermes, and Ge; a sacrifice is to be performed annually on the Hill of Erchia and is to include one sheep for each deity ("the nymphs" are counted as one). This was one of the larger sacrifices in the Erchian calendar and one of only three days during the year when at least five victims were sacrificed. The larger number of victims probably ensured a larger turnout of demesmen, since more portions of meat would be available for distribution. The deities are those we constantly find associated with the nymphs: Acheloös; Alochos, whose name indicates that she is a deity of birth like Artemis or Iphigeneia; Hermes, another representative of youth and the nymphs' companion in their pastoral functions; and Ge, the nymphs' mother in some accounts and a patron of pasturing as Demeter is of agriculture.[30] These are gods of the life cycle, who ensure the successful conception, birth, and rearing of babies and youths; at the same time, they are rural gods who govern the herdsmen's pursuits and the multiplication of kids and lambs. The importance of this conceptual sphere to the demesmen (and, presumably, women) is illustrated by the prominence given to the diety Kourotrophos ("Nourisher of Youths,"

Figure 4.5 Bendis relief from the Peiraieus. Ny Carlsberg Glypototek.

an epithet given to Ge at Athens) in three of the extant deme calendars (Thorikos, Erchia, Marathon). A slightly different connotation is found in the sacrifice on another day to Apollo Nymphagetes (one male goat) and the nymphs (one female goat). Here, the rural, pastoral associations are still clear in the goat sacrifice, but the focus is upon the nymphs as chorus, with Apollo as the chorus leader and musician. This cult of Apollo as the "leader of the nymphs" is also attested widely in the rest of the Greek world.

The calendar of the Marathonian Tetrapolis mentions one sacrifice of a goat to a nymph, Euis, perhaps associated with Dionysos, but nothing more.[31] There is, however, another document, possibly recording cults practiced by a *trittus* (a tribal subgroup) of Marathon. The gods and heroes of this group include Eros, Hippolytos, Poseidon, Zeus Tropaios, Herakles, Glaukos, Apollo Pythios, and the nymphs with Acheloös. The choice of gods addresses various aspects of the lives of young men who will soon be enrolled as citizens. Zeus Tropaios is known from ephebic inscriptions, and the choices of Eros, Hippolytos, Herakles, and the nymphs with Acheloös also have clear significance for ephebes.[32]

These sacrifices are of interest because they confirm that the extraurban cults of the nymphs were not confined to cave sites, numerous in Attica by this period. We do not know whether any of the cave sites, such as Vari, were included in official lists of cults administered by demes. A large proportion of the cults and festivals celebrated by the demes must have come down from archaic times rather than being newly instituted with Kleisthenes' arrangements of 508–7.[33] Would nearby demesmen have considered the cave sites to be under their purview, or were the caves, for the most part archaeologically recognizable as cult sites only after 480, considered too recent or minor a development for inclusion in the calendars of ancestral traditions? The appearance of the cave cults in the wake of Marathon suggests that they were part of a devotional wave encouraged by the state, so that these sites attracted pilgrims and wealthier outside dedicators of stone votive reliefs. Though the cave cults were rural, they might not have been deme cults per se, in that their administration was not a concern of the demes.

In the neighborhood of Lamptrai, southeast of Hymettos, was found an inscription (c. 440–30) that contained a sacred law said to originate from the Delphic oracle.[34] It is somewhat surprising to find the oracle taking an interest in the detailed administration of a cult of the nymphs, particularly as the cult in question belongs to an obscure spring rather than a famous one, such as Kallirhoë or Klepsydra. According to Bousquet, the actual directive from Delphi must have specified nothing more than a regular sacrifice to the nymphs, while the local functionaries added a regulation that concerned fees to be paid for the use of the spring water of Halykos. Residents were to pay one obol per year for drinking water, while for other more intensive uses, a surcharge was to be paid to the nymphs' shrine. This law concerning spring water can be compared with others from Attica and Kos, but seems to be unique in its concern with generating income rather than with the need to prevent fouling of the spring with offal or other impurities.[35]

The deme of Phlya was the site of an old mystery cult. Pausanias describes altars there of Dionysos Antheios, Apollo Dionysodotos with Artemis Selasphoros, and the Ismenides nymphs with Ge, whom they called Great Goddess. This deme was the home of the Lykomidai, a family involved in various mystery cults. Themistokles, who was affiliated with the Lykomidai, caused the shrine at Phlya to be restored after it was burned by the Persians, while another member of the family was said to have reorganized the rites of the Theban Kabeiroi. This Theban connection may expain the presence of the Ismenides nymphs, who properly belong in Boiotia.[36]

4.3 Central Greece

4.3.1 *Boiotia*

More than in any other part of the Greek world, cults of female pluralities were concentrated in Boiotia. The Boiotian nymphs were part of a local tradition, stemming ultimately from sources in the areas of the north whence the Boiotoi migrated, of female pluralities concerned, on the one hand, with springs and, on the other, with the inspiration of mantic and other poetic utterances. These pluralities include the Leibethrian and Sphragitic nymphs, the Charites of Orchomenos, and, most famous of all, the Muses of Helikon. The Parthenoi of Eleon and the Praxidikai of Haliartia probably also should be included in this group. The tradition of divine female pluralities extends into the realm of heroines and manifests itself in an unusual concentration of female sacrifical sisters in Boiotian and Attic myths.[37] Boiotia is also the home of nymph-inspired oracles, the supposed birthplace of the nympholept prophet Bakis (1.3).

The mountains of Boiotia are well supplied with female divinities. Mount Helikon is the home of Hesiod's Muses but also of the springs Hippokrene and Aganippe and the cave of the Leibethrian nymphs, according to Strabo. In the literary tradition, the Muses are sometimes conflated with these nymphs.[38] There is also a Mount Leibethrion, about five miles from Koroneia, which Pausanias describes. He says the site had statues of the nymphs and Muses, and two springs called Leibethrias and Petra, "like a woman's breasts with water flowing like milk." Mount Leibethrion is one of the peaks of the Helikon range, which explains why Strabo locates the cave of the Leibethrian nymphs on Helikon, when we would naturally expect it to be on Leibethrion. Pausanias does not mention a cave, but in modern times a cave was found, which contained an assemblage of terra-cottas consistent with the presence of a cult of the nymphs (5.1.10). Mount Thourion, east of Chaironeia, had its own cult of the Muses, and Mount Kithairon had a cave of the Sphragitid nymphs.[39]

Many of the place names connected with the Boiotian cults of the Muses and nymphs are duplicated from the Macedonian district of Pieria, the birthplace of the Muses in Hesiod: Leibethron, Helikon (a river of the Macedonian city Dion), Thourion, and so on. Tradition has it that Thracians, who lived in the district of Pieria from a very early period, established the cult of the nine Muses and the associated cult of the Leibethrian nymphs in Boiotia (4.7.1). We may not wish to accept Strabo's statement that Thracians actually came to Boiotia; the Boiotoi themselves could have brought these ideas to the area when they migrated from their earlier homes in the north.[40]

Helikon and, more specifically, the Hippokrene fountain was the locale associated with the blinding of Teiresias, the famous seer and son of the nymph Chariklo. According to Callimachus' account, Teiresias unwittingly came upon Athena at her bath. By the law of the gods, he was blinded, but Athena gave him divinatory powers because of her love for her companion Chariklo. Callimachus' source might have been the fifth-century mythographer Pherecydes of Athens, who tells the same story.[41]

Like many other Greeks, the Boiotians closely associated the nymphs with local rivers, in particular the Asopos River, which was and is something of a natural boundary between Attica and Boiotia. The Asopos River was a great progenitor of daughter nymphs, though ancient sources disagree on whether the river in question is the Peloponnesian Asopos of Phlious and Sikyon or the Boiotian Asopos. Stories about both rivers seem to have been merged into one set of myths claimed by both districts; most agree that Asopos' bride, Metope, was herself a nymph, the daughter of the Arkadian (or Boiotian) river Ladon.[42] Most sources also agree that Korkyra, Aigina, and Thebe were among their daughters. The earliest source is Homer, who says that Antiope, daughter of Asopos, bore Amphion and Zethos to Zeus. While Homer certainly referred to Boiotian Asopos, the Peloponnesians found a way to lay claim to Antiope. In later versions, she was supposed to have fled to Sikyon or been abducted by its king Epopeus, who fathered one of her twins.[43] Thus the Sikyonians were able to assert their own role in one of the founding myths of Thebes.

Similarly, Pausanias reports that the Thebans objected to the Phliasian characterization of Thebe as the daughter of the Peloponnesian river but that the Phliasians nevertheless dedicated at Olympia a statue group of Asopos with Nemea, Harpina, Korkyra, and Thebe, and Aigina being abducted by Zeus. They also presented a statue group of Zeus and Aigina at Delphi.[44] (The parentage of Aigina was hotly disputed, for from this nymph arose the prestigious lines of Achilles and Ajax.) Pindar, while avoiding an overt statement about the identity of Asopos, also wished to emphasize the mythical kinship of Thebes and Aigina, which shared similar political and social ideologies. This point is illustrated by Herodotus, who describes the oracle received by the Thebans when they wished to avenge themselves upon Athens: they were told to ask their "nearest" to help them. The oracle caused confusion until it was interpreted as a reference to the kinship of the sisters Aigina and

Thebe, and the Thebans accordingly applied to the Aiginetans for help. Similar themes are sounded in Bacchylides' account of Asopos' daughters. The deeds of Telamon, Peleus, Achilles, and Ajax are celebrated, and the poet continues:

στείχει δι' εὐρείας κελε[ύ]θου
μυρία πάνται φάτις
σᾶς γενεᾶς λιπαρο-
    ζώνων θυγατρῶν, ἃς θε[ο]ί
σὺν τύχαις ὤικισσαν ἀρχα-
    γους ἀπορθήτων ἀγυιᾶν.

τίς γὰρ οὐκ οἶδεν κυανοπλοκάμου
    Θήβας ἐΰδμα[τον πόλι]ν,
ἢ τὰν μαγαλώνυ]μον Αἴγιναν, μεγ[ίστ]ου
Ζην]ὸς [ἃ πλαθεῖσα λ]έχει τέκεν ἥρω . . . (Bacchyl. 9.47–56)[45]

On a wide path travel in all directions the countless reports of your family, the bright-belted daughters whom gods settled with happy fortunes as founders [archagoi] of inviolate cities. Who does not know of the well-built town of dark-haired Thebe or of renowned Aigina, who came to the bed of great Zeus and bore the hero . . .

Bacchylides speaks unabashedly of the Peloponnesian Asopos, writing as he is for a Phliasian patron.

Unlike Theban Pindar, whose foreign patronage meant that he must employ ambiguity where Asopos was concerned, Corinna of Tanagra came down firmly on the side of the Boiotian river. Evidence of Boiotia's local traditions about Asopos comes from a fragment of Corinna, who wrote of Asopos' anger at the abduction of his nine daughters by the lustful Olympian gods (1.4.2). Zeus was said to have taken Aigina and two others (Thebe and, possibly, Plataia); Poseidon took three, including Korkyra and Salamis; Apollo took Sinope and Thespeia; and Hermes took one daughter, probably Tanagra. The tradition of Asopos' anger was also preserved in the Peloponnesian versions of the myth, in which Corinthian Sisyphos betrayed Zeus as the ravisher of Aigina, and Zeus was forced to drive the outraged father back to his stream with thunderbolts.[46]

The majority of the attested daughters fall into two main groups, which correspond to the dispute over the identity of Asopos: those associated with the Peloponnese, especially its eastern half, and those who can be assigned to Boiotia and Euboia.[47] The Peloponnesian group includes Kleone, from the town Kleonai between Argos and Corinth; Peirene, from the fountain at Corinth; Ornia, from the Phliasian town Orneai; Harpin(n)a, from the town in Elis; Nemea; and Korkyra, a colony of Corinth.[48] The Boiotian/ Euboian group includes Thebe, Tanagra, Thespeia, and Plataia, all Boiotian towns; Ismene, perhaps a nymph of the Ismenos River at Thebes; Oinoë, or

Oeroë (the latter is a Boiotian river); Antiope, the mother of the Theban founders, Amphion and Zethos; Chalkis, or Kombe, a Euboian city; and Euboia herself. The name Asopis is appropriate to either group, having been used for both the district around Phlious and the island of Euboia.[49] Aigina and Salamis, the disputed islands of the Saronic gulf, should perhaps make up a third group. One important, early-attested daughter who does not fit these categories is Sinope, the eponym of the Milesian colony (founded c. 600) on the south coast of the Black Sea, who is supposed to have borne Syros to Apollo. She is mentioned by the epic poet Eumelus and seems to represent an early Corinthian attempt to stake territorial claims (perhaps purely mythical in this case) in the Black Sea. Two additional daughters who cannot be geographically fixed with certainty are Eurynome and Pronoë.[50]

Several of the cities adjacent to the Boiotian Asopos river, including Thespiai,[51] Plataia, Thebes, and Tanagra,[52] were considered his daughters. There is some evidence linking each of these towns to cults of the nymphs, though often no clear connections can be drawn to the eponymous nymphs themselves. In most cases, the mythological brides of the gods did not have corresponding cults. Instead, the cults tended to be directed at the traditional female pluralities, with little or no differentiation of individual nymphs. Everywhere in the Greek world, but especially in Boiotia, Thessaly, and the western colonies, can be found a certain tension between the need to recognize individual nymphs as ancestors and eponyms and the cultic tendency toward worship of nymphs in the plural.

A boundary stone from Thebes attests a classical sanctuary of the nymphs in that city. Thebe, daughter of Asopos, was honored at Thebes, at least in the forms of coin, statue, and choral ode. Pindar mentions an armed statue (*agalma*) in a fine chariot, "most sacred, with gold chiton." In Pindar's sixth Olympian, Thebe takes on the role of inspiratrix: "Horse-driving Thebe, whose welcome water I drink as I weave the varied song for the spearmen."[53] For Pindar, Thebe is both nymph and city, mother and Muse; the concepts are inextricably melded. Thebe and her sister Asopid Ismene also appear on a number of Attic and Italian vases; they sit or stand beside the serpent of Ares as Kadmos approaches.[54]

The celebration at Plataia of the great Boiotian festival in honor of Hera, the Daidala, and its connection with the nymphs, is discussed in 3.2.4. Not far from the spot where the Daidala bonfire was held, a cave on Kithairon housed the Sphragitid nymphs. An oracle, received from Delphi on the eve of the battle of Plataia, directed the Athenians to make sacrifices to Zeus, Hera Kithaironia, Pan and the Sphragitid nymphs, and seven local heroes (1.3). The true gods of Kithairon are Hera and the nymphs; Zeus is included in his role as husband of the Bride, and Pan as the regular companion of the nymphs after 490. Plataia makes an appropriate local rival for Hera, as one of the daughters of Asopos whom Zeus abducted. She gained in importance after the great battle, of course, and Pausanias mentions her shrine in the city itself. He calls her shrine a *herôon* and characterizes her as the daughter of an early king Asopos, but he notes that the Plataians themselves thought of her as the daughter of the river. Near Plataia was the fountain Gargaphia, where Artemis was interrupted at her bath by the ill-fated hero Aktaion. Ovid describes the site as a picturesque, shady grotto of the nymphs, quite in contrast to Herodotus, who prosaically describes how the spring was choked and spoiled by the invading Persians. A personified Gargaphia appears on Italian vases that illustrate the Aktaion myth.[55]

While several of the Boiotian towns to the south drew their names from Asopos' daughters, others seem to have been named for the fifty sons whom Orion fathered with nymphs, according to Corinna (1.4.2). These nymphs were perhaps the daughters of the Kephisos River of northern Boiotia and Phokis, referred to as an ancestor (*archagos*) in the same fragment. Corinna seems to subscribe to the tradition that Orion was fathered by Hyrieus, the son of the Pleiad Alkyone and Poseidon and the eponym of the town Hyria near Aulis. Hyrieus is elsewhere said to have married a local nymph, Klonia, and fathered Lykos and Nykteus.[56]

Tradition held that Ismenos, eponym of the Theban river and hill, and his brother Teneros, the seer of Apollo Ptoös and eponym of the Teneric plain, were offspring of Apollo and the Okeanid Melia. The name Melia has an ancient association with nymphs in Boiotia, for Hesiod says that nymphs called Meliai were born along with the Erinyes and giants from the drops of blood shed on the earth when Kronos castrated his father. "Melia" is also the ash tree; Callimachus makes the Melia of Thebes not an Okeanid but an earthborn nymph who dwells in a tree.[57] Because of her seat at the great shrine of Apollo at Thebes, Melia seems to have an older, more exalted position than the daughters of Asopos, more so than Thebe herself. The relationship between Apollo and Melia, as depicted by Pindar, has much about it of the sacred marriage. In the fragmentary ninth *Paean*, the couch or bed (*lechos*) of Melia is mentioned twice, in the contexts of intercourse with Apollo and of birthing the heroes. And in *Pythian* 11.1–16, Melia acts as the hostess when local heroines are bidden to visit the shrine of Apollo Ismenios.

According to Pausanias, Melia's brother, Kaanthos, was sent by their father, the river Okeanos, to look for her after she was abducted. Kaanthos attempted to set fire to the Ismenion and was shot by the god. His tomb was located by a spring near the Ismenion; his story is clearly a doublet of the better-known myth of Kadmos, who was sent to find his sister, Europe, after her abduction by Zeus. (It also reminds us of the stories of Asopos as the outraged father who attempts to regain his abducted daughters.) The spring by which Kaanthos' tomb lay belonged perhaps to his sister, Melia; it is identified by Pausanias as the famous spring of Ares, once guarded by a great serpent. There is much disgreement in both ancient and modern sources about the springs and rivers of Thebes. The city had two roughly parallel rivers, the Ismenos and the Dirke, joined by a third smaller rivulet. The Ismenos was fed entirely by one spring, now known as Agianni. Dirke was fed by several springs, among them one at the foot of the Kadmeia, now called Pege.[58] Ismenides nymphs are attested at Phlya in Attica (4.2.2), while Dirke herself has been considered both a nymph and a heroine (1.1).

At Lebadeia was the cult complex of the oracular hero Trophonios and his cult partner, Herkyn(n)a. Trophonios' grove was separated from the town by a river called Herkyna, upon the bank of which stood her shrine (naos); and the spring feeding the river emerged in a cave, where Pausanias saw statues of the pair. Herkyna too has characteristics of both heroine and nymph. She was considered the daughter of Trophonios, but this appears to have been a relatively late development. Her pairing with a hero belongs to a cult pattern more typical of heroines, though the combination of nymph and hero is found elsewhere in Boiotia (for example, Melia's association with her sons at the Ismenion of Thebes). Features of the cult that suggest Herkyna was at some time considered a nymph include her identification with the river (and perhaps also the spring); the grotto on the site; and the local legend that Herkyna was a playmate of Kore. Furthermore, we know that nymphs and Pan were worshiped at the site from a rupestral inscription at the mouth of a cave there, perhaps the same one mentioned by Pausanias.[59]

Several other nymph eponyms and cults are mentioned in various sources. Anthedon and Thisbe are recorded as nymph eponyms. Boiotian spring nymphs include Aganippe, daughter of the river Permessos, whose spring was sacred to the Muses; Tilphossa, who came into conflict with Apollo; the nymphs of the fountain Kissoëssa near Haliartos, to whom the doomed girl Aristokleia made a prenuptial sacrifice and who bathed the infant Dionysos at his birth; and those of the northern town Kyrtones, who had a shrine (hieron) by a spring and a grove of Apollo.[60]

We can end our survey of Boiotia with the district around Oropos, which lies on the Attic side of the Asopos and has at various times in history been counted as territory of both Boiotia and Attica. Oropos is most famous for the oracle of Amphiaraos. On the great fourth-century stone altar of Amphiaraos, which is described by Pausanias, was a section dedicated to the nymphs, Pan, Acheloös, and Kephisos (the Phokian/Boiotian river to the north, not the smaller Attic river). This combination recalls the iconography of contemporary Attic votive reliefs and might have been influenced by them.[61]

Another important cult in the district was that of Halia Nymphe. This deity, whose name means Sea Nymph, was honored with regular athletic competitions, and several marble tripod bases with inscribed dedications by chorêgoi (sponsors) have been recovered, dating from the fourth century through the Hellenistic period. Halia Nymphe has been connected with Halia of Rhodes, a sister of the Rhodian Telchines, who was raped by her sons, then threw herself into the sea, and was worshiped as Leukothea.[62] Unfortunately, we know nothing about the Oropian Halia except her name, so that it is impossible to be certain whether the identification with Leukothea is correct.

4.3.2 Euboia

Both Euboia and Chalkis, daughters of Asopos, appear on Euboian coins.[63] Chalkis had a special status as the mother of the Euboian Korybantes and Kouretes, the earliest inhabitants of Chalkis, and there was a sanctuary at Chalkis dedicated to her as *archêgetis* (founder or ancestor). For her part, Euboia was beloved of Poseidon and bore a local hero, Tychios.[64] The affinity between Boiotia and Euboia suggested by the inclusion of these Euboian nymphs among Asopos' daughters is also reflected in a Hesiodic genealogy of the hero Abas, eponym of the Abantes (a synonym for Euboians). He was born of Arethousa, whom Poseidon abducted from Boiotia to Chalkis, where Hera transformed her into a spring. This story seems to have been recounted in the *Ehoeae,* and it creates a genealogical link between Boiotia and Euboia, for Arethousa's father was Hyperes, brother to Boiotian Hyrieus, and they were both sons of Poseidon and the Pleiad Alkyone.[65]

Euboia had its own Dionysiac tradition, according to which the infant god was reared on that island by Aristaios, with the help of nymphs and Euboian women (2.5.3). Another version had Aristaios' nymphlike daughter, Makris (an alternative name for Euboia), rearing the child and moistening his lips with honey (4.5.2).

A stele marking the boundary of a shrine to the nymphs and Acheloös was found on a hill at Oichalia (modern Kymi). With the inscription was a small bronze statue of Acheloös, a bearded, draped figure standing stiffly and holding a cornucopia (c. 460).[66] Finally, a Hellenistic epigram records a youth's dedication of his hair, along with a golden cicada hairpin and an ox, to "the Amarynthian maidens [*kourai*]." These are certainly local nymphs, and the golden cicada reminds us of that found in the nymph cave at Phyle on Mount Parnes (5.1.9). Amarynthos was a Euboian town located near Eretria, and these nymphs may be associated with the cult of Artemis Amarynthia, who had a temple there.[67]

4.3.3 Saronic Gulf

The most celebrated of Asopos' daughters was, of course, Aigina, whose importance to Pindar and the Thebans has already been mentioned. The special relationship of Thebes and Aigina was expressed mythically through the idea that the nymphs Thebe and Aigina were twins, the youngest of Asopos' daughters. The story of Aigina's descendants is the most coherent and well attested of the Asopid genealogies, and it appeared in the Hesiodic *Catalogue,* though Homer characteristically restricts the genealogy to the male line.[68] Aigina, abducted by Zeus, gave birth to Aiakos, whose people were the Myrmidons. Aiakos captured the Nereid Psamathe, sired Phokos, and had additional sons Peleus, Telamon, and Menoitios. The latter three were the respective fathers of Achilles, Ajax, and Patroklos. How this family with so many Thessalian connections was assigned to the island of Aigina is a historical riddle. West surmises that Aigina was originally the daughter of yet another Asopos River, one in Thessaly. The Aiginetans seem to have appropriated the genealogy (albeit at a very early period) on the strength of the duplicate names Aigina and Asopos (4.6).[69]

Scenes of Aigina's pursuit by Zeus appear on Attic vases during the first half of the fifth century; sometimes the pursuit is observed by her sisters and her father. During this period, scenes of divine pursuits and abductions reached a peak of popularity in Athens, but Aigina is the only one of the Asopids to be firmly identified in the paintings. Stewart has suggested that these pursuit scenes may be erotic metaphors for the growing self-assertion of the Athenian male citizenry during the period. Certainly, the long Athenian conflict with Aigina came to a climax in these decades, ending with the subjugation of the Aiginetans as tributary "allies" in 457–56 and their eventual expulsion from the island in favor of Athenian colonists in 431. It is likely that the vase paintings reflect the contemporary hostilities with Aigina, expressing the view that the island Aigina's eventual submission to Athens was as inevitable as the nymph Aigina's submission to Zeus. At least one of the examples includes a figure of Nike holding a fillet and dates to the decade of Aigina's final subjugation.[70]

On Aigina itself, near the temple of Aphaia, is a crudely carved rupestral inscription, probably dating to the fifth century. It consists of the words AIGINA PAIS, LERN[A PAIS] and a few other letters, mostly worn away. Here, the term *pais* ("child," "girl") is used as an alternative to *korê* or *numphê*, and whoever carved the inscription seems to be invoking Aigina, Lerna, and perhaps a third name as tutelary deities. The Aiginetans also instituted a ritual in honor of the nymph, in which a maiden chorus sang of Aigina, Endaïs (nymph bride of Aiakos), and their descendants.[71]

The identity of Salamis as one of Asopos' daughters is clearly secondary to that of Aigina; Salamis is connected with the Aiakids through Telamon and Ajax. The nymph Salamis was abducted by Poseidon and brought to the island where she bore Kychreus, who became the first inhabitant and then king of the island, just as Aiakos had been the first to inhabit Aigina. Also in the Saronic gulf is the small island of Kalaureia, or Eirene, with its ancient temple of Poseidon. The god abducted Melantheia, daughter of the river Alpheios, to this island, where their child, Eirene, was born.[72]

4.3.4 *Megara*

The tyrant Theagenes gained power in Megara in the last third of the seventh century. He built the famous conduit and fountain house of Megara with riches apparently confiscated from aristocrats. A version of the fountain house was still standing in Pausanias' day, and he comments that it was worth seeing for "its size, ornament, and the number of columns." The scale of the project was unprecedented and coincided with an influx of common people, who dramatically increased the urban population. The attitude of the aristocrats toward this development is reflected well in the poems of the Megarian noble Theognis. The fountain of Megara was home to the Sithnid nymphs, who played a role in the mythic past of the area. According to the Megarians, the primordial hero Megaros had been a child of Zeus and one of these "native" (*epichôreios*) Sithnid nymphs. At the time of Deukalion's flood, Megaros and his mother escaped the waters by swimming to the heights of Mount Gerania.[73] This story is designed to legitimize the Megarians' claim to the land: the nymph who bears the local hero is autochthonous; the hero himself belongs to the pre-Flood generation of men and is hence the earliest claimant. The mythic past of Megara involved many occupations of the city by outsiders: there was successive rule by the Athenians, the Dorians of the Peloponnese, Lelex the Egyptian, Minos the Kretan, and others. Even the Megarian king Alkathous was a son of Pelops, who married into the royal family when it lacked a male heir. Thus, Theagenes' practical need for a fountain house might have coincided with a need for a legitimizing myth that belonged to all the Megarians and had no specific aristocratic ties. The tendency for tyrants to reach into the pre-Dorian past for mythic and religious propaganda has been well recognized.[74]

It is probable that the Sithnid nymphs existed as the deities of the spring before the construction of the fountain house, but they subsequently became tools in the tyrant's public relations strategy. The power to define and control the water supply, whether physically or conceptually, was a potent one, especially in the water-poor Megarid. Theagenes also left his mark on another spring at a place called Rhous ("stream"), where water used to run from the mountains above the city. After diverting the water to his fountain house, the tyrant made an altar to Acheloös, a deity closely connected with the nymphs and, like them, primordial. Both the site of Rhous and the fountain house of Theagenes have been excavated. Part of the fountain decoration is a sixth-century poros relief slab that shows a seated female who may well be the unnamed mother of Megaros. Hesychius, however, mentions a sacrifice carried out in honor of the Sithnids as a group.[75]

One also wonders what significance the nymphs, as important pastoral deities, might have held in a state where the principal industry was wool production. Theagenes is said to have risen to power by slaughtering the flocks of the aristocrats, and it is at least possible that his valorization of the nymphs was important to the "goatskin-clad" herdsmen, whom Theognis so despised. At the period of the fountain's construction, the neighboring Athenians seem to have offered few durable or valuable objects to the nymphs (5.1). If the veneration of the nymphs was considered a habit of the poor during the archaic period, its rise to prominence under Theagenes might have had political significance.[76] At Athens, too, the tyrants later created waterworks. The natural spring Kallirhoë was incorporated into the famous Enneakrounos, the nine-spouted fountain of the Peisistratids (4.2.1).

In the topography of Megara, nymphs also appear at the *pulai Numphades*, or Gates of the Nymphs, which seem from Pausanias' description to be the southernmost gates that led to the port, Nisaia. Two votive reliefs of the fourth century, clearly inspired by Attic models, have been found at Megara, and at least one cave, apparently dedicated to Pan, is known in the area.[77]

4.3.5 Phokis

In Phokis, we find the same type of relationship between the river Kephisos and his daughters as between Asopos and his daughters in Boiotia or Phlious, though the details are not as well attested. Several of the towns in Phokis have nymph eponyms, in particular, Daulis and Lilaia, the daughters of Kephisos. Both towns are mentioned in the Homeric *Catalogue of Ships*, and both are associated there with "immortal Kephisos." The sources of the Kephisos were located at Lilaia, whose eponym Pausanias describes as a naiad nymph. Kephisos was also the father of Narkissos with the nymph Leiriope, "Lily face," in a tale best known from Ovid.[78]

Other nymphs were associated with Mount Parnassos and the general area of Delphi. The eponym of the town Tithorea was a nymph of the mountain, said to be "one of those nymphs who, as the poets say, used to grow out of trees, especially oaks." Several myths associate nymphs with the earliest period of the mountain's history. The primordial oracular shrine that belonged to Ge had as its prophet, according to one story, a mountain nymph named Daphnis. On the other hand, nymphs allied themselves with the new master of the shrine, Apollo, when he fought the monster Delphyne. The Korykian nymphs, daughters of the Parnassian river Pleistos, cheered Apollo and brought him gifts. And a nymph, Korykia, bore to Apollo the hero Lykoros, who founded the early settlement of Lykoreia on the mountain. Alternatively, the hero Parnassos, son of the nymph Kleodora, founded the earliest town, which was swept away in the flood of Deukalion's time.[79]

The Korykian cave on Parnassos was the most popular cave of the nymphs in antiquity, and the number of votives there by far exceeds those of any other excavated cave (5.1.5). A fourth-century relief found at Delphi has two registers: the lower, large scene is one of sacrifice, and the small upper register shows several deities, who seem to be the local gods of Delphi. These include Apollo with his lyre, Hermes, an unidentifiable figure (perhaps Pan), and a group of three frontal females seated behind an offering table and wearing *poloi*. These are reminiscent of the representations of triple nymphs found in Sicily and Magna Graecia and almost certainly depict the Korykian nymphs.[80]

The Delphic springs Kastalia and Kassotis also had their nymphs. Kassotis, named for a nymph of Parnassos, had the power to "make women prophetic in the god's holy places." The Kastalian spring had an ancient, though strictly mythical link to the Kephisos River and Lilaia; it was said the water of Kastalia was a gift from Kephisos and that, on certain days, sweet cakes thrown into the springs at Lilaia would surface in the Kastalian spring. This tradition is attested as early as the archaic poet Alcaeus, who mentioned Kephisos and

Kastalia together in a lost hymn to Apollo. As for Kastalia herself, the epic poet Panyassis, clearly subscribing to a different tradition than that of the Lilaians, called her a daughter of Acheloös. The desire to forge connections with Delphi and the famous spring probably explains the Lilaian story. Rivers can and do run underground in Greece, a convenient geological feature that permitted the fabrication of ties between specific locales; another example is the story of Alpheios' journey under the sea to the spring of Arethousa at Syracuse (4.10.1).[81]

4.4 Peloponnese and Corinth

4.4.1 *Corinth*

Continuing across the Isthmos, we come to the eastern Peloponnese. I have already discussed the Asopos River of Phlious, a strong rival to the Boiotian Asopos for the distinction of having fathered so many nymphs beloved of the gods (4.3.1). At Corinth, the famous fountains Peirene and Glauke were supplied by the tyrants with fountain houses roughly contemporary to Theagenes' fountain house in Megara.[82] Diodorus Siculus makes Peirene one of the daughters of Phliasian Asopos, while Pausanias makes her a daughter of Acheloös. She is supposed to have borne to Poseidon two sons, the eponymous heroes of the two Corinthian ports, Lechaion and Kenchreai. Pausanias adds that she was transformed into a spring as she wept for her dead son Kenchrias, who was killed by Artemis.[83]

Though there is no evidence for a cult until the Roman period, it is likely that Peirene, with its plentiful waters, played a role in early Corinth similar to that of Kallirhoë in Athens or the Sithnid spring in Megara.[84] Peirene was so well known in the archaic period that it was a common metonymy for Corinth; the spring was particularly noted as the site of Bellerophon's taming of Pegasos. Two other major springs at Corinth are also associated with female figures. The name Glauke, which seems to mean "gleaming, silvery," has a probable association with spring water but has been traditionally given to the king's daughter, whom Medeia poisoned and who threw herself into the spring in search of relief from her agony. Glauke, then, is one of the many hybrid figures, like Dirke, who possess characteristics of both heroine and nymph. The "sacred spring" appears to have been the center of a cult to an unidentified female figure, and the diversity and abundance of oil containers found in the votive deposits there have close parallels in the Leokoreion and the shrine to Nymphe, both at Athens, and in the Korykian cave of the nymphs at Delphi.[85]

A cult of the nymphs has been more conclusively identified at a spring outside the defenses of the city, beside the road leading to Sikyon. Here were found a statue base and a pit that contained a votive deposit of terra-cottas, mostly of dancers around a syrinx player. This motif, whether fully molded or on plaques, is well attested at shrines of the nymphs. Fragments of fourth-century nymph reliefs, both the familiar Attic type and an unusual type that shows Pan as a youth with throwing-stick and dog, have also been discovered at Corinth.[86] Near Sikyon itself, the city most closely associated with the Peloponnesian Asopos, is Saftulis cave, celebrated for its unique panel paintings of sacrifices to the nymphs (5.1.4, 5.2.1). Pliny mentions what is probably a different nymphaion at Sikyon, where an ancient clay portrait head was preserved until the city's destruction by Mummius.[87]

4.4.2 *Argolis*

We turn now to the Argolid peninsula. The mythic reputation of the river Inachos was much more impressive than its actual appearance, as it was a dry riverbed except when swollen by the rains.[88] Inachos is a primordial father figure, who gives rise to the great Argive heroes Phoroneus, Danaos, and, ultimately, Perseus and Herakles (not to mention the Boiotian line that leads to Kadmos and Oedipus). The daughters of Inachos are invoked in a cultic context in an Aeschylean play, the *Xantriae* (3.2.4). One daughter, "fair-crowned Mykene," is mentioned by name in Homer and the Hesiodic *Great Ehoeae*, presumably as the eponymous nymph of Mycenae.

The second book of Apollodorus' *Bibliotheca* gives the Inachid genealogy, probably derived from the Hesiodic *Ehoeae*. The genealogy begins with Inachos and the nymph Melia, both offspring of Okeanos and Tethys. Their sons were Aigialeos, who died childless, and Phoroneus, who begat Apis and Niobe with a nymph (Teledike or Laodike).[89] Argive sources presented Phoroneus as a local rival to Prometheus and Deukalion: he was the first man or first inhabitant and king of Argos, and he lived in the time of the Flood. He first established Hera's cult in Argos, and with Inachos and other local river gods, he awarded the land to Hera in the contest with Poseidon. According to the Argive epic *Phoronis*, he was the "father of mortal men."[90] Thus, his Okeanid mother, Melia, calls to mind the "Melian race of mortal men" in Hesiod. In a fragment of the *Ehoeae*, we hear of another daughter of Phoroneus, who joined with a descendant of Deukalion (probably Doros) to produce five daughters. These in turn bore "the divine mountain nymphs and the race of worthless satyrs, unsuited for work, and the Kouretes, divine sportive dancers." The fragment contains the earliest attested literary reference to satyrs. This daughter of Phoroneus might be Iphthime, who appears both in the papyrus context of this fragment and in Nonnos as a daughter of Doros and mother of satyrs with Hermes. The local tradition, then, associates the nymphs, satyrs, and Kouretes with the Dorian Peloponnese and, particularly, with Argolis.[91]

Niobe's son by Zeus was Argos, the eponym of the city, and his wife was Evadne, a daughter of the Thracian river Strymon. His namesake descendant, the "all-seeing" monster Argos, was said to have fathered Iasos with a daughter of the Asopos River, Ismene. Iasos, Inachos himself, and other candidates are put forward as the father of Io (Hesiod names Peiren as her father, but sources of classical date usually favor Inachos).[92] Io herself seems thus to have been envisioned as a mortal woman by the author of the *Ehoeae*, but it is possible that she was later perceived as a nymph. The persistence of her identification as Inachos' daughter and her position early in the Argive genealogy as a primordial "foremother" are consistent with such a perception.

Nymphs again are not lacking in the subsequent genealogy leading to the Danaids, who themselves have some interesting associations with water sources.[93] The lack of water in "thirsty Argos" was attributed to the enmity of Poseidon, who punished the Argives because Inachos had rejected him in favor of Hera as the patron deity of Argolis. Thus Danaos, having taken possession of the country, sent his daughters to draw water in the drought-stricken land. According to a fragment of Hesiod, "waterless Argos the Danaids made well-watered."[94] Historically, this was accomplished by the sinking of numerous wells; in myth, the Danaid Amymone was pursued by a lustful satyr but rescued by Poseidon. She had a sexual liaison with the god, after which he ended his punishment by providing access to water. According to Apollodorus, he "revealed to her the springs at Lerna," while Pausanias reports that a spring and the river it fed at Lerna were called Amymone. At Argos itself, there was also a water source called Amymone, held in special reverence along with three others important to Hera's cult and likewise identified with Danaids (1.4.4). Amymone, then, and at least some of her sisters were probably water nymphs attracted into the Danaid saga.[95]

Between the old palaces of Mycenae and Tiryns, across the Inachos River from Argos itself, the Argives built the Heraion, the chief cult center of the district. Local myth associated Hera with the surrounding landscape: according to Pausanias, "the mountain opposite the Heraion is called after Akraia, the country below it after Prosymna, and the ground around it after Euboia." Akraia and Euboia, the two large peaks, along with Prosymna, the plain, were the daughters of the Asterion River, which runs past the Heraion, and the nurses (*trophoi*) of Hera.[96]

Lerna, on the coast south of Argos, was a marshy area fed by many springs and the home of the notorious Hydra. This serpent was reared, according to local tradition, under a plane tree by the spring, a tradition reminiscent of the serpent at Thebes, who is likewise associated with spring and nymph. Lerna was also a lake in the district. She appears in the form of a nymph on a band cup of c. 550; she holds her arms out to Herakles while he attacks the Hydra, just as other vases show Thebe and Ismene watching while Kadmos approaches the serpent of Ares.[97]

Nemea, yet another of Asopos' daughters, was a river that formed the boundary between the territories of Sikyon and Corinth. A female figure, probably Nemea, appears on sixth-century Attic vases that show Herakles with the Nemean lion, and Nemea brings water to Herakles after the fight with the lion on a classical scaraboid gem. According to a lost play by Aeschylus,

Nemea was the mother of Archemoros, in whose honor the Nemean games were founded on the banks of the Asopos.[98]

Nymphs play a role in the saga of the Argive hero Perseus, though the nymphs he meets seem to belong to the underworld or some other inaccessible land. Perseus first visited the Graiai, daughters of Phorkys, who shared one eye and one tooth. Seizing these, Perseus refused to return them unless the sisters told him the way to the nymphs, who possessed the magic items he needed in order to succeed against the Gorgons. This myth is attested as early as c. 560 on an Athenian loutrophoros and slightly later on a Chalkidian amphora (figure 4.6). On the latter vase, Perseus, accompanied by Athena, meets a group of three nymphs. Each holds one of the magic objects in her right hand (winged sandals, cap, and kibisis, or wallet) and greets the hero with her left. The vase painter has labeled them Neïdes. This scene is probably similar to the one Pausanias saw worked in bronze on the archaic "bronze house" of Athena at Sparta: "There is Perseus setting out for Libya to meet Medousa, with the nymphs giving him his cap and the sandals to travel through the air." We also hear that Perseus considerately returned the objects to the nymphs when he was finished with them.[99]

4.4.3 Lakonia, Messenia, and Arkadia

Important figures in the Lakonian genealogical tradition are the mountain Taygetos and the river Eurotas. Taygete was one of the seven Pleiades, the daughters of Atlas, who appear in the Hesiodic *Ehoeae* and are prominent in

Figure 4.6 Chalkidian amphora: Perseus and three nymphs. Photo copyright British Museum.

the mythology of the Peloponnese. Like the daughters of Okeanos, the Pleiades were of Titan stock and thus primordial. Like the daughters of Asopos, they were much desired by the gods. All but one mated with a god, and they bore various heroes. The star of Merope, who bore Glaukos to the mere mortal Sisyphos, was supposed to have been dimmer than the others on account of her shame.[100] (One is reminded of Thetis' shame at being forced to marry the mortal Peleus.) Taygete's son with Zeus was Lakedaimon, who fathered Amyklas (eponym of the city Amyklai), who in turn sired the Amyklaian cult hero Hyakinthos. The great throne of the statue of Apollo at Amyklai included reliefs of Zeus and Poseidon abducting Taygete and Alkyone (Paus. 3.18.10).

Amyklas' line led to the Spartan king Tyndareos, Helen, and the Dioskouroi. During the eighth century, when Amyklai came under the influence of Sparta, this genealogy was expanded and adapted to reflect Spartan interests. Lakedaimon's wife was said to be the nymph Sparte, daughter of the river Eurotas. Eurotas himself was the son or grandson of the autochthonous first inhabitant of the land, Lelex. In Apollodorus' account, Lelex has a naiad wife, Kleocharia. Another daughter of Eurotas was Tiasa, one of the streams encountered on the road from Amyklai to Sparta.[101]

For the Spartans, Helen's prominent cult fulfilled many of the functions elsewhere performed by the nymphs, Artemis, or Hera with regard to women's rites of passage. Sparta was, of course, famous for its female choruses; the wedding of Helen was celebrated by maidens dancing beside the Eurotas, and Alcman's fragments give us a glimpse of Lakonian choruses.[102] Helen's cult, however, was quite localized, and just to the north of Sparta we find choruses of girls dancing in honor of Artemis at Karyai. Artemis Karyatis and Karyai are named for a nut tree that must have been locally abundant, though the common term *karuon* could refer to any of several types of nut. Perhaps it is this connection with trees that brought together the cults of Artemis and the nymphs, normally kept separate in spite of their overlapping functional concerns (3.2.2). A tree nymph, Karya, is attested, while the famous dance of the Lakonian girls was called Karyatis and was the source of the architectural term Karyatid.[103]

The southern coast of Lakonia is defined by two large projections: the Malean cape and the Tainaran cape, or the Mani. Here, Silenos was associated with a spring in Pyrrhichos, and the inhabitants considered him their founder. They said that Silenos had come from Malea to build their town, and Pausanias quotes a Pindaric fragment in support of their claim: "The ecstatic one, the stamping-footed dancer whom Mount Malea reared, Silenos, husband of Naïs [naiad]." He further describes a harbor known as Nymphaion at the Malean cape, which probably derived its name from the cave there containing a freshwater spring.[104]

The most striking Peloponnesian tradition about the nymphs, attested in both Messenia and Arkadia, is that they acted as attendants at the birth of the infant Zeus. Arkadia and Krete made strong rival claims for recognition as

Zeus' birthplace. The Messenian tradition, which is probably derived from the Arkadian, cited as nurses of the infant Zeus the mountain Ithome, itself an important cult site of the god, and the river Neda. These two nymphs washed the baby Zeus in a spring called Klepsydra at Messene, having received him from the Kouretes. Water from the spring was taken daily to Zeus' sanctuary.[105] The river Neda was somewhat unusual, though not unique, in its designation as a female, for Greek river gods are normally male.

Originating on the southern slopes of Mount Lykaion, the Neda also played a crucial role in the Arkadian versions of Zeus' birth. Lykaion was, of course, the center of Zeus' Arkadian cult, and testimonies to the local tradition of his birth and the nymphs' role in it were to be found throughout the district. Associated with Lykaion itself, in addition to the Neda, were the territory of Theisoa, on the northern part of the mountain, and the spring Hagno, which the priest of Lykaian Zeus stirred with an oak branch in times of drought.[106] Pausanias reports in his description of Lykaion that these three nymphs (Neda, Theisoa, and Hagno) reared Zeus. At Tegea, the altar of Athena Alea showed Rhea and a nymph, Oinoë, with the baby Zeus, accompanied by four other nymphs on each side: Glauke, Neda, Theisoa, and Anthrakia to one side, and Ide, Hagno, Alkinoë, and Phrixa on the other. At Megalopolis, a table dedicated to the Great Goddesses showed Neda carrying the infant, while Anthrakia carried a torch, Hagno held a water jar and cup, and two other nymphs, Anchiroë and Myrtoëssa, carried water jars with water pouring from them.[107]

The Neda is joined by the Lymax river at Phigalia. Pausanias learned from the Phigalians that the Lymax took its name from Rhea's purification: "When she had given birth to Zeus and the nymphs cleaned her up, they flung the water they used into this river; the ancient word for it was *lumata*, as Homer proves when he speaks of the Greeks being purified to put an end to the plague and says they threw the *lumata* into the sea." A similar story prevailed at the town of Theisoa (already mentioned as one of the Lykaian nymphs), where the springs of the Lousios, "the Wash," rose. This river, also called the Gortys, was said to have been used for washing the infant Zeus. Finally, Rhea was associated with a cave on neighboring Mount Methydrion, which locals claimed as the spot where the deception of Kronos by the substitution of a stone took place.[108]

Though Neda and Hagno, both associated with Lykaion, are the most prominent nymphs in the Peloponnesian traditions of Zeus' birth, it is clear that several local traditions came into conflict, and the list of kourotrophic nymphs multiplied, as the story of Zeus' birth on Lykaion gradually became canonical for the Arkadians. Neda's importance is emphasized by Callimachus, whose *Hymn to Zeus* reconciles the claims of Krete and Arkadia by asserting that Zeus was indeed born in Arkadia, then hidden on Krete for protection from his father. When Rhea bore Zeus, she looked for a stream in which to cleanse herself and the baby, but no water then flowed in Arkadia. Rhea called upon the earth to give birth as she had just done and struck the ground with her staff. A stream burst forth and, having made use of its waters, she named it for Neda, the eldest of the nymphs who attended her childbed. Neda was also entrusted with the responsibility of carrying the child to Krete.[109]

A noticeable feature of these Peloponnesian traditions is their preoccupation with water and its role in purification after birth and the cleansing of the infant. They contrast with most other myths about nymph nurses, which concentrate upon the nourishment or education of the young god or hero. The nymphs are represented as important providers of water, which has a very specific purpose in the myth of Rhea's delivery, corresponding to its ritual and practical uses at human births. Yet this purifying water is also understood in the broader context of the entire district's need for water. The nymphs who assisted at Zeus' birth hold hydriai in the Megalopolitan relief; Neda is the first stream in a hitherto waterless, uninhabitable land; Hagno can ease droughts when called upon by Zeus' priest and has the special quality of always producing a steady flow of water in winter and summer alike.[110]

The nymphs' function is similarly understood in another Arkadian birth myth, that of Hermes. A hill near Pheneos was called Trikrena, "Three Springs," after the springs where the local nymphs washed the infant god Hermes. Nearby was the much more imposing peak Kyllene, generally acknowledged as Hermes' birthplace. Among the daughters of Atlas, or the Pleiades, was Hermes' mother, Maia, who appears on coins of Pheneos. In the Homeric *Hymn to Hermes*, which deals with the god's birth and precocious theft of Apollo's cattle, Maia is described as a mountain nymph and a "lovely-haired nymph, modest, for she avoided the company of the blessed gods, living in a deep, shady cave." In Sophocles' satyr play *Ichneutae*, which farcically handles the same subject (3.1.1), we meet not Maia but the mountain nymph Kyllene, who acts as Hermes' nurse.[111]

In the Arkadian genealogy of the *Ehoeae*, two strands can be distinguished. One is that of the descendants of Pelasgos, the earthborn first inhabitant, and his son, Lykaon. Pelasgos had the reputation of hoary antiquity, and a lyric fragment refers to him as *proselênaios*, "before the moon." The Arkadians themselves could be called *proselênoi*, and the Proselenides were a group of Arkadian nymphs. Pelasgos' wife was said to be either an Okeanid Meliboia or the mountain nymph Kyllene (the latter was probably the Hesiodic version). The *Ehoeae* contained a catalogue of Lykaon's fifty sons, mostly eponyms of Arkadian towns. Their wives, like the wife of Pelasgos, will have been nymphs.[112]

After the destruction wrought by Zeus upon Lykaon and his sons, a new Arkadian genealogy appeared with the union of Kallisto and Zeus. While there were several accounts of Kallisto's human parentage, the *Ehoeae* made her "one of the nymphs." Others call her a daughter of Keteus, Nykteus, or Lykaon himself. In some accounts, Kallisto was shot by Artemis, a version of the myth consistent with the presence of a tomb of Kallisto, topped by a sanctuary of Artemis, near Trikolonoi. Fourth-century coins of Orchomenos show Artemis shooting a girl, undoubtedly Kallisto.[113] Thus, Kallisto in most accounts, particularly the Arkadian ones, must be considered a heroine, but the Hesiodic account might have made her a nymph because of the prominence of nymphs in the Arkadian genealogies. Her son, Arkas, married a tree nymph, either the hamadryad Chrysopelia or the dryad Erato (2.4.1). According to the epic poet Eumelus, Chrysopelia gave Arkas the sons Elatos ("Fir tree," associated with the region of Kyllene) and Apheidas (a deme of Tegea). Pausanias calls Arkas' wife the nymph Erato and adds another son, Azan (eponym of the district Azania). Stymphalos, Aleos, and other local heroes were descended from these sons. At Lykosoura, "the first city the sun ever saw," was a sanctuary of Pan with verse oracles by Erato.

We might expect Pan's homeland to be especially rich in mythic and cultic links between that god and the nymphs, given their usual strong association. This expectation is only partly fulfilled. We do not find in Arkadia the type of cave cults of Pan and the nymphs familiar in Attica and elsewhere. Instead, Pan seems to have been honored in his own exclusive sanctuaries, which sometimes included a temple, as on Lykaion. As Borgeaud has shown, Pan was celebrated outside of Arkadia in cave cults because the cave was felt to be an analogue for the Arkadian landscape and thus an appropriate home for the rustic god (3.1.2). Pan's oracle with Erato at Lykosoura is the primary example of a cultic link with a nymph.[114] Among the numerous traditions of Pan's genealogy and birth, the Tegeate version seems to have made Oinoë his mother (presumably the same Oinoë who supplants Neda as the primary nurse of Zeus on the Tegean altar of Athena Alea).[115] Finally, south of Lykosoura in the Nomian mountains was a sanctuary of Nomian Pan, where Pan first played his pipes in company with a nymph, Nomia (there is a pun here on the dual meanings of *nomos*: pasturage and a musical mode). Nomia reappears as a companion of Kallisto in Polygnotos' great painted gallery at Delphi.[116]

Also set in Arkadia are the myths of the nymphs Syrinx, Echo, and Pitys, stories of Pan's unsuccessful loves. Syrinx fled Pan and was swallowed by Ge, the Earth; reeds grew up at the spot where she disappeared, and Pan, in his anger, tore them apart. His mournful sighs then caused the fragments to emit a sound, and thus he invented the Pan flute, or syrinx. Echo's myth exists in several versions. In that given by Longus, she was a nymph, desired by Pan because of her beauty and envied by him because of her musical skill. He sent a madness upon the herdsmen, who tore her to pieces. The Earth received her broken limbs (*melê*), which even after burial continued to make songs (*melê*). Pitys fled Pan and was metamorphosed into a pine tree; she now sings her sad fate when the wind blows through her branches. These tales exist only in late versions and are generally thought to have been invented during the Hellenistic period. They do, however, draw upon folk traditions of much earlier date: the association of both Pan and the nymphs with pastoral music; the primordial relation of the nymphs with Ge; the concept of futile, "panic" sexuality; and so on.[117] Perhaps the lost story of Nomian

Pan and the nymph Nomia near Lykosoura was similar to those of Syrinx or Echo.

Syrinx was a daughter of the Ladon River, which rises in Arkadia and flows into the Alpheios at the border with Elis. Other daughters of the Ladon are recorded, including Metope, the mother of all Asopos' celebrated daughters; Thelpousa, eponym of the Arkadian district best known for its cult of Demeter Erinys; and Daphne, who is discussed below (4.4.4, 4.9.8).[118]

Of the other nymphs of Arkadia, the most famous is Styx, eldest daughter of Okeanos and Tethys. Like the rivers Acheron and Kokytos, Styx has a dual identity as both an underworld and an earthly river. Hesiod says that Styx's famous role as guardian of oaths came about because she with her children was the first to support Zeus' reign. He describes Styx herself as inhabiting in Hades "a glorious house apart from the gods, roofed with huge rocks," but when an oath is to be sworn, Iris fills a jug from "far away, the famous cold water which flows down from a high overhanging rock." This is a fair description of the Arkadian Styx, which boasts a 600-foot waterfall. Styx was also among the Okeanids who gathered flowers with Persephone before her abduction.[119]

The nymphs seem to be omnipresent in Arkadia, yet there are few examples of cult sites devoted to them as a plurality. Tegea yielded an aniconic triple herm pillar once used to mark a sanctuary of the nymphs, and a cave at Glyphai on the Alpheios River with Glyphian nymphs is mentioned by lexicographical sources.[120] An epigram of Crinagoras, who flourished in the late first century, records the thank offering of a hunter at Bassai near Phigalia (best known for its temple of Apollo):

σπήλυγγες νυμφῶν εὐπίδακες αἱ τόσον ὕδωρ
  εἴβουσαι σκολιοῦ τοῦδε κατὰ πρεόνος,
Πανός τ᾽ ἠχήεσσα πιτυστέπτοιο καλιή,
  τὴν ὑπὸ Βασσαίης ποσσὶ λέλογχε πέτρης,
ἱερά τ᾽ ἀγρευταῖσι γερανδρύου ἀρκεύθοιο
  πρέμνα, λιθηλογέες θ᾽ Ἑρμέω ἱδρύσιες,
αὐταί θ᾽ ἱλήκοιτε καὶ εὐθήροιο δέχοισθε
  Σωσάνδρου ταχινῆς σκῦλ᾽ ἐλαφοσσοΐης. (Crinagoras 43,
  Anth. Pal. 6.253)[121]

Caves of the nymphs with many springs, from which an abundance
of water trickles down this winding slope, and you echoing cabin of
Pan crowned with pine leaves, his home under the foot of Bassai's
crags, stumps of juniper holy to hunters, and you stone heap raised in
Hermes' honor: accept the spoil of fortunate Sosander's swift chase of
the deer.

This description is consistent with what we have already observed about the cult of Pan in Arkadia: he is not an occupant of caves but has separate accommodations from the nymphs, even when they are, as here, closely associated with him. The north metopes from the temple of Apollo at Bassai illustrate Apollo's return from the Hyperborean lands; he is greeted by Zeus, Arkas, and a chorus of local nymphs.[122]

4.4.4 Elis and Achaia

The Alpheios and the Ladon both rise in Arkadia; they flow together at the border and continue west into Elis, the home of the Olympic games. In a myth common to the Arkadians and Eleans, the youth Leukippos fell in love with Daphne, daughter of the Ladon River. Since Leukippos was growing his hair long in order to dedicate it to Alpheios, he joined Daphne's companions disguised as a girl. One day, when they had decided to swim in the Ladon, the huntresses stripped Leukippos, discovered his true sex, and stabbed him to death with their spears. The Daphne of this story is difficult to distinguish from Daphne, the daughter of the Thessalian river Peneios; each was said to be the beloved of Apollo, changed into the bay tree as she fled his pursuit.[123]

The god of the Alpheios River, the largest river in the Peloponnese, is famed for his sexual aggressiveness, though he cannot boast of numerous progeny. His pursuit of the nymph Arethousa to the Sicilian island of Ortygia is discussed below (4.10.1). Strabo's description of the area where the river reached the sea is worth repeating:

πρὸς δὲ τῇ ἐκβολῇ τὸ τῆς Ἀλφειονίας Ἀρτέμιδος ἢ Ἀλφειούσης ἄλσος ἐστί (λέγεται γὰρ ἀμφοτέρως), ἀπέχον τῆς Ὀλυμπίας εἰς ὀγδοήκοντα σταδίους. ταύτῃ δὲ τῇ θεῷ καὶ ἐν Ὀλυμπίᾳ κατ᾽ ἔτος συντελεῖται πανήγυρις, καθάπερ καὶ τῇ Ἐλαφίᾳ καὶ τῇ Δαφνίᾳ. μεστὴ δ᾽ ἐστὶν ἡ γῆ πᾶσα Ἀρτεμισίων τε καὶ Ἀφροδισίων καὶ Νυμφαίων ἐν ἄλσεσιν ἀνθέων πλέως τὸ πολὺ διὰ τὴν εὐυδρίαν . . . (Strabo 8.3.12, 343)

Near the mouth of the river is the sacred grove of Artemis Alpheionia or Alpheiousa (for it is spelled both ways), about eighty stades from Olympia. In honor of this goddess there is also an annual festival at Olympia, as well as for [Artemis] Elaphia and Daphnia. The whole country is full of shrines of Artemis, Aphrodite, and the nymphs in groves full of flowers, due to the plentiful water.

Pausanias tells us the myth attached to the sanctuary of Artemis at Letrinoi: the river Alpheios conceived a passion for Artemis and decided to attempt rape. He came to a night festival (*pannuchis*), which the goddess was holding along with the nymphs who dance (*paizein*) with her, but Artemis suspected his intentions and smeared her own face and those of the nymphs with mud. Alpheios could not tell which one of them was Artemis, so he went away disappointed. This myth seems to reflect a ritual setting involving a chorus of girls; it is one among many examples of the motif of a chorus invaded by a sexually threatening outsider. The abduction of the young virgin from the chorus, where her lover had spotted her among the other girls, was a mythic paradigm for marriage. The institution of the chorus exposed the girls to the view of both potential suitors and potential rapists; likewise, marriage was seen simultaneously as a socially desirable goal and a forceful violation. In the Peloponnese, nymphs were also associated with the goddess Artemis at Karyai, where members of the Karyatid chorus were said to have been abducted by the Messenian hero Aristomenes and nearly raped by his men.[124] As at Karyai, which was named for the nut trees (4.4.3), the environment at Letrinoi was characterized by lush vegetation, groves of trees, and abundant flowers. Flowers, trees, and other vegetation are particularly prominent in the myths and cults of the Peloponnesian nymphs.

Strabo says that at Herakleia, a town about forty stades from Olympia on the Kytherios River, was the sanctuary (*hieron*) of the Ionides nymphs, whose waters cured diseases. Pausanias calls the river Kytheros and he mentions a spring that runs into the river with a sanctuary of the Ionides nymphs nearby: Kalliphaeia, "lovely shining"; Synallasis, "intercourse"; Pegaia, "she of the spring"; and Iasis, "healer." He adds that washing in the spring could cure all kinds of aches and pains and that the nymphs were collectively named after Ion, son of Gargettos, who migrated there from Athens.[125]

Scholars have suggested several possible etymologies for Ion's name, relating it to the ritual cry for the Ionian god Apollo (*ia*), a verb for healing (*iaomai*), an arrow (*ios*), and so on. The most popular view seems to be that Ion (*Iawôn*) was an early name for Apollo in his capacity as healing deity. No scholar accepts the folk etymology of Ion's name from the word for violet or gillyflower (*ion*), though this is of interest to us as a reflection of local beliefs. According to Nicander, the nymphs were filled with love for Ion and offered him a garland of the flowers when he stopped to wash himself after killing a wild boar. He then "passed the night with the Ioniad nymphs."[126]

At the Panhellenic sanctuary of Olympia, there were three altars to the nymphs, where as primordial deities they received special wineless libations, just as they did in Attica. Near the temenos of Pelops were altars of the Muses, the nymphs, and Dionysos with the Charites. Southwest of the temple of Zeus grew the wild olive from which the crowns of the Olympic victors were cut; here was an altar of the Kallistephanoi, the lovely wreathed nymphs. At the horse-racing track, inside the entrance to the "Beak," or starting place, was a group of altars, including those of Good Fortune, Pan, Aphrodite, and the nymphs called Akmenai. Their name, derived from *akmê*, can be understood in various senses; the term could refer to the "outermost edge" of the starting place itself, the "critical moment" when the race begins, or the "high point" of bloom and growth, as in the Odyssean description of the olive tree around which the hero built his bedchamber: *akmênos thalethôn*, "in its prime and vigorous."[127]

Moving south into Triphylia, we find another cult of healing nymphs near Samikon on the river Anigros. There are two caves, once accessible by foot but now flooded, where people still bathe in the foul-smelling, sulfurous waters. Pausanias describes the bathing procedure used in antiquity:

Ἔστι δὲ ἐν τῶι Σαμικῶι σπήλαιον οὐκ ἄπωθεν τοῦ ποταμοῦ, καλούμενον Ἀνιγρίδων νυμφῶν. ὃς δ᾽ ἂν ἔχων ἀλφὸν ἢ λεύκην ἐς αὐτὸ ἐσέλθηι, πρῶτα μὲν ταῖς νύμφαις εὔξασθαι καθέστηκεν αὐτῶι καὶ ὑποσχέσθαι θυσίαν ὁποίαν δή τινα, μετὰ δὲ ἀποσμήχει τὰ νοσοῦντα τοῦ σώματος· διανηξάμενος δὲ τὸν ποταμὸν ὄνειδος μὲν ἐκεῖνο κατέλιπεν ἐν τῶι ὕδατι αὐτοῦ, ὁ δὲ ὑγιής τε ἄνεισι καὶ ὁμόχρως. (Paus. 5.5.11)[128]

There is near Samikon a cave of the nymphs called Anigrides not far from the river. Whoever comes to it afflicted with *alphos* or *leukê* [leprosy or similar skin diseases] must first pray to the nymphs and promise whatever the sacrifice is, and afterward he wipes the sick parts of his body. When he swims across the river, he leaves the disgrace in its waters, and he emerges healthy and clear-skinned.

The earliest testimony to the cult may be an epigram of Moero of Byzantium, which dates to the late fourth century:

Νύμφαι Ἀνιγριάδες, ποταμοῦ κόραι αἲ τάδε βένθη
    ἀμβρόσιαι ῥοδέοις στείβετε ποσσὶν ἀεί,
χαίρετε καὶ σώζοιτε Κλεώνυμον ὃς τάδε καλά
    εἴσαθ᾽ ὑπαὶ πιτύων ὕμμι, θεαί, ξόανα. (Moero 2, *Anth. Pal.* 6.189)

You Anigriades, daughters of the river, ambrosial beings who ever tread these depths with rosy feet, greetings! And cure Kleonymos, who set up for you these lovely images under the pines.[129]

Another feature of Triphylia is the unusual cult and temple of the god Hades. Associated with this cult is nearby Mount Minthe, named for the nymph Minthe, who became the lover of Hades, enraging Persephone. She or Demeter trampled Minthe underfoot, and the nymph was transformed into the garden mint, which releases its sweet aroma when people tread on it.[130]

To conclude this survey of the Peloponnese, we move to the northern coastal area known as Achaia. A spring Argyra and a town of the same name lay near the Selemnos River there. Pausanias reports that Selemnos was a beautiful shepherd beloved of Argyra, a nymph of the sea. She eventually tired of him when his youthful bloom faded, and he died of love. Aphrodite turned him into a river and gave him the gift of forgetfulness; the water cures the wounds of love for those who wash in it. This story combines some ancient themes, such as the mating of herdsman and nymph beside a river, and the

Eos/Tithonos motif of the goddess who tires of her lover when he is no longer young, with elements that seem to cater to Hellenistic tastes (dying of love followed by metamorphosis). One other story concerns another river and town in the same vicinity as Argyra: the Bolinaios and the town Bolina. Apollo fell in love with a maiden, Bolina, and she threw herself into the sea there to escape him. By the favor of Apollo, she became immortal; presumably, she was transformed into a nymph in the same fashion as Dryope or Kyrene, other maidens beloved of Apollo (4.6).[131]

4.5 Northwestern Greece

4.5.1 *Aitolia and Akarnania*

The major river of this area and, indeed, the longest river in Greece is the Acheloös (3.1.3). The river god and one of his daughters appear in the myth of the matricide Alkmaion, who killed Eriphyle because she betrayed his father, Amphiaraus, for the sake of a coveted necklace and robe. Exiled, Alkmaion arrived in Aitolia and married Acheloös' daughter Kallirhoë, who bore two sons, Akarnan and Amphoteros. Like Alkmaion's mother, she coveted the necklace and robe of Harmonia and forced Alkmaion to attempt to retrieve the items from his previous wife in Psophis, whereupon he was ambushed and killed. Kallirhoë prayed to Zeus that her sons might magically grow old enough to avenge their father, and Zeus granted her prayer. After killing Alkmaion's slayers, the sons colonized Akarnania. Thucydides, who neglects to mention Kallirhoë, says that Alkmaion settled in the Echinades, the islands formed near the mouth of the river, that he became a ruler there, and that his son Akarnan gave the country its name. It is likely that in early local versions of the tale the nymph Kallirhoë was simply Alkmaion's wife and mother of the eponymous heroes; it is in this connection that Kallirhoë appears with Acheloös on fifth-century coins of the city Stratos.[132] The melodramatic avenging of Alkmaion's death is probably an elaboration by the tragedians to reconcile the many conflicting versions of Alkmaion's activities.

4.5.2 *Epeiros, the Ionian Islands, and Korkyra*

Farther north, we find nymphs represented on the coins of both Ambrakia and nearby Anaktorion. On the Ambrakian coin, an unnamed nymph plays a drinking game called *kottabos*, while the Anaktorian coins (after 350) show the nymph Aktias, who personifies the famous promontory of Actium. Anaktorion and Leukas were two leading cities of the Akarnanian league, both colonies of Corinth. Certain coins of the latter, which show the head of the nymph Leukas adorned with a chaplet, closely resemble those of Anaktorion.[133] At Ambrakia (modern Arta), as well as on the islands Leukas, Meganisi, Kephallenia, and Ithake, caves with dedications to the nymphs have been discovered (5.1.8). The dedications bear witness to a shared taste for plaques that depict the chorus of the nymphs. The topographical lore of Ithake, as described in the *Odyssey*, associates the aboriginal heroes with nymphs (1.4.1). It is also worth noting that the poet of the *Ehoeae* (Hes. fr. 150.30–31) made "the lady [*potnia*] nymph Kalypso" and Hermes parents of the Kephallenians.

Korkyra (modern Corfu) was yet another Corinthian foundation. The numismatist Imhoof-Blumer argues that many of the female heads identified as Aphrodite on its silver coinage should instead be understood as the nymph Korkyra. Some support is lent to his claim by the fact that Korkyra is one of the best and earliest attested daughters of Asopos. According to Hellanicus, Poseidon and Korkyra, daughter of Phliasian Asopos, were the parents of Phaiax, the eponymous ancestor of the Phaiakians.[134] The people of Korkyra doubtless shared this view insofar as it established their island's claim to be the Homeric Scheria visited by Odysseus. On the other hand, having quickly become rivals and enemies to their old mother city, they would have rejected the political claims of Corinth implicit in the story. Anti-Corinthian sentiment is expressed in the local myth of the heroine or nymph Makris, daughter of Aristaios, who was driven out of Euboia by Hera because she nursed the infant god Dionysos. Makris, who settled in a cave on the island in earliest times and gave prosperity to the inhabitants, represents the tradition of a Euboian settlement antedating the arrival of the Corinthians.[135]

Another local tradition preserved by Apollonius of Rhodes is the tale that Herakles came to the island to be purified in Makris' cave and fell in love with the naiad Melite, daughter of the river Aigaios. The son born of this union was Hyllos, and he led a colony of settlers, the Hyllaians, into Illyria. It was also in Makris' cave, bedecked with flowers by the nymphs, that Jason and Medeia consummated their marriage. Using topographical categories that first appeared in Homer, Apollonius describes these nymphs (*Argon.* 4.1143–52), sent by Hera to show her approval of the union, as belonging to the river Aigaios, the mountain Meliteion, and the local groves.[136]

Nymphs are associated with the ancient oracle of Zeus at Dodone, where Pherecydes says the Dodonides (Ambrosia, Koronis, Eudore, Dione, Phaisyle, Phaio, and Polyxo) were the nurses of Zeus. Clearly, Dodone at some point entered the competition with Krete and Arkadia to be recognized as the god's birthplace. Zeus' ties to the oak tree at Dodone (as at Lykaion, where the priest stirred the spring Hagno with an oak branch) and his title Naïos, "of flowing springs," make the introduction of nymphs unsurprising. An eponymous nymph, the Okeanid Dodone, is also attested.[137]

4.5.3 Apollonia in Illyria

Outside the bounds of Greece proper, another oracle lay in the territory of Apollonia, a joint colony (founded during the seventh or sixth century) of Corinth and Korkyra. The site had already been occupied by Illyrians, and it is likely that the nymphaion, close to the asphalt mines at Selenike, was already a cult site because of its strange physical properties. In the district, there were numerous springs of hot water that exuded inflammable gases. The nymphaion seems to have consisted of a continuous flame, fueled by the bituminous deposits. According to Cassius Dio:

ὅ τε μάλιστα διὰ πάντων ἐθαύμασα, πῦρ πολὺ προς τῷ Ἀώῳ ποταμῷ ἀναδίδοται, καὶ οὔτε ἐπὶ πλεῖον τῆς πέριξ γῆς ἐπεξέρχεται, οὔτ᾽ αὐτὴν ἐκείνην ἐν ᾗ ἐνδιαιτᾶται ἐκπυροῖ ἢ καὶ κραυροτέραν πῃ ποιεῖ, ἀλλὰ καὶ πόας καὶ δένδρα καὶ πάνυ πλησία θάλλοντα ἔχει· πρός τε τὰς ἐπιχύσεις τῶν ὄμβρων ἐπαύξει καὶ ἐς ὕψος ἐξαίρεται. καὶ διὰ τοῦτο αὐτό τε Νυμφαῖον ὀνομάζεται καὶ δὴ καὶ μαντεῖον τοιόνδε τι παρέχεται. λιβανωτὸν δὴ λαβών, καὶ προσευξάμενος ὅ τι ποτὲ καὶ βούλει, ῥίπτεις αὐτὸν τὴν εὐχὴν φέροντα. κἂν τούτῳ τὸ πῦρ, ἂν μέν τι ἐπιτελὲς ᾖ ἐσόμενον, δέχεται αὐτὸν ἑτοιμότατα, κἂν ἄρα καὶ ἔξω που προπέσῃ, προσδραμὸν ἥρπασε καὶ κατανάλωσεν· ἂν δὲ ἀτέλεστον ᾖ, οὔτ᾽ ἄλλως αὐτῷ προσέρχεται, κἂν ἐς αὐτὴν τὴν φλόγα φέρηται, ἐξαναχωρεῖ τε καὶ ἐκφεύγει. καὶ ταῦθ᾽ οὕτως ἑκάτερα περὶ πάντων ὁμοίως, πλὴν θανάτου τε καὶ γάμου, ποιεῖ· περὶ γὰρ τούτων οὐδὲ ἔξεστί τινι ἀρχὴν αὐτοῦ πυθέσθαι τι. (Cass. Dio 41.45)

What I have marveled at above all is that a great fire issues from the earth near the Aoös River and neither spreads much over the surrounding land nor sets on fire even the place where it dwells nor dries it out, but has grass and trees flourishing close by. In pouring rains, it increases and rises high. For this reason it is called a nymphaion, and provides an oracle in this way: you take incense and after making whatever prayer you wish, cast it in the fire to carry the prayer. And if your wish is to be fulfilled, the fire accepts it readily, and even if it falls outside, runs out, snatches the incense and burns it up. But if the wish is not to be fulfilled, the fire does not go to it, but even if the incense is carried near, it recedes and flees. It acts in this way with regard to all matters except death and marriage; concerning these, one is absolutely not permitted to inquire.

Dio's wonder at the greenness and moistness of the place in spite of its fire is reflected in other accounts. Pliny's description, drawn from the fourth-century historian Theopompus, describes a public rather than private form of divination, according to which the welfare of the Apolloniates was linked to the steadiness of the fire spring.[138] The asphalt mines were of economic importance to the area, and Apollonia provides another example of how nymphs are regularly associated with profitable natural resources: timber, bees and honey, water, marble, pasturage, and so on.

Coins of Apollonia from about 100 B.C.E. through the Imperial period depict three nymphs dancing about the fire of the nymphaion; the obverse shows Apollo (figure 4.7). Epigraphic evidence reveals that games were held in honor of the nymphs. These are not attested until the Hellenistic period, when the athlete Menodotos set up inscriptions at Athens and Delos to record his feats, including his wrestling and pankration victories in the Nymphaia at Apollonia.[139]

Plutarch's *Life of Sulla* recounts an interesting tale in connection with the nymphaion: a live satyr fell asleep beside it and was captured. The creature was brought to Sulla and questioned through many interpreters. When he proved unable to make any sound but a hoarse cry, Sulla sent him away in disgust. As in Herodotus' story of the capture of Silenos in the gardens of Midas, the creature is drawn to a beautiful, lush spot, the natural home of the nymphs.[140]

4.6 Thessaly

The great Pindos range separates the eastern and western halves of northern Greece: Epeiros and Thessaly. To the north, Mount Olympos marks the traditional border with Pieria, or the larger district of Macedonia. Between Olympos and the chain of mountains on the coast (Ossa, Pelion, Othrys) is the vale of Tempe, where the river Peneios, having risen in Pindos and run through the Thessalian plain, finally reaches the sea. This Peneios, like the Inachos or the Asopos rivers, is considered the progenitor of the land's earliest inhabitants and its local nymphs.[141]

Figure 4.7 Coin from Apollonia: three nymphs. Photo copyright British Museum.

One of the primordial inhabitants of Thessaly was Hypseus, the son of Peneios and the naiad Kreousa, whom Gaia bore. Pindar gives us this gene-alogy, which he drew from the *Ehoeae*. Hypseus is usually identified as king of the Lapithai, the aboriginal race that was perpetually at war with the Kentauroi (centaurs) until the latter were driven from Mount Pelion. As West notes, there seems to be no systematized genealogy of the Lapithai until a late period, in spite of their early appearances in vase paintings and sculp-ture. In making the eponymous ancestors Lapithes and Kentauros sons of Apollo and Hypseus' sister (the nymph Stilbe), Diodorus Siculus separates Hypseus from the Lapiths by at least a generation.[142] All the same, it is safe to assume that the Lapithai, like Hypseus, are in some way descended from the river, perhaps through nymphs.

Similarly, the origins of the Kentauroi are murky, but they are closely associated both with nymphs and with mountains, especially Mount Pelion. Pelion was thickly forested, and its famous timber was used in the construc-tion of the ship *Argo*. Thus, it is fitting that Apollonius of Rhodes has the Peliades, or nymphs of Pelion, see off the *Argo* as it sets out on its long jour-ney. Diodorus relates that the Kentauroi were reared by nymphs on Mount Pelion. They consorted with mares, and in this way the Hippokentauroi, horse-human hybrids, came into being. Another version of their origin in-volves the intercourse of the Lapith Ixion with the cloud woman Nephele; their son, Kentauros, then mates with mares on Mount Magnesia.[143] Thus, the Lapithai and Kentauroi, while reliably hostile to each other, are by all accounts related. The Lapithai belong to the river and the lowlands, while the Kentauroi are a mountain race.

The most famous of the Kentauroi, Cheiron, is called by Hesiod the son of Phil(l)yra. He is often named using the matronymic, presumably because the appellation "son of Kronos" was reserved for Zeus. (Kronos, taking the form of a horse, had mated with the Okeanid Philyra.) Mount Pelion is the location of Cheiron's cave and is also called "the bridal chamber of Philyra," *Philurês numphêion*.[144] According to Pindar, the family consisted of Philyra and Cheiron's wife, Chariklo, in addition to *kourai hagnai*, "pure daughters," who reared Jason in their cave. Similarly, in Apollonius of Rhodes' account, Achilles is nursed in the cave by naiads, presumably Cheiron's daughters. Chariklo is quite prominent on the sixth-century vases that depict the wed-ding of Peleus and Thetis, where she forms a stately triad with Demeter and Hestia. Another Kentauros, Pholos, was the offspring of Silenos and a Melian nymph. Clearly, a certain kinship or affinity existed between the nymphs and these horse-human hybrids, just as it did between nymphs and silens or satyrs. Cheiron, in particular, shared with the nymphs the role of nurturer of heroes and habitation in a cave.[145]

Ancient sources attribute a number of offspring to the *Urmensch* Hypseus, but the most famous is Kyrene, the beloved of Apollo and mother of Aristaios. Kyrene's story appeared in the *Ehoeae*, though it is unclear to which geneal-ogy she was attached or exactly what form the story took (4.8.8). In Pindar's account, Cheiron is on hand to predict Apollo's marriage to Kyrene and her removal to Libya, where she will bear the culture hero, Aristaios.[146] In general, Apollo is the most prominent lover of Thessalian nymphs, including Stilbe, Kyrene, Dryope, and Daphne.

A rival to Hypseus as the primordial man of Thessaly is Pelasgos. Other districts of Greece also claimed Pelasgos, including Arkadia (4.4.3) and Argos. He is the eponymous hero of a mythic people, the Pelasgians, whom the Hellenes considered their predecessors in mainland Greece. Pelasgos is associated with cities called Larissa in both Argos and Thessaly. According to Hellanicus (4 F 4), the sons of Poseidon and (Argive) Larissa were Achaios, Phthios, and Pelasgos. They migrated into Thessaly and divided the land into three districts named for themselves. Pelasgos married Menippe, the daughter of the river Peneios. In the fourth generation after Pelasgos, they were driven out by the Hellenes and reappeared in Italy as the Tyrrhenians.

The heroine or nymph of Thessalian Larissa, however, was said to be Pelasgos' daughter, and the city founded by Akrisios, the grandfather of Perseus. Larissa is another of those daughters of primordial kings who fall somewhere between the status of heroine and nymph. In the Thessalian city, she seems to have been regarded as a fountain nymph, for she is depicted on Larissan coins (from about 480 onward) beside a fountain with a lion's head spout or posing with a hydria, as well as in more ambiguous poses (figure 4.8).[147] The city was situated on the banks of the Peneios, and there is a story that Larissa was playing ball beside the river when she fell in and was drowned. The coins seem to allude to this episode by showing Larissa with her ball, yet we cannot be certain that the sequel of drowning is implied (the motif of a nymph playing with a ball appears elsewhere, as at Trikka). Hence, we may conclude either that Larissa was thought to have drowned and been reborn as a water nymph, in the manner of Ino/Leukothea, or that the drowning story is a later rationalization intended to explain the name of the fountain and city. Pliny mentions a bronze statue of Larissa by the fifth-century sculptor Telephanes; this, if we accept the identification of certain marble copies, depicted her seated upon a rock.[148]

Figure 4.8 Coin from Larissa: nymph Larissa seated with wreath. Photo copyright British Museum.

Other relatives of Peneios appear in the lore of Thessaly, and several make appearances on coins of the fifth and fourth centuries. The Thessalian coins that show nymphs are similar to those of Sicily and bear witness to cultural exchange between these two areas. In particular, the third-century coins of Larissa that show the nymph's head are lovingly copied from Kimon's famous Syracusan tetradrachms with the head of Arethousa.[149] The coins are particularly important as evidence for the role of the nymphs in Thessaly, because written sources are quite scanty by comparison with, for example, the large amount of material on Asopos' daughters.

Late authors identify Trikka as another of Peneios' daughters. Fifth-century coins show her in a variety of poses: seated, holding a phiale or mirror; playing with a ball; leaning on a column; opening a box; sacrificing at an altar.[150] The contrast with the attributes on coins of Larissa suggests that Trikka, though a city eponym, was not a fountain nymph. After 400, the coins show only Trikka's head (on the obverse); the trend away from full-figure representations is probably again the result of Kimon's success with his head of Arethousa. The lion's head spout appears again on coins of Pherai, where Hypereia is featured.[151] Hypereia, like Peirene, was a famous fountain: in book 6 of the *Iliad*, Hector fears that Andromache may be enslaved and forced to draw water "from Messeis or Hypereia" in far-off Greece. The coins show Hypereia's head or the standing nymph in association with the lion's head spout and sometimes with a fish. That Hypereia was a daughter of Peneios is nowhere attested but is a reasonable guess.[152]

More nymphs figure in the genealogy of the sons of Hellen, which is geographically tied to Phthia and the north side of the Malian gulf. Hellen's wife is Othreïs or a nymph, Orseïs; West suggests that both are corruptions of Othryis, a nymph of Mount Othrys.[153] Their descendants, the Hellenes, spread far and wide, in the process displacing the Pelasgians resident in Thessaly. Aiolos, who is supposed to have remained in Thessaly, especially interests us. There are several conflicting traditions about the name of Aiolos' wife. The earliest attested is that of Hellanicus (4 F 125), who says she was Iphis, daughter of Peneios and mother of Salmoneus.

The Thessalian city Kierion claimed that it was once known as Arne, after another member of Aiolos' family. This Arne, or Melanippe as she is sometimes called, was the offspring of Aiolos' union with a daughter of Cheiron. Arne herself became pregnant by Poseidon and bore the twins Aiolos and Boiotos. The latter is the eponymous hero of the Boiotians, and the story reflects the historical movement of the Boiotoi from their home in Thessaly to what is now called Boiotia. The myth exists in several versions: according to Pausanias' Boiotian sources, Boiotos was the son of Itonos and a nymph, Melanippe. West suggests that the *Ehoeae* made Arne a daughter of Asopos; she bore Boiotos to Poseidon. (Both of these bits of information support the possibility that Melanippe/Arne was considered a nymph in local Boiotian traditions.)[154]

The city of Kierion issued coins that showed Arne, who is usually described as a nymph by numismatic scholars. These show her playing with astragaloi, a scene that can be interpreted in two different ways. First, the astragaloi may indicate the presence of an oracle at Kierion; this would be all the more plausible if Arne were, indeed, regarded as a nymph (1.3). Head suggests, however, that the scene is merely a decorative one in the manner of contemporary terra-cottas, showing an attractive girl playing a popular game.[155] I tend to agree with the latter view, for nothing else in Thessalian Arne's genealogy or the iconography of the coins points toward her identification as a nymph.

The foolish herdsman Kerambos (2.5) was descended from another nymph of Mount Othrys, Eidothea. Ovid diverges from Nicander's tale that Kerambos was transformed into a beetle as punishment; instead, he speaks of

Othryn et eventu veteris loca nota Cerambi:
hic ope nympharum sublatus in aera pennis,
cum gravis infuso tellus foret obruta ponto,
Deucalioneas effugit inobrutus undas. (Ov. Met. 7.353-56)

Othrys and the regions made famous by the adventure of old
Cerambus. He, by the aid of the nymphs borne up in the air on
wings, when the heavy earth had drowned in the flooding sea,
escaped Deucalion's waves undrowned.

According to a fragment of Hellanicus, Deukalion's ark (*larnax*) came to rest not, as usually stated, upon Mount Parnassos but upon Othrys. This mountain, like Gerania in the Megarid, was part of a local flood tradition, according to which an indigenous hero escaped the flood on a mountain top with the aid of the nymphs.[156]

In the southern part of Thessaly, the river Spercheios flows past Oite and Othrys into the Malian gulf, the shores of which were the home of Achilles and the people known as the Myrmidons. The genealogy Zeus-Aiakos-Peleus-Achilles originated in Thessaly, though it was appropriated by the Aiginetans. A small river Asopos flowed into the Malian gulf beside Spercheios, and it is probable that in Thessalian tradition, Aiakos' mother, the nymph Aigina, was the daughter of this river, not of the Peloponnesian or Boiotian Asopos.[157] Aiakos and his son Peleus both took sea-nymph wives, Psamathe and Thetis (2.3.3). Peleus' story is closely intertwined with that of Cheiron, who protected him when Akastos abandoned him to the Kentauroi on Mount Pelion, attended his wedding to Thetis, and cared for the young Achilles. A further hint that betrays the Thessalian origin of the Aiakids is that Peleus' mother is sometimes said to be Endeïs, daughter of Cheiron.[158]

In the Malian gulf area, the eponymous hero Dryops was a son of the river Spercheios. His daughter, Dryope, herded flocks and became a companion of the hamadryad nymphs. Seeing Dryope dancing with the nymphs, Apollo conceived a desire for her and coupled with her in the form of a serpent. Her son was Amphissos, founder of the city Oite at the foot of the mountain, as well as a shrine to the nymphs who had spirited away his mother and replaced her with a poplar and a spring. The names Dryopes, Dryops, and Dryope all share the root *dru*, "tree" or "oak," with the words for tree nymphs: dryad or hamadryad. In the story from Nicander, Dryope's special relationship with the hamadryads is emphasized.[159] In Ovid's version, Dryope is the daughter of Eurytos of Oichalia. While gathering garlands for the nymphs, she plucks flowers of the lotus, offending the nymph of that plant, and is herself then transformed into a lotus tree.

In both Nicander and Ovid, Dryope joins the tree nymphs by becoming a tree (poplar/lotus). A similar but better known story is that of Daphne, another nymph who was loved by Apollo. We have already seen an Elean-Arkadian version of Daphne's myth, in which she killed her would-be lover, Leukippos. In that myth, she was characterized as a daughter of the Peloponnesian river Ladon, whereas Ovid makes her the daughter of Peneios. When she is pursued by the amorous Apollo, it is Peneios who answers Daphne's plea for help by transforming her into the laurel tree.[160]

Mount Oite was also famous as the scene of Herakles' death and the home of Philoktetes, who lit the great hero's funeral pyre. In Sophocles' play *Philoctetes*, the hero anticipates his return to "the haunt of the Maliad nymphs, beside the banks of Spercheios" and touchingly bids farewell to the nymphs of his temporary island home (1.4.3). That the nymphs were, in fact, the object of a cult on Mount Oite is attested, at least for a later period, by a marble base with a dedication to the nymphs, from Hypata at the foot of Oite on the south bank of the Spercheios.[161] The main archaeological evidence for the nymphs' cult in Thessaly are the two caves devoted to the nymphs, one in Mount Ossa on the north coast and one inland near Pharsalos (5.1.6).

4.7 Northern Aegean

For our purposes, I have divided the northern Greek areas into Macedonia, extending from Mount Olympos to the Strymon River and including the Chalkidike peninsula; Aegean Thrace, the coastal area extending from the Strymon to the Hebros River and including Thasos; Pontic Thrace, which includes the Greek colonies on the coast of the Black Sea, as well as selected sites farther inland (modern Bulgaria); and the northern Aegean islands of Lemnos, Imbros, and Samothrace. The northern Aegean was thickly settled by Greeks, a fact belied by the paucity of literary evidence concerning their culture and activities. In the regions under discussion, archaeological, numismatic, and epigraphic evidence have necessarily played key roles in scholarship.[162] The place of the Thracian peoples in our understanding of the cult of the nymphs is important but enigmatic. As we will see, cultural conditions permitted the association of the Thracian goddess Bendis with the nymphs in the fourth century, but there are indications of much earlier Thracian interactions with the Greeks, crucial to later conceptions of the nymphs.

4.7.1 Macedonia

Thracians seem to have occupied the district of Pieria in northern Greece from the late Bronze Age through about 650, during which time they exerted a strong cultural influence on the eastern portion of mainland Greece. The abundance of parallel place names associated with Muses and nymphs in Pieria and Boiotia has already been mentioned. This duplication is attributed by ancient and some modern authors to early Thracian influence in both areas (4.3.1). As we will see, the Muses also have important roles to play in the traditions about Thrace proper. Macedonia had cults of the Muses at several sites in Pieria: Pimpleia, Olympos, Leibethra, and perhaps Thourion. Leibethra and Pimpleia were also associated with the Thracian singer Orpheus; both had well-known springs and memorials to that hero.[163] Leibethra means "the pouring places," apparently with reference to springs. Clearly in force here is the juxtaposition of poetic or prophetic utterance, female deity, and spring, common to the concepts of both Muse and nymph. It is probable that the early people of Pieria did not sharply distinguish between "Muse" and "nymph." According to Hammond, the term *Thourides*, glossed by Hesychius and referring to nymphs or Muses associated with the Macedonian Thourion, is one of the few words that can be confidently attributed to the Makedones in the preclassical period.[164] It is likely also that the concept of the nymphs as providers of musical and prophetic inspiration was a contribution to mainland Greece from this geographical area, whatever the exact ethnic makeup of the peoples there.

At Mieza (Naoussa) in Macedonia was a nymphaion that served as a school for Aristotle and his pupil Alexander. According to Plutarch, Philip provided this facility at Mieza, "where even now they show the stone seats and shady walkways of Aristotle." The three unexcavated caves there are unusual because architectural façades were placed over their entrances. The interiors of the caves were left in their natural state; Pliny refers to their stalagmites. It is unclear when the caves were first used for the cult of the nymphs, but terracing of the site dates as far back as the sixth century.[165] That a nymphaion was considered an appropriate spot for learning should not surprise us if we think of Sokrates and Phaidros' dialogue at the shrine of the nymphs and Acheloös beside the Ilissos River; yet the story shows a nymphaion officially put to secular use, a phenomenon that would become commonplace in the Hellenistic and Roman periods.

The Chalkidike peninsula is separated from Macedonia proper by Lake Bolbe (modern Volvi), whose reedy marshes are mentioned by Aeschylus.

A Hellenistic story tells how the nymph Bolbe sent shoals of fish down the river on an annual basis as a memorial to her son, Olynthos. The genealogy probably arose from the desire to justify the Greek possession (from the fifth century on) of Olynthos, whose eponym was accordingly born of an indigenous nymph and a Greek hero.[166] Another local genealogy says that a nymph, Mendeïs, bore Pallene to Sithon, son of Poseidon and Ossa. Sithon, who held a contest of suitors for the hand of his daughter in the manner of the Elean king Oinomaos, is the eponym of a Thracian tribe east of the Axios River. Coins of the city Potidaia show a nymph who has been identified as Pallene.[167] Also on Pallene was the city of Aphytis, with its cave devoted to the nymphs and Dionysos from as early as the eighth century (5.1.6). Inscriptions and reliefs further attest the cult of the nymphs in Macedonia, though these are primarily of Roman date.[168]

4.7.2 Aegean Thrace and Thasos

On Thasos was an important early fifth-century monument, now in the Louvre, dedicated to the nymphs and Apollo Nymphagetes (figure 4.9). Apollo's main manifestation at Thasos was as Pythios, the Delphic god who ordained the colonization of the island from Paros. But on the southeast side of the agora, a major street culminates in a marble walled passageway known as the "Passage of the Theoroi" from the catalogue of religious magistrates inscribed on the walls. Here was a bas-relief of the nymphs and Apollo with his *kithara*, arranged about a central niche and accompanied by an inscription: "To the nymphs and Apollo Nymphagetes, sacrifice whatever you wish, male or female, except sheep or pig. The paian is not sung. For the Charites neither goat nor pig is lawful." Other panels from the facing wall, where an altar was installed, show Hermes greeting a group of female figures, who may be interpreted as the Charites. The inscription emphasizes the distinction between Charites and nymphs, a point that would otherwise be ob-

Figure 4.9 Thasian relief: Apollo with kithara, four nymphs. Photo by M. and P. Chuzeville. Louvre Museum.

scured, because no iconographical differences are visible among the female figures on the reliefs. The sacrificial rule is paralleled in part by the sacrifice to Apollo Nymphagetes and the nymphs in the Attic deme of Erchia, where the victims were a male goat for the god and a female goat for the nymphs. Apollo's usual hymn, the *paian*, is here forbidden; it might have been restricted to his main cult on the Thasian akropolis as the Pythian god. A *bothros*, or sacrificial pit, beneath the monument showed that the cult there preceded the construction of the walls in the fifth century.[169]

The more recent excavations have shown that the monument did not mark the entrance to the prytaneion, as once was thought. Instead, the passageway might have marked the archaic entrance to the city itself. The appearance of the nymphs in this civic, urban context is unusual, but their stately procession to Apollo's music is appropriately dignified for the decoration of the passageway, clearly a focal space for civic ceremony. It is perhaps due to this special role of the nymphs in Thasian civic cult that, when Pan made his appearance, as on the fourth-century rock relief at his sanctuary on the Thasian akropolis, his cult was kept separate from theirs, contrary to the usual practice.[170]

The nymphs also appear in another Thasian civic context, that of the family gods (*Patrôoi*). On the north side of the town, a sanctuary was set up for these gods, probably at the founding of the colony. They were worshiped by the *patrai*, or gentilician subdivisions of the colonists, during the Ionian celebration of the Apatouria, the festival at which youths were admitted to citizenship. The gods included Zeus Patroös, Ktesios, and Alastoros; Athena Patroia and Mykesia; Artemis Orthosia; and the Nymphai Kourades Patrooi. The epithet *Kourades* is related to the *koureion*, the sacrifice and ritual haircut performed as part of the rites of passage. These nymphs will have been primarily concerned with the successful transition of the city's youths from boyhood to manhood, though it is also possible that they had to do with new wives of members of the *patrai*. The inscriptions also indicate that certain gods "belonged" to individual *patrai*; the nymphs are specified as being "of the Amphoteridai." There are parallels to this familial manifestation of the nymphs, particularly on other Aegean islands, whether ethnically Ionian or Dorian.[171]

The earliest coins to depict nymphs are those of Greek colonists and Thraco-Macedonian peoples living in the ore-rich area of coastal Thrace.[172] The first coins of the Thasians, who quickly settled the shore opposite their island, belong to the second half of the sixth century and depict ithyphallic silens, who approach or carry off resistant nymphs. That these had religious significance on Thasos is suggested by a late sixth-century Thasian relief of an ithyphallic silen holding a kantharos, with an accompanying niche for offerings. The silen-nymph motif was enthusiastically used by local tribes and dynasts around Mount Pangaion, some of whom also used a centaur and nymph. For the Thraco-Macedonians themselves as well as for the Greeks, the silen-nymph images can be interpreted as a reflection of Dionysiac cult.

Dionysos was an important deity in the area of Pangaion, and one theory holds that he is Thracian or part-Thracian in origin (though, as we learn from the Linear B tablets, he was known to the Greeks at least since the end of the Bronze Age). Many of the early coins, it has been suggested, should be attributed to the tribe of the Satrai, who administered the oracle of Dionysos on Pangaion. A tribe called the Diony(sii?) were early beneficiaries of the mines in the region east of Philippoi and issued staters that showed a centaur and nymph.[173] In addition to mining, wine making was of economic importance both for Thasos and the coast opposite.

On all the coins, whether issued by native peoples or colonists, the attitudes of the silen and nymph change over time. The earlier coins (c. 550–10) show the nymphs violently resisting the silens, while the later coins (c. 510–480 and 435–11) depict nymphs who seem to welcome their lovers' advances. (Interestingly, this reverses the sequence seen on Attic vases, which begins in the early sixth century with cordial relations between nymph and silen but eventually deteriorates into molestation.)[174] As for the centaurs, their association with the nymphs is more difficult to explain but is paralleled in Thessaly (4.6). In the case of the Orreskioi, there might have been a direct association between their tribal name and the Homeric characterization (*Il.* 1.268) of the centaurs as *oreskôoi*, "mountain dwelling" (though other tribes also used the centaur motif).[175] Hammond suggests that the centaur-nymph coins represent a fertility cult analogous to that of the Dionysiac silens and nymphs.

The Pangaion area was closely associated with the myth of Lykourgos, a Thracian king who was punished when he attacked the young god Dionysos. This tale appears first in Homer, who tells of the enraged king

ὅς ποτε μαινομένοιο Διωνύσοιο τιθήνας
σεῦε κατ᾽ ἠγάθεον Νυσήιον· αἱ δ᾽ ἅμα πᾶσαι
θύσθλα χαμαὶ κατέχευαν, ὑπ᾽ ἀνδροφόνοιο Λυκούργου
θεινόμεναι βουπλῆγι· Διώνυσος δὲ φοβηθεὶς
δύσεθ᾽ ἁλὸς κατὰ κῦμα, Θέτις δ᾽ ὑπεδέξατο κόλπῳ
δειδιότα· κρατερὸς γὰρ ἔχε τρόμος ἀνδρὸς ὁμοκλῇ. (Hom. *Il.*
6.132–37)

who once chased the nurses of maddened Dionysos down holy Nysa.
And they all cast down their *thusthla* [*thursoi*, or sacred staffs] to the ground, beaten with the ox goad by man-killing Lykourgos.
Dionysos in a panic leapt down into the sea, and Thetis received him terrified into her bosom, for a powerful trembling seized him at the man's rebuke.

As we learn from later sources, Lykourgos was king of the Edonoi, who lived beside the Strymon; and it has been suggested that Nysa, the mountain where the god was nursed, is to be understood as Pangaion. Homer clearly envisions the god as a young child, seeking refuge in Thetis' arms when his nymph nurses are scattered on the slopes of Nysa by the threatening king. In the Homeric version, Dionysos remains passive while Zeus punishes Lykourgos by blinding him, but in later versions Dionysos avenges himself quite ably.[176]

Archaeological evidence in the area suggests a further association of the nymphs with a local goddess called Parthenos, who seems to be a Hellenized version of the Thracian goddess Bendis. At both Neapolis (modern Kavala) and Oisyme, Thasian possessions on the mainland, archaic sanctuaries of Parthenos are attested.[177] A cave near Oisyme (5.1.6) contained dedications to the nymphs beginning in the sixth century, though prehistoric sherds were also present. The appearances together of Bendis and the nymphs on a fourth-century relief from Peiraieus in Athens (4.2.2) and on a Parian relief dedicated by the Thracian Adamas (4.8.1) support the interpretation that the deities of the sanctuary and cave at Oisyme were cultically linked.

Of the Thracian rivers, the Strymon appears most prominently in archaic Greek literature and was endowed with the richest mythology. In Aeschylus' *Suppliants*, King Pelasgos of Argos declares that he rules the land all the way to "the holy Strymon." That Strymon's daughter, Evadne, appears in the Argive genealogy and marries the eponymous hero Argos may be a reflection of this concept of a wide Pelasgian domain in primordial times. Rhodope, eponym of the Thracian mountain, is in one account a daughter of Strymon; she and Poseidon produced the giant Athos. We also hear of Kallirhoë, daughter of the river Nestos east of the Strymon, who bore to Ares various Thracian eponymous heroes.[178] Here is the pattern, familiar from the myths of Asopos and Peneios, of a god mating with the river's daughter but with the Thracian favorite, Ares, substituted for Poseidon or Zeus as the divine progenitor. A nymph, Thraike, appears in the fourth-century historian Andron of Halikarnassos as one of four Okeanids, who represent the four quarters of the known world, the others being Asia, Libya, and Europe. A Titanid (probably again signifying Okeanid) nymph, Thrake, is mentioned by the lexicographer Stephanus as the mother of various Thracian peoples.[179] Her Titanid status and her sexual liaisons with Kronos and the giant Obriareus reflect the Greek perception of the Thracians as a cognate but uncivilized people. These genealogies are of relatively late date, but it is probable that some have their roots in classical authors, such as the historian Hecataeus.

Strymon's best-known offspring is the hero Rhesos, who was killed by Diomedes at Troy. The play *Rhesos*, attributed to Euripides, tells how Strymon sexually violated Rhesos' mother, an unnamed Muse. The outraged goddess flung her offspring into the river, where he was reared by the "spring maidens," *pēgaiai korai*, to become the king of Thrace. Rhesos' name appears to contain the Thracian root for "king," and he has been linked to the heroic rider so prominent in Thracian religious iconography. The fifth-century founding of Amphipolis was tied to an injunction to install Rhesos' bones there; a sanctuary of the Muse Klio was established facing the tomb.[180] The Muse has a relationship with the Thracian hero similar to that of Achilles with his divine mother, Thetis. Muses are mentioned in various sources as mothers of the Thracian heroes Orpheus, Linos, and Thamyris, which shows that in Thracian contexts, Muses may take the usual place of nymphs as the mothers of primordial heroes.[181] The fact that Rhesos has the same genealogy but is a warrior rather than a singer like the others supports this conclusion. At least one source, though late, says that Oiagros, the father of Orpheus, was himself a river, thus strengthening the parallels between Rhesos and Orpheus. Moschos' *Lament for Bion* speaks of Bistonian nymphs and Oiagrides, who can be understood as nymphs of the river Oiagros.[182]

The singer Thamyris, whose famous contest with the Muses is set in Thrace, was at some point appropriated by Delphi, and a story of a migrating nymph was used to explain his Thracian connections. Thamyris was said to be the son of the singer Philammon, who won an early victory in the singing contests at Delphi and was the first to train choruses of maidens. The Parnassian nymph Argiope became Philammon's lover, but Philammon repudiated her after she became pregnant, and she went to the Odrysians in Thrace to bear her son.[183]

The hero Abderos was a native of Opous in Lokris and went to Thrace with Herakles to capture the mares of Diomedes. When he was killed by the mares, Herakles founded the city Abdera beside his tomb. From Hellanicus, we learn that Abderos was the son of Hermes, but Pindar tells a different story. In his *Paean for the Abderitans*, he addresses the hero as "son of Poseidon and the naiad Thronia." Since Thronion was a town in Opous, this is an allusion meant to remind us of Abderos' Lokrian origins. The Abderitan coins, on the other hand, show a nymph or heroine who has been identified as Abdera, daughter of Kyrene and sister of Thracian Diomedes.[184]

4.7.3 *Pontic Thrace and Bulgaria*

Most of the evidence from these regions is of Roman date, but its sheer volume requires comment here. The cult of the nymphs was so popular and widespread in Roman Thrace that we must assume its presence in earlier times. Kazarow explains the phenomenon as the result of syncretism of Greek nymphs with a thriving cult of indigenous spring deities. The great impetus for this blending of cults must have occurred in the Hellenistic period, but as we have seen, its origins lie even further back in the period of Greek colonization. The region under consideration here boasts a number of thermal springs; Robert observes that whenever the coins of cities in Thrace or Moesia depict nymphs or Charites, there is invariably a hot spring at or near the location (Anchialos, Apollonia, Hadrianopolis, Traianopolis, Augusta Traiana, etc.).[185] At this period, there appears to be little distinction between nymphs and Charites, and the late iconography of the three nude Charites is often used on reliefs dedicated to the nymphs.

On the Black Sea north of Salmydessos lay the Greek colony Anchialos, with a bathing establishment known as Aquae Calidae close by. During the heyday of the shrine in the first centuries B.C.E. and C.E., people came from far and wide to be healed in the hot waters provided by the nymphs. Excavation of Aquae Calidae revealed that nearly 3,000 coins had been thrown into the springs, most falling within the period between the fourth century B.C.E. and the first century C.E. The coins represented a range of distant homes for the pilgrims in various cities of the Black Sea, Macedonia, Thrace, and Asia Minor. Other items recovered included bronze fibulae, a large number of gold and silver rings, and fragments of votive reliefs and statues of the nymphs. Two inscribed reliefs from the site are similar in iconography to those of Ognyanovo (below); one is dedicated to the Nymphs of Anchialos, *Numphai Anchialeai*. In the Imperial period, games in honor of the nymphs were held and commemorated on coins of the Severans and later emperors.[186]

The best-documented cult site of the nymphs in Bulgaria is Ognyanovo (formerly Saladinovo), on the left bank of the Hebros not far from Plovdiv (ancient Philippopolis). Here was the nymphaion of Bourdapa, where Dobrusky found ninety-five votive plaques dedicated to the nymphs and a few others dedicated to the enigmatic Thracian Rider; all appeared to date from the second and third centuries C.E.[187] Foundations of a simple structure about six meters square were uncovered. Along the walls of this shrine were arranged the marble plaques, most of which are no more than twenty-five centimeters tall. Some are roughly square in shape, with the pictorial frame rounded at the top; others are rectangular. All depict three nymphs, but there is a wide variety in the exact iconography and in the quality of workmanship. One type shows the nymphs in a pose reminiscent of the Charites: two nude nymphs face forward, each holding an object, such as an apple or a mirror, while the central nymph stands with her back to the viewer, turning her head to peek over her shoulder. To each side of the group lie vessels with water pouring from their mouths (figure 4.10). A second type has nude nymphs dancing exuberantly as they toss scarves above their heads; urns gush beside them. A third type shows the trio dressed in long chitons, either dancing in a sedate row or simply facing the viewer. In one of the latter examples, the central nymph holds a large scalloplike shell, which covers her abdomen. The two nymphs on the sides hold vases from which they pour water to the ground.

Two further reliefs, unique at this site, show the nymphs accompanied by a priest (of the same size as they), who pours a libation, and the nymphs with Zeus and Hera (of larger size) standing to their right. The latter motif is paralleled at other Bulgarian sites.[188] Lamps, mirrors, and coins were also found. The site was revisited in 1985, and more plaques were found, along with coins and ceramics that push the date of the sanctuary back into the Hellenistic period. Some of the new plaques represent a pair of ears and, in conjunction with the epithet *epêkoos*, "listening one," also attested at the site, contribute further to the evidence that the nymphs here were assisting gods, probably healers.[189] The site is generally considered an example of a thriving yet strictly local cult, whose dedicants virtually all had Thracian names. The

Figure 4.10 Nymph relief from Bourdapa. National Archaeological Museum, Sofia.

dedications often call the nymphs *Bourdapênai*, "nymphs of Bourdapa." Yet, for all its Thracian character, many basic elements, such as the use of votive tablets, their iconography, and even the parochial quality of the shrine itself, closely parallel Greek practices. The dedication of lamps is of particular interest, because lamps are regularly deposited at Greek cave sites of the nymphs, where they might be interpreted as more utilitarian than votive. Here, however, no cave or grotto is reported.

In Bulgarian inscriptions, the nymphs are often called *kuriai*, the feminine plural form of a title meaning "lord" or "master." This is part of a widespread phenomenon of the Hellenistic and Roman periods, according to which the gods, particularly the assisting gods like Asklepios or the nymphs, began to be named in votive inscriptions with the titles given to absolute monarchs. Nock, in his classic explanation of the phenomenon, argues that the rise of absolute rulers in the Hellenistic kingdoms affected the religious mentality of worshipers, who began to see their relationships with the deities as analogous to those between master and servant or ruler and subject. The inscriptions show them applying the terms *kurios* and *despotês* ("master") to deities and terms like *latris* and *hupourgos* ("servant") to themselves. Pleket has recently qualified Nock's view by pointing out that some roots of this collective mentality lie in the classical period and that we can see hints of such a relationship between worshiper and deity in the phenomenon of nympholepsy as experienced by Archedamos (1.3), for example.[190] In the fourth century, this type of relationship seems to have been manifested only with certain deities and perhaps only in times of acute personal distress or among more devout individuals; gradually, it became paradigmatic under the impetus of the changing social structure.

Other sites in Thrace, Moesia, and Dacia are too numerous to discuss, and interesting discoveries continue to be made. The thermal springs at Hissar, north of Plovdiv, yielded similar nymph reliefs, and the sanctuary contained silver surgical instruments, a dedication paralleled in classical Attica (5.1.9).[191]

4.7.4 *Lemnos, Imbros, and Samothrace*

Strabo recognized the affinity of the Kabeiroi, Korybantes, Kouretes, Daktyls, and Telchines, all of whom are Greek manifestations of a cult type that was shared by peoples of Thracian, Anatolian, and Hellenic stock throughout the Aegean. These *daimones* appear either as ministers of greater gods and goddesses or as gods in their own right. The character of their cult tends to be ecstatic yet secretive. They vary in number but normally are plural. They preside over various trades, particularly metallurgy, and are often characterized as culture heroes and aboriginal inhabitants of the land. Finally, they tend to have female counterparts, who are often characterized as nymphs.

Lemnos, Imbros, and perhaps Samothrace, together with the Thraco-Phrygian mainland opposite them, shared the cult of the Kabeiroi (also found in other places, most notably Thebes).[192] Strabo quotes myths that recount the genealogy of the Lemnian Kabeiroi from two fifth-century historians, Acusilaus and Pherecydes. According to the former, Kabeiro and Hephaistos had a son, Kadmilos (or Kamillos), who fathered the three Kabeiroi, and these in turn fathered the nymphs called the Kabeirides. Pherecydes' account adds that Kabeiro was a daughter of Proteus and says that she and Hephaistos produced both triads, the three Kabeiroi and the three Kabeirid nymphs.[193] Sacred rites were conducted in honor of each triad, but their individual names were kept secret as part of the mysteries. These accounts show that, at least during the classical period, the Lemnian cult had a symmetrical male-female structure, one that was to be modified later as the nymphs lost their importance in the cult. (No more is heard of these Kabeirid nymphs, though perhaps they are the Lemnian nymphs to whom Medeia prayed in order to assuage the famine in Corinth.) This shift apparently took place during the Hellenistic period, when the Kabeiroi were assimilated to the Dioskouroi.[194]

One question that comes to mind is how much these figures have in common with other Greek nymphs, if they are essentially non-Hellenic deities who have been adopted and reclassified as nymphs. The role of the male Kabeiroi, as sons of Hephaistos and patrons of metallurgy, is more easily understood, though it is possible that the nymphs had to do with the actual extraction of ores. Nymphs are elsewhere connected with quarries and regularly with economic activities that involve the collection of raw materials. On the other hand, the basic concept of nymphs as attendants upon the gods, with or without male counterparts such as Kouretes or silens, is firmly embedded in Greek religion from the earliest times, so that no such distinction between "Greek" and "non-Greek" may be possible.

As for Samothrace, the particulars of the cult there are less clear, since the Samothracians did not refer to their gods as Kabeiroi but as Great Gods. Sources differ on the exact number of these gods and their genders. According to Mnaseas, they were Kabeiroi, and their number was four: two female and two male. One of the latter he calls Kasmilos, which is reminiscent of the Lemnian Kamillos-Kadmilos.[195] There are several tales about the first inhabitants of Samothrace. According to Diodorus Siculus, the five tribes (*phulai*) of the island were named for the sons of Saon, the local *Urmensch* who survived the Great Flood. The Black Sea had burst from its confines and inundated the island, and a few inhabitants survived by praying to the native gods and running to the higher regions of the island. The survivors set up boundary stones around the island and altars to these native gods, who must be the same as the Great Gods for whom the island was famed. Saon, the lawgiver and progenitor, was said to be the son either of Zeus and a nymph or of Hermes and a nymph of Kyllene named Rhene. Saon is also the eponym of the Saoi, a pre-Hellenic people of Lemnos, but the name would have sounded to Greek speakers like "the saved one," a reference to the salvation from drowning offered through initiation into the mysteries.[196] We have already seen in Megara and Thessaly the motif of the primordial inhabitant, son of a nymph, who survives a flood; the Samothracian account is paralleled in several respects by the Rhodian saga of the Telchines (4.9.4).

To return to Lemnos, excavation of Hephaistia, the principal city, yielded two archaic terra-cotta models of fountains. Both of these include human figures that could conceivably be interpreted as fountain nymphs.[197] The first is a small figure, who sits on the edge of the water basin with his/her feet in the water, which also contains turtles and a snake or eel. The scene, according to one report, is one of healing at a sacred spring. On the other model, the architectural scheme of the fountain includes human figures attached to the façade; one of the two extant figures is seated on a throne, and one is standing. These might well be cult images of the nymphs pre-dating the canonical triad iconography; one is reminded of the limestone relief of a seated female from the fountain of Theagenes at Megara (4.3.4). Terra-cotta models of fountains, each with a single head of a nymph affixed to its face, are also found at a later period in Lokroi in Italy (4.10.7).

Also tied to Lemnos is the myth of Philoktetes, the unfortunate hero who was bitten by a snake en route to the Trojan war and abandoned by his companions because of the festering wound (1.4.3). The snakebite is associated with a place called Chryse, either on Lemnos itself or a small island nearby. Accounts of the myth explain the reason for Philoktetes' wound in different ways, but one has the nymph Chryse desiring sex with Philoktetes and sending the snake to bite him when he rejects her. The name Chryse, "Golden," suggests some connection with metallurgy or with the abundant mines of the northern Aegean.[198]

4.8 Southern Aegean and Northern Africa

4.8.1 Paros

Of the Cyclades, the richest in nymph lore is Paros, the mother island of the Thasian colonists. Paros is most famed for its ancient cult of the Charites, and the Thasian colonists undoubtedly took with them this cult (4.7.2), though it is unclear at what point the nymphs were added.[199] Another link to the northern Aegean is the Parian quarry relief noted by travelers since the time of Cyriacus of Ancona in the fifteenth century. Now sadly weathered and damaged by attempts to remove it from its rock face, the relief was carved in an irregular shape, possibly meant to evoke the mouth of a cave, at the entrance to a subterranean gallery in the quarry. It was dedicated by Adamas the Odrysian to the nymphs sometime in the second half of the fourth century. The Odrysians were a prominent family of Thrace, and Adamas brought with him (via Thasos?) some cultic observances evocative of the north.[200]

Drawings made by travelers in the eighteenth century are helpful now in reconstructing the damaged relief (figure 4.11). The scene can be divided roughly into three sections: on the left, a small upper and a large lower register display the gods; on the lower right, a crowd of worshipers (including one kneeling figure) is assembled. The relief is remarkable for its profusion of gods, who are depicted in different sizes and squeezed together into a relatively small space. Several of the gods are merely disembodied heads floating above the other figures. The use of registers and the depiction of a variety of gods together are attested in other nymph reliefs, but the Parian relief is the most extreme example of this phenomenon. The upper register of the quarry relief contains several of the iconographic elements seen in fourth-century Attic reliefs to the nymphs, but the composition is different, and

Figure 4.11 Paros relief as drawn by J. Stuart. Line drawing from Stuart and Revett (1882) vol. 4, pl. 51.

other features are introduced. The common elements are the mask of Acheloös (at center instead of to one side); the seated Pan playing the syrinx (though this Pan is corpulent and large in relation to the other figures); and the nymphs with Hermes (here, there appear to be only two nymphs). To the left of this group are a head rising from the earth (probably Ge) and a seated, silenlike figure; to the far right is a heavily weathered group that looks like three heads behind a large circular object. These heads, to judge from similar scenes elsewhere, represent the Korybantes.[201] If the upper register was intended to roughly approximate an Attic votive relief, we might compare it to the inset of Hermes, nymphs, and Acheloös on the upper left corner of a contemporary Bendis relief from Peiraieus, which served the same function (see figure 4.5).[202]

The main register depicted four full-length standing figures: three nymphs stepping to the right and facing the worshipers and, beside them but facing away, a figure in a short tunic. These four are the largest figures in the composition. The companion of the three nymphs seems to be the Thracian goddess Bendis, who wears her characteristic cap and leans on a hunting spear. One likely theory has it that the scene represents Bendis' introduction to the gods of Paros. This helps to explain the identity of some of the other gods in the lower register: a seated female figure and her younger companion could then be identified as Demeter and Kore, who were important deities of Paros. A girl standing behind them, from the torches in her hands, should be Hekate. The disembodied heads above this group could be various gods: Zeus Kynthios, Herakles, Apollo. As a Thracian, Adamas must have felt that

Bendis and the nymphs ought to be honored together, but the nymphs of the Parian relief are probably the local denizens, mistresses of the quarry, not Bendis' Thracian partners.

Alternatively, the appearance of Demeter and Kore on the relief suggests a connection with the story of Demeter's introduction of her mysteries on Paros. After the abduction of her daughter, according to a fragment of Apollodorus, Demeter brought Persephone's workbasket to the nymphs. She also went to Paros, where she was received by King Melissos and his sixty daughters. She bestowed on these daughters the cloth woven by Persephone and taught them her mysteries. Thus, the women who perform the ritual of the Thesmophoria are called bees, *Melissai*. The fragment leaves unclear exactly what the relationship between the nymphs and the daughters of Melissos was; both are described as recipients of Persephone's maidenly possessions. The equation bee = nymph = priestess is known from other contexts; here, the etiological myth of the Parian Thesmophoria traces its origin to maiden daughters, who must become *numphai*, brides, as part of their transformation into the sexually aware, yet chaste, wives who celebrate the goddess's festival of fertility.[203] A similar king, Melisseus, and his daughters figure in a Kretan myth of Zeus' birth and nurture: they feed the infant Zeus with honey. Parian tradition held that the island had been colonized from Krete, and this was expressed mythically in the story that a Kretan nymph, Pareia, bore four sons to Minos; they became the first colonists: Eurymedon, Nephalion, Chryses, and Philolaos.[204]

In the area of Myrsine (Psychopiana), a block was found with an inscription that identified it as the altar of the *Dorpophoroi Numphai*, "Meal-bringing Nymphs." The altar is of Roman date, but a boundary stone for a sanctuary of the Dorpophoroi, dating to the fourth century, was also recovered a few kilometers away in Paroikia. Thus, these nymphs enjoyed a long-lived cult on Paros; the epithet is appropriate for deities of prosperity and abundance and is analogous to Demeter's titles of Karpophoros and Malophoros.[205] The cult of the nymphs is also attested in various other inscriptions, including a tablet found in some caves east of Paroikia, inscribed "of the nymphs" with letters of fifth-century date (the earliest archaeological evidence for their cult here), and a tablet of the Christian era with a dedication to the nymphs and a relief carving of two breasts. At least in the late period, then, the nymphs were approached as healers or, perhaps, to aid new mothers with nursing. Two similar Parian reliefs with breasts were dedicated to Eileithyia.[206]

4.8.2 Naxos

Naxos had its own myth about Dionysos' birth, which naturally located that event on the island itself. Zeus is said to have taken the infant god from his thigh and entrusted him to the local nymphs (*enchôrioi numphai*) Philia, Koronis, and Kleide. Naxos was beloved of the god and favored by him because of his upbringing there. According to Porphyry, the Naxians consecrated a cave to Dionysos; this was probably the supposed site of Dionysos' nurture by the Naxian nymphs.[207] The location of this Dionysiac cave is unknown, though three caves, one of which is now an underground church, are reported in the Lakkos region. A rough marble stele, which marks the shrine of the "Inner Nymphs," *Muchiai Numphai*, dates to the fourth century and was probably removed from one of these caves. The stele lends itself to two possible interpretations. First, the term *muchos* is used in the *Odyssey* to describe the innermost recess of Kalypso's cave, where she and Odysseus make love, and the recess of the Ithakan cave of the nymphs, where Odysseus stores his treasure.[208] It makes an appropriate epithet for nymphs, evoking as it does the ideas both of the cave and of sexual intimacy. Another approach is suggested by an ancient passage about the Roman household gods: "As for these gods, the Romans call them Penates. Some who translate the name into Greek render it Patrooi, others Genethlioi, Ktesioi, or Mychioi, and still others Herkeioi." These epithets all describe gods who protect the prosperity and fecundity of individual households or larger kinship groups. Based on this interpretation, the Nymphai Mychiai would be protectors of the storeroom, *muchos*, and similar to the domestic god Zeus Ktesios.[209] Nymphai Patrooi are attested on Thasos (4.7.2).

4.8.3 *Delos*

Delos, center of the Ionian worship of Apollo, was the home of a famous female chorus, which performed on ritual occasions. The Homeric *Hymn to Delian Apollo*, which calls the chorus *kourai Dêliades* and servants of the Far Shooter, says they sing the praises of Apollo, Leto, and Artemis, as well as songs about the men and women of days long past. These Delian maidens were a professional group, renowned as a sort of ideal chorus during the classical period in much the same way as the Karyatid maidens of the Peloponnese.[210] And, as with the Karyatides, the mythic model for the Deliades was a group of nymphs, those who sang the chant of Eileithyia at the birth of Apollo. In the case of the Deliades, it may be that the human chorus pre-dated the myth of the nymphs, for in the Homeric *Hymn*, the attendants at the birth are "all the goddesses" except Hera: Rhea, Themis, Amphitrite, and others. But by the third century, Callimachus' *Hymn to Delos* gives a different account, making the birth attendants Delos herself and the *numphai Deliades*, offspring of an ancient river. This river is presumably the Inopos, prominent in both *Hymns* because Leto gave birth beside its banks.[211]

Already in the Homeric *Hymn*, Delos is personified and speaks to Leto, offering her refuge if she swears an oath that Delos will not be forgotten once Apollo is born. Callimachus elaborates this personification, making Delos a nymph who was once called Asteria, since she leapt like a star from heaven into the deep sea as she fled from Zeus. Delos then wandered without moorings over the sea until she gave shelter to Leto and became fixed in the midst of the Cyclades, which dance about her like a chorus.[212] For Callimachus, as for Pindar, geographical locale and divine personification cannot be separated. Delos does seem to have possessed a cult on the island in the Hellenistic period, which may correspond chronologically to Callimachus' special emphasis on Delos as kourotrophos of Apollo.[213] A nymphaion is also amply attested from inscriptions that begin at the end of the fourth century, though its location is unknown. One likely suggestion is that it lay near the theater beside one of the marble quarries.[214]

One of the more unusual monuments to the nymphs is that dedicated ca. 400 by the Athenian *genos* of the Pyrrhakidai.[215] This noble family, also active at Delphi, dedicated two circular marble structures, one for the Tritopator, an ancestral spirit, and one for the "Nymphai of the Pyrrhakidai." The monument of the nymphs, somewhat smaller than that of the Tritopator, was situated beside the Inopos River. The design of these two structures is unique but has characteristics of both *abaton* (a restricted sacred area) and altar. The area beneath the Tritopator monument was excavated and yielded abundant signs of sacrifice conducted on the spot, apparently long before the monument itself was built. The nymphs are similarly attested as patrons of the Amphoteridai on Thasos (4.7.2). The phenomenon might have arisen because the nymphs had the power to aid in conception and birth, so that certain families came to rely on specific groups of nymphs as guarantors of the family's posterity. Such nymphs are exceptional in that their association is more with a particular kin group than with a geographical location.

In the sanctuary of Apollo was the Krene Minoë, a fountain of the archaic type (also found at Delphi) in which the cistern is sunk into the ground and is reached by a stairway. The oldest parts of the fountain date from the fifth century, and a fourth-century inscription forbids anyone from washing in the water. At the end of the second century, the fountain house was rebuilt, perhaps as part of a private dwelling, and incorporated a relief sculpture dedicated to the nymphs of Minoë.[216] This sculpture is unique, depicting three frontal, seated female figures who hold vessels in their hands. To their left is a large bearded head, facing the viewer, which must be either a hornless Acheloös or Zeus. The latter possibility is supported by a second-century C.E. relief, found on Mykonos but thought to come from Delos, which is inscribed "to Zeus Dimeranos and the divine nymphs," *numphai theai*.[217]

4.8.4 *Keos*

Keos was celebrated in antiquity both for its nymphs and for its cult of Zeus Ikmaios, said to have been founded by the hero Aristaios (2.5.3). The sources give conflicting accounts about the nymphs but agree that nymphs were the earliest inhabitants of the island. According to Callimachus, who draws upon the fifth-century Kean chronicler Xenomedes, the history of the island begins with the Korykian nymphs, whom "a great lion drove away from Parnassos; for that reason they called it [the island] Hydrous(s)a." The Keans' claim to have received the famous Korykian nymphs indicates some connection, either real or desired, with Delphi, perhaps colonization from Phokis. The arrival of the nymphs also explains the island's early name: Hydroussa, "well-watered." A fragment of Aristotle's *Constitution of the Ceians* gives a different story. In the Aristotelian account, "The island used to be called Hydrousa and nymphs are said to have inhabited it earlier, but since a lion frightened them, they went to Karystos. For this reason, the promontory of Keos is called Leon." A third source, Ovid, describes the island as "once frequented by the Korykian nymphs." He thus agrees with Xenomedes in identifying the nymphs as Korykian and also with Aristotle in suggesting that the nymphs left the island.[218]

Much of the early mythological history of Keos is concerned with the water supply. That the nymphs arrive first on the island is a mythic way of expressing its suitability for human habitation: water is a prerequisite for colonization. The myth that the nymphs were frightened away from Keos expresses the concept of drought, possibly even conserving the memory of historical drought(s). Aristaios, nurtured and taught by the nymphs, appears at a later stage in the island's history, when his sacrifices to Rainy Zeus (Ikmaios) and Seirios bring about the yearly appearance of the Etesian winds, which ease the late summer heat and drought. Bee nymphs, or *Brisai*, appear in connection with Aristaios in both Euboia and Keos, bringing to mind the daughters of the bee king (Melissos or Melisseus) on Krete and Paros.[219]

As for the lion who chased the nymphs, there are several possible ways, none entirely satisfactory, of explaining its role in the myth. Near Ioulis, a large lion of archaic date is carved from the rock; its presence might have influenced the story. It is not, however, located on a promontory.[220] Second, the lion is the zodiac sign that corresponds to the period of late summer (but also to the arrival of the cooling Etesian winds) so that the entry of the sun into Leo might correspond either to the onset or the relief of drought, that is, the departure or arrival of the nymphs. It is questionable, though, whether the Keans could have been influenced by knowledge of the zodiac at such an early date.[221] Finally, the lion–nymph association could have been prompted by the ubiquitous use of lion heads as fountain spouts.

4.8.5 *Andros*

Elsewhere in the Cyclades, Palaiopolis on Andros yielded the largest extant votive relief to the nymphs, measuring approximately a meter in height and width. In both size and style, the relief is more akin to grave monuments than other votive reliefs, and it dates to the last quarter of the fourth century. The arrangement of the figures is also different from standard Attic types: a frontal Hermes stands at left, while on the right, two standing nymphs flank an older, seated one. An Acheloös mask is carved in the center of the upper border, and a tiny reclining Pan is in the upper right corner. The cult of the nymphs at Palaiopolis is also attested by an inscription of the first century C.E.[222]

4.8.6 Krete

The birth myth of Kretan Zeus unfolds in a cave, either the Idaian cave or the Diktaian. The birth cave on Ide has been identified and shows evidence of cult activity from the late Minoan period onward; the Diktaian cave has long been identified as Psychro in the Lasithi range (primarily because of its proximity to Lyktos, the Hesiodic site of Zeus' birth), but the cult there ended before the historical period. It is possible, if one accepts the idea that Kretan Zeus was in origin a Minoan god, to suppose that the cult at Psychro was superseded by that at Ide. In 1904, an inscribed hymn to Diktaian Zeus was discovered at Palaikastro, far from Lasithi on the eastern end of the island. It and other inscriptions indicate that the cult of Diktaian Zeus, which represented him as a young man rather than an infant, was to be found throughout eastern and central Krete.[223]

Several districts in the Aegean considered Zeus their fosterling, the most ancient claims being those of Arkadia and Krete. Because of the homology of Kretan with Phrygian Ide and Kretan Rheia with the Phrygian Great Mother, the Troad was also able to enter the competition at a relatively late period. The birth myths are characterized by the presence of supernatural attendants, both male and female, upon Rheia and the infant god. Contrary to the prevailing motifs in Arkadia, which emphasized the birth attendants' role in bathing the mother and child, the Kretan myths tell how Rheia's helpers nourished and protected the infant.

Therotrophic myths, in which animals feed human children, are known worldwide and, in the Mediterranean context, are especially common in Krete. Many of the nurses of Zeus must at an early period have been simply goat, dog, bear, or bee.[224] Later, they were understood as nymphs, and finally, many of them were identified with constellations. The most famous is Amaltheia, who is variously described as a goat, a nymph, or in Euhemeristic fashion, as a nymph who owned a goat. The familiar combination of bee, nymph, and cave is found in other versions, in which bees or nymphs, daughters of Melisseus, feed Zeus with honey. According to one Hellenistic account, Zeus was born in the "cave of the bees," *antron melissôn*. Four men tried to steal the bees' honey and were punished by being transformed into birds. A black-figure vase from Vulci seems to depict this myth, thus pushing the story of the bee nurses back to the sixth century. The nurses Kynosoura and Helike were transformed into constellations as Ursa Minor and Major; Kynosoura is also perhaps to be associated with Kydonian coins that show an infant fed by a dog.[225]

Some sources speak of the nurses as nymphs with no discernable animal qualities: in the rationalized account of Diodorus Siculus, the nurses are nymphs who feed Zeus with honey and milk from the goat Amaltheia. Zeus rewards the bees by giving them their gold color and making them impervious to the cold air of the mountains. At Gortyn, not far from Ide, Nymphai Geraistiai are attested as nurses of Zeus. Ide herself, personification of the mountain, often figures as one of the nurses, as does Adrasteia. The sources for these myths are unfortunately late, but in spite of the absence in Hesiod's account of nurses other than Gaia, there is general agreement about the ancient origins of the stories.[226] Callimachus gives us a detailed and relatively early account:

Ζεῦ, σὲ δὲ Κυρβάντων ἑτάραι προσεπηχύναντο
Δικταῖαι Μελίαι, σὲ δ᾽ ἐκοίμισεν Ἀδρήστεια
λίκνῳ ἐνὶ χρυσέῳ, σὺ δ᾽ ἐθήσαο πίονα μαζόν
αἰγὸς Ἀμαλθείης, ἐπὶ δὲ γλυκὺ κηρίον ἔβρως.
γέντο γὰρ ἐξαπιναῖα Πανακρίδος ἔργα μελίσσης
Ἰδαίοις ἐν ὄρεσσι, τά τε κλείουσι Πάνακρα.
οὖλα δὲ Κούρητές σε περὶ πρύλιν ὠρχήσαντο
τεύχεα πεπλήγοντες, ἵνα Κρόνος οὔασιν ἠχήν
ἀσπίδος εἰσαΐοι καὶ μή σεο κουρίζοντος. (Callim. *Hymn* 1.46–54)

The Diktaian Meliai, companions of the Kyrbantes, took you into their arms, Zeus, and Adrasteia laid you in a golden *liknon*, and you sucked the rich teat of the goat Amaltheia, and with it you ate the sweet honeycomb. For suddenly there appeared the works of the Panakrian bee, on the Idaian hills which men call Panakra. And the Kouretes danced the war dance rapidly about you, clashing their armor, that Kronos might hear with his ears the din of the shield, but not your cries.

Here, the poet, like many later authors, seems to conflate Ide and Dikte, as well as the Kyrbantes and Kouretes, while combining several traditions of Zeus' nurses. The Meliai, or ash-tree nymphs, are mentioned by Hesiod but are otherwise unattested as nurses of Zeus. The god partakes not of nectar and ambrosia but of the products of mountainous pasture lands: goat's milk and honey. The nymphs are companions of the Kyrbantes/Kouretes, a relationship described as early as the *Ehoeae*, in which the nymphs, satyrs, and Kouretes are all siblings. The earliest source to connect the Kouretes with the birth of Zeus, however, is Euripides. The Kouretes are paradigmatic "youths," *kouroi*, just as the nymphs are maidens, *kourai*. Appearing in multiples of three, they are, according to West, the male counterparts of nymphs, spirits of burgeoning growth in the natural world. Diodorus Siculus makes them early inhabitants of Krete, culture-bearing gods who taught herding and beekeeping (elsewhere, the nymphs themselves or their fosterlings perform this civilizing role; see, for example, 2.5.3).[227]

In the cave of Zeus' birth, the roles of the attendants are strictly gender segregated: the nymphs are kourotrophic, providers of the motherly attentions required by an infant, while the Kouretes perform the exaggeratedly masculine war dance and provide the paradigm for the growth of the Diktaian god into the supreme Kouros, as he is addressed in the hymn found at

Palaikastro. Both Kouretes and nymphs appear in the oath formulas of treaties between Kretan cities in the central and eastern parts of the island, which correspond to the sphere of Diktaian Zeus' cult. These inscriptions date to the second century but are probably copies of older exemplars, with the formulas themselves perhaps reaching back to the archaic period. The cave on Ide was the site of a mystery cult, and it is possible that the cult was served by groups of priestly Kouretes and bees, who emulated the divine attendants.[228]

Another group of attendants at the birth of Zeus is the Daktyloi, "Fingers." They were born from soil that fell from the hands of a nymph, either the mountain nymph Ide or the nymph Anchiale in the Diktaian cave. According to Sophocles, there were ten of them, five male and five female (just as the Kabeiroi had their female counterparts, the Kabeirid nymphs). Other sources also separate them into a male group (those of the right hand) and a female group (those of the left). Like the Kabeiroi, they are associated with a mother goddess and have knowledge of metalwork and sorcery. Their number, usually multiples of five, and their function as attendants of the Mother distinguish them from the Kouretes, who appear in multiples of three and are more closely associated with Zeus himself. Jeanmaire has compared them to Cheiron, on the basis of the etymological similarity between *cheir* (hand) and *daktulos* (finger), the similarity in their function as mentors, and the rapports between the cults at Ide and the cave of Cheiron on Pelion.[229]

Owing partly to the strong residue of pre-Hellenic religion in Krete, the island supported the cults of several female figures whose status (goddess, heroine, nymph) is indeterminate. Akakallis, Diktynna, Britomartis, and Kynosoura might fall into any of these categories, depending on a given context. Akakallis, for example, is described by mythographers as the daughter of Minos or as a nymph. Different versions of her myth make her the mother, by Apollo and Hermes, of as many as five Kretan eponyms or founders and two other sons connected with northern Africa. The therotrophic motif so prominent in myths of Zeus' birth is also found in connection with Akakallis: a wolf nursed her son Milatos, while a goat nursed her twins, Phylakides and Philandros. Her name among the Kretans meant "narcissus," and her cult, according to Fauré, was celebrated in Lera cave near ancient Kydonia (5.1.7).[230] This identification is based primarily on the location of the cave and dedications to a nymph or nymphs and to Kydon, the son of Akakallis. Fauré has further linked Kynosoura to the cave Arkoudia ("Cave of the She Bear"), where her associations with the bear made her an analogue of Greek Artemis. Diktynna and Britomartis were also assimilated to Artemis, though their origins were clearly as local goddesses.[231]

Like the borderland of Arkadia and Lakonia, Krete is one of the areas where Artemis is more closely associated with the nymphs, blending her identity with that of figures like Diktynna in the cult sphere, while Hellenistic poets surround her with a bevy of nymph companions. Callimachus and Apollonius of Rhodes both describe the nymphs of the river Amnisos, near Knossos, as Artemis' companions. This association is probably due to yet another assimilation of Artemis with the birth goddess Eileithyia, whose cave on the Amnisos is mentioned as early as the *Odyssey*.[232]

Finally, there is some evidence that the nymphs acted as healing deities on the island, as they often did elsewhere. At Lebena in south-central Krete, an inscription recorded the fourth-century installation of Asklepios' cult from Epidauros, apparently in the old shrine of the nymphs and Acheloös. In spite of the new god's advent, the Lebenians were required to continue their sacrifices of a piglet to Acheloös and a kid to the nymphs. This superimposition of Asklepios' cult onto that of the nymphs must have been fairly commonplace, as both were concerned with healing, and a convenient water source was a necessity for Asklepios' shrines.[233] The same phenomenon probably took place at Athens (4.2.1).

4.8.7 *Thera*

On the island of Thera, the city of the same name was situated on a hilltop. The southeast portion of the hillside was a sacred space dominated by the temple of Apollo Karneios, a broad terrace used for the Karneian festival, and small shrines of other deities. There was also a gymnasium of the ephebes, and in the area between this structure and the temple were carved a large number of rupestral inscriptions. South of the temple and dating to the fourth century is a prescription for sacrifice to the nymphs of the Hylleis. A similar, damaged inscription in the same area appears to provide for sacrifice to the nymphs of the Dymanes. The Hylleis and Dymanes, with the Pamphyloi, made up the three early tribes (*phulai*) of the Dorians, attested from the seventh century onward. According to Roussel, the appearance of the inscriptions at this late date probably means that the groups making sacrifice were cultic associations that had adopted the prestigious names of the now-defunct tribes.[234] On the other hand, the fact that the inscriptions were found at the sanctuary of Apollo Karneios, a Dorian god par excellence whose cult must date to the colonization of the island, is suggestive. Sacrifices to nymphs of the Dymanes are also attested from Hellenistic Kos (4.9.4).

4.8.8 *Kyrene*

Kyrene, founded from Thera in the late seventh century, adopted as one of its central myths the story of Kyrene's abduction by Apollo from Thessaly, her installation in Libya on the hill site of the future city, and the birth of the hero Aristaios (2.5.3). Kyrene's story must have been confined to Thessaly in the beginning; ancient sources agree that she was either the daughter or granddaughter of the river Peneios. The sixth-century account in the *Ehoeae* is too fragmentary for us to ascertain whether it included the abduction to Libya. By the time of Pindar's ninth *Pythian Ode* (probably performed in 474), the Libyan version was well established, and Pindar seamlessly blends elements from both Thessalian and Kyrenaic traditions. Apollo is smitten when he sees Kyrene wrestling a lion in defense of her father's herds, a motif that Pindar sets in Thessaly, but one that is equally if not more at home in a northern African context. According to Acesandrus of Kyrene, the cattle of the Libyan king Eurypylos were being ravaged by a lion. He offered the kingdom to anyone who could kill the lion, and Kyrene, upon successfully completing this task, became the queen and bore Aristaios and Autychos to Apollo.[235]

The reasons for the Kyrenaic appropriation of a Thessalian heroine or nymph are obscure, but it should be noted that both areas play an important role in the saga of the Argonauts. In the mythology of the city, Kyrene's arrival is one of three successive stages: first, the advent of Kyrene the huntress with the city god Apollo ensures the fertility of the land and its freedom from savage beasts, hence its suitability for colonization. Second is the Argonauts' visit to the area, which sets in motion the events leading to the third stage, the (historical) arrival of Battos and Greek colonists from Thera.[236] According to Chamoux, the similarity in name between nymph and city is probably coincidental. The city name might have been derived from Kyra, the indigenous name for the asphodel that grew there abundantly. The name Kyra appears in ancient accounts of both the spring and the hill where the city was founded. Once the name Kyrene (Doric Kyrana) was adopted, the colonists would have associated it with Thessalian Kyrene and developed the myth of Kyrene's journey to Africa.[237]

Kyrene is unusual among female city eponyms because she is characterized as a queen, not merely as the mother of a primordial king. Her status as queen or ruler is already emphasized by Pindar, who calls her *archepolis*, "city ruler," and *despoina chthonos*, "mistress of the land." It is further developed in the Hellenistic accounts of Kyrene, which describe her as ruling the land. This regal identity is probably due to more than one factor: Kyrene's name, to Greek ears, might have suggested the root that gives us *kuros*, "authority," and *kurios*, "lord or master."[238] Kyrene's Libyan myth, moreover, was first propagated under the Battiad dynasty, who ruled as kings until the mid-fifth century; surely, her royal qualities were linked with theirs. She appears on archaic coins of the city, seated before the silphium plant, which was an important source of revenue.[239] Her usurpation of masculine roles in killing the lion, ridding the land of its menace, and taking the throne from Eurypylos is surprising; it could reflect the influence of an indigenous goddess of the mistress of animals type.

Pindar, following Hesiod, makes Kyrene of mortal origin: she is the daughter of the Lapith king Hypseus (4.6). According to Apollonius of Rhodes, Apollo, because of his love, "entrusted her to the indigenous nymphs who inhabited Libya beside the Hill of Myrtles" and "made her one of the long-lived nymphs, a huntress." Kyrene's cult dates from at least the late sixth or early fifth century, when an altar inscribed with her name was placed in the sanctuary of Apollo.[240] The symbolic center of the city was the "spring of Apollo," or Kyra, to which the Libyans had led the first Greek settlers; to see this spring once again was the heart's desire of Pindar's client, Damophilos, who had been exiled.[241] Kyrene would naturally have been closely associated with the spring that seemed to bear her name, and by the Roman period she seems to have been regarded as a fountain nymph. Near the spring of Apollo, a fountain was topped with a statue of Kyrene holding the lion in a headlock; the water spouted from the lion's mouth. The spring, the temple of Apollo Karneios, and the Hill of Myrtles, which was popularly identified as the spot where Kyrene wrestled the lion, were all contiguous.[242]

Kyrene, then, was linked by the Hellenistic period with the group of indigenous nymphs (*chthoniai numphai*) who inhabited the Hill of Myrtles beside the spring of Apollo, or Kyra. It is probably these nymphs who are mentioned in a number of graffiti scratched inside the tunnel from which the spring emerged. The water poured out of a passageway in a small waterfall and was caught in cisterns below. The actual spring lay at the end of a 300-meter tunnel, the inner half of which served as a sanctuary of the nymphs. The inscriptions, primarily of Roman date, speak of priests of Apollo "coming in" to the nymphaion or to the nymphs. At some point, a shrine was cut in the rock directly east of the spring; this collapsed, but there remained an altar dedicated to the nymphs. In addition, there is epigraphic evidence that Apollo was worshiped in the sanctuary as Nymphagetes.[243] In general, the archaeological evidence corresponds quite closely to the picture we get from the poets: both portray an intimate relationship between Apollo, his bride, Kyrene, and the indigenous nymphs whose number she joined. A stray reference in the *Suda*, however, shows that the picture was more complicated: the nymphs and Dionysos were worshiped together at Kyrene in a festival called Theodaisia.[244] Cult links might have also existed with Artemis, whose temple stood near that of Apollo (3.2.2).

An interesting question is whether these Kyrenaic nymphs are to be identified with another plurality that inhabited the northern African coast, the Heroines of Libya. These are mentioned in other sources of Hellenistic date; Callimachus called them the "heroine mistresses [*despoinai*] of Libya, who watch over the home and the long shores of the Nasamones." The most detailed description is preserved in Apollonius of Rhodes' *Argonautica*, in which the Heroines appear to Jason as he and his fellow Argonauts wander in the desert. Here, they are the "Succoring Heroines of Libya, who once met and anointed Athena beside the waters of Triton when she had leapt resplendent from the head of her father." They appear before Jason at noon and identify themselves as "desert herders, indigenous [*chthoniai*] goddesses with human speech, succoring heroines and daughters of Libya." Jason describes them to his companions as three in number, like young maidens, and dressed in goat skins.[245]

These Heroines have several nymphlike characteristics: they attend the birth of another deity; they appear as a group of three; and their epiphany occurs at the magical hour of noon. The primary reason for identifying the companions of Kyrene in book 2 of the *Argonautica* with the Libyan Heroines of book 4 is that both are given the epithet *chthonios*, "indigenous." The language used to describe the Heroines makes them mistresses of the land in much the same way Kyrene herself is described by Pindar; furthermore they, like Kyrene, are concerned with the protection of livestock. Finally, the description of the Heroines as goatskin-clad seems to be reflected in the dress of female figures in a deposit of terra-cottas found about 300 meters from the Hill of Myrtles.[246] On the other hand, the two pluralities can be distinguished geographically, since the companions of Kyrene are native to the Hill of Myrtles, the center of the city, and the Heroines appear to Jason in the desert south of Euhesperis. The cult title of Heroines is attested from Thera and must have been bestowed by the Greek colonists. Yet, their goatskin cloaks, their concern for the lands of the Nasamones, a local tribe, and their epithet of *chthonios* point to a strong association with the native peoples.[247]

4.8.9 *Egypt*

Already in Hesiod, the Nile is named as one of the river gods who are children of Okeanos and Tethys. The Greek mythographers incorporated the Nile into their comprehensive genealogies; in Apollodorus, Io bears her son, Epaphos, beside the Nile, and Epaphos' bride is Memphis, the daughter of the river god. Their daughter in turn is Libya. Euripides' *Helen* opens with a description of the Nile as a "stream of lovely maidens" (*kalliparthenoi rhoai*).[248] In Egypt itself, of course, native belief reigned supreme well into the Hellenistic period, and it is only in the Roman period that we see evidence of the cult of the nymphs. On the other hand, the evidence points not to a superficial adoption of Greco-Roman concepts at a late period but to a process of gradual syncretism during which Egyptian and Greek beliefs were inextricably blended.

Egyptian popular religion recognized both male and female river spirits; the latter seem to have conformed to the worldwide motif of the water sprite who is alternately seductive and horrific.[249] Servius, the commentator on Vergil, speaks of a rite in which children were "given to the nymphs" by priests during the festival of the river god. When they reached adolescence and were returned to their parents, they spoke of the woods beneath the earth and the great body of water from which all earthly things had their origin.[250] This initiatory rite combined Greek lore of the nymphs (their desire for human children and their role in rites of passage) with the Egyptian theology of the Nile. In Egyptian thought, the Nile was supplied by a great subterranean ocean, the source of all creation; the sacredness of Nile water was further emphasized by the special funerary treatment given to those who drowned in its waters, which conferred immortality.

These themes are brought together in the second century C.E. monument of Isidora at Hermoupolis.[251] The tomb itself and the accompanying inscriptions combine Greco-Roman and Egyptian beliefs and tastes. Isidora's mummy rested on a couch in a funerary chamber (*thalamos*), in the decoration of which the focal point was a large, white stucco scallop shell.[252] The first epigram reads:

Ὄντως αἱ Νύμφαι σοι ἐτεκτήναντ᾽, Ἰσιδώρα,
    Νύμφαι τῶν ὑδάτων θυγατέρες, θάλαμον·
πρεσβυτάτη Νίλοιο θυγατρῶν ἤρξατο Νιλώ,
    κόγχον τευξαμένη, βένθεσιν οἷον ἔχει,
πατρὸς ἐνὶμ μεγάροισι θεηδῆ οἷον ἰδέσθαι·
    Κρηναία δε, Ὕλα σύνγαμος ἁρπαγίμου,
κείονας ἀμφοτέρωθεν ἅτε σπέος, ἧχι καὶ αὐτὴ
    πηχύνασα Ὕλαν καλποφόρον κατέχει·
κρεινάμεναι δ᾽ ἄρα χῶρον Ὀρειάδες ἱδρύσαντο
    ἱερόν, ὡς αὐτῶν μηδὲν ἀφαυρὸν ἔχης.

In truth, it was the nymphs, daughters of the water, who built the chamber for you, Isidora. Nilo, the eldest of the daughters of Nile, began by fashioning a shell such as the river holds in its depths; such one might see, a marvelous thing, in her father's palace. And Krenaia, mate of Hylas who was snatched away, built the columns on both sides, like the grotto where she herself keeps Hylas, who carried the water jar, in her arms' embrace. And the Oreiads, having chosen the spot, founded a sanctuary, that you might have nothing less than the best.

The second inscription is composed in the voice of Isidora's father:

Οὐκέτι σοι μέλλω θύειν, θύγα[τερ, μετ]ὰ κλ[α]υθμοῦ,
    ἐξ οὗ δὴ ἔγνων ὡς θεὸς ἐξεγένου.
Λοιβαῖς εὐφημεῖτε καὶ εὐχωλαῖς Ἰσιδώραν,
    ἣ νύμφη Νυμφῶν ἁρπαγίμη γέγονεν.
Χαῖρε, τέκος· Νύμφη ὄνομ᾽ ἐστί σοι, ἰδέ τε Ὧραι
    σπένδουσιν προχοαῖς ταῖς ἰδί[α]ις κατ᾽ ἔτος·
χειμὼν μὲν γάλα λευκόν, ἀλείφατον ἄνθος ἐλαίης,
    ναρκίσσωι δὲ στέφει, ἄνθει ἀβροτάτωι·
Εἶαρ δ᾽ αὐτομάτης πέμπει γόνον ἔνθα μελίσσης,
    καὶ ῥόδον ἐκ καλύκων, ἄνθος Ἔρωτι φίλον·
Καῦμα δ᾽ ἀρ᾽ ἐκ ληνοῦ Βάκχου πόμα καὶ στέφανόν σοι
    ἐκ σταφυλῆς, δῆσαν βότρυας ἀκρεμόνων.
Ταῦτά νυ σοί· τάδε πάντα ἐτήσια ἔνθα τελεῖται
    τεθμὸς ἅτ᾽ ἀθανάτοις· τούνεκα δ᾽ αὐτὸς ἐγὼ
οὐκέτι σοι μέλλω θύειν, θύγατερ, μετὰ κλαυθμοῦ.

No longer shall I come to make sacrifice with lamentation, daughter, now that I have learned that you have become a goddess. With libations and vows praise Isidora, who as a *nymphê* was snatched away by the nymphs. Greetings, child! Nymph is your name, and the

Horai pour you their own libations throughout the year. Winter brings white milk, the rich flower of the olive, and crowns you with the delicate narcissus flower. Spring sends the produce of the industrious bee and the rose from its bud, flower beloved of Eros. Summer heat brings the fruit from the vat of Bakchos and a crown of grapes for you, having tied back the clusters from the branches. These things are for you. All will be performed here annually, as is the custom for the immortals. Therefore, daughter, no longer with lamentation shall I come to make sacrifice.

The epigrams draw explicitly upon the Greek cult and folklore of the nymphs: Isidora has been taken away to join the daughters of the river, just as Hylas was snatched by the spring nymphs. Having died as a *numphê*, at the peak of her beauty, she thus remains a *numphê* forever. The offerings brought to her tomb closely resemble the offerings to nymphs in Hellenistic epigrams: milk, oil, wine, and flowers. At the same time, commentators have stressed that the epigrams for Isidora are not inconsistent with native Egyptian belief. The statement that Isidora has been taken by the nymphs, just as Hylas was, strongly suggests that she died by drowning; alternatively, it has been suggested that Isidora was one of the children "given to the nymphs" at the festival of the Nile. Moreover, Nilo, the eldest daughter of Nile, who builds Isidora's tomb, might have Egyptian counterparts. Daughters of the Nile god Hâpi and other plural goddesses associated with the Nile are attested in texts as early as the Pharaonic period.[253]

Though the cult of the nymphs was not especially prominent in Hellenized Egypt, where it did exist, it followed familiar patterns. An inscription from Ptolemaïs declares that Pan and the nymphs aided Isidoros in the discovery of a quarry.[254] The nymphs of Nysa also appeared as part of the celebration of Dionysos in the Grand Procession of Ptolemy Philadelphos (3.1.1).

4.9 Asia Minor, Associated Islands, and Syria

4.9.1 *Troad and Bithynia*

The Troad is the northwest corner of Asia Minor, dominated by the Ide massif, from which flow the rivers Skamandros, Satnioeis, Simoeis, Granikos, and others. "Many-fountained" Ide was a mountain sacred to both Zeus and the Great Mother, and its nymphs play an important role in the epic tradition. These are the nymphs whom Aphrodite designates as the guardians of her son Aineias: "But him, as soon as he sees the light of the sun, the deep-breasted mountain nymphs shall rear, those who inhabit this great and holy mountain." And in the *Cypria*, Aphrodite is described as adorning herself with flower garlands on Mount Ide in the company of the Charites and nymphs, probably in preparation for the Judgment of Paris. Ide is imagined as a place of crystal fountains and lovely spring flowers, where the goddesses bathe before their competition in the waters provided by the nymphs.[255] This concept of the nymphs as attendants upon the great goddesses, with special regard to the provision of springs, is similar to the outlook in Sicily and Magna Graecia.

The royal herdsman is a mythic figure characteristic of the Troad and the Ide range. Stinton has examined the tension between Paris' dual identities as herdsman and prince; this same duality is present throughout the entire royal genealogy.[256] Anchises (2.5.2) and Ganymedes are herdsmen, Aineias meets Achilles as he is herding cattle on Ide, and so on. Indeed, Homer personifies this combination in Priam's half brother, Boukolion, born of a nymph (1.4.1). Among the Trojan allies, we find the same pattern of a heroic son born to the herdsman Enops and a nymph.[257] These tales of illicit love are sternly excluded from the formal genealogy of the royal family, which Homer places in the mouth of Aineias. Here, neither the nymphs nor any other female progenitors are mentioned. The male line is traced from Dardanos through the three sons of Tros: Ilos, Assarakos, and Ganymedes. Ilos begat Laomedon, the father of Priam, and Assarakos begat Kapys, the father of Anchises and grandfather of Aineias. Boukolion, presumably because of his illegitimate status, is not mentioned, though Laomedon's five other sons are. The nymphs, here conspicuously absent, appear instead in the "pathetic genealogies" of individual heroes as each meets his fate. This separation perhaps suggests a popular as opposed to an aristocratic source for the nymph material, as do the anonymity of the nymph who visits Enops and the universality of the name Boukolion.[258]

The pattern of bucolic unions with nymphs recorded by Homer is applied only to the Trojans and their allies, not to the Greeks. Of course, many Greek mythic genealogies included nymphs, but among these the characteristic liaison with a solitary herdsman is usually absent. Instead, they tend to involve the abduction of a nymph by Poseidon, Apollo, or Zeus. The myth of the hero Dardanos, who is supposed to have arrived at Troy from either the Peloponnese or Samothrace, follows this pattern: he is the son of the Pleiad Elektra and Zeus. The herdsman–nymph pattern, characteristic of the Troad, seems to be a piece of local lore that was incorporated into the epic.[259] It recurs in Sicily in the myth of Daphnis, though he is not a royal herdsman as the Trojan heroes are.

The gaps left by Homer in the genealogy were filled in at least as early as the fifth-century historian Hellanicus, probably through a combination of local sources and extrapolation from what Homer does say. The prominence of nymphs in the resulting Trojan genealogy is unparalleled in Greek myth. Hellanicus and other compilers of genealogies caused the Trojan royal line to be intimately connected with the local rivers through their daughters, the naiad nymphs. The rivers Simoeis, Granikos, and Skamandros have their sources in the range of Ide, and the earliest mother of the race is thus an

Idaian nymph who unites with Skamandros to produce the first king, Teukros.[260] In every generation except that of the immigrant Dardanos, who marries Teukros' daughter Bateia, one of the royal princes marries or has intercourse with a nymph.

The most detailed source for the Trojan genealogy is Apollodorus, who draws on Hellanicus' lost *Troica*. In his account, Dardanos' son Erichthonios marries Astyoche, daughter of the river Simoeis;[261] their son, Tros, marries Kallirhoë, daughter of Skamandros;[262] their son, Assarakos, marries Hieromneme, daughter of Simoeis; and their descendants include Anchises and Aineias. Assarakos' brother is Ilos, the founder of Troy; Ilos' son is Laomedon, whose wife is usually said to be Strymo, daugher of Skamandros.[263] Laomedon has five legitimate sons, including Priam, and three daughters. His illicit union with the nymph Kalybe produces Boukolion, who himself sires twin sons with the naiad Abarbareë, as we have seen. According to Ovid, Priam repeated the act of Laomedon, secretly fathering a son, Aisakos, with Alexirhoë, daughter of the river Granikos, though other sources give a mortal Arisbe as Aisakos' mother. Aisakos, in turn, loved a daughter of the river Kebren: Hesperia or Asterope. His pursuit of her ended disastrously when she was bitten by a serpent and died, much like Eurydike in the better-known Vergilian tale of her pursuit by Aristaios. In his grief, Aisakos was then metamorphosed into a bird.[264] The parentage of Hekabe, Priam's queen, was much disputed. According to Pherecydes, Hekabe was descended from the river Sangarios and a naiad nymph, Euagora, and her parents were Dymas and the nymph Eunoë. Homer, typically neglecting to mention the mother, merely says she was a daughter of Dymas, who dwelt by the Sangarios River.[265]

To what extent these mythic genealogies were related to cult is a difficult question. Late sources give a few hints that there were correspondences, but we cannot determine whether they were present at an early period. For example, a class of nymphs called Abarbareai, clearly related to Boukolion's nymph consort, is attested, and coins of the town Skamandreia show the head of the nymph Ide, wreathed with fir.[266]

Further examples of the localization of the herdsman–nymph pattern on Ide are the myth of Paris and Oinone (2.5.2) and the tradition surrounding the birth of the Sibyl Herophile at Marpessos in the Troad. According to Pausanias, one of the oracles traditionally attributed to her stated that her mother was a nymph of Ide and her father a mortal. At Alexandria Troas, her tomb was located beside a spring in the grove of Sminthian Apollo; the spot was simultaneously a shrine of the nymphs and Hermes, whose statues stood beside the grave. At Erythrai in Ionia, they disputed the Marpessans' account, saying that Herophile was born in a cave on Mount Korykos to a nymph and a local shepherd called Theodoros.[267]

Just as the myth of erotic union between herdsman and nymph is prominent in the Troad, the related motif of a man's erotic abduction by the nymphs is specific to Mysia-Bithynia, the coastal region east of the Troad and home of the myths of Hylas and Bormos. For complex historical reasons, the name of the town Astakos, which was near the site of Hylas' abduction, came to be associated with the local nymphs.[268] Thus, Callimachus uses the epithet Astakides to describe a Kretan herdsman who, like Hylas, was abducted by the nymphs (2.3.1).

We find further testimony to the special connotations of the name Astakos in books 15 and 16 of the *Dionysiaca*, where Nonnus gives a baroque account of the nymph Nikaia, eponym of the Bithynian city. Nikaia is one of a group of nymphs called Astakides. She is loved by the oxherd Hymnos but spurns his advances, devoting herself to chastity and the hunt. When Nikaia, having scornfully compared Hymnos to Daphnis, shoots an arrow into his throat, the dead oxherd is mourned by the local nymphs, including "the naiad Abarbareë, not yet having come to Boukolion's pallet." Nonnus demonstrates an awareness of the ways in which local traditions about herdsmen and nymphs, beginning with Homer, were absorbed into the pastoral genre. In book 16, Nikaia becomes the unwilling beloved of Dionysos, who intoxicates and violates her after changing her water source into wine.[269]

Plentiful mention of local nymphs in Mysia and Bithynia is to be found in other postclassical sources. The hero Astakos was described as the son of a local nymph in Arrian's *Bithyniaca*, and the nymph Arganthone is named as the mother of the eponymous heroes Mysos and Thynos.[270] In addition to the account of Hylas' abduction, Apollonius of Rhodes' epic of the Argonauts' journey incorporates many local nymphs, often imbuing their myths with the pastoral associations so characteristic of the region: Kleite, the wife of Kyzikos, is mourned by the woodland nymphs; Amykos, the king of the Bebrykes, is (like Astakos) the son of Poseidon and a Bithynian nymph; the father of Paraibios offends a Thynian nymph by cutting her tree; Dipsakos, a local herdsman-hero whose tomb the Argonauts pass by, is the son of an unnamed meadow nymph and the river Phyllis.[271]

The cult of the nymphs, primarily focused upon healing waters, is well attested in the region only for the Hellenistic period and later. North of the Arganthonios range at Pythia Therma was found a series of reliefs that depict Herakles and the nymphs, with dedications to them. These votives are stele-shaped, with three draped, dancing nymphs in the lower register and Herakles in the upper. They date from the late Hellenistic and early Imperial periods. The cult association of Herakles with the nymphs is due, as usual, to their common interest in thermal springs.[272] Pythia Therma was a healing establishment, and on one of the reliefs, Asklepios stands beside an altar to the left of Herakles. According to the second-century C.E. sophist Aelius Aristides, who spent a great deal of time at the healing shrines of Mysia, Herakles gave his name to springs and was placed in charge of them along with the nymphs. Another spa was at Prousa near the Asian Mount Olympos. An anonymous epigram on a fountain declares its healing virtues: "I yield to the nymphs of Prousa, and hail to the Pythiades [nymphs of Pythia Therma], my superiors. But let all naiads after Pythia and Prousa give way to my nymphs." The cult of the Pythiades was transmogrified in Christian times into a legend of three virgins, Menodora, Metrodora, and Nymphodora, who were martyred under Galerius. Doubtless, these saints presided over the healing operations at the thermal baths.[273]

4.9.2 Aiolis and Lesbos

Immediately south of the Troad is the area colonized by the Aiolian Greeks, which for our purposes will be defined as the coastal area south to Kyme and the Hermos River, along with the island of Lesbos. The fifth- and fourth-century coins of Mytilene, the chief city of Lesbos, are often adorned with the head of an eponymous nymph; the same is true for the Lesbian town of Pyrrha.[274] Issa is attested as an early name of Lesbos, and Issa, a nymph and/or daughter of the primordial king Makar, is said to have born a son with Apollo, who appeared to her in the guise of a shepherd, and another son, the seer Prylis, with Hermes Kadmilos. Local nymphs called Ennesiades, "nymphs of the island," are attested, and Longus' romance of Daphnis and Chloë, though late, gives further evidence for a Lesbian cult of the nymphs (1.4.5).[275]

Of the mainland Aiolian cities, a nymph eponym is recorded only for Pitane; Kyme and Myrina were thought to be named for Amazons. The latter city is famous for the large numbers of Hellenistic terra-cottas taken from its necropolis. Among these is a unique grave gift, a model nymph grotto (figure 4.12). It stands upon a base decorated with rosettes and bucrania; above this rises the cave opening, perfectly symmetrical but molded to give the appearance of rustic, unworked stone. Within the grotto are three dancing nymphs; a mask of Pan or a satyr appears behind them, while Erotes are placed to each side. The closest parallel for this grotto is to be found in the model nymphaia from Lokroi Epizephyroi, also of Hellenistic date (5.1.12).[276] Yet, they are quite different in that they appear to have been made specifically as dedications for the Caruso cave shrine, while the Myrina piece was taken from a tomb. This find spot need not imply a funerary significance for the iconography. Whether purchased as personal possessions or as grave gifts, the terra-cottas from the Myrina tombs reflect the taste and religious sensibilities of their occupants during their lifetimes. The Myrina grotto was probably a devotional object that served its owner as a domestic shrine of the nymphs.

The Hellenistic capital Pergamon, in the valley of the Kaikos, was famed among other things for its Asklepieion, where the nymphs were worshiped in conjunction with the healing god, according to Aelius Aristides, the connoisseur of healing shrines. A Pergamene law provides for punishment of those who water animals or wash clothing in the public fountains, with half of the proceeds from fines going toward the upkeep of the sanctuary (hieron) of the nymphs, but it is unclear whether the sanctuary in question was part of the Asklepieion. Finally, other votive fragments have been found at

Figure 4.12 Terra-cotta grotto model from tomb at Myrina. Photo by M. and P. Chuzeville. Louvre Museum.

Pergamon, including a statue base with dedications to Hermes and the nymphs, and two votive reliefs to the nymphs in the neo-Attic style, one from the area of the Asklepieion.[277]

4.9.3 Ionian Cities and Lydia

The great peninsula between the Hermos and Kayster rivers, along with the islands Chios and Samos, was the home of the twelve cities of the Ionian league. According to the tragic poet Ion of Chios, Poseidon came to the island when it was still uninhabited and had intercourse with a nymph. While she was in labor, snow fell on the island, so Poseidon named his son Chios. This hero (or Poseidon) then sired with another local nymph the sons Agelos and Melas. Another early king of Chios was Oinopion, who is supposed to have married a nymph, Helike. Archaeological evidence for the cult of the nymphs on Chios is scanty, but it is attested by an inscription on a boundary stone of uncertain date.[278]

Among the mainland cities, Aelius Aristides mentions choruses of the nymphs in conjunction with the Muses at Smyrna; the city also yielded a votive relief of the round dance of Hermes and the nymphs.[279] Erythrai, as we have noted, disputed the claim of Marpessos near Mount Ide to be the birthplace of the Sibyl Herophile. At the Sibyl's Erythraian shrine, which took the form of a grotto with a spring, she was worshiped in conjunction with her mother, a naiad nymph who is called *presbugenês*, "eldest born," and with Demeter Thesmophoros.[280] The dedicatory inscriptions from this shrine date to the second century C.E., but considering the antiquity of the rivalry between the cities, it is likely that the cult is much older. The identification of the Sibyl's mother as a nymph at both Marpessos and Erythrai illustrates the close association of the nymphs with divination and prophecy (1.3).

A recent find from Ephesos, on a spot near the temple of Domitian, is of particular interest. A block, carved in relief on three sides and slightly over a meter long, depicts a total of forty-three small figures in two registers (of the two small faces, one shows a rider and the other a reclining couple). In the upper left corner of the top register, three female figures labeled NYMPHAI stand within a grotto; above the grotto float three disembodied heads, probably to be identified by the inscription HORAI. There follows a large number of unidentifiable figures (one, probably Artemis/Hekate, is labeled PHOSPHOROS), but the general theme seems to be a gathering of the gods for a banquet. Kybele and Zeus are seen enthroned, while other gods stand in male-female pairs. In the lower register, three labeled dedicants appear with a sacrificial ox. Beside them stands a female trio labeled CHARITES and other figures, including SOTERA, PANAKEA, and HYGIEA. Among the unlabeled figures, we can identify the Dioskouroi and Helen, as well as Herakles. The inscriptions date the piece to the third century, and it was probably part of a larger votive monument.[281] The relief has been aptly compared to the dedication of Adamas in the quarry at Paros (4.8.1). Both compositions squeeze in a maximum number of divine figures, including Olympian gods, but both focus in particular on the assisting deities, those whom the dedicators perceive to be the most accessible and likely to answer their personal petitions. The three dedicators of this block, all male, seem to have felt that female triads, such as the nymphs, Charites, and Horai, and the female associates of Asklepios (Hygieia and Panakea) belonged to this category.

Mount Sipylos is famous as the setting of the myths of Tantalos and Niobe but was also a home of the nymphs. In the last book of the *Iliad*, Achilles tells of the Acheloios River of Sipylos, where the nymphs have their beds and dancing grounds (1.4.1). The scholiast identifies Homer's Acheloios with the Achelesios River between Sipylos and Smyrna, which the epic poet Panyassis mentions. Herakles fell ill and was cured by the warm springs of the rivers Hyllos and Achelesios; nymphs called Acheletides also figured in the story. Herakles thus named two of his sons Hyllos and Acheles.[282]

Nymphs appear in Lydian royal and heroic genealogies. In the *Iliad*, we learn that the Lydian hero Iphition, slain by Achilles, was "born to Otrynteus, sacker of cities, and a naiad nymph, beneath the snow of Tmolos in the rich land of Hyde." Under the epithet of Karios, Zeus was a principal god of the region around Mount Tmolos, the territory of the Torrhebian ethnic group. Zeus and the nymph Torrhebia were the parents of Karios, the eponym of the Karians. The line then continues with the kings Manes, Atys, and Torrhebos.[283]

Lydia was celebrated for its contributions to Greek music. A myth about king Torrhebos, attributable to the fifth-century historian Xanthus of Lydia, gives us some idea of the role the nymphs played in the Hellenized culture of the peoples there. One day, Torrhebos was wandering beside a lake, when he heard the voices of the nymphs "whom the Lydians also call Muses" and so learned music and himself taught it to the Lydians. Therefore, certain melodies were called Torrhebian (as was the lake where the encounter took place). Other sources say that Toroibos [*sic*], king of the Lydians, added a fifth string to the lyre, and they confirm that the Lydians called the Muses nymphs.[284] We have already noted the overlapping of Muse and nymph in Thrace, and a similar phenomenon will be observed farther south in the Lykian-Pamphylian district.

Nymphs played a significant role in the legends that surround the early history of Samos. A genealogy followed by later authors was provided by the seventh- or sixth-century epic poet Asius of Samos. He recorded that the first king of the island was Ankaios, son of Poseidon, who ruled over the Leleges, a pre-Hellenic people who are sometimes identified with the Karians. Ankaios, famed as a member of the Argonauts, married Samia, the daughter of the river Maiandros. Samos was an early center of Hera's cult, and the alternative names Parthenia, "Maiden's Isle," for the island and Parthenios for the river Imbrasos are tied to the myth that Hera's first intercourse with Zeus occurred here. According to a local historian, Greek presence on the island began with Admete, the priestess of Argive Hera, who came to administer the Samian sanctuary, already founded by "Leleges and nymphs." This legend is perhaps echoed in Anacreon's description of Samos as "city of the nymphs," though the designation might also refer to the construction of the famous Samian aqueduct.[285]

The most important topographical features of Samos, from a mythographic point of view, were the river Imbrasos and Chesias, either a promontory on the coast or perhaps a peak of Mount Kerketes. Nicander's poem on poisons and antidotes recommends the use of "Parthenian earth . . . the snow-white earth of the Imbrasos which a horned lamb first revealed to the Chesiad nymphs beneath the rush-grown riverbanks of snow-capped Kerketes." The same combination of river and peak recurs in a Hellenistic fragment, which says that the Imbrasos River and Chesias produced the nymph Okyrhoë, upon whom the Horai bestowed infinite beauty. Apollo attempted to abduct her, but she entreated the help of a man, Pompilos, to ferry her across the channel to Miletos during a festival of Artemis. Apollo finally seized her and turned Pompilos into a fish. The widely diffused cult of Apollo Nymphagetes is also attested on Samos.[286]

Immediately opposite Samos was the promontory of Mykale, and Callimachus speaks of the Mykalessides, the "neighbor nymphs of Ankaios." A fourth-century ritual law from Thebes at Mykale shows that these nymphs were the object of a cult. Established to regulate tithes by herdsmen who pastured their flocks on lands owned by a sanctuary, the law stipulates offerings, including cheeses, on specific days of the month for Mykale, the nymphs, the Maiandros River, and Hermes Ktenites. In addition, the shepherds and goatherds are required to swear by these gods as to the number of their flocks, and tithe individual animals accordingly. As is often the case, the nymphs are patrons of pastoralism and associated with a non-elite segment of society; the carefully organized tithing schedule, however, indicates that an unusually large amount of resources was being placed at the disposal of the nymphs' sanctuary. The deity Mykale is probably identified with a specific spring, perhaps a tributary of the Maiandros, which debouched south of the promontory.[287] The nymphs of Mykale are linked geographically and in cult with Maiandros, just as the nymph Samia, wife of Ankaios, is the river's daughter.

Also from Mykale, a century or so after the cult inscription, is a votive relief that displays considerable charm despite its crude carving (figure 4.13). Within a cave frame are two female figures; the one on the left, naked, kneels beside a washbasin. On the right, a draped nymph, seated on a rocky outcropping, pours water into the basin from a jug. High up in the rocks, a tiny head of Pan peers lasciviously down at the pair of nymphs. The bathing nymph as a votive type must have become conventional in Asia Minor, for it is also found on a votive of the early Imperial period from Tralleis. This shows a naked nymph kneeling with small basin before a herm statue of Pan, and the inscription records a dedication to the nymphs and Pan in accordance with a dream, *kat' oniron*.[288]

Important examples of archaic devotion to the nymphs are the sixth-century inscribed votive sculptures of female figures from the area of Miletos. The first, a fragmentary kore preserving a dedication to the nymphs by the son of Mandris, has often been assigned to Samos (figure 4.14). The second, a seated figure inscribed to the nymphs from the son of Euagoras, was found on the Sacred Way, which passes from Miletos to Didyma.[289] It seems to have belonged to a sanctuary to the nymphs situated on the Stephania hill, where a spring and the remnants of buildings were found in addition to the statue. Use of the sanctuary is attested in an inscription that describes the activities

Figure 4.13 Relief from Mykale: two nymphs bathing while Pan looks on. Staatliche Museen zu Berlin, Preussischer Kulturbesitz, Antikensammlung.

of the Molpoi, religious and civic officials of Miletos who specialized in ritual song. They passed in an annual procession along the Sacred Way, stopping at designated spots to sing the paian for various deities, including Hekate, Dynamis (Power), the nymphs, and Hermes. The inscription stipulates that the paian is to be sung "at the meadow on the hill by the nymphs," apparently the very hill where the seated figure was discovered. The extant copy of the inscription dates to the late Hellenistic period, but scholars have determined that most of its content pre-dates 450.[290]

These early, relatively large-scale examples of Greek votive sculpture show that, as at Mykale, significant resources could be invested in the cult of the nymphs. This phenomenon is quite different from the contemporary state of the cult in mainland Greece, where it appears to have been the province of the poor, agrarian population, or at least not to have inspired the presentation of durable or valuable dedications. Again, since the ritual procession seems to have enjoyed its heyday during the archaic period, the time when our statue was dedicated, it follows that state sponsorship of a nymph cult was in effect at an earlier period in Miletos than in Attica. Although individual seated figures of nymphs are elsewhere attested in the archaic period, for example, from Megara and perhaps Vari, no special meaning should be detected in the seated pose of the Milesian figure, because the type was used extensively for dedications there.

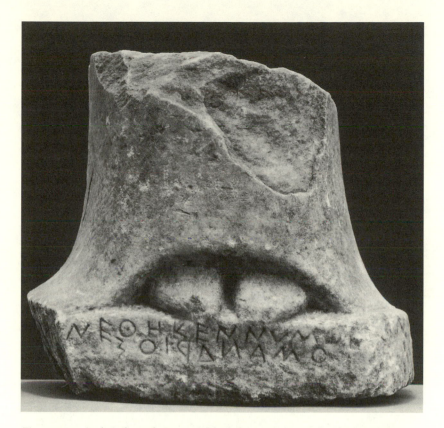

Figure 4.14 Archaic kore fragment with dedication to nymphs, from Miletos. Staatliche Museen zu Berlin, Preussischer Kulturbesitz, Antikensammlung.

A similar caveat applies to a marble votive relief from Miletos, which depicts two frontal standing figures in the style of contemporary east Greek korai (figure 4.15). Dressed in Ionic chitons, each holding her skirt with the right hand and a small object before her chest in the left, they stand within a simple naiskos frame. The inscription reads, "Sames dedicated me to the nymphs," and the piece dates to the mid–sixth century. Several other examples of this votive type are known, including one with only a single female figure. It is unlikely, however, that all are votives to the nymphs. As with other types of archaic votive sculpture, including korai, the same category of object could be dedicated to a variety of deities as needed.[291]

The Milesians claimed that their eponymous hero, a son of Apollo, came from Krete. He married a native, either the daughter of the local king or a nymph, Kyaneë, daughter of the Maiandros River. The offspring of this union were the twins Kaunos and Byblis, tortured by an incestuous love for one another. In the various versions of the tale, Byblis attempts suicide by hang-

Figure 4.15 Archaic votive relief with two female figures, from Miletos. Staatliche Museen zu Berlin, Preussischer Kulturbesitz, Antikensammlung.

ing herself or throwing herself from a rock, but the nymphs take pity on her. In Nicander's version, she is transformed into a hamadryad, while Ovid says that the Lelegian nymphs gave her unlimited tears, which formed a fountain. Most versions agree that a fountain or stream in the area of Miletos was known as the Tears of Byblis. As for Kaunos, Conon relates that, after Byblis' death, he married a prophetic naiad nymph appropriately named Pronoë ("Foresight"), who rose out of the river as he was wandering on the Lykian borderlands. Their son, Aigialos, built the city Kaunos and named it for his father.[292]

4.9.4 Dorian Hexapolis and Karia

South of the Maiandros was the territory of the Karians, a people who appear as Trojan allies in the *Iliad*, and of Dorian Greek colonists, who occupied the coast and islands. The Dorian hexapolis was composed of Knidos, Halikarnassos, Kos, and the three cities of Rhodes; its members met at a periodic festival of Triopian Apollo in Knidos.

The prominence of the cult of the nymphs on Kos was due to several factors, the most obvious being the presence of the sanctuary of Asklepios, in conjunction with the famous Hippokratic school of medicine. A fourth-century inscription from the Asklepieion is intended to safeguard the purity of the water:

Φίλιστος Αἰσχίνα εἶπε· ὅσσα
κα θύωντι ἐν τῶι ἱερῷ τοῦ Ἀσ-
κλαπιοῦ ταῖς Νύμφαις θυόν-
τω ἐπὶ τῶν βωμῶν, εἰς δὲ τὰς
κράνας τὰς ἐν τῶι ἱερῶι μὴ ἐξέ-
στω μηθενὶ πέμμα μηθὲν ἐνβάλ-
λειν μηδὲ ἄλλο μηθέν· εἰ δέ τις
κα ἐνβάληι, καθαράτω τὸ ἱερον
τᾶν Νυμφᾶν ὡς νομίζεται. (*LSCG* no. 152)

Philistos, son of Aischines, said, Whoever sacrifices in the sanctuary of Asklepios to the nymphs, let him sacrifice on the altars, but nobody is to throw either a cake or anything else whatsoever into the springs in the sanctuary. If anyone does throw something in, he must purify the sanctuary of the nymphs as is customary.

Philistos discourages practices that were otherwise common in the cult of the nymphs, particularly in rural shrines: the use of cheap sacrificial cakes in preference to more expensive blood sacrifices and the tossing of offerings into springs.[293] The votives in the Koan nymph cave of Aspripetra (5.1.11) included a head of Asklepios, which indicates that the association of the nymphs with the god was also made outside of the Asklepieion itself.

As at Thera, sacrifices for the nymphs in connection with the Dorian tribe of the Dymanes are attested for the Hellenistic period. A list records the cult officials who "sacrificed the victims according to tradition for the nymphs and welcomed worthily the tribesmen of the goddesses." Paton and Hicks speculate that the nymphs were so honored because the tutelary god of the Dymanes was Apollo. Another Hellenistic inscription, a sacrificial calendar, prescribes offerings for Apollo and the nymphs, though it is unknown on whose behalf the sacrifices were made.[294]

Theocritus' seventh *Idyll*, set on Kos, describes a visit to the agricultural district of Haleis for a festival of Demeter. Near her altar is a cave of the nymphs with a spring issuing forth, surrounded by aspens and elms. An archaic sanctuary of Demeter and Kore on the northern outskirts of the town had a spring as its focal point, so it is possible that Theocritus' association of the goddess and the nymphs represents an ancient local tradition.[295]

The Koan cult of the Charites is of particular interest because their iconography is almost indistinguishable from that of the nymphs. Two reliefs from Mesaria, perhaps the site of a rural shrine to the Charites, date respectively to the early fourth and the third centuries. The earlier depicts three maidens dancing behind a carefully carved altar; a half-size worshiper greets them with upraised arm, while a small head of Pan peers down from the upper left corner. The relief bears a close resemblance to the Archandros relief, the earliest Attic nymph relief, and is clearly based on Attic prototypes, though the usual rustic stone altar of the nymphs is replaced by a carefully finished one. The inscription shows that it was dedicated to "the fair-haired Charites." The later relief owes far less to Attic iconography. Within an architectural frame, four frontal figures are preserved. The two on the left stand in relaxed poses while the head of Pan looks on overhead; the two on the right dance as one of them plays the *krotala*. The relief is broken on the right side, possibly indicating that a third dancer was part of the original composition. A small cave, which originally would have been in a central position, is depicted in front of the first dancer. Within this grotto reclines a tiny male figure. The inscription indicates that the relief was dedicated to the Charites by Daikrates. It is possible that Daikrates himself is the tiny figure within the cave and that the scene represents a dream vision. The iconography, however, recalls vases from the Attic cave of Vari and similar terra-cottas, which show a child in a grotto—undoubtedly, the infant Dionysos. The Charites were normally worshiped as pluralities of two or three; hence it seems likely that this relief shows the Charites (the two standing figures) together with a triad of dancing nymphs.[296]

Rhodes, which had seen both Minoan and Mycenaean colonization before the arrival of the Dorians during the Dark Age, possessed a rich store of traditions about the island's ancient history. Diodorus Siculus recounts several of these myths, drawing upon Zenon of Rhodes' Hellenistic history. In the first stage, the island was occupied by the magical race of the Telchines, inventors of metalworking, who produced miraculous statues and controlled the weather. The Telchines, children of the sea (Thalatta), supposedly nurtured the infant Poseidon with the help of Kapheira, daughter of Okeanos. Kapheira is related to Kabeiro, the daughter of Proteus who played an important role in Lemnian genealogies of the metalworking Kabeiroi (4.7.4). Several ancient cult statues on Rhodes were called Telchinian in reference to their manufacture by the Telchines; these included a Hera and a group of nymphs at Ialysos. Zeus' three sons with a nymph, Himalia, enter the saga at this point: Spartaios, Kronios, and Kytos, born "at the time of the giants."[297] The Telchines foresaw the Great Flood and left Rhodes forever, but the sons of Zeus survived the Flood by fleeing to the upper parts of the island.

The Flood myth is also associated with the first arrival of Helios, the patron god of Rhodes. Becoming enamored of Rhodos, the daughter of Poseidon and the Telchines' sister Halia-Leukothea, Helios dried up the waters of the Flood, and his seven sons with Rhodos, the Heliadai, took possession of the island. Pindar, our oldest source for the Rhodian myths, ignores the Telchines and makes the history of the island begin with the love affair of Helios and Rhodos, an eponymous nymph. Helios is absent when the lands of the earth are apportioned among the gods, but he claims as his own the island nymph Rhodos, which has newly risen from the sea. Pindar calls her "child of Aphrodite, Rhodos of the sea" and says she bore the seven Heliadai, who carried out the first sacrifice to Athena on the island but forgot to bring fire. One of the Heliadai fathered the eponymous heroes of the three principal Rhodian cities: Ialysos, Kameiros, and Lindos. Pindar's version is in accord with the rest of Diodorus' account, which also tells of the fireless sacrifice and the seven Heliadai. Of these, Ochimos married a local nymph, Hegetoria, and their daughter, Kydippe or Kyrbia, married her uncle Kerkaphos and bore the three city founders.[298]

When Ialysos, Kameiros, and Lindos combined about 408 to form one city called Rhodes, the emblem of the rose (*rhodon*) was chosen for the coins. While best known for their magnificent facing heads of Helios, some of the coins also show the head of the nymph Rhodos. On the akropolis of Rhodes, a spring cave has been identified as a cave of the nymphs and Pan because of its numerous votive niches. Rhodes was a prolific producer of neo–Attic style votive reliefs to the nymphs in the second and first centuries; two examples come from the akropolis of Lindos. Finally, Hesychius records the existence of Makrobioi, "long-lived nymphs" at Rhodes, and a late metrical inscription from Loryma near Lindos was dedicated at a sanctuary of Helios and the nymphs.[299]

From Halikarnassos comes an interesting inscribed votive relief of the second century. On it, Hermes leads a group of three mantled nymphs to the left, where a bull-shaped Acheloös stands, his hindparts hidden by the architectural frame. The scene recalls Attic votive reliefs of two centuries earlier. The inscription states that Apelles of Myndos, son of Apollonios, servant (*hypourgos*) of the gods, dedicated the naiad nymphs Periklymene, Naiousa, and Panope; Acheloös; and Hermes to the Anakes. Thus, a representation of the rustic gods is dedicated as a gift to other gods, the Anakes, or Lords. Their identity is unclear, though the Dioskouroi were often called Anakes.[300]

In the area of Knidos, the Dorians of the hexapolis (later the pentapolis, when Halikarnassos was excluded) held their games at the Triopion, the promontory where the temple of Apollo was located. Only Dorians of the member cities were permitted to participate, and the games were held in honor of Apollo, Poseidon, and the nymphs.[301] Myths of tree nymphs are associated with Knidos; both Triopas, cutter of Demeter's grove, and Rhoikos, who saved a nymph's tree, were Knidians (2.4.1–2).

Excavations at Knidos in the area of the circular temple of Aphrodite Euploia uncovered the so-called Altar of the Nymphs, a monumental structure comparable to the famous Pergamene altar but on a smaller scale and lacking a colonnade. The foundations of the altar and several blocks from its frieze are preserved. One of the blocks shows Hermes standing in front of a chariot; the word NYMPHAI is inscribed above his head. Another is a landscape that shows a half-nude male figure at the feet of a draped female, who reclines on the rocks above; a tree is carved behind her. Under the male figure, the name INOPOS is carved. A third block is sculpted on three sides: two of the faces depict a single draped female, while the third shows a female figure standing beside an enthroned female deity. Two other blocks were discovered, each with triads of females. One of the latter is inscribed "Theon of Antioch made the three figures [zôdia]." Theon's signature dates the altar to the second century. It is tempting to associate this altar with the cult of Aphrodite and to identify the female triads as the nymphs, Charites, and Horai, the groups who traditionally acted as attendants upon Aphrodite, bathing and dressing her. Inopos could be the river god of Delos (4.8.3) or, more likely, a homonymous local river.[302]

4.9.5 Sporades

Moving to the smaller islands off the coast of Karia, we find that a statue base from Astypalaia bears a metrical inscription mentioning the sanctuary of Pan (theos nomios) and the Nymphai Meilichiai. The epithet Meilichios, "kindly, gentle," is applied to various gods, especially Zeus in his chthonic, snake form. It is propitiatory, helping to ward off a god's possible anger, while simultaneously announcing the same deity's power to provide good things. At Athens, we have seen Zeus Meilichios associated in cult with the nymphs (4.2.1); here, the nymphs themselves have his epithet and presumably carry out a similar function of dispensing wealth and health.[303]

From Karpathos is reported an unusual relief that depicts six figures dancing to the left with clasped hands. The leader is a male wearing a short tunic and cloak; he leads five chiton- and himation-clad women. Beaudouin interprets the scene as Hermes leading five nymphs. We cannot be certain whether he is correct, since the relief apparently offered no other clues to its iconography, such as a mask of Acheloös; it was also badly damaged.[304]

At Kasos, on the eastern shore facing Karpathos, were a number of rupestral inscriptions, several of which were effaced by the island's inhabitants in the nineteenth century. The surviving inscriptions seem to be dedications worded as greetings to the gods. One, by a man named Eudemos, addresses the gods in general, and the other greets the nymphs using two different spellings (Chairete nunphai and Chairete numphai).[305]

4.9.6 Lykia and Hinterlands

While Lykia, unlike its neighbor districts of Karia, Lydia, and Mysia, remained outside the early parameters of Greek colonization, it held an important position in the Greek imagination from early times. The Lykian kings Glaukos and Sarpedon are prominent in the *Iliad*, and the mythical poet Olen of Lykia is supposed to have celebrated the Lykian patron god, Apollo, in the oldest Greek hymns. Delian tradition said that Apollo spent the winter months in Lykia giving oracles and returned for the summer to Delos. The legends of Patara held that its founder had been the son of Apollo and a nymph, Lykia, daughter of the river Xanthos.[306] Another Lykian genealogy appears in the epic poet Panyassis, who recounts the line of the eponymous hero Termiles, or Tremiles: "There great Tremiles dwelled and married a daughter, an Ogygian nymph whom they call Praxidike, at the eddies beside the silvery Sibros river. Her deadly sons were fair-haired Tlos, Pinaros, and Kragos, who mightily plundered all the fields."[307] The three sons, of course, are eponyms of places in Lykia, Tlos being a city and Kragos a hill.

Both Glaukos and Sarpedon had Lykian cults, and both their bodies were magically wafted to burial places in Lykia after they were killed at Troy. Sarpedon's journey is described in the *Iliad*, while that of Glaukos is not attested until Quintus of Smyrna; yet Glaukos was counted an ancestor of the ruling Ionian families by Herodotus, and the story of his burial is likely to be ancient. According to Quintus, Apollo caused the winds to carry Glaukos to a lovely glade of high Telandros, where the nymphs made water flow from the great stone that marked his tomb, forming the river Glaukos. Robert has suggested that the Turkish toponyms for the village Nif and the river Nifçay correspond to this local legend.[308]

The most prosperous Lykian city was Xanthos, located north of Patara in the fertile valley of the Xanthos River. Here, excavations have shed light on the process of religious syncretism and the influence of Hellenic culture on the Lykians. While retaining their own language through the classical period, they showed an increasing degree of Hellenization in art and religion beginning in the sixth century. The most important sanctuary at Xanthos was that of Leto, where she was worshiped in conjunction with her children, Apollo and Artemis and, rather surprisingly, with the nymphs. In the mid–fourth century, under the satrap Pixodaros, a trilingual stele (Lykian, Greek, Aramaic) was set up at the Letoön, which detailed the introduction of new cults in the territory. It includes threats against any who might transgress the stipulations on the stele, to be carried out by the resident deities "Leto, her children, and the nymphs." Later inscriptions show that the cult continued in this form through the Hellenistic and Imperial periods. Leto appears to be the name given to the local mother goddess inherited from the Bronze Age Luwian pantheon. Interestingly, the inscription shows that the Lykian language had its own word for nymphs, *eliyâna*. The nymphs, like

Leto, had their counterpart in the old pantheon, but their functions need not have been radically different from those familiar in Greek religion. Their presence tends to support the hypothesis that the early cult at Xanthos was centered around a spring sanctuary, which the excavators traced back to the sixth century. In the late period, an elaborate nymphaion was an important part of the cult complex and contained dedications to Leto and the nymphs.[309]

The central and eastern area of Lykia, Hellenized much later than the southwest, nevertheless developed a thriving cult of the nymphs (or rather, local deities who were identified as nymphs after Hellenization). In its material manifestations, this cult is strikingly similar to, and roughly contemporary with, that at Ognyanovo and other Thracian sites (4.7.3), belonging to the first centuries of the Roman empire. Numerous votive reliefs were dedicated at small rural sanctuaries; the Lykian names of the dedicants indicate the strictly local nature of the cult.[310] The reliefs, carved in a crude local style, depict the nymphs in Muselike groups of three or nine, playing musical instruments (syrinx, aulos, tympana). In at least one case, the nymphs are *epêkooi*, "listening ones," and in another, they receive credit for curing a quartan fever; as in Thrace, the focus of the cult was on the nymphs as assisting deities, who could provide healing and help with the struggles of daily life. The epithet Trageatides appears, probably as a local designation parallel to that of the Bourdapenai at Ognyanovo, while a Tragasia is attested as the mother of Kaunos and Byblis.[311]

4.9.7 *Cyprus*

The lexicographer Hesychius mentions two classes of nymphs in Cyprus: the Endeïdes and the Peirethoi. The name of the former seems to mean "they who bind," perhaps in the sense of female entrapment; the singular nymph name Endeïs is elsewhere attested.[312] The name of the Peirethoi comes from the verb *peiraô*, "to test" or "to try one's luck." More concrete evidence of the nymphs' cult is found in a bowl inscribed with a dedication in the classical Cypriot syllabary. The provenance of the bowl is unknown, but the painted inscription reads, "Diveiphilos gave to the nymphs during the war up to twenty [of these], when Aristas and Onasilos, having like Diveiphilos profited, gave to the Tamassian twenty-two spears, [taken] from Aristokles whom Aristogenes[?] wounded."[313] Thank offerings to the nymphs in return for success in war are otherwise unattested, but it is clear that the main motivation for thanks is not that honor was preserved or lives saved. Instead, the gods are thanked for providing a profit, the spoils or ransoms that the men divided and a part of which they returned as ex-votos. Diveiphilos, unlike his colleagues, chose to make dedications to the nymphs, perhaps reflecting a personal devotion the others did not feel. Also, Diveiphilos gave the nymphs bowls rather than spears, which are reserved for the Tamassian city god. The dedication was made sometime in the fourth century, probably before the period of Cypriot kingship ended.

In Hellenistic Cyprus, the cult of the nymphs seems to have been syncretized to some degree with that of Arsinoë Philadelphos. On an altar from Chytri, she is called a naiad. On the ceramics from the Hellenistic nymph cave at Kafizin (5.1.13), the nymph is often referred to as "sister," *adelphê*, and once as *philadelphos*. Also of early Hellenistic date is a sherd from the village of Troulli with a dedication to the nymphs.[314]

4.9.8 *Syria*

Near Antioch was the celebrated grove of Daphne, where the most important deities were Apollo and the nymphs. This shrine had been founded by one of Alexander's generals, Seleukos Nikator. The Arkadian myth of Daphne was transferred wholesale to this site; here, it was said, the daughter of Ladon metamorphosed into a laurel tree, and the tree itself was proudly displayed. The river running nearby was called the Ladon. The springs here were the main water source for the city of Antioch, and the nymphs of Daphne are mentioned several times by the fourth-century C.E. orator Libanius. In a lament for the emperor Julian, he regrets that he and his companions were at Daphne, "worshiping the nymphs with dances and other delights," when the emperor's death occurred. The three goddesses of Daphne, he writes, are as at home there as Zeus is in Pisa or Poseidon at the Isthmos. Libanius' special fondness for the nymphs might have been due to his poor health, much as his predecessor Aelius Aristides had been fond of the nymphs because of the healing qualities of their baths.[315]

4.10 Sicily and Southern Italy

Whoever studies the coins of Sicily will be impressed by the frequent appearance of river gods and nymphs. The situation is analogous to that in Thessaly, where local nymphs, who might otherwise have been obscure, are prominently displayed on the coinage. Both areas began producing coins that showed nymphs in the early fifth century, but the impetus for the custom seems to have come from Sicily, and common aspects of the iconography (such as a nymph sacrificing at an altar) seem to have traveled from west to east. On the other hand, river gods appear often on Sicilian coins, both independently and in conjunction with the nymphs, but not on Thessalian ones. The difference might be due in part to the fact that Sicily was colonized late, whereas Thessaly was an ancient Greek stronghold. For the Sicilian Greeks, there had been a pressing need to establish claims upon the soil and the all-important water sources, the first priority in choosing the site of a new settlement.[316] Belief in the intimate relationship between river gods and nymphs, though its roots lie in the Greek homelands, is imbued with a new freshness and immediacy in the Sicilian (and Italian) colonies, where myriad small rivers irrigated the soil, and each city recognized its own minor river gods. For the western Greeks, the representation of nymphs and river gods was also a way of advertising the extraordinary fertility of the new lands; ears of grain, wreaths made of grainstalks, and individual grains are common motifs on the coins. Thessaly, by contrast, was dominated by the majestic Peneios and a few other major rivers. Though Thessaly too was a rich land, cities such as Larissa, Kierion, and Trikka were relatively more interested in the genealogical significance of local nymphs and less interested in their role as guarantors of fertility.

The western nymphs have, on the one hand, close ties to river gods and local topography; on the other, they seem to have been closely linked to major goddesses: Athena, Artemis, and Persephone in Sicily; Hera, Aphrodite, and Persephone in Italy. This characteristic feature of the western colonies demands further examination. The earliest evidence for the presence of the nymphs in Sicily is a group of sixth-century terra-cotta antefixes in the shape of female heads. These are to be found primarily in the southeast portion of the island, at sites such as Syracuse, Kamarina, and Akrai, though a similar group of heads comes from Himera. Mertens-Horn has interpreted these objects as the heads of nymphs, once the primary adornment of the temples of the goddesses.[317]

Scholarly consensus holds that the Sicilian nymphs were already in some sense present when the historical wave of Greek colonization began. This means either that Greek nymphs had already been introduced to the island, probably during the Mycenaean period, or that Sicily already contained a thriving cult of native spring goddesses, who were easily assimilated as nymphs upon the arrival of the Greek colonists.[318] The nymphs themselves were not traditionally worshiped in temples, but in Mertens-Horn's interpretation, they figure as protective, beneficial presences who welcomed the Olympian goddesses. The antefix is an appropriate way of expressing this relationship: the use of heads as architectural ornaments demonstrates the role of local nymphs as attendants upon the major goddesses and might also have had a protective, apotropaic purpose. (The reverse trend has also been detected, for the cults of Demeter and Kore are also to be found installed in rupestral sanctuaries with springs, where the nymphs might naturally be expected to reside.)[319] As we will see below, much of the archaeological evidence from the western colonies supports this hypothesis of cult links between the nymphs and the goddesses, especially in the cases of Persephone and Hera.

The theory also finds support in Diodorus, the first-century historian who was himself a native of Sicily. The island tradition held that the sacred inland site of Enna, abundant in flowers, was the spot where Persephone's abduction took place:[320]

μυθολογοῦσι δὲ μετὰ τῆς Κόρης τὰς τῆς ὁμοίας παρθενίας
ἠξιωμένας Ἀθηνᾶν τε καὶ Ἄρτεμιν συντρεφομένας συνάγειν μετ᾽
αὐτῆς τὰ ἄνθη καὶ κατασκευάζειν κοινῇ τῷ πατρὶ Διὶ τὸν πέπλον.
διὰ δὲ τὰς μετ᾽ ἀλλήλων διατριβάς τε καὶ ὁμιλίας ἁπάσας στέρξαι

τὴν νῆσον ταύτην μάλιστα, καὶ λαχεῖν ἑκάστην αὐτῶν χώραν, τὴν
μὲν Ἀθηνᾶν ἐν τοῖς περὶ τὸν Ἱμέραν μέρεσιν, ἐν οἷς τὰς μὲν
νύμφας χαριζομένας Ἀθηνᾷ τὰς τῶν θερμῶν ὑδάτων ἀνεῖναι
πηγὰς κατὰ τὴν Ἡρακλέους παρουσίαν, τοὺς δ᾽ ἐγχωρίους πόλιν
αὐτῇ καθιερῶσαι καὶ χώραν τὴν ὀνομαζομένην μέχρι τοῦ νῦν
Ἀθήναιον· τὴν δ᾽ Ἄρτεμιν τὴν ἐν ταῖς Συρακούσαις νῆσον λαβεῖν
παρὰ τῶν θεῶν τὴν ἀπ᾽ ἐκείνης Ὀρτυγίαν ὑπό τε τῶν χρησμῶν
καὶ τῶν ἀνθρώπων ὀνομασθεῖσαν. ὁμοίως δὲ καὶ κατὰ τὴν νῆσον
ταύτην ἀνεῖναι τὰς νύμφας ταύτας χαριζομένας τῇ Ἀρτέμιδι
μεγίστην πηγὴν τὴν ὀνομαζομένην Ἀρέθουσαν. . . . τὴν Κόρην
λαχεῖν τοὺς περὶ τὴν Ἔνναν λειμῶνας· πηγὴν δὲ μεγάλην αὐτῇ
καθιερωθῆναι ἐν τῇ Συρακοσίᾳ τὴν ὀνομαζομένην Κυάνην.
(Diod. Sic. 5.3.4–4.2)

They tell the story that both Athena and Artemis, having made the
same choice of maidenhood as Kore, were reared with her and joined
her in gathering flowers and weaving a robe for their father, Zeus.
And because of their time together and their fellowship, they all
loved this island the best, and each one received a portion of it.
Athena's district was that around Himera, where the nymphs, to
please Athena, caused springs of warm waters to appear when
Herakles visited, and the inhabitants consecrated a city to her and a
place even now called Athenaion. And from the gods Artemis
received the island named Ortygia after her by both oracles and men.
Likewise at this island the nymphs, to please Artemis, caused the great
spring called Arethousa to flow. . . . Kore took the meadows about
Enna. But a great fountain was consecrated to her in Syracuse, the
one called Kyane.

Thus, all three of the virgin goddesses were assigned springs, and their fellowship on the island sprang from their early experience in the flowery
meadows at the time of Kore's abduction. This version is closely related to
that in the Homeric *Hymn to Demeter*, in which Persephone gathered flowers
with Athena, Artemis, and a list of Okeanid nymphs whose names form a
catalogue (Hom. *Hymn Cer.* 2.418–24). This is the ancient narrative of the
maiden's abduction from a chorus of agemates. The myth takes on added
significance in the Sicilian context, where the agemates are also indigenous
deities who welcome the new goddesses by creating springs.

4.10.1 *Syracuse*

Ortygia, the small island in the harbor at Syracuse, was sacred to Artemis.
Delphi was said to have given an oracle to Archias the Corinthian, the leader
of the colonists: "A certain Ortygia lies in the misty sea above Thrinakia, where
the mouth of Alpheios bubbles, mixing with the springs of fair-flowing

Arethousa." If authentic, the oracle will have been delivered in the eighth century, when the first settlement was installed on Ortygia.[321] Arethousa is a common spring name derived from the verb *ardô*, "to water"; the name might have been bestowed on the spring by the Chalkidians, who explored Sicily at an early date and who had a famous Arethousa in their home town (4.3.2). The Alpheios River was known to dive underground and resurface farther along its course; the oracle simply takes the observable fact one step further in making Alpheios resurface in Sicily. Ortygia and Sicily thus become extensions of the mother land, and the oracle serves an important dual purpose of establishing political claims and forging affective ties between old land and new. In particular, the salient link seems to have been the one between Syracuse and the Panhellenic sanctuary of Olympia. According to a persistent legend, a cup thrown in the Alpheios at Olympia resurfaced in Ortygia, and sacrifices of oxen at Olympia discolored the waters of Arethousa.[322] The victory odes of Pindar, including the first six Olympian odes, amply demonstrate the desire of the Sicilian elites to maintain ties with the centers of Hellenic culture.

In Elis, there existed a myth of Artemis' attempted rape by Alpheios (4.4.4); at the mouth of the river was a sanctuary of Artemis Alpheiousa, and at Olympia itself she shared an altar with the river god. Thus Artemis' worship was transferred from Elis along with that of the river god. Pindar calls the Ortygian goddess "river Artemis." As for Arethousa herself, the early sources say only that Alpheios emerged in the spring by that name on Ortygia, but the myth of the nymph Arethousa's pursuit from Elis by an amorous Alpheios (so that both spring and river resurface in Sicily) is not attested until the Augustan age.[323] It is probable that an early version of the myth had Artemis herself fleeing to Sicily to escape Alpheios, who followed and emerged in the spring. The development of Arethousa's cult in Sicily then stimulated the creation of the myth that it was she, not Artemis, whom the river pursued.[324]

Early Syracusan coins show a female head within an incuse square; it is impossible to tell whether this should be taken as Artemis or Arethousa. By the early fifth century, the coins show Arethousa's head circled with dolphins, a reference to the paradox of a copious freshwater spring surrounded by the salt waters of the harbor (figure 4.16). The plentiful fish in Arethousa's spring were considered sacred and forbidden as a food source. The head of Arethousa continued to be used on coins through the fourth century, culminating in Kimon's famous facing head of Arethousa with dolphins swimming about her.[325]

Also at Syracuse was the fountain of Kyane, "Dark Blue," which was sacred to Kore. According to Diodorus, Pluton caused the fountain to gush forth as he sped beneath the earth with Kore in his chariot. At the fountain, he says, "The Syracusans hold a notable annual festival, and private individuals offer the lesser victims. But on behalf of the state they plunge bulls in the pool, since Herakles introduced this mode of sacrifice when he made the

Figure 4.16 Coin from Syracuse: head of nymph Arethousa with dolphins. Photo copyright British Museum.

circuit of the island driving the cattle of Geryon." Ovid's account makes Kyane protest the rape of Proserpina. Dis smites her pool and opens the path to the underworld there; Kyane then dissolves into tears at the violation of her pool. Both Ovid and Aelian mention the local tradition that Kyane was the wife of the river Anapos, which flows into the harbor at Syracuse. Images of a female head beside a lion's head fountain spout on Syracusan coins have been interpreted as representations of Kyane.[326]

A different side of the cult of the nymphs at Syracuse is attested by the historian Timaeus, who relates an anecdote about the tyrant Dionysios II. It was customary throughout Sicily to offer sacrifices to the nymphs from house to house, spending the night in a drunken condition around their images (*agalmata*) and dancing around the goddesses. Damokles the parasite, however, maintained that one should not bother with lifeless divinities and danced around Dionysios instead. The results of this blasphemous attempt at flattery are not recorded, but the passage does provide some interesting information about the cult. The all-night revel, with its feasting from house to house, drinking, and dancing, sounds like a night of carnival, a popular phenomenon not sponsored by the state, as the dignified sacrifices to Kyane were.[327] The use of alcohol in the festivities suggests Dionysiac cult, but the wine god is not mentioned in Timaeus' description. Finally, the cult seems to have been celebrated in the urban area, where images of the nymphs provided its focal point. Cult images of the nymphs are not widely attested, but the few clear examples belong to Sicily and Magna Graecia (5.1.12). A votive relief from Syracuse gives some idea of the images' appearance. Radically different from Attic votive reliefs, it depicts three nymphs standing in identical frontal poses, wearing *poloi* and grasping the borders of their mantles in their hands. They are flanked by two small Pans, each playing the syrinx. The relief is difficult to date but has been plausibly assigned to the late fourth or early third century.[328] The frontality of the three figures suggests that the votive sculptor was merely reproducing a group of cult images. Alternatively, since votive reliefs themselves qualify as *agalmata*, reliefs such as this one might have served as focal points for the celebrations.

The cult of the nymphs and Pan thrived in the area of the theater at Syracuse. An archaic cult, thought to have superseded that of indigenous deities, has been detected in the area of the west pylon, where there are votive niches and hollowed water basins. The nymphaion on the terrace above the theater, once highly ornamented, dates to the third century, though channels were dug at an early period to facilitate the city's use of its spring water.[329] Also from Syracuse are an altar with a fourth-century inscription to Apollo and the nymphs, and from a cave outside the city, a rupestral inscription recording the dedication to the nymphs of an altar and *trikleina*, or banqueting couches. Apparently, groups met in the cave for ritual banquets, a practice paralleled in a cave of the nymphs at Oisyme in Thrace (5.1.6).[330]

4.10.2 *Kamarina*

Pindar's fourth and fifth Olympian odes celebrate the victories of Psaumis, a wealthy citizen of Kamarina, which was located on the southern shore between Akragas and Syracuse. In *Olympian* 5 (1.4.2), the poet addresses Kamarina, the nymph of the lake beside the city, as "daughter of Okeanos." The rivers Oanos and Hipparis, as well as the goddess Athena, complete the tally of important local deities. The iconography of the fifth-century coinage of Kamarina corresponds closely to Pindar's evocation of the city's religious landscape. Athena (on earlier coins), the river god Hipparis, and Kamarina are the most prominent figures. One example displays the horned head of Hipparis over a border of waves; on the reverse, the nymph Kamarina skims over the waves on a swan, her veil billowing behind her (figure 4.17). Swan riders are not rare in ancient iconography; other attested examples are Apollo, Hyakinthos, and Aphrodite. The swan rider of Kamarina has sometimes been called Aphrodite, but the goddess had no cult at Kamarina so far as we know, and the consensus is that the image represents the local nymph.

Figure 4.17 Coin from Kamarina: nymph Kamarina on swan. Photo copyright British Museum.

She is generally shown together with Hipparis because that river flowed into her lake.[331]

4.10.3 *Mount Aitne*

The area of Mount Aitne, watered by the river Symaithos, teemed with nymphs. This was the home of the legendary Daphnis, who was raised by nymphs and, to his sorrow, loved a nymph (2.5.1). Thermal springs, here as in other parts of Sicily, were associated with nymphs. An epigram describes the healing of an old woman in the thermal waters below Aitne:

οἶκτος δὲ νύμφας εἶλεν, αἱ τ᾽ ὀρεινόμοι
Αἴτνης παρωρείησι Συμαίθου πατρός
ἔχουσι δινήεντος ὑγρὸν οἰκίον·
καὶ τῆς μὲν ἀμφίχωλον ἀρτεμὲς σκέλος
θερμὴ διεστήριζεν Αἰτναίη λιβάς,
νύμφαις δ᾽ ἔλειπε βάκτρον, αἱ δ᾽ ἐπήινεσαν
πέμπειν μιν ἀστήρικτον ἠσθεῖσαι δόσει. (Philip no. 76 = *Anth. Pal.* 6.203.5–11)

Pity seized the mountain-roaming nymphs, who inhabit the watery house of their father, eddying Symaithos, on the foothills of Aitne. The hot spring of Aitne restored the strength of her lame legs, and she left the nymphs her stick. They, rejoicing in the gift, consented to send her home without its support.[332]

A number of sources mention an eponymous nymph Aitne, the earliest being Simonides, who told how she decided the dispute between Hephaistos and Demeter for possession of the land. Hephaistos, who is, of course, closely associated with the volcano, seems to have been the victor. The local historian Silenos made Aitne, daughter of Okeanos, the mother by Hephaistos of the subterranean deities known as the Palikoi (4.10.5).[333]

The myth of Galateia also belongs to this area. Although Galateia appears as a Nereid in the catalogues of both Homer and Hesiod, her Sicilian myth was widely disseminated only as a result of a well-known poem by Philoxenus of Cythera, who wrote in the fifth century of the Kyklops Polyphemos' love for the Nereid. Some of the sources say that Philoxenus invented the story, but it seems to have been based upon a local cult. There was a shrine to Galateia near Mount Aitne, reputedly built by Polyphemos in thanks for his abundant supply of milk (*gala*); Philoxenus bypassed this pedestrian explanation of the shrine in favor of a love story.[334] Polyphemos' love is also mentioned in the Greek bucolic poets, but the most detailed version is that of Ovid, who makes the jealous Polyphemus kill Galatea's lover, Acis, the son of Faunus (Pan) and a nymph of Symaethus. Acis, crushed by a boulder, is transformed into a river.[335] Whatever the origins of the Polyphemos story, the myth of Galateia and Akis is consistent with the Sicilian pattern of amorous relationships between river and nymph (Kyane-Anapos, Segeste-Krimisos, and perhaps Kamarina-Hipparis or Selinous-Eurymedousa).

4.10.4 *Himera and Messana*

Himera and Messana, unlike Dorian Gela, Syracuse, and Kamarina, were Chalkidic colonies. Their nymph lore and iconography are quite in keeping with those in the south of the island but show particular affinities with the west as well. Himera was noted for its thermal baths, which the nymphs opened in order that Herakles might be refreshed during his journey around the island. Throughout the Greek world, "Herakleian" baths were understood to be heated, and Herakles is often associated with the nymphs by reason of their common worship at baths.[336] Simultaneously with the plural nymphs, whom Pindar mentions as deities of the warm baths, the eponymous nymph Himera was honored. She appears on the reverse of Himeran coins, pouring a libation from a phiale onto an altar as a small silen bathes in the stream from a lion's head fountain spout (figure 4.18). Above Himera, a single cereal grain hovers in the background. On other coins, Himera is given the epithet Soter, "Savior," showing that she was regarded as protector of the city's safety and prosperity or perhaps as a deity of healing.[337] In 408, however, Himera was destroyed by the Carthaginians, though a small remnant of its population was allowed to resettle at the location of the baths. This new town was known as Thermai Himereiai. Cicero mentions that Scipio restored several bronzes to Thermai after the destruction of Carthage, among which was a statue of Himera as the city goddess. A coin issued by Thermai in the first century shows Himera as one of three standing nymphs; she is set off from the two flanking her by her veil and turreted crown (see figure 1.2).[338]

Figure 4.18 Coin from Himera: nymph Himera sacrificing by fountain. Photo copyright British Museum.

Messana lay at the extreme northeast corner of Sicily. At the edge of the sea was a long sandy spit known as Peloris or Pelorias; the eponymous nymph of this area, as well as Messana herself, appears on the coins (figure 4.19). (Pan, Poseidon, and the local hero Pheraimon, son of Aiolos, are also important local figures.) Messana appears as the charioteer of a mule car, while on the reverse, a naked Pan is seated upon rocks as a hare leaps up before him. The head of Pelorias, wreathed in grainstalks, is complemented on the reverse by the naked, charging warrior Pheraimon. The emblem of the shell, which often appears in conjunction with Pelorias, might be a reference to her name; besides identifying the promontory of Messana, it also refers to the giant whelk.[339] In a Hellenistic epigram, Theodoridas refers to a shell taken from the cape as a dedication to the nymphs:

-Εἰνάλι' ὦ λαβύρινθε, τύ μοι λέγε, τίς σ' ἀνέθηκεν
ἀγρέμιον πολιᾶς ἐξ ἁλὸς εὑρόμενος;
-Παίγνιον Ἀντριάσιν Διονύσιος ἄνθετο Νύμφαις
δῶρον δ' ἐξ ἱερᾶς εἰμι Πελωριάδος
υἱὸς Πρωτάρχου· σκολιὸς δ' ἐξέπτυσε πορθμός
ὄφρ' εἴην λιπαρῶν παίγνιον Ἀντριάδων. (Theodoridas 5; *Anth. Pal.* 6.224)

Labyrinth of the sea, tell me, who found you, spoil from the gray sea, and dedicated you? Dionysios, son of Protarchos, dedicated me as a plaything for the cave nymphs, for I am a gift from holy Pelorias. The curved strait spit me out that I might be a plaything of the sleek cave nymphs.

A limestone votive relief found outside Messana is similar to the Syracusan example described above (three standing frontal figures with *poloi*) but lacks the small flanking Pans.[340]

Figure 4.19 Coin from Messana: head of the nymph Pelorias. Photo copyright British Museum.

In the interior of the island were many settlements of the native Sikels, and in the west were the cities of the Elymoi, as well as the westernmost Greek colony, Selinous. The coins of the latter city, founded by Dorians from Megara Hyblaia, prominently feature the river gods Selinous and Hypsas. Paired with Selinous is a nymph labeled Eurymedousa (the name means "wide ruling" with the connotation of guardianship), who appears with a marsh bird or seated on a rock beside a large, coiled snake.[341] The snake motif also appears on the coins of Segeste (below) and is usually thought to imply a healing function. It might also be that the snake is a *genius loci*, or guardian spirit of the place, and thus properly associated with the local nymph who ensures prosperity.

I have already mentioned the importance of the Sikel town Enna in the cult of Demeter and Persephone. Morgantina, another Sikel settlement, was contested by Greek and Sikel in the fifth century and was thereafter ruled by Greeks. It has yielded a series of terra-cotta votive deposits, all from sanctuaries and all consistent in types and subjects. The content of the deposits (for example, standing figures with *polos*, torch, and piglet) shows that the town had a number of sanctuaries serving different neighborhoods, yet all were primarily devoted to the same deity, Persephone. Included among the offerings in these sanctuaries of Persephone were eight plaques that show a triad of musical nymphs. They wear chiton, himation, and *polos*, and they play the double flute, cymbals, and tambourine. This type of plaque recurs elsewhere in Sicily, as well as at Lipari and Lokroi. Most examples are of early Hellenistic date, though a fragment from Granmichele, of the fifth century, seems to belong to this type.[342]

Readers of bucolic poems set in Sicily know that the nymphs were "rustic Muses," but the most convincing interpretation of these musical nymphs is that of Bell. As he observes, the majority of the plaques do not come from identified sanctuaries of the nymphs. Many, like eight of the examples from Morgantina, are indisputably associated with Persephone. Thus it is plausible to interpret these plaques in the context of the nuptial narrative with which so much of the western Persephone cult is concerned. The nymphs provide music for the wedding of the archetypal bride; their choice of instruments seems to reflect local Sikeliote marriage customs.[343] One plaque did come from a votive deposit at the fountain house in Morgantina, showing that the nymphs could also appear in the familiar context of the spring. In fact, the Hellenistic nymph cult at Morgantina might have been connected with the spring nymph whom the Greeks called Arethousa and the Sikels called Kupara.[344]

The Sikel twin gods known as the Palikoi were deities of the bituminous pools near Menaion. The Greeks devised their own myth and folk etymology for these gods, thus appropriating an indigenous tradition in the service of colonization: a nymph, either Aitne or Thalia, had become pregnant by

Zeus. In fear of Hera's vengeance, she begged to be swallowed by the earth. She then bore twins who made their way back up (*palin hikesthai*) through the pools. Other traditions made Hephaistos the father of the Palikoi.[345]

The cities of the Elymoi, including Segeste (also spelled Egesta, Aigeste), Entella, and Eryx, were highly Hellenized. The Elymoi claimed to be descended from Trojans, and this belief was reflected in the myth of the eponymous heroine or nymph who appears on the coins of Segeste. According to Servius, Segeste was one of the maidens sent away from Troy to escape being given to the sea monster who was threatening the town (Laomedon, king of Troy, had brought on this disaster by making a bad bargain with Apollo and Poseidon). Segeste came by chance to Sicily, where she was met by the river god Krimisos. He took the form of a dog, mated with her, and she gave birth to their son, Akestes/Aigestes, who subsequently named the town he founded for his mother.[346] Many of the coins show Segeste: sacrificing at an altar as she is crowned by Nike; seated, receiving a large serpent to her bosom; or simply as a head in profile, set off by an ear of grain. The obverse usually shows Krimisos, either in the shape of a dog or as a youthful hunter accompanied by a dog.[347] The town, like Himera and Aitne, possessed hot springs created by the nymphs, with which Segeste might have been associated as a healing deity. In origin, she was probably an important goddess of the Elymoi, the same one who was known to the Romans as Venus Erycina.[348]

A coin of Eryx shows a female figure standing at an altar, with a dog on the reverse; a similar type from Entella again has the sacrificing female figure, this time with the river god Hypsas, in the form of a man-headed bull, on the reverse. In the latter example, the sacrificing figure is probably Entella, the wife of Akestes/Aigestes; she is accompanied by a crane to show her affinity with water.[349]

4.10.6 *Akrai*

There was a tradition of Kretan colonization on Sicily, according to which the Kretans, who were stranded on the island after Minos' abortive expedition to punish king Kokalos, founded a settlement at Engyon in the interior. This they named after the local spring, and they instituted a cult to "the Mothers," for whom they built a temple. The Mothers, or Meteres, were said to be the very nymphs who had nurtured Zeus in the Kretan cave and were set into the sky as the greater and lesser Bears. Diodorus comments that the cult spread and became so popular that it was still quite active in his own time. Along with the Meteres, we find other nymphlike pluralities under the names Paides, Theai Paides, and Hagnai Theai, above all in the area of Akrai and the nearby sanctuary at Buscemi.[350]

At Buscemi, the sanctuary consisted of three chambers cut into the rock to form an artificial cave. This shows signs of use from the third century B.C.E. through the Byzantine period, but the feature of greatest interest is a number of rupestral inscriptions, generally dating to the first century C.E.[351] These indicate that the cave was a sort of pilgrimage site, devoted to deities called the Paides and Anna. In at least two of the inscriptions, the name Paides ("Girls") appears to be interchangeable with nymphs. Apollo is sometimes part of the cult group, and a priestess of the Paides is mentioned. A sacrificial banquet can be inferred from the verb *euphrainesthai*, "to enjoy oneself," which also appears in the inscription set up by Pantalkes at the cave of the nymphs in Pharsalos (1.3). Anna is enigmatic but has been compared to the Italian goddess Anna Perenna; she seems to be a central figure to whom the Paides are subordinate. This general pattern is one we have observed throughout Sicily and will find again in Italy. Also noticeable is a tendency for these plural deities to be given generic names corresponding to social categories: Girls, Mothers, Brides. Pythagoras is supposed to have made a similar observation, that each female social category corresponds to the names of divinities: *korai, numphai, mêteres*.[352]

4.10.7 *Medma and Lokroi Epizephyroi*

As in Sicily, river gods and water nymphs are much in evidence on Italian coins. Colonies often shared their names with the local spring; Strabo tells us that this was the case for Lokroi Epizephyroi, Medma, Elea, and Thurioi.[353] All of these towns except the first displayed eponymous nymphs on their coins. Medma is thought to be an indigenous name. The head of the nymph appears on the obverse of fourth-century coins with a hydria to indicate her status as a spring deity. She is paired with a male figure, who is seated on a rock with a dog; he must be either the local river Metauros or a youthful Pan.[354] Medma was a colony of Lokroi Epizephyroi, and the two sites share a particular type of terra-cotta mask votive that resembles a gorgon. The two examples from Medma have small horns, bovine ears, and a diadem, while the Lokrian example lacks these features but was found in the Caruso nymph cave. All three of the masks are attractive female faces, the most gorgonlike feature being the serpentine curls on their heads. It is possible that they represent a local iconography of the nymphs, in which the bovine characteristics of the river god have been transferred to a female figure.[355]

At Lokroi itself, the Caruso cave was the site of an important cult of the nymphs from the fifth century through the Hellenistic period, apparently in conjunction with the cults of Persephone and Aphrodite (5.1.12). One of the most abundant categories of terra-cotta votive from Caruso is the triple herm, which shows the heads of three nymphs. This general type has a distribution throughout the western colonies. In Sicily, it is attested on a coin, where the three nymphs appear as busts set side by side on an ornamental base. A similar arrangement with busts rather than heads appears on a Hellenistic terra-cotta thought to be from Rhegion. The tiny busts are framed within a miniature grotto; above them sits a nymph, nude to the waist. A similar piece was found in a tomb at Rhegion.[356]

Thourioi was established on the site of the old city Sybaris, famous for its luxury, which had been destroyed in 510. Sybaris was an Achaian foundation; it and the nearby Sybaris River derived their name from the spring Sybaris in the homeland of Achaia. When the new city was founded, it took its name from the spring Thouria, who appears personified on a coin of Thourioi.[357] The fourth-century local historians Lycus and Timaeus both speak of a cave shrine of the nymphs in this district. According to Timaeus, "In summer the young men of the Sybarites, traveling out of town to the caves of the Lousiad nymphs, used to occupy themselves with every kind of luxury." This suggests that the caves of the nymphs, which must have offered welcome relief from the summer heat, were the site of feasting or perhaps the kind of orgiastic celebration of the nymphs attested at Syracuse. The caves are perhaps to be identified with the large complex of caves at the foot of Mount Sellaro in the Cerchiara district, which contain abundant thermal springs.[358] Aelian confirms the existence of a Lousias River, "the Wash," from which the nymphs took their name. A variant name, Alousias, appears in Lycus' anecdote:

Λύκος φησὶ τῆς Θουρίας ὄρος Θάλαμον, ὑφ' ὃ ἄντρον τῶν νυμφῶν· καλοῦσι δὲ αὐτὰς Ἀλουσίας οἱ ἐπιχώριοι ἀπὸ τοῦ παραρρέοντος Ἀλουσίου ποταμοῦ. ἐν τούτωι ποιμὴν ἐπιχώριος δεσπότου θρέμματα βόσκων, ἔθυεν ἐπίσυχνα ταῖς Μούσαις, οὗ χάριν δυσχεράνας ὁ δεσπότης εἰς λάρνακα κατακλείσας ἀπέθετο αὐτόν. ἐν τούτωι ἐδίσταξεν ὁ δεσπότης [βουλευόμενος], εἰ σώσειαν αὐτὸν αἱ θεαί. ἐξηκούσης δὲ διμήνου, παραγενόμενος καὶ τὰ ζύγαστρα τῆς λάρνακος διανοίξας, ζῶντα κατείληφε, καὶ τὴν λάρνακα κηρίων πεπληρωμένην εὗρεν. (Lycus 570 F 7)

Lycus says there is a mountain Thalamos of Thouria, beneath which is a cave of the nymphs; the locals call them Alousiai after the Alousias River flowing nearby. Now, a local shepherd was feeding his master's flocks here, and he used to sacrifice occasionally to the Muses. The master, being annoyed because of this, shut him up in a chest and put it away. The master wished to see whether the goddesses would save him. After two months had passed, he had the chest opened and found the man alive, and the chest filled with honeycombs.[359]

It is probable that the Timaean passage and not that of Lycus preserves the correct name, since Alousias would mean something like "unwashed," a curious name for a river. Rivers called Lymax and Lousios, whose names suggest purification and washing, are attested in Arkadia (4.4.3). More difficult is the question of the emended reading *Lousiai* (Lousiad nymphs) versus the manuscript reading *Mousai* (Muses) in the description of the sacrifice. A corruption of the text to *Mousai* is certainly suggested by the abrupt transition from the mention of the nymphs, who are the local goddesses, to a sacrifice for the Muses, whose presence is unexplained.[360] Again, it is the nymphs, so often associated with bees, who might be expected to send the insects to nourish the hapless shepherd with honey during his incarceration in the chest. On the other hand, the distinction between Muse and nymph is not necessarily clear-cut. An alternative account, given by Theocritus (*Id.* 7.78–89), helps to explain how the Muses might have found their way into the story. In his version, an evil king shut up a goatherd named Komatas in a chest, and the bees fed him from the flowers because he was a poet: "because the sweet Muse poured nectar in his mouth." Similarly, both nymphs and Muses are said in variant stories to have sent bees to feed the infant Plato on the slopes of Hymettos, signaling his future literary skills (5.1.1).

At Francavilla, in the territory of Sybaris, stood a shrine to Athena Promachos, which accommodated a minor cult of Pan and the nymphs for a period of about a hundred years beginning in the late fifth century. The terra-cotta votives there show Pan or Silenos and a nymph. It is possible that the nymph cult extended back to the time before the arrival of Pan, because the site also contained a large number of miniature hydriai of the sixth and fifth centuries.[361]

4.10.9 *Taras and Other Cities*

The coins of the Spartan colony Taras show the eponymous hero riding on a dolphin. Taras, who was also the eponym of the river, was the son of Poseidon and a local nymph, whom some sources call Satyra. A district or neighboring town Satyron and a spring of Satyra are also attested. Satyra herself is thought to be the female visage on other Tarentine coins, paired with either Taras or a cockle shell. The coins of Elea/Velia pair the spring nymph Hyele, who is identified by the coin legend, with a lion or lion's head. Various female heads, which are unidentified but probably represent local nymphs, also adorn the coins of Kyme, Laos, Pandosia, and Metapontion. The latter town is also associated with the exile of Melanippe/Arne, the mother of Aiolos and Boiotos (4.6).[362] One of the more splendid coinages of Magna Graecia is that of Terina. There, the eponymous nymph Terina, who often appeared with Nike on the coins, was assimilated to her in the mid–fifth century, so that the iconography depicts a winged city goddess, Terina-Nike. Indications of Terina's origin as a water nymph, however, are plentiful. She fills a hydria at a spring, or sits upon a hydria, or is accompanied by water birds. In other designs, she makes an offering at an altar or plays a ball game.[363]

From Ischia at the entrance to the bay of Naples comes a series of twelve marble reliefs dedicated to the Nymphai Nitrodes, patrons of the healing cult at the thermal springs on the island.[364] The earliest of these dates to the first century; the majority are from the early Imperial period. It is likely, however, that the cult originated during the period of Greek tenure at

Neapolis. The nymphs' title comes from the Greek *nitron* (carbonate of soda) and refers to the mineral content of the water; the form *nymphae* (for *lymphae*) is normally used even when the inscriptions are in Latin. The clientele appears to be a mixture of Latin and Greek speakers; they include a freedwoman of Poppaea, Augusta, and a Greek physician, Menippos. The reliefs, unlike classical Attic examples, make little attempt to evoke a natural setting or a grotto. They depict Apollo and three nymphs, who appear in various poses, often holding shells or hydriai from which water flows in a motif typical of Roman nymph iconography.

At Poseidonia (Paestum), a curious underground shrine, or hypogaeum, was built in the sixth century and dedicated to Nymphe. Possible interpretations of the shrine are discussed in 3.2.4.

5 | CAVES OF THE NYMPHS AND VOTIVE ICONOGRAPHY

5.1 Caves of the Nymphs

The distinctive landscape of Greece and the Aegean is characterized by abundant limestone and marble, types of stone that easily dissolve in and crystallize from water. When the concentration of carbon dioxide dissolved in water is high, an acid is produced, which enlarges fissures to form caves. When the concentration of carbon dioxide drops, calcite is crystallized from the water, which produces cave formations such as stalactites and stalagmites. This landscape, which geologists call karst, is full of caves and sinkholes. Rain or snow melts, sinks down into the rocks, and reemerges as spring water.[1]

Caves that have hosted the cult of the nymphs are broadly distributed throughout mainland Greece, on the Greek islands, and in the western colonies. Some sites are known only from ancient authors; some have yielded a single inscription or a few sherds; several have been excavated. This section will focus on the latter group (for literary caves, see 1.4.5). Many more cave sites than those we now know of must have existed. Some, like the Polis cave at Ithake and the cave at the summit of Mount Pentelikon in Attica, collapsed partially and were sealed. Others, like the famous Korykian cave at Delphi, have been frequented since antiquity. Attica alone has at least six rural cave sites of the nymphs and several more sites in the urban area. During the classical period, Attica experienced a revival of nymph worship, which helps account for the preponderance of sites there, but this abundance is also due to the fact that Attica has been more thoroughly explored than other areas.

Cave shrines are unlike most other sanctuaries in that their location is dictated first by nature: manmade caves were used only rarely. The rural Attic examples are relatively inaccessible, and the visitor must exert some effort to reach them. The entrances are usually inconspicuous and difficult to find unless one knows the way or has a guide.[2] What factors contributed to the establishment of a shrine of the nymphs in a particular cave? The mountains in Attica contain hundreds of caves, but most show no sign of use in antiquity, much less of cult. A primary factor seems to have been the presence of potable water, which would have drawn the attention of herdsmen and reminded them of the nymphs. Another is the size and comfort of the cave. Was the mouth large enough to permit easy access? Was the interior large enough to stand in, and could it be used as an animal pen? Caves that could provide convenient water, shelter, and shade for herdsmen or passersby were more likely to be visited often, and more frequent visits contributed to the likelihood that the cave might become a shrine. Wickens' survey of cave sites in Attica demonstrated that peaks in cave use, including cult use, coincide with times of higher population density in the Neolithic, late Bronze Age, late Roman, and, above all, the classical periods.[3] Another factor that drew visitors, and eventually votaries, to individual caves must have been the presence of interesting cave formations. Pausanias' description of the cave at Marathon mentions rocks known as "the goats of Pan" and "baths," *loutra*, probably the rimstone pools found in the cave.

It is important to note that the nymphs and Pan were not the only gods worshiped in caves. Any particularly good cave site might become the precinct of a local god or goddess. At Eleusis, the caves that make up the Ploutoneion were part of Demeter's sanctuary, and Iphigeneia's tomb site in a cave was part of the sanctuary of Artemis Brauronia. (Interestingly, however, these sites were altered by decorating the mouths of the caves with a temple façade, whereas caves of the nymphs and Pan only rarely received that sort of embellishment.) Nor must the deity have some particularly chthonic aura in order to be honored in a cave. Apollo himself, that most Olympian of gods, had a cave site on the north slope of the Akropolis, in association with a nearby cave of Pan.

How can we recognize a given cave as a cult site of the nymphs? Lacking votive reliefs or inscriptions that identify the site, we must rely on the presence of characteristic votive deposits from the periods when nymph worship was conducted in caves. For Attica, the classical period is the most important of these, owing to the introduction of Pan's cult (3.1.2). It is probable that the rural cave sites were in use from the late sixth century but were visited only by herdsmen or other rustics, who made such archaeologically invisible offerings as wreaths or sprigs of greenery, flowers, libations of milk in wooden bowls, and wooden figurines. This "rustic votive" tradition was remembered even when the cult of the nymphs and their companion, Pan, became newly popular, and the shrines began to be visited by a greater variety of people, including city folk, who brought mass-produced votive objects. In the fourth-century comedy *Dyscolus*, we see a marked contrast between Knemon's daughter, the local girl who regularly "crowns" the nymphs, presumably with greenery or flower garlands, and Sostratos' mother, a wealthy pilgrim who brings an entire entourage to sacrifice at the shrine (1.4.3). Evidence concerning the nature of the offerings, and the state of mind of the worshipers, is provided by dedicatory epigrams of varying date in the *Palatine Anthology*. The information in the epigrams meshes well with archaeological evidence to provide a generalized portrait of the cults. Epigrams preserve evidence of homemade votives, "images of the nymphs carved by a shepherd's hand," and "wooden images," or *xesmata*, as well as the customary offerings of fruit and flowers.[4]

Nevertheless, without a deposit of clearly archaic votive objects, it is impossible to be certain that the cult activity at these sites extends back into the archaic period. The same problem exists for caves with only a few reported sherds of classical material. Do sporadic visits, perhaps by a few individuals, constitute a cult? How long a period should the deposit cover before we can refer to the site as a cult site? These questions are debatable. For the majority of the cave sites discussed here, the issue is moot, because as a general rule, only the sites clearly identified by reliefs or inscriptions as cult sites have received attention from excavators. Wickens' survey of Attic cave sites has added some ambiguous cases to the catalogue of nymph caves. Some of the doubtful sites may yield further deposits if excavated, but could deposits alone identify the site as one consecrated to the nymphs? Identifying deities by their votive deposits alone is notoriously difficult. The comparative evidence of nymph caves in Attica, as well as other areas, however, does offer some aid.[5] In Attica, the presence of loutrophoroi in caves is diagnostic, for these had a special function relating to the nymphs. A fair idea of the characteristic deposits can be gained from the descriptions below. In combination with the distinctive locations of the deposits in caves, these can indicate the likelihood, though not the certainty, of the nymphs' presence.

Few cave sites were part of a state-sponsored program of regular sacrifice. Though local nymphs are mentioned in the extant Attic deme calendars (4.2.2), they cannot be tied reliably to cave sites. The cave sanctuaries were more likely to receive frequent small offerings (flowers, libations) than periodic expensive ones. For the most part, the votives in nymph caves are of poor quality. The ceramics tend to be the cheapest available; valuable metal objects, though found regularly, are a very small proportion of the offerings. There is also an unusual tendency, as we have seen, for the clientele to create their own, homemade votives and to add "amateur" rock-cut features and rupestral inscriptions to the caves. Though some local and chronological variation is inevitable, the cult of the nymphs both at cave sites and other types of sites seems to have been conservative, preserving throughout the Hellenistic period the same basic motifs first found in Homer. Some of the cave sites held uninterrupted cults of extremely long duration.

People visited nymph caves for a variety of reasons. Simple piety toward the neighborhood gods is the most obvious, though certainly herdsmen had special reason and opportunity to honor their patrons.[6] On the eve of a wedding, Greek girls visited the nymphs or other goddesses in order to make a *proteleia*, or prenuptial dedication; in Attica, this dedication often included a loutrophoros (3.2.3). We also hear of girls dedicating their toys as a sign that they are leaving the period of childhood, and jointed clay dolls have been found in several caves. A much-quoted line from Euripides' *Electra* (1.4.3) shows that the nymphs could be honored before birth as a protective measure, or after birth in thanks for a safe delivery. At Pitsa, though not at other nymph caves, terra-cottas of pregnant women were found. The nymphs also helped ensure the safe nurture of the young. One of the apocryphal stories of Plato's life is that his parents brought him to a cave on Mount Hymettos to be blessed by Pan, the nymphs, and Apollo Nomios; upon returning from the sacrifice, Periktione found her child's mouth filled with honey by the bees, the agents of the nymphs. In modern times, the custom of bringing premature babies to caves as a sort of helpful incubation has continued.[7]

Other uses were varied and corresponded to local needs. Certain nymph caves are known to have been centers of healing, especially those containing springs or those associated with a nearby water source. After the rise in the classical period of Asklepios' cult, which made regular use of water for healing purposes, he and the nymphs were often cult partners. The cave of the Anigrid nymphs in Elis, with its associated river, was well known for its healing properties. In Boiotia, the cave of the Sphragitic nymphs on Kithairon was a center of divination, as was the Korykian cave at Delphi. Especially after the advent of Pan in the fifth century, hunters made dedications to this god in conjunction with the nymphs. An epigram records the dedication of the head, hide, and feet of a boar to Pan of Akroria and the nymphs by a hunter at Sikyon.[8]

Finally, certain individuals felt particularly drawn to the nymphs. Their special devotion might be manifested in beautification of a particular site, as in the case of certain nympholepts, or in regular pilgrimages to area shrines, as in the case of Sostratos' mother in the *Dyscolus*. The unusually intense piety of such people was recognized and commented upon by their contemporaries. There also existed groups dedicated to the nymphs, who pooled money to purchase expensive votives or to hold banquets. In some cases, the groups had a common economic interest and considered the nymphs their patrons.

5.1.2 *A Visit to a Nymph Cave*

After a long climb, devotees might have paused to admire the gardens often cultivated outside a cave, using water supplied from a spring within.[9] They would come equipped with lamps if the interior of the cave were very dark. Once within, they gazed about them at the dimly lit handiwork of generations: niches cut into the rock to receive votive objects, channels and basins placed to collect spring water, perhaps a paved dancing floor for the nymphs. Votive reliefs that depict cave sanctuaries usually include an altar, either a carved block of stone or a rustic pile of small boulders. Literary evidence suggests that other furnishings, such as seats or beds, might have been provided, or that natural formations were viewed as furnishings (1.4.1, 1.4.5).

The worshipers, as shown on votive reliefs, raised their right arms in a reverent gesture and must have greeted the divine inhabitants of the cave with a prayer. Perishable offerings, such as flowers, fruit, greenery, and animal parts, such as trophy heads, were common, as were libations of various liquids: milk, oil, water, or wine. In Attica, during the fourth-century vogue for marble votive reliefs, these gifts to the gods were set up inside the caves on cylindrical bases or placed in niches. Before the fourth century, there were terra-cotta plaques and figurines and painted wooden panels like those found at Pitsa. Plaques, protomes, musical instruments, and other dedications, such as animal skins, were suspended from the walls or ceiling of the cave.

Many visitors came prepared to sacrifice. A large number of the vessels left in the caves must have been used as ritual implements for libation and sacrifice, rather than as simple dedications. Usually the victim was a goat or sheep. Finds of bones and ash-filled cooking sites show that the sacrifice might take place within or just outside the cave, depending on the topography. Such a sacrifice was a festive occasion, probably a full day's expedition, and the participants might include musicians, porters, and other attendants.

It is unclear whether the caves regularly contained cult images of the nymphs as a focus for worship. The evidence seems to be against this, for no identifiable images have been discovered nor are they mentioned unambiguously in the literature. I suggest below that the large rock-cut figure in the Vari cave might have been a cult image of a nymph; and cult images in the form of a triple herm appear in the terra-cotta votives from Caruso cave at Lokroi. Yet these seem to be exceptions.

Extant votive offerings from the caves consist primarily of inexpensive pottery. Miniature pots are common, probably as cheaper (and lighter) alternatives to the full-size articles. Tiny jugs might contain a small amount of perfumed oil or other liquid intended as a gift, though miniature jugs, particularly loutrophoroi with narrow necks, are often nonfunctional. As at other cult sites, pots sometimes carry a graffito to indicate the intended recipients. The second most common offerings are terra-cotta figurines. A majority of these are standing or seated female figures and female heads. Also typical are Pans, Dionysiac figures such as silens, and comic figures wearing masks and phalloi. Other shapes include animals, birds, and fruit. Masks are not unusual, perhaps indicating a ritual use. Clay votive plaques, mass produced in molds, were popular in some areas. A favorite motif for gifts to the nymphs, repeated in terra-cotta figurines, plaques, and marble reliefs, is the circle dance of the nymphs with Pan or another musician in the center. Metal objects tend to be rings, pins, or coins, though larger objects, such as bronze vases and mirrors, have been found. Earrings, beads, combs, and other objects of female adornment are well attested, as are utilitarian objects like surgical tools or flutes. There are a few unique or valuable objects, such as the gold cicada and miniature gold bed from Phyle cave on Mount Parnes.

Finally, large deposits of lamps are found in many of the caves. These appear in such great numbers that they were clearly left as offerings, but some might simply have been disposable light sources, discarded in the cave after use. A few date to the classical and Hellenistic periods, but most were left in late Roman times. Prevailing opinion has been that the bearers of these lamps were Christians, perhaps meeting secretly, who would destroy and deface any remnants of pagan cult. The reliefs found in the cave at Vari in Attica and those at Phyle were deliberately mutilated. Virtually all the figures' heads had been gouged out, and the reliefs themselves were broken up and placed on rubbish heaps. Wickens has recently suggested, however, that the evidence for Christian presence in the caves is ambiguous.[10] Some of the lamps bear Christian symbols, but many also have pagan representations of Pan or Eros. Would the defacers of the reliefs have brought these to the caves? A plausible alternative explanation is that the third and fourth centuries C.E. saw a revival of paganism, particularly in Attica, and that the people, including some Christians, brought lamps to the caves and lit them there as votive gifts to the old gods. The mutilation of the reliefs could have been done by anti-pagans of earlier or, more likely, later periods. Many other Roman and Byzantine visitors were tourists, perhaps following a guidebook like that of Pausanias. They too often left lamps and coins.

The following discussion adheres to a roughly chronological framework, beginning with the caves that show the earliest signs of activity (excluding the Neolithic and Mycenaean periods), continuing with the caves where cults are identifiable from the sixth century onward but most of the evidence is classical, and ending with examples best illustrating the Hellenistic period. Within this general scheme, however, caves from the same regions are grouped together. The archaeologists whose work is summarized here employed widely varying standards of excavation and reportage, some providing great detail and others very little. For this reason, it is impossible to make detailed numerical or typological comparisons of the finds from the caves.

5.1.3 *Ithake and Polis Cave*

At Ithake, Benton excavated a collapsed cave in Polis Bay, which had seen activity in the Mycenaean period. In the ninth and eighth centuries, numerous bronze tripod cauldrons were dedicated there; Benton has suggested that word of this cave inspired the Homeric description of Odysseus' arrival and the stowing of his Phaiakian treasure in the cave of the nymphs. More recently, the relationship of the Polis cave to the Odysseus myth has been vigorously debated, for the name Odysseus is not attested on a dedication from the cave until the Hellenistic period. Yet the highly unusual collection of valuable geometric tripods, found in no other nymph cave, indicates the presence of another important cult figure in the cave, and this cave was undoubtedly considered by some ancients to be the cave described in the *Odyssey*. It is unlikely that the cave's association with nymphs pre-dates the epic account.[11]

The cave contained a large number of geometric and archaic vase fragments. The terra-cottas, beginning in the sixth century, are mainly of local manufacture, including a fifth-century relief of the Judgment of Paris and numerous masks, which continue through the Hellenistic period. One of the masks has a dedication to Odysseus. Dedications continue until the first century C.E. The earliest certain indication of the cult of the nymphs is a graffito on a plate belonging to the late third century, though the Homeric account must have reinforced the idea of the cave as the abode of nymphs from a relatively early date. There are two other inscribed dedications to the nymphs, and among the terra-cottas are three plaques: one shows female figures in a cave, and two other disk-shaped reliefs show the nymphs dancing around a flutist.[12] The Polis cave is atypical of nymph caves because of its focus upon the hero Odysseus and the wide range of other gods attested there, factors that account for its unusual abundance of valuable metal objects: besides the tripod cauldrons, there were weapons, pins, and other objects of bronze and iron. Polis cave, then, is not the best exemplar for a discussion of pre-Marathon nymph caves. The best early sites are Saftulis cave at the village of Pitsa west of Sikyon and the famous Korykian cave at Delphi.

5.1.4 *Saftulis Cave (Pitsa)*

The discovery in 1934 of Saftulis cave near Sikyon created a sensation when it was found to contain unique examples of archaic painting on wood panels.[13] The four votive tablets, or pinakes, had been preserved in the dry atmosphere of the cave, though two were fragmentary. The best-preserved one (figure 5.1) shows a sacrificial scene, with three adult women, younger flute and lyre players, and a slave with the necessary sacrificial wares approaching an altar. A sheep is the intended victim, and the tablet is inscribed with the names of two women, Euthydika and Eucholis, and the words "dedicated to the nymphs." The other well-preserved tablet shows three standing women whose bodies overlap (probably the nymphs themselves) and has another dedication to the nymphs (figure 5.18).

One important question is whether similar tablets would have been placed in other nymph caves, or if they were characteristic only of the Sikyon-Corinth area, which was noted for its skilled painters in this period. Indications are that wooden votives were an important part of the rustic cult tradition, and it is most likely that wooden artifacts, including pinakes, have been

Figure 5.1 Archaic panel from cave at Pitsa: sacrifice to the nymphs. National Archaeological Museum, Athens.

lost in large numbers from cave sites.[14] These tablets (the two best-preserved examples were dated 540–30) provide us with some interesting information about the cult of the nymphs in the sixth century in the eastern Peloponnese. First, the nymphs receive a typical blood sacrifice like that offered to the Olympian gods. There was nothing unusual about such a sacrifice except its value. Other evidence shows that while blood sacrifices for the nymphs were not unknown, lesser offerings were more common. These votive tablets probably commemorated some special occasion that called for a richer-than-usual offering to the nymphs. The prominence of the female dedicators in the sacrificial scene is also suggestive. They invite comparison with the mother of Sostratos in Menander's *Dyscolus*, who is described as particularly enthusiastic in her devotions to local deities and who makes pilgrimages to their shrines with an entourage of musicians and servants similar to that shown in the tablet.

Terra-cottas and pottery from the Pitsa cave date as early as the seventh century and continue through the Hellenistic period, a long and unbroken tenure for the cult. There is a significant number of satyr, or silen, figures, which fits well with the early affinity between these creatures and the nymphs, illustrated on black-figure vases (3.1.1). Female figures and masks predominate, including female dancers in a chorus. A wide variety of animal figurines is also present, including roosters, doves, dogs, sheep, goats, turtles, a cicada, and a sphinx. Pottery includes Corinthian and Attic wares, with many miniature skyphoi and a few larger vases like amphoras and kraters. This cave and its nymphs must have been revered, because many metal objects, including valuable bronze vases, a mirror, and jewelry, were also recovered. There is no sign that Pan was ever worshiped at this cave, which makes it unique among caves of the nymphs.

5.1.5 *Korykian Cave*

High above the temples of Delphi on Mount Parnassos lies the Korykian cave (figure 5.2).[15] This cave, like many others in Greece, was used in Neolithic and Mycenaean times. Whether the early use represents cult activity is difficult to say. Clear evidence of cult activity begins in the sixth century, though scattered objects are present from the geometric period and the seventh century. Because of its association with the Panhellenic site of

Figure 5.2 Korykian cave entrance. Photo by P. Amandry. Copyright EFA.

Delphi, this cave received more attention than its less-celebrated counterparts, and the heavy deposits reflect its fame. It is also the subject of far more references in ancient literature than other caves (many, like that at Pitsa, are not mentioned at all in extant texts).[16] A meticulous excavation by French archaeologists has added much to our knowledge of the cult.

At the entrance to the cave, flanked by a niche in the rock, there was once a stone and earth platform used for sacrifices. The entrance opens into a huge vaulted room sixty meters deep and twenty-six meters high. The ceiling, the walls, and parts of the floor are covered with cave formations (figure 5.3), and spring water was plentiful when Pausanias made his visit.[17] The most numerous offerings at the cave, drawn from both exterior and interior deposits, were pottery, terra-cottas, and astragaloi, knucklebones of sheep or goats, which were tossed like dice for gaming or divination. The terra-cottas comprised some 50,000 fragments, spanning the sixth through third centuries, though the great majority belonged to the classical period. They included examples from all the mainland centers of coroplastic production: Corinth, Boiotia, Attica. Eighty to ninety percent were female figures, seated or standing women, often wearing *poloi*. The figures were generalized enough to be appropriate for virtually any goddess. Other shapes included female protomes, sphinxes, gorgons, animals (including pigs, tortoises, doves, and roosters), Pans, silens, comic and grotesque figures, female figures carrying hydriai, and articulated dolls.[18]

More than half of the pots, again most numerous in the fifth and fourth centuries and including Corinthian, Attic, and various Hellenistic wares, were miniature skyphoi and perfume containers, most of mediocre quality. Other common shapes were pyxides, oinochoai, and plates. One black-figure plaque depicts dancing nymphs and silens. A few better pots were dedicated and inscribed; at least three fine kraters were gifts from one Hieronymos in the fourth or third century.[19]

The 23,000 astragaloi (figure 5.4) are not paralleled at other cave sites, though they are sometimes found in lesser numbers at shrines and tombs. At Pitsa, a small number of dice was found, but they were probably dedicated as toys by a few individuals. The huge number of astragaloi at the Korykian cave seem to have functioned as a poor man's oracle for the visitors to the cave (1.3). Another characteristic offering at this cave is seashells. Some 400 were found, including bronze and lead models of shells. The excavator concluded that the shells were intended as amusing and pleasing gifts for the nymphs (4.10.4). Many were brought from the shores of the Corinthian gulf when pilgrims began their journey inland to Delphi. Among the other offerings were nearly a thousand bronze and iron signet rings (found primarily in the exterior deposits around the altar and dating from the geometric through the Hellenistic periods); other jewelry, including earrings and glass beads; miniature, nonfunctional combs made of bone; 129 coins primarily of the fourth and third centuries; and five fragments of *auloi*, or double flutes. About a hundred lamps date primarily from the Roman period.[20] Seven

Figure 5.3 Korykian cave interior. Photo by P. Amandry. Copyright EFA.

inscribed blocks, each large enough to support only a small statue, were inscribed with dedications of varied date to Pan, the nymphs, or Apollo Nymphagetes; one rupestral inscription at the entrance to the cave, much worn, names the nymphs and Pan.[21]

The earliest representation of the nymphs' circle dance was found at the Korykian cave, a clay spoked wheel around the perimeter of which nymphs stand with their hands joined (figure 5.5). At the center of the wheel stands Pan, playing his pipes. This terra-cotta group, c. 450, is also important be-

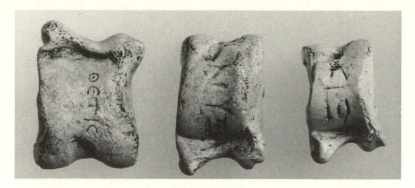

Figure 5.4 Korykian cave: astragaloi. Photo by Ph. Collet. Copyright EFA.

Figure 5.5 Korykian cave: terra-cotta chorus. Photo by E. Sérof. Copyright EFA.

cause it is one of the earliest known images of Pan subsequent to his famous role in the battle of Marathon. It is reasonably certain that during the sixth century, the Korykian cave was dedicated to the nymphs alone; the earliest dedications and testimonies do not mention Pan.[22] Another fragmentary ring in the same style and date was found in the cave, but the figures upon it seem to have been seated nymphs (the two rings together perhaps reflect *Od.* 12.316–18: "there were the dancing floors and seats of the nymphs"). Later, the same subject of the nymph chorus was produced more quickly and cheaply in relief on circular or rectangular clay plaques, most notably on islands of the Ionian sea, Ithake, Kephallenia, and Leukas (5.1.8).

An Attic or Attic-inspired nymph relief was found at the cave, along with fragments in marble, including an archaic female bust; a miniature altar and two marble eggs; late classical statuettes of Pan and a draped woman; and two Hellenistic statues of silens.[23] Inscriptions detailing offerings are not unusual in nymph caves, but statues are. The dedication of several statues here is certainly due to the cave's celebrity. The Korykian cave remained in use until the second century C.E., although its period of greatest popularity was the fifth, fourth, and third centuries.

5.1.6 *Thessaly, Macedonia, and Thrace*

Several nymph caves are known from the northern Aegean area. The most celebrated is a cave near Pharsalos, which contained varied pottery fragments that dated from the sixth century.[24] The other finds included archaic terra-cottas of seated female figures, female protomes, and clay votive plaques, which clearly pre-date Pan's introduction to the cave. There were numerous fragments of votive tablets from different periods; those of archaic style show a female figure or figures walking to the left. Later examples also show female figures; at least one shows the lower half of a figure striding to the left in drapery reminiscent of fourth-century Attic nymph reliefs. There were hydrophoroi and bearded silen heads of archaic or classical date, and Hellenistic items included Pans, naked youths, and doves (presumably indicating the cult of Aphrodite or its influence). Metal objects were present but few: a ring, a belt hook, a fragment of a vase, a coin, all in bronze. There was also a tiny bronze pendant of a vase with a lid, found inside a small votive lekythos. The cave is famous because of two inscriptions attributed to the nympholept Pantalkes (1.3).

On Mount Ossa, overlooking the vale of Tempe, a cave was reported to contain several marble stelai with dedications to the nymphs. The stelai, the earliest of which dated to the fourth century, had once been painted, probably with scenes similar to those on the clay and wooden votive tablets we have already noted. All that remains, however, are the inscriptions. One of these, of Hellenistic date, thanks the Oreiades, or mountain nymphs, for the birth of a child. Surprisingly, there was no overt evidence of Pan's worship. A preliminary excavation brought to light fragments of black-glazed pottery and terra-cottas of the fourth and third centuries, a bronze ring showing Eros, and a copper coin of the Antonine period.[25]

At Aphytis (Nea Kallithea) in the Pallene peninsula of Chalkidike, a cave was dedicated to Dionysos and the nymphs.[26] Dionysos' association with the nymphs is, of course, a given, and the numerous terra-cottas with Dionysiac themes found in nymph caves reflect it. But the dedication of the cave itself to both Dionysos and the nymphs is unusual and apparently is due to the presence nearby of a sanctuary of Dionysos. Also nearby was a celebrated temple of Zeus Ammon, raising the possibility that this combination of cults was intended to reflect the myths of Dionysos' birth and nurture by the nymphs in the Libyan cave of Nysa.[27] The finds from areas immediately outside the cave included pottery beginning in the eighth century, probably contemporary with the founding of Aphytis by Euboians, and Attic black- and red-figure vases, including a black-figure krater with a dedication to the nymphs (supplied from the final letters]si) on its lip. Terra-cottas included a silen and a lion, both of archaic date. Xenophon describes how, when Agesipolis became ill, he conceived a longing for the "shadowy resting places and clear, cool waters" of this cave sanctuary.[28]

Farther east along the Thracian coast, overlooking the port of ancient Oisyme (Nea Herakleitsa), is a cave filled with stalactites. Here, there were Neolithic sherds, with the first evidence of cult use in the sixth century attested by Corinthian and Attic wares and lamps of similar date. A preponderance of the vessels were those designed for storing, serving, and drinking wine, including amphoras, a krater, kylikes, kantharoi, skyphoi, and miniature cups called kotyliskoi. The ceramic evidence continued through the Hellenistic period; terra-cottas were not especially numerous but included seated female figures of archaic style. This site is notable for the two inscriptions left by cult societies calling themselves *hetairoi*, "companions," and *sumpotai*, "fellow drinkers," which met at the cave in the fourth century to sacrifice and consume a ritual meal in honor of the nymphs. Evidence of these meals was left in the form of burnt bones and oyster shells, in addition to the ceramics already described. The offering of a *pelanos*, a ritual mixture of grain, honey, and oil, is mentioned.[29] Oisyme was a settlement of Thasos, which itself has some caves that are likely cult sites of the nymphs. These are located at Aliki, which was an important quarry (thus suggesting a parallel with the quarry and nymph relief on Paros, the mother city of the Thasians). So far, however, the only god known to have been worshiped at the Aliki caves is Apollo.[30]

5.1.7 Krete

Other caves with cult evidence beginning in the sixth century are Lera in Krete and Asbotrypa cave on the Ionian island of Leukas. Because caves were focal points of worship in Minoan religion and retained their relatively high status in the historical period, the study of Kretan cave use is virtually a discipline in itself.[31] This also means that particularly stringent standards must be used in identifying cults of the nymphs, since so many deities claimed caves there. Northwest of the Akrotiri peninsula, Lera cave was used for various purposes from Neolithic to Byzantine times.[32] At the cave entrance are niches and polished spaces on the rocks for the placement of dedications and altars. One of the four rooms contained a body of water, in the vicinity of which large numbers of ceramic fragments belonging to the archaic, classical, and Hellenistic periods were found. Among these were forty-seven fragments of Attic kotylai from the sixth and fifth centuries, with inscriptions that indicate the cult of a nymph or nymphs, kraters, skyphoi, and lekythoi. Lamps, present in the hundreds, appeared in the sixth century and continued through the Roman period. A silver fibula was also found here.

In another room, three stalagmites, which according to Fauré resemble veiled figures, were the focus of much sacrificial activity indicated by ashes and dedications. These included a Kydonian coin, fragments of terra-cotta plaques with floral decoration, lamps and ceramics of the same dates as in the lake room, and about fifty terra-cotta statuettes of female figures, mainly of classical date. These stand or sit and hold a rectangular object at chest level or a round bundle, which resembles an infant. There were also a few fragments of masculine or childlike figures, including one silen or Pan. Fauré has argued that the Kretan nymph Akakallis was worshiped here (4.8.6). Because nymph reliefs were found in the vicinity of Vasiliki and Lappa, it is likely that other caves on Krete were likewise cult sites of the nymphs and Pan.[33]

5.1.8 Ionian Islands and Epeiros

The islands Leukas, Meganisi, Kephallenia, and Ithake in the Ionian sea all boast caves of the nymphs, and all have yielded terra-cotta pinakes, or plaques, that show the chorus of the nymphs. We have seen that the Polis cave in Ithake was used as a shrine of Odysseus and was considered by some ancients to be the nymph cave described in the *Odyssey*. Asbotrypa cave on Leukas was used in Neolithic and Mycenaean times and was the site of a cult dating from the end of the sixth century to the Hellenistic. Excavation here brought to light terra-cotta female figures and protomes beginning in the fifth century, silens, fragmentary pinakes that show nymphs and Pan playing the syrinx (figure 5.6), and a terra-cotta group of the nymphs' chorus, with a flute player in the center. Chorus pinakes were also found by Dörpfeld in two other grotto sites on Leukas.[34] Two basic types of the terra-cotta chorus pinax were produced: one is rectangular, with the figures, holding hands and stepping sideways, arranged inside a cave frame. This detail is reminiscent of Attic votive reliefs. The other type is a disk with the dancing figures arranged around the perimeter and the musician in the center. The pinakes are dated by the excavators from the classical period to the Hellenistic. There are interesting variations, such as a pinax pierced with holes for hanging, which

Figure 5.6 Pinax with nymphs and silen or Pan, Asbotrypa cave, Leukas.
Ephoreia Proistorikôn kai klassikôn Archaiotêtôn Iôanninôn.

shows a nymph standing beside a comic figure with mask, padding, and
phallos. Once again, we are reminded of the Dionysiac character of the
nymphs' cult.

On Kephallenia, the flooded cave of Melissani was found to contain a small
yet diagnostic deposit of objects dating to the fourth and third centuries.[35]
One is a disk that shows the dance of the nymphs around Pan, who plays the
syrinx at the center. Another pinax has a unique scene of three nymphs
walking to the left, carrying torches, and holding hydriai on their heads. They
are led by a tiny figure of Pan. Two other plaques show a female head, which
the excavators called "the nymph Melissane." Melissani is the modern name
of the cave, yet such a conjecture is not farfetched, considering the close
affinities between nymphs and bees (*melissai*). The other finds there were a
terra-cotta statuette of Pan holding a kantharos and a "horn of Amaltheia,"
three lamps, and a few fragments of storage vessels, including a wine amphora. Benton mentions the find of "Hellenistic terra-cotta plaques showing nymphs, satyrs and a krater" at the entrance to a cave near Spartochori
village on the island of Meganisi, east of Leukas. The other finds from this
cave appear to be of Neolithic and Roman date.[36]

Koudounotrypa cave at Arta (Ambrakia in Epeiros) yielded a small number of terra-cottas beginning in the sixth century, including female protomes,
silen heads, and again a pinax, this time showing four frontally posed women
holding birds in their right hands in front of their chests and fruits(?) in their
left hands (figure 5.7). Later figurines included standing, seated, and dancing women, and fragments of plaques with architectural details (capitals,
pediments) were also found. Like the cities of the Ionian islands, Ambrakia
was a Corinthian colony. Tzouvara-Souli has pointed out the affinities among
the votive objects found in the Ionian islands, Ambrakia, and Apollonia
(4.5.3), tracing their influence to Corinth and noting similarities to objects
from the Pitsa cave near Sikyon.[37]

Figure 5.7 Pinax with nymphs, Koudounotrypa cave, Arta. Ephoreia
Proistorikôn kai klassikôn Archaiotêtôn Iôanninôn.

5.1.9 *Attic Caves*

As discussed above, there is only minimal archaeological evidence for cave
cults of the nymphs in Attica during the archaic period, though this is no
reason to conclude that they did not exist. The best known Attic cave is that
at Vari on the south end of Mount Hymettos, known today as Nympholiptou
because of its association with the nympholept Archedamos.[38] It may be the
cave to which, according to the legend, Plato's parents brought him as an
infant to be blessed by the nymphs, Pan, and Apollo Nomios (5.1.1). Its lowest
stratum was an earth platform built on a layer of stone, probably a dancing
floor. This was said by the excavator to be of the sixth century or earlier,
though no objects found in the excavation supported this dating. As at the
Korykian cave, the nymphs were envisioned in a manner consistent with
Homer's account, which mentions their dancing floors on Mount Sipylos.

The artifacts indicate use from c. 500 B.C.E. to 150 C.E. and in late antiquity. Vari, like most of the other Attic caves, contained deposits of minia-

ture loutrophoroi left by brides. The earliest of these was dated 460. The other ceramics, about 400 fragments, included "ointment pots," aryballoi and lekythoi, cups and small flat bowls, pyxides, baby feeders, and several large kraters, many of the latter containing inscribed dedications. Two of these dedications are by women. Some eighty-five terra-cottas also begin in the mid–fifth century and include the familiar female figures and a female mask, supplemented by Pans, silens, a dove, a tortoise, and a frog. The later examples are Tanagra figures. There were also twenty jugs with terra-cotta applied decorations in various shapes, including, notably, seven examples of a naked child in a grotto.[39] These probably have a Dionysiac connotation and refer to the nurture of the infant god by nymphs. Other objects include three articulated dolls, 147 coins primarily of Roman date, rings, a strainer, bells, nails, glass fragments, and almost a thousand late Roman lamps. Goat horns and various animal bones attest to sacrifices at the site.

As at the Korykian cave, the poor quality of the offerings led the excavators to conclude that the place was frequented by the humbler members of society. As if to confirm this view, we find an inscribed dedication, one of the earliest in the cave (early fifth century) by a man who identifies himself as "Skyron the goatherd." One of the fourth-century votive reliefs from this cave was dedicated by a group of twelve men, several of whose names were commonly borne by slaves. They might also have been herdsmen who depended on the water and shelter of the cave for their flocks.[40]

The interior of the cave displays an unusual number of rock-cut features, though these are fairly crude. The cave is divided into two main rooms: Room 1 contains most of the worked areas. Crude steps are carved at the mouth of the cave and lead down into room 1, where the first features to greet the visitor are niches in the form of temple façades and inscribed with the name Pan. Nearby is a monumental seated figure, apparently female, now headless (figure 5.8). There is a large amorphous object compared by the excavators to a schematic, ithyphallic torso or an omphalos. In other areas of room 1 are banks of shelves for votives, another apparent shrine with an inscription to Apollo Hersos(?), and a natural water channel with votive shelves and a reservoir. The author of at least some of these works depicted himself in shallow relief, wearing a short chiton and carrying carving tools (figure 5.9). This was Archedamos, an immigrant from Thera (or perhaps Arkadian Therai), who seems to have adopted the cave and its cults around 400 as his private obsession (1.3).

In room 2, where the votive material was found, there is a rock-cut feature that seems to be a cistern, and near it an inscription specifies that entrails (presumably those from sacrifice) are to be cleaned of dung outside the cave, a regulation to protect the quality and sanctity of the cave's spring water.[41] Also in room 2 were found a rock protruberance shaped to resemble a head, with the legend "of the Charis," and nearby, a lion's head. The lion is usually associated with the large seated figure in room 1, who is identified as Kybele. Though this identification is, of course, possible, it is based only

Figure 5.8 Vari cave: steps, Pan shrine, and seated figure. Deutsches
Archäologisches Institut, Athens.

Figure 5.9 Vari cave: Archedamos. Photo courtesy H. R. Goette.

on the traditional association of Kybele with lions. One of the inscriptions recording Archedamos' deeds refers to a nymph in the singular, and it could be that the seated statue represents one nymph.[42] Very likely it was carved before the standard representation of three nymphs, as seen on the votive reliefs that begin about 400, became canonical in Attica. As for the lion, its location near a cistern recalls the widespread use of lion heads as spouts or adornments for fountain houses. During or slightly after the time of Archedamos came the great resurgence of interest in Pan and the nymphs, and at least seven marble votive reliefs were dedicated in the cave, only to be broken up by hostile Christians centuries later and placed as rubbish in a smaller room at the back of the cave.[43]

The cave of Phyle on Mount Parnes (figure 5.10), now known as Lychnospilia because of the large number of lamps found there, was used in Mycenaean times, then from the classical period to Roman times.[44] This cave, a relatively inaccessible and inconspicuous spot, is identified by scholars with the shrine of the nymphs and Pan used by Menander as the setting for his *Dyscolus*. The earliest objects from Phyle were some archaic-looking terracottas and black-figure sherds, so this cult is one of those that probably pre-dated Pan's arrival. Attic vases were present in many shapes, including lekythoi, kraters, and loutrophoroi. Several had representations of Pan. A large krater, possibly depicting the Judgment of Paris, and an oinochoe had

Figure 5.10 Cave of nymphs and Pan at Phyle, interior. Photo courtesy H. R. Goette.

been dedicated with inscriptions to Pan and the nymphs. No Hellenistic or Roman pottery is mentioned in the published reports, though some was probably present at the site. The terra-cottas were relatively few in number, and the types included seated females, silens, a nude youth, and Pan. Two stone objects that appear to be lustral basins bear inscribed dedications of the fourth century; one of these mentions shepherds. There were eight marble votive reliefs, which had been deliberately mutilated in late antiquity.[45] Among the other finds here were about fifty Athenian coins, assorted small objects, such as copper needles, metal plaques from a wooden pyxis (of Roman date), surgical instruments, and two small gold objects: a cicada and a miniature bed fashioned of golden wire (both of uncertain date). Gold cicadas are mentioned by Thucydides as ornaments of the old-time, autochthonous Athenians.[46] The golden bed is unique, though it has possible analogues in a clay bed from the Caruso cave, a "bed" in the Paestum hypogaeum (3.2.4), and beds of the nymphs mentioned in literary sources (1.4.1, 1.4.5). Two finger rings, of uncertain date, were decorated with bees, as were two lamps; these details might refer to the nymphs' association with bees. The cave had twelve rupestral inscriptions of late Roman date, contemporary with some 2,000 lamps. The inscriptions record prayers and thanks to Pan, supporting Wickens' suggestion that the pagan cult was revived in this period and that the lamps were brought to the cave as part of pagan observances.

A cave on Mount Pentelikon, sealed after a collapse in the early centuries C.E., is now merely a pit full of debris, though it still contains dripping water. This cave was the source of two splendid fourth-century votive reliefs, including the "relief of three donors," which was found standing on its cylindrical base as it had for the past two millennia.[47] It shows three nymphs, Hermes, Pan, and three donors of smaller size, all standing within an architectural frame. The contrasting Agathemeros relief (see figure 5.20) displays the same assemblage of deities in a cave frame, with widely differing poses drawn from various classical models.

Only five terra-cottas were recovered, including an early fifth-century seated female, a Pan, and some hermlike pillars. There was also a shallow marble basin, some marble slabs that could have been used either as flooring or as an offering table, and pieces of terra-cotta conduit, which had once belonged to the spring. Zorides suggested that *lekanê* divination (using a basin of water to see visions) had taken place here, a theory difficult to prove or disprove. There were also roofing tiles and clay tiles, which might have come from repairs made after a partial collapse. These were found in groupings, one in front of the relief of three donors, and seemed to show signs of burning; the excavator believed that they were used for burnt offerings before the gods' images. Some thirty lamps found here date from the first century B.C.E. to the first century C.E. The cave is in the area of the ancient quarries.

At Marathon itself, two and a half kilometers west of the modern town, a cave (figure 5.11) had been used as a cult place in the Neolithic period.[48]

Figure 5.11 Marathon, Oinoe: entrance of Pan cave. Photo courtesy H. R. Goette.

Cult activity began again in the fifth century, clearly in association with the victory at Marathon. This cave is probably the one seen by Pausanias (1.32.7), which was located near ancient Oinoë and which, with Vari, is one of the two largest Attic nymph caves. Like Vari, it is composed of two main rooms and contains many cave formations, which probably correspond to the "baths" and "goats" mentioned by Pausanias, as well as carved niches. The materials from the historical period, not surprisingly, begin in the fifth century. Among some twenty-five terra-cottas were many female figures and a few Pans. The pottery included kylikes and skyphoi, and there was a pair of gold hoop earrings assigned to the fifth century.

Outside the east entrance was a stone wall with an inscribed marble stele (dated 60–61) on which three ephebes recorded a dedication to Pan and the nymphs; it cited an unusual prohibition on bringing dyed, colored clothing into the cave.[49] This type of law attempted to preserve a sense of immeasurable antiquity in the sanctified atmosphere of the shrine, a simplicity belonging to the old ways and symbolizing the way of life of rustics, who could not afford dyed cloth but wore the natural colors of wool as it came off the sheep. Vergil's fourth *Eclogue*, written roughly twenty years before this inscription, speaks of dyed wool as one of the perquisites of luxurious, civilized humanity.

Daphni cave is located on the Sacred Way to Eleusis, about 500 meters west of the Daphni monastery.[50] Unlike most other Attic nymph caves, it is relatively conspicuous and accessible. Predictably, it contained loutrophoroi and terra-cottas of female figures, Pans, and silens, though in small numbers. In Wickens' opinion, one of the loutrophoroi might be dated as early as 540, and other black-figure sherds were present, raising the possibility of a cult pre-dating the Persian wars. Red-figure material included a loutrophoros, lekythoi, a plate, and a kylix. There were animal bones and horns in an ancient stratum and the remains of sacrificial fires. There were no inscriptions to confirm the identity of the cult recipients, but the votives are similar enough to those at other caves of the nymphs and Pan to leave little doubt. The cult at this cave, however, was of relatively short duration and seems to have ended with the classical period.

A cave near Eleusis, the likely provenance of at least two votive reliefs to the nymphs, yielded an assortment of hundreds of votives beginning in the fifth century and continuing through every period to the late Roman.[51] There were miniature vessels, including loutrophoroi and lekythoi; at least three full-size, red-figure loutrophoroi; and terra-cottas of Pan and female figures. One of the reliefs assigned to the site is unique in that its center is pierced for use as a water spout (figure 5.12).[52] This cave was quite unusual in that the opening was too small to enter standing upright. The cave's orientation, moreover, was essentially vertical, so that it was necessary to crawl down a steep, narrow passageway in order to reach the main chamber. It has been plausibly suggested that this particular cave was used as a dump for votive deposits from another nearby shrine of Pan and the nymphs. Another small cave is known to have existed nearby, but it, as well as the cave in question, has been quarried away.

Other caves in rural Attica might also have been cult sites of the nymphs and Pan. One possibility is an unexcavated cave on the north end of Mount Hymettos, known as the Lion cave. Here, a large number of sherds was found, including classical, Roman, and possibly archaic material. This could be the cave of "Pan at Paiania" mentioned in the *Dyscolus*. Another candidate is a cave in Rapedosa gorge, east of the sanctuary of Dionysos at Ikarion, where a nymph relief was found. Though sherds have not been found in the cave itself, many have been found in the area below it, including miniature vessels of the fifth and fourth centuries. The cave itself also seems to have artificial

Figure 5.12 Votive relief from Eleusis. National Archaeological Museum, Athens.

niches, though these are too worn to make identification certain. A votive relief to the nymphs was found in the area of the Dionysos sanctuary.[53]

In general, the rural Attic caves reveal a lack of archaeologically visible attention during the seventh and sixth centuries, followed by two surges of activity: one after the Persian wars, stimulated by Pan's cult, and another during the fourth century when marble votive reliefs had their greatest vogue. Activity continues somewhat abated through the Hellenistic period and tapers off in the early Roman period, only to surge again in the third and fourth centuries C.E., when the lamps were deposited. In contrast to Attica, caves in other Greek areas (Korykian cave, Pharsalos, Lera on Krete, Leukas, Kavala in Macedonia) show cult activity beginning in the sixth century or even in the seventh, as at Saftulis cave.

I treat the cave sites in Athens itself separately, along with the other Athenian cult sites (4.2.1), because they share certain features not common to the rural caves. The urban caves themselves were not as important as the water sources found within them and were often little more than artificially enlarged clefts, incorporated into the architecture around them. They do not contain diagnostic votive deposits, since any such objects were cleaned out over the centuries, either to make room for new objects in heavily used areas or, later, by hostile Christians and souvenir hunters. Marble votive reliefs and inscriptions, often moved from the immediate area of the cave, and waterworks are the only remaining artifacts. The Athenian sites, then, are identified through topographical study, using the remarks of ancient authors and whatever identifying inscriptions may be available.

5.1.10 *Boiotia and Euboia*

A cave in the range of Helikon, first noted in 1984 through a find of terra-cotta figurines, yielded artifacts mainly from the classical and Hellenistic periods, including a large number of female figurines, standing and seated. The pots included amphoras, skyphoi, and pyxides. Smaller numbers of objects were attributed to the archaic and Roman periods. The cave is probably the one dedicated to the Leibethrian nymphs as noted by Strabo. The same nymphs are also mentioned by Pausanias, who says that a site on Leibethrion, a peak in the Helikonian range, had statues of the nymphs and Muses (4.3.1).[54]

Skoteini cave, about three kilometers from Tharrounia in central Euboia, is the largest known cave in Euboia. It shows much evidence of use in the late Neolithic period and smaller numbers of sherds from every subsequent period. In the historical period, terra-cottas, pots, and lamps suggest that the cave was used as a shrine, but the number of objects was not large enough to imply a systematic cult. Sampson attributed the cult to the nymphs or similar rustic deities, noting that local traditions reported the presence of *neraïdes* in the cave.[55]

5.1.11 *Aegean Islands*

On the Aegean islands, only one cave has been excavated, Aspripetra on Kos. The inner parts of the cave showed signs of extensive use in the Neolithic period, while the later deposits were concentrated in an area near the entrance. A variety of terra-cottas from the fourth and third centuries included standing, seated, and dancing female figures (one holding an infant), female heads, nude male children and youths, many Pans, an ithyphallic herm, and a head recognizable as that of Asklepios from similar examples found in the Asklepieion. There was also a hydrophoros (water carrier), a motif that in this context, as on the pinax from Melissani on Kephallenia, refers to the nymphs as providers of spring water. A third-century stele was inscribed on both sides with lists of names, perhaps members of a religious association devoted to the nymphs. There were some Mycenaean sherds and several geometric cups and bowls. The cave also contained a large deposit (over 150 examples) of miniature votive vases in varying shapes. These objects are remarkable in that they appear to have been amateur efforts by visitors to the cave rather than the products of professional potters. From the Roman period, there were a small number of lamps.[56]

On Siphnos, a cave on the western shoreline contained a rock-cut altar with an inscription identifying a sanctuary of the nymphs (*nupheôn hieron*).

The inscription is of particular interest because of its relatively early date, c. 500.[57]

5.1.12 Caruso Cave (Lokroi Epizephyroi)

In Magna Graecia, we find the nymphs worshiped in Caruso cave (Lokroi Epizephyroi), but the cultic context, the physical appearance of the cave sanctuary, and the votive traditions are quite different from the fairly uniform pattern we have seen in mainland Greece and the Aegean. Excavated by Arias in 1940, after which it was destroyed in a landslide, the cave and its contents have received more detailed scholarly attention than any other cave sanctuary of the nymphs except the Korykian cave at Delphi.[58] The site is outside the walls of the city, indicating that the shrine was initially of a rural, agrarian character. The earliest votive objects, terra-cottas of a seated female, belong to the end of the sixth century. At this period, the site was probably in daily use by the locals as a water source. It might have begun as a small natural grotto, but it received extensive artificial embellishment, first an ornamental façade, then improvements to facilitate the supply of water, and finally, a large semicircular basin with steps leading into the water. That these changes had begun by the mid–fifth century is attested by a sima with a lion's head protome; silen head antefixes dating to the fourth century are also thought to be remains of the portico-like early façade.[59] The embellishments took place primarily from the fourth to the second centuries, at which point the shrine was damaged by fire, then abandoned.

These kinds of changes were alien to the classical concept of the nymphs' cave in mainland Greece, where embellishment was limited to utilitarian necessities, such as access steps and votive niches, and ornamentation, such as gardens or rupestral sculpture and inscriptions, which would not substantially alter the rustic, natural setting. The embellishments were, however, in keeping with the growing fashion for artificially worked nymphaia in the Hellenistic period. Caruso cave has been seen as an important "missing link" between the Alexandrian nymphaia known only from literary sources and the first Roman examples of the artificial grotto.[60] Ultimately, the trend would lead to the entirely architectural (and increasingly secular) Roman nymphaea, which drew inspiration from the natural grotto but no longer imitated it.

Of special interest to architectural historians are the twelve terra-cotta models of the grotto façade, dating from the fourth to the second centuries (figure 5.13).[61] These vary considerably in design (the only element common to all is the lion's head spout), and to some degree, they record physical changes to the sanctuary over the two centuries. An exact chronology is not possible, however, because the terra-cotta artisans were not concerned with providing a historical record of the shrine's appearance. Instead, they wished to convey the essence of the place and to evoke its charm. Ritual considerations probably also played a role in the design, since several of the examples were designed as working models, with reservoirs for liquids (libations?),

Figure 5.13 Model of nymphaion from Caruso cave, group B. Museo di Reggio Calabria.

which would pour through the miniature lion's head spouts into the cisterns below. The models have been divided into four groups. Those designated A and B, presumably the earlier examples, attempt to depict the elements of the shrine that mark it as "natural" and cavelike: walls textured to appear rustic, water vegetation, and stalactites. Groups C and D convey a much more architectural and less grotto-like picture of the sanctuary.

Two features of interest, found in all the groups except D, are the use of scallop shells as decorative motifs and the appearance of a single female protome, usually located above the entry to the grotto on the façades. Though shells make sporadic earlier appearances as emblems of or dedications to the nymphs, as at the Korykian cave, the scallop shell was first closely linked with the nymphs during the Hellenistic period and was common thereafter. Presumably, this association arose as a result of contact with the cult of Aphrodite; as we will see, such contact is well attested at Caruso cave. The female head included on several of the models may be an eponymous nymph, Lokria.[62] According to Strabo, the colonists first pitched camp at a spring called Lokria. The presence of an individual nymph's cult at the cave is perhaps also signaled by the terra-cottas of draped seated females, which appear in the sixth and second centuries, both before and after the heyday of the triple-nymph iconography.[63] Whether or not the Caruso spring is to be identified with Lokria, it is probable that the head represents a local nymph, whose cult was superseded later by that of the plural nymphs.

A large and diverse collection of terra-cottas was recovered; the pottery and other types of dedications have not been described in detail but included miniature hydriai. A distinctive terra-cotta style is the triple herm, of which about 200 examples were found (figure 5.14).[64] This consists of a broad pillar or base, at the top of which sit three female heads wearing low *poloi*. The

Figure 5.14 Triple herm with Pan from Caruso cave. Museo di Reggio Calabria.

frontal, hieratic quality of the goddesses is striking and duplicates the effect seen in reliefs from Syracuse and Messana (4.10.1, 4.10.4). In the oldest examples of the type, which date from the second quarter of the fifth century, the herm base is free of adornment and stands behind an offering table on which are placed three separate vessels for offerings. One example has a goat affixed to the side, indicating the role of the nymphs as protectors of livestock. On other examples, the herm is framed within two upright poles, perhaps Dionysiac thyrsoi, or an object like a thyrsos rises in phallic fashion up the central portion of the herm base.

We can be fairly confident that these terra-cottas depict the cult images housed in the cave. Besides the examples with triple heads receiving offerings, there are a few that have an attached female figure playing the *aulos*, presumably the music that accompanied sacrifice. Other variations on the triple herm show an ancillary scene on the base of the herm; often a symbolic grotto is depicted within which Pan sits, playing the syrinx. Several examples show the foreparts of a bearded, man-headed bull, who turns his head to face the onlooker. This is either Acheloös or some local river god (figure 5.15). Most surprising of all are the herms on which the ancillary scene depicts another man-headed bull, clearly distinguished from the Acheloös type by his lack of a beard. He bends toward an altar-shaped basin as if to drink and stands on a platform labeled "Euthymos." These were dedications to the Lokrian athlete Euthymos, who was apparently heroized in the form of a man-headed bull and whose cult was associated with that of the nymphs.[65]

The triple herm of the nymphs is not unique to Caruso cave; examples were also found at the theater in Lokroi. A coin of c. 300, thought to be Sicilian, shows on the reverse three busts of nymphs standing on an ornamented base, before which Pan plays his syrinx.[66] An aniconic marble example of a triple herm dedicated to the nymphs is attested from Arkadia (4.4.3), so it is possible that the Lokrian herms had mainland antecedents. On the other hand, the abbreviation of female figures to simple heads or busts is typical of the votive culture and iconography of the western colonies, particularly in the worship of Persephone.

Another important terra-cotta group, represented by several hundred examples, depicts seated females, nude except for a *polos* and interpreted as wedding offerings (3.2.5). The dedication of similar figures to Persephone is attested, and this raises the question of what relationship existed between the famous sanctuary of Persephone at Lokroi and the cult at Caruso. The cult at Persephone's sanctuary was declining just as the grotto cult reached its acme in the fourth and third centuries, so it is possible that the grotto became the focus of certain rituals that had previously been attached to the older shrine. This transfer would have involved a certain blending of votives and iconography, perhaps even the worship of Persephone herself at the grotto (where a few busts of the type usually dedicated to Persephone were found). Cult ties between nymphs and goddesses, particularly Persephone, are well attested in Sicily (4.10) and are likely to have been in effect at Lokroi as

Figure 5.15 Triple herm with Acheloös from Caruso
cave. Museo di Reggio Calabria.

well. Several plaques that depict the nymphs as musicians were found here
(figure 5.16), which have close parallels in examples from a Persephone
sanctuary on Lipari; they too seem to have nuptial connotations. In addition, the Persephone and Aphrodite cults at Lokroi were closely intertwined, and Aphrodite's cult begins to be well attested at the grotto around
the time the nude "nuptial" terra-cottas appear. Another object with nuptial connotations is the terra-cotta model of a bed, of which a single example
was found.[67]

Other terra-cottas from the cave can be divided into erotic, Dionysiac,
and miscellaneous groups, all belonging to the Hellenistic period from the

Figure 5.16 Group of musicians from Caruso cave.
Museo di Reggio Calabria.

fourth to the second centuries. The subjects in the erotic group include
Aphrodite nude, leaning on a pillar; a winged youth, presumably Eros, in a
similar pose; Eros sleeping and in other poses; hermaphrodites; two types of
a girl holding a goose; and doves. One interesting example from the Dionysiac
group is a fat Silenos reclining in a grotto setting; below him in the rock a
niche holds a tiny version of the triple herm (figure 5.17). Both Silenos and
Pan appear as musicians seated on a rock. Other Dionysiac subjects are busts
of silens, silen or satyr masks, maenads sleeping and in other poses, and comic
actors. The miscellaneous group includes various animals, such as pigs and
horses; standard herms; female figures playing the flute; and assorted figures
of Athena, Zeus, and standing korai.[68]

The divergence of Caruso cave from mainland and Aegean Greek patterns is quite clear in several respects. First and most important, the most
active period at this site was the Hellenistic rather than the classical. The
artificial enhancements to the sanctuary reflect this Hellenistic aesthetic, as
does the unusually large variety of terra-cotta subjects. The cult links with
Persephone and Aphrodite are typically western, though a similar group of
erotic terra-cottas was deposited during the Hellenistic period at the Pharsalos
cave.

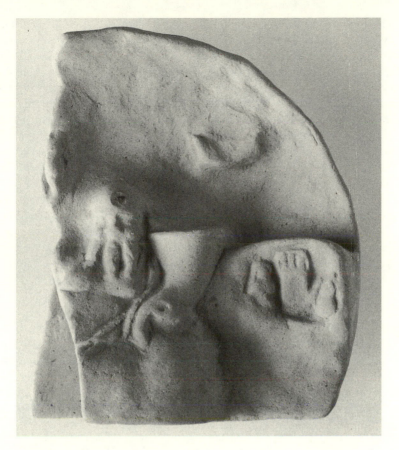

Figure 5.17 Silen in grotto with triple herm from Caruso cave. Museo di Reggio Calabria.

5.1.13 Cave at Kafizin (Cyprus)

The last of the excavated caves is also one of the more unusual. On Cyprus, a grotto in a cone-shaped hill at Kafizin was used for dedications by one Onesagoras and his business associates.[69] The object of the cult was a single nymph, "she upon the pointed hill." Onesagoras and others made hundreds of dedications of pottery, which was one of the commodities they were engaged in selling. These were inscribed in many instances to the patron nymph, sometimes using the alphabet and sometimes the classical Cypriot syllabary. Onesagoras himself seems to have shared a fervor similar to that of the fourth-century nympholepts Archedamos and Pantalkes, though he was active nearly two centuries later. The cult is unusual in that the object of Onesagoras' devotion was a single nymph, not a plurality. The nymph is many times called "sister," *adelphê*, or "his own sister," *hê autou adelphê*, probably reflecting the influence of the Hellenistic cult of Arsinoë Philadelphos.

The epithet Philadelphos, again recalling the Ptolemies, is attested once. The nymph is also referred to as "his own daughter," *hê autou thugatêr*, and Onesagoras once even seems to call himself her "suitor," *mnêstêr*, though this reading is uncertain. In any case, he shows a certain possessiveness about the nymph, and his use of kinship terms seems to be a way of expressing the intimacy of his relationship with her. On a few of the vases, the inscriptions are accompanied by an incised male head and other decorations, which look like plant vines; the heads are thought to be self-portraits of Onesagoras.[70] Other epithets of the nymph are occasionally used: she is "mistress of the mountains," *oreôn despotis*; "mountain ranging," *oreonomos*; "listener," *epêkoos*; and "she who loves vows," *philorkeios*.

The dedications were almost exclusively ceramic vessels, though the inscriptions speak of a statuette (*azalma*) of Themis and a plaque or panel (*ikôn*), which were not recovered. The only other object found in the cave was a fragment of a gold diadem. The dedications were overwhelmingly made to the nymph, though there are scattered mentions of Zeus, Themis, plural nymphs, Agathe Tyche, and Agathos Daimon. Sacrifices are mentioned, and one inscription suggests that a festival was held in honor of the nymph.[71]

Activity ceases after a period of about seven years (225–18), and Onesagoras, perhaps in retirement, leaves a dedication calling himself the faithful steward of the nymph. This site is unique because of its seeming use as a religious locus for a commercial enterprise and because of the large number of inscribed pots, which with other inscriptions found at the site, tell a detailed story of its use during a small window of time. The cult seems to have been of interest primarily to Onesagoras and his circle, rather than to an entire community of people living nearby.

5.2 Attic Votive Reliefs and the Iconography of Pluralities

The most spectacular artifacts associated with the worship of the nymphs are the Attic votive reliefs (see figures 3.1, 4.2, 4.3, 5.12). These belong to a broader religious phenomenon of the late fifth and fourth centuries, a rise in the popularity of marble reliefs as gifts to the gods, especially to Asklepios and Hygeia, the nymphs, and local heroes and heroines. This vogue began at Athens as the Parthenon was completed in 438 and quickly spread outward. Such reliefs, particularly the more finely carved examples, involved an expense much greater than had been customary for minor local deities. Their popularity indicates prosperity and revived interest in Athenian cults, probably encouraged by the authorities as Athens began to rebuild its walls after 400. Neoptolemos, the dedicant of a relief found in the agora in 1971, for example, is known to have been a rich benefactor of local cults (3.1.1).[72] He and others who began to dedicate reliefs in the Attic cave shrines as the fourth century opened were socially and economically far above the humble herdsmen and rural folk, who had been the primary visitors at the nymphs' shrines in previous centuries.

This type of activity contrasts with the earlier amateur attempts of Archedamos to carve images pleasing to the nymphs and with the home-made wooden votives and perishable objects we know were typical gifts. The votive activities of the rich impressed the less well-off, who now wished to dedicate similarly permanent tokens. Sometimes, the reliefs were purchased by a group, and each contributor's name was added in the dedicatory inscription. The reliefs also display wide variations in quality. Some are carved in high relief with great detail, and others are rather crudely and shallowly carved. Ironically, the lesser examples often appear to modern eyes to fit better within the rustic atmosphere of the cave shrines. All are charming witnesses to the ancient, specifically Attic, fourth-century idea of the nymphs' appearance. The nymphs are always shown as a group of three; they either dance about an altar as Hermes leads them or sit and stand about the cave in various poses. They wear heavy draperies as if to keep off the chill of the mountain air. They often appear within a rough frame, like a stage proscenium, carved to resemble a cave mouth.

5.2.1 Archaic Antecedents: Processions and Dances

Many of the reliefs appear to be based upon specific models drawn from monumental sculpture or painted votives, but the representation of grouped maidens in processions and round dances (both of which may be interpreted as choruses) has a long history that stretches back to the geometric period and beyond.[73] If we look at the Attic votive reliefs in the context of previous iconographic conventions for female pluralities, we can better understand how they incorporate some earlier traditions and depart from others.

Greek religion and myth abounded with female pluralities, often, but not always, trinities: the Charites, the Horai, the Moirai, the Muses, the nymphs, and many others. Representations of dual goddesses also appear, usually identified as Demeter and Persephone or Leto and Artemis. These, however, share the semiotic elasticity of the trinities and, depending on context, may represent not only mother-daughter pairs but doubled goddesses (attested for Kybele, Athena, and others) or deities who nearly always appear in a double or triple context, such as the Charites.[74] These pluralities are a firmly embedded conceptual feature of Greek religious thought, one that is applicable most often to female figures, though male pluralities are not unknown (Panes, Kouretes, Kabeiroi, Dioskouroi, and so on). Duplication or multiplication seems to have strengthened the functional potency of the particular figure; two heads (or three) were truly better than one. Various functional aspects could be assigned to different members of a plurality, as with the Muses. Also significant is the correspondence between many of these pluralities and the ubiquitous choruses and cult societies of the ancient Greek world. Groups that came together for ritual purposes, especially groups of girls, had their mythic counterparts in the choruses of Horai, nymphs, Charites.[75]

Such pluralities present an obvious iconographic challenge, particularly in the archaic period, when there was usually no attempt to differentiate one plurality from another by attributes. The concept of one goddess who is split off into several aspects is widespread in modern assessments of Greek mythology and religion (an archetypal Great Goddess is thought to have manifested herself in various contexts as Hera, Artemis, Leto, Kybele, and so on), and such a phenomenon is observable in, for example, Hindu religion, where many goddesses are explicitly acknowledged as emanations of one.[76] Yet, whatever the historical reality, there is no evidence that the Greeks themselves regularly thought in this way of their dyads and triads, much less of the Olympian goddesses.

On the François vase and on two dinoi by Sophilos is depicted the wedding of Peleus and Thetis; all three vases (c. 570) show female triads walking in the procession. One of the triads on the François vase is labeled Horai, and the figures appear to be under one mantle. Sophilos' dinoi include groups called, respectively, nymphs and Nysai (a reference to the nymph nurses of Dionysos), the earliest firmly identified depictions of nymphs.[77] The specific motif of triads of females at weddings, however, seems to have appeared first on Corinthian vases; an example c. 600 showing the wedding of Herakles and Hebe has two figures labeled Charites and two groups of three Muses, each set of three covered by one mantle. On another Corinthian vase, we see a wedding procession with three female triads, each of which is covered by one mantle.[78] The latter are of interest because of their similarity to a fragmentary wooden votive panel (c. 540–30) found in the nymphs' cave at Pitsa and probably painted by a Corinthian artist (figure 5.18). The panel shows clearly the lower two-thirds of a female triad with overlapping bodies, covered by one mantle in exactly the same fashion as in the vase painting; it is inscribed to the nymphs.[79] Though there is a slight possibility that the panel depicts women going in procession to meet the nymphs, the probability is greater that this is our earliest representation of the nymphs as a plurality in a devotional context.

The correspondence between the iconography of female pluralities and early black-figure representations of the Judgment of Paris was long ago noted by Harrison. She describes a patera on which the three goddesses, not differentiated but wearing individual mantles, are led by Hermes toward Paris, who attempts to run away. The Attic black-figure Xenokles cup showed a triad led by Hermes which has been interpreted both as the three goddesses of the Judgment and as three nymphs.[80] The Judgment was a popular subject, and although Hermes nearly always appears as the goddesses' guide, Paris is sometimes absent. This led Harrison to suggest that the schema of Hermes leading a female trinity pre-dates the Judgment story and that the type of

Figure 5.18 Archaic panel from cave at Pitsa with overlapping figures. National Archaeological Museum, Athens.

Hermes and the Charites was the model for the black-figure painters of the Judgment. While Harrison's view has not met with full acceptance from modern scholars, she was certainly correct to point out the curious similarities between the Judgment of the vase paintings and the sculptural iconography of female trinities—not only Hermes and the Charites but the grouping of Hermes and nymphs so often depicted on later Attic votive reliefs.

The most important source for the Judgment, whether portrayed on vases or in literature, must have been the *Cypria* (though, of course, not necessarily in written form). It included a description of Aphrodite's adornment for the contest, aided by Charites, Horai, and nymphs. Another detail of the Judgment as described by Euripides, the baths of the goddesses in the mountain springs before their contest, probably also goes back to the *Cypria*. According to Proclus' summary, the *Cypria* included Hermes in the story as the guide and set the scene as the flowery, abundantly springfed (*polupidax*) slope of Ide, where Paris played the lyre while tending his flocks.[81] The *Cypria* itself, like the vase paintings of the Judgment, might have drawn attention to the similarity of the goddess triad with other triads who were more at home in the setting, particularly the nymphs (2.5.2).

Plural nymphs in procession also appear on an early black-figure vase in another mythic context: the Perseus saga. On a Chalkidian amphora, Perseus receives the winged boots, hat, and wallet from three kore-like maidens labeled Neïdes (4.4.2, fig. 4.6).[82] The three are lined up in identical poses, but their bodies do not overlap as in the Sophilos dinoi and the wooden panel from Pitsa. Overlapping bodies reminiscent of the painted examples can be observed in an archaic votive relief inscribed "Sotias [dedicated] the *korai*," which depicts three maidens holding, respectively, a flower, a fruit, and a garland.[83]

From the fifth century, we have the well-known bas-relief from Thasos (4.7.2, fig. 4.9, c. 470), with its groups of Apollo and the nymphs and Hermes and the Charites. Each figure has a space of her own, as they walk in a stately manner toward the central niche or altar. All, except for one figure, who crowns Apollo as he holds his lyre, carry typical objects (fruit or wreaths), and all are shown in profile. A similar scene is preserved on the *polos* of an archaic karyatid from Delphi.[84] More archaic looking, but of about the same date as the Thasian relief, is the procession of three maidens from the Harpy tomb at Xanthos in Lykia. Like the nymphs and Charites at Thasos, these maidens carry small offerings and walk in procession; the Lykian maidens approach a seated female figure, perhaps a goddess.[85]

Returning to our original distinction between walking and dancing maidens, we possess several archaic and early classical examples of the latter. From Paros comes the well-known Charites relief (c. 550), with the middle of the three dancers distinguished from the others by the frontal pose of her head, a feature notable for its later appearance on the Attic nymph reliefs. The maidens on a relief from the Athenian Akropolis (c. 500, figure 5.19), which depicts Hermes followed by three energetic dancers and a smaller boy or worshiper, have been interpreted as Charites, nymphs, Aglaurids, or simply as women dancing at a festival.[86] The presence of Hermes certainly indicates that the group is a divine one; nothing points conclusively to either the Charites or nymphs, except that the small figure could be interpreted as a juvenile or adult nympholept. A late black-figure skyphos in Leningrad, however, gives some support to the identification of the Akropolis dancers as nymphs because of its close correspondence to certain details of the relief. It shows four nymphs clad in short chitons dancing to the music of Hermes,

Figure 5.19 Akropolis relief of Charites or nymphs. Akropolis Museum 702. Line drawing by author.

who plays the double flute. Meanwhile, a silen grasps the hand of the last nymph, joining in the dance.[87] The appearance of Hermes, his instrument, the way the dancers grasp each others' wrists, and the addition of an extra figure to the dance are all noticeably similar on the vase and the relief. On the other side of the skyphos, Apollo plays the lyre for five standing figures, who appear to be Muses. One plays the double flute, while the others hold castanets. The painter of this vase, then, attempts to distinguish two groups of divine females, who previously lacked recognizable attributes. Other vases dated 525–500 show Apollo and Hermes, sometimes accompanied by Dionysos, with groups of dancing women, who seem to be nymphs or Muses.[88]

Another well-known relief depicting dancing women is the so-called Charites of Sokrates. Pausanias mentions a carving of the Charites near the Propylaia "made by that Sokrates who as the Pythian priestess testified was the wisest of all human beings." Scholars today attribute the work instead to a Boiotian sculptor named Sokrates. The Chiaramonti relief, which shows three dancing maidens, is thought to be a later copy of this work, and there are other late copies. The date of the original has been variously estimated from as early as c. 470 to as late as the early fourth century.[89] Also of the fifth century are the groups called the Horai and Aglaurids, now known only from neo-Attic copies. The originals of these groups have been interpreted as figures from the base of the cult statues of Athena and Hephaistos once located in the Athenian Hephaistaion.[90]

Terra-cotta groups and plaques representing the round dance are well attested from the sixth century onward, and have Bronze Age antecedents. The groups often include a musician, who sits or stands at the center of the ring. One such group (see figure 5.5, c. 480), with Pan as the musician, was discovered in the Korykian cave; others have been found at Corinth, Korkyra, Leukas, and Apollonia.[91]

5.2.2 *Attic Nymph Reliefs*

In this cultural context, then, one in which the female plurality was already familiar in both literature and art, the Attic votive reliefs to the nymphs appeared.[92] The fourth century was the heyday for both gravestone and votive reliefs. Examples began in the last quarter of the previous century and were prolific until the anti-luxury decree of Demetrios of Phaleron in 317. Lavish sculpted funerary monuments were no longer permitted, and the loss of the market for these had a damping effect on the production of votive reliefs as well (presumably because sculptors were forced to leave Athens in order to find work). While grave reliefs end abruptly after 317, votive reliefs continue to flourish until 300 or so; yet they are all but absent from Attica after the fourth century, until the neo-Attic examples of the late Hellenistic period. The apparent exodus of stone workers from Attica coincides neatly with the dissemination of Athenian styles to other parts of the Greek world, where the Attic iconographic tradition is carried into the Hellenistic and Roman Imperial periods and becomes increasingly secularized.[93]

The popularity of stone votive reliefs seems to have been due to several factors, in particular the stimulus of the great building programs of the previous century. Many of those who had learned the stone-cutting trade must have turned to the production of grave and votive reliefs when the great public buildings were completed. At the same time, the religious climate had begun to move toward the cultivation of gods who addressed the daily concerns of individuals, a trend that was to continue in the Hellenistic period. These gods, including Asklepios and Hygeia, Artemis, the nymphs and Pan, Zeus in various chthonic forms, and Demeter with Kore, were chosen most often as the recipients of votive reliefs.[94]

The two main modes of presentation for archaic pluralities, as we have seen, were processions and dances. Some of the Attic votives use the old procession/dance motifs; others depict the nymphs standing and sitting in various poses (figure 5.20). Interestingly, most of the earliest Attic votive reliefs to the nymphs, those belonging to the end of the fifth century and the beginning of the fourth, do not show the dance or procession. They seem, instead, to be inspired by classical monuments that show seated and standing figures, in particular the Parthenon frieze with its serene gods. The earliest

Figure 5.20 Agathemeros relief. Archaeological Museum, Athens.

example of the dancing group in these reliefs seems to be the Quirinal relief (see figure 3.1), dated by Edwards to 400–390.

According to Edwards, the Quirinal relief and other examples showing the dance were directly inspired by the lost originals of the Horai and Aglaurids.[95] This is possible, though as we have seen, other models for the iconography of the reliefs were not lacking, in particular the archaic Akropolis relief of c. 500 (and whatever models it drew upon). While figural types for individual nymphs might have been copied from monuments in vogue at the time the reliefs were carved, the basic scheme of Hermes leading the dancers is much older (Hermes, moreover, appears in the archaic Akropolis relief but not on the reliefs of the Horai and Aglaurids). Again, Acheloös appears as a man-faced bull on the early Xenokrateia and Quirinal reliefs; his front half protrudes into the scene. We do not know the origin of this element of the composition, but it ties together the examples with standing/seated nymphs and those with dancers. The Acheloös protome must have been considered proper to the iconography of the nymphs before the introduction of the stone reliefs (3.1.3). Finally, the case of Pan is similar to that of Acheloös. He appears in the reliefs from the beginning, but his position is usually peripheral: he sits to one side of the scene or above in the rocks of the cave frame. Pan had been introduced to the Attic cult of the nymphs after 490 and was added to the preexisting scheme of the nymph triad and its leader, Hermes. Fuchs argued in his study of Attic nymph reliefs that the iconography goes back to a fifth-century archetype located in Pan's cave on the northwest slope of the Akropolis.[96]

The direct predecessors of stone votive reliefs were painted tablets and plaques of terra-cotta or wood and hammered metal reliefs similar to the *tamata* found in modern Greek Orthodox churches.[97] Since so few of these have survived from fifth-century Athens, little can be said about their influence upon the reliefs. One of the archaic painted tablets from sixth-century Pitsa bears a clear relationship to the iconography of many Attic votive reliefs, in that it depicts a group of worshipers bringing to the altar a sacrificial animal and the necessary utensils for the feast. Yet it is different from virtually all the fourth-century stone examples in that it shows worshipers but does not depict the deities who are to receive the sacrifice. The painters of the Pitsa examples seem to have represented the nymphs on a tablet separate from that showing the worshipers. Attic votive reliefs, by contrast, are notable for the way the relationship between worshiper and deity is depicted in concrete form, as the worshiper comes face to face with the gods. As the fourth century ends, and in later reliefs, a process of distancing can be observed, in which worshipers are separated from the diety by an altar or cave wall or are placed on a separate register of the relief. Finally, in the Imperial period, the worshipers may be absent altogether.[98] In spite of the paucity of examples, the influence of votive tablets on the stone examples should not be underestimated. It is probable that the basic formula of the nymph reliefs (three nymphs, Hermes, Acheloös, and Pan) was drawn from these tablets and reinterpreted by sculptors. In particular, the topographic and landscape features so prominent in the reliefs to the nymphs (the peripheral areas where Pan usually appears) can be attributed to painterly models, since these are absent from most classical funerary and architectural reliefs.

In several of the earlier votive reliefs to the nymphs, architectural elements are used to frame the scene. These could have been borrowed from grave monuments or, indeed, from earlier votive sculptures, such as the Akropolis Hermes and nymphs/Charites, which has a pediment. A symbolic meaning for the architectural elements—the stoa as meeting ground for human and divine—has been suggested.[99] In the second half of the century, however, the figures are usually surrounded by a cave frame. The origin of this frame has been variously explained. Edwards, who most recently studied and catalogued the corpus of nymph reliefs, attributed the cave frame to two factors. One was, of course, that the cave is a suitable setting for these deities. The second factor had to do with Edwards' belief that the reliefs were strongly influenced by the sculptures of the statue base of Dionysos Eleutherios, which he reconstructed as showing the delivery of the infant Dionysos to the nymphs of Nysa.[100] Dionysos is closely associated with caves (both in the context of his birth and in the iconographic depiction of his marriage to Ariadne) and with nymphs. Yet the vast majority of the fourth-century reliefs show no Dionysiac iconography, and the cave setting can be explained without reference to Dionysos.[101] Ridgway suggests that the cave frame could have come about as a result of the common placement of such reliefs in stone niches, as dedicators and artists attempted to make the reliefs blend in, so to speak, with the rough rocks of the surrounding niche. A third possibility is that the cave frame reflects the contemporary popularity of the Attic cave cult of the nymphs. At least sixteen of the Attic examples were, after all, found in caves, and thus the cave frames probably began as an attempt to depict the actual scene of worship. It is also possible that painted tablets showed nymphs in caves, since the landscape features of the stone votives are those most likely to derive from painted scenes.

AFTERWORD

At an unknown date, perhaps during the second or third century c.e., the Orphic *Hymns* were composed for a religious association in western Asia Minor. Some of the hymns show knowledge of Orphic theogonies, hence their name, but there is little else about them to connect them with Orphism as a movement, except the mention of *mustai*, "initiates," and the association's apparent preoccupation with Dionysos.[1] What is most interesting about the hymns is that they were certainly in liturgical use, something we might suspect for other preserved hymns, such as the Homeric *Hymns* or those of Callimachus, but could rarely demonstrate. The Orphic *Hymns*, often dismissed because of their mediocrity, were not intended to draw attention to themselves but to the gods they praised and invoked. Each hymn includes a notation of the correct offering to accompany it, usually incense. The gods hymned include the Olympians, various nature gods and personifications (Boreas, Proteus, Ether, Physis, Dike), and three local Phrygian goddesses (Mise, Hipta, Melinoë). Many of the hymns are composed in the age-old devotional style of the litany, a recital of epithets and phrases that describe the deity and enumerate his or her characteristics and glories. In particular, the hymn to the nymphs is a long string of epithets, cleverly strung together to form hexameters:

Νυμφῶν, θυμίαμα ἀρώματα.
Νύμφαι, θυγατέρες μεγαλήτορος Ὠκεανοῖο,
ὑγροπόροις γαίης ὑπὸ κεύθεσιν οἰκί᾽ ἔχουσαι,
κρυψίδρομοι, Βάκχοιο τροφοί, χθόνιαι, πολυγηθεῖς,

καρποτρόφοι, λειμωνιάδες, σκολιοδρόμοι, ἀγναί,
ἀντροχαρεῖς, σπήλυγξι κεχαρμέναι, ἠερόφοιτοι,
πηγαῖαι, δρομάδες, δροσοείμονες, ἴχνεσι κοῦφαι,
φαινόμεναι, ἀφανεῖς, αὐλωνιάδες, πολυανθεῖς
σὺν Πανὶ σκιρτῶσαι ἀν' οὔρεα, εὐάστειραι,
πετρόρυτοι, λιγυραί, βομβήτριαι, οὐρεσίφοιτοι,
ἀγρότεραι κοῦραι, κρουνίτιδες ὑλονόμοι τε,
παρθένοι εὐώδεις, λευχείμονες, εὔπνοοι αὔραις,
αἰπολικαί, νόμιαι, θηρσὶν φίλαι, ἀγλαόκαρποι,
κρυμοχαρεῖς, ἀπαλαί, πολυθρέμμονες αὐξίτροφοί τε,
κοῦραι ἁμαδρυάδες, φιλοπαίγμονες, ὑγροκέλευθοι,
Νύσιαι, μανικαί, παιωνίδες, εἰαροτερπεῖς,
σὺν Βάκχωι Δηοῖ τε χάριν θνητοῖσι φέρουσαι·
ἔλθετ' ἐπ' εὐφήμοις ἱεροῖς κεχαρηότι θυμῶι
νᾶμα χέουσαι ὑγεινὸν ἀεξιτρόφοισιν ἐν ὥραις. (Orph. *Hymn* 51)

To the Nymphs: incense, aromatic herbs.
Nymphs, daughters of great-hearted Okeanos, you who have your
homes in the moist recesses beneath the earth; you of secret paths,
nurses of Bakchos, chthonic, joyful; growers of fruits, you of the
meadows, of the winding paths, pure; delighting in caves, lovers of
grottoes, wandering the air; you of the springs, roaming ones, dewclad
with light steps; visible, invisible, you of the glens, with many blooms;
leaping with Pan on the mountains as you cry out; flowing from rocks,
clear-voiced, buzzing like the bee, mountain haunting; girls of the
wilds, you of the gushing water and the woodlands; sweet-smelling
maidens, clothed in white, fragrant in the breezes; you of the
goatherds, you of the pasture, dear to the beasts, you of splendid fruit;
lovers of frost, tender ones, you nurture and foster growth; girls joined
with the trees, you delight in play, you of the wet paths; you of Nysa,
ecstatic, healers, you who love spring, who bring grace to mortals with
Bakchos and Deo. Come with joyful heart to the holy offerings,
pouring wet streams in the seasons of full growth.

Though composed in all likelihood at a time when Christianity was rapidly
gaining popularity, this hymn, like the others in the collection, is resolutely
pagan in its outlook, and nothing in it would have been out of place in a
hymn composed 500 years before. At the same time, it is unlike any other
extant description of the nymphs, and only a few of its epithets are the standard literary ones (*leimôniades, pêgaiai, nomiai, hamadruades*). It subtly anticipates the later folkloric view of nymphs or *neraïdes* as beings who frequent
the paths, the springs, the trees, and air, white-clad maidens whom a trav-
eler in the wilds might glimpse or hear singing. But these nymphs are addressed as givers of good things, especially in their capacity as deities of
moisture, who foster animal and vegetable growth.

The author of the hymn understands the nymphs primarily as nature deities, without the social functions relating to rites of passage and local identity that we explored earlier in this book. In fact, this is a universalized portrait of the nymphs and probably does not correspond to a local shrine. In this respect, it differs from most of the cults we have examined and might be characteristic of the later period. The intellectual and pagan apologist Porphyry, for example, drew the universal meaning from the specific by interpreting cave cults allegorically (1.4.5). Yet even in the time of Libanius, when the pagan revival under Julian took place, the nymphs inhabited and were worshiped according to tradition in special places of their own, such as the grove of Daphne at Antioch (4.9.8). It is certain that worship of the nymphs continued to exist at all levels of society up to and beyond the triumph of Christianity, though the form and nature of this worship was manifold.

ABBREVIATIONS AND EDITIONS
OF PRIMARY SOURCES

Abbreviations for primary texts and authors follow S. Hornblower and Antony Spawforth, eds., *The Oxford Classical Dictionary*, 3d ed. (Oxford: Oxford University Press, 1996). Abbreviations of periodicals follow *L'Année philologique*. Fragments of the Greek historians are cited from *FGrHist* in the following format: Hellanicus 4 F 10.

Abbreviations

ARV	J. D. Beazley. *Attic red-figure vase-painters.* 2d ed. Oxford: Clarendon, 1963.
BE	*Bulletin épigraphique.* Paris: Belles Lettres, 1938–.
BMC Italy	British Museum Department of Coins and Medals. *Catalogue of Greek coins, Italy.* Ed. R. S. Poole. London: Trustees [of the British Museum], 1873. Repr. Bologna: A. Forni, 1963.
BMC Sicily	British Museum Department of Coins and Medals. *Catalogue of Greek coins, Sicily.* Ed. R. S. Poole. London: Trustees [of the British Museum], 1876. Repr. Bologna: A. Forni, 1963.
BMC Thessaly	British Museum Department of Coins and Medals. *Catalogue of Greek coins, Thessaly to Aetolia, by Percy Gardner.* Ed. R. S. Poole. London: Trustees [of the British Museum], 1883. Repr. Bologna: A. Forni, 1963.

CIL   *Corpus inscriptionum Latinarum.* Berlin: Reimer, 1869–.

Coll. Alex.   J. U. Powell, ed. *Collectanea Alexandrina.* Oxford: Clarendon, 1925.

CVA   *Corpus vasorum antiquorum.* Paris: E. Champion, 1923–.

DK   H. Diels and W. Kranz. *Die Fragmente der Vorsokratiker,* 6th ed., 3 vols., 1952. Repr. Berlin: Weidemann, 1961.

EAA   *Enciclopedia dell'arte antica, classica e orientale.* Rome: Istituto della enciclopedia italiana, 1958–.

EGF   M. Davies, ed. *Epicorum Graecorum fragmenta.* Göttingen: Vandenhoeck and Ruprecht, 1988.

Epigr. Gr.   G. Kaibel, ed. *Epigrammata Graeca ex lapidibus conlecta,* 1878. Repr. Hildesheim: G. Olms, 1965.

Ergon   Το Ἔργον της Αρχηαιολογικής Εταιρείας. Athens, 1955–.

FGrHist   F. Jacoby. *Die Fragmente der griechischen Historiker.* Leiden: Brill, 1923–58.

FHG   C. Müller. *Fragmenta historicorum Graecorum.* 5 vols. Paris: F. Didot, 1841–70.

FGE   D. Page, ed. *Further Greek epigrams.* Cambridge and London: Cambridge University Press, 1981.

GDI   F. Bechtel, H. Collitz, et al. *Sammlung der griechischen Dialektinschriften.* Göttingen: Vandenhoeck and Ruprecht, 1884–1915.

GLP   D. L. Page, ed. *Select papyri. Vol. 3: Literary papyri, poetry,* 1942. Cambridge, MA: Harvard University Press; London: Heinemann, 1950.

GP   A. S. F. Gow and D. Page, eds. *The Greek anthology: The garland of Philip and some contemporary epigrams.* 2 vols. London: Cambridge University Press, 1968.

GVI   W. Peek. *Griechische Vers-Inschriften. I: Grab-Epigramme,* 1955. Repr. Berlin: Akademie-Verlag, 1988.

HE   A. S. F. Gow and D. L. Page, eds. and trans. *The Greek anthology: Hellenistic epigrams.* 2 vols. Cambridge: Cambridge University Press, 1965.

IC   M. Guarducci. *Inscriptiones creticae.* Rome: Libreria dello Stato, 1935–50.

IDélos   F. Durrbach et al. *Inscriptions de Délos.* Paris: H. Champion, 1923–.

IE   M. L. West, ed. *Iambi et elegi Graeci.* 2d ed. Oxford: Clarendon, 1989.

IG   *Inscriptiones graecae.* Berlin: W. de Gruyter, 1873–.

IGBulg   G. Mihailov, ed. *Inscriptiones graecae in Bulgaria repertae.* Sofia: Academia Litterarum Bulgarica, 1956–71.

IK Bd. 2   H. Engelmann and R. Merkelbach. *Die Inschriften von Erythrai und Klazomenai,* vol. 2 of Inschriften griechischer Städte aus Kleinasien. Bonn: R. Habelt, 1973.

IK Bd. 15   C. Börker and R. Merkelbach. *Die Inschriften von Ephesos*, vol. 5 of Inschriften griechischer Städte aus Kleinasien. Bonn: R. Habelt, 1980.

IK Bd. 32   T. Corsten. *Die Inschriften von Apameia (Bithynien) und Pylai*, vol. 32 of Inschriften griechischer Städte aus Kleinasien. Bonn: R. Habelt, 1987.

IK Bd. 41   W. Blümel. *Die Inschriften von Knidos*, vol. 41 of Inschriften griechischer Städte aus Kleinasien. Bonn: R. Habelt, 1992.

Lex.   W. H. Roscher. *Ausführliches Lexicon der griechischen und römischen Mythologie.* 10 vols., 1884–1937. Repr. Hildesheim: G. Olms, 1965–68.

LIMC   *Lexicon Iconographicum Mythologiae Graecae.* Zurich: Artemis Verlag, 1981–.

LSAM   F. Sokolowski. *Lois sacrées de l'Asie Mineure.* École française d'Athènes travaux et mémoires, fasc. 9. Paris: E. de Boccard, 1955.

LSCG   F. Sokolowski. *Lois sacrées des cités grecques.* École française d'Athènes travaux et mémoires. Paris: E. de Boccard, 1969.

LSCG Suppl.   F. Sokolowski. *Lois sacrées des cités grecques. Supplément.* École française d'Athènes travaux et mémoires, fasc. 11. Paris: E. de Boccard, 1962.

LSJ   H. G. Liddell and R. Scott. *A Greek-English lexicon.* 9th ed., 1940. Repr. Oxford: Clarendon, 1966.

MI   S. Thompson. *Motif index of folk literature.* 6 vols. Bloomington: Indiana University Press, 1955–58.

OCT   Oxford Classical Texts. Oxford: Clarendon Press.

OGI   W. Dittenberger. *Orientis Graeci inscriptiones selectae: Supplementum sylloges inscriptionum Graecum,* 1903. Repr. Hildesheim: G. Olms, 1960.

PG   J. P. Migne. *Patrologiae cursus completus [Patrologiae graecae].* Paris: Migne, 1844–1904.

Praktika   Πρακτικά της εν Αθήναις Αρχηαιολογικής Εταιρείας. Athens, 1837–.

RE   A. Pauly, G. Wissowa, and W. Kroll. *Real-Encyclopädie der klassischen Altertumswissenschaft.* Stuttgart: J. B. Metzler, 1893–.

SEG   *Supplementum epigraphicum Graecum.* Alphen aan den Rijn: Sijthoff & Noordhoff, 1923–.

Suppl. Hell.   H. Lloyd-Jones and P. Parsons, eds. *Supplementicum Hellenisticum.* Berlin and New York: W. de Gruyter, 1983.

TAM   E. Kalinka et al. eds. *Tituli Asiae Minoris*. Vienna: Hoelder-Pichler-Tempsky, 1901–.

Editions of Authors Cited

Each author's name is followed by his or her *floruit*. Dates for authors and texts are as given in L. Berkowitz and K. A. Squitier, *Thesaurus Linguae Graecae: Canon of Greek Authors and Works*, 3d ed. (New York: Oxford University Press, 1990).

Acesandrus, 4?/2 B.C.E. *FGrHist*, vol. 3B, no. 469.

Achilles Tatius, 3 C.E. S. Gaselee. 1969. Cambridge, MA: Loeb.

Acusilaus, 5 B.C.E. *FGrHist*, vol. 1A, no. 2.

Aelian, 2–3 C.E.
   De natura animalium: A. F. Scholfield. 1958. Cambridge, MA: Loeb.
   Varia Historia: N. G. Wilson. 1997. Cambridge, MA, and London: Loeb.

Aeneas Tacticus, 4 B.C.E. W. A. Oldfather. 1923, repr. 1948. Cambridge, MA: Loeb.

Aeschylus, 6–5 B.C.E.
   Fragments: S. L. Radt. 1985. Göttingen: Vandenboeck and Ruprecht.
   Plays: M. L. West. 1990. Stuttgart: Teubner.

Agathocles, 3 B.C.E.? *FGrHist*, vols. 3B, F, no. 472.

Aglaosthenes, 4–3 B.C.E.? *FGrHist*, vol. 3B, no. 499.

Alcaeus, 7–6 B.C.E. D. A. Campbell. 1982. Cambridge, MA, and London: Loeb.

Alcaeus of Messene, 3–2 B.C.E. *HE.*

Alcimus of Sicily, 4 B.C.E. *FGrHist*, vol. 2B, no. 560.

Alcman, 7 B.C.E. D. A. Campbell. 1988. Cambridge, MA, and London: Loeb.

Alexander Polyhistor, 2–1 B.C.E. *FGrHist*, vol. 3A, no. 273.

Amelesagoras, 4–3 B.C.E. *FGrHist*, vol. 3B, no. 330.

Ampelius (Lucius), 3–4 C.E. E. Assmann. 1935, repr. 1976. Stuttgart: Teubner.

Anacreon, 6 B.C.E. D. A. Campbell. 1988. Cambridge, MA, and London: Loeb.

Anacreontea, 1?/6 C.E. D. A. Campbell. 1988. Cambridge, MA, and London: Loeb.

Andron of Halikarnassos, 4 B.C.E.? *FGrHist*, vol. 1A, no. 10.

Anecdota Graeca. I. Bekker. 1814. Berlin: Nauck.

Anonymous lyric fragments. D. A. Campbell. 1993. Cambridge, MA, and London: Loeb.

Antipater of Sidon, 2 B.C.E. *HE.*

Antiphilus of Byzantium, 1 C.E. *GP.*

Antoninus Liberalis, 2 C.E.? E. Martini. 1896. Leipzig: Teubner.

Anyte of Tegea, 4 B.C.E. *HE.*

[Apollodorus], 1/2 C.E. J. G. Frazer. 1921, repr. 1989. Cambridge, MA: Loeb.

Apollodorus of Athens, 2 B.C.E. *FGrHist*, vol. 2B, no. 244.

Apollonius of Rhodes, 3 B.C.E. F. Vian and E. Delage. 1976–81. Paris: Budé.

Araethus of Tegea, ante 2 B.C.E.? *FGrHist*, vol. 3B, no. 316.

Aratus, 4–3 B.C.E. D. Kidd. 1997. Cambridge: Cambridge University Press.

Aristides (Publius Aelius), 2 C.E. F. W. Lenz and C. Behr. 1976–81. Leiden.

Aristophanes, 5–4 B.C.E. V. Coulon and H. van Daele. 1954. Paris: Budé.

Aristotle, 4 B.C.E.

    Constitution of Athens: H. Rackham. Rev. ed. 1952. Cambridge, MA: Loeb.

    Constitution of the Ceians: M. R. Dilts. 1971. Durham, NC: Duke University Press.

    [*De mirabilibus auscultationibus*]: G. Westermann, 1839. London: Black and Armstrong.

    Fragments: V. Rose. 1886. Leipzig: Teubner.

    Politics: J. Aubonnet. 1973. Paris: Budé.

    Problems: P. Louis. 1994. Paris: Budé.

Arrian, 1–2 C.E.

    Fragments: A. G. Roos and G. Wirth. 1967. Leipzig: Teubner.

    Indica: P. Chantraine. 1927. Paris: Budé.

Artemidorus, 2 C.E. R. Pack. 1963. Leipzig: Teubner.

Asclepiades of Tragilos, 4 B.C.E. *FGrHist*, vol. 1A, no. 12.

Asius of Samos, 6 B.C.E.? *EGF*.

Athenaeus, 2–3 C.E. C. B. Gulick. 1928–50. New York: Loeb.

Bacchylides, 5 B.C.E. D. A. Campbell. 1992. Cambridge, MA, and London: Loeb.

Bion, 2 B.C.E. A. S. F. Gow. 1952. *OCT*.

Callias of Syracuse, 4–3 B.C.E. *FGrHist*, vol. 3B, no. 564.

Callimachus, 4–3 B.C.E. R. Pfeiffer. 1949–53. Oxford: Clarendon.

Callistratus (Domitius), 1 B.C.E.? *FGrHist*, vol. 3B, no. 433.

Cassius Dio, 2–3 C.E. E. Cary. 1916, repr. 1954. Cambridge, MA: Loeb.

Certamen Homeri et Hesiodi, 3 B.C.E./2 C.E. T. W. Allen. 1912. *OCT*.

Charon of Lampsakos, 5 B.C.E. *FGrHist*, vol. 3A, no. 262.

Cicero, 2–1 B.C.E.

    De divinatione: A. S. Pease. 1920–23, repr. 1963. Darmstadt: Wissenschaftliche Buchgesellschaft.

    Verrines: L. H. G. Greenwood. 1928, repr. 1959. Cambridge, MA, and London: Loeb.

Cleidemus of Athens, 4 B.C.E. *FGrHist*, vol. 3B, no. 323.

Clement of Alexandria, 2–3 C.E. O. Stählin. 1905. Leipzig: Hinrich.

Columella, 1 C.E. E. S. Forster and E. H. Heffer. 1954. Cambridge, MA: Loeb.

Conon, 1 B.C.E.–1 C.E. *FGrHist*, vol. 1A, no. 26.

Corinna, 5/3 B.C.E.? D. A. Campbell. 1992. Cambridge, MA, and London: Loeb.

Crinagoras, 1 B.C.E.–1 C.E. *GP*.

Cypria, 7–6 B.C.E.? *EGF*.

Demetrius of Kallatis, 3–2 B.C.E. *FGrHist*, vol. 2A, no. 85.

Diodorus Siculus, 1 B.C.E. F. Vogel. 1888–1906. Leipzig: Teubner.

Diogenes Laertius, 3 C.E. H. S. Long. 1964. *OCT.*

Dionysius of Halikarnassos, 1 B.C.E. E. Cary. 1937–50. Cambridge, MA: Loeb.

Dionysius Scytobrachion, 2 B.C.E. *FGrHist*, vol. 1A, no. 32.

Duris of Samos, 4–3 B.C.E. *FGrHist*, vol. 2A, no. 76.

Empedocles, 5 B.C.E. *DK.*

Ephorus, 4 B.C.E. *FGrHist*, vol. 2A, no. 70.

Epimenides of Krete, 6–5 B.C.E. *FGrHist*, vol. 3B, no. 457.

[Eratosthenes], post 3–2 B.C.E. A. Olivieri. 1907. Leipzig: Teubner.

Etymologicum Magnum, 12 C.E. F. Sylburg. 1816. Leipzig: Weigel.

Euanthes, ante 2 C.E. *Suppl. Hell.*

Eudoxus, 4 B.C.E. F. Lasserre. 1966. Berlin: de Gruyter.

Euhemerus, 4–3 B.C.E. M. Winiarczyk. 1991. Stuttgart and Leipzig: Teubner.

Eumelus, 8 B.C.E.? *EGF.*

Euphorion, 3 B.C.E. *Coll. Alex.* Oxford. New fragments: *Suppl. Hell.*

Euripides, 5 B.C.E.

> *Erechtheus: Nova fragmenta Euripidea.* C. Austin. 1968. Berlin: de Gruyter.
> Fragments: A. Nauck. 1889. Leipzig: Teubner.
> *Helen:* R. Kannicht. 1969. Heidelberg: C. Winter, Universitätsverlag.
> Other plays: J. Diggle and G. Murray. 1981. *OCT.*

Eustathius, 12 C.E.

> *Eustathii Commentarii ad Homeri Iliadem.* 1827–30, repr. 1960. Hildesheim: Olms.
> *Eustathii Commentarii ad Homeri Odysseam.* 1825–26, repr. 1960. Hildesheim: Olms.

Festus, 2 C.E. C. O. Mueller. 1839, repr. 1975. Hildesheim and New York: Olms.

Geoponica, 6 C.E. H. Beckh. 1895, repr. 1994. Stuttgart and Leipzig: Teubner.

Greek Anthology: see *Palatine Anthology.*

Harpocration, 1/2 C.E.? W. Dindorf. 1853. Oxford: Oxford University Press.

Hecataeus of Miletos, 6–5 C.E. *FGrHist*, vol. 1A, no. 1.

Hegesandrus of Delphi, 3 C.E. *FHG*, vol. 4.

Hegesippus of Mekyberna, 4 B.C.E.? *FGrHist*, vol. 3B, no. 391.

Hellanicus of Lesbos, 5 B.C.E. *FGrHist*, vol. 1A, no. 4.

Hermocreon (incertum), *HE.*

Herodotus, 5 B.C.E. C. Hude. 3d ed. 1927. *OCT.*

Hesiod, 8/7 B.C.E.? F. Solmsen, R. Merkelbach, and M. L. West. 3d ed. 1993. *OCT.*

Hesychius, 5 C.E. M. Schmidt. 1858–68, repr. 1965. Amsterdam: Hakkert.

Hippocrates, 5–4 B.C.E. W. H. S. Jones. 1923. New York: Loeb.

Homer, 8 B.C.E.

> *Iliad:* D. B. Monro and T. W. Allen. 3d ed. 1912. *OCT.*
> *Odyssey:* T. W. Allen. 2d ed. 1912. *OCT.*

Homeric *Hymns,* 8–6 B.C.E. T. W. Allen. 1912. *OCT.*

Hyginus, 2 C.E.

    De Astronomia: G. Viré. 1992. Stuttgart and Leipzig: Teubner.

    Fabulae: P. K. Marshall. 1993. Stuttgart and Leipzig: Teubner.

Iamblichus, 3–4 C.E. L. Deubner and U. Klein. 2d ed. 1975. Stuttgart: Teubner.

Ibycus of Rhegion, 6 B.C.E. D. A. Campbell. 1991. Cambridge, MA, and London: Loeb.

Ion of Chios, 5 B.C.E. *FGrHist*, vol. 2B, no. 392.

Isidore of Seville, 7 C.E. W. M. Lindsay. 1911. *OCT*.

Junius Philargyrius: see Scholia, Vergil.

Leonidas of Tarentum, 4–3 B.C.E. *HE*.

Libanius, 4 C.E. R. Foerster. 1903–23, repr. 1963. Hildesheim: Olms.

Longus, 2 C.E.? G. Thornley, rev. J. M. Edmonds. 1916, repr. 1955. London and Cambridge, MA: Loeb.

Lycophron, 4–3 B.C.E. E. Scheer. 2d. ed. 1908. Berlin: Wiedmann.

Lycurgus, 4 B.C.E. N. Conomis. 1970. Leipzig: Teubner.

Lycus of Rhegion, 4–3 B.C.E. *FGrHist*, vol. 3B, no. 570.

Marsyas of Philippi, post 4 B.C.E. *FGrHist*, vol. 2B, no. 136.

Meleager, 2–1 B.C.E. *HE*.

Memnon of Herakleia, 1 B.C.E.–1 C.E. *FGrHist*, vol. 2B, no. 434.

Menander, 4–3 B.C.E. F. H. Sandbach. 1990. *OCT*.

Menodotus of Samos, 3 B.C.E.? *FGrHist*, vol. 3B, no. 541.

Mnaseas, 3 B.C.E. *FHG*, vol. 3.

Mnesimachus of Phaselis, 4/3 B.C.E.? *FGrHist*, vol. 3C, no. 841.

Moero of Byzantium, 4–3 B.C.E.

    Epic fragments: *Coll. Alex.*

    Epigrams: *HE*.

Moschus, 2 B.C.E. A. S. F. Gow. 1952. *OCT*.

Myrtis, 5/3 B.C.E.? D. A. Campbell. 1992. Cambridge, MA, and London: Loeb.

Nicaenetus, 3 B.C.E. *Coll. Alex.*

Nicander, 3–2 B.C.E. A. S. F. Gow and A. F. Scholfield. 1953, repr. 1979. Cambridge: Cambridge University Press.

Nicolaus of Damascus, 1 B.C.E. *FGrHist*, vol. 2A, no. 90.

Nonnus, 5/6 C.E. W. H. D. Rouse. 1940. London and Cambridge, MA: Loeb.

Nymphis of Herakleia, 4–3 B.C.E. *FGrHist*, vol. 3B, no. 432.

Oppian, 2 C.E. A. W. Mair. 1928. London and New York: Loeb.

Orphic *Argonautica*, 4 C.E.? F. Vian. 1987. Paaris: Budé.

Orphic *Hymns*, 2–3 C.E.? W. Quandt. 1955. Berlin: Weidmann.

Ovid 1 B.C.E.–1 C.E.

    Fasti: E. H. Allen et al. 1978. Leipzig: Teubner.

    Heroides: H. Dörrie. 1971. Berlin and New York: de Gruyter.

    Metamorphoses: W. S. Anderson. 1991. Leipzig: Teubner.

Palaephatus, 4 B.C.E.? N. Festa. 1902. Leipzig: Teubner.

Palatine Anthology (poets discussed by name are listed separately). W. R. Paton. 1916–18. London and New York: Loeb.

Panyassis, 5 B.C.E. *EGF.*

Parthenius, 1 B.C.E. E. Martini. 1902. Leipzig: Teubner.

Pausanias, 2 C.E. M. H. Rocha-Pereira. 1989–90. Leipzig: Teubner.

Persius, 1 C.E. W. V. Clausen. 1959. *OCT.*

Pherecydes of Athens, 5 B.C.E. *FGrHist*, vol. 1A, no. 3.

Philochorus of Athens, 4–3 B.C.E. *FGrHist*, vol. 3B, no. 328.

Philostephanus of Kyrene, 3 B.C.E. *FHG*, vol. 3.

Philostratus, 2–3 C.E.
> *Heroicus*: L. de Lannoy. 1977. Leipzig: Teubner.
> *Vita Apollonii*: F. C. Conybeare. 1912. London and New York: Loeb.

Philoxenus of Kythera, 5–4 B.C.E. D. A. Campbell. 1993. Cambridge, MA, and London: Loeb.

Phoronis, 7 B.C.E.? *EGF.*

Photius, 9 C.E.
> *Bibliotheca:* R. Henri. 1959–91. Paris: Budé.
> *Lexicon*: R. Porson. 1823. Leipzig: Hartmann.

Phylarchus of Athens, 3 B.C.E. *FGrHist*, vol. 2A, no. 81.

Pindar, 6–5 B.C.E. B. Snell and H. Maehler. 1975–80. Leipzig: Teubner.

Plato, 5–4 B.C.E.
> Epigrams: *FGE.*
> *Laws*: E. des Places. 1951. Paris: Budé.
> *Phaedrus*: L. Robin and C. Moreschini. Trans. P. Vicaire. 1985. Paris: Budé.
> *Republic*: E. Chambry. 1959. Paris: Budé.

Pliny the Elder, 1 C.E. H. Rackham et al. 1938–63. Cambridge, MA: Loeb.

Plutarch, 1–2 C.E.
> [*De fluviis*]: F. Deubner. 1855. Paris: Didot.
> *Lives*: B. Perrin. 1916–28. Cambridge, MA: Loeb.
> *Moralia*: F. C. Babbitt et al. 1927–69. Cambridge, MA, and London: Loeb.

Polemon of Ilium, 3–2 B.C.E. *FHG*, vol. 3.

Pollux, 2 C.E. E. Bethe. 1900–1937. Leipzig: Teubner.

Porphyry, 3 C.E. A. Nauck. 1886. Leipzig: Teubner.

Posidippus, 3 B.C.E. *HE.*

Pratinas, 6–5 B.C.E. D. A. Campbell. 1991. Cambridge, MA, and London: Loeb.

Probus: see Scholia, Vergil.

Quintus of Smyrna, 4 C.E. F. Vian. 1963–69. Paris: Budé.

Sappho, 7–6 B.C.E. D. A. Campbell. 1982. Cambridge, MA, and London: Loeb.

Scholia, Apollonius of Rhodes. C. Wendel. 2d ed. 1935. Berlin: Wiedmann.

Scholia, Aristophanes. G. Dindorf. 1837. Oxford: Oxford University Press.

Scholia, Clement of Alexandria. O. Stählin. 1905. Leipzig: Hinrich.

Scholia, Euripides. E. Schwartz. 1887–91. Berlin: Reimer.

Scholia, Hesiod. L. Di Gregorio. 1975. Milan: Università Cattolica Milano.

Scholia, Homer. W. Dindorf. 1875. Oxford: Clarendon. H. Erbse. 1969. Berlin: de Gruyter.

Scholia, Lycophron. E. Scheer. 2d ed. 1908. Berlin: Weidmann.

Scholia, Pindar. A. B. Drachmann. 1903–27. Leipzig: Teubner.

Scholia, Statius (Lactantius), 5–6 C.E. R. D. Sweeney. 1997. Stuttgart and Leipzig: Teubner.

Scholia, Theocritus. C. Wendel. 1914, repr. 1967. Stuttgart: Teubner.

Scholia, Vergil.

    Aeneid: G. Thilo and H. Hagen. 1881–84. Leipzig: Teubner.

    Eclogues and Georgics: G. Thilo. 1887. Leipzig: Teubner.

Semonides of Amorgos, 7 B.C.E. *IE.*

Servius: see Scholia, Vergil.

Silenus, 3 B.C.E. *FGrHist*, vol. 2B, no. 175.

Silius Italicus, 1 C.E. J. D. Duff. 1934, repr. 1961. Cambridge, MA: Loeb.

Simonides, 6–5 B.C.E. D. A. Campbell. 1991. Cambridge, MA, and London: Loeb.

Sophocles, 5 B.C.E.

    Fragments: S. Radt. 1977. Göttingen: Vandenhoeck and Ruprecht.

    Plays: H. Lloyd-Jones and N. G. Wilson. 1990. *OCT.*

Stephanus of Byzantium, 6 C.E. W. Dindorf et al. 1825. Leipzig: Kuehn.

Stesichorus, 7–6 B.C.E. D. A. Campbell. 1991. Cambridge, MA, and London: Loeb.

Stesimbrotus, 5 B.C.E. *FGrHist*, vol. 2B, no. 107.

Strabo, 1 B.C.E.-1 C.E. H. L. Jones. 1917–32. London and New York: Loeb.

Suda, 10 C.E. A. Adler. 1928–38. Leipzig: Teubner.

Suidas of Thessaly, 4/3 B.C.E. *FGrHist*, vol. 3B, no. 602.

Telegonia, 7–6 B.C.E. *EGF.*

Telesilla, 5 B.C.E. D. A. Campbell. 1992. Cambridge, MA, and London: Loeb.

Theocritus, 4–3 B.C.E. A. S. F. Gow. 2d ed. 1952. Cambridge: Cambridge University Press.

Theodoridas, 3 B.C.E. *HE.*

Theognis, 6 B.C.E. *IE.*

Theopompus of Chios, 4 B.C.E. *FGrHist*, vol. 2B, no. 115.

Theseus, 1 C.E.? *FGrHist*, vol. 3B, no. 453.

Thucydides, 5 B.C.E. H. S. Jones and J. E. Powell. 1942. *OCT.*

Timaeus of Tauromenion, 4–3 B.C.E. *FGrHist*, vol. 3B, no. 566.

Titanomachia, post 7 B.C.E. *EGF.*

Trogus (Pompeius), 1 B.C.E.-1 C.E. O. Seel. 1972. Stuttgart: Teubner.

Valerius Maximus, 1 B.C.E.–1 C.E. J. Briscoe. 1988. Stuttgart and Leipzig: Teubner.

Varro, 2–1 B.C.E.

    De lingua Latina: R. G. Kent. 1938, repr. 1977. Cambridge, MA: Loeb.

    De re rustica: J. Heurgon. 1978. Paris: Budé.

Vergil, 1 B.C.E. R. A. B. Mynors. 1969. *OCT.*

Xanthus of Lydia, 5 B.C.E. *FGrHist*, vol. 3C, no. 765.
Xenagoras of Herakleia, 4/1 B.C.E. *FGrHist*, vol. 2B, no. 240.
Xenomedes of Keos, 5 B.C.E.? *FGrHist*, vol. 3B, no. 442.
Xenophon, 5–4 B.C.E. E. C. Marchant. 1900. *OCT*.
Xenophon of Ephesus, 2/3 C.E. G. Dalmeyda. 1962. Paris: Budé.
Zenon of Rhodes, 2 B.C.E. *FGrHist*, vol. 3B, no. 523.

NOTES

CHAPTER I

1. The etymology of *numphē* is unknown but is thought to be related to Latin *nubo*, "I marry": Chantraine (1968–80) s.v. νύμφη; Andò (1996) 48–49. The basic reference works on nymphs are Ballentine (1904); Roscher *Lex.*, vol. 3.1, cols. 500–567 s.v. Nymphen; Wilamowitz-Moellendorf (1931) 185–95; *RE* 17.2 (1937) 1527–99 s.v. nymphai (Herter-Heichelheim); *EAA*, vol. 5, s.v. Ninfe (Sichtermann); Nilsson (1967) 244–55; Muthmann (1975) 77–165; Gantz (1993) 139–43; Andò (1996) 47–79; *LIMC* s.v. Nymphai (Halm-Tisserant and Siebert).

2. Andò (1996) 52.

3. On gender-specific death narratives, see Larson (1995b) 16, 131–44.

4. Larson (1995b) 19–20.

5. Heroines as facilitators in childbirth and childcare: Kearns (1989) 21–36.

6. For the Arrhephoria and Arkteia, see Larson (1995b) 39–40 with bib., and 3.2, n. 29.

7. Kearns (1989) 19.

8. Gate nymphs are attested at Megara (Paus. 1.44.2). Antinoë: Paus. 8.8.4, 8.9.5. See Larson (1995b) 194 n. 61.

9. Contrary to Nock (1944), who argues that "heroine" is often synonymous with "nymph."

10. Larson (1995b) 101–9.

11. Daughter of Acheloös: Eur. *Bacch.* 519–20. Tomb in Thebes: Plut. *Mor.* 578b (*De gen.*).

12. For the Okeanids, see Hes. *Theog.* 337–70, with commentary by West (1966); Hom. *Hymn Cer.* 2.418–24, with commentary by Foley (1994).

13. Barringer (1995); on Thetis, see Slatkin (1991).

14. Ap. Rhod. *Argon.* 4.1411–14. Hesperides: their names and number vary, though Hes. fr. 360 has three: Aigle, Erytheia, Hesperethousa. Arethousa and

several other names are attested on vase paintings: *LIMC* s.v. Hesperides, nos. 1, 3, 29, etc. (McPhee).

15. Muse and nymph: see Kambylis (1965) 31–49; Otto (1956) 9–91. For the terms *mousolêptos* and *mousagetês*, parallel to *nympholêptos* and *nymphagetês*, see Plut. *Mor.* 452b (*De virtute morali*); Sappho fr. 208 (= Himer. *Or.* 46.6); Pind. fr. 94c.

16. On the Charites, see Schwarzenberg (1966), esp. 7, 8, 15–16; Rocchi (1979, 1980); Pirenne-Delforge (1996); Schachter (1981–94) 1.140–44; *LIMC* s.v. Charis, Charites (Sichtermann). Charites and nymphs together: *Cypria* fr. 5; reliefs from Thasos (4.7.2, 5.2.1), Kos (4.9.4), and Telos (n. 296).

17. Hom. *Il.* 5.749–51. On the Horai, see *LIMC* s.v. Horae (Machaira); Muthmann (1975) 104. See also Hes. *Op.* 75 (wedding of Pandora); Pind. *Pyth.* 9.60 (nurses of Aristaios); Hom. *Hymn Ap.* 3.194–96 (chorus).

18. Carnoy (1956) 187–95.

19. *Hudriades, ephudriades: Anth. Pal.* 6.57; 9.327, 329, 823; Schol. Hom. *Il.* 20.8 Dindorf. *Potamêides, epipotamioi:* Ap. Rhod. *Argon.* 3.1219; Schol. Ap. Rhod. 4.1412–14; Schol. Hom. *Il.* 20.8 Dindorf. *Heleionomoi:* Ap. Rhod. *Argon.* 2.821, 3.1219; Schol. Hom. *Il.* 20.8 Erbse and Dindorf. *Limnades, limnaiai:* Theoc. *Id.* 5.17; Orph. *Arg.* 646; Schol. Ap. Rhod. 4.1412–14. *Kranaiai, kranides:* Theoc. *Id.* 1.22; Mosch. 3.29; Schol. Hom. *Il.* 20.8. *Pêgaiai:* Orph. *Hymns* 51.6; Porph. *De antr. nymph.* 13.

20. For *naïs* and *numphê*, see Chantraine (1968–80) s.v. For the formulaic phrase "naiad nymph," see Hom. *Il.* 6.21–22, 14.444, 20.384, *Od.* 13.348, 356; Eur. *Cycl.* 430, *Hel.* 187; Apollod. *Bibl.* 1.9.6; *Anth. Pal.* 9.328, 814; Porph. *De antr. nymph.* 8–10. *Naïs* for *numphê:* Pind. *Pyth.* 9.16, fr. 156; Eur. *Hipp.* 550. *Krênaiai* also has a Homeric pedigree: *Od.* 17.240; possibly also Sappho fr. 214.

21. On water and the nymphs, see Borthwick (1963) 225–43; Cole (1988) 161–65.

22. Buxton (1992) 1–15, (1994) 80–96; Fowden (1988) 48–59.

23. Georgoudi (1974) 82, 171; on transhumance cf. Whittaker (1988) 35–74, 75–86.

24. Hom. *Il.* 6.420. *Orestiades, oreades:* Hom. *Hymn Pan* 19.19; Ar. *Av.* 1098; Bion 1.19; Eust. *Od.* 1.14 (1384.37); Schol. Hom. *Il.* 20.8 Dindorf; Serv. on Verg. *Ecl.* 10.62. *Oressigonoi:* Arist. *Ran.* 1344. Nymphs are also "of the wild places," *agronomoi:* Hom. *Od.* 6.106 cf. Hsch. s.v. ἀγρωστῖναι, ἀγριάδες.

25. Buxton (1994) 104–8 describes caves as "good to think with" in the Lévi-Straussian sense.

26. Among the voluminous literature on landscape and the *locus amoenus*, see esp. Parry (1957) 3–29; Schönbeck (1962) 61–87; Motte (1971); Elliger (1975), esp. 27–147; Thesleff (1981) 31–45.

27. Later, it is also the hour of greatest danger from malevolent *daimones*, male or female: Caillois (1937a) 142–73, (1937b) 54–186.

28. Pl. *Phdr.* 238d. Motte (1971) 26–37 discusses the *puissance hiérophanique* of meadows and gardens.

29. Dion. Hal. *Ant. Rom.* 1.38.1; Wycherley (1937) 2–3.

30. Female genitalia: Motte (1971) 45–48, 85. *Numphê* also refers to the clitoris: Phot. *Lex.* and Suda s.v. νύμφη. On Aphrodite and gardens (Elis, Paphos, Athens, etc.), see Motte (1971) 122–66 and Calame (1999) 153–74, who makes a typological distinction among the meadow, garden, and *locus amoenus*. A class

of nymphs called *leimoniades* ("meadow nymphs"): Soph. *Phil.* 1454; Ap. Rhod. *Argon.* 2.655; Orph. *Hymn* 51.4; Eust. *Od.* 1.14 (1384.37); Hsch. s.v. Λειμονιάς; Serv. on Verg. *Ecl.* 10.62.

31. Poplars: Hom. *Od.* 17.208–11; Ant. Lib. *Met.* 22, 32. Hamadryads and dryads: Paus. 8.4.2; Eust. *Od.* 1.14 (1384.37); Schol. Hom. *Il.* 20.8 Dindorf; Orph. *Hymns* 51.14; Serv. on Verg. *Ecl.* 10.62; Murr (1890) 14, 17–22, 26, 28. Elm nymphs: Hsch. s.v. πτελεάδες. Ash nymphs: Hes. *Theog.* 187 (Meliai). Meliai later became a synonym for dryads or tree nymphs in general: Callim. *Hymn* 1.47, 4.80; Nonnus *Dion.* 14.212. Laurel nymphs or *daphnaiai*; Nonnus *Dion.* 24.99. *Alsêides* or grove nymphs: Ap. Rhod. *Argon.* 1.1066; Schol. Hom. 20.8 Dindorf. Hamadryas bore the tree nymphs Karya (nut), Balanos (acorn), Kraneia (cornel), Moria (oleaster), Aigeiros (poplar), Ptelea (elm), Ampelos (vine), and Syke (fig); Pherenicus in Ath. 3.78b. See also Pitys (4.4.3) and Daphne (4.4.4, 4.9.8).

32. Syrinx (4.4.3); Leiriope (4.3.5); Ionides (4.4.4); Rhodos (4.9.4); Hsch. s.v. πτερίδες.

33. Mnesimachus of Phaselis 841 F 2.

34. Aesch. fr. 168. Proteus: Hom. *Od.* 4.349. Nereus: Hes. *Theog.* 235. Nereid name: Hes. *Theog.* 262; Hom. *Il.* 18.46.

35. Amandry (1984) 375–78.

36. Hom. *Hymn Merc.* 4.552–66. Thriai: Philochorus 328 F 195. Cf. *Suda* and Hsch. s.v. θριαί; Callim. *Hymn* 2.45 with schol.; Pherecydes 3 F 49. Variant story: Steph Byz., *Etym. Magn.* s.v. θρῖα; Wilamowitz-Moellendorff (1931) 379–81.

37. For bee maidens, bees, nymphs, see Larson (1995a) and 2.5.3, 4.8.6.

38. Apollod. *Bibl.* 3.10.2.

39. On Bakis and chresmologues, see Fontenrose (1978) 145–65. Boiotian Bakis: Theopompus 115 F 77; Paus. 10.12.11; Cic. *Div.* 1.18.34; Ael. *VH* 12.35; Schol. Lycoph. 1278. See also Schol. Ar. *Eq.* 123; Philetas in Schol. Ar. *Pax* 1071, *Av.* 963; *Suda* s.v. βάκις; Bouché-Leclercq (1879–82) 2.105–7.

40. Hdt. 8.20, 8.77 (Salamis), 8.96, 9.43.

41. Hierokles: Ar. *Pax* 1046–1126. Kleon/Paphlagon: Ar. *Eq.* 1003–99.

42. Schol. Ar. *Pax* 1071; *Suda* s.v. Βάκῖς.

43. This section on nympholepsy owes a great deal to the seminal article on the subject, Connor (1988). Verbal skills and prophecy: Plato *Phdr.* 238d, 263d; Aristid. *Or.* 21.15; Hsch. s.v. νυμφόληπτος. Amelesagoras: 330 T 2, c. 300 B.C.E., according to Jacoby, but earlier according to the testimonia. On this shadowy figure, see Pearson (1942) 87–89, 161.

44. Epimenides and the cave: Epimenides 457 T 1. *Hieron* of the nymphs: Theopompus 115 F 69 = Diog. Laert. 1.115. Food from the nymphs: Epimenides 457 T 1; Timaeus 566 F 4 = Diog. Laert. 1.114. For a red-figured vase shaped like a hoof, see Himmelman-Wildschütz (1980) figs. 12, 13. See also Plut. *Vit. Sol.* 12.4; Poljakov (1987).

45. Plut. *Mor.* 421a–b (*De def. or.*). Apollonios: Philostr. *VA* 2.37. Apollonios also made a miraculous appearance to his disciples in a nymphaion at Dikaiarchos (Puteoli): *VA* 8.11–12.

46. Connor (1988) 171–72; Arist. *Pr.* 954a 35–36.

47. Archedamos inscriptions: *IG* I³ 977–80; Connor (1988) 178, 184–85; Purvis (1998) 70–89.

48. For the Pharsalos inscriptions, see Giannopoulos (1912, 1919); Comparetti (1921–22); *SEG* (1923) 1.247–48, 1.2, (1925) 357; von Gaertringen (1937); Peek

(1938) 18–27, pl. 2, 3; McDevitt (1970) nos. 166, 171; Connor (1988) 162–63; Decourt (1995) nos. 72–73 with a new text.

49. Peek (1938) 22 reads "Athanippa raised the laurel," with Athanippa as either a female dedicator or, perhaps, a nymph.

50. My translation owes a debt to that of Connor (1988) 163; the text is that of Peek (1938) 18–27.

51. Decourt (1995) 88–93 argues that Pantalkes was a herdsman, responsible for the earlier inscription but not the later. Onesagoras: Mitford (1980) 263, no. 291.

52. E.g., Comparetti (1921–22) 158–59.

53. Pleket (1981) 163; *GVI* no. 378. Compare the verse inscription left by a physician, Timokleides (Thasos, first century), recording his establishment of a cave sanctuary of Dionysos and the nymphs: École française d'Athènes (1968) 172.

54. Verg. *Aen.* 6.46–51, 77–80. This understanding of possession, though by no means universal, exists across many cultures; see Lewis (1971) 58–64.

55. On gender and nympholepsy, see Connor (1988) 178 n. 75; 186 n. 107.

56. Paus. 9.3.9. Hdt. 9.43 quotes an oracle of Bakis that he considered fulfilled by the victory at Plataia.

57. Cleidemus 323 F 22 = Plut. *Vit. Arist.* 11.2–4.

58. Theognis 19–30. Schachter (1981–94) 2.186–87 reviews various explanations of the name; he follows Maass's derivation from an original *sphrâgos*, which refers to the process of cave formation. See Maass (1922) 272–76.

59. Ford (1985). I use the name "Theognis" as a convenience; part of Ford's thesis is that the "seal" was placed on a body of traditional and new material in order to impose unity and authority on the corpus as a whole.

60. Onomakritos: Hdt. 7.6.3–5. *Theoros*: Theognis 21, 809–10. See Ford (1985) 88.

61. Bride: e.g., Hom. *Il.* 18.492–93. *Numpha philê*: Hom. *Il.* 3.130, *Od.* 4.743. Cf. Callim. fr. 788 and, for the dear nymphs, *numphai philai*, Ar. *Thesm.* 977–78.

62. Daughters of Zeus: Hom. *Il.* 6.420, *Od.* 6.105, 9.154, 13.356, 17.240. Daughters of Helios: Hom. *Od.* 12.131–33.

63. Aisepos River: Hom. *Il.* 2.285, 12.21. Pedasos: Hom. *Il.* 6.35, 20.92.

64. The epic poem called the *Telegonia*, which continued Odysseus' story, began with Odysseus sacrificing to the nymphs and sailing to Elis to inspect his herds there: *Telegonia* T 5.

65. Another Ithakan fountain, Arethousa, is mentioned at Hom. *Od.* 13.407–8. Arethousa is a common spring name (4.10.1), and it is not clear whether a homonymous nymph was identified with the spring.

66. Eumaios: Hom. *Od.* 14.435. Hill of Hermes: Hom. *Od.* 16.471. On the details of Eumaios' sacrifice, see Kadletz (1984); Petropolou (1987).

67. Kalypso as *numphê*: Hom. *Od.* 5.14, 153, 196, 230. *Numphê potnia*: Hom. *Od.* 1.14, 5.149. *Numphê euplokamos*: Hom. *Od.* 5.57–8. *Dia, thea*: Hom. *Od.* 5.78, 85, 97, 116, 173, 180, 202.

68. Kalypso is *deinê theos*: Hom. *Od.* 7.246; *deinê theos audêessa*: 12.449. On the "dread goddess with human speech," see Loraux (1992) 20–21; Nagler (1996). Kalypso's island called Nymphaia: Steph. Byz. s.v. Νυμφαία.

69. Kirke is *potnia*: Hom. *Od.* 8.448, 10.394, 549, 12.36. *Dia theaôn*: Hom. *Od.* 10.400, 503, 12.20, 155. *Thea*: Hom. *Od.* 10.220, 310, 481. *Athanatê*: Hom.

Od. 12.302. *Euplokamos*: Hom. *Od.* 11.8. *Deinê theos audêessa*: Hom. *Od.* 11.8, 12.150. *Polupharmakos*: Hom. *Od.* 10.276. *Numphê*: Hom. *Od.* 5.230, 10.543–45. Amphipoloi: Hom. *Od.* 10.348–51; Eust. *Od.* 10.348 (1660.53–61). Cf. the naiad servants of Kirke in Ap. Rhod. *Argon.* 4.711.

70. Schol. Hes. *Theog.* 187; Palaephatus 35; Eust. *Il.* 20.321 (1210.39). On Melia, see 4.3.1 and below on Pindar. Human origins: see Hom. *Od.* 19.163 and further sources in West (1978) on lls. 145–46.

71. No nymphs: with the possible exception of Sappho fr. 214, restored as κραννίαδες παρθενίκαις. Sappho's brother: fr. 5 cf. fr. 213c.

72. Sappho T 45 (= Demetrius *On Style* 132). On nymphs and weddings, see 3.2.3.

73. Translations of lyric by Campbell (1982–93).

74. Leukothea, "white goddess," is the name of the sea goddess in the *Odyssey*, who saved Odysseus from drowning. Here, the name is used in plural form, probably as an honorific for these nymphs or minor goddesses, who have to do with a river not the sea.

75. Aggressors: Stehle (1996). For Sappho and Phaon, see Sappho fr. 211; Nagy (1996). For vase paintings, see Burn (1987) 26–44. The female figures who accompany Aphrodite have an intermediate status between personification and nymph. The paradise garden setting belongs as much to the nymphs as to Aphrodite (who was worshiped in a garden setting on the south slope of the Akropolis, Paus. 1.19.2). Pan appears with Phaon and adoring females on MM13 (Burn).

76. Alcm. fr. 63. The Lampads who follow Hekate seem to be otherwise unknown.

77. It has been suggested that this is a dramatic fragment, perhaps from one of Pratinas' satyr plays. See Sutton (1980) 7–11; Seaford (1977–78).

78. Translations of Pindar by Race (1997).

79. E.g., Pind. *Ol.* 5.2–4, 8.1, *Nem.* 1.1–6, *Isth.* 1.1–4, 7.1; cf. Pind. fr. 33c, 52b.1, 52g, 76, 195. See Mullen (1982) 79 n. 37.

80. See Norwood (1956) 36.

81. For dating, see Mullen (1982) 82.

82. Nagy (1990) 177. On the importance of heroic genealogies in the odes, see 144 n. 43, chap. 6, esp. 153, 175–78, 205.

83. On Pindar's consciousness of civic ideology, see Kurke (1991) 163–94.

84. Aigina, however, might have been listed in the Hesiodic *Ehoeae*: West (1985) 100–101.

85. Aigina and Thebe: Pind. *Isthm.* 8.16–20. See Nisetich (1980) 11, 12; Nagy (1990) 205, 381. Metope: Pind. *Ol.* 6.84.

86. Cf. Melia: Pind. *Pyth.* 11.4, fr. 52g.4, 52k.35, 43. Thronia: fr. 52b.1.

87. Vivante (1972) 47.

88. It is in the prose works of the classical logographers, now fragmentary, that we find continued interest in nymphs (4.1).

89. Tragedy reflects cult practice by associating the nymphs with Pan (Eur. *Bacch.* 951–52, *Hel.* 187–90; Soph. *OT* 1098–1100), with river gods (Eur. *Hel.* 1, *Heracl.* 785–86, Eur. [*Rhes.*] 929; Soph. *Philoc.* 725–26; Aesch. fr. 168), and with Dionysos (Eur. *Bacch.* 519–21, *Cycl.* 3–4, 68–69, 430; Soph. *OC* 679–80, *OT* 1105–9). Or they are mentioned in their natural contexts of mountains (Eur. *Helen* 1324) and springs (Eur. *IA* 1291–99; Soph. *Phil.* 1454–61). The same applies

to mentions of nymphs in comedy: Ar. *Pax* 1070–73 (the prophet Bakis), *Nub.* 271 (Okeanos), *Thesm.* 326 (catalogue of gods; mountains), 990–94 (Dionysos), 977–81 (Hermes Nomios and Pan), *Ran.* 1344, *Av.* 1097–98 (Charites, Okeanos); Men. *Dys.* 36–39 (Pan). Mentions of nymphs in Aesch. include fr. 168 (3.2.4), two fragments in which he refers, respectively (fr. 204b.4–6, 15), to a chorus of nymphs and a mysterious *despoina numphê*, who rules the mountains (Artemis?), and the reference to the Korykian nymphs and their cave in the Pythia's enumeration of Delphic gods in *Eum.* 122–23. See also fr. 312 for the Peleiades, daughters of Atlas, and the chorus of Okeanids, who leave their cave to come to Prometheus' aid (*PV* 133–34).

90. "Fairy" infants in other cultures: MI F321.1 (changelings).

91. Eur. *Hipp.* 545–52. For this difficult passage, see Barrett (1964) 263.

92. Arnott (1981).

93. For discussion, see Wilamowitz-Moellendorff (1895) on line 781.

94. For the dramatic presentation of Philoktetes' cave, see Jobst (1970) 38–44.

95. Cf. Men. *Dys.* 197 where the devout girl expresses her trust in the nymphs: *ô philtatai numphai*.

96. Dover (1968) on line 271.

97. On the staging of the *Dyscolus*, see Jobst (1970) 78–82.

98. Statues: Men. *Dys.* 51, 572. Pan and nymphs mentioned: Men. *Dys.* 444, 643, 947.

99. Gutzwiller (1998) 54–74. On Anyte, see also Snyder (1989) 67–77. Aesthetic: Fowler (1989) 4, 70–71, 110–36.

100. Gutzwiller (1998) 91, 100–101.

101. *Anth. Pal.* 9.823, attributed to Plato and quoted here, is of Hellenistic date. For nymphs who "tread with rosy feet," cf. an early epigram, Moero *Anth. Pal.* 6.189 and, similarly, *Anth. Pal.* 9.327. For other epigrams, see *Anth. Pal.* 6.43, 154, 224, 253, 324; 7.55, 196; 9.330, 334, 341, 826; *Anth. Plan.* 226. Later examples are quite derivative of Anyte and Leonidas, e.g., *Anth. Pal.* 6.25, 57, 176; 9.142, 663–64; 11.194.

102. For nymphs invoked in musical contexts, cf. Theoc. *Id.* 1.12, 4.29, 5.140.

103. Amymone and Automate appear in Apollod. *Bibl.* 2.1.5. Hippe and Physadeia are attested with Amymone in Schol. Eur. *Phoen.* 188. Cf. Hsch. s.v. Ἵππειον τὸ Ἄργος. For other Callimachean nymphs, see esp. *Hymns* 1.35 (Neda), 5.57 (Chariklo), 6.38 (in Demeter's grove), and *Hymns* 3 and 4 passim; *Aet.* fr. 26.10 (Psamathe), 75.56 (Korykian n.), incert. fr. 788. Callimachus wrote a book on nymphs: fr. 413.

104. Vian and Delage (1976–81) 2.137 n. 869. Cf. Ap. Rhod. *Argon.* 1.1222–29; Callim. *Hymn* 3 passim.

105. Jason's horror at his near-meeting with Hekate is amplified by the reaction of the nymphs: Ap. Rhod. *Argon.* 3.1218–20. Cf. Callim. *Hymn* 4.79–80. For the motif of fearful nymphs, see also Ap. Rhod. *Argon.* 2.821; Callim. *Hymn* 3.51, 62–63.

106. Mourning: Bion 1.19; Mosch. 3.17–18, 29.

107. For Nereids, see Barringer (1995) 141–51. Cf. Eur. *Andr.* 1254–69 (death of Peleus).

108. Antiphilus 23 = *Anth. Pal.* 7.141; cf. Philostr. *Her.* 9.1–4 (141); Quint. Smyrn. 2.585–92 (Memnon), 4.1–12 (Glaukos), 10.362–66, 458–59 (Paris). For discussion, see Janko (1992) 372. For Euphorion, see Phot. *Bibl.* 149a.

109. Cf. Nic. *Alex.* 65, 266, 321; *Ther.* 623. See also Aristid. *Or.* 41.11.

110. Cf. *Anth. Pal.* 9.406, 9.587, 11.49.

111. There is archaeological evidence of renewed interest in the Attic caves of the nymphs during the third and fourth centuries, perhaps indicating a resurgence of pagan devotions in response to the growth of Christianity (5.1.2).

112. According to Merkelbach (1988) 137, 140–41, the Lesbos of the novel is a *Märchenlandschaft,* yet there is a religious dimension to the work.

113. Diodorus' source for this fantastic tale of Nysa is thought to be the parody author Dionysius Scytobrachion (second century B.C.E.), so it is unlikely that this description corresponds to a historical cave site.

114. Quintus' cave is probably that better known as the *specus Acherusia,* used for necromancy (e.g., Plut. *Vit. Cim.* 6.6) and thought to contain an opening to Hades. For a description of the cave, which is flooded and contains votive niches, see Hoepfner (1972) 44–45, pl. 5. Cf. Ap. Rhod. *Argon.* 2.353–56, 735–51; Nymphis 432 F 3 (with no mention of nymphs).

115. Trans. Lamberton (1983).

CHAPTER 2

1. Danforth (1984) 53–85. Discussion by classicists has also been very cautious: Winkler (1990) 10 calls the issue of continuity a "red herring" but maintains that "certain deep premises (protocols) about social life, widely shared and with very significant variations around the Mediterranean, can be used to frame and illuminate ancient texts, bringing out their unspoken assumptions." Ideology: Danforth (1984); Herzfeld (1986). For a discussion of Politis' work, see Herzfeld (1986) 101.

2. Lawson (1904) 35. In his introduction to Megas (1970), Richard Dorson gives a helpful summary of Greek folklore scholarship by classicists.

3. Information about the *neraïdes* can be found in the following works: Pashley (1837) 2.214–18, 232–34; Schmidt (1871) 98–131; Politis (1904) 387–490; Lawson (1910) 130–62; Argenti and Rose (1949) 1.266–31, 245–49; Dawkins (1950) 346–49; Blum and Blum (1970); Stewart (1985) 219–52, (1991). For convenience, I use the term *neraïda* throughout, but many dialectal variants exist. See Schmidt (1871) 98–99; for euphemisms, see Schmidt (1871) 100–101; Stewart (1991) 162–63. The name *neraïda* is associated through folk etymology with νερό, "water": Argenti and Rose (1949) 30; Schmidt (1871) 100.

4. Belief in the *exôtika* in modern times is, of course, rapidly disappearing. A sharp drop in the rate of infectious diseases, which were often attributed to *neraïdes,* and the obsolescence of windmills, watermills (cf. Schmidt [1871] 102), and threshing floors (Politis [1904] nos. 700, 701), major points of contact with them, have done much to speed this process. See Stewart (1991) 108–10, 174.

5. For the relationship between the devil, the *exôtika,* and the church, see Stewart (1991) 137–61, esp. 151. Though the church sometimes disavows the *exôtika* as non-Christian, in practice they are and historically have been an integrated part of the system.

6. For *neraïdes* and water sources, see Politis (1904) nos. 663, 666, 672; Blum and Blum (1970) nos. 68, 72, 75, 77, 83, 85, 88. Caves: Politis (1904) nos. 704, 705, 745, 768, 775. Appearance at midday or night: Politis (1904) nos. 657, 718,

724, 728, 732. Interest in children: Blum and Blum (1970) nos. 72, 79, 78. Sexual allure: Blum and Blum (1970) nos. 29, 66, 70. Propitiation with honey and milk: Schmidt (1871) 124–25, 127; Dawkins (1950) 393; Stewart (1985) 238–39. Both dress in white: Orph. *Hymns* 51.11; Stewart (1991) 97, 176.

7. Arist. *Pr.* 954a.35–38. See Connor (1988) 172 n. 56. The author of the Hippocratic treatise *On the Sacred Disease* (4) heaps scorn on quacks who attribute convulsions and other violent symptoms to possession by various gods.

8. Festus s.v. *lymphae* (second century C.E.). Cf. Varro *Ling.* 7.87; Poll. 1.19; Isid. *Etym.* 10.161–62. Festus echoes Varro's comparison of *nympholêptos* and *lymphaticus*. Varro, however, merely notes that people of this description have an agitated or disturbed mind (*commota mente*), while Festus speaks of insanity caused by an apparition. The similarity of ancient and modern terms for those affected by the nymphs/*neraïdes* is striking: compare νυμφόληπτος with modern νεραϊδοπαρμένος, νεραϊδοπιασμένος, ἀνεραϊδοβαρημένος. See Schmidt (1871) 119–20; Politis (1904) nos. 725, 736, 748; Lawson (1910) 142–44; Dawkins (1950) 392; Stewart (1985) 228–29. For the relationship of nymphs and other figures of Greek myth to the widespread idea of the "midday demon," see Caillois (1937a) 142–73, (1937b) 54–83, 143–86, esp. 68–83.

9. For the Byzantine period, see Greenfield (1988) 182–95. On Christian demonology and earlier Near Eastern demons, like Lamashtu, see Barb (1966) 1–23. *Testament of Solomon*: McCown (1922) 18★-19★, 83★. The text is of Byzantine date, though some parts are probably earlier: Greenfield (1988) 159. Several versions of varying date and length exist; see Delatte (1927) 211; McCown (1922) 10–28. For Ornias, a similar demon of the succubus type, see McCown (1922) 16★; Caillois (1937) 76 n. 3. Protective spell: Delatte (1927) 122.27, with Caillois (1937) 76 n. 1. Delatte's collection of manuscripts dates from the fifteenth to the nineteenth centuries, but much of the material is clearly of antique and Byzantine origin. Other spells in Delatte's collection mention Nereids (119.3, 132.9) and include a fifteenth-century reference to a personage called Ἀνεράδα βασίλισσα (460.17, 462.2). Fair One of the Mountains: Lawson (1910) 162–73; Politis (1904) no. 660 cf. Aesch. fr. 204b 15. *Neraïdes* are part beast: Schmidt (1871) 105; Lawson (1910) 133; Stewart (1985) 245; Politis (1904) nos. 654, 680.

10. Gautier (1980) 165–69, ll. 545–48. Cf. Greenfield (1988) 182–95. The same dialogue describes the Onoskeleis as male in form, but see Gautier (1980) n. 61. For the date and author of the text, see Gautier (1980) 128–31, who makes a cautious attribution to Nicholas of Modon (twelfth century). In any case, the earliest manuscripts provide a *terminus antequem* of the late thirteenth to early fourteenth centuries.

11. Bryennios: Oeconomos (1930) 1.225–33 cf. Vryonis (1971) 419 n. 42. Canabutzes: cited by Lobeck (1829) 2.1204 cf. McCown (1922) 12 n. 1. On Canabutzes, see Lehnerdt (1890) v–xiii.

12. Giustiniani: Argenti (1943) 175–76. Argenti was able to locate the original Italian manuscript; a French version is cited by Lawson (1901) 167–68.

13. Allatius: cited by Argenti and Rose (1949) 27 cf. Politis (1904) no. 671.

14. Nilsson (1940) 21.

15. Nock (1933) 104–5.

16. *RE* 17.2 (1937) 1531 s.v. *nymphai* (Herter). The Kouretes sometimes seem to play this role as well (4.8.6).

17. Folklorists distinguish between *types* (entire tales that preserve the main events of the narrative in the same sequence wherever they are found) and *motifs* (the building blocks of folktale types). Thus, the Cinderella story is a type, while having a fairy godmother is a motif. In order to classify and compare folktale material from cultures worldwide (where tale types are not always constant), it is necessary to break down the tales into their constituent parts as in Thompson's *Index*. For the material discussed here, I cite corresponding motif numbers from the *Index*. Folktale types, mostly European, are listed in Aarne and Thompson (1961). The only clearly recognizable type in my collection of material is the swan maiden (types 313, 400, 465a) of which the myth of Peleus' capture of Thetis is an example. Therefore (and in order to avoid discussion of whether each example is a myth or a folktale), I refer to my examples as *narratives* or *stories*. I do, however, cite other types where they seem relevant.

18. For example, some modern stories depict *neraïdes* as requiring the services of a human midwife: Stewart (1985) 222–23; Politis (1904) nos. 794–96, a motif that is extremely common in European fairy stories (*MI* F 372.1) but reverses the ancient practice whereby nymphs aided human mothers in childbirth. Similarly, the *neraïdes* are sometimes depicted not only as abducting human infants but leaving changelings in their place: Pashley (1837) 216; *MI* F 321, 321.1. Turkish influence is also visible in Greek folklore, though to what extent the experts do not agree. For a view that emphasizes the Turkish contributions, see the chapter written by Halliday in Dawkins (1916) 215–83, esp. 216, 219. Dawkins himself, however, saw only a slight Turkish influence in his collection of material from the Dodecanese: Dawkins (1950) 20.

19. Pindar warns against the hubris of aspiring to sex with a goddess (Ixion: *Pyth.* 2.28–30; Tityos: *Pyth.* 4.90–92), as does Alcm. fr. 1.17: "let no man strive to marry Aphrodite."

20. Winkler (1990) 203.

21. Abduction: Vermeule (1979) 168. *MI* F 320–29 describe variations on the theme of abduction by supernatural beings. Ganymedes: Hom. *Il.* 20.232–35. Beauty is often mentioned as a factor in abductions; cf. Eos' abduction of Kleitos, Hom. *Od.* 15.249–51. Likewise, it is the most beautiful individuals who are chosen by the nymphs and the modern *neraïdes*.

22. Eos seems to typify goddess-mortal relationships in an epic context, since her case is cited by both Kalypso (Hom. *Od.* 5.121–24) and Aphrodite (Hom. *Hymn Ven.* 5.218–19), would-be lovers of mortals. For Eos as Indo-European dawn goddess and her relations with mortals, see Boedeker (1974) 64–84; Slatkin (1991) 28–31; Vermeule (1979) 163–65. Eos carries off Orion (Hom. *Od.* 5.121), Kleitos (*Od.* 15.250), Kephalos (Hes. *Theog.* 986), and Tithonos (*Theog.* 984, Hom. *Hymn Ven.* 218–19). For abductions by goddesses, see Stehle (1996) 219, who argues that the motif was popular because it "opened space for fantasies of uncodified erotic relationships."

23. On abduction and heroization, see Vermeule (1979) 163; Nagy (1979) 174–210; Larson (1995b) 16–18.

24. Wilamowitz-Moellendorf (1931) 187–88.

25. Ap. Rhod. *Argon.* 1.1324–25. *MI* F 324.3: youth abducted by fairy; F 302.3.1.4: fairy abducts whomever she falls in love with; F 420.5.2.1.1: water maiden enamors youth, then draws him under water; type 316: the nix of the mill pond pulls youth under water after he is promised to her in marriage.

26. Trans. Gow (1952).

27. Theoc. *Id.* 13.53–54. On the setting, see Mastronarde (1968) 272–80. On bodily abduction by nymphs, see Borgeaud (1988) 118–19.

28. Bormos: Nymphis 432 F 5a–b. Hsch. s.v. Βῶρμον. θρῆνον ἐπὶ Βώρμου νυμφολήπτου Μαριανδυνοῦ; Poll. 4.54–55 (Βώριμος). Variant: Aesch. *Pers.* 935–40 with schol. (= Callistratus 433 F 3a). For Hylas' cult, see Strabo 12.4.3, 564; Ap. Rhod. *Argon.* 1.1354–56 with schol.; Serv. on Verg. *Ecl.* 6.43; Nic. in Ant. Lib. *Met.* 26.

29. Hylas and Echo: Nic. in Ant. Lib. *Met.* 26. Salmakis: Ov. *Met.* 4.285–388.

30. Echo: Ov. *Met.* 3.341–507. Galatea: Ov. *Met.* 13.740–897. See also 4.4.3; Borgeaud (1988) 56, 118–19. Hylas is mentioned as early as the fifth century in Hellanicus (4 F 131).

31. On Astakides as abductee, see Larson (1997a).

32. Five-year-old: *IG* XIV 2040 = *GVI* no. 1595 (Rome): παῖδα γὰρ ἐσθλὴν ἥρπασαν ὡς τερπνὴν Ναῖδες, οὐ θάνατος. In l. 2, the girl is referred to as a πενταέτη νύμφη. Cf. *Anth. Pal.* 7.170 on a child drowned in a well, where the nymphs are mentioned but not directly named as the culprits. Two-year-old: *IG* XIV 2067 = *GVI* no. 952 (Rome): Νύμφαι κρηναῖαί με συνήρπασαν ἐκ βιότοιο. An eight-year-old Roman male was *raptus a nymphis*, *CIL* VI 29195. See Cumont (1942) 401–3 with n. 3.

33. Ino's transformation into a Nereid perhaps should also be mentioned in this category (Hom. *Od.* 5.333–35; Hyg. *Fab.* 2; Apollod. *Bibl.* 3.4.3). Cf. Byblis, who upon her suicide is changed to a hamadryad in Ant. Lib. *Met.* 30.

34. Dawkins (1950) no. 36. *MI* F 302.3.4.2: fairies dance with youth until he dies or goes mad.

35. *(H)arpazô*: Stewart (1991) 279 n. 17; cf. Politis (1904) nos. 653, 736, 738. Man found dead by fountain: Blum and Blum (1970) 115. Forced to dance: Blum and Blum (1970) 113; Politis (1904) nos. 657, 730. Men carried off or "seized": Politis (1904) nos. 657, 672, 723, 766.

36. Adolescent girl: Schmidt (1871) 122; cf. Lawson (1910) 141; Politis (1904) nos. 751, 752. Abducted children: Politis (1904) nos. 739, 745. Exorcism: Blum and Blum (1970) no. 78. Wells: Lawson (1910) 160; Argenti and Rose (1949) 1.252.

37. *MI* F 387: fairy captured.

38. Hes. *Theog.* 1003–5; Pind. *Nem.* 5.12–13; Apollod. *Bibl.* 3.12.6; Schol. Eur. *Andr.* 687. Seal women captured by fishermen appear in the folklore of the Shetland islands. See Hartland (1925) 265–66.

39. Differing accounts are given of the reason for the unusual marriage: Peleus was being rewarded for his virtue (Pind. *Nem.* 5.25–37); Thetis, having refused Zeus, was condemned to a mortal husband (Hes. fr. 210; Apollod. *Bibl.* 3.13.5); Themis' oracle or Prometheus drove off all divine suitors (Hyg. *Fab.* 54; Apollod. *loc. cit.*). In all versions, however, Thetis is unwilling (Hom. *Il.* 18.434, οὐκ ἐθέλουσα) For Thetis' shapeshifting, see Pind. *Nem* 4.62–64; Ov. *Met.* 11.235–64; Apollod. *loc. cit.*; Paus. 5.18.5 (depicted on the chest of Kypselos). On Thetis' cosmogonic significance, see Slatkin (1991), esp. 53–84.

40. Physical struggle: Schefold (1966) pl. 28, 70 b–c; 43 figs. 11–12 illustrate archaic representations of Thetis' transformation scene. The subject was popular on Attic vases; see Beazley (1956, 1963, 1971) s.v. Peleus; Reeder (1995) 340–51. For Pindar's accounts, see *Nem.* 4.57–65, 5.25–37.

41. *MI* D 361.1 = types 313, 400, 465a. For a discussion of the folkloric context of Peleus and Thetis, see Séchan (1967) 91–109. Hartland (1925) 255–83 includes a useful discussion of the swan maiden theme, in which he observes that it is a gender reversal of Psyche and Amor.

42. ἀφθόγγους γάμους: Soph. fr. 618. Cf. Frazer (1921) app. 10.

43. Blum and Blum (1970) 112, 114–15; Argenti and Rose (1949) 246, 251; Lawson (1910) 136–37; Politis (1904) nos. 772, 773, 779, 781. On the scarf or veil, see Schmidt (1871) 104. Shapeshifter: Megas (1970) no. 76 = Politis (1904) no. 775 (Krete). Cf. Schmidt (1871) 115–17. Lawson (1910) 136–37 gives a version from Messenia that includes the shapeshifting motif. Thetis' departure: Ap. Rhod. *Argon.* 4.866–79; Apollod. *Bibl.* 3.13.6.

44. Exceptions exist, particularly in the ritual sphere. Certain Greek rituals attempted to persuade or gain power over a deity (usually Ares) by binding representative statues. See Faraone (1991) 165–205.

45. Plut. *Mor.* 415d (*De def. or.*), and Pind. fr. 165; for nymph and tree, see also Mnesimachos of Phaselis 841 F 3; Callim. *Hymn* 4.80–85; Schol. Hom. *Il.* 6.22 Erbse; Nonnus *Dion.* 2.92–108, 14.209–12, 16.245; Ov. *Fast.* 4.231–32.

46. *MI* F 304.5: mortal chooses to sleep with fairy as boon for saving her life. *MI* C 43.2: cutting trees offends spirits; C 51.2.2: taboo against cutting sacred trees or groves. On the taboo against tree cutting, see Henrichs (1979) 85–108.

47. Charon of Lampsakos 262 F 12a; Cf. *Etym. Magn.* s.v. Ἁμαδρυάδες, which repeats Charon's version. See Pearson (1939) 148–50. The term used to describe Rhoikos' punishment, πηρωθῆναι, is a vague word used to describe some form of incapacitation, most often in respect to the limbs (*LSJ* s.v.; Ar. *Ran.* 623). It can also refer to blindness or even sexual function, though qualifying words may be added in these cases.

48. Plut. *Mor.*, *Quaest. Nat.* 36 (from Longolius): *Parvula favorum fabricatrix quae Rhoecum pepugisti aculeo domans illius perfidiam.* Pind. fr. 165 probably belonged to Pindar's account of Rhoikos: ἰσοδένδρου τέκμαρ αἰῶνος θεόφραστον λαχοῖσα ("having been allotted a term as long as the years of a tree").

49. Plut. *Mor.* 144d (*Conjugalia Praecepta*): "these insects are thought to be irritable and hostile towards men who have been with women." Cf. Columella *Rust.* 9.14.3; Ar. [*Mir. ausc.*] 21; Detienne (1974) 99–101.

50. Eumelus fr. 11 = Charon of Lampsakos 262 F 12b. Apollod. *Bibl.* 3.9.1 gives two alternative mortal mothers in addition to the nymph and lists the sons as Elatos and Apheidas. Paus. 8.4.2, 8.37.11. Compare Egeria and King Numa: Dion. Hal. *Ant. Rom.* 2.60.5; Ogilvie (1965) 102–3. For nymphs as teachers of civilized skills see 2.5.3.

51. Thamyris: Apollod. *Bibl.* 1.3.3; Schol. Hom. *Il.* 2.595 Erbse (intercourse with one only). For other versions, see Devereux (1987) 199–201.

52. Hom. *Hymn Ven.* 5.267–68. Lawson (1910) 152, 155, 158–59.

53. Ap. Rhod. *Argon.* 2.456–89. Schol. Ap. Rhod. *Argon.* 2.456–57 alludes to other accounts in which Paraibios is a slave of Phineus. See Vian and Delage (1976–81) 1.198.

54. Poplars: see 1.2. *MI* F 261.3.1: fairies dance under tree. The myth is possibly represented on a fifth-century pelike: Erysichthon raises his ax to strike a tree while a female figure rises from the earth to protest: Gantz (1993) 69; *LIMC* s.v. Erysichthon I, no. 1 (Kron).

55. Dawkins (1950) no. 33. Dawkins translated *neraïda* as "fairy"; I use his translation but retain the term *neraïda*.

56. Also, in Callim. *Hymn* 6.53, Erysichthon threatens to strike Nikippe, the representative of Demeter, just as the king's son strikes Dimitroula, the representative of the *neraïda*. For other points of similarity between the modern and the two ancient versions, see Hopkinson (1984) 28; McKay (1962) 53. Dawkins does not find the common name "Dimitroula" significant in relation to "Demeter," though such a connection seems plausible.

57. Dawkins (1950) 347. The legend may be Thessalian in origin: Callim. *Hymn* 6.24–26; Diod. Sic. 5.61. See Wilamowitz-Moellendorf (1924) 2.34–44; McKay (1962) 36–37; Hollis (1970) 128–32. For links between Thessaly and Kos (where the modern folktale was collected), see Paton and Hicks (1891) xiv, 344–48; Hsch. s.v. Θεσσάλαι (Koan women were called Thessalians). For arguments that the *Hymn* was performed on Kos, see Fraser (1972) 2.916–17, n. 290; Sherwin-White (1978) 306–11. *Contra*: Hopkinson (1984) 38.

58. Fehling (1972) 173–96; Hopkinson (1984) 26–30; Henrichs (1979) 87 n. 11.

59. For this theory, see Kenney (1963) 57. Planudes was a Byzantine of the late thirteenth century.

60. Fehling (1972) 187 with n. 60, 193.

61. For Demeter and Triopion, see Callim. *Hymn* 6.30; *RE*, ser. 2, vol. 7.1 (1939) col. 174 s.v. Triopas (Wüst). Henrichs (1979) 86 n. 5 comments that "by substituting gods of wider appeal such as Demeter . . . for the anonymous and undifferentiated tree-sprites, the polis-religion eventually absorbed the tree cult."

62. For herdsmen and the syrinx, see Duchemin (1960) 19–56.

63. Nic. in Ant. Lib. *Met.* 22 cf. 4.6. On Kerambos and transhumance, see Georgoudi (1974) 171. *Neraïdes* will gather to dance around a herdsman who plays music: Schmidt (1871) 110–11; Politis (1904) no. 779; Stewart (1985) 230.

64. Another of Nicander's stories (Ant. Lib. *Met.* 31) is that of the Messapian youths who challenged the Epimelid (i.e., herd-guarding) nymphs to a dance; after being defeated, they were changed to trees. Cf. Ov. *Met.* 14.514–26.

65. For Pan's lack of erotic success, see Borgeaud (1988) 75–81. For Pan as *duserôs*, see *Anth. Pal.* 9.825; Nonnus *Dion.* 48.489.

66. Timaeus 566 F 83 (= Parth. *Amat. Narr.* 29); Diod. Sic. 4.84 and Ael. *VH* 10.18 use Timaeus either directly or indirectly. *MI* F 302.3.3.1: fairy avenges self on inconstant lover or husband; Q247: punishment for desertion of fairy mistress.

67. Stesichorus and Daphnis: Ael. *VH* 10.18. Daphnis invented bucolic song: Diod. Sic. 4.84.2–4; Ael. *VH* 10.18; Schol. Theoc. *Id.* 1.141a. See van Groningen (1958) 293–317; Halperin (1983) 75–84, 249–57. Other versions: in addition to Theoc. *Id.* 1, see *Id.* 8.43, 92–93 (Daphnis marries a nymph, Naïs), *Id.* 7.72–77 (Daphnis is wasting with love of Xenea, and the oaks sing his dirge); Schol. Theoc. 8.82–85e (Daphnis is maimed, ἐπηρώθη), 8.93a (Daphnis falls off a cliff after being blinded); Serv. on Verg. *Ecl.* 5.20 (Daphnis is blinded then translated to heaven by Hermes and replaced by a spring at which the Sicilians sacrifice), 8.68 (Daphnis is blinded then turned to stone); Junius Philargyrius on Verg. *Ecl.* 5.20 (Daphnis is blinded); Ov. *Met.* 4.276–78 (Daphnis is changed to stone). On relationships among the various versions, see Gow (1952) 2.1–2, 30.

68. Theoc. *Id.* 1.97–98, 103, 140. The view that Daphnis drowns himself, though not universally accepted, has a certain plausibility in view of Daphnis' association with the nymphs in this *Idyll* (66, 141). For the drowning hypothesis, see especially Ogilvie (1962) 109 with Williams (1969) 121–23 and Segal (1974a) 20–38.

69. For a summary of scholarship, see Gutzwiller (1991) 95–101 with notes. Gow (1952) 2.2 and Lawall (1967) 18–27 favor the Hippolytos analogy; cf. Schmidt (1968) 539–52. Ogilvie (1962) 106–7, followed by Williams (1969) 121–23, argued that the Timaean and Theocritean versions could be reconciled.

70. Misanthropic Daphnis: cf. Parth. *Amat. narr.* 29. Similarly, Aisakos, son of Priam and the nymph Alexirhoë: Ov. *Met.* 11.761–63. See Gutzwiller (1991) 96–97, 100.

71. Serv. on Verg. *Ecl.* 5.20. Hounds: Nymphodorus in Schol. Theoc. *Id.* 1.65–66b–c; cf. Ael. *NA* 11.13.

72. Devereux (1973) 36–49; Buxton (1980) 22–37. For another critique of the Freudian view, see Bernidaki-Aldous (1990) 60, 78 n. 5.

73. Hom. *Od.* 10.301, 341; Hom. *Hymn Ven.* 5.188; Giacomelli (1980) 1–19. Also pertinent is the strange story reported by Plut. *Mor.* 417e (*De def. or.*) in which Molos, a local hero of Krete, is said to have been found headless after raping a nymph: νύμφῃ συγγενόμενος ἀκέφαλος εὑρεθείη.

74. Illness follows encounter with *neraïda*: Lawson (1910) 139; Politis (1904) no. 653; Stewart (1991) 4–5. This motif is also found in northern European folklore: Christiansen (1958) 123. Taboo of sexual infidelity: Schmidt (1871) 112. *MI* F 302.6: fairy mistress leaves man when he breaks taboo; F 302.3.3.1: fairy avenges self on inconstant lover or husband; C 31.5: taboo against boasting of supernatural wife; C 942.3: weakness from seeing woman or fairy naked; C 943: loss of sight for breaking taboo.

75. Herdsmen: Politis (1904) nos. 681, 722, 779. Naxos: Stewart (1991) 4–5, 106.

76. Hom. *Hymn Ven.* 257–72. Mediation: Segal (1974b) 205–19, (1986) 37–47; Clay (1989) 193–98; Podbielski (1971) 77; Smith (1981) 93–94. Bickerman (1976) 234–36 sees the parallel to folklore and speculates that "the original history of Anchises as told among the mountaineers of Mysia" involved an affair with a nymph.

77. Oinone: Hellanicus 4 F 29; Hegesianax 45 F 2, 6; Conon 26 F 1.23; Apollod. *Bibl.* 3.12.6; Ovid *Her.* 5; *Anth. Pal.* 2.1.221 ("Oinone, Kebrenid nymph"). For the herdsman-nymph pattern and the relations between saga and folktale in the case of Paris, see Stinton (1965) 44, 59.

78. E.g., Segal (1974, 1986); Clay (1989) 194.

79. Charon of Lampsakos 262 F 5 gives Kybebe as the "Phrygian and Lydian" name of Aphrodite; see Burkert (1979) 99–122. For Kybele with fawning animals, see, e.g., Ap. Rhod. *Argon.* 1.1144–45. For Aphrodite's similarity to Kybele, see Wilamowitz-Moellendorff (1920) 83; Rose (1924) 11–16; Nilsson (1967) 1.522–23; Cassola (1975) 231–43. For the more general question of Aphrodite's origins, see sources in Penglase (1994) 160–161 n. 2; Boedeker (1974).

80. Duchemin (1960) 71–73.

81. The pattern also appears to be present in some versions of the Attis myth, as in Ov. *Fast.* 4.223–44.

82. This important point is noted by Bickerman (1976) 235. In Hes. *Theog.* 987, Aphrodite carries off Phaethon; according to Apollod. *Bibl.* 1.9.25, she carried off the mortal Boutes, and in Ael. *VH* 12.18, she hides Phaon among the lettuces.

83. Hom. *Hymn Ven.* 286–90 (punishment), 247 (shame). Cf. Hom. *Il.* 5.311–13, 375–78. Anchises' punishment, like that of Daphnis, is variously described: he is killed by lightning after bragging to his friends (Hyg. *Fab.* 94); enfeebled (Virg. *Aen.* 2.647–49, 2.707); blinded (Serv. on Verg. *Aen.* 1.617); paralyzed (*semper debilis vixit*) by lightning after boasting (Serv. on Verg. *Aen.* 2.649). Cf. Gow (1952) 2.24. See Podbielski (1971) 78–79; Lenz (1975) 144–52.

84. In Homer, Aineias is reared in the house of Alkathoös (*Il.* 13.466), but Servius on Verg. *Aen.* 1.617 mentions the tale of Aineias' birth beside the Simoeis River and his connection with nymphs.

85. Okeanids: Hes. *Theog.* 346–48. *MI* F 345; fairies instruct mortals; A 511.8: culture hero reared by supernatural woman. In Hom. *Od.* 4.383–93, Eidothea sends Menelaus to consult her father, Proteus, on how to return home. Compare *Od.* 10.487–95 (Kirke-Tiresias); Verg. *G.* 4.387–414 (Kyrene-Proteus); and Pherecydes 3 F 16a; Apollod. *Bibl.* 2.5.11 (Eridanos nymphs–Nereus). On the "consultation myth" as it applies to Kirke and Kalypso, see Nagler (1996) 145. Perseus received magical objects (sandals, wallet, and helmet) from the nymphs (4.4.2).

86. This consensus is based primarily on a lack of any evidence to the contrary. For a different view, see Jacobsen (1984) 285 n. 38; Detienne (1974) 95–100.

87. The fullest extant account is Diod. Sic. 4.81–82. Aristaios' cults involved his identification with Apollo and Zeus, while several later sources associate him with Dionysiac themes. Cf. Pind. *Pyth.* 9.64–65; Ap. Rhod. *Argon.* 2.498–527 with schol.; Serv. on Verg. *G.* 1.14; Callim. fr. 75.32–37; Storck (1912) 14.

88. In all the Thessalian-Libyan accounts, Aristaios is descended from the nymphs and rivers of Thessaly on his mother's side. On Pindar's probable use of Hesiod's account, which therefore would have belonged in the Thessalian category, see West (1985) 86.

89. *RE* 2 (1896) no. 854 s.v. Aristaios (von Gaertringen). The connection between Euboia and Keos is explained historically by early Eretrian control of the island: Strabo 10.1.10, 448.

90. Ar. *Constitution of the Ceians* nos. 26–27, trans. Dilts (1971). Cf. Ar. fr. 511. Both Diod. Sic. 4.81.2–3 and *Etym. Magn.* s.v. βρίσαι say that Aristaios was taught about honey and/or bees by nymphs. Honey discovered by Aristaios in Thessaly or Keos: Euhemerus T 24.

91. Oppian [*Cynegetica*] 4.265–72. Boiotian Ino: according to Hesiod, Aristaios was the husband of Kadmos' daughter Autonoë, best known as one of Pentheus' maddened killers in Eur. *Bacch.* By her, he became the father of the ill-fated Aktaion. Hes. *Theog.* 977 mentions Ἀρισταῖος βαθυχαίτης; cf. Hes. fr. 217.1, where he is associated with Hermes and called *episkopos* of herdsmen. For the Karyai-Karystos equation, see Hollis (1991) 11–13. Yet another set of accounts has Aristaios' daughter Makris rearing Dionysos and feeding him with honey on Euboia (Aristaios himself is mentioned in the passage as the discoverer of honey and olive oil): Ap. Rhod. *Argon.* 4.1131–40. Euboia itself was also called Makris: Callim. *Hymn* 4.20 with schol. Dionysus is reared by *Kroniê numphê* Makris on Euboia: Nonnus *Dion.* 21.193–95.

92. Ar. *Constitution of the Ceians* nos. 26–27. Another version of the nymphs' journey (Callim. *Aet.* fr. 75.56–59) contradicts the Aristotelian fragment by making the "Korykian nymphs" travel from Parnassos to Keos (cf. Ov. *Her.* 20.223–24).

93. Diod. Sic. 3.70.1. Scytobrachion is generally thought to be a satirical writer, and the story might be a fabrication rather than authentic Libyan material. The mythic parallel, however, remains valid.

94. Hom. *Hymn Merc.* 4.555–57. Cheiron and Asklepios: Pind. *Pyth.* 3.45–46; Apollod. *Bibl.* 3.10.3. Jason: Pind. *Nem.* 3.53–55. Medos: Hes. *Theog.* 1001–2. Achilles: Pind. *Nem.* 3.43.

95. Mnaseas *FHG* fr. 5. For the folklore and mythology of the bee, see Cook (1895) 1–24; Ransome (1937); Bodson (1978); Davies and Kathirithamby (1986) 47–73; Fraser (1951).

96. Note that the scholiast here quoted conflates various meanings of the word *melissa*: bee, nymph, priestess (of Demeter and certain other deities). On the relationship between Demeter and *melissai*, see Detienne (1974) 100. In the founding legend of Keos itself (Callim. *Aet.* fr. 75.55–56; Ar. *Constitution of the Ceians*, nos. 26–29), the nymphs are transitional colonizers of the island before the advent of men, while Servius (on *G.* 1.14) states that Aristaios himself was the first inhabitant of Keos.

97. Cherry (1988) 8–9 cf. Hodkinson (1988) 35. For the Kyklopes as an intermediate stage, see Guthrie (1957) 80–81.

98. Plut. *Mor.* 657e 8 (*Quaest. conv.* 3), trans. Babbitt (1927).

99. Among the other mortal offspring nursed by nymphs are Achilles (Ap. Rhod. *Argon.* 4.812–13), Aineias (Hom. *Hymn Ven.* 5.273–75), and Rhesos (Eur. [*Rhes.*] 928–31).

100. This category of civilizing nymphs is the only one without plentiful modern parallels, though the *neraïdes* are occasionally benefactors of humans: for healing, see Politis (1904) no. 683; for music lessons, see Politis (1904) no. 779; Stewart (1985) 230. In Dawkins (1950) no. 32, a man who has been blinded and cast into the sea is healed and given food and clothing by the *neraïdes*.

101. Stewart (1991) 108, 175.

102. Herzfeld (1979) 295–96.

103. Panaghia: Stewart (1991) 156. Accomplished: Schmidt (1871) 103, 106; Argenti and Rose (1949) 26; Blum and Blum (1970) 114–15; Stewart (1985) 243. Brides: Pashley (1837) 217–18, 232–34; Stewart (1985) 230, (1991) 176 n. 20.

104. Blum and Blum (1970) 218–19; Stewart (1991) 107–8.

105. Blum and Blum (1970) 219. Attribution of unstated fears and desires, whether to ancients or moderns, must of course remain speculative.

106. E.g., Politis (1904) no. 653: impotent men on Samos are said to have been snatched by the *neraïdes* when they were younger.

107. For a recent discussion, see Versnel (1993) 253–57, 277–83.

108. Blum and Blum (1970) 218.

109. Blum and Blum (1970) 113.

CHAPTER 3

1. Hedreen (1992) 9, 163, (1994) 47 n. 1. This section as a whole owes an obvious debt to the important work of Hedreen (1986) and Carpenter (1997). For the words *saturos* and *silênos*, see Brommer (1937).

2. Midas and silen: Hdt. 8.138; *LIMC* Suppl. s.v. Midas nos. 7–41 (Miller). Amymone and silen: Apollod. *Bibl.* 2.14. Rampaging satyrs or silens: Apollod. *Bibl.* 2.1.2; Philostr. *VA* 6.27. Satyrs on unknown island: Paus. 1.23.6. For discussion and other examples, see Hedreen (1992) 72–73. For satyrs or silens as exemplars of the folkloric "wild man," see Seaford (1976).

3. Hom. *Hymn Ven.* 5.256–63; Hes. fr. 10a 17–18; Pind. fr. 156; Xen. *Symp.* 5.7 (naiads are mothers of silens); Theopompus 115 F 75c (Seilenos is child of a nymph); Apollod. *Bibl.* 2.5.4; Paus. 3.25.2; Strabo 12.4.8, 566, 14.5.29, 681; *Anth. Pal.* 16.8, 9.826; *Anth. Plan.* 8; Ov. *Fast.* 3.409–10; Phot. *Lex.* s.v. νυμφόβας (Seilenos as husband of the nymphs). On similar relationships with centaurs, see 4.6.

4. On the nature of silens, see Sutton (1980), esp. 134–45. Cave mouths: Sutton (1980) 141 cf. Jobst (1970) 50–59.

5. *Oineus*: Soph. fr. 1130.6–8. For discussion of the attribution, see Sutton (1980) 57; Carden (1974) 135–39. *Ichneutae*: Soph. fr. 314.41, 147–49. On Silenos, see Sutton (1980) 139. Roughly a quarter of Sophocles' *Ichneutae* (The Trackers) is preserved. It deals with the same myth related in the Homeric *Hymn to Hermes*, the birth of the god in a cave on Mount Kyllene and how the infant Hermes stole Apollo's cattle. The silens are charged with the task of finding the cattle, and they create such a racket outside the cave that Kyllene herself, the nymph of the mountain, emerges to reprove them.

6. Antipater of Sidon 48 = *P. Oxy.* 662.

7. Eur. *Cycl.* 1–4, 68–71, 429–30. For the *Dionysiscus*, see Sutton (1980) 40–41; Carpenter (1997) 35–38; Apollod. *Bibl.* 3.5.1; Pl. *Leg.* 672b.

8. Hedreen (1992) 67–103.

9. Literary sources: Hom. *Hymn Bacch.* 26.3–10 (nymphs received him in a cave and followed him when he grew to adulthood); Soph. *OC* 678–80 (divine nurses, *theai tithênai*); Eur. *Cycl.* 4. For vases, see, e.g., Boardman (1989) figs. 22, 126; Carpenter (1997) 54–62. A fragmentary dinos by Sophilos showing the wedding of Peleus and Thetis includes ΝΥΣΑΙ among the guests, though in a matching scene on another Sophilan dinos, they are labeled ΜΟΣΑΙ. See Carpenter (1986) 9. Plaster cast: Richter (1960). Votive relief: Shear (1973); Thompson (1977) 73–84; Edwards (1985) no. 14; Stewart (1990) 192–93, figs. 581–83.

10. For the Dionysiac portion of Ptolemy's procession, see Ath. 5.196e–203b (= Callixenus 627 F 2); Rice (1983) 62–68, 81–82.

11. Early black figure: Carpenter (1986) 80. For discussion of the François vase, see Hedreen (1994) 48. For the dropped nasal in the common form *nuphai*, see Threatte (1980) 1.486, 2.755; Robert (1980) 384.

12. For nymphs vs. maenads, see Edwards (1960); Henrichs (1987) 91–124; Hedreen (1994).

13. For historical maenadism, see Henrichs (1978) 121–60; Versnel (1990) 131–55.

14. For Dionysiac nymph names, see Carpenter (1997) 57–62; Fränkel (1912). The obvious nymph names Naïs, Nynphaia, and Antro are also attested (Fränkel [1912] 13, 21, 44).

15. Carpenter (1997) 70–84 even goes so far as to argue that the females who dance around statues of Dionysos on the famous series of Lenaia vases are intended as nymphs rather than as mortal celebrants.

16. The *polos* from a sixth-century karyatid from the Siphnian treasury at Delphi has a scene of revelry with uncooperative nymphs: Themelis (1992) 56 and fig. 5.

17. According to Aristid. *Or.* 53.4, "Hermes as *chorêgos* always leads the nymphs." Hermes as companion (συνοπάων) of the naiads: *IG* II/III² 4728; Semonides fr. 20. Herding nymphs include *epimêlides numphai* (Schol. Hom. *Il.* 20.8 Dindorf; Ant. Lib. *Met.* 31), *perimêlides* (Serv. on Verg. *Ecl.* 10.62), and *hamamêlides* (Eust. *Od.* 1.14 [1384.37]).

18. Pastoral wedding songs: Eur. *Alc.* 576–77. Hom. *Hymn Ven.* 5.256–63. For Apollo and Pan, see 4.4.3–4, 4.9.8.

19. Larson (1995b) 26–57.

20. Wickens (1986) 166–67.

21. Parker (1996) 165; Borgeaud (1988) 4, 51 n. 54.

22. Borgeaud (1988) 47–73.

23. Ar. *Thesm.* 977–78.

24. For a discussion of panolepsy and nympholepsy, see Borgeaud (1988) 88–116.

25. Son of Okeanos: Acusilaus 2 F 1; cf. Hes. *Theog.* 340; Plut. [*De fluviis*] 22.1 (son of Okeanos and naiad nymph). Nymph daughters: Pl. *Phdr.* 263d. Dirke: Eur. *Bacch.* 520. Kastalia: Panyassis F 15.

26. Hes. *Theog.* 346–48. Oracle: Ephorus 70 F 20. See Parke (1967) 153–57. On Acheloös' cults and iconography, see Isler (1970); Gais (1978); Weiss (1984). Attic boundary stone of nymphs and Acheloös: *IG* I³ 1061 (500–450). *Koureion*: Cole (1984b).

27. For a shrine to the Attic river Kephisos and the nymphs cofounded by a man named Kephisodotos, see 4.2.2.

28. Antefixes: Mertens-Horn (1991) fig. 11. Jewelry: Isler (1970) nos. 279–310. For Acheloös protomes and the fifth-century mask from Marathon, see Gais (1978) 357; Isler (1970) 37, no. 51, 113–15.

29. The literature on this topic is abundant; for recent surveys of the issues involved, see the introduction in Reeder (1995) 13–16; Calame (1999) 125–29, 153–64. Rituals of maturation: Dowden (1989); Calame (1997); etc. The Arkteia has no explicit associations with the nymphs, though some *krateriskoi*, the distinctive vases connected with the rite, were found in the cave of Pan and the nymphs at Eleusis. See Kahil (1965) 23, 31.

30. Reilly (1997). For previous views of the figures in the reliefs as dolls, see bib. in Reilly (1997) 166–67 nn. 6–9; especially Elderkin (1930) 464–65; Dörig (1958) 45–46, pl. 23; Schmidt (1971) 40–41. See also Arguriade (1991) 18. For jointed dolls, see also Stillwell et al. (1952) 145–51; Higgins (1954–) nos. 683, 702, 909, 941. Most extant examples are of either Attic or Corinthian manufacture.

31. Stele of Melisto: Sackler Mus. Inv. 1961.86; Pedley (1965) 259–67, pls. 1–3; Clairmont (1993) 204–5; Reilly (1997) 158 fig. 36, 166 n. 4. Boys at play: Clairmont (1993) 140 and nos. 0.869, 0.870. Clothed doll on relief: Clairmont (1993) no. 0.780, in which a girl holds a seated, clad doll in her raised left hand while a dog leaps at a bird she holds in her lowered right hand.

32. On the uses of terra-cottas, see Higgins (1954–) 1.7–8. Stylistic parallels between dolls and votive figurines: see, e.g., Higgins nos. 903–7 (standing votives

on bases) compared to no. 909 (articulated doll), all from Corinth; no. 1500 (seated woman) compared to no. 1501 (seated doll) from the area of Kyrene.

33. For the variety of objects used as dolls, see the classic article Ellis and Hall (1907). Elderkin (1930) 457 fig. 2 illustrates an Egyptian doll with the lower limbs rounded off.

34. According to a recent study of American dolls and girls' socialization, one of the most common fantasies during play with Barbies is the staging of weddings. See Markee (1994) 190.

35. Erinna: Bowra (1936) 325–42. For text, see *Suppl. Hell.* no. 401; West (1977). *Plangôn*: cf. Callim. *Hymn* 6.91–92; Schol. Theoc. *Id.* 2.110f; Hsch. s.v. δατύς; Clem. Alex. *Protr.* 4.58 with schol. 45, 22.

36. Schol. Theoc. *Id.* 2.110d.

37. For dancing dolls with string attachments, see Higgins (1954–) nos. 701, 721, 734, 909. Musical instruments and *poloi*: Elderkin (1930) 461–62, figs. 7, 14, 15; Arguriade (1991) 20, figs. 5, 7, 8, 12; Higgins (1954–) nos. 909–11, 924–29 (Corinth), 1437–39, 1501 (Kyrene).

38. *Anth. Pal.* 6.280. Daux (1973a, 1973b). Following Daux are Reilly (1997) 159 and Oakley and Sinos (1993) 14. Dedications of dolls to Venus are attested for Rome: Pers. 2.70 (*Veneri donatae a virgine pupae*).

39. As in *Anth. Pal.* 6.309: Philokles dedicates to Hermes his ball, rattle, astragaloi, and top.

40. Hom. *Od.* 6.102–9; Burkert (1985) 150; Ap. Rhod. *Argon.* 3.882; Verg. *Aen.* 1.499–500. For other epic associations of Artemis with the nymphs, see Ap. Rhod. *Argon.* 1.1221–25; Verg. *Aen.* 11.532–38. Artemis and a chorus of (mortal) maidens also appear at Hom. *Il.* 16.179.

41. In extant lyric poetry, the main association of the nymphs seems to be with Dionysos and Aphrodite or Eros: Anac. fr. 357; Alcm. fr. 63; Pratin. fr. 708. This may be due to the fragmentary nature of lyric; Philostr. and Menander Rh. mention hymns to Artemis by Sappho, which conceivably could have linked her with nymphs (Sappho T21, T47). For Dionysos and the nymphs, see 3.1.1. On Sappho and the nymphs, see Winkler (1981) 63–89.

42. Soph. *Trach.* 214–15. *Numphê* as bride in tragedy: Eur. *Med.* 150, 163, 555–56; *Heracl.* 476, 481, 801, *Hel.* 725; *Or.* 1147; Soph. *Ant.* 797. The fact that in the passage from the *Trachiniae* the nymphs are called neighbors, *geitones*, suggests that their cult is spatially contiguous with that of Artemis but not integrated with it: Rusten (1983) 291 n. 11.

43. Callim. *Hymn.* 3.13–15, 40–43; Ov. *Met.* 3.155–98. It is unclear whether a swarm of nymphs was present in earlier versions of the Aktaion myth. Lacy (1990) cites two Italian vases that show the death of Aktaion at the spring of Gargathia, with a personifying nymph present.

44. Artemis and water sources: Croon (1956) 193–220; Nilsson (1967) 492–95; Morisot (1994).

45. On the Echelos relief (4.2.2) is a group thought to include Artemis and three nymphs, but the dedication is to Hermes and the nymphs. Epigrams: the nymphs are usually addressed as spring deities (*Anth. Pal.* 6.43, 189; 7.170; 9.142, 326–29) and are associated with Pan (9.142, 330, 823), Pan and Dionysos (6.154, 158), or Pan and Hermes (6. 253, 334). Epigrams on Artemis deal with the hunt (6.268), childbirth (6.271–73), maidenhood (6.276, 77, 80).

46. These are the only two examples adduced by Nilsson (1967) 499. Other possible but ambiguous cult links between Artemis and the nymphs: Strabo 8.3.12, 343 mentions the many Artemisia, Aphrodisia, and nymphaia in the countryside at the mouth of the Alpheios River. The Chesiad nymphs of Mount Kerketes on Samos (Nic. *Alex.* 151) are perhaps connected with Artemis Chesias (Callim. *Hymn* 3.228). The Amnisos nymphs are mentioned in relation to Artemis by both Callim. (*Hymn* 3.15) and Ap. Rhod. (*Argon.* 3.877) but the cult connection, if any, is unclear. Finally, "Amarynthian maidens," who are mentioned in Theodoridas 2 = *Anth. Pal.* 6.156, might be associated with the cult of Artemis at Amarynthos in Euboia. See *GP* 2.538–39. On Artemis and choruses, including nymphs, see Calame (1997) 90–113.

47. Cf. the night dances of the nymphs in honor of Artemis at Ap. Rhod. *Argon.* 1.1221–25. Paus. 3.10.7 does not speak of a *hieron* or *temenos* but calls Karyai a *chôrion* of Artemis and the nymphs. Artemis on the hunt accompanied by nymphs has connotations similar to those of Artemis with her chorus, since the hunt belongs to the subadult, sexually pure Hippolytos type whether male or female; see Vidal-Naquet (1986) 118–20. This is implicit in the simile at Hom. *Od.* 6.102–9; for the choral features of the simile, see esp. Lonsdale (1993) 208. Though the subject of the simile is the hunt, the verb *paizô*, the element of competition in beauty, and the proud mother looking on are more suggestive of a chorus than a hunt.

48. Wright (1957) 301–10; Goodchild (1971) 123; Chamoux (1953) 314–20. For the cathartic inscription, see *SEG* 9.72, 20.717; translation, commentary, and bib. in Parker (1983) 332–51. Another possible "bride room": Paus. 2.11.3.

49. Burkert (1985) 173, 150; Dowden (1989) 62, 102–5. On the indispensable role of dance in courtship, see Lonsdale (1993) 206–33; Burkert (1985) 151; Pl. *Leg.* 771e-772a; Plut. *Mor.* 254a (*De mul. virt.*).

50. Chantraine (1968–80) s.v. νύμφη; Burkert (1985) 151; Dowden (1989) 105.

51. Nilsson (1967) 499–500. Against this is her seeming origin in Asia Minor and kinship with Eastern mother goddess types, such as Kybele: Burkert (1985) 149.

52. Callim. *Hymn* 3.19–22, 36–39, 225. For Artemis at the borders of the polis, see Cole (1998) 27–30; de Polignac (1995) 25–26.

53. Hussey (1890) 59–64.

54. For the bathing of images, see Ginouvès (1962) 283–94; Kahil (1994) 217–23.

55. Cf. Dowden (1989) 123 on the relations among rivers, initiations, fertility, and civic identity.

56. Priam painter: Hurwit (1991) 40–41, fig. 5 and 58 nn. 45–46; Moon (1983b) 97–118, fig. 7. Voyeurism: as on the Chalkidian cup by the Phineus painter, Boardman (1998) no. 479; Rumpf (1927) no. 20, pls. 40–44. See also Ginouvès (1962) 115–17.

57. Plut. *Mor.* 772b (*Am. narr.*); Ginouvès (1962) 269. Hsch. s.v. γάμων ἔθη lists *proteleia*, first fruits, and hair offerings.

58. Artemis: Eur. *IA* 433–34, 718; Poll. 3.38; Xenophon of Ephesus 1.8.1; Plut. *Vit. Aristid.* 20.6 (in Boiotia, the sacrifice is made to Artemis Eukleia). See Oakley and Sinos (1993) 12. Other deities: Oakley and Sinos (1993) 12; Paus. 2.32.1 (Hippolytos). See also *Suda* s.v. προτέλεια and προτέλειον (*proteleia* may

refer either to the sacrifices or the day on which they are performed). Ginouvès (1962) 269–70.

59. Oakley and Sinos (1993) 6; Ginouvès (1962) 257–58; Ballantine (1904) 97–106. Most of our information on the custom comes from the lexicographers: Harp. s.v. λουτροφόρος; Hsch. and Phot. *Lex.* s.v. νυμφικὰ λουτρά; Poll. 3.43; *Etym. Magn.* s.v. Ἐννεάκρουνος. Cf. Thuc. 2.15; Eur. *Phoen.* 346–48 with schol.; Porph. *De antr. nymph.* 12.

60. Sanctuary of Nymphe: *IG* I³ 1064; Travlos (1971) 361 with bib., figs. 464–67; Brouskari (1974) 84–118; Wycherley (1978) 197–98.

61. Stele: Daux (1958) 366–67. For other links between nymphs and Zeus Meilichios, see 4.2.1.

62. Priestess of Nymphe: *SEG* 39 (1979) 135.2, 8; Vanderpool (1979). For the seat of the priestess of Aphrodite Pandemos and Nymphe, see Daux (1958) 367; *IG* II/III² 5100, 5149.

63. Calame (1997) 113, 120 cf. Clark (1998) 13–15.

64. On the Daidala: Paus. 9.3.1–9 (Plataia); Plut. in Euseb. *Praep. Evang.* 3.1.85c–86b, text in Donohue (1988) 137, app. 1.104, 108 (Daidale). Cf. Burkert (1979) 132–34; Schachter (1981–94) 1.242–50; O'Brien (1993) 19 n. 5; Clark (1998) 22–25.

65. O'Brien (1993) 9–76.

66. Simon (1972) 210–11, fig. 6.

67. Simon (1972) 216.

68. Simon (1972) 210–11; for bib., see Schachter (1981–94) 1.244 n. 3.

69. Elderkin (1930) 458–60, figs. 5–6; Dörig (1958) 42–44, pl. 22.1; Arguriade (1990) 19. For similar early articulated dolls, made by potters rather than coroplasts, see Higgins (1967) 19–20, pls. 6E, 7C (Kos, Rhodes, and Attica).

70. Aesch. fr. 168, attributed by Asclepiades to the *Xantriae*, has been assigned by some modern scholars to the *Semele* or *Hydrophori*. See Robertson (1983) 153–62, who makes a convincing argument for the original attribution. For an opposing view, see Gantz (1993) 475. Nilsson (1955) interpreted the ritual begging on behalf of the nymphs as a form of rain magic.

71. Hes. fr. 130–33. Cf. Pherecydes 3 F 114 (Hera, madness, cure by Melampous, and marriage); Apollod. *Bibl.* 2.2.2.

72. Robertson (1983) 158–62. Cure of Proitids, spring of Anigrid nymphs: Strabo 8.3.19, 346 cf. Paus. 5.5.3, 10. Lousoi: Paus. 8.18.7. Azania: Eudoxus fr. 313. Cure through institution of choruses to Artemis: Bacchyl. 11.85–112. See also Callim. *Hymn* 3.233–36; Calame (1997) 117–18. On the girl's resistance to marriage as a central theme of Bacchyl. 11, see Seaford (1988). On the Proitids, see also Dowden (1989) 71–95.

73. Bath of the Palladion and *numphai* or *gunaikes* who wash it: Callim. *Hymn* 5 with schol. Hera's Argive bath: Hsch. and *Etym. Magn.* s.v. Ἡρεσίδες. Hera Parthenia at Argos: Schol. Pind. *Ol.* 6.149 b, g. Bath of Hera at Nauplia: Paus. 2.38.2.

74. Brommer (1938–39) 172.

75. Pedley (1990) 36–39; Saflund (1981); Kron (1971) with bib.; Neutsch (1957) 7–29; Sestieri (1956).

76. Sestieri (1956) 22–23.

77. The latter theory is favored by Sestieri (1956); Kron (1971); and Saflund (1981).

78. Sestieri (1956) 23–24.

79. Kron (1971) 147–48.

80. Ath. 12.521e.

81. Costabile et al. (1991) 114–27. For the cave, see 5.1.12.

82. Higgins (1954–) nos. 702, 1501, 1528. Dörig (1958) pls. 24–26; Elderkin (1930) 470–71, figs. 20–22; Arguriade (1991) figs. 13–15. See Winter (1903) 1.87, 88, 165–68.

83. The largest group is that from Lokroi; others are from Taras, Rhegion, Fontana Calda, Medma, Metapontion, and Morgantina. Outside the western colonies, examples are found at Kyrene and Myrina. See Bell (1981) 95 and nn. 158–67; Costabile et al. (1991) 122–24 and nn. 114–33 for bib.

84. Costabile et al. (1991) 125–27; Bell (1981) 94–96 ; Zuntz (1971) 168–70.

85. Pottier and Reinach et al. (1887) 1.262; Mollard-Besques (1954–) vol. 2, pls. 9, 11; Elderkin (1930) 469–70; Arguriade (1991) 22. See also Dörig (1958) 47–48.

CHAPTER 4

1. For the logographers, see esp. Pearson (1939); Luce (1997) 10–14.

2. Hellanicus 4 F 4; Hdt. 1.57. For this point, see Pearson (1939) 158–59.

3. Huxley (1969) 91.

4. Dougherty (1993) 61–102.

5. Naiad nymphs: Apollod. *Bibl.* 3.14.6, 8. Praxithea: Eur. *Erechtheus* fr. 65.63; Lycurg. *Leoc.* 22, 98. Granddaughter of Kephisos: Apollod. *Bibl.* 3.15.1.

6. Klepsydra: Schol. Ar. *Lys.* 910–12, *Vesp.* 853; Hsch. s.v. Κλεψύδρα; Parsons (1943). Mycenaean remains in the area of the East Cutting are consistent with use as a shrine: Smithson (1982).

7. *IG* I³ 1063; Travlos (1971) 323. See also *Hesperia* 10 (1941) 38 no. 3.

8. Empedo: Parsons (1943) 203. Caves: Eur. *Ion* 938; Ar. *Lys.* 911; Travlos (1971) 417; Wickens (1986) nos. 66–67, 2.361–92. For Pan, see 3.1.2.

9. Daughters of Kekrops: Eur. *Ion* 10–24, 268–74, 492–509; Paus. 1.18.2; Apollod. *Bibl.* 3.14.6; Philochorus 328 F 105; Larson (1995b) 39–42, 101–9 with notes; Shapiro (1995) 39–48; Lefkowitz (1996) 78–91. The remains of the *Erechtheus* (fr. 65.71–74) show that the daughters received worship at their tomb in a fashion reserved for heroic cults, not those of nymphs. I do not, however, wish to push the distinction too far, and it was most likely to be blurred in cases such as this, involving a primordial king's daughters. For vase paintings of the Aglaurids (sixth and fifth centuries), see *LIMC* s.v. Aglauros nos. 1–4 (Kron).

10. For the testimonia concerning Kallirhoë-Enneakrounos, see Wycherley (1957) 137–42. Thuc. 2.15; *Etym. Magn.* s.v. Ἐννεάκρουνος; Poll. 3.43; and Harp. s.v. λουτροφόρος specifically refer to the nuptial baths.

11. Travlos (1971) fig. 267 = Beazley (1956) 261, no. 41. See also Dunkley (1935–36) 153–71.

12. Ay. Photeini site: Travlos (1971) 204; Wycherley (1978) 171–72; Wickens (1986) no. 58, 2.313–19. Southeast Fountain House: Travlos (1971) 204, with figs. 269–71.

13. Corruption: see, for example, Parsons (1943) 192 n. 1 with bib. Two springs: Wycherley (1978) 171–72, 248 cf. Broneer (1949) 58. Removal to agora: Robertson (1992) 13.

14. Brommer (1979) 52 pl. 129; *LIMC* s.v. Ilisos 649–50, no. 1 (Prosynitopolou).

15. Pl. *Phdr.* 230b–d; Travlos (1971) 289; Wycherley (1963b). There is some disagreement as to whether the shrine was on the north (city) or south (stadium) side of the river.

16. For votive reliefs as *agalmata*, see Van Straten (1981) 75. Dates: Wycherley (1963b) 90.

17. Launderer relief: *IG* II/III² 2934; Edwards (1985) no. 30. The launderers bore slave names.

18. Philochorus 328 F 5b (fourth to third centuries). Horai and nymphs inscription: *IG* II/III² 4877. The same combination (Dionysos, Horai, nymphs) appears on Paros: *IG* XII 5.445.

19. On Telemachos, see Edelstein and Edelstein (1945) T720, 2.120; Parker (1996) 175–87, esp. 177 with n. 85. For the topography of the site and extensive bibliography, see Aleshire (1989) 21–36; Wickens (1986) no. 60, 2.324–35. The site of Telemachos' building has been much debated, with many arguing for the site of the sixth-century spring house rather than that of the Doric stoa and the cave spring. Archandros relief: Edwards (1985) no. 1 with bib. (c. 410–400). Priest of Asklepios: *IG* II/III² 4371.

20. Travlos (1971) 138. Isis inscription: *IG* II/III² 4994; Aleshire (1989) 28–32; see also Walker (1979) 246.

21. Nymphs and Demos: *IG* I³ 1065. For Demos, see Hamdorf (1964) 30–32, 93–95; Schwarzenberg (1966) 33–39; Kron (1979). Hamdorf suggests that the personification Demos had its origin in the late fifth century in Attic comedy and was then transferred to cult. Another possible interpretation is that the inscription refers to a specific phratry or genos, such as the Demokleidai. See Bourriot (1976) 2.1163 n. 232. Charites and Demos: *IG* II/III² 4676, 4775.

22. Boundary of Zeus: *IG* I³ 1055; Ervin (1959) 156–57. See also Wycherley (1978) 188. Zeus Meilichios: *IG* II/III² 4677–78 (third century). *Ompniai*: *IG* II/III² 4647; Edwards (1985) no. 11 with bib.

23. Sanctuary of Kephisos: Stais (1909); *IG* I³ 986–87 (reliefs); *IG* II/III² 4547 (cult regulation). See Edwards (1985) no. 3 with bib., esp. Linfert (1967), who summarizes identifications of the figures made in previous scholarship. See Purvis (1998) 24 n. 1.

24. Pythios: Wycherley (1963a) 166–67. For Geraistian nymphs as nurses in Krete, see 4.8.6.

25. Quirinal relief: Edwards (1985) no. 5 with bib. (c. 400–390).

26. Alternatively, Hermes might be present simply as a guide for Xenokrateia and a conventional companion of the nymphs. It could be that the separate altar belonged to Echelos.

27. Kephisodotos' interest in Echelos could be attributed to membership in a group of orgeones, or sacrificial associates, of that hero. An orgeonic association of Echelos is attested in an inscription from the Areopagos; see Ferguson (1944) 73–79.

28. Bendis: *IG* II/III² 1283.17–20 (third century); Pl. *Rep.* 327a; *IG* II/III² 1256 (fourth century). On Bendis and Deloptes, see Ferguson (1949) 131–62. Other votive reliefs: Edwards (1985) nos. 31, 34, 57 with bib. Zeus Meilichios is also popular here: *IG* II/III² 4617–20 (fourth century).

29. Men: Lane (1971) 1.3–4, nos. 5–6; Perdrizet (1896) 79–80. Well inscription: *IG* II/III² 4876. For Antioch, see Lane (1971) 3.107, 4.62, no. 136.

30. For Erchia, see *SEG* 21 (1965) 541; Dow (1965); Jameson (1965); White-head (1986) 199–204. See also Mikalson (1977). Ge: Robertson (1992) 29–30.

31. Euis' name is reminiscent of the Bacchic festal cry εὐοι: Richardson (1895) 211, col. I.45. Kirchner in *IG* II/III² 1358 read Νυμφαγέτης. This sacrifice belongs to col. 1 of the inscription, probably a list of sacrifices made by the Tetrapolis as a whole (Marathon, Oinoë, Probalinthos, Trikorynthos) rather than by an individual deme. See Whitehead (1986) 190 n. 75.

32. *LSCG* 11.17, c. 421. Not a *trittus*: Parker (1996) 103 n. 4.

33. Parker (1996) 143; Whitehead (1986) 177, citing Thuc. 2.16.

34. *IG* I³ 256; *LSCG* 178; *SEG* 23 (1968) 76. Original publication and discussion in Mitsos (1965) 80–83 pl. 46. The document is not demonstrably a deme document in the strict sense; see Whitehead (1986) 383.

35. Bousquet (1967) 92–94. Compare *LSCG* 152 (fourth century, from Kos); 4.9.4.

36. Mystery cult: Nilsson (1967) 671. Altars: Paus. 1.31.4. Themistokles: Plut. *Vit. Them.* 1.3. See Schachter (1981–94) 2.105–6, 190. An Attic nymph relief of the fourth century, Edwards (1985) no. 28, was dedicated by a demesman of Phlya: *IG* II/III² 4886.

37. Parthenoi and Praxidikai: Schachter (1981–94), 2.199; 3.6–7. On Boiotian trinities, see Schachter (1972) 17, (1981–94) s.v. Muses, Charites, Nymphai, Parthenoi; Larson (1995b) 101–10.

38. Strabo 9.2.25, 410. Aganippe: Paus. 9.29.5 (daughter of Termessos or Permessos, a stream of Helikon); Catullus 61.26. Euphorion of Chalcis (fr. 416 Lloyd-Jones and Parsons) used the term *parthenikai Leibêthrides*, or *gaiês parthenikai Leibêthridos*, for his Muses. For the textual issues, see Maas (1935). Vergil (*Ecl.* 7.21) follows Euphorion with his "Nymphae . . . Libethrides." See Schachter (1981–94) 2.188 n. 3.

39. Paus. 9.34.4. For Helikonian nymphs as mothers of foundling children, see Soph. *OT* 1108 with the manuscript reading of Ἑλικωνιάδων for Wilamowitz-Moellendorff's ἑλικωπίδων. Mount Thourion: Plut. *Vit. Sulla* 17.6; Schachter (1981–94) 2.146. For the Sphragitid nymphs, see 1.3.

40. Muses born at Pieria: Hes. *Theog.* 53; Strabo 9.2.25, 410; 10.3.17, 471, probably from Hecataeus; Paus. 9.29.2–5. Thracians occupied district of Pieria: Hammond (1972) 416–18; occupied Boiotia: Burn (1949) 322–23; Buck (1969) 289–91, (1979) 50, 67–68, 78; Schachter (1981–94) 2.187–88. See also 4.6 (Arne/Melanippe).

41. Callim. *Hymn* 5.57–130; Pherecydes 3 F 92.

42. An Arkadian river Metope: Callim. *Hymn* 1.26 with schol. Boiotian Ladon: Corinna fr. 684; Paus. 9.10.6.

43. Hom. *Od.* 11.260; Asius of Samos fr. 2; Paus. 2.6.1–2; Ap. Rhod. *Argon.* 1.735. Other links between Theban and Sikyonian legend are discussed by Vian (1963) 194–95. For Asius, see Huxley (1969) 89–98, esp. 92. For the alternative genealogies of Antiope (usually her father is Nykteus), see Gantz (1993) 215–16, 483–88; West (1985) 97–98.

44. Paus. 5.22.6, 10.13.6. The Olympia group asserts the Phliasians' claim with one representative from each of the major geographical divisons found among Asopos' daughters: Nemea (Argolis); Harpina (Elis); Korkyra (colonies); and Thebe (Boiotia). Aigina herself is the crown jewel.

45. Trans. Campbell (1982–93), vol. 4.

46. Corinna fr. 654 with Bowra (1938). Sisyphos: Paus. 2.5.1–2; Apollod. *Bibl.* 3.12.6.

47. Diod. Sic. 4.72, who favors the Peloponnesian Asopos, gives the most complete account of Asopos' daughters, listing twelve. These are Korkyra (cf. Hellanicus 4 F 77; Timaeus 566 F 79), Salamis, Aigina, Peirene, Ornia, Kleone, Thebe, Tanagra, Thespeia, Asopis, Sinope, and Chalkis. He adds two sons, Pelasgos and Ismenos. Apollod. neglects to specify the Boiotian or Peloponnesian river but says there were twenty daughters. Of these, he names Ismene (*Bibl.* 2.1.3), Salamis (3.12.7), and Aigina (1.9.3, 3.12.6) in addition to two sons (3.12.6). Paus., for his part, lists, from Phliasian sources (2.5.1–2, 5.22.6, 10.13.6) Nemea, Aigina, Harpina, Korkyra, Thebe, and Kleone, and from Boiotian sources (9.1.1, 9.4.4, 9.20.2, 9.26.6) Thespeia, Plataia, Oeroë, and Tanagra. Schol. Pind. *Ol.* 6.144e excludes the Boiotian daughters except for Thebe: Korkyra, Aigina, Salamis, Thebe, Kleone, Harpin(n)a, Nemea. Late sources add Euboia: Eust. *Il.* 2.536 (278.31); Hsch. s.v. Εὐβοίης.

48. Kleonai: Strabo 8.6.19, 377. Orneai: 8.6.24, 382. Harpinna: 8.3.32, 357.

49. Oeroë a Boiotian river: Hdt. 9.51. Asopis used of Phlious: Plin. *HN* 4.13; of Euboia, *HN* 4.64. Chalkis, daughter of Asopos, identified with Kombe: Hecataeus 1 F 129.

50. Eumelus fr. 7 (before 700). As a native, Eumelus promoted the interests of Corinth. See Huxley (1969) 67–68. Sinope, however, was also said to be abducted from (Boiotian) Hyria: Schol. Ap. Rhod. 2.946–54c. For Sinope, see also Diod. Sic. 4.72; Plut. *Luc.* 23. Eurynome: Clem. Rom. *Rec.* 10.23 (cited in Bowra 1938). Pronoë: Schol. *Il.* 2.517 Dindorf.

51. Nymph Thespeia and nymphaion: Paus. 9.26.4; Colin (1897) 553–57 (third century); *SEG* 13 (1956) 343; the sanctuary was on land leased by the state. Votive reliefs: Edwards (1985) nos. 79, 80, 82; Schachter (1981–94) 1.193.

52. Corinna made Tanagra a daughter of Asopos: Paus. 9.20.2. Coins: Schachter (1981–94) 3.37 n. 1, 2. Tanagran nymph Eunoste: Myrtis fr. 716. Soros relief with Meter and nymphs: Schachter (1981–94) 2.132–37.

53. Boundary stone: *IG* VII 2.2453 (fourth century); Schachter (1981–94) 2.190. For coins with the head of Thebe, see Head (1911) 350; Imhoof-Blumer (1908) 84. *Agalma*: Pind. fr. 195 cf. *Isthm.* 1.1, "My mother Thebe of the golden shield"; Soph. *Ant.* 844–45, "O Dirkaian springs and grove of well-armed Thebe." Horse-driving Thebe: Pind. *Ol.* 6.85.

54. Vases: Vian (1963) 38.11, 39.13, 39.15, 40.19, 40.20; Aellen (1994) 2 pls. 81, 88, 89. For Ismene, see *LIMC* s.v. Ismene II nos. 1–4 (Berger-Doer).

55. Paus. 9.2.7 cf. 9.1.2. Gargaphia: Hdt. 9.25, 49–52; Ov. *Met.* 3.155–72; Hyg. *Fab.* 181. For Apulian and Lucanian vases, see *LIMC* s.v. Gargaphia nos. 1–3 (Kossatz-Derssman); Lacy (1990).

56. Orion's sons: e.g., Akraiphen, eponym of the town near Mount Ptoion (but the reading of Akraiphen's name in Corinna fr. 654 has been disputed; see Schachter [1981–94] 1.61). On Orion's ancestry, see Gantz (1993) 212–19, 271–73. Klonia: Apollod. *Bibl.* 3.10.1. Hom. *Il.* 2.495 mentions a Klonios among the heroes of Hyria and Aulis.

57. For Ismenos and Teneros, see Paus. 9.10.6, 9.26.1 (sons of Melia and Apollo); Pindar fr. 52k.41 (Teneros only); Schol. Pind. *Pyth* 11.5–6 (Melia is sister of Ismenos and mother of Teneros). See also Hsch. s.v. Πτῷΐδες; these nymphs presumably inhabited Mount Ptoion. Melia: Hes. *Theog.* 187; Callim. *Hymn* 4.79–85. Cf. Callim. *Hymn* 1.47 (Diktaian Meliai care for the infant Zeus);

Hes. *Op.* 145 (bronze race sprang from "meliai," either nymphs or trees); Hes. *Theog.* 563 (the "Melian race" of mortal men); Callim. fr. 598 (Okeanid Melia and Meliai). An Okeanid Melia also plays a role as progenitor in the Argive saga: Apollod. *Bibl.* 2.1.1. On Melia, see Vivante (1972).

58. Kaanthos: Paus. 9.10.5–6. According to Schol. Pind. *Pyth.* 11.6, at the site of the Ismenion there is a spring with the name of "the heroine" Melia. Theban rivers and springs: Symeonoglou (1985) 180–81; Vian (1963) 83–85.

59. Herkyna: Paus. 9.39.2–3. Daughter of Trophonios: Schol. Lyc. 153; see also Schachter (1967, 1981–94) 2.38–39; Larson (1995b) 78–100. Inscription: *IG* VII 2.3092, date unknown. A man and his wife made a dedication to the nymphs and Pan; the man made a separate dedication to Pan and Dionysos.

60. Anthedon: Paus. 9.22.5. Thisbe: Paus. 9.32.3. Tilphossa: Hom. *Hymn. Ap.* 3.244–76, 375–87; Schachter (1990). Kissoëssa: Plut. *Mor.* 772b (*Am. narr.*); Plut. *Vit. Lys.* 28.4. Kyrtones: Paus. 9.24.4.

61. Paus. 1.34.3. On the altar of Amphiaraos, see Petrakos (1968) 98, 122–23.

62. Diod. Sic. 5.55.4; see also 4.9.4. For Halia Nymphe, see Petrakos (1968) 54–58 pl. 40b; *SEG* 24 (1969) 352, 355; 31 (1981) 453, 446–51. The term *halia* is used as a synonym for sea nymph, or Nereid, as early as Hom. *Il.* 18.432 and *Od.* 24.55.

63. Euboia on Eretrian coins: Imhoof-Blumer (1908) nos. 240–42; Head (1911) 362–63, c. 411–378, 378–38 (the nymph motif is perhaps related to the fact that Euboia regained its autonomy from Athens in 411); Franke and Hirmer (1964) 122. Nymph Chalkis on Chalkidian coins, beginning in the fourth century: Imhoof-Blumer (1908) nos. 243–44; *LIMC* s.v. Chalkis et Euboia nos. 1–4 (Picard). There is also a Bacchic nymph, Histiaia, on a coin from northern Euboia: Imhoof-Blumer (1908) nos. 380–83.

64. Chalkis/Kombe: Eust. *Il.* 2.537, 279.7–8 (Euboia, formerly Chalkis, got its name from a daughter of Asopos: Kombe or Chalkis); Schol. Hom. *Il.* 14.291 Erbse (Chalkis as mother of the Korybantes); Nonnus *Dion.* 13.146–47 (Kombe as mother of Korybantes by Sochos); Hsch. s.v. Κόμβη and Σωχός (father and mother of the Kouretes); Steph. Byz. s.v. Χαλκίς (Kombe as daughter of Asopos). The sanctuary is attested in *IG* XII 9.906, an inscribed stele of the third century C.E. This is very late, but nothing about it is inconsistent with an earlier origin. Euboia, daughter of Asopos: Eust. *Il.* 2.536–37, 278.30–31; see also Hsch. s.v. Εὐβοίης (mother of Tychios); Nonnus *Dion.* 42.411 (Poseidon rooted Euboia in the sea).

65. Hes. fr. 188a and 244 with West (1985) 99. Hyg. *Fab.* 157 (cf. praef. 8) makes Arethousa a Nereid. An early Delphic oracle singled out for praise "the men who drink the water of fair Arethousa," i.e., the Chalkidians: Parke and Wormell (1956) 1.82, 2 no. 1. Arethousa is a common spring name meaning "waterer"; it appears on Ithaka (Hom. *Od.* 13.408) and in Syracuse, Boiotia, Argos, Smyrna, etc. See *RE* 2 (1896) col. 679 s.v. Arethusa (Hirschfeld).

66. *IG* XII 9.135; Gais (1978) 359; Papabasileos (1912) 133, fig. 15; Isler (1970) 60, 112, no. 264.

67. *Anth. Pal.* 6.156; *GP* 2.538–39. For Amarynthos and the cult of Artemis, see Strabo 10.1.10, 448; Paus. 1.31.5. This cult of Artemis was also known at Athens.

68. Twins: Pind. *Isthm.* 8.17 cf. Hdt. 5.81. Hesiodic *Catalogue*: West (1985) 100–101. Aiakid genealogy: Hom. *Il.* 21.189. Other sources on Aigina: Apollod. *Bibl.* 3.12.6; Diod. Sic. 4.72.5; Paus. 2.29.2; Hyg. *Fab.* 52.

69. Aigina, like many other islands, is said to have once had a different name, Oinopia or Oinone (Pind. *Isthm.* 5.34, 8.21, *Nem.* 4.46, 8.7), presumably associated with the period before the nymph Aigina's arrival (Paus. 2.5.2).

70. *LIMC* s.v. Aigina (Kaempf-Dimitriadou): nos. 12–17 (Zeus, Aigina, and sisters); nos. 18–20 (Zeus, Aigina, and Asopos); nos. 21–27 (Zeus, Aigina, sisters, Asopos); Stewart (1995) 85, 87. For Athens and Aigina, see Figueira (1985; 1991) 104–5. For the arguments in favor of the equation Zeus = Athens, see Arafat (1997) 110–15. Arafat dates the Aigina vases to between 490 and 440, while Stewart (1995) prefers 475–50. Vase with Nike: Arafat (1997) 114; *ARV* 495.6. The myth of Aigina was treated in the Aeschylean satyr play *Sisyphos Drapetes* (fr. 225–34); this fact may also be related to the popularity of the subject in vase painting.

71. Inscription: Marabini (1949–51) 135–40; *BE* (1955) 97. Parallel in the cult of the Paides in Sicily: see 4.10.6. Chorus: Bacchyl. 13.77–99.

72. Telamon and Ajax: Hom. *Il.* 2.557; Strabo 9.1.9, 394. On Kychreus (also called Ophis), see West (1985) 103, 164; Plut. *Vit. Thes.* 10.2–3; Diod. Sic. 4.72.4; Apollod. *Bibl.* 3.12.7; Paus. 1.35.2; *Etym. Magn.* s.v. Σαλαμίς (Salamis d. of Asopos); Strabo 9.1.9, 393 (= Hes. fr. 226); Schol. Lycoph. 451. Kalaureia: Plut. *Mor.* 295d–e (*Quaest. Graec.*).

73. Sithnid nymphs: Paus 1.40.1. On the construction of the fountain house, see Dunkley (1935–36) 145–46. See also *AJA* 62 (1958) 323–24 with pl. 86.6; *BCH* 82 (1958) 688–92 with figs. 35–36. On Theagenes, see also Arist. *Pol.* 1305a 9; Figueira and Nagy (1985) 112–58. For the Flood, see also 4.6, 4.7.4.

74. On this point, see Snodgrass (1980) 115.

75. Altar to Acheloös: Paus. 1.41.2. For Rhous, see Muller (1981) 203–7. Figueira (1985) 145 tentatively associates the Rhous with the *potamos*, or "river" where Theagenes' slaughter of the flocks took place. Hsch. s.v. σιτνίδες· θυσία τις νύμφαις ἐπιτελουμένη.

76. Figueira (1985) 139 speaks of an opposition at Megara between the aristocratic ideology, represented by Theognidean elegy, and the democratic/populist ideology represented by comedy.

77. Gates: Paus. 1.44.2. On the topography of Megara cf. Bohringer [de Polignac] (1980). Reliefs: Edwards (1985) nos. 77–78. Cave: Zervoudakis (1965) 3–11. I have not been able to obtain a copy of the latter.

78. Hom *Il.* 2.519–23. Daulis as daughter of Kephisos: Paus. 10.4.5. District of Daulia in Phokis: Thuc. 2.29; Apollod. *Bibl.* 3.14.8. Naiad Lilaia: Paus. 10.33.4. Leiriope: Ov. *Met.* 3.341–46 cf. Paus. 9.31.7–8. *Leirion* is a synonym for *narkissos*: Ath. 15.681e.

79. Tithorea: Paus. 10.32.8. Daphnis: Paus. 10.5.5. Apollo and nymphs: Ap. Rhod. *Argon.* 2.711–13; hypothesis C of Schol. Pind. *Pyth.* Korykia: Paus. 10.6.3, 32.2. Kleodora: Paus. 10.6.1.

80. Amandry et al. (1984) 398–99.

81. Nymph Kassotis: Paus. 10.24.7. Kastalia: Panyassis fr. 15; Alc. fr. 307; Paus. 10.8.4–5. For underground rivers, see Baladié (1980) 92–115; Brewster (1997) 62, 80. Late sources make Kastalia either a spouse of Delphos and mother of Kastalios and Phemonoë (Schol. Eur. *Or.* 1094) or a maiden who threw herself into the spring in order to escape Apollo's pursuit (Schol. Stat. *Theb.* 1.698).

82. Dunkley (1935–36) 145–50.

83. Peirene: Diod. Sic. 4.72. Cf. *Anth. Pal.* 9.225 (*Asôpis krênê*); Paus. 2.2.3. Hes. fr. 258 makes Peirene the daughter of Oibalos, who is presumably the father of Spartan Tyndareos, but nothing further is known of this version.

84. The earliest reference is Pind. *Ol.* 13.61: "city of Peirene." Cf. Hdt. 5.92, where the Delphic oracle refers to those who dwell around Peirene and (Akro) Korinthos. The spring and its waters are described as hallowed (*semnos*): Eur. *Med.* 68–69; *Tro.* 205–6. Pegasos is the Peireneian colt: Eur. *El.* 475. For the spring house, see Hill (1964) 8–115. Roman cult: Blegen and Broneer (1930) 59; Hill (1964) 99–100. Coins: Head (1911) 405; Imhoof-Blumer (1908) nos. 247–69. Imhoof-Blumer (1908) 86 argues that the head of Peirene appears on Corinthian coins as early as the fifth century.

85. Sacred spring: Hill (1964) 116–99; Steiner (1992). The spring is usually identified as the cult site of the Thracian Kotyto or the related heroine, Hellotis. For the latter, see Larson (1995b) 138–39.

86. Votive deposit: Williams (1981) 409; *BCH* 87 (1963) 724, figs. 9 and 88, (1964) 704, 708. Reliefs: Ridgway (1981) 427–28, pls. 91c, 92a.

87. Pliny *HN* 35.151–52. Among the early kings of Sikyon in the account of Pausanias (2.6.7) is Zeuxippos, a son of Apollo and the nymph Syllis or Hyllis.

88. Brewster (1997) 59–60. Paus. 2.15.5 (cf. Apollod. *Bibl.* 2.1.4) explains that the rivers Kephisos, Asterion, and Inachos chose Hera over Poseidon as the patron of Argos, so the angry god dried up their waters.

89. For Apollod. and the *Ehoeae*, see West (1985) 32–45. There are conflicting traditions about Phoroneus' family; for example, his wife was Peitho (Schol. Eur. *Or.* 632) or Kerdo (Paus. 2.21.1). For discussion, see Waldstein (1902–5) 1.33–34.

90. Phoroneus founds Hera's cult: Apollod. *Bibl.* 2.1.3. The fifth-century Argive Acusilaus (2 F 23a) and the *Phoronis* (fr. 1) put Phoroneus forward as "the first man"; cf. Gantz (1993) 198. For the *Phoronis*, see Huxley (1969) 31–38. Contest with Poseidon: Paus. 2.15.5; Apollod. *Bibl.* 2.1.4.

91. Melian race: Hes. *Theog.* 563–34. For the fr. of the *Ehoeae*, see the new papyrus in Solmsen, Merkelbach, and West (1990), fr. 10 a–b = Hes. fr. 123 Merkelbach and West (1967). Iphthime: Nonnus *Dion.* 14.105–17. See Gantz (1993) 135; West (1985) 59; Carpenter (1986) 78.

92. Peiren: Hes. fr. 124. See West (1985) 76; Dowden (1989) 118–24. For Io as daughter of Inachos, see Bacchyl. 19.18; Aesch. *PV* 590, 663; Hdt. 1.1. See also Gantz (1993) 199–203. Schol. Pind. *Nem.* 10.8 makes her the child of Inachos and a nymph.

93. Genealogy: Apollod. *Bibl.* 2.1.4 (Memphis and Anchinoë as daughters of Nile). Danaos' wives included hamadryad nymphs Atlantia and Phoibe and the naiad nymph Polyxo, whose twelve daughters married the twelve sons of Aigyptos and the naiad nymph Kaliadne (Apollod. *Bibl.* 2.1.5 cf. Hyg. *Fab.* 170).

94. Hes. fr. 128. A variant of the line has *Danaos* instead of *Danaai*.

95. Amymone: Apollod. *Bibl.* 2.1.4; Paus. 2.37.4. Satyr play *Amymone*: Aesch. fr. 13–15; Sutton (1974) 193–202. Wells at Argos: Strabo 8.6.8, 371; Callim. fr. 66.7. Cf. Eur. *Phoen.* 186–89 with schol.; Hyg. *Fab.* 169. Amymone's pursuit by the satyr is reminiscent of archaic depictions of nymphs and satyrs, e.g., on the François vase and Thasian coins. Danaids as nymphs: Kaempf-Dimitriadou (1979) 28 n. 210; *LIMC* s.v. Danaides 337–41 (Keuls), Amymone nos. 742–52

(Simon); see these sources for numerous vases. On springs and Danaids, see Detienne (1988) 165, 168–70; on Amymone as river, see Dowden (1989) 152–53. For the hydrology of the Argolid, see Baladié (1980) 110–15.

96. Mykene: Hom *Il.* 2.120 with schol. (Argos was her son with Arestor); also cited by Paus. 2.16.4; Hes. fr. 246 (Arestor's wife). Heraion: Paus. 2.17.2. On the topography, see O'Brien (1993) 123–25; Waldstein (1902–5) 1.10–20. We also hear of the daughters of the Erasinos River (near Lerna), Anchiroë, Byze, Melite, and Moira: Ant. Lib. *Met.* 30. For Erasinos, see Paus. 2.36.6–7; Brewster (1997) 61–62.

97. Schefold (1992) 102. Lake Lerna: Strabo 8.6.8, 371. Cf. the river Lerna in the district of Temenion, distinct from the marsh of Lerna: Strabo 8.6.2, 368. Thebe and Ismene: see 4.3.1. For Lerna, see 4.3.3.

98. Nemea: Paus. 5.22.6; Strabo 8.6.25, 382. Vases: *LIMC* s.v. Nemea nos. 2–7 (Fracchia); Schefold (1992) fig. 110, c. 530–20. Gem: Jacobsthal (1931) 151, fig. 30.156; *LIMC* s.v. Nemea no. 9; Aesch. fr. 149a; Mette (1963) 38–39; cf. Bacchyl. 9.10–20. Euripides' *Hypsipyle* gave a different version: Gantz (1993) 510–11.

99. Perseus and nymphs: Apollod. *Bibl.* 2.4.2; Pherecydes 3 F 11; Schol. Lycoph. 838. Loutrophoros: *LIMC* Suppl. s.v. Nymphai, no. 55 (Halm-Tisserant and Siebert). Hydria: Carpenter (1991) no. 148; Rumpf (1927) 66, pl. 15. Aeschylus' *Phorkides* appears to have omitted the episode with the nymphs, so that Perseus proceeds directly from the Phorkides to the Gorgons: Aesch. fr. 261–62; Mette (1963) 155–56. Bronze house: Paus. 3.17.3. Herakles consults with nymphs of the Eridanos: Pherecydes 3 F 16a.

100. Pleiades: Hes. fr. 169. The source here, Schol. Pind. *Nem.* 2.17, calls them nymphs; cf. Davies in *EGF* 19, who attributes the lines to the *Titanomachia*. The other Pleiades, according to Hes. and Hellanicus 4 F 19, are Maia, who bore Hermes with Zeus; Taygete, who bore Lakedaimon with Zeus; Elektra, who bore Dardanos with Zeus; Alkyone, who bore Hyrieus with Poseidon; Kelaino, who bore Lykos with Poseidon; and Sterope/Asterope, who bore Oinomaos with Ares. See Gantz (1993) 212–14. The Pleiades are mentioned in Alcman's *Partheneion* as a rival chorus; the name might have to do with the importance of the Atlantid genealogy in the Peloponnese and, particularly, in Lakonia.

101. Eurotas: Apollod. *Bibl.* 3.10.3. Cf. Paus. 3.1.1–2, which rationalizes Eurotas by making him a king who drained the marshes, thus creating the river. Apollodorus' account is sprinkled with naiads who do not appear in other sources, including Oibalos' naiad wife, Bateia (*Bibl.* 3.10.4); Ikarios' naiad wife, Periboia (*Bibl.* 3.10.6). On Spartan influences in the genealogy, see West (1985) 156. Tiasa: Paus. 3.18.6 = Alcm. fr. 62.

102. For Helen's role at Sparta, see Charachidzé (1992); Calame (1997) 191–206. For Helen in choruses, see Ar. *Lys.* 1296–1315; Eur. *Hel.* 1465–77. Chorus beside Eurotas: Theoc. *Id.* 18.22–25; Alcm. fr. 11.

103. Dances at Karyai: Paus. 3.10.7. Karya: Ath. 3.78b. Cf. the story of the Lakonian king's daughter, Karya, who was turned into a nut tree by Dionysos: Serv. on Verg. *Ecl.* 8.29. On Artemis Karyatis, see Calame (1997) 149–56.

104. Silenos: Paus. 3.25.2 = Pind. fr. 156. Nymphaion: Paus. 3.23.2.

105. Springs of Pamisos: Paus. 4.31.4. Ithome and Neda: 4.33.1. Cult of Kouretes: 4.31.9.

106. Theisoa: Paus. 8.38.9. Hagno: 8.38.3. For the excavation of the spring of Hagno on Mount Lykaion, see *AE* (1904) 162; *Praktika* (1909) 198–200, fig. 21; for a more recent discussion, see Jost (1985) 181–82; 251–52.

107. Tegea: Paus. 8.47.3. The presence of Ide is a nod to the Kretan accounts of Zeus' birth (4.8.6). Anthrakia's name refers to the fact that the heavily wooded mountains are a source of charcoal; like herdsmen, charcoal burners were associated with rural, especially mountainous, areas; see Buxton (1992) 3. Anthrakia's torch is part of the iconography of birth scenes; cf. Eileithyia with torch at her sanctuary at Aigion (Paus. 7.23.5). Phrixa is a town on the Alpheios River in Triphylia; see Baladié (1980) 52–53. Megalopolis: Paus. 8.31.4. The sanctuary of Hekate at Lagina had a relief similar to the Tegean birth of Zeus, dating to the second century: Laumonier (1958) 350.

108. Lymax: Paus. 8.41.2. Phigalia took its name either from a dryad nymph or from one of Lykaon's fifty sons: Paus. 8.39.3. Theisoa: Paus. 8.38.9; Brewster (1997) 85–86. *Lumata*: Hom. *Il.* 1.314. Methydrion: Paus. 8.36.4.

109. Callim. *Hymn* 1.10–45 cf. Strabo 8.3.22, 348.

110. Hagno: Paus. 8.38.3. On baths and childbirth see Ginouvès (1962) 235–6; 3.2.2.

111. Trikrena: Paus. 8.16.1. Maia: Hes. fr. 169–70; Hom. *Hymn Merc.* 4.4–6, 244. For coins, see Imhoof-Blumer (1908) nos. 275–78. Philostephanus of Kyrene *FHG* fr. 9 made Hermes' nurses Kyllene and Helike; see Jost (1985) 442. Kyllene is cited as the birthplace of the Pleiades by Apollod. *Bibl.* 3.10.1.

112. *Proselênaios*: Anon. fr. 985 (Campbell). See Borgeaud (1988) 6, with notes. Nymphs: Hsch. s.v. Προσελήνιδες. Lykaon's sons: note the similarity to the fifty sons of the nymphs and Orion, who were eponyms of Boiotian towns (1.4.2). Pelasgos' wife: Pherecydes 3 F 156; Apollod. *Bibl.* 3.8.1; Schol. Eur. *Or.* 1646. See West (1985) 91–92; Hes. fr. 160, 161–62, 167. See also Steph. Byz. s.v. Κυλλήνη (naiad nymph).

113. *Ehoeae*: Hes. fr. 163 with West (1985) 92. Lykaon was the father in Eumelus, Nykteus in Asius of Samos, and Keteus in Pherecydes (Apollod. *Bibl.* 3.8.2). Kallisto's fate is variously described: Sale (1962, 1965); Gantz (1993) 725–29; Dowden (1989) 182–90. Tomb of Kallisto: Paus. 8.35.8; Larson (1995b) 90, 178 n. 75; *LIMC* s.v. Arkas nos. 609–10 (Trendall); Head (1911) 451 (coins of Orchomenos and Methydrion, after 370); Jost (1985) 407. Trendall suggests that the appearance of the fourth-century representation is connected with the founding of the Arkadian league in 370.

114. See also Paus. 8.30.3 (a nymph nurse, Sinoë), 8.37.2, 8.38.5.

115. Jost (1985) 462–63. Araethus of Tegea (316 F 4 = Schol. Eur. [*Rhes.*] 36) gave as Pan's parents Aither and a nymph, Oinoë (cf. Schol. Theoc. *Syrinx* 1); the local legend might have been attached to the cult of Pan on Mount Parthenion (Paus. 8.54.6). The scholiast mentions that Pan was called *numphagenês* and that a nymph, Orsinoë, and Hermes were also reputed to be his parents.

116. Nomian Pan: Paus. 8.38.11. Nomia and Kallisto: Paus. 10.31.10.

117. For these nymphs and "panic" sexuality, see Borgeaud (1988) 74–83. Syrinx: Ov. *Met.* 1.690–712; Longus 2.34; Achilles Tatius 8.6; Serv. on Verg. *Ecl.* 2.31. Echo: Ov. *Met.* 3.356–401; Longus 3.23. Pitys: *Geoponica* 11.10 cf. Nonnus *Dion.* 2.108, 16.363, 42.258–60.

118. Thelpousa: Paus. 8.25.2; Steph. Byz. s.v. Τέλφουσσα. Ladon River: Brewster (1997) 74–77.

119. Styx: Hes. *Theog.* 361, 383–403, 775–806; Brewster (1997) 69–70. Styx and Persephone: Hom. *Hymn Cer.* 2.423.

120. Jost (1985) 476. Tegea herm: *IG* V 2.65; Mendel (1901) 276 no. 14; Rhomaios (1911) 154, no. 11; Nilsson (1967) 206, pl. 33.2. Glyphai: Hsch. s.v. Νυμφαῖον ὄχθον and Γλυφεῖον· ἄντρον τι; *Etym. Magn.* s.v. Γλύφιον· ἄντρον τι καὶ ὄρος· ὅθεν νύμφαι γλυφίαι.

121. See Gow and Page (1968) 254–55; Paus. 8.41.7–10 does not mention these caves. Jost (1985) 91 suggests that this shrine at the foot of Bassai might be that of Pan Sinoëis (Paus. 8.30.3); compare *IG* V 2, 429.9–13 (fourth century: Apollo Bassitas and Pan Sinoëis).

122. Madigan (1992) 16–28.

123. Daphne as daughter of Ladon: Paus. 8.20.1–3. Palaephatus 49 (fourth century) makes Daphne's parents Gaia and the river Ladon; when Apollo chases her, she calls on her mother, is swallowed into the earth, and replaced by the tree. Cf. Schol. Lycoph. 6. Phylarchus 81 F 32 makes her daughter of the Spartan king Amyklas. For the myth, see Gantz (1993) 90–91; Dowden (1989) 174–79. For Syrian Daphne, see 4.9.8.

124. Alpheios and Artemis: Paus. 6.22.8–11. Aristomenes: Paus. 4.16.7–10. On the role of the chorus, see Calame (1997), esp. 92. Abductions from chorus: Hom. *Il.* 16.179–86 (Polymele); Hom. *Hymn Ven.* 5.92–106; Hom. *Hymn Cer.* 2.417; Eur. *Hel.* 1301–7 (Persephone); Plut. *Vit. Thes.* 31.2 (Helen); Hyg. *Fab.* 79; Calame (1997) 335–67. Rape of the maidens at Karyai: Paus. 4.16.9. Rape of Leukippides on a vase by the Meidias painter (*ARV* 1313): Burkert (1985) 150 n. 16.

125. Strabo 8.3.32, 356; Paus. 6.22.7. Hsch. glosses ἰατροί as "some nymphs at Elis"; he might have in mind the Ionides or the Anigrid nymphs of Triphylia (below).

126. For these and other etymologies, see Sakellariou (1956), who suggests that Ion was an early name of the Alpheios River. Ion and the nymphs: Nic. fr. 74. Similar etymology of the Elean seers called the Iamids: Pind. *Ol.* 6.30–57.

127. Three altars: Paus. 5.15.4–10. Wineless libations or *nêphalia* in Attica for the Muses, Eos, Selene, the nymphs, and Heavenly Aphrodite: Polemon of Ilium *FHG* fr. 42; Henrichs (1983). Temenos of Pelops: Paus. 5.5.11. Kallistephanoi: Paus. 5.15.3. Akmenai: Paus. 5.15.6. Odysseus' chamber: Hom. *Od.* 23.191.

128. Cf. Strabo 8.3.19, 346–47, where the nymphs are called Anigriades. He associates the second cave with the daughters of Atlas, or the Pleiades, and particularly with the birth of Dardanos.

129. The widely accepted emendation Ἀνιγριάδες for Ἀμαδρυάδες seems plausible here, since hamadryads are unlikely to be invoked as water nymphs. See Gow and Page (1965) 2.415.

130. Strabo 8.3.14, 344. Cf. Ov. *Met.* 10.728–30; Oppian *Halieutica* 3.485–86 (Minthe was a nymph of Kokytos).

131. Selemnos: Paus. 7.23.1–2. Bolina: Paus. 7.23.4.

132. Alkmaion: Apollod. *Bibl.* 3.7.5–7; Paus. 8.24.8–10; Gantz (1993) 526. The earliest attestation of this myth is Thuc. 2.102, but Apollod. and Paus. seem to draw on lost tragedies of Sophocles and Euripides. For Kallirhoë, see also Ov. *Met.* 9.413–14. Coins of Stratos: Imhoof-Blumer (1908) 236–37; Head (1911) 331–33. For nymphs of the Echinades, see Ov. *Met.* 8.580–89; *Anth. Pal.* 9.684.

133. Coins of Ambrakia: Imhoof-Blumer (1908) 221. Anaktorion: Imhoof-Blumer (1908) 222–27; Head (1911) 329. Leukas: Imhoof-Blumer (1908) 228–29, 230–35.

134. Imhoof-Blumer (1908) 78, no. 220. Korkyra and Phaiax: Hellanicus 4 F 77; Diod. Sic. 4.72; Steph. Byz. s.v. Φαίαξ. Ap. Rhod. *Argon.* 4.566–71, probably observing the local anti-Corinthian bias, transfers the story to Black Korkyra. See Vian and Delage (1976–81) 3.29–30, 35.

135. Makris: Ap. Rhod. *Argon.* 4.1130–40 with schol. For the Euboian settlement, attested only in Plut. *Mor.* 293a–b (*Quaest. Graec.*), see Vian and Delage (1976–81) 3.30 and n. 4. Euboia = Makris: Callim. *Hymn* 4.20 with schol. cf. Strabo 10.1.1, 444. Dionysos reared by *Kroniē numphē* Makris on Euboia: Nonnus *Dion.* 21.193–5.

136. Melite: Ap. Rhod. *Argon.* 4.537–43 cf. Schol. Ap. Rhod. 4.1149–50. Altar to Moirai and nymphs founded by Medeia on Korkyra: Ap. Rhod. *Argon.* 4.1217–19. Timaeus 566 F 88 also mentions this altar but specifies Nereids rather than Moirai.

137. Pherecydes 3 F 90. Hyg. *Fab.* 182 calls the nurses daughters of Okeanos or of Melisseus and names them Idyia, Althaia, and Adrasta (with apparent influence from the Kretan versions). He further notes that these nymphs were called Dodonides and seems later to identify them with the Hyades; thus Hyg. *Poet. astr.* 2.21 says that the stars known as Hyades were also formerly called Dodonides. Okeanid nymph Dodone: Epaphroditus (first century C.E.) in Steph. Byz. s.v. Δωδώνη; cf. Schol. Hom. *Il.* 16.233 Erbse; Eust. *Il.* 2.750 (335.44); *Etym. Magn.* s.v. Δωδωναῖος. On Zeus at Dodone, see Parke (1967).

138. Strabo 7.5.8, 316; Plin. *HN* 2.237, 3.145; Ael. *VH* 13.16; Arist. [*Mir. ausc.*] 127; Ampelius *Liber Memorialis* 8.1. The latter, a late source, speaks of a Mount Nymphaeum, where fire issues from the earth, and of Pan's music (*Panis symphonia*), which can be heard from the neighboring wood. Public divination: Theopompus 115 F 316 (= Pliny *HN* 2.237).

139. Coins: Head (1911) 314; Imhoof-Blumer (1908) 506–13. Menodotos: Bizard and Roussel (1907) 432–34 no. 26; Dow (1935) 81–90 no. 38; Tzouvara-Souli (1988–89) 21–46. Cult of nymphs: *IG* II/III² 3147, 3149a. Priest of the nymphs (Roman period): Demitsas (1879) 233. On Apollonia and the nymphaion, see also Hammond (1967) 231–34, 426.

140. Plut. *Vit. Sulla* 27.1–2. Gardens of Midas: Hdt. 8.138 cf. Ael. *VH* 13.15. Archaic bronze silenos, possibly dedicated at the nymphaion: Hammond (1967) 436; Neugebauer (1931) no. 215, 109, pl. 39. Also, two votive reliefs are reported from Dyrrachion: Praschniker and Schober (1919) 41–42, fig. 49; Saria (1926) fig. 40; Tzouvara-Souli (1988–89) 48–49. Neither is listed in Edwards (1985), but the style of the dancing nymphs is close to that of his no. 60, which supports the suggested dating to the fourth century.

141. For Peneios as father of nymphs, see Callim. *Hymn* 4.105-52 and below.

142. Kreousa: Pind. *Pyth.* 9.15-18 with schol. cf. Pherecydes 3 F 7. See West (1985) 85. Stilbe ("brilliance"): Diod. Sic. 4.69; Schol. Hom *Il.* 1.266 Erbse, 12.128 Dindorf; Schol. Ap. Rhod. 1.948 (Aineus is the son of Apollo and Stilbe). A Kyrenaic account (Acesandrus 469 F 2) made Hypseus the son of Peneios and Philyra, daughter of (Thessalian?) Asopos.

143. Peliades: Ap. Rhod. *Argon.* 1.549-50 cf. *Etym. Magn.* s.v Ἰτωνὶς καὶ Ἰτωνία. Kentauroi reared by nymphs: Diod. Sic. 4.70. Ixion: Pind. *Pyth.* 2.25-48.

144. Cheiron: Hes. *Theog.* 1001-2. Kronos and Philyra: *Titanomachia* fr. 9; Pind. *Pyth.* 3.1-4, 4.102-3, 115, 9.30; Pherecydes 3 F 50; Apollod. *Bibl.* 1.2.4; Ap. Rhod. *Argon.* 2.1232-41. Hyg. *Fab.* 138 connects Philyra with the lime tree, *philyra*. Nymphaion or chamber of Philyra: Callim. *Hymn* 4.118 cf. Ov. *Met.* 7.352 (*Philyreia tecta*). See Guillaume-Courier (1995).

145. Family of Cheiron: Pind. *Pyth.* 4.102-3; Ap. Rhod. *Argon.* 4.812-13. For Chariklo on the Sophilos *dinoi* and the François vase, see Gantz (1993) 145-46. Pholos as son of Silenos: Apollod. *Bibl.* 2.5.4. Cheiron as kourotrophos: West (1966) on Hes. *Theog.* 1001. On the Kentauroi, see Gantz (1993) 143-47.

146. Kyrene: Hes. fr. 215 makes Kyrene herself the daughter of Peneios. Cf. Schol. Ap. Rhod. 2.498-527c; Hyg. *Fab.* 161. See West (1985) 85-89; Pind. *Pyth.* 9.1-70. For Libyan Kyrene, see 4.8.8.

147. Thessalian Larissa: Hellanicus 4 F 91. Head of Larissa on coins: *BMC* Thessaly nos. 3, 47-52, 55; Imhoof-Blumer (1908) nos. 163-70. Larissa holding hydria, spring nearby: *BMC* no. 14; Imhoof-Blumer (1908) no. 184. Larissa with ball: *BMC* nos. 23-24, 41, 46; Imhoof-Blumer (1908) nos. 185-88. Larissa with hydria in other poses: *BMC* nos. 42-44; Imhoof-Blumer (1908) nos. 195-200. Head (1911) 297-99 dates the coins that show Larissa's head on the obverse from c. 400-344; the coins with a full figure of Larissa, normally on the reverse, date c. 480-400. See also Rogers (1932) 92-101; Biesantz (1965) 114-16; Moustaka (1983) nos. 34, 83, 95, 111-22, 130-32.

148. Drowning of Larissa: Suidas of Thessaly 602 F 2. Statue: Pliny *HN* 34.68; Langlotz (1951).

149. Oddly, however, the Thessalians do not display in their coinage the interest shown in local river gods by Sicilians. Peneios, for example, does not appear. Moustaka (1983) nos. 52-53. Kimon: Head (1911) 297–99.

150. Trikka as Peneios' daughter: Steph. Byz. s.v. Τρίκκη; Eust. *Il.* 2.729 (330, 26-27). Coins: *BMC* Thessaly nos. 12-15; Imhoof-Blumer (1908) nos. 211-15; Head (1911) 310-11 (dated by Head c. 480-400 and 400-344); Rogers (1932) 176-78; Lacroix (1953) 19; Moustaka (1983) nos. 124-26. Biesantz (1965) 143 suggests that the type depicting Trikka seated may correspond to a cult statue.

151. Hypereia: Hom. *Il.* 2.734; Pind. *Pyth.* 4.125. For coins, see Imhoof-Blumer (1908) nos. 175-77, 216; Head (1911) 306-7; Rogers (1932) 162-63; Moustaka (1983) no. 72.

152. Other nymphs may appear on Thessalian coins, as of Atrax: *BMC* Thessaly no. 1; Head (1911) 292, c. 400-344; Rogers (1932) 64-65. Gyrton: *BMC* nos. 1-2; Moustaka (1983) nos. 77, 130. Perrhaibia: *BMC* no. 8; Moustaka (1983) nos. 81, 123. Magnesia: Moustaka (1983) no. 103. From Atrax, see also a Hellenistic dedication to Dionysos and nymphs: *SEG* 45 (1995) 554.

153. West (1985) 57. Ὀθρηίς in Hellanicus 4 F 125 and νύμφη Ὀρσηίς in Apollod. *Bibl.* 1.7.3 should be read as Ὀθρυίς, a nymph of Mount Othrys in Phthiotis. Compare Nic. in Ant. Lib. *Met.* 22.

154. The myth was recounted in Euripides' plays *Melanippê Sophê* and *Melanippê Desmôtis*; the latter described the exile of Melanippe and her sons to Metapontion in Italy. See Gantz (1993) 734-35 for details. See also West (1985) 102-3. Hellanicus 4 F 51 makes Boiotos the son of Poseidon and Arne without mention of Aiolos. Boiotoi: Thuc. 1.12; for Boiotian Arne, see Hom. *Il.* 2.507. Boiotos as son of Melanippe: Paus. 9.1.1. A nymph, Arne, is attested as the nurse of Poseidon and eponym of the Boiotian town: Theseus 453 F 1.

155. Arne: *BMC* Thessaly (Cierium) nos. 1-3, 5; Imhoof-Blumer (1908) nos. 179-83; Head (1911) 293, c. 400-344; Rogers (1932) 66-68; Moustaka (1983) nos. 3, 16, 110; cf. Biesantz (1965) 140-41. Not an oracle: Head (1911) 293; *LIMC* s.v. Arne nos. 613-14 (Arnold-Biucchi).

156. Kerambos: Nic. in Ant. Lib. *Met.* 22. Deukalion: Hellanicus 4 F 117. For Megara, see 4.3.4.

157. For Achilles and the Spercheios, see Hom. *Il.* 23.140-51; cf. 16.168-78. Thessalian Asopos: Hdt. 7.199-200; Strabo 8.7.1, 383. See West (1985) 163-64. Another daughter of Thessalian Asopos, Philyra, appears in Acesandrus 469 F 2 as Hypseus' mother.

158. For Cheiron and Peleus, see Gantz (1993) 226, 230-31; for Achilles nursed by naiads in Cheiron's cave, see Ap. Rhod. *Argon.* 4.812-13. Endeïs: Pind. *Nem.* 5.11-12 with schol.; Bacchyl. 13.96-99. In Hyg. *Fab.* 14.8 and Schol Hom. *Il.* 16.14 Dindorf, her father is Cheiron; in Apollod. *Bibl.* 3.12.6; Plut. *Vit. Thes.* 10; and Paus 2.29.9, her father is Skiron of Megara.

159. Dryope: Nic. in Ant. Lib. *Met.* 32; Ov. *Met.* 9.326-91. An Arkadian Dryope becomes the mother of Pan in the Homeric *Hymn* to that god (19.34).

160. Daphne: Ov. *Met.* 1.452-567; see also 4.4.3, 4.9.8.

161. According to Apollod. *Bibl.* 2.7.7, it was Philoktetes' father, Poias, who lit the pyre. Dedication: Daux and de la Coste-Messelière (1924) 365-66, no. 2; *SEG* 3 (1929) 453, dated conjecturally at the end of the second century. Lebrun (1989) 83-85 adduces a parallel between Greek Μαλίς -Μαλιάδες and Anatolian Maliya-Maliyanni. Pronoë, a nymph of Oite, bears a son, Melaneus, to Apollo: Hes. fr. 26.25-26.

162. Isaac (1986) xi–xiv.

163. Hammond (1972) 416–17; Aesch. fr. 23–25; Mette (1963) 138. On the Pierian, Pimpleian, and Leibethrian cults of the Muses, see Otto (1956) 63.

164. Hammond and Griffith (1979) 48. Seuré, cited by Kazarow in *RE* 6.1, ser. 2 (1936) col. 509 s.v. Thrake (Religion) relates Thourion and Thourides to Thracian ζβερθουρδος.

165. Mieza: Plut. *Vit. Alex.* 7.3; Pliny *HN* 31.30. Hammond (1972) 162–64; *Ergon* (1965) 21–28, (1968) 59–63; *BCH* 90 (1966) 867–70; *AR* (1965–66) 15, (1968–69) 24.

166. Lake Bolbe: Aesch. *Pers.* 496; Hegesandrus of Delphi *FHG* fr. 40. Different genealogy: Conon 26 F 1.4 cf. Hammond and Griffith (1979) 38, 39 n. 1.

167. Mendeïs and Pallene: Conon 26 F 1.10 cf. the city Mende on Pallene. According to Schol. Lycoph. 1161, Pallene was the daughter of Sithon and Anchiroë, daughter of Nile. Cf. Hegesippus 391 F 1, 2. Nonnus *Dion.* 48.90–237 has a wrestling contest between Pallene and Dionysos. Pallene on coins: Imhoof-Blumer (1908) 150–52.

168. First-century dedication to Dionysos mentioning a nymphaion: *SEG* 42 (1992) 587. Votive relief from Stobi: Edwards (1985) no. 65 (first century). Relief of Imperial date with three hydria-bearing nymphs: *SEG* 24 (1969) 496. Coins with two nymphs, who represent the Axios and Erigon rivers: Hammond (1972) 175 n. 1.

169. *IG* XII, 8.358; *LSCG* 114 with bib.; Seyrig (1927) 178–85; École française d'Athènes (1968) 37–39, figs. 12, 104; Pouilloux (1979) 134. A votive relief from Thasos shows Hermes with three figures, who could be interpreted as either nymphs

or Charites, probably the latter in view of the cult inscriptions in the Passage of the Theoroi: École française d'Athènes (1968) fig. 105; not in Edwards (1985).

170. Pouilloux (1979) 138. For Pan on Thasos, see Brommer (1949–50) 30–32, figs. 40–42; Lazaridis (1971) 39; École française d'Athènes (1968) 57–58.

171. École française d'Athènes (1968) 49, 171; Rolley (1965) 457–58. Koureion: Cole (1984b). Cf. the nymphs of the Pyrrhakidai on Delos (4.8.3), the nymphs of the Hylleis and Dymaneis on Thera (4.8.7), and Kos (4.9.4).

172. Imhoof-Blumer (1908) nos. 362–69; Head (1911) 197–98; Schaeffer (1939) 464–69; Franke and Hirmer (1964) 123; École française d'Athènes (1968) 185–86; pl. 1; Hammond (1983) 245–58. The attribution of the earliest satyr-nymph coins to the Thraco-Macedonian town of Lete has been questioned by Picard, who assigns them to Thasos: Picard (1982a) 418 n. 27, (1982b) 10; Oikonomidou (1990) 533–39.

173. Silen relief: École française d'Athènes (1968) 58–62, fig. 23; Boardman (1978) fig. 223. Thracian origin of Dionysos: Nilsson (1967) 564–68. Dionysos' cult around Pangaion: Perdrizet (1910) 36–81. Coins attributed to the Satrai (usually assigned to Lete): Kraay (1976) 148. An oracle of Dionysos belonging to the Satrai: Hdt. 7.111. For the Diony(sii?), see Hammond and Griffith (1979) 77–91, 111; Isaac (1986) 11, 83; Head (1911) 194–97.

174. The northern Aegean and Attic scenes of nymphs and silens might draw upon a common source: Carpenter (1997) 44. See 3.1.1.

175. Price and Waggoner (1975) 32–35.

176. Edonoi: Apollod. *Bibl.* 3.5.1. Pangaion: Perdrizet (1910) 49–50. For Lykourgos, see Gantz (1993) 113–14. Aesch. wrote a tetralogy on the subject. Cf. Stesich. fr. 234; Pherecydes 3 F 90; Soph. *Ant.* 955–65. One version has Lykourgos attacking the nymph nurse Ambrosia, who changes into a vine and strangles him: Asclepiades of Tragilos 12 F 18 with Casson (1926) 247; Perdrizet (1910) 33–34.

177. For general information, see Isaac (1986) 10, 66–70; Lazaridis (1971), esp. 38, 56, and figs. 26, 29. Sanctuary of Parthenos at Neapolis: *AD* 17 (1961–62) chron. 235–38, pl. 279–84; *BCH* 86 (1962) 830–40. The evidence does not appear to support Isaac's statement (1986) 69 that the cult of the nymphs is attested at Neapolis.

178. Aesch. *Suppl.* 255–59. Evadne: Apollod. *Bibl.* 2.1.1; Hyg. *Fab.* 145. Rhodope: Schol. Theoc. 7.76–77d. Differently, Ov. *Met.* 6.87–89. See also Tereine as daughter of Strymon in Ant. Lib. *Met.* 21. Tereine sounds suitably Thracian (similar to Teres, king of the Odrysians, or Prokne's Tereus). Kallirhoë: Steph. Byz. s.v. Βιστωνία.

179. Andron of Halikarnassos 10 F 7; Steph. Byz. s.v. βιθυνία and θρᾴκη. Cf. *Etym. Magn.* s.v. Ἴσμαρος.

180. Eur. [*Rhes.*] 915–31. In Hom. *Il.* 10.435, Rhesos' father is named Eioneus, with reference to the city at the mouth of the Strymon, and Conon 26 F 1.4 gives this name as an old designation of the Strymon. Thracian rider: Borgeaud (1991); see also Perdrizet (1910) 17–18; Casson (1926) 248; Otto (1956) 49–53. Tomb: Marsyas of Philippi 136 F 7; Isaac (1986) 55–58. Sanctuary with fifth-century dedication to Klio: *Ergon* (1959) 37–44; *BCH* 84 (1960) 793–98.

181. Lists of the Muses' offspring: Schol. Eur [*Rhes.*] 346; Schol. Hom. *Il.* 10.435 Dindorf; Schol. Lycoph. 830. For Orpheus, whose mother is usually identified as Kalliope and whose father is Oiagros or Apollo, see also Pind. fr.

128c; Schol. Pind. *Pyth.* 4.313a; Ap. Rhod. *Argon.* 1.23–34; Apollod. *Bibl.* 1.3.2; Gantz (1993) 721–25. For Linos, see Hes. fr. 305; Apollod. *loc. cit.*; Phot. *Lex.* s.v. Λίνον.

182. Schol. Verg. *G.* 4.523; Vergil *loc. cit.* speaks of the Oeagrius Hebrus; cf. Schol. Lycoph. 830, where Oiagros seems to be a river god. For Rhesos and Orpheus, see Borgeaud (1991). Bistonian nymphs: Mosch. 3.18.

183. Philammon and Thamyris at Delphi: Paus. 10.7.2. Cf. on Philammon Eur. [*Rhes.*] 915–18; Pherecydes 3 F 26, 120. Argiope: Paus. 4.33.3; Apollod. *Bibl.* 1.3.3. A similar story is in Conon 26 F 1.7. On red-figured Attic vases, Argiope is shown with her son or prays for him in a sanctuary of the Muses: *LIMC* s.v. Argiope nos. 1–4 (Nercessian).

184. Founding of Abdera: Apollod. *Bibl.* 2.5.8; Hellanicus 4 F 105; Pind. fr. 52b.1–2. Coins: Imhoof-Blumer (1908) 146.

185. Kazarow (1936) 509; Robert (1974) 58–59; (1962) 398 n. 1.

186. Anchialos was founded by its neighbor to the south, Apollonia, most likely in the fifth century. See Isaac (1986) 247–49. Excavation: Filow (1911) 350–57; Kazarow (1936) 510–11. Inscribed reliefs: *IG* Bulg. I 380–81; *RA* (1914) 475 no. 95. Coins: Robert (1959) 223–25.

187. Dobrusky (1897); Hoddinott (1975) 196–97.

188. *SEG* 3 (1927) 536; Dobrusky (1897) 138, fig. 17; Velkov and Gerassimova-Tomova (1989) 1354; see also pl. 7.14 from Madara, which depicts a reclining Herakles with a nymph relief at his feet.

189. New excavation: Goceva (1989) 114, (1990) 74–75, figs. 1–2. The term *epêkoos* is common at this period, especially in the cult of the assisting goddess Isis; see Versnel (1981b) 26–37.

190. Nock (1925) 47; Pleket (1981) 155, 161–63.

191. Velkov and Gerassimova-Tomova (1989) 1353. For a summary of Thracian sites, see Kazarow (1936), supplemented by Velkov and Gerassimova-Tomova (1989).

192. On the Theban Kabeiroi, Schachter (1981–94) 2.66–110 with bib. On the Thracian identity of the Samothracian and Lemnian (Sintian) people, see Strabo 10.2.17, 457.

193. Strabo 10.3.1–23, 463–474; Acusilaus 2 F 20; Pherecydes 3 F 48. From later sources, we can conclude that Pherecydes' account identified two daughters of Proteus, who gave rise to different groups of *daimones*. Kabeiro, with Hephaistos, produced the two triads outlined above, plus Kadmilos; Rhetia (or Rhoiteia) with Apollo produced the Kyrbantes, who lived in Samothrace. See Schol. Lycoph. 583, 1161; Schol. Ap. Rhod. 1.929; Steph. Byz. s.v. Καβειρία; Jacoby (1923–58) on *FGrHist* 3 F 48; Hemberg (1950) 82, 165–66.

194. Lemnian nymphs: Schol. Pind. *Ol.* 13.74g. Dioskouroi: Hemberg (1950) 144. Nonnus *Dion.* 14.17–22 speaks of "Thracian Kabeiro," mother of two Kabeiroi who were skilled at the forge. Goceva (1991) emphasizes the putative Thracian origins of the cult and links the Kabeirid nymphs to the voluminous evidence for the worship of a nymph triad in Thrace.

195. Mnaseas *FHG* fr. 27. For a discussion of whether the Samothracian gods can properly be called Kabeiroi, see Cole (1984a) 1–3.

196. Diod. Sic. 5.47–48 gives both of these versions; Dion. Hal. *Ant. Rom.* 1.61.3 makes Samon, son of Hermes and the nymph Rhene, the first settler of Samothrace. Salvation from drowning: Burkert (1985) 284.

197. Lemnos fountains: *AA* 45 (1930) 139–46, figs. 22–23; Muthmann (1975) 98.

198. Chryse on vases: Hooker (1950); *LIMC* s.v. Chryse nos. 6–7 (Froning). Cf. Soph. *Phil.* 268–70, 1326–28. Nymph Chryse spurned by Philoktetes: Schol. Lycoph. 911; Schol. Soph. *Phil.* 194. See Gantz (1993) 589–90; Bernabò-Brea (1961).

199. Parian cult of Charites: Apollod. *Bibl.* 3.15.7.

200. *IG* XII 5.245; Bodnar (1973); Muthmann (1975) 122–23, pl. 18; Berranger (1983) with bib.; Edwards (1985) no. 89.

201. Walter (1939) 53, 70–71.

202. At this period, the cult of Bendis, in concert with the nymphs, was active at Peiraieus in Athens; the appearance of Bendis' cult in Athens and its ally Paros has been linked to Lykourgan support for the Odrysians against Macedonia. For the Bendis relief, see Bodnar (1973) 275; Edwards (1985) no. 20.

203. Demeter on Paros: Apollodorus of Athens 244 F 89; Detienne (1974) 100–101; Andò (1996) 64–69. For bee, nymph, and priestess, see 2.5.3; Schol. Pind. *Pyth.* 4.106c; Hsch. s.v. μέλισσαι; Schol. Theoc. 15.94–95a; Porph. *De antr. nymph.* 18.

204. Apollod. *Bibl.* 2.5.9, 3.1.3. Nephalion's name refers to the local use of wineless libations in the sacrifices to Zeus Endendros; a Parian inscription (*IG* XII 5.1027) specifies the use of honey. Such libations (*nêphalia*) are also attested for sacrifices to the nymphs in Attica and Elis (4.4.4).

205. *IG* XII 5.244; *SEG* 28 (1978) 708–9; Tiverios (1975). Berranger (1992) 133–35 argues convincingly that "Dorpophoroi" is to be understood as an epithet of the nymphs, not as a separate group of deities. Karpophoros in Tegea and Malophoros in Selinous: Nilsson (1967) 478, 412. For Karpophoros on Paros, see *RE* 18.4 (1949) 1845 s.v. Paros (Rubensohn). *Numphai Karpodoteirai* from Nisyra in the Imperial period: *TAM* 5 (1981) 426.

206. *IG* XII 5.1028 (tablet from cave in region of Kapitan Markos), 247 (column fragment of uncertain date inscribed "Of the nymphs; do not move"), 248 (fragment of marble block with metrical inscription). Cf. Rubensohn's description of a cave southwest of Paroikia: *RE* 18.4 (1949) 1854–55 s.v. Paros. *IG* XII 5.246 (tablet with breasts) was originally described by Rubensohn as an anatomical votive of a foot but was corrected by Forsen and Sironen (1991) 176–80, no. 7. They also describe the breast dedications to Eileithyia, nos. 5, 6.

207. Local nymphs: Diod. Sic. 5.52. Cave of Dionysos: Porph. *De antr. nymph.* 20. For Naxos, see also 3.1.1.

208. *Muchiai Numphai*: *IG* XII 5.53; Hom. *Od.* 5.226, 13.363. Compare *Od.* 4.304 and 7.346, where the *muchos* is the sleeping chamber of husband and wife.

209. Dion. Hal. *Ant. Rom.* 1.67.3. See Rolley (1965) 456–57. For Zeus, see Nilsson (1967) 402–6.

210. Hom. *Hymn Ap.* 3.157–64; Calame (1997) 104–10. Some sources (e.g., Thuc. 3.104) speak of *gunaikes* rather than *kourai*; one suspects the professionalism of the chorus eventually took precedence over the marital status of the participants.

211. Callim. *Hymn* 4.256. For the Inopos River, see Bruneau (1990) 554–57; another Inopos River associated with nymphs is attested at Knidos (4.9.4).

212. Hom. *Hymn Ap.* 3.79–88; Callim. *Hymn* 4.37–40, 300–301, 323. Cf. Apollod. *Bibl.* 1.4.1; Schol. Lycoph. 401; Hyg. *Fab.* 53; Serv. on Verg. *Aen.* 3.73.

213. Bruneau (1970) 448–94. An Attic vase depicts Delos seated on an *omphalos*, receiving libations from Artemis and Apollo: *LIMC* s.v. Delos no. 1 (Bruneau); Gallet de Santerre (1976). Callim. *Hymn* 4.312, 321, addressing Delos, speaks of "your altar." See Cahen (1923) 14–25.

214. Nymphaion: *IG* XI 2.144 A 91, 159 A 39; Bruneau (1970) 435–38. A *manteion* mentioned in *IG* XI, 2.165.44 was perhaps that of Glaukos, who gave oracles in company with the Nereids at Delos (Ar. fr. 490). Glaukos was the son of Poseidon and a naiad nymph: Euanthes fr. 409.

215. Roussel (1929) 166–79; Bruneau and Ducat (1983) 221. The monument is located at the spot where the flow of the Inopos was collected into a reservoir. On the Pyrrhakidai and other *genê*, see Parker (1996) 308; Bourriot (1976) 2.1161–67.

216. For the fountain Minoë, see Courby (1912) 114–15, figs. 151–52; *IDélos* (1950) 69; Dunkley (1935–36) 180–81; Ginouvès (1962) 333–34; Bruneau and Ducat (1983) 142–43, fig. 29. For the Minoïd nymphs and the relief, see Edwards (1985) 88; Bruneau (1970) 436, and pl. 5.5.

217. *IDélos* (1937) 2413; Bruneau (1970) 437, pl. 2.1. Zeus Dimeranos is also attested in Roman Moesia.

218. Callim. fr. 75.56–58 (= Xenomedes 442 F 1); Ar. *Constitution of the Ceians* no. 26. See Ov. *Her.* 20.223, *Met.* 10.109 ("nymphs who possess the Karthaian fields" on Keos/Kea).

219. Aristaios and Etesian winds: Ap. Rhod. *Argon.* 2.516–27. For the bee on coins of Ioulis, see Head (1911) 484.

220. For this view, see Jebb (1905) 6–7; Storck (1912) 6–7.

221. The Etesian winds are closely associated with the entry of the sun into Leo, as in Aratus *Phaen.* 150–55; Schol. Ap. Rhod. 2.498–527a, v. Aratus' source was Eudoxus, who was active at Athens in the fourth century. For the fifth century, the activities of Euktemon and Meton at Athens make it just possible, though not likely, that knowledge of the zodiac was available on Keos. Euktemon and Meton were concerned, like the religious specialists on Keos, with the relationship of the weather to the risings and settings of stars, particularly Seirios.

222. Edwards (1985) no. 87. Inscription: *IG* XII 5.731.

223. On the Idaian and Diktaian cults, see Fauré (1964) 94–109; Verbruggen (1981) 71–75 with bib.; Willetts (1962) 144–45, 199–218, 239–43. On the hymn from Palaikastro, the original of which is dated to the third or fourth century, see *IC* III (1942) 2.2; Verbruggen (1981) 101–11 with bib.; West (1965) 149–59.

224. Amaltheia as a nymph or naiad: Ov. *Fast.* 5.111–28; Hyg. *Poet. astr.* 2.13. As a goat: Callim. *Hymn* 1.45–53; Apollod. *Bibl.* 1.1.6–7; Diod. Sic. 5.70; Hyg. *loc. cit.* Bees: Callim. *loc. cit.*; Boio in Ant. Lib. *Met.* 19; Verg. *G.* 4.149; Diod. Sic. *loc. cit.* Daughters of Melisseus: Apollod. *loc. cit.*; Hyg. *Fab.* 182; Hyg. *Poet. astr.* 2.13; Schol. Eur. [*Rhes.*] 342. Doves and an eagle bring nectar and ambrosia to Zeus: Moero fr. 1. A sow nourishes Zeus: Agathocles 472 F 1a. For bees, see Ransome (1937) 91–11; 1.3, 2.4.1. For therotrophism, see Verbruggen (1981) 39–44.

225. Honey thieves: Boio in Ant. Lib. *Met.* 19; *CVA* Great Britain, fasc. 4, pl. 32.1; Nilsson (1950) 543; Verbruggen (1981) 42. Bears Kynosoura and Helike: Aratus *Phaen.* 36–37; Aglaosthenes 499 F 1. Kydonian coins with a nursing dog: Verbruggen (1981) 43; Fauré (1964) 146; Head (1911) 463–64 (c. 400–300). The obverse shows a female head, possibly a nymph.

226. Diod. Sic. 5.70. Nymphai Geraistiai: *Etym. Magn.* s.v. Γεραιστιάδες. Geraistion is a spot in Arkadia where Zeus was swaddled: *Etym. Magn.* s.v. Γεραίστιον. Similar toponyms and legends in Arkadia and Krete suggest that the birth myth of Zeus in both areas had a common source; the most probable explanation is that Peloponnesian settlers carried the myth to Krete. See Fauré (1964) 123; Paus. 8.53.4. Ide and Adrasteia as nymph nurses: Apollod. *Bibl.* 1.1.6–7 (daughters of Melisseus); Ap. Rhod. *Argon.* 3.133; Schol. Eur. [*Rhes.*] 342; Gantz (1993) 42. Gaia alone: Hes. *Theog.* 478–80. See also Hadzisteliou-Price (1978) 81–82.

227. *Ehoeae*: Hes. fr. 10 a, b = Hes. fr. 123 Merkelbach and West (1967); Eur. *Bacch.* 120–25 (or Cor. fr. 654.12); Diod. Sic. 5.64; West (1965) 155.

228. Treaties: *IC* I (1935) Lato 5.76 (Lato and Olous); *SEG* 23 (1968) 563.21 (Axios and Gortyn), 26 (1976–77) 1049.85 (Hierapytna and Lato), 33 (1983) 134.4, 638 (Lyttos and Olous). See Willetts (1962). Mystery cult: Fauré (1964) 116.

229. Daktyloi born from nymph: Stesimbrotus 107 F 12; Ap. Rhod. *Argon.* 1129–31 with schol. Male and female: Soph. fr. 364–66. Right and left: Pherecydes 3 F 47; Hellanicus 4 F 89; Jeanmaire (1949) 255–65. See also Fauré (1964) 112 n. 2.

230. For Akakallis, see Ant. Lib. *Met.* 30 (Milatos); Paus. 10.16.5 (Phylakides and Philandros), 8.53.4 (Kydon); Steph. Byz. s.v. Κυδωνία (Kydon); Schol. Theoc. 7.12c (Kydon); Ap. Rhod. *Argon.* 4.1489–97 (Amphithemis or Garamas). Akakallis is the narcissus: Eumachus in Ath. 15.681e; Hsch. s.v. Ἀκακαλλίς. See Fauré (1961–62); Hadzisteliou-Price (1978) 83.

231. Kynosoura: Fauré (1964) 144–46. Diktynna, Britomartis: Nilsson (1967) 311–12. For Britomartis/Diktynna as a nymph see Callim. *Hymn* 3.189–200.

232. Callim. *Hymn* 3.15, 162; Ap. Rhod. *Argon.* 3.877; cf. Steph. Byz. s.v. Ἀμνισός. Eileithyia: Hom. *Od.* 19.188.

233. *IC* I (1935) Lebena 7.1, 4; Guarducci (1932) 215–29; Ginouvès (1962) 350; Bultrighini (1993) 82. Letter forms date the inscription itself to the second century. From eastern Krete (Itanos), a Hellenistic nymphaion is attested: *IC* III (1942) Itanos 18; Bultrighini (1993) 55.

234. Hylleis: *IG* XII 3.378; *LSCG* 132. Two victims are specified, and the meat from the sacrifice is not to be carried away from the spot. Dymanes: *IG* XII 3.377. For the topography of the site, see Sperling (1973) 73–76; Roussel (1976) 25.

235. Kyrene in the *Ehoeae*: West (1985) 85–89; Acesandrus 469 F 4; cf. Callim. *Hymn* 2.91–92.

236. On the foundation myths of Kyrene, see Dougherty (1993) 146–52; Calame (1996) 99–109.

237. Chamoux (1953) 126–27. Kyra as spring: Callim. *Hymn* 2.88; Steph. Byz. s.v. Κυρήνη; *Anecdota Graeca* 1173. Trogus in Just. *Epit.* 13.7 speaks of the *mons Cyra*.

238. Pind. *Pyth.* 9.7, 54; Acesandrus 469 F 4; Phylarchus 81 F 16. Cf. Schol. Ap. Rhod. 4.1561c; Isid. *Etym.* 15.1.77 (*Cyrene regina fuit Libyae, quae e suo nomine civitatem Cyrenem condidit*). As a historical etymology for Kyrene, however, the root *kur-* is unlikely, since the upsilon is long in *kurios* but generally short in Kyrene. See Chamoux (1953) 126. On the epithets *despoina* and *kuria*, often applied to Kybele, see Henrichs (1976) 253–86.

239. Imhoof-Blumer (1908) nos. 347–53; Head (1911) 866–67 (530–480). Identification disputed by Chamoux (1953) 276. Later, her head appears or that of Libya: Head (1911) 867–71. For a fifth-century terra-cotta of Kyrene with the silphium plant, see Higgins (1954–) no. 1447.

240. Pind. *Pyth.* 9.12; Ap. Rhod. *Argon.* 2.504. Altar: Laronde (1987) 367 cf. Paus. 10.15.6; Chamoux (1953) 199.

241. Spring of Apollo: Hdt. 4.158; Pind. *Pyth.* 4.294–95.

242. Stucchi (1975) 117 n. 6 identifies the Hill of Myrtles with the terrace of the sanctuary of Apollo; see also Bacchielli (1995) 136–37. Callim. *Hymn* 2.90–95 calls the hill "horned Myrtoussa, where the daughter of Hypseus killed the lion that harried Eurypylos' cattle."

243. *Chthoniai numphai:* Ap. Rhod. *Argon.* 2.504–5 cf. Orph. *Hymns* 51.3; Callim. *Hymn* 4.80. Graffiti: Boehringer (1929) 396–400; Goodchild (1971) 111–12. Apollo: Laronde (1987) 426–27 (second-century marble base inscribed to Apollo Nymphagetes and the nymphs). A calendar fragment, *LSCG* Suppl. 116 (second century), mentions among other civic gods the nymphs, Apollo and the nymphs, or Apollo Nymphagetes and prescribes a goat as an offering. Cf. *SEG* 9 (1944) 175.5, 38 (1988) 1900 (both second century).

244. *Suda* s.v. Ἀστυδρομία. See also Willetts (1962) 202 n. 23.

245. Heroines: Callim. fr. 602 cf. *Anth. Pal.* 6.225, where they are *despotides.* Ap. Rhod. *Argon.* 4.1309–11, 1322–23, 1347–50. On the double meaning of *oiopolos,* "solitary" as in desert dwelling and "shepherd," see Vian and Delage (1976–81) 3.192 n. 1322; Livrea (1973) 373–74. See also Vian and Delage (1976–81) 3.191–92. Hsch. mentions a group of nymphs called Λιβυσάτιδες or Λιβυστίδες (s.v.).

246. Bacchielli (1995) 135–36, citing Norton and Curtis (1911) 156–57, pls. 65–66; their attributes are gazelles and silphium. The heroines might also be represented in a series of Hellenistic reliefs that show an assemblage of local gods, including Zeus Ammon; see Fabricotti (1987).

247. The genealogy given in Ap. Rhod. *Argon.* 4.1494–96 makes Nasamon and Kaphauros the sons of Amphithemis/Garamas and a "Tritonian nymph."

248. Nile: Hes. *Theog.* 338; Apollod. *Bibl.* 2.1.4; Eur. *Hel.* 1.

249. Kákosy (1982) 294: a herdsman meets in the marsh a terrifying woman whose body is covered with hair but who later becomes attractive.

250. Serv. on Verg. *G.* 4.363.

251. Graindor (1932) 97–108; Bernand (1969) 342–56, nos. 86–87; Hani (1974); Nock (1961) 919–27; Kàkosy (1982). Text is from Bernand (1969), and my translations are adapted from his French.

252. For statues of nymphs with scallop-shell vessels, based on an original of the fourth century, see *LIMC* s.v. nymphe nos. 13–17 (Halm-Tisserant and Siebert).

253. Hani (1974) 215, 217, 221; Kàkosy (1982) 294–96.

254. Bernand (1969) 464 no. 116 (first century); Kàkosy (1982) 296.

255. Zeus' altar on the peak of Gargaron: Hom. *Il.* 8.47–48. Idaia as epithet of Meter: Eur. *Or.* 1453; Strabo 10.3.2, 469. Aineias: Hom. *Hymn Ven.* 5.256–58; *Cypria* fr. 4–5. Muses, nymphs, and Aphrodite: Hes. fr. 26.10–13.

256. For a detailed account of Paris as herdsman, see Stinton (1965) 16, 28. For ancient analogies between herdsman and hero, king, or poet, see Gutzwiller (1991) 24–65.

257. Aineias as herdsman: Hom. *Il.* 20.86–92. Boukolion: Hom. *Il.* 6.20–26. Enops: Hom. *Il.* 14.442–45. See Griffin (1992) 197.

258. Homeric genealogy: Hom. *Il.* 20.215–40. Just as Enops' partner is simply a naiad nymph, Daphnis' lover is called "Naïs" in Theoc. *Id.* 8.43, 93; see Stinton (1965) 48.

259. Bucolic unions: Griffin (1992) 201. Gutzwiller (1991) 27 n. 20 comments that the only non-Asiatic noble herdsman in Homer is the disguised Athena at *Od.* 13.221–24. Other examples of nymph-mortal genealogies from Asia Minor: Hom. *Il.* 20. 382–85 (naiad nymph); Ov. *Met.* 9.450–53 (Cyaneë, daughter of Maeandrus). Quintus of Smyrna gives several pathetic genealogies in imitation of Homer, all of Trojan allies: *Posthomerica* 1.291–93 (Neaira); 3.300–302 (Pegasis); 6.464–70 (unnamed nymph and Pronoë); 11.36–39 (Okyrroë).

260. Apollod. *Bibl.* 3.12.1; Diod. Sic. 4.75; Schol. Lycoph. 29; Steph. Byz. s.v. Τευκροί.

261. Apollod. *Bibl.* 3.12.1–6 cf. Schol. Lycoph. 29. Dion. Hal. *Ant. Rom.* 1.62.1–2 makes Erichthonios marry Kallirhoë, daughter of Skamandros, and has Kapys rather than Assarakos marry the naiad nymph Hieromneme.

262. Cf. Hellanicus 4 F 138; Diod. Sic. 4.75.3; Schol. Lycoph. 29.

263. Cf. Hellanicus 4 F 139. Schol. Lycoph. 18 makes Strymo or Rhoio, daughter of Skamandros, the mother of Tithonos only.

264. Aisakos: Ov. *Met.* 11.769; Apollod. *Bibl.* 3.12.5; Schol. Hom. *Il.* 24.497 Erbse. For Alexirhoë, see also Schol. Hom. *Il. loc. cit.*; Plut. [*De fluviis*] 12.1 (mother of the Phrygian river Sagaris by Mygdon); Imhoof-Blumer (1908) no. 313.

265. Hekabe: Pherecydes 3 F 136a–b; Apollod. *Bibl.* 3.12.5; Hom. *Il.* 16.718.

266. Hsch. s. v. ἀβαρβαρεῖαι. Nymph Ide: Head (1911) 548. A votive relief from Lampsakos: Edwards (1985) no. 111, second century.

267. Paus. 10.12.1–4; Larson (1995b) 125–28 with bib.; *Epigr. Gr.* 1075 (dedication to naiad nymphs on a fountain by the Sibyl's cave).

268. For Astakos and the nymphs, see Larson (1997a).

269. Nonnus *Dion.* 15.170, 380 (Astakides), 15.308–10, 376–77 (Hymnos). Nonnus did not invent the nymph Nikaia, daughter of the Sangarios River and Kybele. The story of her parentage and liaison with Dionysos is recorded by Memnon of Herakleia 434 F 1.28.9.

270. Arrian's *Bithyniaca*: a nymph attendant of Kybele is the eponym of the dance called Sikinnos, fr. 10; the Mysian town Abrettene is named for a nymph, fr. 12; a local nymph, Thrake, knows the healing arts, fr. 13; Astakos is the son of a nymph, fr. 5; the nymph Arganthone bore Mysos and Thynos, fr. 21. (Jacoby in *FGrHist*, however, assigns these fragments differently.)

271. Hylas: Ap. Rhod. *Argon.* 1.1221–39. Kleite: Ap. Rhod. *Argon.* 1.1066–69, an example of the "pathetic fallacy," characteristic of pastoral verse, e.g., Theoc. *Id.* 1.70–75, 7.74–75; see Griffin (1992) 205. Amykos: Ap. Rhod. *Argon.* 2.1–4. Paraibios: Ap. Rhod. *Argon.* 2.476–86, 2.4.2. Dipsakos: Ap. Rhod. *Argon.* 2.652–65; on the bucolic flavor of this passage, see Fränkel (1968) 221–22.

272. Reliefs: Mansel (1936) 67–71, pls. 1–5; Robert (1958) 103–8; *IK Bd.* 32, nos. 138–40, pl. 7 (second century B.C.E. to second century C.E.). For first-century coins of Pythia Therma, which show Herakles and the three nymphs, see Imhoof-Blumer (1908) nos. 483–84. For Roman examples of reliefs that show Herakles with the nymphs, see Bieber (1945) 273–77.

273. Herakles: Aristid. *Or.* 40.20; *Anth. Pal.* 9.676. Christian cult: Mansel (1936) 56, 79; *IK* Bd. 32.143; Migne, *PG* 115.654–56. For the baths at Pythia Therma and Prousa, see Robert (1946).

274. Mytilene: Head (1911) 561–62 (c. 440–400, 400–350, 350–250); Imhoof-Blumer (1908) nos. 328–31. Pyrrha: Head (1911) 563 (fourth century); Imhoof-Blumer (1908) nos. 332–33.

275. Issa, like Larissa, is a "Pelasgian," non-Hellenic name. For Makar(eus), see Hom. *Il.* 24.544; Diod. Sic. 5.81. For Issa, see Steph. Byz. and Hsch. s.v. Ἴσσα; Ov. *Met.* 6.124; Schol. Lycoph. 219. See also Hsch. s.v. Ἐννησιάδες; *IG* XII 2.129 = *Epigr. Gr.* 828.

276. Pitane: Steph. Byz. s.v. Πιτάνη. For Amazons, see Larson (1995b) 114–15. Grotto: Pottier and Reinach (1883) pl. 16; Mollard-Besques (1954–) vol. 2, pl. 106b. See comparative discussion in Costabile et al. (1991) 58, where the possible function of the Myrina terra-cotta in funerary ritual is emphasized. The two archaic model fountains from a necropolis on Lemnos (4.7.4) provide another parallel.

277. Asklepios: Aristid. *Or.* 39.9, see also 53.4. Fountain law: *OGI* no. 483, l. 190. The inscription dates to the second century C.E., but the law itself is some centuries earlier. Statue base: *SEG* 28 (1978) 967 (late Hellenistic). Votives: Edwards (1985) nos. 109–10 (second century). See also Habicht (1969) no. 124 (nymphs and Moirai). As for the Kaikos itself, a Mysian nymph, Okyrrhoë, is supposed to have born the river god to Hermes: Plut. [*De fluviis*] 21.1.

278. Ion of Chios 392 F 1. For the possible significance of the names Agelos and Melas, see Vidal-Naquet (1986) 106–28. Oinopion and Helike: Parth. *Amat. narr.* 20. Boundary stone: *MDAI(A)* 13 (1888) 178 no. 26.

279. Aristid. *Or.* 20.21. Relief: Edwards (1985) no. 107, first century.

280. Buresch (1892); Bean (1966) 156–57; *IK* Bd. 2, nos. 224–28; Paus. 10.12.7. For the Sibyls, see bib. in Larson (1995b) 125–28. In Callim. *Hymn* 1.35, the nymph Neda is πρεσβυτάτη. *Numphai presbuterai* and *neôterai: IK* Bd. 15, nos. 1600.27, 36 (Ephesos, Imperial period).

281. Atalay (1985); *SEG* 35 (1985) 1115.

282. Panyassis fr. 17a; Schol. Hom. *Il.* 24.616 Erbse. Cf. Panyassis fr. 17b; Huxley (1969) 178. Paus. 8.38.9–10 discusses the similar river names Acheloös and Acheloios.

283. Lydian genealogies: Xanthus 765 F 16; Nicolaus of Damascus 90 F 15; Bengisu (1996) 3–6. Iphition: Hom. *Il.* 20.382.

284. Torrhebos: Nicolaus of Damascus 90 F 15 with Pearson (1939) 121 n. 3. Toroibos the musician: Plut. *Mor.* 1136c [*De mus.*]. Lydians conflate Muse and nymph: Schol. Theoc. *Id.* 7.92; Phot. *Lex.* s.v. νύμφη. For lake Torrhebos, modern Gölcük, see Bengisu (1996) 3 n. 7.

285. Asius of Samos fr. 7. Hera and Zeus: Schol. Hom. *Il.* 14.295–96 Erbse; Vian and Delage (1976–81) 1.248 n. 188. Admete: Menodotus of Samos 541 F; Anac. fr. 448. The reading "Leleges and nymphs" in Menodotus has been questioned, but I see no reason to reject it. Parallels are perhaps to be found in the welcoming of the goddesses Athena, Artemis, and Persephone by the Sicilian nymphs (4.10).

286. Chesiad nymphs: Nic. *Alex.* 151. Okyrhoë: Ap. Rhod. or Naucratis in Ath. 7.283d. Chesias, an *akrôtêrion* of Samos: Callim. *Hymn* 3.228 with schol. See also Laumonier (1958) 698, 704. For the medicinal properties of Samian earth,

see Pliny *HN* 28.194, 248; 31.117; 35.37, 191. Block inscribed to Apollo Nymphagetes and nymphs: *GDI* 5707.

287. Mykalessides: Callim. *Hymn* 4.48–50. Law: *LSAM* no. 39. For this and similar regulations, see Robert (1949) 152–60. Mykale spring: Paus. 5.7.5. Though there is no obvious connection, it should also be noted that Mount Mykale was the site of the Panionian festival.

288. Reliefs: Blümel (1960) figs. 1–2. Artemidorus' dream manual states (2.44) that three clothed women are to be interpreted as Moirai, three naked women as Horai, and women washing themselves as nymphs.

289. Ehrhardt (1993). See also Tuchelt (1970) 217; Gödecken (1986). The seated figure is no longer extant, but Tuchelt's photographs of similar dedications (e.g., pl. 42) give a good idea of its original appearance. For the kore, see also Richter (1968) no. 64, figs. 209, 211, here attributed to Samos (second quarter of the sixth century).

290. For the law of the Molpoi, see *LSAM* no. 50; for discussion and recent bib., see Robertson (1987) 359–78; Fontenrose (1988) 28–44. A Hellenistic relief shows the gods of Didyma, including the nymphs: Tuchelt (1972).

291. Richter (1968) nos. 70, 71; Graeve (1986) 21–25, pl. 6.

292. Byblis: Nic. in Ant. Lib. *Met.* 30; Ov. *Met.* 9.447–665; Conon 26 F 1.2. Cf. Parth. *Amat. narr.* 11. For Miletos' origin in Krete, cf. Apollod. *Bibl.* 3.1.2; Paus. 7.2.5. There was a town Milatos in Krete: Strabo 10.4.14, 479; 4.8.6. Pronoë's river was perhaps the Kalbis, which flowed past the city of Kaunos: Strabo 14.2.2, 651.

293. *LSCG* no.152; see also Segre (1937–38) 191–92; Sherwin-White (1978) 328–29. For *pemmata* as offerings, see, e.g., *Anth. Pal.* 6.324.

294. Dymanes inscription: Paton and Hicks (1891) no. 44, probably third century. Calendar: *LSCG* no. 153; Segre (1937–38) 193; Sherwin-White (1978) 328–29.

295. Theoc. *Id.* 7.135–37, 154–55; Sherwin-White (1978) 53, 329.

296. Daikrates: Van Straten (1976); Edwards (1985) no. 98 (c. 390–80), 99 (early third century). Cf. Edwards nos. 100, 101 (first century). A parallel for the inclusion of Charites and nymphs in the same relief is Edwards no. 102, a third-century work possibly from Telos between Kos and Rhodes. It shows seven frontal dancers, the endmost of whom is smaller in size, and is inscribed to Euphrosyne, Aglaia, Thalia (i.e., the Charites), Ismene, Kykaïs, Eranno, and Telonnesos (the island Telos).

297. Zenon of Rhodes 523 F 1; Diod. Sic. 5.55–56. The names of Himalia and her sons have to do with agriculture: Hsch. s.v. ἱμαλιά (an abundance of wheat meal). Spartaios recalls sowing, and Kytos means a basket or jar. Kronios denotes a descendant of Kronos, the god of the golden age.

298. Pind. *Ol.* 7.13–14, 54–76 cf. Strabo 14.2.7–8, 653–54. Eust. *Il.* 2.656 (315.29): Kerkaphos, son of Helios and the nymph Rhodos. Hellanicus 4 F 137 gives the same list of seven Heliadai as Diodorus.

299. Coins: Imhoof-Blumer (1908) nos. 337–39; Head (1911) 639 (c. 333–304, 189–66). Cave on akropolis: *AA* (1930) 166. Reliefs: Edwards (1985) nos. 90–97, nos. 95–96 from Lindos. Hsch. s.v. Μακρόβιοι. Loryma: *IG* XII 1, 928.

300. Bean and Cook (1955) 99 no. 4.

301. Schol. Theoc. *Id.* 17.68–69 a, d. Hdt. 1.144 speaks only of Apollo. Nilsson (1906) 178 attributes the addition of Poseidon and the nymphs to Ptolemy Philadelphos.

302. Love (1972) 404–5, (1973) 421–23, pls. 76–77; *BE* 87 (1974) 289, no. 549. See also Stampolidis (1984), who suggests a cult association with Demeter, and Bruns-Özgan (1995), who argues that the altar is dedicated to Apollo Karneios and that the nymphs are his attendants. For the altar inscription, see *IK* Bd. 41, nos. 166–68. Votive relief from sanctuary of the Muses: Edwards (1985) no. 103 (second century).

303. *IG* XII 3.199; Peek (1978) 258–60; date unknown. On Zeus Meilichios, whose cult is widespread, see Nilsson (1967) 413–15.

304. Beaudouin (1880) 282–83. Not in Edwards (1985).

305. *IG*, 1.1042a, b; date unknown.

306. Olen of Lykia: Hdt. 4.35; Paus. 9.27.2; Callim. *Hymn* 4.305. Apollo's stay in Lykia: Verg. *Aen.* 4.143–46. Nymph Lykia: Hecataeus 1 F 256; Serv. on Verg. *Aen.* 3.332. For discussion of Patara, see Parke (1985) 185–93.

307. Panyassis fr. 18. The phrase "wedded a daughter [*thugatra*]" has caused difficulties for editors. Panyassis possibly meant that Praxidike was a daughter of Ogygos or even of the Sibros River. For discussion, see Huxley (1969) 181–82; Schachter (1981–94) 3.6 n. 4. Alexander Polyhistor 273 F 58: Kragos is son of Tremiles and a nymph, Praxidike.

308. Glaukos: Hdt. 1.147; Quint. Smyrn. 4.1–12; Robert (1980) 377–92; 1.4.4. The form νύφη is widely found for νύμφη, at both early and late periods: Robert (1980) 384–85; Threatte (1980) 1.486, 2.755.

309. Metzger et al. (1974a) 333–40 deals with the nymphaion and the stele. For the text of the stele, see Metzger et al. (1974b). For other Xanthian inscriptions that mention the nymphs and Leto, see *SEG* 31 (1981) 1316, 39 (1989) 1414. On the cult at Xanthos, see Bryce (1978) 115–27; LeRoy (1988), (1993) 245–46.

310. Metzger (1952) 44, nos. 19–20, app. 2, nos. 36–41. To these, add Pace (1916–20) 62, 69–71. On the nymphs in Lykia, see Robert (1955) 217–20.

311. *Epêkooi*: Pace (1916–20) 69–70, no. 77. *Numphai Trageatides* and quartan fever: Susini (1952–54) 354–55 no. 11, from Gagae. Tragasia: Nicaenetus fr. 1.

312. Endeïs is the daughter of Cheiron and Chariklo and mother of Peleus and Telamon: Schol. Pind. *Nem.* 5.12b; Schol. Hom. *Il.* 16.14 Dindorf; Hyg. *Fab.* 14.

313. Mitford (1958) 266–73. The translation is Mitford's.

314. Altar: Myres (1914) 547 no. 1900; Mitford (1980) 261. On Arsinoë as nymph, see also Tondriau (1948) 20–21. Sherd: Mitford (1980) 261.

315. For Daphne, see Strabo 16.2.6, 750; Philostr. *VA* 1.16; Lib. *Or.* 11.94; *RE* 4.2 (1903) cols. 2138–39 s.v. Daphne (Waser); Lib. *Or.* 17.22, 11.240–41. Also at Antioch was an important sanctuary of the god Men, who was worshiped in conjunction with the nymphs; see 4.2.2.

316. Nymphs and colonization: Lacroix (1965) 115. On nymphs and coins, see also Gabrici (1959) 10–20.

317. Mertens-Horn (1991) 9–28. The use of antefixes in the shape of female heads is attested in northwest Greece on temples of Apollo, Hera (Corfu), and

Artemis and seems to have spread to Sicily and Italy from there. It might have originated in Sikyon: Winter (1993) 110–12, fig. 12, 287. Popular companion pieces for the female heads are heads of silens and river gods; gorgoneia also appear.

318. Ciaceri (1911) 242; Pugliese Carratelli (1977) 14; Mertens-Horn (1991) 20.

319. Pace (1935–49) 3.480–81: examples at Agrigentum, Enna, Megara Hyblaea.

320. Abduction: Diod. Sic. 5.3.2. Diod. here draws upon the early Hellenistic historian Timaeus of Tauromenium (566 F 164.4), who introduced the idea that Enna was the site of Persephone's abduction into the mainstream of literature. See Pearson (1987) 57–58.

321. Oracle: Paus. 5.7.3. Parke and Wormell (1956) 1.67–68 no. 2 consider the oracle authentic; Fontenrose (1978) 138 classifies it as quasi-historical.

322. Alpheios underground: Paus. 8.54.2–3. Syracuse-Olympia link: Ibycus of Rhegium fr. 323; Timaeus 566 F 41; Strabo 6.2.4, 270–71.

323. Altar of Artemis and Alpheios: Paus. 5.14.6. River Artemis: Pindar *Pyth.* 2.7. Arethousa: Early sources are Pind. *Nem.* 1.1–6; Ibycus of Rhegium fr. 323; Timaeus 566 F 41; and, if authentic, the oracle recorded in Paus. 5.7.3. Cf. Verg. *Aen.* 3.694–96. The story of the nymph Arethousa's pursuit by the river is told in Ov. *Met.* 5.487–508, 572–641. *Anth. Pal.* 9.362 assumes a marriage of Alpheios and Arethousa, punning on the double meaning of *numphê*: nymph and bride.

324. The fifth-century Argive poet Telesilla (fr. 717) mentions Artemis fleeing from Alpheios. On Artemis' relation to springs and rivers, see Nilsson (1967) 492.

325. Fish: Diod. Sic. 5.3.6. Arethousa on coins: *BMC* Sicily (Syracuse) nos. 188, 200, 208; Hill (1903) 105–9; Imhoof-Blumer (1908) nos. 115–45; Head (1911) 171–78 (c. 485–317).

326. Kyane: Diod. Sic. 4.23.4–5, 5.4.2, 14.72.1 (hieron); Ov. *Met.* 5.409–37; Ael. *VH* 2.33 (spring Kyane honored with statue). Coins: *BMC* Sicily (Syracuse) nos. 273–75; Imhoof-Blumer (1908) nos. 143–45; Head (1911) 179 (c. 357–15). The reverse shows Pegasos. For Kyane, see also Ciaceri (1911) 103–6.

327. Timaeus 566 F 32. For Damokles, also the protagonist of the famous anecdote of the sword, see Pearson (1987) 207–8, who suggests that the nymph story and the other material in Athenaeus fit the elder Dionysios better than the younger.

328. Relief: Arias (1936).

329. Cult in the theater: Anti (1948) 23, 58, 69–70; Polacco and Anti (1981) 155–56; Polacco (1992) 9, 12, 14.

330. Altar to Apollo and nymphs: Manganaro (1985) 155; *SEG* 34 (1984) 978. Late Hellenistic dedication of altar and *trikleina* by Aristoboula, from Sella cave: *IG* XIV 4; Manganaro (1992) 450–52.

331. Kamarina: *BMC* Sicily nos. 16–19; Imhoof-Blumer (1908) nos. 73–79; Head (1911) 128–30 (c. 461–405); Hill (1903) 125–26; Westermark and Jenkins (1980). For discussion of the swan rider motif, see Westermark and Jenkins (1980) 66–71.

332. With the suggested ὀρεινόμοι for the manuscript's garbled ἐρινόμου; see Gow and Page (1968) 2.369.

333. Aitne: Silenus 175 F 3; Serv. on Verg. *Aen.* 9.581 (Aitne or Thaleia conceives the Palikoi with Zeus); Hellanicus 4 F 199 (the city and river of Gela

took their name from a son of Aitne); Alcimus 560 F 5 (Mount Aitne was named after a daughter of Ouranos and Ge); Demetrius of Kallatis 85 F 4 (Sikanos and Aitne are children of the Kyklops Briareus). Coin of Aitne with head of a nymph: Imhoof-Blumer (1908) no. 62; *LIMC* s.v. Aitne no. 1 (Arnold-Biucchi), fourth century.

334. Galateia: Hom. *Il.* 18.45; Hes. *Theog.* 250. Shrine: Duris of Samos 76 F 58. For the claim that the poem was based on Philoxenus' own love for the tyrant Dionysios' mistress, see Philoxenus fr. 815, 819.

335. Polyphemos: Theoc. *Id.* 6.6, 11.8; Bion 2.3; Ov. *Met.* 13.738–897. Cf. Serv. on Verg. *Ecl.* 9.39, in which Galatea turns into a spring.

336. On Herakleian baths, see Ar. *Nub.* 1051; Ibycus fr. 300; Ath. 12.512f. Baths at Himera: Aesch. fr. 25a.

337. Plural nymphs: Pind. *Ol.* 12.19. The Himeran motif of the sacrificing nymph or river god is also found on coins of Selinous, Entella, Eryx, and Leontini as well as Terina in Italy; for discussion, see Lacroix (1965) 125–26. For Himera, see also *BMC* Sicily nos. 31–36, 48; Hill (1903) 67–68. Soter: Imhoof-Blumer (1908) nos. 68–72; Head (1911) 143–46; Lacroix (1965) 126–27.

338. Thermai: Cic. *Verr.* 2, 2.35 (87). Coin: *BMC* Sicily (Thermai Himeraeae) no. 5; Imhoof-Blumer (1908) nos. 483–84; Head (1911) 147.

339. Pelorias: *BMC* Sicily (Messana) nos. 58, 70–72, 81; Hill (1903) 69–70, 130–31; Imhoof-Blumer (1908) nos. 83–88; Head (1911) 151–55 (c. 461–396, 357–288). For the shell, see Imhoof-Blumer (1908) nos. 83–85. Ath. 1.4c, 3.92d, 3.92f speaks of Pelorian, or "giant" whelks. Cf. the etymology in Diod. Sic. 4.85. See Ciaceri (1911) 97–101. Another Chalkidian foundation, Katana, issued coins that showed an unidentified nymph, perhaps the consort of the river god Amenanos, who appears prominently on the coins: Imhoof-Blumer (1908) nos. 80–88; Head (1911) 133, c. 413–404; *LIMC* s.v. Aitne nos. 2–3 (Arnold-Biucchi). Similarly, for the ancient Chalkidian colony of Naxos: Head (1911) 160, c. 413–404.

340. Relief: Orsi (1912) fig. 31; Boardman et al. (1967) pl. 287; Arias (1936) fig. 2.

341. Eurymedousa: *BMC* Sicily (Selinous) nos. 39–43, cf. 38; Imhoof-Blumer (1908) nos. 112–14; Head (1911) 167–69 (c. 466–15).

342. Plaques from Lipari: Bernabò-Brea (1958) 126–27, pl. 47. For the debate over the identity of the three figures (whether they are nymphs, gods, or mortals) see bib. in Bell (1981) 107 n. 119. Granmichele: Zuntz (1971) 109–10, pl. 14a; Pace (1935–49) 3, fig. 124. Other examples from Akragas, Syracuse, Butera: Bell (1981) 93, nn. 127–28. Example from Ciminna: Pace (1935–49) 3.623, fig. 166.

343. Bell (1981) 92–93 nos. 253–64. For the nuptial contexts of Persephone's cult, see Zuntz (1971); Sourvinou-Inwood (1978).

344. Bell (1988) 333–4, fig. 27. Fountain houses are unusual in the western Greek colonies; Bell notes that the only other known Greek example is that at Syracuse. For Kupara, attested on a krater graffito and possibly on coinage of Morgantina, see Antonaccio and Neils (1995); Antonaccio (1999) 177–85.

345. For the Palikoi, see Ciaceri (1911) 9–10, 23–37; Pace (1935–49) 3.520–25; Aesch. fr. 6; Mette (1963) 14–15; Dougherty (1993) 79–92 with fig. 5.1 of a Paestan amphora that illustrates Thaleia's rape by Zeus in the form of an eagle; Callias 564 F 1; Diod. Sic. 11.88.6; Serv. on Verg. *Aen.* 9.581; Hsch. s.v. Παλικοί.

346. Hellenization: Galinsky (1969) 89–91. Segeste: Serv. on Verg. *Aen.* 1.550, 5.30. Cf. Verg. *Aen.* 5.35–39; Lycoph. *Alex.* 951–77 (probably drawing on Timaeus); Schol. Lycoph. 952. Different version: Serv. on Verg. *Aen.* 5.73; Dion. Hal. *Ant. Rom.* 1.52–53. See also Ciaceri (1911) 122–33; Pearson (1987) 87–88.

347. Coins: *BMC* Sicily nos. 1–46, 49–64; Hill (1903) 86–87, 90; Imhoof-Blumer (1908) 98–111; Head (1911) 164–67 (c. 480–61); *LIMC* s.v. Aigeste nos. 1–15 (Arnold-Biucchi). See also Lacroix (1965) 61–62.

348. Croon (1956) 201 accepts Segeste's connection with the hot springs but identifies her with Artemis. There was an important cult statue of Artemis at Segeste: Cic. *Verr.* 2, 4.33–34 (72); see also Galinsky (1969) 68.

349. Eryx: *BMC* Sicily nos. 6–9; Hill (1903) 91; Imhoof-Blumer (1908) 65. Entella: *BMC* Sicily nos. 1–2; Imhoof-Blumer nos. 63–64; Head (1911) 137 (c. 450). Entella as Akestes' wife: Schol. Lycoph. 953, 964; Sil. *Pun.* 14.205.

350. Diod. Sic. 4.79–80. For the Meteres, see Mertens-Horn (1991) 20; Ciaceri (1911) 5–6, 239–41. Limestone base with inscription to the Hagnai Theai, from Akrai: *IG* XIV 204; Bernabò-Brea (1956) 158–59 no. 12.

351. Orsi (1899); Pace (1935–49) 3.483–86; *SEG* 42 (1992) 825–36; Manganaro (1992).

352. Pythagoras: Timaeus 566 F 17 cf. Iambl. *VP* 11.56; Andò (1996) 47. Metrical inscriptions from Akrai, possibly related to the cult of Anna and the Paides: *IG* XIV 219; *SEG* 28 (1978) 793, 31 (1981) 821 (see also 823); Manganaro (1992) 473–87.

353. Strabo 6.1.1, 252 (Elea). 6.1.5, 256 (Medma), 6.1.7, 259 (Lokroi), 6.1.13, 263 (Thourioi). For Medma cf. Hecataeus 1 F 81, who says the name is from "a certain maiden Medma."

354. Coins: Head (1903) 105 (after 350); Imhoof-Blumer (1908) nos. 36–37; Giannelli (1963) 216.

355. Costabile et al. (1991) 107–8, 110–14. A parallel in Ael. *VH* 2.33: the Stymphalians give both (the river) Erasinos and (the nymph) Metope bovine forms.

356. Sicilian coin of an unknown city Therai: Imhoof-Blumer (1908) 482; Head (1911) 190; Pace (1935–49) 3.487, fig. 122. Terra-cottas from Rhegion: Costabile et al. (1991) figs. 185–86. For the significance of such items found in a tomb, see 4.9.2.

357. Sybaris: Strabo 8.7.5, 386. Coin: Imhoof-Blumer (1908) no. 29. For the founding of Thourioi, see Diod. Sic. 12.9.1, 12.10.6; Steph. Byz. s.v. θούριοι; Schol. Theoc. 5.1a–d. Thouria has been identified with the modern Fonte del Fico; see De Santis (1960) 53–55, pl. 16.

358. Timaeus 566 F 50. The suitability of the haunts of the nymphs for recreation in the summer season is also mentioned by Diod. Sic. 4.84.1. Cerchiara caves: De Santis (1960) 29–30, 52, 56–57, pl. 22. An archaic column and scattered terra-cottas were recovered, perhaps remnants of a shrine to the nymphs. The collection in the Cosenza museum includes terra-cottas, lamps, and coins of Roman date from the caves, but they remain unexcavated.

359. Lousias: Ael. *NA* 10.38.

360. The emendation of the text was first suggested by Müller; see discussion in *FGrHist* 570 F 7; Giannelli (1963) 114–15.

361. Stoop (1979) 179–83; Costabile et al. (1991) 104. See also Camassa (1993) 584–86.

362. Satyra: Paus. 10.10.8; Schol. Verg. G. 2.197; Probus on Verg. G. 2.197 (Satyra as wife of Tarentus and name of lake); Serv. on Verg. *Aen.* 3.551 (previous name of Taras); Giannelli (1963) 40. For coins, see Imhoof-Blumer (1908) 12–17; Head (1911) 54–55 (c. 500, 473–20). Kyme: Head (1911) 36 (c. 490); Imhoof-Blumer (1908) nos. 9–11. Laos: Imhoof-Blumer (1908) nos. 18–21. Pandosia: Imhoof-Blumer (1908) no. 38; Head (1911) 105–6 (c. 450–400). Metapontion: Imhoof-Blumer (1908) nos. 22–28; Head (1911) 75–80 (c. 400–350). For Melanippe's Italian myth, see Diod. Sic. 4.67; Giannelli (1963) 80–86. In Italy, she is regarded as a heroine rather than as a nymph.

363. Imhoof-Blumer (1908) 39–59; Head (1911) 113–14 (c. 480–25); Regling (1906) 61–68, pls. 1–3; Lacroix (1953) 16–17; Giannelli (1963) 171–73.

364. *IG* XIV 892; Forti (1951). For the healing thermal waters of the area, see Strabo 5.4.9, 248; Pliny *NH* 31.5. See also *IG* XIV 893 from Ischia.

CHAPTER 5

1. Higgins and Higgins (1996) 13–14; Wickens (1986) 1.244–46.

2. Wickens (1986) 1.172.

3. Wickens (1986) 1.98–103, 107–229.

4. Homemade images, *xoana*, and *xesmata*: *Anth. Pal.* 9.326, 328. Fruit and flowers: *Anth. Pal.* 6.154. In the late classical and Hellenistic periods, when these epigrams were produced, the rustic life was idealized, but there is no reason to doubt the details of cult practice they provide.

5. Wickens (1986) 1.171.

6. E.g., the dedication by Skyron the goatherd at Vari (5.1.9); *Anth. Pal.* 9.326; *Anth. Plan.* 291.

7. Plato: There are several versions of this story; Val. Max. 1.6 ext. 3 and Ael. *VH* 10.21, 12.45 speak of Muses or Muses and nymphs, while Olympiodorus *In Alcib.* 2.24–29 and the anonymous *Prolegomena to Plato* 2.16–22 have nymphs and Apollo Nomios (the former adds Pan). For these texts and discussion, see Riginos (1976) 17–21. Modern use of caves: Sampson (1992) 95.

8. Leonidas 51 and Antipater of Sidon 48 (both *P. Oxy.* 662).

9. *Anth. Pal.* 9.329.

10. Wickens (1986) 1.211–16.

11. Benton (1934–35). See also Antonaccio (1995) 152–55; Malkin (1998) 94–119.

12. Odysseus: Benton (1934–35) 54, 55 fig. 7, (1938) 350. Plaques: Benton (1938–39) 45, figs. 65–66.

13. Orlandos (1965) 204–5 s.v. Pitsa; *AA* 50 (1935) 198; Hausmann (1960) 15–16 fig. 4; Neumann (1979) 27, pl. 12a; Amyx (1988) 2.604–5. The third and fourth tablets show groups of female figures. Tablet inscriptions: *BCH* 91 (1967) 644–46; *SEG* 23 (1968) 264.

14. For the popularity of wooden tablets, see Van Straten in Versnel (1981a) 78–79; Ar. *Thesm.* 770–75; Aen. Tact. 31, 15; Van Straten (1995) 57–58.

15. Fully published except for terra-cottas in Amandry et al. (1981, 1984). The first volume contains the geological background, literary testimonials, in-

troduction to the excavation, and Neolithic material; the second contains Mycenaean and later material. Cf. preliminary reports in *BCH* 95 (1971) 771–76; *BCH* 96 (1972) 906–11; Amandry (1972); Pasquier (1977). Ten of the terracotta protomes from the cave are described in Croissant (1983) 1.386.

16. For the Korykian cave, see, e.g., Aesch. *Eum.* 22–23; Hdt. 8.36; Soph. *Ant.* 1126–30; Eur. *Bacch.* 559; other sources in Amandry et al. (1984) 29–35.

17. Péchoux in Amandry et al. (1981) 17–26; Amandry (1972) 257; Paus. 10.32.5.

18. *BCH* 95 (1971) 773; Amandry (1972) 260; Amandry et al. (1981) 80–85, (1984) 401–2, n. 14, 403.

19. Jacquemin in Amandry et al. (1984) 96–97 (pinax), 149–53 (kraters), 155. Jacquemin's catalogue describes some 774 fragments, but these are merely a representative selection of the pots; the total number of fragments was about 16,000.

20. Shells: Amandry et al. (1984) 347–80. Some thirty-two species were represented. Flutes: in Amandry et al. (1984): Jacquemin 166–75, Bélis 176–81, Zagdoun 183–260, Picard 281–306. Lamps: Jacquemin 158–65. For similar deposits of lamps, see 5.1.2, 5.1.6.

21. Inscriptions: Empereur in Amandry et al. (1984) 339–46. Inscriptions date from the fifth to the second centuries. See also *SEG* 34 (1984) 418, 435, 438, 440–43, 446, 450, 454–57.

22. Pasquier (1977); Amandry et al. (1984) 398.

23. Marcadé in Amandry et al. (1984) 307–37; Edwards (1985) no. 83.

24. Levi (1923) 27–42; Connor (1988) 162–64.

25. Wace and Thompson (1908–9). The Oread inscription reads Ὀρει[άσιν] Ἐνπεδόκλεια Φιλοδαμεία πὲρ γενεᾶς.

26. Iouri (1971, 1974) cf. *BCH* 96 (1972) 730–36.

27. Zeus Ammon: Plut. Vit. *Lys.* 20.5; Paus. 3.18.3. On Nysa, see 3.1.1.

28. Xen. *Hell.* 5.3.19 cf. Paus. 2.23.1.

29. Bakalakis (1938); Jameson (1956). Similar activity is attested in the late Hellenistic period at Syracuse in Sicily (4.10.1).

30. *BCH* 86 (1962) 959; 89 (1965) 964–67 (third-century inscription to Apollo); École française d'Athènes (1968) 87–88.

31. Fauré (1964); Nilsson (1967) 261–62.

32. Fauré (1964) 140–44, (1961–62); Hood (1965) 110; *AD* 22 (1967) chron. 495–97, pls. 368–70. Inscriptions: *SEG* 31 (1981) 815–16.

33. Fauré (1964) 148–51, (1962) 42, (1956) 95–103; Edwards (1985) no. 113.

34. Pinakes: *AD* 23 (1968) chron. 321, pl. 259; Dörpfeld (1927) 323–24, 330–31, pl. 76c; Andreou (1980); Tzouvara-Souli (1988–89).

35. Marinatos (1964) 17–22; Dontas (1964).

36. Benton (1931–32) 230–31.

37. *AD* 2 (1916) chron. 52–54; *AE* (1952) chron. 1–3; Hammond (1967) 140; Tzouvara-Souli (1988–89) 10–21.

38. Weller et al. (1903); Travlos (1988) 446–48, 461–65, figs. 581–87; Wickens (1986) no. 20, 2.90–121. Inscriptions: *IG* I³ 974–81.

39. Weller et al. (1903) 332 nos. 45–48. A similar type, from a fourth-century deposit in the Athenian agora, is illustrated in *Hesperia* 8 (1939) 242–43, fig. 43.

40. Skyron: *IG* I³ 974; Mitsos (1953) 349 argues that the word *aipolos* is a proper name, not an occupation. Relief: *IG* II/III² 4650; Dunham in Weller et al. (1903) 290–91; Edwards (1985) 572–76.

41. *IG* I³ 982. For similar prohibitions, see 4.9.4 (Kos), 4.9.2 (Pergamon), and *Anth. Pal.* 9.330.

42. Connor (1988) 186.

43. Edwards (1985) nos. 15, 16, 23, 29, 33, 40, 51. All belong to the mid-to-late fourth century.

44. Rhomaios (1905, 1906); Skias (1918) 1–28; Travlos (1988) 319–20, 325–26 figs. 408–9; Wickens (1986) no. 47, 2.245–69. Cf. Skias (1900, 1901).

45. Basins: *IG* II/III² 4833 (*poimenes*), 4835. Reliefs: Edwards (1985) nos. 13, 21, 22, 26, 36, 37, 54, 76. Inscriptions from cave: *IG* II/III² 4826–48. They range in date from the early fourth century to the late Hellenistic period.

46. Thuc. 1.6. Cf. *Anth. Pal.* 6.156, a dedication of a cicada hairpin to the Amarynthian *kourai* (Euboia) by a youth. On the *tettinx*, or cicada, see Studnitzka (1896) 272–84. For the cicada as "songster of the nymphs," see *Anth. Pal.* 7.196, 9.373.

47. Zorides (1977); Travlos (1988) 329–30, 332–34 figs. 416–20; Wickens (1986) no. 39, 2.202–11; *BCH* 77 (1953) 202; *AJA* 57 (1953) 281; *JHS* 73 (1953) 112, pl. 1.3. Reliefs: Edwards (1985) nos. 20 (three donors), 22 (Agathemeros), both c. 330–20.

48. Papadimitriou (1958); Deligeorghi-Alexopolou (1982) 36–40; Travlos (1988) 218, 246 figs. 302–3; Wickens (1986) nos. 43, 44, 2.223–40; *AJA* 62 (1958) 321–22; *BCH* 82 (1958) 681–86, figs. 27–28, 83 (1959) 587–89.

49. *SEG* 36 (1986) 267; *BCH* 83 (1959) 587.

50. Travlos (1937) 391–408, (1988) 177, 186 figs. 235–36; Wickens (1986) no. 53, 2.287–98.

51. *AD* 16 (1960) chron. 52–55, pls. 41–43; Travlos (1988) 96, 151 figs. 182–83; Wickens (1986) no. 51, 2.275–79; Edwards (1985) nos. 38, 49, both c. 320–300.

52. Edwards (1985) no. 38, c. 320–300.

53. Lion cave: Vanderpool (1967) 309–11; Wickens (1986) no. 33, 2.175–83. Rapedosa: Wickens (1986) no. 40, 2.212–18; Edwards (1985) no. 43, c. 320–300.

54. *AD* 42 (1987) 703, figs. 14–15; Strabo 9.2.25, 410; Paus. 9.34.4.

55. Sampson (1992) 95–96.

56. Levi (1925–26).

57. *IG* XII 5.483; Jeffery (1961) 296. A female head on a Siphnian coin, Imhoof-Blumer (1908) no. 297, has been identified as that of a nymph.

58. The essential publications are those of Arias, including 1941, 1946, and 1947. The most recent and comprehensive study is Costabile et al. (1991) with full bib. See also Costamagna and Sabbione (1990) 154–56; Pugliese Carratelli (1996) catalogue nos. 349 I–VI, 350.

59. Earliest votives: Costabile et al. (1991) 94, figs. 161–65. Embellishments: Costabile et al. (1991) 3–55. Sima and antefixes: Costabile et al. (1991) 15–20.

60. Lavagne (1988) 149–54.

61. Costabile et al. (1991) 45–93; Arias (1941) 195.

62. Costabile et al. (1991) 107–10.

63. Strabo 6.1.7, 259; Costabile et al. (1991) 94, 108–9. The later examples depict the nymph seated upon a rock; similar examples were found at Rhegion (figs. 185–86).

64. Hydriai: Costabile et al. (1991) 104. Triple herms: Costabile et al. (1991) 97–103, 195–226.

65. Euthymos defeated the Hero of Temesa: Strabo 6.1.5, 255; Paus. 6.6.4.

66. Head (1911) 190; Imhoof-Blumer (1908) no. 482; Pace (1935–49) 3.487, fig. 122.

67. Persephone busts: Costabile et al. (1991) 127–31. Musician plaques: Costabile et al. (1991) 179–84. Bed model: Costabile et al. (1991) 104–5. For Persephone and Aphrodite at Lokroi, see Sourvinou-Inwood (1978).

68. Costabile et al. (1991) 137–89.

69. Mitford (1980) esp. 256–63; Masson (1981).

70. E.g., Mitford (1980) nos. 262, 266; Masson (1981) 631 fig. 9.

71. Mitford (1980) nos. 292 (statuette), 227 (panel). Other deities: Masson (1981) 635. Sacrifice: Mitford (1980) nos. 121, 285. Games: Mitford (1980) no. 227.

72. Shear (1973); Thompson (1977); Edwards (1985) no. 14; Stewart (1990) 192–93, figs. 581–83.

73. For geometric examples, see Tölle (1964). For lists of examples, see Brinkmann (1925); Wegner (1968). For the chorus represented as either "circularity" or "procession," see Calame (1997) 36–37, 66.

74. Hadzisteliou-Price (1971). The Charites were worshiped by different communities and at different times as either two or three: Paus. 9.35.1.

75. Burkert (1985) 173–74.

76. Kearns (1992) 193–203. Isis was viewed as a universal goddess with many names during the Imperial period: Nock (1933) 149–53.

77. On the François vase in the scene depicting the return of Hephaistos, we also find figures labeled "nymphs" cavorting with silens (3.1.1). See also Stewart (1983); Carpenter (1986) 1–12, who argues (9) that Sophilos' NYSAI is a misspelling for MOUSAI.

78. Triads: Carpenter (1991) fig. 233; Guarducci (1928) 57 no. 6, pl. 20.4, 5. Additional examples in Clairmont (1951) 116.

79. Orlandos (1965) 204 fig. 225; see also on Pitsa 5.1.4.

80. Harrison (1922) 294 fig. 77 cf. Harrison (1886) 198 fig. 2. For artistic and literary versions of the judgment, beginning in the seventh century, see Gantz (1993) 567–71. Xenokles cup: Clairmont (1951) 26, K 32, c. 575–50. Cf. the triad of nymphs and Hermes on Munich 1490, Clairmont (1951) 115, pl. 40.

81. Baths of the goddesses: Eur. *Andr.* 274–92; *Cypria* fr. 4–5. Cf. the description of the springs, flowers, and nymphs of Ide in Eur. *IA* 1291–99 and the scene attributed to the Dolon painter, this vol., fig. 1.4; Muthmann (1975) 85 fig. 8.

82. Carpenter (1991) fig. 148; Rumpf (1927) pl. 15, c. 540.

83. Tyszkiewicz (1892) pl. 16; Harrison (1922) 289. The provenance is no more specific than Greece, the date probably sixth century. Fröhner describes the twenty-seven-centimeter plaque as showing signs of water wear, perhaps as part of a fountain. The hairstyle of the outermost *korê* is unusual, a sort of ponytail.

84. Thasos: Michaelis (1889) reconstructed the relief with nine nymphs and three Charites. See École française d'Athènes (1968) figs. 11, 12, 104; Salviat (1979); Pouilloux (1979); Boardman (1985) 67, fig. 43. Karyatid: École française d'Athènes (1909) 60–63, which shows Apollo with *kithara* and four female figures plus Hermes with syrinx and three female figures.

85. Harpy tomb: Boardman (1995) 189, fig. 211.

86. Calame (1997) 66–72. Charites relief: Hausmann (1960) 21–23; Schwarzenberg (1966) 5 n. 6, pl. 1. Akropolis relief: Stewart (1990) vol. 2, fig. 162; Boardman (1978) fig. 257; Mitropolou (1977) 22–23 n. 8 with bib.

87. The silen and the boy or worshiper on the Akropolis relief may belong to a category identified as "the late arrival" by Crowhurst in a 1963 unpublished thesis cited by Calame (1997) 68. The late arrival joins the end of the line but is described as executing acrobatic steps, which does not seem to be the case for the boy or the silen.

88. Zanker (1965) pls. 1, 2, 56–59 cf. examples in Clairmont (1951) 117.

89. Paus. 1.22.8. Chiaramonti relief and other copies: Ridgway (1970) 115–18; LIMC s.v. Charis, Charites no. 25 (Harrison).

90. Paus. 1.14.6. See Harrison (1977); Edwards (1985) 48–49. Neither the identification of the figures as Horai and Aglaurids nor their association with the Hephaistaion is certain. Harrison considers the figures Charites and Aglaurids and reconstructs Hermes standing beside the Charites (not leading them) and Aphrodite standing beside the Aglaurids.

91. For summaries of the evidence, see Pasquier (1977) 375–79; Stillwell et al. (1952) 42–43. See also Tölle (1964) 59, 62, pl. 28a and, for the Corinthian colonies, Tzouvara-Souli (1988–89).

92. For votive reliefs to the nymphs, see Feubel (1935); Himmelman-Wildschütz (1957); Hausmann (1960); Isler (1970); Fuchs (1962); Edwards (1985).

93. Ridgway (1997) 193–94; Edwards (1985) 58; Stewart (1990) 1.49. For an introduction to the difficult subject of neo-Attic reliefs, see Richter (1925); Havelock (1964) with bib.; Edwards (1985) 156–241; Ridgway (1993) 445–73.

94. Stewart (1990) 1.48–49; see also Pleket (1981).

95. Quirinal relief: Edwards (1985) no. 5. Horai and Aglaurids as models: loc. cit. 48–49.

96. Fuchs (1962) 244.

97. On votive tablets, see Rouse (1902) 80–83; Ridgway (1983) 204–5.

98. Van Straten (1993) 251–52.

99. Neumann (1979) 50–51, 78–79 cf. Ridgway (1997) 195–99.

100. One problem with this view, as Ridgway (1997) 198 points out, is that while Edwards derives the figural types from his reconstruction of the statue base, the reconstruction does not include a cave.

101. It is true, however, that the finds from Attic and other caves often include objects with Dionysiac associations, such as terra-cottas of silens or comic figures.

AFTERWORD

1. A further point is that animal sacrifices seem to be excluded in favor of libations and incense. For the cult combination of Bakchos, Demeter (Deo), Pan, and the nymphs as presented in the hymn below, see Merkelbach (1988) 31–32, 34. On the Orphic Hymns, see Quandt (1955); Athanassakis (1977); West (1983) 28–29, 252.

BIBLIOGRAPHY

Aarne, A., and S. Thompson. 1961. *The types of the folktale: A classification and bibliography*. Helsinki: Academia Scientarum Fennica.

Aellen, C. 1994. *A la recherche de l'ordre cosmique: Forme et fonction des personnifications dans la céramique italiote*. 2 vols. Kilchberg/Zürich: Akanthus.

Aleshire, S. 1989. *The Athenian Asklepieion: The people, their dedications, and the inventories*. Amsterdam: J. C. Gieben.

Alexiou, M., and V. Lambropoulos, eds. 1985. *The text and its margins: Post-structuralist approaches to twentieth-century Greek literature*. New York: Pella.

Amandry, P. 1972. "L'Antre corycien près de Delphes." *CRAI* 255–67.

Amandry, P. et al. 1981. *L'Antre corycien*. *BCH* Suppl. 7.

Amandry, P. et al. 1984. *L'Antre corycien II*. *BCH* Suppl. 9.

Amyx, D. A. 1988. *Corinthian vase painting of the archaic period*. 2 vols. Berkeley and Los Angeles: University of California Press.

Andò, V. 1996. "Nymphe: La sposa e le ninfe." *QUCC* 52:47–79.

Andreou, E. 1980. "Archaeological collection of Leukas." Αρχαιολογικά Ανάλεκτα εξ Αθηνών (*Athens Annals of Archaeology*) 13:74–84.

Anti, C. 1948. *Guida per il visitatore del Teatro Antico di Siracusa*. Florence: Sansoni.

Antonaccio, C. M. 1995. *An archaeology of ancestors*. Lanham, MD: Rowman and Littlefield.

———. 1999. "Kypara, a Sikel nymph?" *ZPE* 126:177–85.

Antonaccio, C. M., and J. Neils. 1995. "A new graffito from archaic Morgantina." *ZPE* 105:261–77.

Arafat, K. 1997. "State of the art, art of the state: Sexual violence and politics in late archaic and early classical vase-painting," in S. Deacy and K. F. Pierce, eds., *Rape in antiquity*, 97–119. London and Swansea: Duckworth, in association with Classical Press of Wales.

Argenti, P. P., ed. 1943. *Hieronimo Giustiniani's history of Chios*. Cambridge: Cambridge University Press.

Argenti, P. P., and H. J. Rose. 1949. *The folk-lore of Chios*. 2 vols. Cambridge: Cambridge University Press.

Arguriade, M. 1991. Η κούκλα. στην ελλενική ζωή και τέχνη από την αρχαιότητα μέχρι σήμερα. Athens: Louse Bratziote.

Arias, P. 1936. "Sul culto delle ninfe a Siracusa." *Rendiconti della reale accademia nazionale dei Lincei*. 605–8.

Arias, P. E. 1941. "Modelli fittili di fontane d'età ellenistica." *Palladio* 5.193–206.

———. 1946. "Scavi di Calabria (dal 1939 al 1942)." *NSA* 138–61.

———. 1947. "Locri. Piani Caruso. Scavi di case antiche." *NSA* 165–71.

Arnott, W. G. 1981. "Double the vision: A reading of Euripides' Electra." *Greece and Rome* 28:179–92.

Atalay, E. 1985. "Un nouveau monument votif Hellénistique a Éphèse." *RA* 195–204.

Athanassakis, A. 1977. *The Orphic hymns*. Missoula, MT: Scholars Press.

Babbitt, F. C. et al. 1927. *Plutarch's Moralia in sixteen volumes*. Cambridge, MA: Harvard University Press.

Bacchielli, L. 1995. "Apollonio Rodio e il santuario Cireneo delle Nymphai Chthoniai." *QUCC* 51:133–37.

Bakalakis, G. 1938. Ανασκαφή του παρά την Ηρακλείτσαν (Καβάλας) άντρου των Νυμφών. *Praktika* 81–97.

Baladié, R. 1980. *Le Péloponnèse de Strabon: Étude de géographie historique*. Paris: Belles Lettres.

Ballentine, F. G. 1904. "Some phases of the cult of the nymphs." *HSCP* 15:77–119.

Barb, A. A. 1966. "Antaura: The mermaid and the devil's grandmother." *Journal of the Warburg and Courtauld Institute* 29:1–23.

Barrett, W. S. ed. 1964. *Euripides Hippolytus*. Oxford: Clarendon.

Barringer, J. 1995. *Divine escorts: Nereids in archaic and classical Greek art*. Ann Arbor: University of Michigan Press.

Bean G. 1966. *Aegean Turkey: An archaeological guide*. New York: F. A. Praeger.

Bean, G., and J. M. Cook. 1955. "The Halicarnassus peninsula." *ABSA* 50:85–171.

Beaudouin, M. 1880. "L'île de Karpathos." *BCH* 4.261:84.

Beazley, J. D. 1956. *Attic black-figure vase-painters*. Oxford: Clarendon.

Bell, M. 1981. *Morgantina studies. Vol. 1: The terracottas*. Princeton, NJ: Princeton University Press.

———. 1988. "Excavations at Morgantina, 1980–1985: Preliminary Report XII." *AJA* 92:313–42.

Bengisu, R. L. 1996. "Lydian Mount Karios," in E. N. Lane, ed., *Cybele, Attis and related cults*, 1–15. Leiden and New York: Brill.

Benton, S. 1931–32. "The Ionian islands." *ABSA* 32:213–46, pls. 38–24.

———. 1934–35. "Excavations in Ithaca. III: The cave at Polis I." *ABSA* 35.45–73.

———. 1938. "A votive offering to Odysseus." *Antiquity* 10:350.

———. 1938–39. "Excavations in Ithaca. III: Polis Cave II." *ABSA* 39:1–51, pls. 1–24.

Bernabò-Brea, L. 1956. *Akrai*. Catania: Società di Storia Patria per la Sicilia Orientale.

———. 1958. "Lipari nel IV secolo A.C." *Kokalos* 4:119–44, pls. 47–51.

———. 1961. "Lemnos." *EAA* 4:542–45. Roma: Istituto della enciclopedia italiana.

Bernand, E. 1969. *Inscriptions métriques de l'Egypte gréco-romaine. Recherches sur la poésie épigrammatique des Grecs en Égypte*. Paris: Belles Lettres.

Bernidaki-Aldous, E. A. 1990. *Blindness in a culture of light*. New York: P. Lang.

Berranger, D. 1983. "Le relief inscrit en l'honneur des nymphes dans les carrières de Paros." *Revue des Études Anciennes* 85:235–59.

———. 1992. *Recherches sur l'histoire et la prosopographie de Paros a l'époque archaïque*. Clermont-Ferrand, France: Association des publications de la Faculté des lettres et sciences humaines.

Bickerman, E. J. 1976. "Love story in the Homeric *Hymn to Aphrodite*." *Athenaeum* 54:229–54.

Bieber, M. 1945. "Archaeological contributions to Roman religion." *AJA* 14:270–77.

Biesantz, H. 1965. *Die thessalischen Grabreliefs*. Mainz am Rhein: P. von Zabern.

Bizard, L., and P. Roussel. 1907. "Fouilles de Délos." *BCH* 31:421–525.

Blegen, C. W., O. Broneer, et al. 1930. *Acrocorinth. Excavations in 1926: Corinth*, vol. 3, pt. 1. Cambridge, MA: Harvard University Press.

Blum, R., and E. Blum. 1970. *The dangerous hour: The lore of crisis and mystery in rural Greece*. London: Chatto and Windus.

Blümel, C. 1960. "Drei Weihreliefs an die Nymphen," in F. Eckstein, ed., *Theoria: Festschrift für W.-H. Schuchhardt*, 23–28. Baden-Baden: B. Grimm.

Blundell, S., and M. Williamson, eds. 1998. *The sacred and the feminine in ancient Greece*. New York: Routledge.

Boardman, J. 1978. *Greek sculpture: The archaic period*. London: Thames and Hudson.

———. 1985. *Greek sculpture: The classical period*. London: Thames and Hudson.

———. 1989. *Athenian red figure vases: The classical period*. London: Thames and Hudson.

———. 1995. *Greek sculpture: The late classical period and sculpture in colonies and overseas*. London: Thames and Hudson.

———. 1998. *Early Greek vase painting*. London: Thames and Hudson.

Boardman, J., et al. 1967. *The art and architecture of ancient Greece*. London: Thames and Hudson.

Bodnar, E. W. 1973. "A quarry relief on the island of Paros." *Archaeology* 26:270–77.

Bodson, L. 1978. *Hiera zoia: Contribution a l'étude de la place de l'animal dans la religion grecque ancienne*. Brussels: Académie Royale de Belgique.

Boedeker, D. D. 1974. *Aphrodite's entry into Greek epic*. Leiden: Brill.

Boehringer, E. 1929. "Bericht über die archäologischen Funde in Tripolitanien, Kyrenaika, Albanien." *AA* 44:368–431.

Bohringer [de Polignac], F. 1980. "Mégare: Traditions mythiques, espace sacré et naissance de la cité." *AC* 49:5–22.

Borgeaud, P. 1988. *The cult of Pan in ancient Greece*. Trans. K. Atlass and J. Redfield. Chicago and London: University of Chicago Press (orig. French publ. 1979).

———. 1991. "Rhésos et Arganthoné," in P. Borgeaud, ed., *Orphisme et Orphée*, 51–59. Recherches et Rencontres 3. Geneva: Droz.

Borthwick, E. K. 1963. "The Oxyrhynchus musical monody and some ancient fertility superstitions." *AJP* 84:225–43.

Bouché-Leclercq, A. 1879–82. *Histoire de la divination dans l'antiquité*. 4 vols. Repr. Brussels: Culture Civilisation, 1963.

Bourriot, F. 1976. *Recherches sur la nature du genos. Étude d'histoire sociale athénienne périods archaique et classique*. 2 vols. Ph.D. diss., Lille. Paris: Librarie Honore Champion.

Bousquet, J. 1967. "Deux inscriptions attiques." *BCH* 91:90–95.

Bowra, C. M. 1936. "Erinna's *Lament for Baucis*," in C. Bailey et al., eds., *Greek poetry and life: Essays presented to Gilbert Murray*, 325–42. Oxford: Clarendon. Repr. Freeport, NY: Books for Libraries Press, 1967.

———. 1938. "The daughters of Asopus." *Hermes* 73:213–21.

Brewster, H. 1997. *The river gods of Greece: Myths and mountain waters in the Hellenic world*. London and New York: I. B. Tauris.

Brinkmann, A. 1925. "Altgriechische Mädchenreigen." *Bonner Jahrbücher* 130:118–46.

Brommer, F. 1937. *Satyroi*. Würzburg: K. Triltsch.

———. 1938–39. "Amymone." *MDAI(A)* 63–64.171–76, pls. 67–70.

———. 1949–50. "Pan im 5. und 4. Jahrhundert v. Chr." *Marburger Jahrbuch fur Kunstwissenschaft* 15:5–42.

———. 1979. *The sculptures of the Parthenon: Metopes, frieze, pediments, cult-statue*. Trans. M. Whittall. London: Thames and Hudson.

Broneer, O. 1949. "Plato's description of early Athens and the origin of Metageitnia," in *Commemorative studies in honor of Theodore Leslie Shear*, 47–59. *Hesperia* Suppl. 8. Baltimore: American School of Classical Studies at Athens.

Brouskari, M. 1974. *The acropolis museum: A descriptive catalogue*. Athens: Commercial Bank of Greece.

Bruneau, P. 1970. *Recherches sur les cultes de Délos a l'époque hellénistique et a l'époque impériale*. Bibliothèque des Écoles françaises d'Athènes et de Rome, fasc. 217. Paris: E. de Boccard.

———. 1990. "Deliaca." *BCH* 114:553–91.

Bruneau, P., and J. Ducat. 1983. *Guide de Délos*. 3d ed. Paris: École française d'Athènes and E. de Boccard.

Bruns-Özgan, C. 1995. "Fries eines hellenistischen Altars in Knidos." *JDAI* 110:239–76.

Bryce, T. R. 1978. "A recently discovered cult in Lykia." *Journal of Religious History* 10:115–27.

Buck, R. J. 1969. "The Mycenaean time of troubles." *Historia* 18:276–98.

———. 1979. *A history of Boeotia*. Edmonton: University of Alberta Press.

Bultrighini, U. 1993. "Divinità della salute nella Creta ellenistica e romana. Ricerche preliminari." *RCCM* 35:49–117.

Buresch, K. 1892. "Die sibyllinische Quellgrotte in Erythrae." *MDAI(A)* 17:16–36.

Burkert, W. 1979. *Structure and history in Greek mythology and ritual*. Berkeley and Los Angeles: University of California Press.

————. 1983. *Homo necans: The anthropology of ancient Greek sacrificial ritual and myth*. Berkeley and Los Angeles: University of California Press.

————. 1985. *Greek religion: Archaic and classical*. Trans. J. Raffan. Oxford: Basil Blackwell.

————. 1992. *The orientalizing revolution*. Cambridge, MA: Harvard University Press.

Burn, A. R. 1949. "Helikon in history: A study in Greek mountain topography." *ABSA* 44:313–23.

Burn, L. 1987. *The Meidias painter*. Oxford: Clarendon.

Buxton, R. G. A. 1980. "Blindness and limits: Sophocles and the logic of myth." *JHS* 100:22–37.

————. 1992. "Imaginary Greek mountains." *JHS* 112:1–15.

————. 1994. *Imaginary Greece: The contexts of mythology*. Cambridge: Cambridge University Press.

Cahen, E. 1923. "L'autel de cornes et l'hymne a Délos de Callimaque." *REG* 36:14–25.

Caillois, R. 1937a. "Les démons de midi." *Revue de l'histoire des religions* 115:142–73.

————. 1937b. "Les démons de midi." *Revue de l'histoire des religions* 116:54–83, 143–86.

Calame, C. 1996. *Mythe et histoire dans l'antiquité grecque: La création symbolique d'une colonie*. Lausanne: Editions Payot.

————. 1997. *Choruses of young women in ancient Greece*. Trans. D. Collins and J. Orion. Lanham, MD, and London: Rowman and Littlefield (orig. French publ. 1977).

————. 1999. *The poetics of Eros*. Trans. J. Lloyd. Princeton, NJ: Princeton University Press (orig. Ital. publ. 1992).

Camassa, G. 1993. "I Culti," in A. Stazio and S. Ceccoli, eds., *Sibari e la Sibaritide: Atti del trentaduesimo convegno di studi sulla Magna Grecia*, 574–94. Taranto: Istituto per la Storia e l'Archeologia della Magna Grecia.

Campbell, D. A. 1982–93. *Greek lyric*. 5 vols. Cambridge, MA, and London: Harvard University Press.

Carden, R. 1974. *The papyrus fragments of Sophocles*. Berlin: W. de Gruyter.

Carnoy, A. 1956. "Les nymphes des sources en Grèce." *Museon: Revue des Études Orientales* 69:187–95.

Carpenter, T. H. 1986. *Dionysian imagery in archaic Greek art: Its development in black-figure vase painting*. Oxford: Clarendon; New York: Oxford University Press.

————. 1991. *Art and myth in ancient Greece*. London: Thames and Hudson.

————. 1997. *Dionysian imagery in fifth-century Athens*. Oxford: Clarendon; New York: Oxford University Press.

Cassola, F. 1975. *Inni Omerici*. Milan: A. Mondadori.

Casson, S. 1926. *Macedonia, Thrace and Illyria*. London: Oxford University Press.

Chamoux, F. 1953. *Cyrène sous la monarchie des Battiades*. Bibliothèque des Écoles françaises d'Athènes et de Rome, ser. 2, fasc. 177. Paris: E. de Boccard.

Chantraine, P. 1968–80. *Dictionnaire étymologique de la langue grecque: Histoire des mots*. 4 vols. Paris: Klincksieck.

Charachidzé, G. 1992. "The cult of Helen and the tribal initiation of women in Greece," in Y. Bonnefoy and W. Doniger, eds., *Greek and Egyptian mythologies*, 174–78. Chicago and London: University of Chicago Press.

Cherry, J. F. 1988. "Pastoralism and the role of animals in the pre- and protohistoric economies of the Aegean," in Whittaker (1988):6–34.

Christiansen, R. T. 1958. *The migratory legends: A proposed list of types with a systematic catalogue of the Norwegian variants*. FF Communications 175. Helsinki: Suomalainen Tiedeakatemia.

Ciaceri, E. 1911. *Culti e miti nella storia dell'antica Sicilia*. Repr. Sala Bolognese: A. Forni, 1981.

Clairmont, C. 1951. *Das Parisurteil in der antiken Kunst*. Zurich: Der verfasser.

———. 1993. *Classical Attic tombstones*. Kilchberg, Switzerland: Akanthus.

Clark, I. 1998. "The gamos of Hera: Myth and ritual," in Blundell and Williamson (1998):13–26.

Clay, J. S. 1989. *The politics of Olympus: Form and meaning in the major Homeric hymns*. Princeton, NJ: Princeton University Press.

Cole, S. G. 1984a. *Theoi Megaloi: The cult of the great gods at Samothrace*. Leiden: Brill.

———. 1984b. "The social function of rituals of maturation: The koureion and the arkteia." *ZPE* 55:233–38.

———. 1988. "The uses of water in Greek sanctuaries," in Hägg, Marinatos, and Nordquist (1988):161–65.

———. 1998. "Domesticating Artemis," in S. Blundell and M. Williamson, eds., *The sacred and the feminine in ancient Greece*, 27–43. London and New York: Routledge.

Colin, G. 1897. "Inscriptions de Thespies." *BCH* 21:551–71.

Collignon, M. 1911. *Les statues funéraires dans l'art grec*. Paris: Ernest Leroux.

Comparetti, D. 1921–22. "Iscrizioni dell'antro delle ninfe presso Farsalos (Tessaglia)." *ASAA* 4–5:147–60.

Connor, W. R. 1988. "Seized by the nymphs: Nympholepsy and symbolic expression in classical Greece." *ClAnt* 7:155–89.

Cook, A. B. 1895. "The bee in Greek mythology." *JHS* 15:1–24.

Costabile, F., et al. 1991. *I ninfei di Locri Epizefiri: Architettura, culti erotici, sacralità delle acque*. Soveria Mannelli, Catanzaro: Rubbettino.

Costamagna, L., and C. Sabbione. 1990. *Una città in Magna Grecia: Locri Epizefiri: Guida archeologica*. Reggio Calabria: Laruffa.

Courby, F. 1912. *Le portique d'Antigone ou du nord-est et les constructions voisines*. Exploration archéologique de Délos, fasc. 5. Paris: Fontemoing.

Croissant, F. 1983. *Les protomés féminines archaïques: Recherches sur les représentations du visage dans la plastique grecque de 550 a 480 av. J.–C.* 2 vols. Athens: École française d'Athènes; Paris: E. de Boccard.

Croon, J. 1956. "Artemis Thermia and Apollo Thermios." *Mnemosyne* 9:193–220.

Cumont, F. 1942. *Recherches sur le symbolisme funéraire des romains*. Paris: P. Geuthner.

Danforth, L. 1984. "The ideological context of the search for continuities in Greek culture." *JMGS* 1:53–85.

Daux, G. 1958. "Notes de lecture." *BCH* 82:358–67.

———. 1973a. "Les ambiguïtés de grec KORH." *CRAI* 389–93.

————. 1973b. "*Anth. Pal.* VI 280 (Poupées et chevelure, Artemis Limnatis)." *ZPE* 12:225–29.

Daux, G., and P. de la Coste-Messelière. 1924. "De Malide en Thessalie." *BCH* 48:343–76.

Davies, M., and J. Kathirithamby. 1986. *Greek insects*. New York: Oxford University Press.

Dawkins, R., ed. 1950. *Forty-five stories from the Dodekanese*. Cambridge: Cambridge University Press.

Dawkins, R. M. 1916. *Modern Greek in Asia Minor*. Cambridge: Cambridge University Press.

Decourt, J. C. 1995. *Inscriptions de Thessalie. I: Les cités de la vallée de l'Enipeus*. Paris: École française d'Athènes.

Delatte, A. 1927. *Anecdota atheniensia*. Bibliothèque de la Faculté de Philosophie et de Lettres de l'Université de Liège, fasc. 36. Liège: Vaillant-Carmanne; Paris: Champion.

————. 1932. *La catoptromancie grecque et ses dérivés*. Liège: Vaillant-Carmanne; Paris: Droz.

Deligeorghi-Alexopolou, H. 1982. "La grotte Inoé de Marathon." *Archeologia* 171:36–40.

Demitsas, M. 1879. Τῆς ἐν Ἰλλυρίδι Ἀπολλωνίας. *MDAI(A)* 4:228–34.

De Santis, T. 1960. *Sibaritide a ritroso nel tempo*. Cosenza: n.p.

Detienne, M. 1974. "The myth of honeyed Orpheus," in Gordon (1981): 95–109.

————. 1988. "Les Danaïdes entre elles ou la violence fondatrice du mariage." *Arethusa* 21:159–75.

Devereux, G. 1973. "The self-blinding of Oidipous in Sophocles: Oidipous Tyrannos." *JHS* 93:36–49.

————. 1987. "Thamyris and the Muses (an unrecognized Oedipal myth)." *AJPh* 108:199–201.

Diehl, E. 1964. *Die Hydria: Formgeschichte und Verwendung im Kult des Altertums*. Mainz am Rhein: P. von Zabern.

Dobrusky, V. 1897. "Inscriptions et monuments figurés de la Thrace." *BCH* 21:119–40.

Donohue, A. A. 1988. *Xoana and the origins of Greek sculpture*. American Classical Studies 15. Atlanta: Scholars Press.

Dontas, G. S. 1964. Εὑρήματα ἀπό τὸ παρά τὴν Σάμην τῆς Κεφαλληνίας σπήλαιον Μελισσάνη. *AE* 28–35, pls. 6–8.

Dörig, J. 1958. "Von griechischen Puppen." *AK* 1:41–52, pls. 22–26.

Dörpfeld, W. 1927. *Alt-Ithaka: Ein Beitrag zur Homer-Frage. Studien und Ausgrabungen aus der Insel Leukas-Ithaka*. Munich: R. Uhde.

Dougherty, C. 1993. *The poetics of colonization: From city to text in archaic Greece*. New York: Oxford University Press.

Dover, K. J., ed. 1968. *Aristophanes' Clouds*. Oxford: Clarendon.

Dow, S. 1935. "Greek inscriptions." *Hesperia* 4.81–90.

————. 1965. "The greater demarkhia of Erchia." *BCH* 89:180–213.

Dowden, K. 1989. *Death and the maiden: Girls' initiation rites in Greek mythology*. London: Routledge.

Duchemin, J. 1960. *La houlette et la lyre: Recherches sur les origines pastorales de la poésie*. Vol. 1: *Hermès et Apollon*. Paris: Belles Lettres.

Dunkley, B. 1935–36. "Greek fountain buildings before 300 B.C." *ABSA* 36:142–204.

École française d'Athènes. 1909. *Fouilles de Delphes IV, I.* Paris: Écoles françaises d'Athènes et de Rome.

———. 1968. *Guide de Thasos.* Paris: E. de Boccard.

Edelstein, E., and L. Edelstein. 1945. *Asclepius: A collection and interpretation of the testimonies.* 2 vols. Baltimore: Johns Hopkins Press.

Edwards, C. M. 1985. *Greek votive reliefs to Pan and the Nymphs.* Ph.D. diss. NYU.

Edwards, M. W. 1960. "Representations of Maenads on archaic red-figure vases." *JHS* 80:778–87.

Ehrhardt, N. 1993. "Zwei archaischen Statuen mit Nymphen-Weihungen aus Milet." *Epigraphica Anatolica: Zeitschrift fur Epigraphik* 21:3–8.

Elderkin, K. 1930. "Jointed dolls in antiquity." *AJA* 34:455–79.

Elliger, W. 1975. *Die Darstellung der Landschaft in der griechishen Dichtung.* Berlin and New York: de Gruyter.

Ellis, A. C., and G. S. Hall. 1907. "A study of dolls," in G. S. Hall, ed., *Aspects of child life and education,* 157–204. Boston: Ginn. Repr. London: Routledge/Thoemmes Press, 1995.

Ervin, M. 1959. "Geraistai Nymphai Genethliai and the hill of the Nymphs." *Platon* 11:146–59.

Fabricotti, E. 1987. "Divinità greche e divinità libie in rilievi di età ellenistica." *Quaderni di Archeologia della Libia* 12:221–44.

Faraone, C. 1991. "Binding and burying the forces of evil: The defensive use of 'voodoo dolls' in ancient Greece." *CSCA* 10:165–205.

Fauré, P. 1956. "Grottes crétoises." *BCH* 80:95–103.

———. 1961–62. "La grotte de Lera (Kydonias) et la nymphe Akakallis." *Kretika Chronika* 1:195–99.

———. 1962. "Cavernes et sites aux deux extrémités de la Crète." *BCH* 86:36–56.

———. 1964. *Fonctions des cavernes crétoises.* Paris: E. de Boccard.

Fehling, D. 1972. "Erysichthon oder das Märchen von der mündlichen Überlieferung." *RhM* 115:173–96.

Ferguson, W. S. 1944. "The Attic orgeones." *Harvard Theological Review* 37:61–140.

———. 1949. "Orgeonika," in *Commemorative studies in honor of Theodore Leslie Shear. Hesperia* Suppl. 8:130–63.

Feubel, R. 1935. *Die attischen Nymphenreliefs und ihre Vorbilder.* Heidelberg: Buchdruckerei A. Lippl.

Figueira, T. J. 1985. "Herodotus on the early hostilities between Aegina and Athens." *AJP* 106:49–74.

———. 1991. *Athens and Aigina in the age of imperial colonization.* Baltimore: Johns Hopkins University Press.

Figueira, T. J., and G. Nagy, eds. 1985. *Theognis of Megara: Poetry and the polis.* Baltimore and London: Johns Hopkins University Press.

Filow, B. 1911. "Bulgarien." *AA* 26:349–70.

Foley, A. 1988. *The Argolid 800–600 B.C.: An archaeological survey.* Studies in Mediterranean Archaeology 80. Göteborg: P. Aström.

Foley, H. P., ed. 1981. *Reflections of women in antiquity.* New York: Gordon and Breach Science Publishers.

————. 1994. *The Homeric Hymn to Demeter: Translation, commentary, and interpretive essays.* Princeton, NJ: Princeton University Press.

Fontenrose, J. 1978. *The Delphic oracle: Its responses and operations with a catalogue of responses.* Berkeley and Los Angeles: University of California Press.

————. 1988. *Didyma: Apollo's oracle, cult and companions.* Berkeley and Los Angeles: University of California Press.

Ford, A. L. 1985. "The seal of Theognis: The politics of authorship in archaic Greece," in Figueira and Nagy (1985):82–95.

Forsen, B., and E. Sironen. 1991. "Parische Gliederweihungen." *ZPE* 87:176–80.

Forti, L. 1951. "Rilievi dedicati alle Ninfe Nitrodi." *Rendiconti della Accademia di Archeologia, Lettere e Belle Arti di Napoli* 26:161–91, pls. 6–11.

Foucart, P. 1882. "Antiquités d'Eski-Zaghra." *BCH* 6:177–86.

Fowden, G. 1988. "City and mountain in late Roman Attica." *JHS* 108:48–59.

Fowler, B. 1989. *The Hellenistic aesthetic.* Madison: University of Wisconsin Press.

Fox, M. 1996. *Roman historical myths: The regal period in Augustan literature.* Oxford: Clarendon.

Franke, P. R., and M. Hirmer. 1964. *Die griechische Münze.* Munich: Hirmer.

Fränkel, C. 1912. *Satyr und Bakchennamen auf Vasenbildern.* Bonn: C. Georgi, Universitäts-Buchdruckerei.

Fränkel, H. F. 1968. *Noten zu den Argonautika des Apollonios.* Munich: Beck.

Fraser, M. 1951. *Beekeeping in antiquity.* 2d ed. London: University of London Press.

Fraser, P. M. 1972. *Ptolemaic Alexandria.* 3 vols. Oxford: Clarendon.

Frazer, J. G., trans. and ed. 1921. *Bibliotheca. Apollodorus: The library.* 2 vols. Cambridge, MA: Harvard University Press. Repr. 1989.

Fuchs, W. 1962. "Attische Nymphenreliefs." *MDAI(A)* 77:243–49, pls. 64–69.

Gabrici, E. 1959. *Problemi di numismatica greca della Sicilia e Magna Greca.* Naples: G. Macchiaroli.

Gaertringen, H. von. 1937. "Theraeische Studien." *AE* 48–60.

Gais, R. M. 1978. "Some problems of river-god iconography." *AJA* 82:355–70.

Galinsky, K. 1969. *Aeneas, Sicily, and Rome.* Princeton, NJ: Princeton University Press.

Gallet de Santerre, H. 1976. "Athènes, Délos et Delphes d'après une peinture de vase à figures rouges du Ve siècle avant J. C." *BCH* 100:291–98.

Gantz, T. 1980. "The Aeschylean tetralogy: Attested and conjectured groups." *AJPh* 101:133–64.

————. 1993. *Early Greek myth: A guide to literary and artistic sources.* Baltimore and London: Johns Hopkins University Press.

Gautier, P. 1980. "Le *De Daemonibus* du Pseudo-Psellos." *REByz* 38:105–94.

Georgoudi, S. 1974. "Quelques problèmes de la transhumance dans la grèce ancienne." *REG* 87:155–85.

Getty Museum. 1987. *Papers on the Amasis painter and his world.* Malibu, CA: J. Paul Getty Museum.

Giacomelli, A. 1980. "Aphrodite and after." *Phoenix* 34:1–19.

Giannelli, G. 1963. *Culti e miti della Magna Grecia: Contributo alla storia più antica delle colonie greche in occidente.* Florence: Sansoni.

Giannopoulos, N. 1912. Ἄντρον νυμφῶν καὶ Χίρωνος παρὰ τὴν Φάρσαλον. *BCH* 36:668–69.

———. 1919. Φαρσάλου ἄντρον ἐπιγεγράμμενον. *AE* 48–53.

Ginouvès, R. 1962. *Balaneutike: Recherches sur le bain dans l'antiquité grecque.* Bibliotheque des Écoles françaises d'Athènes et de Rome, fasc. 200. Paris: E. de Boccard.

Goceva, Z. 1989. "Neue thrakische Namen und Epithete." *Linguistique Balkanique* 32:113–17.

———. 1990. "Les plaques votives du Nymphée pres du village d'Ognjanovo." *Archeologia* 41:73–76.

———. 1991. "Le culte des Cabires et des nymphes en Asie Mineure et en Thrace." *Eos* 79:199–202.

Gödecken, K. B. 1986. "Beobachten und Funde der Heiligen Strasse zwischen Milet und Didyma, 1984." *ZPE* 66:217–53.

Goodchild, R. G. 1971. *Kyrene und Apollonia.* Zurich: Raggi.

Gordon, R. L., ed. 1981. *Myth, religion and society: Structuralist essays.* Cambridge: Cambridge University Press.

Gow, A. S. F. 1952. *Theocritus.* 2 vols. Cambridge: Cambridge University Press.

Gow, A. S. F., and D. Page, eds. 1968. *The Greek anthology: The Garland of Philip and some contemporary epigrams.* 2 vols. London: Cambridge University Press.

Graeve, V. 1986. "Neue archaische Skulpturenfunde aus Milet," in H. Kyrieleis, ed., *Archaische griechische Plastik*, 21–29, pls. 6–10. Mainz am Rhein: P. von Zabern.

Graindor, P. 1932. "Inscriptions de la nécropole de Touna-el-Geher, Hermoupolis." *Bulletin de l'Institut Français d'Archéologie Orientale* 32:97–119.

Greene, E., ed. 1996. *Reading Sappho: Contemporary approaches.* Berkeley and Los Angeles: University of California Press.

Greenfield, R. P. H. 1988. *Traditions of belief in late Byzantine demonology.* Amsterdam: Hakkert.

Griffin, J. 1992. "Theocritus, the *Iliad* and the East." *AJPh* 113:189–211.

Groningen, B. A. van. 1958. "Quelques problèmes de la poésie bucolique grecque." *Mnemosyne* 11:293–317.

Gruben, G. 1964. "Das Quellhaus von Megara." *AD* 19:37–41, pls. 22–28.

Guarducci, M. 1928. "Due o più donne sotto un solo manto in una serie di vasi greci arcaici." *MDAI(A)* 53:52–65, pls. 19–20.

———. 1932. "I predecessori di Asclepio." *Studi e Materiali di Storia delle Religioni* 8:215–29.

Guillaume-Courier, G. 1995. "Chiron Phillyride." *Kernos* 8:113–22.

Guthrie, W. K. C. 1957. *In the beginning: Some Greek views on the origins of life and the early state of man.* Ithaca, NY: Cornell University Press.

Gutzwiller, K. 1998. *Poetic garlands: Hellenistic epigrams in context.* Berkeley and Los Angeles: University of California Press.

Gutzwiller, K. J. 1991. *Theocritus' pastoral analogies.* Madison: University of Wisconsin Press.

Habicht, C. 1969. *Die Inschriften des Asklepieions.* Altertümer von Pergamon, bd. 8:3. Berlin: W. de Gruyter.

Hadzisteliou-Price, T. 1971. "Double and multiple representations in Greek art and religious thought." *JHS* 91:48–69, pls. 1–10.

———. 1978. *Kourotrophos: Cults and representations of the Greek nursing deities.* Leiden: E. J. Brill.

Hägg, R., N. Marinatos, and G. Nordquist, eds. 1988. *Early Greek cult practice: Proceedings of the fifth international symposium at the Swedish Institute at Athens, 26–29 June 1986.* Stockholm: Swedish Institute at Athens.

Halperin, D. 1983. Before pastoral: Theocritus and the ancient tradition of bucolic poetry. New Haven: Yale University Press.

Hamdorf, F. M. 1964. *Griechische Kultpersonifikationen der vorhellenistischen Zeit.* Mainz: P. von Zabern.

Hammond, N. G. L. 1967. *Epirus.* Oxford: Clarendon.

———. 1972. *A history of Macedonia,* vol 1. Oxford: Clarendon.

———. 1983. "The lettering and iconography of 'Macedonian' coinage," in Moon (1983a):245–58.

———. 1989. *The Macedonian state: Origins, institutions and history.* Oxford: Clarendon.

Hammond, N. G. L., and G. T. Griffith. 1979. *A history of Macedonia,* vol 2. Oxford: Clarendon.

Hani, J. 1974. "Les nymphes du Nil." *AC* 43:212–24.

Harrison, E. 1977. "Alkamenes' sculptures for the Hephaisteion. Part II: The base." *AJA* 81:265–87.

Harrison, J. E. 1886. "The judgment of Paris: Two unpublished vases in the Graeco-Etruscan museum in Florence." *JHS* 7:196–219.

———. 1922. *Prolegomena to the study of Greek religion.* 3d ed. Repr. New York: Meridian, 1955.

Hartland, F. S. 1925. *The science of fairy tales: An inquiry into fairy mythology.* 2d ed. London: Methuen.

Hausmann, U. 1960. *Griechische Weihreliefs.* Berlin: W. de Gruyter.

Havelock, C. M. 1964. "Archaistic reliefs of the Hellenistic period." *AJA* 68:43–58, pls. 17–22.

Head, B. V. 1911. *Historia numorum: A manual of Greek numismatics.* Oxford: Clarendon. Repr. Chicago: Argonaut, 1967.

Hedreen G. 1992. *Silens in Attic black-figure vase painting.* Ann Arbor: University of Michigan Press.

Hemberg, B. 1950. *Die Kabiren.* Uppsala: Almqvist and Wilksells Boktryckeri.

Henrichs, A. 1976. "Despoina Kybele: Ein Beitrag zur religiösen Namenkunde." *HSCP* 80:253–86.

———. 1978. "Greek Maenadism from Olympias to Messalina." *HSCP* 82:121–60.

———. 1979. "Thou shalt not kill a tree." *Bulletin of the American Society of Papyrologists* 16:85–108.

———. 1983. "The 'sobriety' of Oedipus: Sophocles OC 100 misunderstood." *HSCP* 87:87–100.

———. 1987. "Myth visualized: Dionysos and his circle in sixth-century Attic vase-painting," in Getty Museum (1987):92–124.

Héron de Villefosse, A., and E. Michon. 1896. *Musée du Louvre: Département des antiquités grecques et romains: Catalogue sommaire des Marbres antiques.* Paris: Museés Nationaux.

Herzfeld, M. 1979. "Exploring a metaphor of exposure." *Journal of American Folklore* 92:285–301.

———. 1986. *Ours once more: Folklore, ideology, and the making of modern Greece.* New York: Pella.

Higgins, M. D., and R. Higgins. 1996. *A geological companion to Greece and the Aegean*. Ithaca, NY: Cornell University Press.

Higgins, R. A. 1954–. *Catalogue of the terracottas in the British Museum*. 3 vols. London: British Museum.

———. 1967. *Greek terracottas*. London: Methuen.

Hill, B. H. 1964. *The springs: Peirene, Sacred Spring, Glauke. Corinth*, vol. 1, pt. 6. Princeton, NJ: American School of Classical Studies at Athens.

Hill, G. F. 1903. *Coins of ancient Sicily*. Westminster: Constable. Repr. Bologna: A. Forti, 1976.

Himmelman-Wildschütz, N. 1957. ΘΕΟΛΗΠΤΟΣ. Marburg-Lahn: n.p.

———. 1980. *Über Hirten-Genre in der antiken Kunst*. Opladen: Westdeutscher Verlag.

Hoddinott, R. F. 1975. *Bulgaria in antiquity: An archaeological introduction*. New York: St. Martin's.

Hodkinson, S. 1988. "Animal husbandry in the Greek polis," in Whittaker (1988):35–74.

Hoepfner, W. 1972. "Topographische Forschungen," in F. K. Dörner, ed., *Forschungen an der Nordküste Kleinasiens. Bd. 1: Herakleia Pontike*, 37–46. Vienna: H. Böhlaus.

Hollis, A. S. 1970. *Metamorphoses*, bk. 8. Oxford: Clarendon.

———. 1991. "Callimachus Aetia Fr. 75.58–59 Pf." *ZPE* 86:11–13.

Hood, M. S. F. 1965. "Minoan sites in the far west of Crete." *ABSA* 60:99–113.

Hooker, E. M. 1950. "The sanctuary and altar of Chryse in Attic red-figure vase-paintings of the late fifth and early fourth centuries B.C." *JHS* 70:35–41.

Hopkinson, N. 1984. *Callimachus: Hymn to Demeter*. Cambridge: Cambridge University Press.

Hurwit, J. 1991. "The representation of nature in early Greek art," in D. Buitron-Oliver, ed., *New perspectives in early Greek art*, 33–62. Washington, DC: National Gallery of Art; Hanover, NH: University Press of New England.

Hussey, G. B. 1890. "The distribution of Hellenic temples." *AJA* 6:59–64.

Huxley, G. L. 1969. *Greek epic poetry from Eumelos to Panyassis*. Cambridge, MA: Harvard University Press.

Imhoof-Blumer, F. 1908. "Nymphen und Chariten auf griechischen Münzen." *Journal International d'Archéologie Numismatique* 11:3–123, pls. 1–12.

Iouri, E. 1971. Το ιερόν του Ἀμμωνος Δίος παρά την Ἀφυτιν. Αρχηαιολογικά Ανάλεκτα εξ Αθηνών (*Athens Annals of Archaeology*) 4:356–67.

———. 1974. Το εν Αφύτει ιερόν του Διονύσου και το ιερόν του Ἀμμωνος Διός, in U. Jantzen, ed., *Neue Forschungen in griechischen Heilgtümern*, 135–50. Tübingen: Wachsmuth.

Isaac, B. 1986. *The Greek settlements in Thrace until the Macedonian conquest*. Leiden: Brill.

Isler, H. P. 1970. *Acheloös: Eine Monographie*. Bern: Francke.

Jacobsen, H. 1984. "Aristaeus, Orpheus and the laudes Galli." *AJPh* 105:271–300.

Jacobsthal, P. 1931. *Die melischen Reliefs*. Berlin-Wilmersdorf: H. Keller.

Jameson, M. 1956. "The vowing of a pelanos." *AJP* 77:55–60.

———. 1965. "Notes on the sacrificial calendar from Erchia." *BCH* 89:154–72.

Janko, R. 1992. *The Iliad: A commentary*, vol. 4. Cambridge and New York: Cambridge University Press.

Jeanmaire, H. 1949. "Chiron," in *Mélanges Henri Grégoire*, 1:255–65. Brussels: Institut de Philologie et d'Histoire Orientales et Slaves.

Jebb, R. C., ed. 1905. *Bacchylides: The poems and fragments*. Cambridge: Cambridge University Press.

Jeffery, L. 1961. *Local scripts of archaic Greece*. Oxford: Clarendon.

Jobst, W. 1970. *Die Höhle im griechischen Theater des 5. und 4. Jahrhunderts v. Chr. Eine Untersuchung zur Inszenierung klassischer Dramen*. Vienna: Österreichischen Akademie der Wissenschaften.

Johnston, S. I. 1995. "Defining the dreadful: Remarks on the Greek child-killing demon," in Meyer and Mirecki (1995):361–87.

Jost, M. 1985. *Sanctuaries et cultes d'Arcadie*. Paris: J. Vrin.

Kadletz, E. 1984. "The sacrifice of Eumaios the pig-herder." *GRBS* 25:99–105.

Kaempf-Dimitriadou, S. 1979. *Die Liebe der Götter in der attischen Kunst des 5. Jahrhunderts v. Chr.* Bern: Francke.

Kahil, L. 1965. "Autour de l'Artémis attique." *AK* 8:20–33.

———. 1994. "Bains de statues et de divinités." *BCH* Suppl. 28:217–23.

Kákosy, L. 1982. "The Nile, Euthenia, and the nymphs." *Journal of Egyptian Archaeology* 68:290–98.

Kalinka, E. 1906. *Antike Denkmäler in Bulgarien*. Vienna: A. Hölder. Repr. Nendeln/Liechtenstein: Kraus, 1976.

Kambylis, A. 1965. *Die Dichterweihe und ihre Symbolik. Untersuchungen zu Hesiodos, Kallimachos, Properz und Ennius*. Heidelberg: C. Winter.

Kazarow, G. 1936. "Thrake (Religion)." *RE* 2.6:472–551.

Kearns, E. 1989. *The heroes of Attica*. *BICS* Suppl. 57. London: Institute of Classical Studies.

———. 1992. "Hindu mythology," in C. Larrington, ed., *The feminist companion to mythology*, 189–226. London: Pandora.

Kenney, E. J. 1963. "Erysichthon on Cos." *Mnemosyne* 16:57.

Koloski-Ostrow, A. O., and C. L. Lyons, eds. 1997. *Naked truths: Women, sexuality and gender in classical art and archaeology*. London and New York: Routledge.

Kontoleon, N. M. 1952. Νέαι επιγραφαί περί του Αρχιλόχου εκ Πάρου. *AE* 32–95.

Kraay, C. 1976. *Archaic and classical Greek coins*. Berkeley and Los Angeles: University of California Press.

Kron, U. 1971. "Zum Hypogäum von Paestum." *Jahrbuch des Deutschen Archäologischen Instituts* 86:117–48.

———. 1979. "Demos, Pnyx und Nymphenhügel: Zu Demos-Darstellungen und zum ältesten Kultort des Demos in Athen." *MDAI(A)* 94:49–75, pls. 7–12.

Kurke, L. 1991. *The traffic in praise: Pindar and the poetics of social economy*. Ithaca, NY: Cornell University Press.

Kurz, G., D. Müller, and W. Nicolai, eds. 1981. *Gnomosyne: Menschliches Denken und Handeln in der frühgriechischen Literatur. Festschrift für Walter Marg zum 70. Geburtstag*. Munich: Beck.

Lacroix, L. 1953. "Fleuves et nymphes eponymes sur les monnaies grecques." *Revue Belge de numismatique* 99:5–21.

———. 1965. *Monnaies et colonisation dans l'Occident grec*. Brussels: Palais des Académies.

Lacy, L. R. 1990. "Aktaion and a lost 'Bath of Artemis.'" *JHS* 110:26–42.

Lamberton, R., trans. 1983. *Porphyry on the cave of the nymphs*. Barrytown, NY: Station Hill.

Lane, E. 1971. *Corpus monumentorum religionis dei Menis*. 4 vols. Leiden: Brill.

Langlotz, E. 1951. "Die Larisa des Telephanes." *Museum Helveticum* 8:157–70.

Laronde, A. 1987. *Cyrène et la Libye hellénistique. Libykai Historiai*. Paris: Editions du Centre National de la Recherche Scientifique.

Larson, J. 1995a. "The Corycian nymphs and the Homeric *Hymn to Hermes*." *GRBS* 86:341–57.

———. 1995b. *Greek heroine cults*. Madison: University of Wisconsin Press.

———. 1997a. "Astacides the goatherd (Callimachus *Ep.* 22 Pf.)." *CP* 92:131–37.

———. 1997b. "Handmaidens of Artemis?" *CJ* 92:249–57.

Laumonier, A. 1958. *Les cultes indigènes en Carie*. Paris: E. de Boccard.

Lavagne, H. 1988. *Operosa Antra: Recherches sur la grotte à Rome de Sylla à Hadrien*. Rome: École française de Rome; Paris: E. de Boccard.

Lawall, G. 1967. *Theocritus' Coan pastorals*. Washington, DC: Center for Hellenic Studies.

Lawler, L. 1964. *The dance in ancient Greece*. Seattle: University of Washington Press.

Lawson, J. 1910. *Modern Greek folklore and ancient Greek religion*. Repr. New Hyde Park, NY: University Books, 1964.

Lazaridis, D. 1971. *Thasos and its Peraia*. Athens: Athens Center of Ekistics.

Lebrun, R. 1989. "À propos des déesses maliades et de quelques épiclèses grécoasianiques." *Kernos* 2:83–88.

Lefkowitz, M. 1996. "Women in the Panathenaic and other festivals," in Neils (1996):78–91.

Lehnerdt, M., ed. 1890. *Ioannis Canabutzae magistri ad principem Aeni et Samothraces in Dionysium Halicarnasensem commentarius*. Leipzig: Teubner.

Lenz, L. H. 1975. *Der homerische Aphroditehymnus und die Aristie des Aineias in der Ilias*. Bonn: R. Habelt.

LeRoy, C. 1988. "La source sacrée du Létoon de Xanthos et son dépôt votif." *BSAF* 125–31.

———. 1993. "Aspects grecs et anatoliennes des divinités vénérées au Létoon de Xanthos," in J. Borchhardt and G. Dobesch, eds., *Akten des II. Internationalen Lykien-Symposiums*, 1:241–47. Vienna: Verlag der Österreichischen Akademie der Wissenschaften.

Levi, D. 1923. "L'Antro delle ninfe e di Pan a Farsalo in Tessaglia: Topografia e scavi." *ASAA* 6–7:27–42.

———. 1925–26. "La Grotta di Aspripetra a Coo." *ASAA* 8–9:235–302.

Lewis, I. M. 1971. *Ecstatic religion: An anthropological study of shamanism and spirit possession*. Harmondsworth, UK, and Baltimore: Penguin.

Linfert, A. 1967. "Die Deutung des Xenokrateiareliefs." *MDAI(A)* 82:149–57.

Livrea, E. 1973. *Apollonii Rhodii Argonautica, liber quartus*. Florence: La Nuova Italia.

Lobeck, C. A. 1829. *Aglaophamus, sive De theologiae mysticae Graecorum causis*. 2 vols. Regimontii Prussorum: Borntraeger.

Lonsdale, S. 1993. *Dance and ritual play in Greek religion*. Baltimore and London: Johns Hopkins University Press.

Loraux, N. 1992. "What is a goddess?" in Pantel (1992):11–44.

Love, I. C. 1972. "A preliminary report of the excavations at Knidos, 1971." *AJA* 76:393–405, pls. 81–84.

———. 1973. "A preliminary report of the excavations at Knidos, 1972." *AJA* 77:413–24, pls. 73–78.

Luce, T. J. 1997. *The Greek historians.* London: Routledge.

Lyons, D. 1997. *Gender and immortality: Heroines in ancient Greek myth and cult.* Princeton, NJ: Princeton University Press.

Maas, P. 1935. "Der neue Euphorion." *Gnomon* 11:102–4.

Maass, E. 1922. "Segnen weihen Taufen." *Archiv für Religionswissenschaft* 21:241–86.

Madigan, B. C. 1992. *The temple of Apollo Bassitas. Vol. 2: The sculpture.* Princeton, NJ: American School of Classical Studies at Athens.

Malkin, I. 1998. *The returns of Odysseus: Colonization and ethnicity.* Berkeley and Los Angeles: University of California Press.

Manganaro, G. 1985. "Per la storia dei culti nella Sicilia greca," in *Il tempio greco in Sicilia: Architettura e culti,* 148–64. Catania: Istituto di Archeologia.

———. 1992. "Iscrizioni 'rupestri' di Sicilia," in L. Gasperini, ed., *Rupes Loquentes: Atti del convegno internazionale di studio sulle iscrizioni rupestri di età romana in Italia,* 447–501. Rome: Istituto Italiano per la Storia Antica.

Mansel, A. M. 1936. *Yalova ve civari. Yalova und Umgebung.* Istanbul Müzeleri Nesriyati, no. 13. Istanbul: n.p.

Marabini, M. T. 1949–51. "Iscrizione rupestri di Egina." *ASAA* 11–13: 135–40.

Marinatos, S. 1964. Ἔρευναι εν Σάμη της Κεφαλληνίας. *AE* 15–22, pls. 1–2.

Markee, N. L. 1994. "What role do fashion dolls play in the socialization of children?" *Perceptual and Motor Skills* 79:187–90.

Masson, O. 1981. "À propos des inscriptions chypriotes de Kafizin." *BCH* 105:623–49.

Mastronarde, D. J. 1968. "Theocritus' *Idyll* 13: Love and the hero." *TAPA* 99:272–80.

McCown, C. C., ed. 1922. *The testament of Solomon.* Leipzig: J. C. Hinricks.

McDevitt, A. S. 1970. *Inscriptions from Thessaly.* Hildesheim and New York: Georg Olms Verlag.

McKay, K. J. 1962. *Erysichthon: A Callimachean comedy. Mnemosyne* Suppl. 7. Leiden: Brill.

Megas, G., ed. 1970. *Folktales of Greece.* Chicago: University of Chicago Press.

Mendel, G. 1901. "Fouilles de Tegée." *BCH* 25:241–81.

Merkelbach, R. 1988. *Die Hirten des Dionysos: Die Dionysos-Mysterien der römischen Kaiserzeit und der bukolische Roman des Longus.* Stuttgart: Teubner.

Merkelbach, R., and M. L. West, eds. 1967. *Fragmenta Hesiodea.* Oxford: Clarendon.

Merritt, B. D. 1941. "Greek inscriptions." *Hesperia* 10:38–64.

Mertens-Horn, M. 1991. "Una 'nuova' antefissa a testa femminile da Akrai ed alcune considerazioni sulle Ninfe di Sicilia." *Bolletino d'Arte del Ministero della Pubblica Istruzione* 66:9–28.

Mette, H. J. 1963. *Der verlorene Aischylos.* Berlin: Akademie-Verlag.

Metzger, H. 1952. *Catalogue des monuments votifs du musée d'Adalia.* Paris: E. de Boccard.

Metzger, H., et al. 1974a. "Fouilles du Létoon de Xanthos (1970–73)." *RA* 313–40.

Metzger, H., et al. 1974b. "La Stèle trilingue récemment découverte au Létoon de Xanthos." *CRAI* 82–149.

Meyer, M., and Mirecki, P., eds. 1995. *Ancient magic and ritual power: Religions in the Graeco-Roman world*. Leiden and New York: Brill.

Michaelis, A. 1889. "The Thasian relief dedicated to the nymphs and to Apollon." *AJA* 4:417–22.

Mikalson, J. D. 1977. "Religion in the Attic demes." *AJPh* 98:424–35.

Mitford, T. B. 1958. "Three documents from classical Cyprus," in E. Grumach, ed., *Minoica: Festschrift zum 80. Geburtstag von Johannes Sundwall*, 260–73. Berlin: Akademie-Verlag.

———. 1980. *The nymphaeum of Kafizin: The inscribed pottery*. Kadmos Suppl. 2. Berlin and New York: W. de Gruyter.

Mitropolou, E. 1977. *Corpus I: Attic votive reliefs of the 6th and 5th centuries B.C.* Athens: Pyli.

Mitsos, M. T. 1953. "Inscriptions from Athens, IV," in G. E. Mylonas, ed., *Studies presented to David Moore Robinson*, 2.349–52. Saint Louis, MO: Washington University.

———. 1965. Εκ του Επιγραφικού Μουσείου (VI). *AD* 20:79–83, pls. 44–46.

Mollard-Besques, S. [Musée du Louvre] 1954–. *Catalogue raisonné des figurines et reliefs en terre-cuite grecs, étrusques et romains*. Paris: Éditions des Musées Nationaux.

Moon, W. G., ed. 1983a. *Ancient Greek art and iconography*. Madison: University of Wisconsin Press.

Moon, W. G. 1983b. "The Priam painter: Some iconographic and stylistic considerations," in Moon (1983a):97–118.

Morisot, Y. 1994. "Artémis, l'eau et la vie humaine." *BCH* Suppl. 28:201–16.

Motte, A. 1971. *Prairies et jardins de la Grèce antique, de la religion à la philosophie*. Brussels: Palais des Académies.

Moustaka, A. 1983. *Kulte und Mythen auf thessalischen Münzen*. Würzburg: K. Triltsch.

Mullen, W. 1982. *Choreia: Pindar and dance*. Princeton, NJ: Princeton University Press.

Muller, A. 1981. "Megarika III–VIII." *BCH* 105:203–25.

Murr, J. 1890. *Die Pflanzenwelt in der griechischen Mythologie*. Innsbruck: Wagnerische Universitäts-Buchhandlung.

Muthmann, F. 1975. *Mutter und Quelle: Studien zur Quellenverehrung im Altertum und in Mittelalter*. Basel: Archäologischer Verlag.

Myres, J. L. 1914. *Handbook of the Cesnola collection of antiquities from Cyprus*. New York: Metropolitan Museum of Art.

Nagler, M. N. 1996. "Dread goddess revisited," in S. Schein, ed., *Reading the Odyssey: Selected interpretive essays*, 141–61. Princeton, NJ: Princeton University Press.

Nagy, G. 1979. *Best of the Achaeans: Concepts of the hero in archaic Greek poetry*. Baltimore: Johns Hopkins University Press.

———. 1990. *Pindar's Homer: The lyric possession of an epic past*. Baltimore: Johns Hopkins University Press.

————. 1996. "Phaethon, Sappho's Phaon, and the white rock of Leukas: 'Reading' the symbols of Greek lyric," in Greene (1996):35–57.

Neils, J., ed. 1996. *Worshipping Athena: Panathenaia and Parthenon*. Madison: University of Wisconsin Press.

Neugebauer, K. A. 1931. *Die minoischen und archaisch griechischen Bronzen*. Berlin: W. de Gruyter.

Neumann, G. 1979. *Probleme des griechischen Weihreliefs*. Tübingen: E. Wachsmuth.

Neutsch, B. 1957. ΤΑΣ ΝΥΝΦΑΣ ΕΜΙ ΗΙΑΡΟΝ [*Ein Vasengraffito*]: *Zum unterirdischen Heiligtum von Paestum*. Abhandlungen der Heidelberger Akademie der Wissenschaften, Philosophisch-historische Klasse. Heidelberg: C. Winter.

Nilsson, M. P. 1906. *Griechische Feste von religiöser Bedeutung*. Repr. Stuttgart: Teubner, 1957.

————. 1940. *Greek folk religion*. New York: Columbia University Press. Repr. New York: Harper, 1961.

————. 1950. *The Minoan-Mycenaean religion and its survival in Greek religion*. 2d ed. Repr. Lund: C. W. K. Gleerup, 1968.

————. P. 1955. "Sur un drame d'Eschyle et la quête dans le culte grec." *AC* 24:336–40.

————. 1967. *Geschichte der griechischen Religion*, vol. 1. 3d ed. Handbuch der Altertumswissenschaft. Munich: C. H. Beck.

Nisetich, F. 1980. *Pindar's victory songs*. Baltimore: Johns Hopkins University Press.

Nock, A. D. 1925. "Studies in the Graeco-Roman beliefs of the empire," in Z. Stewart (1972):33–48.

————. 1933. *Conversion: The old and the new in religion from Alexander the Great to Augustine of Hippo*. Repr. Baltimore and London: Johns Hopkins University Press, 1998.

————. 1944. "The cult of heroes," in Z. Stewart (1972):575–602.

————. 1961. "Nymphs and Nereids," in Z. Stewart (1972):919–27.

Norton, R., and C. D. Curtis. 1911. "The excavations at Cyrene (1910–11)." *Bulletin of the Archaeological Institute of America* 2:141–63.

Norwood, G. 1956. *Pindar*. Berkeley: University of California Press.

Oakley, J. H., and R. H. Sinos. 1993. *The wedding in ancient Athens*. Madison: University of Wisconsin Press.

O'Brien, J. V. 1993. *The transformation of Hera: A study of ritual, hero, and the goddess in the Iliad*. Lanham, MD: Rowman and Littlefield.

Oeconomos, L. 1930. "L'état intellectuel et moral des Byzantins vers le milieu du XIVe siècle d'après une page de Joseph Bryennios," in *Mélanges Charles Diehl*, 1:225–33. Paris: E. Leroux.

Ogilvie, R. M. 1962. "The song of Thyrsis." *JHS* 82:106–10.

————. 1965. *A commentary on Livy, books 1–5*. Oxford: Clarendon.

Oikonomidou, M. 1990. Αρχαϊκός θησαυρός αργυρών νομισμάτων από το Ποντολίβαδο (1971), in G. Bakalakis, ed., Μνήμη Δ. Λαζαρίδη, 533–39. Thessalonica: Το Υπουργείο and L'École française d'Athènes.

Orlandos, A. K. 1965. "Pitsa." *EAA* 6:200–206.

Orsi, P. 1899. "Buscemi. Sacri spechi con iscrizione greche, scoperti pressi Akrai." *Notizie degli scavi di antichita*. Accademia nazionale dei Lincei 455–71.

————. 1912. "Messina: Rilievo ieratico di Camaro." *Notizie degli scavi di antichita*. Accademia nazionale dei Lincei 456–58.

Otto, W. F. 1956. *Die Musen und der göttliche Ursprung des Singens und Sagens.* Düsseldorf and Cologne: Eugen Diederichs Verlag.

Owens, E. J. 1982. "The Enneakrounos fountainhouse." *JHS* 102:222–25.

Pace, B. 1916–20. "La zona costiera da Adalia a Side." *ASAA* 3:29–71.

———. 1935–49. *Arte e civiltà della Sicilia antica.* 4 vols. Milan: Editrice Dante Alighieri.

Page, D. L. 1981. *Further Greek epigrams.* Cambridge and London: Cambridge University Press.

Pantel, P. S., ed. 1992. *A history of women in the west. I: From ancient goddesses to Christian saints.* Cambridge, MA: Belknap Press of Harvard University Press.

Papabasileos, G. A. 1912. Ανασκαφαί και έρευναι εν Εύβοια. *Praktika* 119–40.

Papadimitriou, J. 1958. Μαραθών, σπήλαιον Πανός. *Ergon* 15–22.

Parke, H. W. 1967. *The oracles of Zeus: Dodona, Olympia, Ammon.* Oxford: Basil Blackwell.

———. 1985. *The oracles of Apollo in Asia Minor.* London and Dover, NH: Croom Helm.

Parke, H. W., and D. E. W. Wormell. 1956. *The Delphic oracle.* 2 vols. Oxford: Blackwell.

Parker, R. 1983. *Miasma: Pollution and purification in early Greek religion.* Oxford: Clarendon.

———. 1996. *Athenian religion: A history.* Oxford: Clarendon.

Parry, A. 1957. "Landscape in Greek poetry." *YClS* 15:3–29.

Parsons, A. W. 1943. "Klepsydra and the paved court of Python." *Hesperia* 12:191–267.

Pashley, R. 1837. *Travels in Crete.* London: J. Murray. Repr. Amsterdam: Hakkert, 1970.

Pasquier, A. 1977. "Pan et les nymphes à l'antre corycien." *BCH* Suppl. 4.365–87.

Paton, W. R., and Hicks, E. L. 1891. *The inscriptions of Cos.* Oxford: Clarendon.

Pearson, L. 1939. *Early Ionian historians.* Oxford: Clarendon. Repr. Westport, CT: Greenwood, 1975.

———. 1942. *The local historians of Attica.* Philadelphia, PA: American Philological Association. Repr. Westport, CT: Greenwood, 1972.

———. 1987. *The Greek historians of the West.* Atlanta: Scholars Press for the American Philological Association.

Pedley, J. G. 1965. "An Attic grave stele in the Fogg Art Museum." *HSCP* 69:259–67, pls. 1–3.

———. 1990. *Paestum: Greeks and Romans in southern Italy.* London: Thames and Hudson.

Peek, W. 1938. "Metrische Inschriften," in J. F. Crome et al., eds. *Mnemosynon Theodor Wiegand*, 14–42, pls. 2, 3. Munich: F. Bruckmann Verlag.

———. 1978. "Zu griechischen Epigrammen." *ZPE* 31:247–64.

Penglase, C. 1994. *Greek myths and Mesopotamia: Parallels and influence in the Homeric hymns and Hesiod.* London and New York: Routledge.

Perdrizet, P. 1896. "Mên." *BCH* 20:55–106.

———. 1910. *Cultes et mythes du Pangée.* Paris and Nancy: Berger-Levrault.

Petrakos, V. C. 1968. Ο Ωρωπός και το ιερόν του Αμφιαράου. Athens: Archaiologike Hetaireia.

Petropolou, A. 1987. "The sacrifice of Eumaios reconsidered." *GRBS* 28:135–49.

Picard, O. 1982a. "Monnayage thasien du Ve s. av. J. C." *CRAI* 412–24.

———. 1982b. "Problèmes de numismatique thasienne." *RA* 7–12.

Pirenne-Delforge, V. 1996. "Les Charites à Athènes et dans l'île de Cos." *Kernos* 9:195–214.

Pleket, H. W. 1981. "Religious history as the history of mentality: The 'believer' as servant of the deity in the Greek world," in Versnel (1981a):152–92.

Podbielski, H. 1971. *La structure de l'hymne Homérique à Aphrodite à la lumière de la tradition littéraire*. Warsaw: Zaklad Narodowy.

Polignac, F. de. 1995. *Cults, territory, and the origins of the Greek city-state*. Trans. J. Lloyd. Chicago and London: University of Chicago Press.

Politis, N. 1904. Μελέται περί του βίου και της γλώσσας του ελλενικού λαού· Παραδόσεις. 2 vols. Repr. Athens: Ιστορική Έρευνα, 1965.

Poljakov, T. 1987. "The nymph Balte, mother of Epimenides." *RhM* 130:410–12.

Polacco, L. 1992. *Il teatro antico di Siracusa*. Syracuse: Edizioni dell'Ariete.

Polacco, L., and C. Anti. 1981. *Il teatro antico di Siracusa*. Rimini: Maggioli Editore.

Pottier, E., and S. Reinach. 1883. "Terre-cuite représentant la grotte des nymphes." *BCH* 7:498–501.

Pottier, E., S. Reinach, et al. 1887. *La nécropole de Myrina: Recherches archéologiques exécutées au nom et au frais de l'École française d'Athènes*. 2 vols. Paris: E. Thorin.

Pouilloux, J. 1979. "Une enigme thasienne: Le passage des théores." *BCH* Suppl. 5:129–41.

Praschniker, C., and A. Schober. 1919. *Archäologische Forschungen in Albanien und Montenegro*. Vienna: A. Hölder.

Price, M., and N. Waggoner. 1975. *Archaic Greek coinage: The Asyut hoard*. London: V. C. Vecchi.

Prinz, F. 1979. *Gründungsmythen und Sagenchronologie*. Munich: Beck.

Pugliese Carratelli, G. 1977. "Tempio e culto nella Sicilia greca." *Cronache di Archeologia* 16:13–20.

Pugliese Carratelli, G., ed. 1996. *The Greek world: Art and civilization in Magna Graecia and Sicily*. Trans. A. Ellis et al. New York: Rizzoli.

Purvis, A. 1998. *Founders and innovators of private cults in classical Greece*. Ph.D. diss. Duke University.

Quandt, W. 1955. *Orphei hymni*. Berlin: Weidmann.

Race, W. H., ed. and trans. 1997. *Pindar*. 2 vols. Cambridge, MA: Harvard University Press.

Ransome, H. 1937. *The sacred bee in ancient times and folklore*. Boston and New York: Houghton Mifflin.

Reeder, E., ed. 1995. *Pandora's box: Women in classical Greece* Baltimore: Walters Art Gallery and Princeton University Press.

Regling, K. 1906. *Terina*. Berlin: G. Reimer.

Reilly, J. 1997. "Naked and limbless: Learning about the feminine body in ancient Athens," in Koloski-Ostrow and Lyons (1997):154–73.

Rhomaios, K. 1905. Ευρήματα ανασκαφής του επί της Πάρνηθος άντρου. *AE* 99–158.

———. 1906. Ευρήματα ανασκαφής του επί της Πάρνηθος άντρου. *AE* 89–116.

————. 1911. Ἀρκαδικοί ερμαί. *AE* 154:149–59.

Rice, E. E. 1983. *The grand procession of Ptolemy Philadelphos*. New York: Oxford University Press.

Richardson, R. 1895. "A sacrificial calendar from the Epakria." *AJA* 10:209–26.

Richter, G. M. A. 1925. "A Neo-Attic krater in the Metropolitan Museum." *JHS* 45:201–9, pls. 6–9.

————. 1960. "An ancient plaster cast in Munich," in F. Eckstein, ed., *Theoria: Festschrift für W.-H. Schuchhardt*, 179–83. Baden-Baden: B. Grimm.

————. 1968. *Korai: Archaic Greek maidens*. London: Phaidon. Repr. New York: Hacker Art Books, 1988.

Ridgway, B. S. 1970. *The severe style in Greek sculpture*. Princeton, NJ: Princeton University Press.

————. 1981. "Sculpture from Corinth." *Hesperia* 50:422–48.

————. 1983. "Painterly and pictorial in Greek relief sculpture," in Moon (1983a):193–208.

————. 1993. *The archaic style in Greek sculpture*. 2d ed. Chicago: Ares.

————. 1997. *Fourth-century styles in Greek sculpture*. Madison: University of Wisconsin Press.

Riginos, A. M. 1976. *Platonica: The anecdotes concerning the life and writings of Plato*. Leiden: Brill.

Robert, L. 1946. "Sur un type monétaire de Prousa de l'Olympe et sur des épigrammes." *Hellenica: Recueil d'Epigraphie de Numismatique et d'Aantiquités Grecques* 2:94–102.

————. 1949. "Épitaphe d'un berger a Thasos." *Hellenica: Recueil d'Epigraphie de Numismatique et d'Antiquités Grecques* 7:152–60.

————. 1955. "Villes et monnaies de Lycie." *Hellenica: Recueil d'Epigraphie de Numismatique et d'Antiquités Grecques* 10:217–20.

————. 1958. "Dédicace à Héraclès et aux nymphes." *Anatolia: Revue Annuelle d'Archéologie* 3:103–8.

————. 1959. "Les inscriptions grecques de Bulgarie." *RPh* 33:11–236, pls. 1–4.

————. 1962. *Villes d'Asie Mineure: Études de géographie ancienne*. Paris: E. de Boccard.

————. 1974. "Des Carpathes à la Propontide." *StudClas* 16:53–88.

————. 1980. *À travers l'Asie Mineure: Poètes et prosateurs, monnaies grecques, voyageurs et géographie*. Athens: École française d'Athènes; Paris: Diffusion de Boccard.

Robertson, N. 1983. "Greek ritual begging in aid of women's fertility and childbirth." *TAPA* 113:143–69.

————. 1987. "Government and society at Miletus 525–442 B.C." *Phoenix* 14:356–98.

————. 1992. *Festivals and legends: The formation of Greek cities in the light of public ritual*. Toronto: University of Toronto Press.

Rocchi, M. 1979. "Contributi allo culto delle Charites." *StudClas* 18:5–16.

————. 1980. "Contributi allo culto delle Charites." *StudClas* 19:19–28.

Rogers, E. 1932. *The copper coinage of Thessaly*. London: Spink and Sons.

Rolley, C. 1965. "Le sanctuaire des dieux Patrôoi et le Thesmophorion de Thasos." *BCH* 89:441–83.

Rose, H. J. 1924. "Anchises and Aphrodite." *CQ* 18:11–16.

Rouse, W. H. D. 1902. *Greek votive offerings*. Cambridge: Cambridge University Press. Repr. New York: Arno, 1975.

Roussel, D. 1976. *Tribu et cité: Études sur les groupes sociaux dans les cités grecques aux époques archaïque et classique*. Paris: Belles Lettres.

Roussel, M. P. 1929. "Deux familles athéniennes a Délos." *BCH* 53:166–84.

Rumpf, A. 1927. *Chalkidische Vasen*. Berlin and Leipzig: W. de Gruyter.

Rusten, J. S. 1983. "ΓΕΙΤΩΝ ΗΡΩΣ: Pindar's prayer to Heracles (N. 7.86–101) and Greek popular religion." *HSCP* 87:289–97.

Saflund, G. 1981. "Beds of the nymphe." *ORom* 13:41–56.

Sahin, S. 1974. *Neufunde von antike Inschriften in Nikomedeia (Izmit) und in der Umgebung der Stadt*. Ph.D. diss. Münster.

Sakellariou, M. 1956. "ΙΑΦΩΝ: Fleuve, dieu fluvial et éponyme des Ioniens," in *Mélanges offerts à Octave et Melpo Merlier*, 2:311–22. Athens: Institut français d'Athènes.

Sale, W. 1962. "The story of Callisto in Hesiod." *RhM* 105:122–41.

———. 1965. "Callisto and the virginity of Artemis." *RhM* 108:11–35.

Salviat, F. 1979. "Les colonnes initiales du catalogue des théores et les institutions thasiennes archaïques." *BCH* Suppl. 5:107–27.

Sampson, A. 1992. "Late Neolithic remains at Tharrounia, Euboea." *ABSA* 87:61–101.

Saria, B. 1926. "Antiken aus Durazzo." *JÖAI* 23:241–46.

Schachter, A. 1967. "A Boeotian cult type." *BICS* 14:1–16.

———. 1972. "Some underlying cult patterns in Boeotia," *Proceedings of the first international conference on Boiotian antiquities: Teiresias*, Suppl. 1, 17–30. Montreal: McGill University.

———. 1976. "Aristiastai: An inscription from Vathy (Boiotia) reconsidered." *ZPE* 23:251–54.

———. 1981–94. *Cults of Boiotia*. 3 vols. London: Institute of Classical Studies.

———. 1990. "Tilphossa: The site and its cults." *Cahiers des Études Anciennes* 24:333–40.

Schaeffer, C. F. A. 1939. "Une trouvaille de monnaies archaïques grecques à Ras Shamra," in *Mélanges syriens offerts à M. René Dussaud*, 1:464–69. Paris: P. Geuthner.

Schefold, K. 1966. *Myth and legend in early Greek art*. London: Thames and Hudson.

———. 1992. *Gods and heroes in late archaic Greek art*. Trans. A. Griffiths. Cambridge and New York: Cambridge University Press.

Schmidt, B. 1871. *Das Volksleben der Neugriechen und das hellenische Altertum*. Leipzig: Teubner.

Schmidt, E. 1971. *Spielzug und Spiele: Der Kinder im klassischen Altertum*. Meiningen: Staatlichen Museen Meiningen.

Schmidt, E. A. 1968. "Die Leiden des verliebten Daphnis." *Hermes* 96:539–52.

Schönbeck, G. 1964. *Der locus amoenus von Homer bis Horaz*. Ph.D. diss. Heidelberg (1962). Cologne: G. Wasmund.

Schwarzenberg, E. 1966. *Die Grazien*. Bonn: Rudolf Habelt Verlag.

Seaford, R. 1976. "On the origins of the satyric drama." *Maia* 28:209–21.

———. 1977–78. "The Hyporchema of Pratinas." *Maia* 29–30:81–95.

———. 1988. "The eleventh ode of Bacchylides." *JHS* 108:118–36.

Séchan, L. 1967. *Sept légendes grecques*. Paris: Belles Lettres.

Segal, C. 1974a. "Death by water: A narrative pattern in Theocritus." *Hermes* 102:20–38.

———. 1974b. "The Homeric *Hymn to Aphrodite*: A structuralist approach." *CW* 67:205–19.

———. 1986. "Tithonus and the Homeric *Hymn to Aphrodite*: A comment." *Arethusa* 19:37–47.

Segre, M. 1937–38. "Due leggi sacre dell'Asclepieo di Coo." *Rivista dell'Istituto Nazionale di Archeologia e Storia dell'Arte* 6:191–98.

Sestieri, P. C. 1956. "An underground shrine at Paestum." *Archaeology* 9:22–33.

Seyrig, H. 1927. "Quatre cultes de Thasos." *BCH* 51:178–233.

Shapiro, H. A. 1995. "The cult of heroines: Kekrops' daughters," in Reeder (1995):39–48.

Shear, T. L. 1973. "A votive relief from the Athenian agora." *ORom* 9:183–91.

Sherwin-White, S. M. 1978. *Ancient Cos. Hypomnemata* 51. Göttingen: Vandenhoeck and Ruprecht.

Simon, E. 1972. "Hera und die nymphen: Ein böotischer Polos in Stockholm." *RA* 2:205–20.

Skias, A. N. 1900. Ανασκαφαί παρά την Φυλήν. *Praktika* 38–50.

———. 1901. Ανασκαφή εν τω άντρω του Πανός. *Praktika* 32–33.

———. 1918. Το παρά την Φυλήν άντρον του Πανός. *AE* 1–28.

Slatkin, L. M. 1991. *The power of Thetis: Allusion and interpretation in the Iliad.* Berkeley and Los Angeles: University of California Press.

Smith, P. 1981. *Nursling of mortality: A study of the Homeric Hymn to Aphrodite.* Frankfurt am Main: P. Lang.

Smithson, E. 1982. "The prehistoric Klepsydra: Some notes," in *Studies in Athenian architecture, sculpture and topography presented to Homer A. Thompson. Hesperia* Suppl. 20:141–54, pls. 21–22. Princeton, NJ: American School of Classical Studies at Athens.

Snodgrass, A. 1980. *Archaic Greece: The age of experiment.* London: J. M. Dent.

Snyder, J. M. 1989. *The woman and the lyre: Women writers in classical Greece and Rome.* Carbondale: Southern Illinois University Press.

Sourvinou-Inwood, C. 1978. "Persephone and Aphrodite at Locri: A model for personality definitions in Greek religion." *JHS* 98:101–21.

———. 1987. "Erotic pursuits: Images and meanings." *JHS* 107:131–53.

———. 1988. *Studies in girls' transitions: Aspects of the Arkteia and age representation in Attic iconography.* Athens: Kardamitsa.

Sperling, J. W. 1973. *Thera and Therasia.* Athens: Athens Technological Organization, Athens Center of Ekistics.

Stais, V. 1909. Αναθηματικόν ανάγλυφον εκ Φαλήρου. *AE* 239–64.

Stampolidis, N. C. 1984. "Der Nymphenaltar in Knidos und der Bildhauer Theon aus Antiochia." *AA* 113–27.

Stears, K. 1998. "Death becomes her: Gender and Athenian death ritual," in Blundell and Williamson (1998):113–27.

Stehle, E. 1996. "Sappho's gaze: Fantasies of a goddess and young man," in Greene (1996):193–225.

Steiner, A. 1992. "Pottery and cult in Corinth: Oil and water at the sacred spring." *Hesperia* 61:385–408.

Stewart, A. 1983. "Stesichorus and the François vase," in Moon (1983a): 53–74.

———. 1990. *Greek sculpture: An exploration.* 2 vols. New Haven and London: Yale University Press.

———. 1995. "Rape?" in Reeder (1995):74–90.

Stewart, C. 1985. "Nymphomania: Sexuality, insanity and problems in folklore analysis," in Alexiou and Lambropoulos (1985):219–52.

———. 1991. *Demons and the devil: Moral imagination and modern Greek culture.* Princeton, NJ: Princeton University Press.

Stewart, Z., ed. 1972. *Essays on religion and the ancient world by Arthur Darby Nock.* 2 vols. Oxford: Clarendon.

Stillwell, A. N., et al., 1952. *Corinth.* Vol. 15, pt. 2: *The Potter's Quarter.* Princeton, NJ: Princeton University Press.

Stinton, T. C. W. 1965. *Euripides and the Judgment of Paris.* London: Society for the Promotion of Hellenic Studies.

Stoop, M. W. 1979. "Conjectures on the end of a sanctuary," in G. Kopcke and M. B. Moore, eds., *Studies in classical art and archaeology: A tribute to Peter Heinrich von Blanckenhagen,* 179–83. Locust Valley, NY: J. J. Augustin.

Storck, K. 1912. *Die ältesten Sagen der Insel Keos.* Ph.D. diss. Geissen. Mainz: O. Schneider.

Stuart, J., and N. Revett. 1882. *Antiquités d'Athènes.* 4 vols. Paris: Didot.

Stucchi, S. 1975. *Architettura cirenaica.* Rome: L'Erma di Bretschneider.

Studnitzka, F. 1896. "Krobylos und Tettiges." *JDAI* 272–84.

Susini, G. 1952–54. "Iscrizione greche di Megiste e della Licia nel Museo di Mitilene." *ASAA* 14–16:341–55.

Sutton, D. F. 1974. "Aeschylus' Amymone." *GRBS* 15:193–202.

———. 1980. *The Greek satyr play.* Beiträge zur klassischen Philologie 90. Meisenheim am Glan: Hain.

Symeonoglou, S. 1985. *The topography of Thebes from the Bronze Age to modern times.* Princeton, NJ: Princeton University Press.

Taylor, M. E. 1955. "Primitivism in Virgil." *AJP* 76:261–78.

Themelis, P. G. 1992. "The cult scene on the polos of the Siphnian karyatid at Delphi," in R. Hägg, ed., *The iconography of Greek cult in the archaic and classical periods. Kernos* Suppl. 1:49–72.

Thesleff, H. 1981. "Man and *locus amoenus* in early Greek poetry," in Kurz, Müller, and Nicolai (1981):31–45.

Thompson, H. A. 1977. "Dionysos among the nymphs in Athens and in Rome." *Journal of the Walters Art Gallery* 36:73–84.

Threatte, L. 1980. *The grammar of Attic inscriptions.* 2 vols. Berlin and New York: W. de Gruyter.

Tiverios, M. A. 1975. Ιερόν Δορποφορών (σημειώσεις από την Πάρο). *AD* 30:140–48, pls. 53–58.

Tölle, R. 1964. *Frühgriechische Reigentänze.* Waldsassen, Bayern: Stiftland-Verlag.

Tondriau, J. 1948. "Princesses ptolémaïques comparées à des déesses." *BSAA* 37:14–33.

Travlos, J. 1937. Σπήλαιον του Πανος παρά το Δαφνί. *AE* 391–408.

———. 1971. *Pictorial dictionary of ancient Athens.* New York: Praeger.

———. 1988. *Bildlexicon zur Topographie des antiken Attika.* Tübingen: Wasmuth.

Tuchelt, K. 1970. *Die Archaischen Skulpturen von Didyma. Beiträge zur frühgriechischen Plastik in Kleinasien.* Berlin: G. Mann.

―――. 1972. "Weihrelief an die Musen." *AA* 87:87–105.

Tyszkiewicz, M. 1892. *La collection Tyszkiewicz: Choix de monuments antiques avec texte explicatif de W. Fröhner.* Munich: Verlagsanstalt für Kunst und Wissenschaft.

Tzouvara-Souli, C. 1988–89. Λατρεία των νυμφών δτην Ηπειρο. Ηπειρωτικά χρονικά 9–65, pl. 1–26.

Vanderpool, E. 1955. "New inscriptions concerning Archilochus." *AJP* 76: 186–88.

―――. 1967. "Pan in Paiania: A note on lines 407–409 of Menander's *Dyskolos*." *AJA* 71:309–11.

―――. 1979. "The genos Theoinidai honors a priestess of Nymphe." *AJP* 100:213–15.

Van Straten, F. T. 1976. "Daikrates' dream: A votive relief from Kos, and some other *kat' onar* dedications." *BABesch* 51:1–38.

―――. 1981. "Gifts for the gods," in Versnel (1981a):65–105.

―――. 1993. "Images of gods and men in a changing society: Self-identity in Hellenistic religion," in A. Bulloch et al., eds., *Images and ideologies: Self-definition in the Hellenistic world*, 248–90. Berkeley and Los Angeles: University of California Press.

―――. 1995. *Hiera kala: Images of animal sacrifice in archaic and classical Greece.* Leiden: Brill.

Velkov, V., and V. Gerassimova-Tomova. 1989. "Kulte und Religionen in Thrakien und Niedermösien." *ANRW* 18.2:1317–61.

Verbruggen, H. 1981. *Le Zeus crétois.* Paris: Belles Lettres.

Vermeule, E. 1979. *Aspects of death in early Greek art and poetry.* Berkeley and Los Angeles: University of California Press.

Versnel, H. S., ed. 1981a. *Faith, hope and worship: Aspects of religious mentality in the ancient world.* Leiden: Brill.

Versnel, H. S. 1981b. "Religious mentality in ancient prayer," in Versnel (1981a):1–64.

―――. 1990. *Ter Unus: Isis, Dionysos, Hermes. Three studies in henotheism.* Leiden: Brill.

―――. 1993. *Inconsistencies in Greek and Roman religion. II: Transition and reversal in myth and ritual.* Leiden: Brill.

Vian, F. 1963. *Les origines de Thèbes: Cadmos et les Spartes.* Paris: C. Klinckseick.

Vian, F., and E. Delage. 1976–81. *Apollonios de Rhodes Argonautiques.* 3 vols. Paris: Belles Lettres.

Vidal-Naquet, P. 1986. *The black hunter: Forms of thought and forms of society in the Greek world.* Trans. A. Szegedy-Maszak. Baltimore and London: Johns Hopkins University Press.

Vivante, P. 1972. "Pindar, Pythian XI, 1–11," in *Proceedings of the first international conference on Boiotian antiquities, Montreal 1972, Teiresias* Suppl. 1:41–50. Montreal: McGill University.

Vryonis, S., Jr. 1971. *The decline of medieval Hellenism in Asia Minor.* Berkeley and Los Angeles: University of California Press.

Wace, A. J. B., and M. S. Thompson. 1908–9. "A cave of the nymphs on Mt. Ossa." *ABSA* 15:243–47.

Waldstein, C. 1902–5. *The Argive Heraeum.* 2 vols. Boston: Houghton Mifflin.

Walker, S. 1979. "A sanctuary of Isis on the south slope of the Athenian acropolis." *ABSA* 74:243–57, pls. 30–32.

Walter, O. 1939. ΚΟΥΡΗΤΙΚΗ ΤΡΙΑΣ. *JÖAI* 31.51–80.

Wegner, M. 1968. *Musik und Tanz*. Archeologia Homerica, bd. 3. Göttingen: Vandenhoeck and Ruprecht.

Weiss, C. 1984. *Griechische Flussgottheiten in vorhellenistischer Zeit: Ikonographie und Bedeutung*. Würzburg: K. Triltsch.

Weller, C., et al. 1903. "The cave at Vari." *AJA* 7:263–349.

West, M. L. 1965. "The Dictaean hymn to the Kouros." *JHS* 85:149–59.

———. 1977. "Erinna." *ZPE* 25:95–119.

———. 1983. *The Orphic poems*. Oxford: Clarendon.

———. 1985. *The Hesiodic catalogue of women: Its nature, structure and origins*. Oxford: Clarendon.

West, M. L., ed. 1966. *Hesiod Theogony*. Oxford: Clarendon.

———. 1978. *Hesiod. Works and days*. Oxford: Clarendon.

Westermark, U., and K. Jenkins. 1980. *The coinage of Kamarina*. London: Royal Numismatic Society.

Whitehead, D. 1986. *The demes of Attica, 508/7–ca. 250 B.C.: A political and social study*. Princeton, NJ: Princeton University Press.

Whittaker, C. R., ed. 1988. *Pastoral economies in classical antiquity*. Cambridge Philological Society, Suppl. vol. 14. Cambridge: Cambridge University Press.

Wickens, J. M. 1986. *The archaeology and history of cave use in Attica, Greece, from prehistoric through late Roman times*. Ph.D. diss. Indiana.

Wilamowitz-Moellendorff, U. von. 1895. *Euripides' Herakles*. 3 vols. Repr. Darmstadt: Wissenschaftliche Buchgesellschaft, 1959.

———. 1920. *Die Ilias und Homer*. 2d ed. Berlin: Weidmann.

———. 1924. *Hellenistische Dichtung in der Zeit des Kallimachos*. 2 vols. Berlin: Weidmann.

———. 1931. *Der Glaube der Hellenen*. 2 vols. Berlin: Weidmann.

Willetts, R. F. 1962. *Cretan cults and festivals*. New York: Barnes and Noble.

Williams, C. K. 1981. "The city of Corinth and its domestic religion." *Hesperia* 50:408–21.

Williams, F. J. 1969. "Theocritus, *Idyll* I, 81–91." *JHS* 89:121–23.

Winkler, J. 1981. "Gardens of the nymphs: Public and private in Sappho's lyrics," in Foley (1981):63–89.

———. 1990. *The constraints of desire: The anthropology of sex and gender in ancient Greece*. New York and London: Routledge.

Winter, F. 1903. *Die antiken Terracotten, im Auftrag des Archäologischen Instituts des Deutschen Reichs*, Vol. 3: *Die Typen der figürlichen Terrakotten*. Berlin: W. Spemann.

Winter, N. 1993. *Greek architectural terracottas from the prehistoric to the end of the archaic period*. Oxford: Clarendon; New York: Oxford University Press.

Woodhead, A. G. 1957. "A votive stele." *ABSA* 52:205–6, pl. 39.

Wright, G. R. H. 1957. "Cyrene: A survey of certain rock-cut features to the south of the sanctuary of Apollo." *ABSA* 77:301–10.

Wycherley, R. E. 1937. "Pêgê and krênê." *CR* 51:2–3.

———. 1957. *Literary and epigraphical testimonia: The Athenian agora*, vol. 3. Princeton, NJ: American School of Classical Studies at Athens.

————. 1963a. "Pausanias at Athens, II." *GRBS* 4:157–75.

————. 1963b. "The scene of Plato's *Phaidros.*" *Phoenix* 17:88–98.

————. 1978. *The stones of Athens.* Princeton, NJ: Princeton University Press.

Zanker, P. 1965. *Wandel der Hermesgestalt in der attischen Vasenmalerei.* Bonn: R. Habelt.

Zervoudakis, T. 1965. Σπήλαιον μέγαρον. Δελτίον της Ελλενικής Σπηλαιολογικής Εταιρείας 8:3–11.

Zorides, P. 1977. Η σπηλία των νυμφών της Πεντέλης. *AE* Chron. 4–11.

Zuntz, G. 1971. *Persephone: Three essays on religion and thought in Magna Graecia.* Oxford: Clarendon.

INDEX OF NYMPHS

Note: As a catalog of nymphs, this index is necessarily incomplete, but the nymphs mentioned in this book have been chosen to demonstrate the group as a whole. For fuller coverage, consult also the entries "cave sanctuaries" and "votive reliefs of the nymphs" in the General Index.

Arne. *See also* Melanippe, nymph of
  Boiotia
    daughter of Aiolos, Thessaly, 166
    nurse of Poseidon, Boiotia, 312n.154
Asopis, daughter of Asopos, 141
Astakides, Bithynia, 196
Asteria. *See* Delos, eponymous nymph
Asterodaia, Kaukasian nymph, 54
Asterope
    daughter of Kebren. *See* Hesperia,
      daughter of Kebren
    Pleiad. *See* Sterope, Pleiad
Astyoche, daughter of Simoeis, 195
Atlantia, hamadryad nymph, 307n.93
Automate, spring/well nymph, Argos, 53

Balanos, acorn nymph, 283n.31
Balte, nymph of Krete, 14
Bassai, nymphs of, Arkadia, 156–57
Bateia, naiad, 308n.101
Bistonian nymphs, 174
Bithynian nymph, mother of Amykos, 196
Bolina, heroine or nymph of Achaia, 187
Bourdapênai, Thrace, 175–76
Brisai, bee nymphs of Keos, 85–86, 184
Britomartis, nymph or goddess of Krete, 7,
  187
Byblis, nymph of Ionia, 203–5, 210,
  290n.33
Byze, daughter of Erasinos, 308n.96

Chalkis, daughter of Asopos, 141, 144
Chariklo, wife of Cheiron, 11, 139, 164
Chesiad nymphs, Samos, 200–201, 299n.46
Choreia, Dionysiac nymph, 95
Chryse, nymph of Lemnos, 179
Chrysopel(e)ia, tree nymph of Arkadia, 74,
  155
chthoniai, Kyrene, 190–91
Cyaneë. *See* Kyaneë, daughter of
  Maiandros

Danaids, 4, 6, 52–53, 150. *See also*
  Amymone, Danaid
daphnaiai, laurel nymphs, 283n.31
Daphne, 96, 310n.123
    daughter of Ladon, Arkadia/Elis,
      156–57
    daughter of Ladon, Syria, 211
    daughter of Peneios, 165, 168
Daphne (Syria), nymphs of, 211
Daphnis, nymph of Delphi, 11, 147
Daulis, daughter of Kephisos, Phokis, 147
Deliades, nymphs of Delos, 182, 316n.210

Delos, eponymous nymph, 182–83,
  317n.213
despoina numphê, 286n.89
Diktynna, nymph or goddess of Krete, 7,
  187
Dione, Dodonid, Epeiros, 161
Dirke, nymph or heroine of Thebes, 6–7,
  98, 142–43
Dodone, daughter of Okeanos, 161
Dodonides, nymphs of Epeiros, 161,
  311n.137
Dorpophoroi, Paros, 181
dryads, 11, 33, 52, 76, 85
Dryope, nymph of Thessaly, 14, 70–71,
  165, 168
Dymanes, nymphs of the, Thera, 188, 205

Echenaïs, nymph of Aitne, Sicily, 79
Echinades, eponymous nymphs, 310n.132
Echo, nymph of Arkadia, 56, 68–69, 96,
  155
Egeria, nymph of Latium, 291n.50
Eidothea, nymph of Othrys, Thessaly,
  167
Elektra, Pleiad, 194, 308n.100
Empedo, spring nymph of Athens, 97,
  126–27
Endeïdes, nymphs of Cyprus, 210
Endeïs, daughter of Cheiron, 38, 145, 167,
  210
Ennesiades, nymphs of Lesbos, 197
Entella, eponymous heroine or nymph,
  Sicily, 221
Ephesos, nymphs at, 199
ephudriades, water nymphs, 8
epimêlides, protectors of herds, 292n.64,
  297n.17
epipotamides, river nymphs, 8
Eranno, nymph of Telos, 322n.296
Erato, nymph of Arkadia, 11, 74, 155
Erchia, nymphs of, Attica, 135
Erytheia, Hesperid, 281n.14
Eridanos river, nymphs of, 294n.85,
  308n.99
Euagora, naiad nymph, Troad, 195
Euboia
    daughter of Asopos, 144
    nymph of Argos, 87, 150
Eudore, Dodonid, Epeiros, 161
Euis, nymph of Attica, 137, 303n.31
Eunika, nymph of Kios, 67
Eunoë, nymph of the Troad, 195
Eunoste, nymph of Tanagra, 304n.52
Eurymedousa, nymph of Selinous, 220

Eurynome, daughter of Asopos, 141
Evadne, daughter of Strymon, 149, 173

Galateia, Nereid, Sicily, 69, 217–18
Gargaphia, spring nymph, Boiotia, 8, 142
Geraistai numphai Genethliai, Attica, 132–33
Geraistiai, Krete, 185
Glauke
    heroine or nymph, Corinth, 148
    nurse of Zeus, Arkadia, 153
Gluphiai, Arkadia, 156, 310

Hagnai Theai, Sicily, 221–22
Hagno, spring nymph, Arkadia, 153–54
halia, a sea-nymph, 305n.62
Halia-Leukothea, Rhodes, 207
Halia Nymphe, Oropos, 143
Halykos, nymphs of, Attica, 137
hamadryads, 52, 70, 73–78, 155, 168, 204,
    310n.129
hamamêlides, protectors of herds, 297n.17
Harpin(n)a, daughter of Asopos, 130–40
Hegetoria, nymph of Rhodes, 207
heleionomoi, nymphs of marshes, 8
Helike
    nymph of Arkadia, 301n.111
    nymph of Chios, 199
    nymph of Krete, 185
Helikon, nymphs of, 303n.39
Helios, daughters of, 21, 27
Herkyn(n)a, heroine or nymph, Boiotia,
    143
Herse, daughter of Kekrops, 6
Hesperethousa, Hesperid, 281n.14
Hesperia, daughter of Kebren, 195
Hesperides, 7, 46, 281–82n.14
Hieromneme, daughter of Simoeis, 195
Himalia, nymph of Rhodes, 206
Himera, nymph of Sicily, 218 fig. 4.18
Himera, nymphs of, Sicily, 37–38, 213,
    218
Hippe, spring or well nymph of Argos, 53
Histiaia, Dionysiac nymph, Euboia,
    305n.63
hudriades, water nymphs, 8, 52
Hyades, 11, 311n.137
Hyele, spring nymph, Italy, 224
Hylleis, nymphs of the, Thera, 188
Hyllis. *See* Syllis, nymph of Sikyon
Hypereia, spring nymph, Pherai, 166

Iasis, Ionid, Elis, 158
iatroi, nymphs of Elis, 310n.125
Idaian nymph, Troad, 194–95

Ide, 87
    nymph of Arkadia, 153
    nymph of Krete, 185–86, 187
    nymph of Troad, 195
Idyia, daughter of Okeanos or Melisseus,
    311n.137
Ilissos, nymphs of, Athens, 13, 19
Ino, heroine or Nereid, 85, 290n.33
Io, heroine or nymph, Argos, 149–50, 191
Ionides, Elis, 158
Iphis, daughter of Peneios, 166
Ismene
    daughter of Asopos, 140, 149
    nymph of Telos, 322n.296
Ismenides, Phlya, 138, 143
Issa, nymph or heroine, Lesbos, 197
Ithake, nymphs of, 10, 24–26

Kabeirides, Lemnos, 177–78, 315n.194
Kabeiro, daughter of Proteus, 177, 206,
    315nn.193–94
Kafizin, nymph of, Cyprus, 257–58
Kaliadne, naiad, 307n.93
Kalliphaeia, Ionid, Elis, 158
Kallirhoë, 8
    daughter of Acheloös, 160
    daughter of Nestos, 173
    daughter of Skamandros, 195
    spring nymph of Athens, 132–33, 146
Kallistephanoi, Olympia, 158
Kallisto, heroine or nymph, Arkadia, 7,
    154–55, 309n.113
Kalybe, nymph of the Troad, 22, 195
Kalypso, daughter of Atlas, 10, 16, 21, 27–
    29, 66, 89, 90, 161, 182
Kamarina, daughter of Okeanos, 37, 41,
    216–17
Kapheira, daughter of Okeanos, 206
Karpodoteirai, Nisyra, 316n.205
Karya, nut-tree nymph, 152, 283n.31,
    308n.103
Kasos, nymphs of, 208
Kassotis, nymph of Parnassos, 147
Kastalia, daughter of Acheloös, 98, 147–48,
    306n.81
Kekrops, daughters of, Attica, 4, 6, 97,
    126–27
Kelaino, Pleiad, 308n.100
Kirke, daughter of Helios, 27–28, 81
Kissoëssa, nymphs of, Boiotia, 143
Kithaironides. *See* Sphragitides, Boiotia
Kleide, nymph of Naxos, 181
Kleocharia, naiad, Lakonia, 152
Kleodora, nymph of Parnassos, 147

Kleone, daughter of Asopos, 140
Klonia, nymph of Euboia, 142
Knidos, nymphs of, 208
Kombe, daughter of Asopos. *See also*
    Chalkis, daughter of Asopos
Korkyra, daughter of Asopos, 139–40, 161
Koronis
    Dodonid, Epeiros, 161
    nymph of Naxos, 181
Korykia, nymph of Parnassos, 147
Korykian nymphs, daughters of Pleistos,
    12, 147, 183–84, 295n.92, 286n.89
Korykos, nymph of, Ionia, 195
Korythaleia, nurse of Apollo, 87
kourades patrôoi, 171
kourai hagnai, daughters of Cheiron, 164
Kraneia, cornel nymph, 283n.31
Krenaia, spring nymph, Egypt, 192
krênaiai, spring nymphs, 8, 290n.32
Kreousa, daughter of Ge, 41, 164
Kupara, nymph of Sicily, 220
kuriai, nymphs of Thrace, 176–77
Kyane, spring nymph, Syracuse, 213, 214–
    15
Kyaneë, daughter of Maiandros, 203,
    320n.259
Kykaïs, nymph of Telos, 322n.296
Kyllene, mountain nymph, Arkadia, 154–
    55
Kynosoura, nymph of Krete, 185, 187
Kyrene, heroine or nymph, Thessaly and
    Libya, 41, 70, 85, 164–65, 189–90,
    318n.238
Kyrtones, nymphs of, Boiotia, 143

Lampetië, daughter of Helios, 21
Laodike. *See* Teledike, nymph of Argos
Larissa, heroine or nymph of Argos,
    Thessaly, 165
Leibethrian nymphs, Boiotia, 138–39, 250,
    303n.38
leimônias numphê, Bithynia, 54, 196
Leiriope, nymph of the lily, 11, 147
Lelegian nymphs, Ionia, 204
Lerna
    eponymous nymph, 150
    nymph of Aigina, 145
Leukas, eponymous nymph, 160–61
Leukothea, 143, 285n.74. *See also* Halia-
    Leukothea, Rhodes
Leukotheai, Lakonia, 35
Libysatides, nymphs of Libya, 245n.319
Libystides. *See* Libysatides, nymphs of
    Libya

Libya, eponymous heroine or nymph, 191
Lilaia, daughter of Kephisos, Phokis, 147
limnades, lake or marsh nymphs, 8
limnaiai, lake or marsh nymphs, 8
Lokria, spring nymph, Lokroi Epizephyroi,
    252
Lousiai, Sybaris, 223–24
Lydia, nymphs of a lake, 200
Lykia, daughter of Xanthos, 209

Maia, Pleiad, 7, 26, 154, 308n.100
Mainas, Dionysiac nymph, 95
Makris, daughter of Aristaios or Kronos,
    144, 161, 294n.91, 311n.135. *See also*
    Euboia
Makrobioi, Rhodes, 207
Maliad nymphs, Thessaly, 168
Malis, nymph of Kios, 67
Medma, spring nymph of Sicily, 222
Megara, nymphs of the gates at, 146
Meilichiai, Astypalaia, 208
Melanippe, nymph of Boiotia, 166
Melantheia, daughter of Alpheios, 145
Melia, daughter of Okeanos, 40–41, 142,
    149
meliai, ash tree nymphs, 11, 29, 283n.31
Meliai, nymphs of Krete, 186
Melian nymph, Thessaly, 164
Meliboia, daughter of Okeanos, 154
Melissa, bee nymph of Peloponnese, 86, 88
melissai, bee nymphs of Peloponnese,
    86–87
melissonomoi, bee nymphs of Euboia, 85
Melite
    daughter of Aigaios, 161
    daughter of Erasinos, 308n.96
Melos, nymphs of, 55
Memphis, daughter of Nile, Egypt, 191
Mendeïs, nymph of Chalkidike, 170
Menippe, daughter of Peneios, 122, 165
Merope, Pleiad, 152
Messana, nymph of Sicily, 219
Methuse, Dionysiac nymph, 95
Metope, daughter of Ladon or Stymphalis,
    39, 139, 156, 326n.355
Minoë, nymphs of, Delos, 183
Minthe, mountain nymph, Triphylia, 159
Moira, daughter of Erasinos, 308n.96
Moria, oleaster nymph, 283n.31
Muchiai, Naxos, 182
Mykalessides, Ionia, 201
Mykene, daughter of Inachos, 149
Myrtoëssa, nymph of Arkadia, 153
Mytilene, eponymous nymph, 197

naiad(s), unnamed, 4, 8, 37, 42–43, 50, 51,
    59–60, 93. *See also* Neides, helpers of
    Perseus
  Ithake, of, 24, 25
  Satnioeis, of, 22
  Tmolos, of, 22
Naiousa, nymph of Halikarnassos, 207
Naïs
  Dionysiac nymph, 296n.14
  nymph of Lakonia, 152
  nymph of Sicily, 292n.67, 320n.258
Neda, nymph of Arkadia, 8, 153–54
Neides, helpers of Perseus, 151
Nemea, daughter of Asopos, 139–40, 150–
    51
neôterai, Ephesos, 321n.280
Nereids, 7, 34, 54. *See also* Psamathe,
    Thetis
Nikaia, eponymous nymph, Bithynia, 123,
    196
Nike-Terina. *See* Terina
Nilo, daughter of Nile, Egypt, 192–93
Nitrodes, Ischia, 224
Nomia, nymph of Arkadia, 155–56
numphai theai, Mykonos or Delos, 183
Nusai, Dionysiac nymphs, 92–94, 260
Nycheia, nymph of Kios, 67
Nymphe
  nymph or goddess, Athens, 97, 148
  nymph or goddess, Paestum, 115–17
Nynphaia, Dionysiac nymph, 296n.14
Nysa, Dionysiac nymph, 57–58, 85, 94,
    172–73, 193, 267, 269

Oiagrides, Thrace, 174
Oinoë
  daughter of Asopos, 140–41
  nymph of Arkadia, 153, 155, 309n.155
Oinoie, naiad, northern Aegean, 54
Oinone, heroine or nymph of Troad, 11, 82
Oite, nymphs of, Thessaly, 168
Okeanids, 7, 173, 286n.89
  nursing function, 30, 98
  Persephone and, 156, 213
Okyr(r)hoë, 8
  daughter of Imbrasos, 201
  nymph of Mysia, 321n.277
ompniai, Athens, 131
oreades, mountain nymphs, 9
Oreiades
  nymph of Egypt, 192
  nymphs of Ossa, 238
oreinomoi, daughters of Symaithos, 217
oressigonoi, mountain nymphs, 9

orestiades, mountain nymphs, 9
Ornia, daughter of Asopos, 140
Orseïs. *See* Othreïs, nymph of Othrys,
    Thessaly
Orsinoë, nymph of Arkadia, 309n.115
Othreïs, nymph of Othrys, Thessaly, 166

Paides, Akrai, 221–22
pais, synonym for *numphê*, 145
Pallene, nymph of Chalkidike, 170
Pandrosos, daughter of Kekrops, 6
Panope, naiad, Halikarnassos, 207
Pareia, nymph of Krete, 181
parthenoi, synonym for *numphai*, 35
Parthenoi of Eleon, nymphs of goddesses,
    Boiotia, 138
patrôoi. See kourades patrôoi
Pegaia, Ionid, Elis, 158
pêgaiai korai, nymphs of Strymon, 173
Peirene, daughter of Asopos, 8, 140, 148
Peirethoi, Cyprus, 210
Pelasgiades, name of Danaids, 53
Peleiades. *See* Pleiades, daughters of Atlas
Peliades, Thessaly, 164
Pelorias. *See* Peloris, nymph of Sicily
Peloris, nymph of Sicily, 219
Periboia, naiad, 308n.101
Periklymene, naiad, Halikarnassos, 207
perimêlides, protectors of herds, 297n.17
Perse, daughter of Okeanos, 28
petraiai, Argos, 43
Phaëthousa, daughter of Helios, 21
Phaio, Dodonid, Epeiros, 161
Phaisyle, Dodonid, Epeiros, 161
Phigalia, dryad, Arkadia, 309n.108
Philia, nymph of Naxos, 181
Phil(l)yra
  daughter of Asopos, 311n.142
  daughter of Okeanos, 164
Phoibe, hamadryad, 307n.93
Phrixa, nymph of Arkadia, 153
Physadeia, spring nymph of Argos, 53
Pitane, eponymous nymph, Aiolis, 197
Pitys, nymph of Arkadia, 96, 155
Plataia, daughter of Asopos, 140–42
Pleiades, daughters of Atlas, 7, 11, 151–52,
    286n.89, 308n.100, 310n.128
Polyxo
  Dodonid, Epeiros, 161
  naiad, 307n.93
potamêides, river nymphs, 8
Praxidikai of Haliartia, nymphs or
    goddesses, Boiotia, 138
Praxidike, nymph of Lykia, 209

Praxithea, daughter of Kephisos, Attica, 126
presbugenês, naiad, Erythrai, 199
presbuterai, Ephesos, 321n.280
Pronoë
 daughter of Asopos, 141
 naiad, Lykia, 204–5
 nymph of Oite, Thessaly, 313n.161
 nymph of Paphlagonia, 58
Proselenides, Arkadia, 154
Prosymna, nymph of Argos, 150
Prousa, nymphs of, 196
Psamathe, Nereid, 71, 72, 144
Ptelea, elm nymph, 283n.31
pteleades, elm nymphs, 11
Pterides, fern nymphs, 11, 283n.31
Ptoïdes, nymphs of Ptoion, Boiotia,
 304n.57
Pyrrha, eponymous nymph, Lesbos, 197
Pyrrhakidai, nymphs of the, Delos, 183
Pythiades, Pythia Therma, 196–97

Rhapso, nymph or goddess, Athens, 132–33
Rhene, nymph of Arkadia or Samos, 178,
 315n.196
Rhodope, daughter of Strymon, 173
Rhodos, nymph of the rose or Rhodes, 11,
 207

Salamis, daughter of Asopos, 140–41, 145
Salmakis, spring nymph of Lykia, 8, 69
Samia, daughter of Maiandros, 123, 200, 201
Satyra, nymph of Taras, 224
Segeste, heroine or nymph, Sicily, 221
Sinope, daughter of Asopos, 123, 140–41,
 304n.50
Sithnides, Megara, 146
Sparte, daughter of Eurotas, 152
Sphragitides, Boiotia, 19–20, 139, 141, 229
Sterope, Pleiad, 308n.100
Stilbe, daughter of Peneios, 164
Strymo, daughter of Skamandros, 195
Styx, daughter of Okeanos, 156
Syke, nymph of the fig tree, 283n.31
Syllis, nymph of Sikyon, 307n.87
Synallasis, Ionid, Elis, 158
Syrinx, daughter of Ladon, 11, 96, 155–56

Tanagra, daughter of Asopos, 140–41
Taygete, Pleiad, 150–51, 308n.100
Telandros (Lykia), nymphs of, 209
"Telchinian nymphs," Rhodes, 206
Teledike, nymph of Argos, 149
Telonnesos, nymph of Telos, 322n.296
Tereine, daughter of Strymon, 314n.178
Terina, 224
Thaleia
 Dionysiac nymph, 95
 nymph of Sicily, 220–21
Theai Paides, nymphs or goddesses, Sicily,
 221–22
Thebe, daughter of Asopos, 39, 139–41,
 304n.53
Theisoa, eponymous nymph, Arkadia,
 153
Thelpousa, daughter of Ladon, 156
Thespeia, daughter of Asopos, 140–41
Thetis, Nereid, 7, 36, 172–73
 Peleus and, 23, 71–73, 89, 164, 260,
 290n.39
Thisbe, nymph of Boiotia, 143
Thoösa, daughter of Phorkys, 31
Thouria, spring nymph, Italy, 223
Thourides, Macedonia, 169
Thraike, daughter of Okeanos, 173
Thrake, Titanid, 173
Thriai, nymphs of Parnassos, 12
Thronia, naiad, Lokris, 174
Thynian nymph, Bithynia, 75, 196
Tiasa, daughter of Eurotas, 152
Tilphossa, spring nymph, Boiotia, 143
Tithorea, tree nymph, Phokis, 147
Torrhebia, nymph of Lydia, 200
Tragasia, heroine or nymph, Lykia, 210
Trageatides, Lykia, 210, 323n.311
tree nymphs, 11, 64, 196, 207–8, 292n.61.
 See also dryads; hamadryads; *meliai*, ash
 tree nymphs
 coeval with tree, 33, 73–78
 Hesperids as, 7
 Peloponnese, in, 152, 155
Trikka, daughter of Peneios, 165–66
Tritonian nymphs, Libya, 319n.247
Tritonides, Boiotia, 113–14

GENERAL INDEX

Note: Ancient authors and works are indexed only when they are directly quoted or when they are the subject of the discussion.

Amyklas, 152
Amynos, 112
Anacreon, 36, 200
Anacreontea, 35
Anaktorion, 160–61
Anatolia. *See* Asia Minor
Anchialos, 174–75
Anchises. *See* Aphrodite, Anchises and
Andromache, 23
Andros, 184
aniconic images, 113, 254
Anna, 222
Antinoë, 5
Antioch, 211, 135
Antiphilus of Byzantium, 55
Anyte of Tegea, 49–50
Apatouria, 171
Apheidas. *See* Aphidamas
Aphidamas, 74, 155
Aphrodite, 9–10, 34, 80, 130, 157–59, 238
  and Anchises, 9, 31–4, 81–84, 105
  Euploia, 208
  and female life cycle, 105, 106, 119–20
  Ide, Mount, 193–94
  Kypris, 40, 67
  Ourania, 310n.127
  Pandemos, 300n.62
Apollo, 17, 147, 152, 205, 209, 211, 222, 225
  Bassitas, 157, 310n.121
  birth of, 182–83
  childcare and, 30, 107
  Dionysodotos, 138
  herding and, 73, 78, 96
  Hermes, relationship to, 12, 154
  Hersos, 243
  Hypakraios, 127, 227
  Ionian god, as, 158, 182
  Ismenios, 142
  Karneios, 188, 190, 323n.302
  Loxias, 42
  as mantic god, 11, 18–19
  Nomios, 85, 229
  Nymphagetes, 96, 109, 137, 170–71, 190, 201, 319n.243
  nymphs, cult relations with, 85–86, 96–98
  nymphs, sexual relations with, 40, 157, 160, 165, 168, 197
  Ptoös, 142
  Pythios, 28, 132–33, 137, 170
  Sminthios, 195
Apollodorus of Athens, 122
Apollonia (Illyria), 12, 162–63

Apollonius of Rhodes, 52–53, 66–67
Apollonius of Tyana, 14, 283n.45
Aquae Calidae, 174–75
archaic period, 12–13, 33–34, 39, 93, 97, 123, 232–33
  iconography in, 259–64
Archedamos, 14–16, 18–19, 134, 177, 243, 244 fig. 5.9
Ares, 173, 291n.44
Argolis, 6, 52–53, 149–51
Argonauts, 66–68, 164, 189, 190, 196
Argos, hero, 149
Ariadne, 93, 96
Aristaios, 84–87, 144, 183–84, 188, 294nn.87, 91
Aristokleia, 111, 143
Aristophanes, 45–46
Aristotle, 169, 184
Arkadia, 7, 49, 75, 97–98, 152–57
Arkas, 74, 78, 155, 157
Arkteia, 5, 100, 297n.29
Arsinoë Philadelphos, 125, 211, 257–58
Arta. *See* Ambrakia
Artemidorus, 322n.288
Artemis, 110, 154–55, 187, 201, 209, 213–14
  Agrotera, 128
  Alpheiousa, 111, 157, 214
  Amarynthia, 144
  bath of, 142
  Brauronia, 112, 227
  chorus of, 5, 53, 21, 27, 53, 65, 90, 107, 109, 157–58
  Daphnia, 157
  Elaphia, 157
  Eukleia, 299n.58
  and female life cycle, 100, 107–11, 112
  Karyatis, 152, 158
  Lochia, 132–34
  Mounychia, 134
  Orthosia, 171
  Selasphoros, 138
Asia Minor, 23, 82, 177, 193–210
Asklepios, 17, 196–98, 205, 229
  absorbs cult of nymphs, 129–30, 188
Asopos river, 38–40, 44, 113
  Boiotian or Peloponnesian, 139–41, 148
  Thessalian, 145, 167
assisting gods, 125, 175–77, 199, 210, 258, 264
Astakides, 196
Astakos, 196
Astarte. *See* Ishtar
astragaloi, 11, 101, 167, 235, 237 fig. 5.4

cave sanctuaries (*continued*)
  Oisyme, 173, 239
  Ossa, Mount, 238–39
  Paphlagonia (Acherusian), 58–59,
    287n.114
  Paros, 181
  Pentelikon, Mount, 246
  Pharsalos, 16–19, 238, 257
  Phyle (Lychnospilia), 47–48, 245–46
    fig. 5.10
  Pitsa (Saftulis), 97, 149, 232–33 fig. 5.1,
    260–61 fig. 5.18
  Rapedosa gorge, 248
  Rhodes, 207
  Samikon (Anigrid nymphs), 159
  Siphnos, 250–51
  Sybaris, 223–24
  Syracuse, 216
  Vari (Nympholiptou), 14–16, 242–45,
    244 figs. 5.8–9
caves of the nymphs, viii, 9, 14–20, 155
  double entrance, 24, 59
  and Homer, 24–25, 123–4
  in literature, 56–60
  models of, 197–98 fig. 4.12, 252 fig. 5.13
  sexual relations in, 32, 92
centaurs, 91, 171–72, 164
Chalkidike peninsula, 169–70
Charites, 7–8. *See also* attendants of deities
  cults of, 131, 138, 158, 179, 199, 208, 243
  iconography of, 174–75, 176 fig. 4.10,
    206, 259–63
chastity, 74, 80, 196
  of Artemisian nymphs, 107–10
  of Dionysiac nymphs, 94, 96
  of wives, 89, 90, 181
Cheiron, 17, 85, 164–67, 187
childbirth, 5, 43, 131–34, 183, 238, 289n.18
childcare. *See* nurses, nymphs as
children, 63, 70, 101–7, 114, 117–20, 191–
    93
Chios, 199
choruses, 46, 100, 107–10, 143. *See also*
    Artemis, chorus of; Persephone,
    chorus of
  in art, 148–49, 161, 233, 237 fig. 5.5,
    259–64
  cult organization as, 5, 6, 91, 96–98, 137
  dolls and, 106–7
  mythic, 34, 52, 199, 157
  in ritual, 145, 158, 182
Christianity, viii, 197, 231, 269–70,
    287n.111
  Orthodox, 62–65, 73, 77–78, 88–90

Chryse, 45, 179
Chrysogonos of Kos, 18
cicada, 10, 144, 246
cities, personification as nymphs, 41, 44,
    124. *See also* coins, nymphs on
  Kyrene, 188–89
  Lesbos, 197
  in lyric poetry, 37–41
  Phokis, 147
  Sicily, 216, 218–19, 221–22
  Thessaly, 165–67
civic functions of nymphs, 5–7, 171
classical period, 41, 46, 95, 112, 125, 177
  cave use in, 227
  concept of nymphaion in, 251
coins, nymphs on, 39, 95, 124, 227, 251
  Arkadia, 154–55
  Epeiros, 160–63
  Italy, 223–24
  Kyrene, 189
  Mytilene, 197
  Potidaia, 170
  Pythia Therma, 320n.272
  Rhodes, 207
  Sicily, 214–19, 221, 254
  Skamandreia, 195
  Thessaly, 124, 165–67, 212
  Thrace, 171–72, 174–75
colonization, role of nymphs in, 4, 39, 91,
    123–24, 241
  Aegean islands, 145, 181, 184, 188
  Africa, 188–91
  Asia Minor, 197, 205–6
  Magna Graecia and Sicily, 99, 211–13,
    220–21
  northern Aegean, 168–69, 170–72, 174
  northwest Greece, 160–62
comedy, Attic, 13, 45–49
consultation myth, 84, 294n.85, 308n.99
contest of gods, 149, 150, 217, 307n.88
continuity, ancient to modern, ix, 65, 77–
    78, 81, 87–90, 197, 209, 269, 287n.1
Corinna, 39–41
Corinth, 148–49. *See also* colonization, role
    of nymphs in, northwest Greece
Cyclades, 179–84
Cypria, 261–62
Cyprus, 16, 211–12

Daidala, Great, 19, 113–14, 141–42
Daktyls, 177, 187
Danaos, 6, 149–50
dance, 24, 62, 71, 90, 95. *See also* choruses
Daphne (Antioch), 211, 270

Daphnis, 19, 52, 69–70, 79–81, 84. 194, 217, 292n.67
Daphnis and Chloë, in Longus, 56–57
Dardanos, 194–95
Dawn. *See* Eos
death narratives, 4, 7, 66, 79–80, 112, 118
Deloptes. *See* Bendis
Delos, 182–83
Delphi, 11, 147–48, 174
    connection desired with, 148, 184
    oracles of, 19, 137–38
demes, Attic. *See* Erchia; Phlya; Phyle; sacrificial calendars
Demeter, 44–45, 66, 128, 129 fig. 4.1, 206, 217, 269
    Erysichthon and, 75–78
    Kore and, 128, 153, 180–81
    Thesmophoros, 199
demons, modern Greek, 62, 64, 73, 88–90, 287n.4
Demos, personified, 131, 302n.21
devotionalism, 52, 125, 134, 197, 199, 201, 257–58, 268–71
    in comedy, 45–48
    definition of, viii
    in Longus' Daphnis and Chloë, 56–57
    nympholepsy and, 14–20, 229
Dimitroula, 76–78
Diodorus Siculus, 57–58
Diomedes
    Greek, 80
    Thracian, 174
Dionysos, 91–96, 128, 158, 190, 206, 243, 268
    Antheios, 138
    Bakchos, 55–56, 93, 192–93, 193
    Bromios, 36, 50, 56
    cave sanctuaries of, 170, 239, 284n.53
    Eleutherios, 267
    Ikarios, 248
    nursed by nymphs, 30, 42, 85–87, 92–94, 96, 143, 144, 181–82
    Orthos, 128
    in poetry, 36, 42, 172, 196
    Thrace, worship in, 172–73
Dioskouroi, 34, 178, 199, 207. *See also* Helen
divination, 5, 10–20, 74, 86, 199, 235, 246. *See also* astragaloi; Bakis; oracles
Dodone, 98, 161
dolls, 101–7, 105 fig. 3.4, 106 fig. 3.5, 114, 117–20, 119 fig. 3.7, 298n.38
    dedicated in caves, 229, 235, 243
    dedicated in fountain, 51 fig. 1.4, 128

Dorian hexapolis, 205–8
Doros, 50, 149
dream visions, 56, 206, 201
Dresos, 22
drowning, 165, 193
    attributed to nymphs or neraïdes, 49, 66, 70, 76
Dryops, 168
Dumuzi, 82–3, 84

Echelos, 131–34
Echidna, 31
Echinades islands, 160
economic activity and nymphs, 9, 178. *See also* herdsmen
    apiculture, 85–87
    asphalt or bitumen, 162–63, 220
    ceramics, 258
    charcoal-burning, 9, 309n.107
    metallurgy, 171–72, 177–79, 187, 206
    quarrying, 9, 179–81, 183, 193, 239, 256
    silphium production, 189, 319n.239
    timber, 9, 75
    wool production, 146
Eëtion, 23, 54–55
Egypt, ix, 191–93
Ehoeae, 39, 144, 149–51, 154–55, 164, 186, 188
Eileithyia, 132–34, 181–82, 188, 309n.107
Elatos, 74, 155
Eleusis. *See* cave sanctuaries
Elis, 157–59, 214
elite populations, vii, 16, 39, 49, 125, 214, 258–59. *See also* non-elite populations
Elymoi, 221
emasculation, 69, 74, 89
    of Anchises, 83, 294n.83
    of Daphnis, 292n.67
    of Rhoikos, 81, 291n.47
Endymion, 83
Enna, 212–13, 220
Enneakrounos. *See* springs, Kallirhoë
Enops, 22, 194
Eos, 24, 27, 289n.22
    affairs with mortals, 35, 65–66, 82, 160
Epaphos, 191
Epeiros, 160–61
epékoos, "listening one," 175, 210, 258, 315n.189
ephebes, 107, 137, 188, 248
Ephesos, 199
epic poetry, 20–34, 107–10
epigrams, dedicatory, 49–52, 92, 107, 125, 144, 156, 159, 193, 228

Epimenides of Phaistos, 14
Epopeus, 139
Erchia, 135–37, 171
Erechtheus, 126
Erichthonios, 126–27
Erinna, 103
Erinyes, 29, 111
Eros, 36, 40, 56–57, 80, 137, 193
Erysichthon, 75–78, 291n.54, 292n.56
Erythrai, 195, 199
Etesian winds, 184, 317n.221
Euboia, 7, 85, 140–41, 144, 161
Eumaios, 26–27
Eumelus, 123
Euphorion, 55
Euripides, 42–45, 92–93
Euryalos, 22
Eurydike, 84, 87, 195
Eurykleia, 3
Eurypylos, 189
Euthymos, 254
exôtika. See demons, modern Greek
exposure of infants, 9, 42

Fair One of the Mountains, 63
familial cults of nymphs, 91, 171, 183
Fates. *See* Moirai
female genitalia, terms for, 10, 282n.30
female life cycle
   adolescence, 100, 107, 109, 111, 118
   brides, 3, 59, 100, 103–6, 107, 111–20,
     254–55
   marriage, 30, 89–90, 158
   pregnancy, 108, 110, 131, 229
   proteleia, 107, 111–12, 143, 229
fertility, 46, 135, 172
   human and animal, 27, 99, 100, 101, 111,
     113
   of land, 189, 212, 218, 269
Festus, 62–63
Flood, Great, 4, 146, 147, 149, 167, 178,
   207
folk etymologies, 158, 220, 287n.3
folklore
   modern Greek, 61–90
   motifs, 64–65, 71–73, 191, 289n.17
   non-Greek, 64, 289n.18
   traditions, ancient, 121, 155, 194, 269
   types, 65, 72–73, 289n.17
fountains, 26, 51, fig. 1.4, 103. *See also*
   springs
   fountain houses, 124, 127, 129–31, 145–
     46, 148
   models of, 178–79, 251–52 fig. 5.13

Freud, Sigmund, 81
funerary art and literature, 14, 49, 70, 101–
   4, 191–93, 264

Gaia. *See* Ge
Ganymedes, 66, 82, 83, 194
gardens, 10, 34–35, 43, 44, 50, 285n.75
   at caves of the nymphs, 14, 16–18, 58, 229
   of Charites, 46
   of Hesperides, 7
   of Kalypso, 28
   of Okeanos, 46
Ge, 28–29, 85, 180
   cults of, in Attica, 128, 135, 138
   as mother of nymphs, 4, 41, 155, 164
gender roles
   normative, 4, 72, 186–87, 222
   resistance to, 95, 100, 115
   reversal of, 4, 9, 18–19, 66–72, 83–84,
     90, 157, 189, 291n.41
   socialization to, 100–107, 113–14, 120,
     298n.34
genealogies, mythic, 4–5, 37–39, 52, 78,
    121–23, 191. *See also* Ehoeae; pathetic
    genealogies
   Arkadian, 154
   Asopid, 39–41, 139–41
   Athenian, 196
   express relationships among peoples, 39,
    122–23, 139–40, 144, 173
   Inachid, 149
   Kabeirid, 177–78
   Lakonian, 151–52
   Lydian, 200
   Lykian, 209
   manipulation of, 123, 152, 170, 174
   Pleiades in, 7, 151–52, 154
   Rhodian, 207
   Trojan, 21–23, 194–95
giants, 29, 92, 173
Gilgamesh epic, 80
Glaukos. *See also* rivers
   Lykian hero, 55, 209
   at Marathon, 137
   sea-god, 67, 317n.214
goddesses. *See also* under individual entries
   demotion to nymphs, 7, 187, 221
   sexual relations with mortals, 28, 35, 65,
    66, 81–84, 289n.19
gods. *See also* under individual entries
   familial relations with nymphs, ix, 98–100
   sexual relations with mortal women, 65
   sexual relations with nymphs, ix, 91, 96–
    100, 152

Graces. *See* Charites
Great Gods (Samothrace), 178

Hades, 159, 214–15
healing by nymphs, 5, 86. *See also* skin
    diseases
    Aegean islands, 178, 181, 188
    Asia Minor, 82, 196–97, 200
    Peloponnese, 5, 158–59
    Thrace, 174–77
    western colonies, 217, 224–25
Hecataeus, 122
Hekate, 132, 180, 202, 285n.76, 309n.107
Helen, 21, 34, 66, 82, 111, 199
Helios, 24, 28, 207
Hellanicus, 122
Hellen, 166
Hellenistic period, 11, 123, 160
    literature in, vii, 49–56, 69, 122
    religious developments in, 64, 94–95,
        110, 174, 176–78, 251, 256
Hellenization, 200, 209–10, 221
Hephaistia, 178
Hephaistos, 93–94, 178, 177, 217, 264
Hera, 8, 90, 92, 175, 200
    at Argos, 115, 149, 150
    and female life cycle, 100, 112–17, 120
    Kithaironia, 19, 141
    Nympheuomene, 112, 114
    Parthenos, 113
    Teleia, 113, 114
Herakleia
    Elis, 158
    Paphlagonia, 59
Herakles, 44, 66–68, 85, 137, 168, 199, 260
    relations with nymphs, 17, 161, 196,
        320n.272
    and thermal springs, 200, 213, 214, 218
herdsmen, 6, 12, 26–27, 49, 83, 224
    concerns of, 9, 96–98, 135, 146, 190–91,
        254
    relations with nymphs, 22, 78–87, 194–96
    as worshipers, 50, 96, 201, 243, 246
herm, triple, 156, 222, 253–55 figs. 5.14–
    15, 257 fig. 5.17
Hermaphroditos, 49, 69
Hermes, 42, 78–79, 107, 110, 149, 161
    as abductor, 40–41, 140
    birth of, 154, 296n.5
    and Charites, 45, 170–71, 261–2, 267
    and Dionysos, 93–94
    Hills of, 27, 45
    in inscriptions, 17, 130, 133, 135, 202,
        208

Kadmilos, 197
Ktenites, 201
Nomios, 46, 98
    relations with nymphs, 12, 26–27, 32,
        96–98, 109, 297n.17
    on votive reliefs, 99 fig. 3.1, 129 fig. 4.1,
        132–34, 136 fig. 4.5, 180, 208, 259–63
        fig. 5.19, 265 fig. 5.20, 266–67
Hermoupolis, 191–93
Herodes Atticus, Odeion of, 112, 127
Herodotus, 121–22
heroic cult, 19, 55, 116, 141, 209, 227,
    231–32
    and tombs, 4–7, 142, 154, 173, 195
heroines, 4–7, 97, 70, 143
Heroines of Libya, 190–91
heroization, 66, 68, 70, 80, 254
Hesiod, 9, 28–31, 54–55
Hippodameia, 6
Hippolyte, 72, 73
Hippolytos, 80, 137, 299n.47
Homer, 4, 54–55, 60
    nymphs in, 20–28, 71–72, 123–24, 172–
        73
Homeric *Hymns*, 31–34, 73, 81–84
honey, 14, 86, 116, 185–86. *See also* bees
Horai, 7–8, 85, 128, 193, 199, 201,
    302n.18
    in art, 259–63
hunting, 9, 92, 189, 229, 299n.47
Hyakinthos, 152
hybrid figures (goddess/heroine/nymph),
    6–7, 143, 150, 154–55, 187, 221
    daughters of kings as, 6–7, 53, 148, 165,
        197, 301n.9
Hydra, 150
Hydroussa. *See* Keos
Hygieia, 17
Hylas, 14, 19, 49, 52, 66–68, 195
Hyllos
    Illyria, 161
    Ionia, 200
Hymnos, 196
Hymns, 36, 268–70. *See also* Homeric
    Hymns
hypogaeum, Paestum, 115–17, 225
Hypseus, 189
Hyrieus, 142, 144

Ialysos, 207
Iapetos, 28
Iasile, 133–34
Iasion, 65, 66
Ibycus, 35

lions, 183–84, 189, 243–44, 248
  on fountain spouts, 165–66, 190, 218,
    251–52
Lipari, 255
locus amoenus, 9–10, 25, 27, 49
logographers, 52, 121–22, 285n.88
Lokris, 55, 174
Lokroi Epizephyroi, 117–20, 251–57
Longus, 56–58
loutrophoros, 112, 228–29, 243, 245, 248
Lydia, 22, 200
Lykaon, 154
Lykia, ix, 55, 209–10
Lykoreia, 147
Lykos, 7, 44, 142
Lykosoura, 155
Lykourgos, 36, 93, 172–73

Macedonia, 169–70
madness, 13, 83, 155, 288n.8. *See also*
    nympholepsy
  Dionysiac, 92, 95
  medical opinions of, 16, 62
maenads, 42, 94–96
magic, 28, 73, 96, 131, 151, 187
Magna Graecia, 117–20
Mantineia, 5
Marathon, 97, 100, 127, 137, 303n.31
Mariandynoi, 68
masks, 99–100, 222, 230, 232, 252
Medeia, 53, 148, 161, 178
Medma, 222
Megalopolis, 153–54
Megara, 124, 145–47
Megaros, 146
Melampous, 115
Melesagoras of Eleusis, 13
melissa, meanings of, 86–87, 181, 295n.96
Melisseus. *See* Melissos
Melissos, 181, 184, 185
Melisto, 101–2 fig. 3.2
Memnon, 55
Men, moon god, 135
Menander, 47–49
Menoitios, 144
Messana, 219
Messenia, 152–53
Metamorphosis, 28. *See also* transformation
    into nymph
  Aisakos, 195
  Akis, 217
  Ambrosia, 314n.176
  Daphne, 157
  Daphnis, 292n.67

Echo, 69, 155–56
Minthe, 159
Niobe, 23–24
Pitys, 155–56
Selemnos, 159–60
Syrinx, 155–56
Midas, 92
midday, hour of epiphany, 9–10, 71, 75,
    88, 190
Mieza. *See* Naoussa
Miletos, 201–2, 203
Minoan religion, 185, 187, 239
Minos, 30, 181
Minyas, daughters of, 7, 94
misanthropy, of herdsmen, 79–80
Mistress of Animals. *See potnia therôn*
models. *See* caves of the nymphs; fountains
Moero of Byzantium, 159
Moirai, 259, 311n.136
Molos, 293n.73
Molpoi, 202
Morgantina, 118, 220
mortality, 4, 29–30, 31, 33, 81, 95. *See also*
    immortality
mother goddesses, 260. *See also* Demeter
  Anatolia (Kybele, Great Mother), 82–83,
    185, 193, 199
  Greece (Meter), 36, 128, 304n.52
  Sicily (Meteres), 221–22
mountains, viii, 8–9, 36, 138
  Aitne 79, 217–18
  Dikte, 185–86
  Gerania, 146
  Helikon, 138–39, 250, 303n.39
  Hymettos, 9. 137, 229, 242
  Ide (Krete), 30, 185–87
  Ide (Troad), 31–34, 45, 81–84, 193–95
  Ithome, 153
  Kerketes, 200–201
  Kithairon, 19–20, 40, 113–14, 138, 141
  Kyllene, 154, 296n.5
  Leibethrion, 138–39
  Lykaion, 153, 155
  Magnesia, 164
  Malea, 152
  Meliteion, 161
  Methydrion, 153
  Minthe, 159
  Neriton, 25
  Oite, 167–68
  Olympos (Asia Minor), 196
  Olympos (Greece), 21, 163, 169
  Ossa, 238–39
  Othrys, 166

mountains (*continued*)
Pangaion, 171–72
Parnassos, 12, 147, 183, 234
Parnes, 9, 40, 47, 245
Pelion, 9, 164
Pentelikon, 9, 246
Ptoion, 304n.57
Sipylos, 23, 199–200, 242
Taygetos, 151
Thourion, 138–39
Tmolos, 22, 200
Muses, 7–8, 52, 75, 85, 158, 199, 250
in art, 259–63
conflated with nymphs, 200, 210, 223–24, 303n.38
Helikonian, 138–39
in Thrace, 169, 173–74
music, 75, 78, 155, 200. *See also* Muses
musical instruments, 12, 106–7, 170
fig. 4.9, 210, 220, 256 fig. 5.16
as dedications, 57, 230, 235
Mykale, promontory, 123, 201, 202
fig. 4.13
Myrina, 119 fig. 3.7, 197, 198 fig. 4.12
"Myrmidonia and Pharaonia," 76–78
Myrsine, 181
Mysia, 195–96
Mysteries, 138, 177–78, 187, 268. *See also*
Demeter, Kore and
Mytilene, 197

Nanas, 122
Naoussa, 169
narcissus, 187, 193, 306n.78
Narkissos, 49, 68–69, 147
Nausikaä, 21, 27, 53, 107, 111
Naxos, 81, 93, 181–82
Neapolis, 173, 224–25
necromancy, 287n.114
neraïdes, viii, 13, 14, 60–90, 250, 269
Nereus, 7, 11, 61
Neritos, 26
New Phaleron, 131–34
Nike, 145, 224
Niobe, daughter of Phoroneus, 149
Niobe, daughter of Tantalus, 23, 199
non-elite populations, viii, 62. *See also* slaves
immigrants, 135
indigenous peoples, 189, 191, 220–21
poor or rural people, 12, 124, 145–46,
201, 243, 259
Nonnus, 196
noon. *See* midday
nudity, 94, 101–7, 117–20, 175–76, 254–55

numphê
etymology of, 281n.1
semantics of, 3, 21, 53, 55–6, 62, 103,
109–10
spelling of, 296n.11
nurses, nymphs as, 5, 7, 30, 33, 42–43, 111.
See also therotrophic myths
Aineias, 33, 193, 294n.84
Apollo, 85, 87, 183
Aristaios, 84–87
Athena, 190
Dionysos, 85–87, 92–94, 172–73, 181–82, 269
Hera, 87, 150
Hermes, 154
Minos, 30
Poseidon, 206, 312n.154
Rhesos, 42, 173
Zeus, 30, 87, 152–54, 161, 185–87, 221.
See also Zeus, birthplace of
Nykteus, 142
Nymphis of Herakleia, 68
nympholepsy, 8, 10, 11–20, 98, 262,
288n.8, 257–8. *See also* Archedamos;
Onesagoras; Pantalkes
mentality of, 16, 18, 134, 177
understood negatively, 62–64, 66–71,
288n.7
nymphs
as ancestors, 4, 38–41, 121–23
called "dear," *philos*, 10, 21, 46, 286n.95
civilizing function of, 84–88
counterparts of, male, 64, 91–93, 186
cult images of nymphs, 51, 178–79, 206, 215,
230, 243, 254. *See also* votive reliefs
as fantasy figures, 89–90
habitations of, 8–11, 23–28, 31–34, 53.
See also caves of the nymphs; trees
as maidservants, 28, 108, 285n.45
mourning, 23, 54–55, 83, 196
as non-Hellenic deities, 178, 187, 210, 212
as nurses. *See* nurses, nymphs as
parentage of, 4, 21, 36, 37, 41, 98, 155, 164
promiscuity of, 4, 32, 34, 92, 94, 95
punishment by, 65, 73–78, 79–84, 90
sexual relations with mortals, 21–23, 65–70, 71–84, 87–90, 158
taxonomy of, 4–11
universalizing interpretations of, 59, 270

oaths, 187, 201
Odysseus, 25–28, 158, 161, 231–32
and Kalypso, 16, 66, 83, 89, 90, 182
Oedipus, 42

Ognyanovo, 175–76
Ogygië, 27
Oiagros, 174
Oichalia, 144
Oinoë, 247
Oinopion, 199
Oite, 167–68
Okeanos, 7, 21, 37, 98, 269
  and Tethys, 28, 30, 98, 149, 156, 191
Olympia, 139, 157–58, 214
Olympian gods, 10, 30, 41, 64, 65, 72
Onesagoras, 6, 18, 20, 257–58
Onoskelis, 63, 288n.10
Opheltios, 22
Opous, 174
oracles, 20, 40, 72, 167, 209, 317n.214
  chresmologues and, 12–13, 20
  Delphic, 139–40, 141, 213–14
  of Dionysos, 172
  of Ge, 147
  of nymphs, 11–13, 162–63
  of Pan, 11, 74, 155
  of Trophonios, 143
  of Zeus, 98, 161
Orestes, 6, 43–44
orgeones, 134–35, 302n.27
Orion, 40, 66, 142
Orpheus, 53, 169, 174
Orphic *Hymn*, 268–70
Ortygia, 213–14
Otrynteus, 22, 200
Ovid, 69, 75–77, 167

Paestum, 115–17
paian, 170–71, 202
Palaikastro, 185, 187
Palikoi, 217, 220–21
Pan, 19, 52, 78, 96–98, 125, 141, 143, 158,
    224. *See also* oracles, of Pan
  Akropolis cave, 6, 97, 126, 127, 129
  Arkadia and, 155–56
  and caves of nymphs, 47–48, 97, 236–38,
    254
  cult predated by nymph cults, 224, 238,
    245, 266
  in inscriptions, 17, 130, 193
  in literature, 34, 42–3, 50, 56–7, 229
  Nomios, 155–56
  Sinoëis, 310n.121
  on votive offerings, 129 fig. 4.1, 130 fig. 4.2,
    180 fig. 4.11, 201, 202 fig. 4.13, 237
    fig. 5.5, 241 fig. 5.6, 265–66 fig. 5.20
Pandion, 126
Pandora, 105

Panolepsy, 98
Pantalkes, 16–19. *See also* cave sanctuaries,
    Pharsalos
Paphlagonia, 58–59
Paraibios, father of, 75, 77, 78, 196
Paris, 11, 44, 55, 82, 194, 262
Parnassos, hero, 147
Paros, 179–81
Parthenius, 79
Parthenon, 127, 131, 258, 265
Parthenos, Thracian goddess, 135, 173. *See
    also* Bendis
passivity, 4, 19, 89
pastoral genre, 49–52, 56–58, 70, 79–80,
    196
pathetic fallacy, 23, 44, 54, 320n.271
pathetic genealogies, 21–23, 53–54, 58, 194
Patroklos, 144
Pausanias, 122, 153, 159
Pedasos, 22, 34
Peiraieus, 131–35
Pelasgos, 122, 154, 165
Peleus, 38, 73, 140, 144
Peloponnese, 7, 115, 149–60
Penelope, 3, 26, 28
Pergamon, 197–98
Persephone, 44–45, 159
  chorus of, 7, 143, 156, 212–13, 214, 220,
    254–55
  female life cycle and, 100, 112, 117–19,
    254–55
Perseus, 149, 151 fig. 4.6, 262
Persian wars, 13, 97, 125
Phaethon, 294n.82
Phaiax, 161
Phaon, 35, 285n.75, 294n.82
Pherai, 166
Phigalia, 153
Philammon, 174
Philoktetes, 45, 168, 179
Phlya, 138
Phokis, 147–48
Phokos, 71, 144
Phoroneus, 149
Phrygia, 135, 193–96
Phyle, 47. *See also* cave sanctuaries, Phyle
    (Lychnospilia)
Pieria, 139, 169
piety (*eusebeia*), 86. *See also* devotionalism
pilgrimage, 18–19, 137, 175, 222, 228–29
Pimpleia, 169
pinakes. *See* votive offerings, terracotta
    plaques; votive offerings, wooden
    panels

Pindar, 37–39, 74, 139–40, 152

plaques. *See* votive offerings, terracotta plaques

Plataia, 133

Plato, 229, 224, 242

pluralities
female, 7–8, 138–39, 190, 221–22, 259–64
male, 177, 186–87, 206–7, 259

Plutarch, 19, 74

polos, 106 fig. 3.5, 147, 215, 219
Caruso cave figurines, worn by, 117, 118 fig. 3.6, 253–54
Delphic karyatid, worn by, 262, 297n.16
Hera and, 113–14

Polyktor, 26

Polymele, 107

Polyphemos, Argonaut, 67

Polyphemos, Kyklops, 31, 52, 92–93, 217–18

polytheism, nature of, 134

Porphyry, 59–60

Poseidon, 137, 150, 206
as adbductor, 40, 41, 91, 140, 144, 145, 152
Amymone and, 6, 53, 115
relations with other nymphs, 31, 144, 148, 166, 173, 174, 198–99, 224

Poseidonia. *See* Paestum

possession. *See* nympholepsy; Panolepsy

potnia therôn, 83, 113–14, 189

Pratinas, 36

Priam, 194–95

priestesses, 109, 111, 112, 115, 187, 200, 222

priests, 130, 153, 154, 175, 187

primordial figures, 126, 174
first inhabitants as, 26, 146, 149, 152, 177–78
kings as, 4, 6, 115, 126, 145, 149, 154, 164, 165, 197, 200
nymphs as, 28, 30, 150, 152, 158, 194–95

Proitos, daughters of, 7, 114–15

prophecy. *See* divination

prosperity, gift of nymphs, 131, 161, 181–82, 208, 210, 218, 220

proteleia. *See* female life cycle

Protesilaus, 23, 55

Proteus, 11, 71

protomes. *See* masks

Prousa, 196

Ptolemaïs, 193

Ptolemies, 94, 125, 193, 258. *See also* Arsinoë Philadelphos

purifications, 113, 115, 153–54, 205

Pyrrhakidai, 183

Pyrrhichos, 152

Pythia, 13, 18

Quintus of Smyrna, 58–59

Rape, 42, 92, 109, 127, 139–41, 143, 173, 196, 293n.73. *See also* abduction
attempted, 84, 87, 155–58

Rhea, 153–54, 182, 185

Rhegion, 222

Rhesos, 42, 173–74

Rhodes, 143, 206–7

Rhoikos, 4, 19, 73–75, 77

Rhous, 146

river gods, 30, 41, 99, 142, 153, 194–95, 254–55 fig. 5.15. *See also* Acheloös
relations with nymphs, 4, 8, 98–100, 173, 211, 218

rivers, 98–99, 148, 214. *See also* Acheloös; Asopos, river
Achelesios. *See* rivers, Acheloios
Acheloios, 24, 199
Aigaios, 161
Aisepos, 55
Alpheios, 99, 156–58, 213–14, 310n.126
Amnisos, 53, 187–88
Anapos, 215
Anigros, 159
Aoös, 162
Asterion, 150
Axios, 170
Bolinaios, 160
Dirke, 44
Erasinos, 208n.96, 326n.355
Eridanos, 294n.85, 308n.99
Eurotas, 152
Glaukos, 209
Gortys. *See* rivers, Lousios
Granikos, 194–95
Hebros, 175
Hipparis, 216
Hyllos, 200
Hypsas, 220
Ilissos, 10, 19, 103, 127–28, 169
Imbrasos, 200–1
Inachos, 114–15, 149–50
Inopos (Delos), 208
Inopos (Knidos), 182–83
Ismenos, 44
Kaikos, 197
Kebren, 82
Kephisos (Athens), 126, 131–34

Kephisos (Phokis), 142, 143, 147
Krimisos, 221
Kytherios, 158
Ladon (Arkadia/Elis), 156
Ladon (Boiotia), 139. *See also* rivers,
    Ismenos
Lousias, 223
Lousios, 153
Lymax, 153
Maiandros, 123, 200, 201, 203
Metauros, 222
Neda, 153–54
Nile, 44, 191–93
Nymphaios, 58
Oanos, 216
Oiagros, 315n.182
Parthenios. *See* rivers, Imbrasos
Peneios, 122, 157, 163, 165–66, 188
Permessos, 138, 143
Pleistos, 147
Sangarios, 195
Selemnos, 159
Selinous, 220
Sibros, 209
Simoeis, 194–95
Skamandros, 194–95
Spercheios, 45, 167–68
Strymon, 149, 172–73
Stymphalis, 39
Styx, 156
Sybaris, 223
Symaithos, 217
Triton, Africa, 57
Triton, Boiotia, 113
Xanthos, 209
Roman Imperial period, cults of, ix, 62,
    121, 174–77, 210, 224–25
rupestral inscriptions, 143, 145, 188, 190,
    208, 216, 221–22, 228, 251
    Attica, 14, 131, 246

sacred laws, 170–71, 201–2, 209, 248. *See
    also* sacrificial calendars
of springs, 137–38, 183, 197, 205, 214, 243
Sacred Way
    Eleusis, 248
    Miletos, 201–2
sacrifices to the nymphs, 26–27, 43–44,
    131–34, 170, 183, 188, 205. *See also
    proteleia*
    at cave sanctuaries, 17, 19, 159, 228–30, 258
    value of, 25, 233–34
sacrificial calendars, 6, 97, 137, 201, 205,
    303n.31

Saladinovo. *See* Ognyanovo
Samos, 113, 200–210
Samothrace, 7, 178
Saon, 178
Sappho, 34–35
Sarpedon, 209
Satnios, 22, 34
satyr plays, 43, 92–93, 95, 285n.77, 306n.70
satyrs. *See* silens and satyrs
Seasons. *See* Horai
secularization, 125, 169, 251, 264
Segeste, 221
Seirios, 184, 317n.221
Selene, 35
Selinous, 220
Semonides, 96
serpents. *See* snakes
sexuality, 3, 10, 18, 55, 78, 155
    female, 35, 63, 65, 88–90
    frustrated, 69, 91–95, 96, 157, 171–72, 179
shapeshifting, 71–73, 291n.43
shells, 175, 192, 219, 225, 235, 252
sibyls, 12, 13, 18–19, 62, 195
Sicily, 79–81, 211–22
signet rings, 20, 235
Sikels, 220–21
Sikyon, 139, 149, 229, 232. *See also* cave
    sanctuaries, Pitsa (Saftulis)
Silenos, 152, 163, 164, 256, 257 fig. 5.17
silens and satyrs, 6, 64, 91–96, 111, 149–50,
    171–72, 218. *See also* satyr plays
    captured, 92, 163
Sisyphos, 140
skin diseases, 115, 159
slaves, 115, 135, 302n.17
snakes, 31, 141, 150, 168, 179, 221
Sokrates, 10, 13, 19, 128, 169
Sophocles, 41–42, 45, 92
sorcery. *See* magic
Sostratos, mother of, 47, 228–29, 233
Sparta, 151–52
Sporades, 208
springs, viii, 8, 67–68, 69. *See also*
    fountains; springs, thermal
    Arethousa, Ithake, 284n.65
    Halykos, 137–38
    Hippokrene, 138–39
    of Ithake, 24–26
    Kallirhoë, 97, 112, 126–27
    Kanathos, 115
    Kissoëssa, 111
    Klepsydra, Athens, 97
    Klepsydra, Messene, 153
    krênai, built springs, 10, 26

springs (*continued*)
    Krene Minoë, 183
    Kyra, 189–90
    of Lerna, 6, 150
    pêgai, natural springs, 10
    Trikrena, 154
springs, thermal
    at Aitne, 217
    at Apollonia, 162–63
    Cerchiara, 223
    at Himera, 37–38, 213
    at Ischia, 224
    Lydian, 200
    Pythia Therma, 196–97
    at Segeste, 221
    Thrace, in, 174–75
star myths, 184, 185
state sponsorship of cult, 6, 19, 124, 202,
    215, 228, 304
Stesichorus, 49, 79
Strabo, 122
structuralism, 65, 87
Stymphalis, 39
surgical instruments, 177, 246
swan maiden type, 72–73, 89, 291n.41
swan riders, 216 fig. 4.17
Sybaris, 116, 223–24
symmetry, male-female. 177–78, 187, 199
syncretism, 125, 174, 187–88, 191–93, 209–
    12
Syria. *See* Antioch

taboos, 83
    boasting, 74–75, 84
    sexual infidelity, 74–75, 79–81
    tree-cutting, 33, 75–78
Tammuz, 82–83
Tanagra, 140–41, 243
Taras, 224
Tegea, 153, 155–56
Teiresias, 11, 96, 139
Telamon, 38, 140, 144
Telchines, 177, 206–7
Telegonia, 284n.64
Telemachos, donor, 130, 302n.19
temples, 110
Teneros, 41, 142
Terina, 224
Termiles. *See* Tremiles
terra-cottas. *See* votive offerings, terracotta
    figurines
territorial claims, 4, 34, 139–40, 146, 211.
    See also genealogies, mythic,
    manipulation of

Tethys. *See* Okeanos
Teukros, 195
Thamyris, 75, 79, 174
Thasos, 170–71, 262
Thebes, 6–7, 44, 142–43, 144
Thebes at Mykale, 201
Themis, 8, 21, 131, 182, 258
Theocritus, 49, 52, 67–68, 79–80
Theodoridas, 219
Theognis, 20
Thera, 14, 188, 189, 191
Thermai Himereiai, 218
therotrophic myths, 185–87
Thesmophoria, 181
Thessaly, 16–19, 70, 78, 85, 163–68, 166,
    292n.57
    coins of, 124, 212
thiasos. *See* choruses
Thourioi. *See* Sybaris
Thourion, 169
Thrace, 135, 179–81
    Aegean, 171–74
    migrations from, 139, 169–70
    Pontic, 174–77
Thrinakia, 24, 213
Thronion, 174
Timaeus, 79–81
Titans, 7, 152. *See also* Atlas; Okeanos
Tithonos, 66, 82, 83
Tityos, 65
Torrhebos, 200
tragedy, Attic, 41–45, 160
transformation into nymph
    Arethousa, Euboia, 144
    Bolina, 160
    Byblis, 204, 290n.33
    Dryope, 14, 70–71, 165, 168
    Ino, 290n.33
    Isidora, 192–93
    Kyrene, 70
trees, 6, 33, 73–78, 155
    ash, 11, 29, 142
    elm, 11, 23
    fir, 83, 155
    laurel, 16, 157, 211
    lime, 312n.144
    lotus, 168
    nut, 11, 152
    oak, 10, 73, 76, 147, 153, 161, 292n.67
    olive, 24, 158
    plane, 10, 128
    poplar, 10, 26, 27, 75, 168
Tremiles, 209
Trikka, 165–66

Trikrena, 154
Triopion, 207
Triphylia, 159
tripods, 231–32
Tritopator(es), 111, 183
Troad, 21–23, 81–82, 193–95
Trojan allies, 21–23, 205, 209
Trophonios, 143
Tychios, 144
Tyndareos, 152
tyrants, 124, 148
   Dionysius II, 215
   Hipparchos, 20
   Peisistratos, 13
   Theagenes, 145–46

vase painting, 35, 151 fig. 4.6
   Asopids in, 123, 141–42, 145, 150
   black figure vases, 32, 94–95, 111, 124,
      164, 185, 260–62, 296n.9
   François vase, 91, 94, 260, 307n.95,
      320n.77
   narrative context in, 93, 94–96
   red figure vases, 95–96, 296n.15
vegetation, 8, 9–11, 78, 129, 158, 162–63.
   See also gardens of the nymphs
virginity, 3, 65, 88, 107–8, 115, 213
votive offerings, 101–3, 227–28, 251, 254
   amateur work, 51, 227–28, 250, 258, 259
   perishable, 124, 227–28, 230, 259
   terracotta figurines, 230–31, 235, 237
      fig. 5.5, 243, 253–56. *See also* dolls
   terracotta plaques, 220, 232, 235, 238,
      240–44, figs. 5.6–7
   value of, 202, 230, 232, 233, 258–59
   wooden panels, 230, 232–33 fig. 5.1,
      260, 261 fig. 5.18, 266–67
votive reliefs, ix, 3, 6, 177
   of Bendis, 173, 179–81, 180 fig. 4.11, 199
   of Charites, 206, 262, 263
   iconography of, 99–100, 133, 264–67
   mutilation of, 231, 245, 246
   Neo-Attic, 198, 207, 264
votive relief(s) of the nymphs, in Attica, 3,
      98–100, 125, 128, 133, 143
   of Agathemeros, 246, 265 fig. 5.20
   Akropolis relief, 262, 263 fig. 5.19, 266,
      267
   of Archandros, 130, fig. 4.2, 206
   Echelos relief, 133–34
   Eleusis, 248–49, fig. 5.12
   Launderers' relief, 128, 129 fig. 4.1
   of Neoptolemos, 93–94, 258–59
   Peiraieus, 134–35

Pentelikon, Mount (relief of three
   donors), 246
Quirinal relief, 99 fig. 3.1, 133, 266
Rapedosa area, 248–49
Sotias, 262
   Xenokrateia, of, 127, 131–34, figs. 4.3–4
votive reliefs of the nymphs, outside Attica
   of Adamas (Paros), 179–81, 180 fig. 4.11,
      199
   Andros, 184
   Corinth, 149
   Delos, 183
   Delphi, 147
   Epeiros, 311n.140
   Halikarnassos, 207
   Ischia, 224–25
   Karpathos, 208
   Kos, 206
   Krete, 240
   Lykia, 210
   Megara, 147
   Messana, 219
   Miletos, 203, 204 fig. 4.15
   Mykale, 201, 202 fig. 4.13
   Pythia Therma, 196
   Smyrna, 199
   Syracuse, 215
   Telos, 322n.296
   Thasos, 96, 170–71 fig. 4.9
   Thrace, Pontic, 174–77
   Tralleis, 201

water, 11, 100. *See also* water supply
water supply, 5, 8, 135, 227
   Antioch, 211
   Argolis, 6, 150
   Arkadia, 154
   Athens, 126–27, 129–30
   Keos, 184
   Lokroi Epizephyroi, 251
   Megara, 146
   Syracuse, 216
weaving, 24, 59, 62
women, 100–120. *See also* female life cycle
   daily lives of, vii, 90
   as dedicants, viii, 127, 131–34, figs. 4.3–
      4, 228–9, 233, 243
   social status of, as wives, 114

Xanthos, 209–10, 262
Xeniades, 131–34
Xenokrateia. *See* votive relief(s) of the
   nymphs, in Attica
Xenomedes of Keos, 183–84

Zethos. *See* Amphion and Zethos

Zeus, 19, 154, 156, 175, 199. *See also* oracles, of Zeus
as abductor, 38–41, 66, 82, 91, 123, 140n.145, 151–52
Alastoros, 171
Ammon, 85, 239
birthplace of, 153–54, 161, 185–87, 318n.226. *See also* nurses, nymphs as
Diktaios, 185–87
Dimeranos, 183
Endendros, 316n.204
as father of nymphs, 4, 21, 23, 25, 36, 41, 78
and Hera, 90, 113, 200
Ikmaios, 183–84
Karios, 200
Ktesios, 171, 182
Kynthios, 180
Meilichios, 112, 128, 131, 208
Naïos, 161
Olympios, 128
Patroös, 171
as ruler, 21, 72, 73
Tropaios, 137